A NEXTEXT ANTHOLOGY

Introduction to
SHAKESPEARE

nextext

Cover, play openers, and icon illustrations: Kris Wiltse

Printed in the United States of America.

ISBN 0-618-22199-9

1 2 3 4 5 6 7 — DCI — 08 07 06 05 04 03 02

Introduction to Shakespeare

Introduction

Plays

Plays

Plays and Poetry

Throughout the anthology, vocabulary words appear in boldface type and are footnoted. Specialized or technical words and phrases appear in lightface type and are footnoted.

Shakespeare's Life and Career

Childhood, Education, and Marriage

William Shakespeare was baptized on April 26, 1564, in Stratford-on-Avon, a small market town about 75 miles northwest of London. He is traditionally said to have been born on St. George's day, April 23; certainly he died on that day in 1616. In Shakespeare's time, Stratford had a population of around 1,200. It was run by a few middle-class families. Shakespeare's father, who had once been Stratford's mayor, made gloves for a living. His mother was from a prosperous farm family in a nearby village.

Although records are lacking, William is presumed to have attended the Grammar School in Stratford. The curriculum was quite different from our idea of education. It consisted largely of Latin language and literature. There are many debts in

▲
Shakespeare attended the Grammar School in Stratford.

Shakespeare's works to classical authors, such as the poet Ovid, the comic playwright Plautus, and the biographer Plutarch. Shakespeare seems to have been a lifelong reader, particularly of history. In addition, he had a deep knowledge of the Bible. His school training in rhetoric (the principles of argument) would have been helpful when he came to express the views of different characters in his plays.

Shakespeare did not go on to a university. He probably left school at 15, the normal age at this time. His father was having money troubles and may have needed extra help at home. In 1582, Shakespeare married Anne Hathaway, whose family were old friends of his parents. He was eighteen and she was twenty-six or twenty-seven. Their first child, Susanna (1583–1649), was followed by twins, Hamnet (1585–1596) and Judith (1585–1662). By an accident of history, no direct descendants of Shakespeare are alive today.

This is one of the bedrooms in the house in Stratford-on-Avon in which Shakespeare was born.
▼

▲
London's playhouses can be seen on the south bank of the Thames in this artist's view of the city in Shakespeare's time.

Actor, Writer, and Businessman

We do not really know what Shakespeare did for several years before he went to London. A longstanding tradition says that he was a country schoolmaster. By 1592, Shakespeare was well enough known as a playwright in London to be attacked in a pamphlet by a rival, Robert Greene. He joined an acting company, the Lord Chamberlain's Men (renamed the King's Men under King James I), and sought the patronage of the Earl of Southampton. He seems to have been a bit-part actor in his own and other authors' plays, but gradually he became a full-time writer.

▲
After becoming a successful playwright, Shakespeare was able to buy New Place in Stratford.

A portrait of Shakespeare appeared in the First Folio, the first collected edition of his plays, which was produced in 1623 by former members of his company. ▶

Shakespeare's contemporaries did not regard drama very highly as literature; they admired poetry more. Of Shakespeare's thirty-eight plays, only half were printed in his lifetime. None of these texts was printed with Shakespeare's permission, and some were full of mistakes. This seems not to have concerned him. His long narrative poems, Venus and Adonis (1593) and The Rape of Lucrece (1594), are the only works whose printing he supervised. He also wrote a large number of sonnets, published in 1609, and a few other short poems.

His income did not come from the sales of books but from his fees for writing plays under exclusive contract to his acting company, and from a percentage of box office takings. He was a coolheaded businessman, and many of the surviving documents concerning him relate to money. In 1597, he was already sufficiently wealthy to buy New Place, a substantial house in Stratford. Two years later, Shakespeare and six others became owners of the new Globe theater.

Retirement, Death, and Reputation

Shakespeare shuttled between Stratford and London during his writing career, producing on average two plays each year. After 1610, he seems to have gone into semi-retirement in Stratford. The exact cause of Shakespeare's death in 1616

▲
Shakespeare's will was dated March 25, 1616, a month before his death. The signature reads, "By me William Shakespeare."

remains unknown; the handwriting on his will is that of a sick man. He was buried on April 25 in the parish church of Stratford, with a threatening inscription on his grave: "Cursed be he that moves my bones." The tomb has never been opened.

Shakespeare the man is notoriously elusive. Famous images of him, such as the portrait in the First Folio of 1623 (the first collected edition of his plays), or the bust in the church in Stratford, look somehow too ordinary. Although he was respected as a playwright in his own time, he was not seen as exceptional. There are frustratingly few reliable accounts of his appearance, character, or life by people who knew him. His own face and voice are hidden behind those of his characters. In the end, we have to follow the advice of his friends, John Heminge and Henry Condell, in their preface to the First Folio: "Read him."

Shakespeare's Theater

The Stage in Shakespeare's Time

It is important to realize that Shakespeare's plays were not written for anything like a modern theater. Many things we take for granted were absent. Theaters were open-air. There was no artificial lighting; performances took place in the afternoon. There was no front-of-house curtain, no fixed scenery. Props were kept to a minimum. Costumes were elaborate, but contemporary. There was little attempt to present the dress of historical periods. Actors playing male characters dressed in a hat, cloak, doublet and hose. Actors playing women wore a headdress with a veil, and a long flowing dress over a hooped petticoat called a farthingale. There would be a few additions for special purposes, such as armor for soldiers or a crown for a king.

▲
In Shakespeare's theater, actors playing female roles wore ordinary Elizabethan female clothing *(left)*. Actors playing male roles wore typical male dress *(right)*.

The Globe

Beginning in the late 1570s, a number of permanent playhouses were built in London and its suburbs. The most famous of these playhouses, Shakespeare's Globe theater, was a multi-sided structure open to the sky. As its name suggests, it was a small-scale model of the universe. The canopy that protected the actors—not the audience—from bad weather was painted with the sun, moon and stars. The bare boards on which the actors stood were the world, and because there was no fixed scenery or backdrop, the stage could represent any time and place. The actors could also come forward on the "thrust" stage, nearer to the audience, to deliver a prologue, epilogue, or soliloquy.

◄ A modern scholar reconstructed this bird's-eye view of Shakespeare's Globe theater.

◀ Today's groundlings watch a performance of The Tempest at London's reconstructed Globe Theatre.

At the back of the stage was a recess that could be covered with a curtain. This probably served as Prospero's "cell" in The Tempest. There was also a gallery above the stage, where musicians could play. This gallery could also be used for actors when an overhead level was needed (as in the balcony scene in Romeo and Juliet). A trapdoor in the stage allowed for the entrances from below of demons or spirits, such as the Weird Sisters in Macbeth or the Ghost of Hamlet's father. Such a simple yet versatile playing space was crucial to Shakespeare's wide-ranging effects in his plays.

◀ A contemporary of Shakespeare made this drawing of London's Swan theater in 1596.

Other Performance Spaces

In addition to the Globe, Shakespeare also produced plays for other kinds of performance spaces. His plays would be performed sometimes at the royal court, in private houses belonging to nobles, or in university college halls. A Midsummer Night's Dream was probably written for a wedding celebration in some noble household. Shakespeare's witty comedy Twelfth Night may have been performed at The Inns of Court, the training schools for lawyers. Educated audiences would be able to appreciate complex ideas and relish sophisticated wordplay. The Tempest may have been written with an indoor theater, such as the Blackfriars, in mind. Such playhouses did have artificial lighting, and permitted "special effects" with stage machinery, which would enable Ariel to fly, for example.

Audiences

The audience would vary with the performance space. Outdoor theaters would have a mixture of social classes. At indoor theaters, higher admission charges ruled out all but the well-to-do. At the Globe, more wealthy patrons had seats on three galleries surrounding the Pit, an open area in front of the stage. The poorer people, known as "groundlings," stood in the Pit. The most expensive seats were actually on the stage, or in the gallery above, if it was not needed for the play. Finally, Queen Elizabeth and King James didn't go to the theater; they saw plays at court or in noble houses.

Actors

All the plays in this volume were performed, as far as we know, by Shakespeare's own company, the Lord Chamberlain's Men (renamed the King's Men after King James I came to the throne). The stars of this company were Richard Burbage in tragic roles, and the clown Will Kemp.

There were no actresses before the Restoration in 1660, because this was felt to be improper, so female roles were taken by boy actors. They could

▲
As was done in Shakespeare's time, male actors play female parts in this production of his play Henry V at the reconstructed Globe Theatre.

perform these parts until the age of sixteen or even older because boys' voices broke later in those days. Having boys playing female roles may seem strange to us, but Renaissance theatergoers seem to have accepted it without difficulty. Younger boys would have taken comic roles such as Maria in Twelfth Night, but the roles of Ophelia or Lady Macbeth are more demanding and must have required older boys.

Acting Style

We know little about acting styles in Shakespeare's time, although Hamlet's advice to the Players gives some clues. If we could have seen an original performance of one of Shakespeare's plays, it would probably have seemed a bit like opera, very formal, and a bit like a sports match, with the audience closely involved and actors addressing them directly. (The modern Globe Theatre in London has attempted to recreate this atmosphere.) The way an actor stood, moved, gestured, and spoke was dictated by the kind of character he was playing and the mood he was expressing.

Plays Within Plays

Something about acting styles is suggested by the "plays within plays" that Shakespeare included as part of the action in some of his plays. In A Midsummer Night's Dream, Bottom and his friends hilariously rehearse and perform a play, "Pyramus and Thisbe," for the wedding of Theseus and Hippolyta. Hamlet stages a play, "The Murder of Gonzago," to try to trap his uncle. In The Tempest, the betrothal of Ferdinand and Miranda is celebrated with an elaborate performance called a masque, which includes music and dancing.

In these "inset" plays, Shakespeare uses a different style from that used in the plays which surround them. Sometimes, as in "Pyramus and Thisbe" and "The Murder of Gonzago," the style is old-fashioned or artificial and is mocked in the plays themselves. The masque, however, was a very popular form in the royal court toward the end of Shakespeare's career, and the one in The Tempest is presented respectfully.

All this shows us that Shakespeare was a highly self-conscious playwright. He was well aware of the power of theater to affect people's feelings, capture their imaginations, and create memorable occasions. All these were reasons why the Elizabethan theater was so popular, and also why some people, such as religious leaders, wanted it suppressed. That was why actors had to have a patron, some powerful person at court who could stand up for them against their enemies. Theater was not just entertainment; it was also part of politics. When Hamlet uses a play to try to trap Claudius, we can see this risky political role at work.

In this scene from the 1995 production of The Tempest by the Artists Repertory Theatre, Ferdinand (Scott Ripley) and Miranda (Jessalyn Gilsig) watch the masque that is a "play within the play."

▼

Reading a Shakespeare Play

Comedies, Tragedies, and Histories

Shakespeare's plays were divided by their first editors into three groups: comedies, tragedies, and histories. Sometimes these categories overlap. Julius Caesar, Hamlet, and Macbeth are just as much history as tragedy. On the other hand, there is comedy early in the tragedy Romeo and Juliet, and painful experiences for some characters in the comedy Twelfth Night. Still, some general distinctions can be made. The comedies tend to celebrate love and marriage and to emphasize society as a whole rather than any single person. The tragedies, by contrast, focus on the struggles, and eventual death, of one or more central characters. Comedy points beyond itself to the future, while tragedy has a stronger sense of closure. The histories are a cycle of plays based on the lives of the English kings. Shakespeare had to keep to the known facts; but he shaped them to his dramatic purpose, inventing characters and episodes on occasion. These plays contain somber reflections on the use and misuse of political power.

Plotting and Structure

Shakespeare took his story material from many places. His originality does not lie in making up stories but in reworking his material into a significant design, involving additions, cuts, and expansions.

Modern editions divide the plays into five acts. This can be misleading. The act is not always a structurally important unit. Shakespeare composed in scenes rather than acts, and his plays were probably performed without an interval. We need to read backwards and forwards across the text, as well as forward in a straight line, to realize how the scenes build into a whole.

In his comedies, Shakespeare often has parallel stories with characters arranged into groups. Thus, A Midsummer Night's Dream follows the adventures of humans and supernatural beings, working people and nobles. There are many pairs of lovers: Demetrius and Helena, Lysander and Hermia, Titania and Oberon, Titania and Bottom, Theseus and Hippolyta, even Pyramus and Thisbe in the play within the play! There are also paired settings—the daylight world of the court, and the moonlit, magical world of the wood.

Tragedy is more concentrated than comedy in its plotting. This is because its effect on our emotions needs to be more direct. We are led through a straight line as we follow the fortunes of Macbeth and Hamlet. We see mounting tension and feel disaster lying in wait. Yet, even here, Shakespeare finds time to develop other stories, such as that of Ophelia's doomed love for Hamlet.

▲
The most mismatched of the pairs of lovers in A Midsummer Night's Dream is Titania and Bottom, played here by Suzanne Bouchard and Geoff Hoyle in a 2001 production of the play by the Seattle Repertory Theatre.

Characters

Shakespeare's plays are not novels. A character may exist simply to advance the plot, and may have little depth. Rosencrantz and Guildenstern in Hamlet *are of this type. At the other extreme, the central figures of the plays are explored in detail through their words, actions, and relationships with other characters. We feel we know them as we know people in real life.*

An important device here is the soliloquy, *in which a character is alone onstage, speaking directly to the audience, sharing his or her thoughts and feelings. However much a character may deceive others, in soliloquy we hear him or her speak the truth. Hamlet's soliloquies are the most famous in Shakespeare, but there are other examples, such as Brutus in Act Two, Scene One, of* Julius Caesar, *or Viola in Act Two, Scene Two, of* Twelfth Night.

▲

The three Witches meet in the all-black production of *Macbeth* staged by Orson Welles in New York City in 1937.

Themes

The plot of a Shakespeare play may seem to include things that do not belong together, but we also need to look for the themes. These are the underlying ideas that bring the various stories together and unify the play. For example, the stories of plots and rebellions in Julius Caesar *and* Macbeth *explore the nature of political ambition and power. The different kinds of magic in* A Midsummer Night's Dream *and* The Tempest *indicate the problem of deciding sometimes what "reality" actually is. Often, Shakespeare will open the play by a sequence of scenes that set up the main themes. A good example is Act Two of* Twelfth Night, *in which we see that Olivia and Viola are linked by the loss of a brother, while Orsino and Olivia are linked by stubborn refusal to accept reality. These attitudes are all criticized by Feste and Sir Toby, whose comic scenes offer another view of the romantic world of the more serious characters.*

Styles of Language

Shakespeare uses four main styles in his plays: prose, rhyming couplets (lines rhyming in pairs), songs, and blank verse. Each of these has several purposes.

Prose is often used when less noble characters are speaking; for example, the tradesmen in Act One of Julius Caesar, *or Bottom and his friends in* A Midsummer Night's Dream. *Prose may convey some piece of information quickly and simply; for example, Macbeth's letter to his wife. Prose may also be used when the conversation is informal or intimate; for example, the talk between Maria and her fellow-conspirators about their plot against Malvolio in Act Two, Scene Five, of* Twelfth Night.

Rhyming couplets are often used to signal the end of a scene. Rhyming couplets may also be used to suggest a special, magical atmosphere; for example, Puck's speech in Act Two, Scene Two, of A Midsummer Night's Dream; *the Weird Sisters' chanting in* Macbeth; *or Prospero's Epilogue to* The Tempest.

▲
Viola (Marin Ireland) talks to Orsino (Justin McCaffrey) in the 2000 production of *Twelfth Night* by the Hartt School at the University of Hartford.

Songs can provide a change of mood in a scene, or they can sum up key themes of the play in a brief, memorable way. Celebrated Shakespearean songs include those of Feste in Twelfth Night *and Ophelia in* Hamlet.

Blank Verse

Shakespeare generally used blank verse in his plays. It is called "blank" because it does not rhyme. The normal blank verse line is ten syllables long. A perfectly regular line has five stresses, on the second, fourth, sixth, eighth, and tenth syllables, forming the following pattern (in which x indicates an unstressed syllable and / a stressed one):

x / x / x / x / x /

This line is also called "iambic pentameter." The iamb is the name for the combination of an unstressed and a stressed syllable, and penta means "five" in Greek, so the term simply means "five pairs of iambs."

If every line were perfectly regular, the rhythm would become boring. Shakespeare thus has to vary the "beat" of the lines to keep our attention. He does this by making the sense of a sentence run across the regular syllable-count of a line, and by moving the stressed syllables around. Here is a small example from Twelfth Night, *Act Two, Scene Four. Viola declares her love for Orsino indirectly. The stressed syllables are printed in* **bold:**

My **fa**ther had a **daugh**ter **loved** a **man**,
As it **might** be, per**haps**, were **I** a **wo**man,
I should your **lord**ship.

The movement of these lines acts out Viola's nervous hesitation. Her last line ends half way through the ten syllables. Orsino completes it:

And **what**'s her **his**tory?

Viola replies:

A **blank**, my lord. She **ne**ver **told** her **love** . . .

The sudden stop in the middle of the line (called a caesura) creates a dramatic pause and makes the short sentence 'A blank, my lord,' even more bleak.

One of the pleasures of reading Shakespeare is noticing how he varies the movement of the lines in this way to convey emotion and atmosphere. It's hard at first, but worth the trouble!

Romeo and Juliet

Introduction

Romeo and Juliet have become the most famous "star-crossed," or ill-fated, lovers in literature. This tale of a young man and woman who come to tragic ends because of a feud between their families has been told many times, before and since Shakespeare's day. That their story still has appeal for audiences is proved by the frequent stage productions and many film versions of Shakespeare's play, as well as by the great success of the musical adaptation, West Side Story. The warring families of Shakespeare's Renaissance Italy seem to translate effortlessly into the warring street gangs of 20th-century New York City. The notion of a love so powerful that it causes two people to kill themselves rather than be separated is ageless.

Romeo and Juliet are secretly married by Friar Laurence.

▼

Plot

Romeo and Juliet meet at a party and fall in love at first sight. Unfortunately, Romeo is a Montague and Juliet is a Capulet. The houses, or extended families, of the Montagues and the Capulets have been feuding for years, and both Romeo and Juliet recognize the danger of loving an enemy. Nevertheless, they are so strongly drawn to each other that they make plans for an immediate and secret wedding.

Their timing is unfortunate because members of their families choose the same time to renew their feud, in spite of the warning of Prince Escalus of Verona that more disturbances of the peace mean death for the family heads. Tybalt, a Capulet, kills Mercutio, a friend of the Montagues. Romeo, despite his efforts to stop the fight, is drawn into it instead and kills Tybalt, who is Juliet's cousin. Prince Escalus exiles Romeo from Verona on threat of death.

◀ The violence of the feud between the Capulets and Montagues is conveyed by this scene from a 1996 production of *Romeo and Juliet* at the Seattle Children's Theatre.

▲
Romeo (Nathan Hinton) and Juliet (Sanaa Lathan) are discovered dead in the tomb in this scene from a 1993 production of *Romeo and Juliet* at the Yale School of Drama.

Meanwhile Juliet's parents have arranged a marriage for her, one that she cannot refuse without revealing her secret marriage to Romeo. To help her, Friar Laurence gives her a drug that will make her appear as dead. His message to Romeo goes astray, however, and Romeo kills himself beside what he thinks is Juliet's corpse. When she revives, Juliet sees her Romeo dead and kills herself in turn. The families' grief over these two young suicides finally prompts them to end the long-standing feud.

Settings and Characters

The action of Romeo and Juliet takes place mostly in the Italian city Verona, in the 1300s. Settings are various streets of Verona, the Capulet household, Friar Laurence's monastery, the Capulet family tomb, and a street in Mantua, a nearby city. The major characters fall into three groups, the members of the two feuding families and the other people of Verona.

The House of Montague	The House of Capulet	Other Townspeople
Lord Montague	Lord Capulet	Escalus, Prince of Verona
Lady Montague	Lady Capulet	Mercutio, Prince Escalus's kinsman and Romeo's friend
Romeo, their son	Juliet, their daughter	Count Paris, Prince Escalus's kinsman and Juliet's suitor
Benvolio, Montague's nephew and Romeo's cousin	Nurse, Juliet's nurse and personal attendant	Friar Laurence, a priest
	Tybalt, Lady Capulet's nephew and Juliet's cousin	

Themes

Romeo and Juliet is about love and the things people will do for love. It is also about hatred and the things people will do to keep alive old wrongs and to avenge themselves on perceived enemies. We never learn what caused the feud between the Montagues and the Capulets in the first place, but that is not important. More important are the tragic consequences of that old hatred.

Modern audiences also may read into the play messages about the dangers of immaturity, of parents' trying to control children's lives, or simply of acting in haste. Juliet is barely fourteen years old, and Romeo not much older. Yet such early marriages were not unusual in Renaissance Europe, where parents often had total control over their children's lives and arranged their marriages, not for love but to increase family fortunes. The danger of haste is clear: Romeo and Juliet's entire story, from their falling in love to their deaths, takes less than one week. Shakespeare does have Friar Laurence tell Romeo, "Wisely and slow. They stumble that run fast." Unfortunately, neither Romeo nor anyone else in the play heeds that good advice.

Characters

Chorus
Escalus, Prince of Verona
Mercutio, the Prince's kinsman and
    Romeo's friend
Paris, a young count and kinsman of
    the Prince
Page to Count Paris
Lord Montague
Lady Montague
Romeo, their son
Benvolio, Montague's nephew and
    Romeo's friend
Abram, a servant of the Montague
    household
Balthasar, a servant of the Montague
    household attending Romeo

Lord Capulet
Lady Capulet
Juliet, daughter of the Capulets
Nurse, Juliet's nurse and personal attendant
Peter, a servant of the Capulet household
    attending the Nurse

SCENE: *Verona, Mantua*

Tybalt, Lady Capulet's nephew
Tybalt's **Page**
Petruchio, Capulet's kinsman
Second Capulet, an old man, Capulet's
    kinsman
Servants of the Capulet household
    Samson
    Gregory
    Anthony
    Potpan
    Clown or **Servant**
    Other Servants
Friar Laurence, a Franciscan priest
Friar John, a Franciscan priest

Apothecary

Three **Musicians (Simon Catling, Hugh
    Rebeck,** and **James Soundpost)**

Three **Watchmen**

**Citizens, Maskers, Torchbearers, Guards,
    Servants,** and **Attendants**

The Prologue

The Chorus, played by a single actor, outlines the events of the play.

Enter Chorus.

Chorus.
> Two households, both alike in dignity,
> In fair Verona, where we lay our scene,
> From ancient grudge break to new mutiny,[1]
> Where civil blood makes civil hands unclean.[2]
> 5   From forth the fatal loins of these two foes
> A pair of star-crossed[3] lovers take their life;
> Whose misadventured[4] piteous overthrows
> Doth with their death bury their parents' strife.
> The fearful passage of their death-marked love
> 10   And the continuance of their parents' rage,
> Which, but their children's end, naught could remove,[5]
> Is now the two hours' traffic of our stage;
> The which, if you with patient ears attend,
> What here shall miss, our toil shall strive to mend.[6]
> [Chorus *exits.*]

---

[1] mutiny—rioting.

[2] civil blood . . . civil hands unclean—Citizens' hands are stained with fellow citizens' blood.

[3] star-crossed—ill-fated. In Shakespeare's day, it was commonly believed that the stars controlled people's lives.

[4] misadventured—unfortunate.

[5] but . . . remove—Nothing could stop their hatred except their children's deaths.

[6] What . . . mend—Whatever is defective in today's performance we will work to improve in the future.

Act One, Scene One

In a public square in Verona, Samson and Gregory, servants of the house of Capulet, meet Abram and another servant of the house of Montague. Renewing the old feud between the families, they start to fight with swords and shields. Tybalt and Benvolio join the fight. Citizens try to stop them. Lord Capulet and Lord Montague try to fight, but they are held back by their wives. Prince Escalus puts an end to the fight. If the families again disturb the peace, the prince threatens, the family heads will pay with their lives. Lord Montague and Lady Montague ask Benvolio if he knows what has made their son, Romeo, so moody lately. When Romeo enters, Benvolio finally persuades him to admit that he is in love with a woman (Rosaline) who does not return his love.

Enter Samson *and* Gregory, *armed with swords and shields.*

Samson. Gregory, on my word, we'll not carry coals.[1]

Gregory. No, for then we should be colliers.[2]

Samson. I mean, an[3] we be in choler, we'll draw.

Gregory. Ay, while you live, draw your neck out of collar.

5   **Samson.** I strike quickly, being moved.

Gregory. But thou art not quickly moved to strike.

Samson. A dog of the house of Montague moves me.

Gregory. To move is to stir, and to be valiant is to stand. Therefore, if thou art moved, thou runn'st away.

10   **Samson.** A dog of that house shall move me to stand. I will take the wall of any man or maid of Montague's.

Gregory. That shows thee a weak slave, for the weakest goes to the wall.[4]

Samson. 'Tis true, and therefore women, being the weaker vessels, are ever thrust to the wall. Therefore I will push Montague's men from

15   the wall and thrust his maids to the wall.

Gregory. The quarrel is between our masters and us their men.

---

[1] carry coals—endure insults.

[2] colliers—coal carriers, persons looked down upon; puns follow on *choler,* "anger," and *collar,* "hangman's noose."

[3] an—if.

[4] take the wall of . . . goes to the wall—get the better of . . . are forced to give way.

Samson. 'Tis all one. I will show myself a **tyrant.**[5] When I have fought with the men, I will be civil with the maids—I will cut off their heads.

Gregory. The heads of the maids?

20 **Samson.** Ay, the heads of the maids, or their maiden-heads. Take it in what sense thou wilt.

Gregory. They must take it in sense that feel it.

Samson. Me they shall feel while I am able to stand, and 'tis known I am a pretty piece of flesh.

25 **Gregory.** 'Tis well thou art not fish; if thou hadst, thou hadst been Poor John.[6] Draw thy tool. Here comes of the house of Montagues.

[*Enter* Abram *and a* Servingman.]

Samson. My naked weapon is out. Quarrel, I will back thee.

Gregory. How? Turn thy back and run?

Samson. Fear me not.

30 **Gregory.** No, marry.[7] I fear thee!

Samson. Let us take the law of our sides.[8] Let them begin.

Gregory. I will frown as I pass by, and let them take it as they list.[9]

Samson. Nay, as they dare. I will bite my thumb[10] at them, which is disgrace to them if they bear it.

[Samson *makes taunting gestures.*]

35 **Abram.** Do you bite your thumb at us, sir?

Samson. I do bite my thumb, sir.

Abram. Do you bite your thumb at us, sir?

Samson [*aside to* Gregory]. Is the law of our side if I say "Ay"?

Gregory [*aside to* Samson]. No.

40 **Samson** [*to* Abram]. No, sir, I do not bite my thumb at you, sir, but I bite my thumb, sir.

Gregory. Do you quarrel, sir?

Abram. Quarrel, sir? No, sir.

Samson. But if you do, sir, I am for you. I serve as good a man as you.

45 **Abram.** No better?

Samson. Well, sir.

---

[5] **tyrant**—absolute ruler.

[6] Poor John—cheap fish, salted and dried to preserve it.

[7] marry—by the Virgin Mary; a mild oath that could indicate surprise, agreement, or indignation.

[8] Let us . . . sides—Let us have the law on our side.

[9] list—please.

[10] bite my thumb—make an insulting gesture.

Shakespeare's warring families, the Montagues and the Capulets, duel in a Verona street at the opening of a 1995 production of *Romeo and Juliet* by the Hartford Stage theatre company.

[*Enter* Benvolio.]

Gregory [*to* Samson]. Say "better." Here comes one of my master's kinsmen.

Samson [*to* Abram]. Yes, better, sir.

Abram. You lie.

50   **Samson.** Draw, if you be men. Gregory, remember thy washing[11] blow.
[*They fight.*]

Benvolio. Part, fools! Put up your swords. You know not what you do.
[*Enter* Tybalt *with sword drawn.*]

Tybalt. What, art thou drawn among these heartless hinds?[12]
    Turn thee, Benvolio. Look upon thy death.

Benvolio. I do but keep the peace. Put up thy sword,
55   Or manage it to part these men with me.

---

[11] washing—forceful.

[12] heartless hinds—cowardly servants; pun on female deer (*hinds*) without a male deer (*hart*).

Tybalt. What, drawn and talk of peace? I hate the word
　　As I hate hell, all Montagues, and thee.
　　Have at thee,[13] coward!
[*They fight.*]
[*Enter three or four* Citizens *with clubs or partisans.*][14]
60　**Citizens.** Clubs, bills, and partisans! Strike! Beat them down!
　　Down with the Capulets! Down with the Montagues!
[*Enter* Lord Capulet, *in his gown, and* Lady Capulet.]
Capulet. What noise is this? Give me my long sword, ho!
Lady Capulet. A crutch, a crutch! Why call you for a sword?
Capulet. My sword, I say! Old Montague is come
　　And **flourishes**[15] his blade in spite of me.
65　[*Enter* Lord Montague *and* Lady Montague.]
Montague. Thou villain Capulet!—[*To* Lady Montague.] Hold me not; let
　　me go.
Lady Montague. Thou shalt not stir one foot to seek a foe.
[*Enter* Prince Escalus, *with his* Followers *and* Attendants.]
Prince. Rebellious subjects, enemies to peace,
70　　Profaners of this neighbor-stainèd steel[16]—
　　Will they not hear? What, ho! You men, you beasts,
　　That quench the fire of your **pernicious**[17] rage
　　With purple fountains issuing from your veins,
　　On pain of torture, from those bloody hands
75　　Throw your mistempered weapons to the ground
　　And hear the sentence of your movèd prince.
　　Three civil brawls, bred of an airy word,
　　By thee, old Capulet, and Montague,
　　Have thrice disturbed the quiet of our streets
80　　And made Verona's ancient citizens
　　Cast by their grave-beseeming ornaments
　　To wield old partisans in hands as old,
　　Cankered with peace, to part your cankered hate.[18]

---

[13] Have at thee—On guard! Here I come!

[14] *partisans*—long-handled bladed weapons.

[15] **flourishes**—waves about grandly.

[16] Profaners . . . steel—You who dishonor your weapons by staining them with neighbors' blood.

[17] **pernicious**—destructive, deadly.

[18] Cankered . . . hate—the weapons, rusty with disuse, to end the destructive family feud.

If ever you disturb our streets again

85   Your lives shall pay the forfeit of the peace.[19]

For this time all the rest depart away.

You, Capulet, shall go along with me,

And Montague, come you this afternoon,

To know our farther pleasure in this case,

90   To old Freetown, our common judgment-place.

Once more, on pain of death, all men depart.

[*Exit all but* Lord Montague, Lady Montague, *and* Benvolio.]

Montague. Who set this ancient quarrel new abroach?[20]

Speak, nephew, were you by when it began?

Benvolio. Here were the servants of your **adversary**,[21]

95   And yours, close fighting ere I did approach.

I drew to part them. In the instant came

The fiery Tybalt with his sword prepared,

Which, as he breathed defiance to my ears,

He swung about his head and cut the winds

100   Who, nothing hurt withal,[22] hissed him in scorn.

While we were interchanging thrusts and blows,

Came more and more, and fought on part and part

Till the prince came, who parted either part.

Lady Montague. O, where is Romeo? Saw you him today?

105   Right glad I am he was not at this fray.[23]

Benvolio. Madam, an hour before the worshiped sun

Peered forth the golden window of the east,

A troubled mind drive me to walk abroad,

Where, underneath the grove of sycamore

110   That westward rooteth from this city's side,

So early walking did I see your son.

Towards him I made, but he was ware of me

And stole into the covert of the wood.

I, measuring his affections by my own,

---

[19] Your . . . peace—The penalty for disturbing the peace will be your deaths.

[20] set . . . abroach—reopened this old quarrel.

[21] **adversary**—enemy.

[22] withal—with it.

[23] fray—fight.

115   Which then most sought where most might not be found,[24]

    Being one too many by my weary self,

    Pursued my humor, not pursuing his,

    And gladly shunned who gladly fled from me.

Montague. Many a morning hath he there been seen,

120   With tears **augmenting**[25] the fresh morning's dew,

    Adding to clouds more clouds with his deep sighs;

    But all so soon as the all-cheering sun

    Should in the farthest east begin to draw

    The shady curtains from Aurora's bed,[26]

125   Away from light steals home my heavy[27] son

    And private in his chamber pens himself,

    Shuts up his windows, locks fair daylight out,

    And makes himself an artificial night.

    Black and portentous[28] must this humor prove

130   Unless good counsel may the cause remove.

Benvolio. My noble uncle, do you know the cause?

Montague. I neither know it nor can learn of him.

Benvolio. Have you importuned[29] him by any means?

Montague. Both by myself and many other friends.

135   But he, his own affections' counselor,

    Is to himself—I will not say how true,

    But to himself so secret and so close,

    So far from sounding[30] and discovery,

    As is the bud bit with an envious worm

140   Ere he can spread his sweet leaves to the air

    Or dedicate his beauty to the sun.

    Could we but learn from whence his sorrows grow,

    We would as willingly give cure as know.

[*Enter* Romeo.]

---

[24] most . . . found—mostly wanted a place where there were no other people.

[25] **augmenting**—adding to.

[26] Aurora's bed—bed of the goddess of the dawn.

[27] heavy—sad.

[28] portentous—threatening evil.

[29] importuned—asked urgently.

[30] sounding—being measured, as the depth of water.

Benvolio. See where he comes.

145   So please you, step aside.

I'll know his grievance or be much denied.[31]

Montague. I would thou wert so happy by thy stay

To hear true shrift.[32] Come, madam, let's away.

[*Exit* Lord Montague *and* Lady Montague.]

Benvolio. Good morrow, cousin.

150 **Romeo.** Is the day so young?

Benvolio. But new struck nine.

Romeo. Ay me! Sad hours seem long.

Was that my father that went hence so fast?

Benvolio. It was. What sadness lengthens Romeo's hours?

155 **Romeo.** Not having that which, having, makes them short.

Benvolio. In love?

Romeo. Out—

Benvolio. Of love?

Romeo. Out of her favor where I am in love.

160 **Benvolio.** Alas, that Love, so gentle in his view,

Should be so tyrannous and rough in proof![33]

Romeo. Alas, that Love, whose view is muffled still,[34]

Should without eyes see pathways to his will!

Where shall we dine?—O me! What fray was here?

165   Yet tell me not, for I have heard it all.

Here's much to do with hate, but more with love.

Why, then, O brawling love, O loving hate,

O anything of nothing first create,[35]

O heavy lightness, serious vanity,

170   Misshapen chaos of well-seeming forms,

Feather of lead, bright smoke, cold fire, sick health,

Still-waking sleep, that is not what it is!

This love feel I, that feel no love in this.

Dost thou not laugh?

---

[31] I'll know ... denied—He will find it hard to refuse to answer me.

[32] shrift—act of confessing to a priest and being absolved (shrived), or forgiven, for sins.

[33] Alas ... proof!—It's sad that Love, who looks so gentle, should be such a harsh master!

[34] Love ... still—Love, who is always blindfolded.

[35] anything ... create—anything created from nothing; one of a series of contradictory figures of speech, such as "heavy lightness."

Benvolio. No, coz,[36] I rather weep.

Romeo. Good heart, at what?

175   **Benvolio.** At thy good heart's oppression.

Romeo. Why, such is love's transgression.[37]

     Griefs of mine own lie heavy in my breast,

     Which thou wilt propagate, to have it pressed

     With more of thine.[38] This love that thou hast shown

180   Doth add more grief to too much of mine own.

     Love is a smoke made with the fume of sighs;

     Being purged, a fire sparkling in lovers' eyes;

     Being vexed, a sea nourished with lovers' tears.

     What is it else? A madness most discreet,

185   A choking gall, and a preserving sweet.

     Farewell, my coz.

Benvolio. Soft![39] I will go along.

     An if you leave me so, you do me wrong.

Romeo. Tut, I have lost myself. I am not here.

     This is not Romeo; he's some other where.

190   **Benvolio.** Tell me in sadness,[40] who is that you love?

Romeo. What, shall I groan and tell thee?

Benvolio. Groan? Why, no, but sadly tell me who.

Romeo. A sick man in sadness makes his will—

     A word ill urged to one that is so ill!

195   In sadness, cousin, I do love a woman.

Benvolio. I aimed so near when I supposed you loved.

Romeo. A right good markman! And she's fair I love.

Benvolio. A right fair[41] mark, fair coz, is soonest hit.

Romeo. Well, in that hit you miss. She'll not be hit

200   With Cupid's arrow. She hath Dian's wit,[42]

     And, in strong proof of chastity well armed,

---

[36] coz—cousin. The term is also used loosely to refer to any family member.

[37] transgression—act of going beyond limits or bounds.

[38] propagate . . . thine—increase by adding your own sorrow on my account.

[39] Soft—Wait.

[40] in sadness—seriously.

[41] fair . . . fair—beautiful . . . clear; a play on words.

[42] Dian's wit—wisdom of Diana, Roman goddess of chastity and the moon.

From love's weak childish bow she lives unharmed.[43]
She will not stay the siege of loving terms,[44]
Nor bide th' encounter of assailing eyes,

205 Nor ope her lap to saint-seducing gold.
O, she is rich in beauty, only poor
That when she dies, with beauty dies her store.[45]

Benvolio. Then she hath sworn that she will still live chaste?

Romeo. She hath, and in that sparing makes huge waste,

210 For beauty, starved with her severity
Cuts beauty off from all **posterity**.[46]
She is too fair, too wise, wisely too fair,
To merit bliss by making me despair.
She hath forsworn[47] to love, and in that vow

215 Do I live dead, that live to tell it now.

Benvolio. Be ruled by me. Forget to think of her.

Romeo. O, teach me how I should forget to think!

Benvolio. By giving liberty unto thine eyes:
Examine other beauties.

Romeo.   'Tis the way

220 To call hers, exquisite, in question more.
These happy masks that kiss fair ladies' brows,
Being black, puts us in mind they hide the fair.[48]
He that is strucken blind cannot forget
The precious treasure of his eyesight lost.

225 Show me a mistress that is passing fair:[49]
What doth her beauty serve but as a note
Where I may read who passed that passing fair?
Farewell. Thou canst not teach me to forget.

Benvolio. I'll pay that doctrine,[50] or else die in debt.

[*They exit.*]

---

[43] From . . . unharmed—She is immune to the arrows of Cupid, who makes people fall in love.

[44] stay . . . terms—listen to words of love.

[45] with beauty . . . store—She will die without children, and so her beauty will die with her.

[46] **posterity**—future generations.

[47] forsworn—vowed to give up; also, untrue to one's vows.

[48] These happy . . . fair—The black masks that women sometimes wear in public remind us of the beauty they hide.

[49] mistress that is passing fair—a woman who is exceedingly beautiful.

[50] pay that doctrine—teach Romeo to forget.

Act One, Scene Two

On a street in front of the Capulets' house, Count Paris asks Capulet for Juliet's hand in marriage. Capulet says his daughter ought to wait a couple of years but suggests that Paris try to win her heart. Capulet gives his servant a list of people to invite to a party that night.

The servant cannot read, however, and when Benvolio and Romeo pass by, he asks Romeo to read the list for him. Benvolio recognizes one of the names as Romeo's beloved and suggests that they attend the party.

Enter Capulet, Count Paris, *and a* Servingman.

Capulet. But Montague is bound as well as I,
In penalty alike, and 'tis not hard, I think,
For men so old as we to keep the peace.
Paris. Of honorable reckoning[1] are you both,
5   And pity 'tis you lived at odds so long.
But now, my lord, what say you to my suit?[2]
Capulet. But saying o'er what I have said before:
My child is yet a stranger in the world;
She hath not seen the change of fourteen years.
10   Let two more summers wither in their pride
Ere we may think her ripe to be a bride.
Paris. Younger than she are happy mothers made.
Capulet. And too soon marred are those so early made.
The earth hath swallowed all my hopes but she;
15   She is the hopeful lady of my earth.[3]
But woo her, gentle Paris, get her heart;
My will to her consent is but a part;[4]
And, she agreed, within her scope of choice
Lies my consent and fair-according voice.
20   This night I hold an old accustomed feast,
Whereto I have invited many a guest

---

[1] reckoning—reputation.
[2] suit—request (for Juliet's hand in marriage).
[3] hopeful . . . earth—my heir and hope for future generations.
[4] My will . . . part—My wishes are not as important as her agreement.

One fire burns out another's burning
One pain is lessened by another's anguish.

Such as I love; and you among the store,
One more, most welcome, makes my number more.
At my poor house look to behold this night
25   Earth-treading stars that make dark heaven light.
Such comfort as do lusty young men feel
When well-appareled April on the heel
Of limping winter treads, even such delight
Among fresh fennel buds shall you this night
30   Inherit[5] at my house. Hear all, all see,
And like her most whose merit most shall be;
Which on more view of many, mine, being one,
May stand in number, though in reckoning none.[6]
Come, go with me. [*To the* Servingman, *giving him a paper.*] Go, sirrah,[7]
         trudge about
35   Through fair Verona; find those persons out
Whose names are written there, and to them say,
My house and welcome on their pleasure stay.
[*Exit* Capulet *and* Paris.]
Servingman. Find them out whose names are written here! It is written
         that the shoemaker should meddle with his yard and the tailor with
40   his last, the fisher with his pencil, and the painter with his nets.[8] But
         I am sent to find those persons whose names are here writ, and can
         never find what names the writing person hath here writ.[9] I must to
         the learned. In good time!
[*Enter* Benvolio *and* Romeo.]
Benvolio. Tut, man, one fire burns out another's burning
45   One pain is lessened by another's anguish;

---

[5] Inherit—receive.

[6] Which . . . none—My daughter will be one of the number of ladies, but she may not be the one you like best.

[7] sirrah—customary form of address for a servant.

[8] shoemaker . . . nets—The servingman confuses various craftsmen and their tools.

[9] can never . . . writ—can't read these names (because he can't read).

Turn giddy, and be holp by backward turning;[10]
One desperate grief cures with another's languish.
Take thou some new infection to thy eye,
And the rank poison of the old will die.

50 **Romeo.** Your plaintain leaf is excellent for that.
Benvolio. For what, I pray thee?
Romeo.   For your broken shin.
Benvolio. Why, Romeo, art thou mad?
Romeo. Not mad, but bound more than a madman is;
Shut up in prison, kept without my food,
55 Whipped and tormented and—Good e'en, good fellow.
Servingman. God gi'good e'en.[11] I pray, sir, can you read?
Romeo. Ay, mine own fortune in my misery.
Servingman. Perhaps you have learned it without book. But, I pray, can
you read anything you see?
60 **Romeo.** Ay, if I know the letters and the language.
Servingman. Ye say honestly. Rest you merry![12]
[*Going.*]
Romeo. Stay, fellow, I can read. [*He reads the letter.*]
"Signor Martino and his Lady Capulet and daughters,
County Anselme and his beauteous sisters,
65 The lady widow of Vitruvio,
Signor Placentio and his lovely nieces,
Mercutio and his brother Valentine,
Mine Uncle Capulet, his Lady Capulet, and daughters,
My fair niece Rosaline, and Livia,
70 Signor Valentio and his cousin Tybalt,
Lucio and the lively Helena."
A fair assembly. Whither should they come?
Servingman. Up.
Romeo. Whither? To supper?
75 **Servingman.** To our house.
Romeo. Whose house?
Servingman. My master's.

---

[10] Turn giddy . . . turning—become lightheaded, and be helped by turning about. Benvolio is advising Romeo to find a new love to cure the old.

[11] God . . . e'en—God give you a good evening.

[12] Rest you merry—Happiness to you (used as a good-bye).

I will make thee think
thy swan a crow.

Romeo. Indeed, I should have asked thee that before.

Servingman. Now I'll tell you without asking. My master is the great
80 rich Capulet; and if you be not of the house of Montagues, I pray,
come and crush a cup[13] of wine. Rest you merry!

[*Exit* Servingman.]

Benvolio. At this same ancient[14] feast of Capulet's
Sups the fair Rosaline whom thou so loves,
With all the admirèd beauties of Verona.
85 Go thither, and with unattainted[15] eye
Compare her face with some that I shall show,
And I will make thee think thy swan a crow.

Romeo. When the devout religion of mine eye
Maintains such falsehood, then turn tears to fires;
90 And these who, often drowned, could never die,
Transparent heretics, be burnt for liars![16]
One fairer than my love? The all-seeing sun
Ne'er saw her match since first the world begun.

Benvolio. Tut, you saw her fair, none else being by,
95 Herself poised with herself in either eye;
But in that crystal scales let there be weighed
Your lady's love against some other maid
That I will show you shining at this feast,
And she shall scant show well that now seems best.

100 **Romeo.** I'll go along, no such sight to be shown,
But to rejoice in splendor of mine own.

[*They exit.*]

---

[13] crush a cup—have a drink.

[14] ancient—traditional.

[15] unattainted—impartial, unbiased.

[16] When . . . liars—When my eyes tell such lies, then let their tears turn to fire, so that they will be burned like heretics (religious nonbelievers who were sometimes burned at the stake for punishment).

Act One, Scene Three

In a room in the Capulets' house, Lady Capulet asks Juliet how she feels about getting married. Juliet has not thought about it, but she agrees to her mother's suggestion that she look Paris over at the party to see how well she likes him.

Enter Lady Capulet *and* Nurse.

Lady Capulet. Nurse, where's my daughter? Call her forth to me.
Nurse. Now, by my maidenhead at twelve year old,
 I bade her come.—What, lamb! What, ladybird!
 God forbid. Where's this girl? What, Juliet!
[*Enter* Juliet.]
5 **Juliet.** How now? Who calls?
Nurse. Your mother.
Juliet. Madam, I am here. What is your will?
Lady Capulet. This is the matter—Nurse, give leave[1] awhile,
 We must talk in secret—Nurse, come back again.
10 I have remembered me, thou's hear our counsel.[2]
 Thou knowest my daughter's of a pretty age.
Nurse. Faith, I can tell her age unto an hour.
Lady Capulet. She's not fourteen.
Nurse.   I'll lay fourteen of my teeth—
 And yet, to my teen[3] be it spoken, I have but four—
15 She's not fourteen. How long is it now
 To Lammastide?[4]
Lady Capulet.   A fortnight[5] and odd days.
Nurse. Even or odd, of all days in the year,
 Come Lammas Eve at night shall she be fourteen.
 Susan[6] and she—God rest all Christian souls!—

---

[1] give leave—leave us alone.
[2] thou's . . . counsel—You shall hear our discussion.
[3] teen—sorrow.
[4] Lammastide—August 1 is Lammas Day; July 31 is Lammas Eve.
[5] fortnight—two weeks.
[6] Susan—the Nurse's own child, who died in infancy. That is why the Nurse was able to breast-feed the infant Juliet.

20	Were of an age. Well, Susan is with God;
	She was too good for me. But, as I said,
	On Lammas Eve at night shall she be fourteen,
	That shall she. Marry, I remember it well.
	'Tis since the earthquake now eleven years,
25	And she was weaned—I never shall forget it—
	Of all the days of the year, upon that day;
	For I had then laid wormwood to my dug,[7]
	Sitting in the sun under the dovehouse wall.
	My lord and you were then at Mantua—
30	Nay, I do bear a brain![8] But, as I said,
	When it did taste the wormwood on the nipple
	Of my dug and felt it bitter, pretty fool,
	To see it tetchy[9] and fall out wi' th' dug!
	"Shake" quoth the dovehouse.[10] 'Twas no need, I trow[11]
35	To bid me trudge!
	And since that time it is eleven years,
	For then she could stand high-lone; nay, by the rood,[12]
	She could have run and waddled all about.
	For even the day before, she broke her brow,
40	And then my husband—God be with his soul!
	He was a merry man—took up the child.
	"Yea," quoth[13] he, "dost thou fall upon thy face?
	Thou wilt fall backward when thou hast more wit,
	Wilt thou not, Jule?" and, by my holidam,
45	The pretty wretch left crying and said "Ay."
	To see now how a jest shall come about!
	I warrant, an I should live a thousand years,
	I never should forget it. "Wilt thou not, Jule?" quoth he,
	And, pretty fool, it stinted[14] and said "Ay."

---

[7] laid . . . dug—put a bitter-tasting plant on my breast; used to wean a child from breast-feeding.

[8] bear a brain—have a good memory.

[9] tetchy—fretful.

[10] "Shake" . . . dovehouse—The dovehouse shook with the earthquake.

[11] trow—believe.

[12] she could . . . rood—She could stand by herself; I swear by the Holy Cross.

[13] quoth—said.

[14] stinted—stopped (crying).

50 **Lady Capulet.** Enough of this. I pray thee, hold thy peace.

Nurse. Yes, madam. Yet I cannot choose but laugh
To think it should leave crying and say "Ay."
And yet, I warrant, it had upon its brow
A bump as big as a young cock'rel's stone—

55 A perilous knock—and it cried bitterly.
"Yea," quoth my husband, "fall'st upon thy face?
Thou wilt fall backward when thou comest to age,
Wilt thou not, Jule?" It stinted and said "Ay."

Juliet. And stint thou too, I pray thee, Nurse, say I.

60 **Nurse.** Peace, I have done. God mark thee to his grace!
Thou wast the prettiest babe that e'er I nursed.
An I might live to see thee married once,
I have my wish.

Lady Capulet. Marry, that "marry" is the very theme

65 I came to talk of.—Tell me, daughter Juliet,
How stands your disposition to be married?

Juliet. It is an honor that I dream not of.

Nurse. An honor? Were not I thine only nurse,
I would say thou hadst sucked wisdom from thy teat.

70 **Lady Capulet.** Well, think of marriage now. Younger than you
Here in Verona, ladies of esteem,
Are made already mothers. By my count
I was your mother much upon these years[15]
That you are now a maid. Thus, then, in brief:

75 The valiant Paris seeks you for his love.

Nurse. A man, young lady! Lady, such a man
As all the world—why, he's a man of wax.[16]

Lady Capulet. Verona's summer hath not such a flower.

Nurse. Nay, he's a flower, in faith, a very flower.

---

[15] much ... years—at almost your age.

[16] a man of wax—handsome enough to be modeled in wax.

As her nurse (Roberta Maxwell) looks on, Juliet (Calista Flockhart) is questioned by her mother (Mary Layne) about her willingness to marry Paris in this scene from the Hartford Stage production.

80 **Lady Capulet.** What say you? Can you love the gentleman?
This night you shall behold him at our feast.
Read o'er the volume of young Paris' face,
And find delight writ there with beauty's pen;
Examine every married lineament,[17]
85 And see how one another lends content;

---

[17] married lineament—perfectly matched part or feature.

And what obscured in this fair volume lies
Find written in the margent[18] of his eyes.
This precious book of love, this unbound lover,
To beautify him, only lacks a cover.
90 The fish lives in the sea, and 'tis much pride
For fair without the fair within to hide.[19]
That book in many's eyes doth share the glory,
That in gold clasps locks in the golden story;
So shall you share all that he doth possess
95 By having him, making yourself no less.

Nurse. No less? Nay, bigger. Women grow by men.

Lady Capulet. Speak briefly, can you like of Paris' love?

Juliet. I'll look to like, if looking liking move;[20]
But no more deep will I endart[21] mine eye
100 Than your consent gives strength to make it fly.

[*Enter* Servingman.]

Servingman. Madam, the guests are come, supper served up, you
called, my young lady asked for, the Nurse cursed in the pantry,
and everything in extremity. I must hence to wait. I beseech you,
follow straight.[22]

105 **Lady Capulet.** We follow thee. [*Exit* Servingman.] Juliet, the
County stays.[23]

Nurse. Go, girl, seek happy nights to happy days.

[*They exit.*]

---

[18] margent—commentary, as written in a book's margin.

[19] 'tis much . . . hide—It is suitable for the beautiful contents of a book to have a beautiful cover.

[20] I'll look . . . move—I'll look on him favorably, if just looking can inspire liking.

[21] endart—look, as if with love's darts or arrows.

[22] I beseech . . . straight—I beg you, come immediately.

[23] the County stays—Paris waits. Count Paris is frequently referred to as "County."

Act One, Scene Four

On a street in Verona, that same evening, Romeo, Benvolio, and their friend Mercutio put on masks as they prepare to attend Capulet's party. Romeo fears that no good will come of it. Mercutio tells a fantastic tale of the fairy queen, Mab, who brings appropriate dreams to various sleepers.

Enter Romeo, Mercutio, Benvolio, *with five or six other* Maskers *and* Torchbearers.

Romeo. What, shall this speech be spoke for our excuse?
    Or shall we on without apology?[1]
Benvolio. The date is out of such prolixity.[2]
    We'll have no Cupid hoodwinked[3] with a scarf,
5   Bearing a Tartar's painted bow of lath,[4]
    Scaring the ladies like a crowkeeper,[5]
    Nor no without-book prologue, faintly spoke
    After the prompter, for our entrance;
    But let them measure us by what they will,
10   We'll measure them a measure,[6] and be gone.
Romeo. Give me a torch. I am not for this ambling.[7]
    Being but heavy, I will bear the light.
Mercutio. Nay, gentle Romeo, we must have you dance.
Romeo. Not I, believe me. You have dancing shoes
15   With nimble soles; I have a soul of lead
    So stakes me to the ground I cannot move.
Mercutio. You are a lover; borrow Cupid's wings,
    And soar with them above a common bound.[8]

---

[1] What . . . apology—Young men could attend a party without being invited if they wore masks. They were expected to give a short speech, apologizing for coming and complimenting the hosts.

[2] The . . . prolixity—Such wordiness is out-of-date.

[3] hoodwinked—blindfolded.

[4] Tartar's . . . lath—that is, a curving bow such as Cupid was pictured using.

[5] crowkeeper—scarecrow.

[6] measure . . . measure—dance a dance for them.

[7] ambling—light dancing.

[8] bound—boundary or limit. Later, there are puns on "*bound*," "tied up" and "leap."

Romeo. I am too sore enpiercèd with his shaft

20   To soar with his light feathers, and so bound

      I cannot bound a pitch above dull woe.

      Under love's heavy burden do I sink.

Mercutio. And, to sink in it, should you burden love—

      Too great oppression for a tender thing.

25 **Romeo.** Is love a tender thing? It is too rough,

      Too rude, too boist'rous, and it pricks like thorn.

Mercutio. If love be rough with you, be rough with love;

      Prick love for pricking, and you beat love down.—

      Give me a case to put my **visage**[9] in.

[He puts on a mask.]

30   A visor for a visor![10] What care I

      What curious eye doth quote deformities?

      Here are the beetle brows shall blush for me.

Benvolio. Come, knock and enter, and no sooner in

      But every man betake him to his legs.[11]

35 **Romeo.** A torch for me. Let wantons light of heart

      Tickle the senseless rushes with their heels,[12]

      For I am proverbed with a grandsire phrase:[13]

      I'll be a candle holder and look on.

      The game was ne'er so fair, and I am done.

40 **Mercutio.** Tut, dun's the mouse,[14] the constable's own word.

      If thou art dun, we'll draw thee from the mire

      Of—save your reverence—love, wherein thou stickest

      Up to the ears. Come, we burn daylight,[15] ho!

Romeo. Nay, that's not so.

Mercutio.   I mean, sir, in delay

45   We waste our lights in vain, like lamps by day.

      Take our good meaning, for our judgment sits

      Five times in that ere once in our five wits.[16]

---

[9] **visage**—face; appearance.

[10] visor . . . visor—a mask for an ugly, masklike face.

[11] betake . . . legs—start dancing.

[12] Let . . . heels—Let lighthearted people dance on the plant fibers (used as floor coverings).

[13] proverbed . . . phrase—informed by an old saying ("A good candle-holder—that is, onlooker—is the best gambler.).

[14] dun's the mouse—keep quiet.

[15] we burn daylight—waste time.

[16] Take . . . wits—Understand what I mean, relying on common sense rather than the five senses.

Romeo. And we mean well in going to this masque,
But 'tis no wit to go.

Mercutio. Why, may one ask?

50 **Romeo.** I dreamt a dream tonight.

Mercutio. And so did I.

Romeo. Well, what was yours?

Mercutio. That dreamers often lie.

Romeo. In bed asleep, while they do dream things true.

Mercutio. O, then, I see Queen Mab[17] hath been with you.
She is the fairies' midwife, and she comes
55 In shape no bigger than an agate stone
On the forefinger of an alderman,
Drawn with a team of little atomi[18]
Over men's noses as they lie asleep.
Her chariot is an empty hazelnut,
60 Made by the joiner[19] squirrel or old grub,
Time out o' mind the fairies' coachmakers.
Her wagon spokes made of long spinners'[20] legs,
The cover of the wings of grasshoppers,
Her traces of the smallest spider web,
65 Her collars of the moonshine's watery beams,
Her whip of cricket's bone, the lash of film,
Her wagoner[21] a small gray-coated gnat,
Not half so big as a round little worm
Pricked from the lazy finger of a maid.[22]
70 And in this state she gallops night by night
Through lovers' brains, and then they dream of love;
O'er courtiers' knees, that dream on curtsies straight;
O'er lawyers' fingers, who straight dream on fees;
O'er ladies' lips, who straight on kisses dream,

---

[17] Queen Mab—the fairy queen.

[18] atomi—tiny creatures.

[19] joiner—furniture maker.

[20] spinners'—spiders'.

[21] wagoner—coachman.

[22] worm . . . maid—reference to the ancient superstition that worms breed in the fingers of the idle.

75   Which oft the angry Mab with blisters **plagues**[23]
      Because their breaths with sweetmeats tainted are.
      Sometimes she gallops o'er a courtier's nose,
      And then dreams he of smelling out a suit.[24]
      And sometimes comes she with a tithe-pig's[25] tail
80   Tickling a parson's nose as he lies asleep;
      Then dreams he of another benefice.[26]
      Sometimes she driveth o'er a soldier's neck,
      And then dreams he of cutting foreign throats,
      Of breaches, ambuscadoes,[27] Spanish blades,
85   Of healths five fathom deep, and then anon[28]
      Drums in his ear, at which he starts and wakes,
      And, being thus frighted, swears a prayer or two
      And sleeps again. This is that very Mab
      That plats the manes of horses in the night,
90   And bakes the elflocks[29] in foul sluttish hairs,
      Which once untangled much misfortune bodes.
      This is the hag, when maids lie on their backs,
      That presses them and learns them first to bear,
      Making them women of good carriage.
95   This is she—
Romeo.   Peace, peace, Mercutio, peace!
      Thou talk'st of nothing.
Mercutio.   True, I talk of dreams,
      Which are the children of an idle brain,
      Begot of nothing but vain fantasy,

---

[23] **plagues**—bothers, annoys.

[24] smelling . . . suit—seeing an opportunity for royal favor.

[25] tithe-pig's—of a pig given to the Church instead of money.

[26] benefice—well-paying position for a clergyman.

[27] ambuscadoes—ambushes.

[28] anon—soon; right away.

[29] elflocks—tangles.

Which is as thin of substance as the air,
100 And more inconstant than the wind, who woos
Even now the frozen bosom of the north,
And being angered, puffs away from thence,
Turning his side to the dew-dropping south.

Benvolio. This wind you talk of blows us from ourselves.
105 Supper is done, and we shall come too late.

Romeo. I fear, too early; for my mind misgives
Some consequence yet hanging in the stars[30]
Shall bitterly begin his fearful date
With this night's revels, and expire the term
110 Of a despisèd life closed in my breast
By some vile forfeit of untimely death.[31]
But He that hath the steerage of my course
Direct my suit! On, lusty gentlemen.

Benvolio. Strike, drum.

[*They exit.*]

---

[30] misgives . . . stars—fears some misfortune yet to come.
[31] expire . . . death—bring my unhappy life to an early end.

Act One, Scene Five

In the Capulets' ballroom, servants hurry to clear the tables after dinner. Capulet welcomes his guests and, as others dance, reminisces with a kinsman about their old dancing days. Romeo, seeing Juliet dance, is struck by her beauty. Tybalt recognizes Romeo's voice and vows to kill the intruder, but Capulet orders him to leave Romeo alone, so as not to disturb the guests. Romeo and Juliet meet, flirt, and kiss. Leaving, Romeo finds out who Juliet is, and Juliet finds out who Romeo is. They both realize they are in love with an enemy.*

Servingmen *enter with napkins.*

First Servingman. Where's Potpan, that he helps not to take away?
    He shift a trencher?[1] He scrape a trencher?

Second Servingman. When good manners shall lie all in one or two
    men's hands, and they unwashed too, 'tis a foul thing.

5 **First Servingman.** Away with the joint stools, remove the court
    cupboard, look to the plate.[2]—Good thou, save me a piece of
    marchpane,[3] and, as thou loves me, let the porter let in Susan
    Grindstone and Nell. [*Exit* Second Servingman.] Anthony
    and Potpan!

[*Enter* Anthony *and* Potpan.]

10 **Anthony.** Ay, boy, ready.

First Servingman. You are looked for and called for,
    asked for and sought for, in the great chamber.

Potpan. We cannot be here and there
    too. Cheerly, boys! Be brisk awhile, and the longest
15   liver take all.[4]

[*Exit all* Servingmen.]

[*Enter* Capulet, Lady Capulet, Juliet, *all the* Guests, *the* Servants *and the* Maskers.]

---

[1] trencher—wooden dish.

[2] plate—silverware.

[3] marchpane—marzipan, a cake made from sugar and almonds.

[4] the longest . . . all—survivor takes all.

Capulet [*to the* Maskers]. Welcome, gentlemen! Ladies that have their toes
Unplagued with corns will walk a bout with you.
Ah, my mistresses, which of you all
Will now deny to dance? She that makes dainty,[5]
20   She, I'll swear, hath corns. Am I come near you now?
Welcome, gentlemen! I have seen the day
That I have worn a visor and could tell
A whispering tale in a fair lady's ear
Such as would please. 'Tis gone , 'tis gone, 'tis gone.
25   You are welcome, gentlemen! Come, musicians, play.
[*Music plays, and they dance.*]
A hall,[6] a hall! Give room! And foot it,[7] girls.
[*To* Servingmen.] More light, you knaves, and turn the tables up,[8]
And quench the fire; the room is grown too hot.
[*To his* cousin.] Ah, sirrah, this unlooked-for sport comes well.
30   Nay, sit, nay, sit, good cousin Capulet,
For you and I are past our dancing days.
How long is 't now since last yourself and I
Were in a mask?

Second Capulet.   By'r Lady,[9] thirty years.

Capulet. What, man? 'Tis not so much, 'tis not so much;
35   'Tis since the nuptial[10] of Lucentio,
Come Pentecost[11] as quickly as it will,
Some five-and-twenty years, and then we masked.

Second Capulet. 'Tis more, 'tis more. His son is elder, sir;
His son is thirty.

Capulet.   Will you tell me that?
40   His son was but a ward two years ago.

---

[5] makes dainty—teasingly refuses to dance.

[6] A hall—Make room.

[7] foot it—dance.

[8] turn . . . up—The tables were flat leaves laid on trestles; when folded up, they took little space.

[9] By'r Lady—by the Virgin Mary (a mild oath).

[10] nuptial—marriage.

[11] Pentecost—five weeks after Easter.

O, she doth teach the torches to burn bright!

Romeo [*to a* Servingman]. What lady's that which doth enrich the hand
 Of yonder knight?

Servingman. I know not, sir.

Romeo. O, she doth teach the torches to burn bright!

45 It seems she hangs upon the cheek of night
 As a rich jewel in an Ethiop's[12] ear
 Beauty too rich for use, for earth too dear!
 So shows a snowy dove trooping with crows
 As yonder lady o'er her fellows shows.

50 The measure done, I'll watch her place of stand,
 And, touching hers, make blessèd my rude hand.
 Did my heart love till now? Forswear it, sight!
 For I ne'er saw true beauty till this night.

Tybalt. This, by his voice, should be a Montague.—

55 Fetch me my rapier, boy. [*Exit* Page.] What dares the slave
 Come hither, covered with an antic[13] face,
 To fleer[14] and scorn at our solemnity?
 Now, by the stock and honor of my kin,
 To strike him dead I hold it not a sin.

60 **Capulet.** Why, how now, kinsman? Wherefore storm you so?

Tybalt. Uncle, this is a Montague, our foe,
 A villain that is hither come in spite
 To scorn at our solemnity this night.

Capulet. Young Romeo is it?

Tybalt.   'Tis he, that villain Romeo.

65 **Capulet.** Content thee, gentle coz, let him alone.
 He bears him like a portly[15] gentleman,

---

[12] Ethiop's—African's.

[13] antic—odd; fantastic (referring to Romeo's mask).

[14] fleer—sneer.

[15] portly—dignified.

And, to say truth, Verona brags of him
To be a virtuous and well-governed youth.
I would not for the wealth of all this town

70 Here in my house do him **disparagement.**[16]
Therefore be patient; take no note of him.
It is my will, the which if thou respect,
Show a fair presence and put off these frowns,
An ill-beseeming semblance[17] for a feast.

75 **Tybalt.** It fits when such a villain is a guest.
I'll not endure him.

Capulet.   He shall be endured.
What, goodman boy? I say he shall. Go to![18]
Am I the master here, or you? Go to.
You'll not endure him! God shall mend my soul,

80 You'll make a mutiny among my guests!
You will set cock-a-hoop![19] You'll be the man!

Tybalt. Why, uncle, 'tis a shame.

Capulet.   Go to, go to,
You are a saucy[20] boy. Is 't so, indeed?
This trick may chance to scathe you, I know what.[21]

85 You must contrary me.[22] Marry, 'tis time.—
Well said, my hearts!—You are a princox,[23] go.
Be quiet, or—More light, more light!—For shame!
I'll make you quiet.—What, cheerly, my hearts!

Tybalt. Patience perforce with willful choler meeting

90 Makes my flesh tremble in their different greeting.[24]
I will withdraw. But this intrusion shall,
Now seeming sweet, convert to bitterest gall.[25]

[*Exit* Tybalt.]

---

[16] **disparagement**—insult.

[17] ill-beseeming semblance—unsuitable appearance.

[18] Go to—Come on, now!

[19] You . . . cock-a-hoop—You will cause an uproar.

[20] saucy—rude, insolent.

[21] This trick . . . what—This misbehavior might injure you; I know what I'm doing.

[22] You must . . . me—You insist on opposing me.

[23] princox—rude youngster.

[24] Patience . . . greeting—Forced patience combined with my great anger makes me tremble.

[25] gall—hatred, ill feeling.

Romeo kneels before Juliet at the ball in this scene from the 1997 production of *Romeo and Juliet* by Boston's Commonwealth Shakespeare Company.

Romeo [*to* Juliet]. If I profane with my unworthiest hand
    This holy shrine, the gentle sin is this:
95   My lips, two blushing pilgrims, ready stand
    To smooth that rough touch with a tender kiss.
Juliet. Good pilgrim, you do wrong your hand too much,
    Which mannerly devotion shows in this;
    For saints have hands that pilgrims' hands do touch,
100   And palm to palm is holy palmers'[26] kiss.

---

[26] **palmers'**—of pilgrims who brought palm leaves back from the Holy Land; puns on *palm*, "hand," and *palmer*, "pilgrim."

Romeo. Have not saints lips, and holy palmers too?

Juliet. Ay, pilgrim, lips that they must use in prayer.

Romeo. O, then, dear saint, let lips do what hands do.

    They pray; grant thou, lest faith turn to despair.

105 **Juliet.** Saints do not move, though grant for prayers' sake.

Romeo. Then move not, while my prayer's effect I take.

[*He kisses her.*]

    Thus from my lips, by thine, my sin is purged.

Juliet. Then have my lips the sin that they have took.

Romeo. Sin from my lips? O trespass sweetly urged!

110   Give me my sin again.

[*He kisses her.*]

Juliet.   You kiss by th' book.[27]

Nurse [*approaching*]. Madam, your mother craves a word with you.

[Juliet *moves toward her mother.*]

Romeo. What is her mother?

Nurse.   Marry, bachelor,

    Her mother is the lady of the house,

    And a good lady, and a wise and virtuous.

115   I nursed her daughter that you talked withal.

    I tell you, he that can lay hold of her

    Shall have the chinks.[28]

Romeo [*aside*]. Is she a Capulet?

    O dear account! My life is my foe's debt.[29]

120 **Benvolio** [*approaching*]. Away, begone! The sport is at the best.

Romeo. Ay, so I fear; the more is my unrest.

[Romeo *and his friends prepare to leave.*]

Capulet. Nay, gentlemen, prepare not to be gone.

    We have a trifling foolish banquet towards.[30]

[*One whispers in his ear.*]

    Is it e'en so? Why, then, I thank you all.

125   I thank you, honest gentlemen. Good night.—

    More torches here!—Come on then, let's to bed.—

---

[27] by th' book—expertly.

[28] chinks—money (inherited by Juliet from her father).

[29] O dear . . . debt—What a costly situation. My life is at my enemy's mercy.

[30] foolish banquet towards—light refreshments ready.

My only love sprung from
my only hate!

[*To his* cousin.] Ah, sirrah, by my fay,[31] it waxes late.
    I'll to my rest.
[*All begin to leave but* Juliet *and the* Nurse.]
Juliet. Come hither, Nurse. What is yond gentleman?

130 **Nurse.** The son and heir of old Tiberio.

Juliet. What's he that now is going out of door?

Nurse. Marry, that, I think, be young Petruchio.

Juliet. What's he that follows here, that would not dance?

Nurse. I know not.

135 **Juliet.** Go ask his name. [*The* Nurse *goes.*] If he be marrièd,
    My grave is like to be my wedding bed.

Nurse [*returning*]. His name is Romeo, and a Montague,
    The only son of your great enemy.

Juliet. My only love sprung from my only hate!

140   Too early seen unknown, and known too late![32]
    Prodigious birth of love it is to me
    That I must love a loathèd enemy.

Nurse. What's this? What's this?

Juliet.   A rhyme I learned even now
    Of one I danced withal.

145 [*One calls within*[33] *"Juliet."*]

Nurse. Anon, anon!
    Come, let's away. The strangers all are gone.
[*They exit.*]

---

[31] fay—faith.

[32] Too early ... late—I saw him too early, when I didn't know him, and I know him now, but it's too late.

[33] within—offstage.

Act Two, Prologue

The Chorus explains that Romeo has forgotten Rosaline and now loves Juliet.

Enter Chorus.

Chorus.
Now old desire doth in his deathbed lie,
And young affection gapes[1] to be his heir;
That fair[2] for which love groaned for and would die,
With tender Juliet matched, is now not fair.
5   Now Romeo is beloved and loves again,
Alike[3] bewitchèd by the charm of looks;
But to his foe supposed he must complain,[4]
And she steal love's sweet bait from fearful hooks.
Being held a foe, he may not have access
10   To breathe such vows as lovers use to swear;
And she as much in love, her means much less
To meet her new-belovèd anywhere.
But passion lends them power, time means, to meet,
Temp'ring extremities[5] with extreme sweet.
[*Exit* Chorus.]

---

[1] gapes—waits eagerly.

[2] fair—beauty; that is, Rosaline.

[3] Alike—Both lovers equally.

[4] complain—declare his love.

[5] Temp'ring extremities—moderating hardships.

Act Two, Scene One

Outside the Capulets' orchard wall, Benvolio and Mercutio search for Romeo. Benvolio has seen Romeo climb over the garden wall, and Mercutio jokingly attempts to make Romeo appear by magic. Giving up, Benvolio and Mercutio go home.

Enter Romeo *alone.*

Romeo. Can I go forward when my heart is here?
  Turn back, dull earth,[1] and find thy center out.
[Romeo *hides.*]
[*Enter* Benvolio *with* Mercutio.]
Benvolio. Romeo! My cousin Romeo! Romeo!
Mercutio.   He is wise
  And, on my life, hath stol'n him home to bed.

5 **Benvolio.** He ran this way and leapt this orchard wall.
  Call, good Mercutio.
Mercutio.   Nay, I'll **conjure**[2] too.
  Romeo! Humors![3] Madman! Passion! Lover!
  Appear thou in the likeness of a sigh.
  Speak but one rhyme, and I am satisfied.
10 Cry but "Ay me!" Pronounce but "love" and "dove."
  Speak to my gossip Venus[4] one fair word,
  One nickname for her purblind son and heir,
  Young Abraham[5] Cupid, he that shot so trim
  When King Cophetua[6] loved the beggar maid.—
15 He heareth not, he stirreth not, he moveth not;
  The ape is dead,[7] and I must conjure him.—

---

[1] dull earth—Romeo himself.

[2] **conjure**—call up a spirit by magic.

[3] Humors—romantic moods.

[4] gossip Venus—intimate friend, the goddess of love.

[5] Abraham—beggarly, thieving (alluding to the so-called "Abraham man," a beggar who wandered through the countryside half-naked, picking up what he could).

[6] King Cophetua—In an old ballad, he falls in love with a beggar maid and makes her his queen.

[7] The ape is dead—The trained monkey is playing dead.

I conjure thee by Rosaline's bright eyes,
By her high forehead and her scarlet lip,
By her fine foot, straight leg, and quivering thigh,
20   And the demesnes[8] that there **adjacent**[9] lie,
That in thy likeness thou appear to us.
Benvolio. An if he hear thee, thou wilt anger him.
Mercutio. This cannot anger him. 'Twould anger him
To raise a spirit in his mistress' circle[10]
25   Of some strange nature, letting it there stand
Till she had laid it and conjured it down;
That were some spite.[11] My invocation
Is fair and honest; in his mistress' name
I conjure only but to raise up him.
30   **Benvolio.** Come, he hath hid himself among these trees
To be consorted with the humorous night.[12]
Blind is his love, and best befits the dark.
Mercutio. If love be blind, love cannot hit the mark.
Now will he sit under a medlar tree
35   And wish his mistress were that kind of fruit
As maids call medlars when they laugh alone.
O, Romeo, that she were, O, that she were
An open-arse, and thou a poppering pear!
Romeo, good night. I'll to my truckle bed;[13]
40   This field bed is too cold for me to sleep.
Come, shall we go?
Benvolio.   Go, then, for 'tis in vain
To seek him here that means not to be found.
[*Exit* Benvolio *with* Mercutio.]

---

[8] demesnes—regions.
[9] **adjacent**—near, close by.
[10] circle—conjuring circle; witches' coven.
[11] spite—injury.
[12] consorted . . . night—associated with the damp night; puns on *humorous* "moody."
[13] truckle bed—bed on wheels to be rolled under a larger bed.

Act Two, Scene Two

In the Capulets' orchard, Romeo sees a light at Juliet's window. When she appears, he praises her beauty. Juliet wonders to herself why her lover has to be an enemy. Romeo reveals himself, and though Juliet warns him of the danger he is in, they speak words of love to each other. Ignoring her Nurse's calls, Juliet tells Romeo that she will send a messenger the next day to learn what arrangements he has made for their marriage.

Romeo *is hiding from* Mercutio *and* Benvolio.

Romeo [*coming forward*]. He jests at scars that never felt a wound.[1]
[*A light appears above, at Juliet's window.*]

But soft, what light through yonder window breaks?
It is the East, and Juliet is the sun.
Arise, fair sun, and kill the envious moon,
5 Who is already sick and pale with grief
That thou, her maid, art far more fair than she.
Be not her maid, since she is envious;
Her vestal livery is but sick and green[2]
And none but fools do wear it. Cast it off.

[*Juliet is visible at her window.*]

10 It is my lady. O, it is my love.
O, that she knew she were!
She speaks, yet she says nothing. What of that?
Her eye discourses. I will answer it.
I am too bold. 'Tis not to me she speaks.
15 Two of the fairest stars in all the heaven,
Having some business, do **entreat**[3] her eyes
To twinkle in their spheres[4] till they return.
What if her eyes were there, they in her head?
The brightness of her cheek would shame those stars

---

[1] He jests . . . wound—He (Mercutio) laughs at love because he has never felt it.

[2] vestal livery . . . green—dress of the priestesses of the moon goddess. Possibly it is referring to "green sickness," anemia thought to affect girls in puberty.

[3] **entreat**—beg.

[4] spheres—orbits in which the planets and stars were believed to travel.

What's in a name? That which we call a rose
By any other word would smell as sweet.

20 As daylight doth a lamp; her eyes in heaven
Would through the airy region stream so bright
That birds would sing and think it were not night.
See how she leans her cheek upon her hand!
O, that I were a glove upon that hand,
25 That I might touch that cheek!

Juliet. Ay me!

Romeo [*aside*]. She speaks.
O, speak again, bright angel, for thou art
As glorious to this night, being o'er my head,
As is a wingèd messenger of heaven
Unto the white-upturnèd wond'ring eyes
30 Of mortals that fall back to gaze on him
When he bestrides the lazy puffing clouds
And sails upon the bosom of the air.

Juliet [*to herself*]. O Romeo, Romeo, wherefore art thou Romeo?[5]
Deny thy father and refuse thy name!
35 Or, if thou wilt not, be but sworn my love,
And I'll no longer be a Capulet.

Romeo [*aside*]. Shall I hear more, or shall I speak at this?

Juliet. 'Tis but thy name that is my enemy;
Thou art thyself, though not a Montague.[6]
40 What's Montague? It is nor hand, nor foot,
Nor arm, nor face, nor any other part
Belonging to a man. O, be some other name!
What's in a name? That which we call a rose
By any other word would smell as sweet;
45 So Romeo would, were he not Romeo called,
Retain that dear perfection which he owes
Without that title. Romeo, doff[7] thy name,

---

[5] wherefore ... Romeo—Why are you named Romeo?
[6] though ... Montague—even if you were not a Montague.
[7] doff—take off, discard.

And for thy name, which is no part of thee,
Take all myself.

Romeo.   I take thee at thy word!
50   Call me but love, and I'll be new baptized.
Henceforth I never will be Romeo.

Juliet. What man art thou that, thus bescreened in night,
So stumblest on my counsel?

Romeo.   By a name
I know not how to tell thee who I am.
55   My name, dear saint, is hateful to myself,
Because it is an enemy to thee;
Had I it written, I would tear the word.

Juliet. My ears have yet not drunk a hundred words
Of thy tongue's uttering, yet I know the sound:
60   Art thou not Romeo and a Montague?

Romeo. Neither, fair maid, if either thee dislike.

Juliet. How camest thou hither, tell me, and wherefore?
The orchard walls are high and hard to climb,
And the place death, considering who thou art,
65   If any of my kinsmen find thee here.

Romeo. With love's light wings did I o'erperch[8] these walls,
For stony limits cannot hold love out,
And what love can do, that dares love attempt;
Therefore thy kinsmen are no stop to me.

70   **Juliet.** If they do see thee, they will murder thee.

Romeo. Alack, there lies more peril in thine eye
Than twenty of their swords. Look thou but sweet,
And I am proof against their enmity.[9]

Juliet. I would not for the world they saw thee here.

75   **Romeo.** I have night's cloak to hide me from their eyes;
And but[10] thou love me, let them find me here.
My life were better ended by their hate
Than death proroguèd wanting of thy love.[11]

Juliet. By whose direction found'st thou out this place?

---

[8] o'erperch—fly over.

[9] proof . . . enmity—protected from their hatred.

[10] And but—If only.

[11] proroguèd . . . love—put off if I don't have your love.

80   **Romeo.** By love, that first did prompt me to inquire.
He lent me counsel, and I lent him eyes.
I am no pilot; yet, wert thou as far
As that vast shore washed with the farthest sea,
I should adventure for such merchandise.

85   **Juliet.** Thou knowest the mask of night is on my face,
Else would a maiden blush bepaint my cheek
For that which thou hast heard me speak tonight.
Fain would I dwell on form—fain, fain deny
What I have spoke. But farewell compliment!¹²

90   Dost thou love me? I know thou wilt say "Ay,"
And I will take thy word. Yet if thou swear'st
Thou mayst prove false. At lovers' perjuries,¹³
They say, Jove¹⁴ laughs. O gentle Romeo,
If thou dost love, pronounce it faithfully.

95   Or, if thou thinkest I am too quickly won,
I'll frown and be perverse¹⁵ and say thee nay,
So thou wilt woo, but else not for the world.
In truth, fair Montague, I am too fond,
And therefore thou mayst think my havior light.¹⁶

100   But trust me, gentleman, I'll prove more true
Than those that have more cunning to be strange.¹⁷
I should have been more strange, I must confess,
But that thou overheard'st, ere I was ware,
My true-love passion. Therefore pardon me,

105   And not **impute**¹⁸ this yielding to light love,
Which the dark night hath so discovered.

---

¹² Fain . . . compliment—I would gladly follow custom and deny what you heard me say. But forget tradition.

¹³ perjuries—lies under oath.

¹⁴ Jove—Jupiter, ruler of the Roman gods.

¹⁵ perverse—stubbornly contrary.

¹⁶ my havior light—my behavior is not modest.

¹⁷ cunning . . . strange—skill at being reserved.

¹⁸ **impute**—attribute.

Romeo. Lady, by yonder blessed moon I vow,
That tips with silver all these fruit-tree tops—
Juliet. O, swear not by the moon, th' inconstant moon,
110   That monthly changes in her circled orb,
Lest that thy love prove likewise variable.
Romeo. What shall I swear by?
Juliet.   Do not swear at all;
Or, if thou wilt, swear by thy gracious self,
Which is the god of my idolatry,
115   And I'll believe thee.

In the balcony scene from the Yale School of Drama production, Romeo (Nathan Hinton) swears his love as Juliet (Sanaa Lathan) listens from above.

My bounty is as boundless as the sea, My love as deep.

Romeo.   If my heart's dear love—

Juliet. Well, do not swear. Although I joy in thee,
I have no joy of this contract[19] tonight.
It is too rash, too unadvised, too sudden,
Too like the lightning, which doth cease to be
120   Ere one can say "It" lightens. Sweet, good night!
This bud of love, by summer's ripening breath,
May prove a beauteous flower when next we meet.
Good night, good night! As sweet repose and rest
Come to thy heart as that within my breast!

125   **Romeo.** O, wilt thou leave me so unsatisfied?

Juliet. What satisfaction canst thou have tonight?

Romeo. Th' exchange of thy love's faithful vow for mine.

Juliet. I gave thee mine before thou didst request it;
And yet I would it were to give again.

130   **Romeo.** Wouldst thou withdraw it? For what purpose, love?

Juliet. But to be frank[20] and give it thee again.
And yet I wish but for the thing I have.
My bounty is as boundless as the sea,
My love as deep. The more I give to thee,
135   The more I have, for both are infinite.

[Nurse *calls from within.*]

I hear some noise within. Dear love, adieu![21]—
Anon, good Nurse!—Sweet Montague, be true.
Stay but a little; I will come again.

[*Exit* Juliet, *above.*]

Romeo. O blessèd, blessèd night! I am afeard,
140   Being in night, all this is but a dream,
Too flattering-sweet to be substantial.

---

[19] contract—exchange of vows.

[20] frank—generous.

[21] adieu—French for "good-bye."

Romeo (Keir O'Donnell) and Juliet (Hannah Mellow) clasp hands in a scene from a 2000 production of *Romeo and Juliet* at the Hartt School at the University of Hartford.

[*Enter* Juliet *above.*]

Juliet. Three words, dear Romeo, and good night indeed.
  If that thy bent[22] of love be honorable,
  Thy purpose marriage, send me word tomorrow,
145   By one that I'll procure[23] to come to thee,
  Where and what time thou wilt perform the rite,
  And all my fortunes at thy foot I'll lay
  And follow thee my lord throughout the world.

---

[22] bent—purpose, intention.

[23] procure—arrange.

Nurse [*within*]. Madam!

150 **Juliet.** I come, anon.—But if thou meanest not well,
　　I do beseech thee—

Nurse [*within*].　　　Madam!

Juliet.　　　　　　By and by, I come—
　　To cease thy strife and leave me to my grief.
　　Tomorrow will I send.

Romeo.　　　　　　So thrive my soul—

Juliet. A thousand times good night!

[*Exit* Juliet *above.*]

155 **Romeo.** A thousand times the worse, to want thy light.
　　Love goes toward love as schoolboys from their books,
　　But love from love, toward school with heavy looks.

[*He starts to leave.*]

[*Enter* Juliet *above again.*]

Juliet. Hist! Romeo, hist! O, for a falconer's voice,
　　To lure this tassel-gentle[24] back again!

160　Bondage is hoarse and may not speak aloud,[25]
　　Else would I tear the cave where Echo[26] lies
　　And make her airy tongue more hoarse than mine
　　With repetition of "My Romeo!"

Romeo. It is my soul that calls upon my name.

165　How silver-sweet sound lovers' tongues by night,
　　Like softest music to attending ears!

Juliet. Romeo!

Romeo.　　My nyas?[27]

Juliet.　What o'clock tomorrow
　　Shall I send to thee?

Romeo.　　　　　By the hour of nine.

Juliet. I will not fail. 'Tis twenty years till then.—

170　I have forgot why I did call thee back.

Romeo. Let me stand here till thou remember it.

---

[24] tassel-gentle—male hawk, used by falconers for hunting.

[25] Bondage . . . aloud—I am watched and can only speak softly.

[26] Echo—a nymph who wasted away for love until only her voice was left.

[27] nyas—fledgling; young bird.

Parting is such sweet sorrow
That I shall say "good night" till it be morrow.

Juliet. I shall forget, to have thee still stand there,
    Remembering how I love thy company.
Romeo. And I'll still stay, to have thee still forget,
175   Forgetting any other home but this.
Juliet. 'Tis almost morning. I would have thee gone—
    And yet no farther than a wanton's[28] bird,
    That lets it hop a little from his hand,
    Like a poor prisoner in his twisted gyves,[29]
180   And with a silken thread plucks it back again,
    So loving-jealous of his liberty.
Romeo. I would I were thy bird.
Juliet.   Sweet, so would I.
    Yet I should kill thee with much cherishing.
    Good night, good night! Parting is such sweet sorrow
185   That I shall say "good night" till it be morrow.
[*Exit* Juliet *above.*]
Romeo. Sleep dwell upon thine eyes, peace in thy breast!
    Would I were sleep and peace, so sweet to rest!
    Hence will I to my ghostly[30] friar's close cell,
    His help to crave, and my dear hap[31] to tell.
[*Exit* Romeo]

---

[28] wanton's—spoiled child's.
[29] gyves—shackles, bonds for holding a prisoner.
[30] ghostly—spiritual.
[31] dear hap—good fortune.

Act Two, Scene Three

In Friar Laurence's monastery garden, at dawn the next morning, he gathers herbs and flowers. Romeo asks the Friar to marry him and Juliet. Friar Laurence wonders that

Romeo has forgotten Rosaline so quickly, but he agrees, thinking that a marriage might end the hatred between the Montagues and Capulets.

Enter Friar Laurence *alone, with a basket.*

Friar Laurence. The gray-eyed morn smiles on the frowning night,
Check'ring the eastern clouds with streaks of light,
And fleckled[1] darkness like a drunkard reels
From forth day's path and Titan's fiery wheels.[2]

5   Now, ere the sun advance his burning eye,
The day to cheer and night's dank dew to dry,
I must up-fill this osier cage[3] of ours
With **baleful**[4] weeds and precious-juicèd flowers.
The earth that's nature's mother is her tomb;

10   What is her burying grave, that is her womb;
And from her womb children of divers[5] kind
We sucking on her natural bosom find,
Many for many virtues excellent,
None but for some,[6] and yet all different.

15   O, mickle[7] is the powerful grace that lies
In plants, herbs, stones, and their true qualities.
For naught so vile that on the earth doth live
But to the earth some special good doth give;
Nor aught so good but, strained from that fair use,

20   Revolts from true birth,[8] stumbling on abuse.

---

[1] fleckled—dappled, spotted.

[2] Titan's . . . wheels—The sun god was thought to drive the chariot of the sun across the sky.

[3] osier cage—basket made of willow twigs.

[4] **baleful**—harmful, poisonous.

[5] divers—various.

[6] None . . . some—Every plant is good for something or other.

[7] mickle—much.

[8] Revolts . . . birth—reveals its own special purpose.

Virtue itself turns vice, being misapplied,
And vice sometime's by action dignified.

[*Enter* Romeo.]

Within the infant rind of this weak flower
Poison hath residence and medicine power:

25 For this, being smelt, with that part cheers each part;
Being tasted, stays all senses with the heart.[9]
Two such opposèd kings encamp them still
In man as well as herbs—grace and rude will;
And where the worser is predominant,

30 Full soon the canker[10] death eats up that plant.

Romeo. Good morrow, Father.

Friar Laurence.   Benedicite![11]
What early tongue so sweet saluteth me?
Young son, it argues a distempered[12] head
So soon to bid "Good morrow" to thy bed.

35 Care keeps his watch in every old man's eye,
And, where care lodges, sleep will never lie;
But where unbruisèd youth with unstuffed brain[13]
Doth couch[14] his limbs, there golden sleep doth reign.
Therefore thy earliness doth me assure

40 Thou art uproused with some distemp'rature;
Or if not so, then here I hit it right:
Our Romeo hath not been in bed tonight.

Romeo. That last is true. The sweeter rest was mine.

Friar Laurence. God pardon sin! Wast thou with Rosaline?

45 **Romeo.** With Rosaline, my ghostly father? No.
I have forgot that name, and that name's woe.

Friar Laurence. That's my good son. But where hast thou been, then?

Romeo. I'll tell thee ere thou ask it me again.
I have been feasting with mine enemy,

50 Where on a sudden one hath wounded me

---

[9] For this . . . heart—This plant, when smelled, pleasures the body with its fragrance, but, when tasted, destroys the body by stopping the heart.

[10] canker—cankerworm, which destroys plants.

[11] Benedicite—Latin for "Bless you."

[12] distempered—disturbed.

[13] unstuffed brain—unworried mind.

[14] couch—rest.

Romeo (Robert Petkoff) consults with Friar Lawrence (Robert Slattel) in the Hartford Stage production.

That's by me wounded. Both our remedies
Within thy help and holy physic[15] lies.
I bear no hatred, blessèd man, for, lo,
My intercession likewise steads my foe.[16]

55 **Friar Laurence.** Be plain, good son, and homely in thy drift.[17]
Riddling confession finds but riddling shrift.[18]

Romeo. Then plainly know my heart's dear love is set
On the fair daughter of rich Capulet.
As mine on hers, so hers is set on mine,
60 And all combined, save what thou must combine
By holy marriage. When and where and how
We met, we wooed, and made exchange of vow
I'll tell thee as we pass; but this I pray,
That thou consent to marry us today.

65 **Friar Laurence.** Holy Saint Francis, what a change is here!
Is Rosaline, that thou didst love so dear,
So soon forsaken? Young men's love then lies
Not truly in their hearts, but in their eyes.

---

[15] physic—medicine; treatment.

[16] My intercession . . . foe—My act of pleading for another person also helps my enemy.

[17] homely . . . drift—simple and direct in your meaning.

[18] shrift—forgiveness (of sins in confession).

Wisely and slow. They stumble that run fast.

	Jesu Maria, what a deal of brine[19]
70	Hath washed thy sallow cheeks for Rosaline!
	How much salt water thrown away in waste
	To season love, that of it doth not taste!
	The sun not yet thy sighs from heaven clears,
	Thy old groans yet ringing in mine ancient ears.
75	Lo, here upon thy cheek the stain doth sit
	Of an old tear that is not washed off yet.
	If e'er thou wast thyself, and these woes thine,
	Thou and these woes were all for Rosaline.
	And art thou changed? Pronounce this sentence then:
80	Women may fall, when there's no strength in men.

Romeo. Thou chid'st[20] me oft for loving Rosaline.

Friar Laurence. For doting,[21] not for loving, pupil mine.

Romeo. And bad'st[22] me bury love.

Friar Laurence.   Not in a grave
To lay one in, another out to have.

85 **Romeo.** I pray thee, chide not. She whom I love now
Doth grace for grace and love for love allow.
The other did not so.

Friar Laurence.   O, she knew well
Thy love did read by rote, that could not spell.[23]
But come, young waverer, come, go with me,
90 In one respect I'll thy assistant be,
For this alliance may so happy prove
To turn your households' **rancor**[24] to pure love.

Romeo. O, let us hence! I stand on sudden haste.

Friar Laurence. Wisely and slow. They stumble that run fast.

[*They exit.*]

---

[19] brine—salty tears.

[20] chid'st—chided, scolded.

[21] doting—being infatuated.

[22] bad'st—bade, urged.

[23] Thy love . . . spell—You merely repeated conventional expressions of love without understanding them.

[24] **rancor**—bitter resentment, hatred.

Act Two, Scene Four

On a street in Verona, later that morning, Benvolio tells Mercutio that Tybalt has sent a letter to Montague, challenging Romeo. When Romeo enters, they tease him about having hidden from them last night, but they appreciate that he has regained his good spirits. The Nurse comes, sent by Juliet, to find Romeo. He tells her of his plans to marry Juliet that afternoon at Friar Laurence's cell.

Enter Benvolio *and* Mercutio.

Mercutio. Where the devil should this Romeo be?
　　Came he not home tonight?
Benvolio. Not to his father's. I spoke with his man.
Mercutio. Why, that same pale hardhearted wench, that Rosaline,
5　　Torments him so that he will sure run mad.
Benvolio. Tybalt, the kinsman to old Capulet,
　　Hath sent a letter to his father's house.
Mercutio. A challenge, on my life.
Benvolio. Romeo will answer it.
10　**Mercutio.** Any man that can write may answer a letter.
Benvolio. Nay, he will answer the letter's master, how he dares,
　　being dared.
Mercutio. Alas poor Romeo! He is already dead,
　　stabbed with a white wench's black eye, run through
15　　the ear with a love song, the very pin of his heart cleft
　　with the blind bow-boy's butt shaft.[1] And is he a man
　　to encounter Tybalt?
Benvolio. Why, what is Tybalt?
Mercutio. More than prince of cats.[2] O, he's the courageous captain
20　　of compliments. He fights as you sing prick song,[3] keeps time,
　　distance, and proportion. He rests his minim rests,[4] one, two, and

---

[1] blind . . . shaft—Cupid's arrow of love.

[2] prince of cats—In a fable, Tybalt was the name of the Prince of Cats.

[3] prick song—music written out.

[4] minim rests—half rests in music.

the third in your bosom. The very butcher of a silk button,[5] a duelist, a duelist, a gentleman of the very first house, of the first and second cause.[6] Ah, the immortal *passado!* The *punto reverso!* The *hay!*[7]

25 **Benvolio.** The what?

Mercutio. The pox of [8] such antic, lisping, affecting phantasimes, these new tuners of accent![9] "By Jesu, a very good blade! A very tall man! A very good whore!" Why, is not this a lamentable thing, grandsire, that we should be thus afflicted with these strange flies, these fashion

30 mongers, these pardon-mes, who stand so much on the new form that they cannot sit at ease on the old bench? O, their bones, their bones!

[*Enter* Romeo.]

Benvolio. Here comes Romeo, here comes Romeo.

Mercutio. Without his roe,[10] like a dried herring. O flesh, flesh, how art

35 thou fishified! Now is he for the numbers that Petrarch[11] flowed in. Laura to his lady was but a kitchen wench—marry, she had a better love to berhyme her—Dido a dowdy, Cleopatra a gypsy, Helen and Hero hildings[12] and harlots, Thisbe a gray eye or so, but not to the purpose.—Signor Romeo, *bonjour!* There's a French salutation to your

40 French slop.[13] You gave us the counterfeit[14] fairly last night.

Romeo. Good morrow to you both. What counterfeit did I give you?

Mercutio. The slip, sir, the slip. Can you not conceive?[15]

Romeo. Pardon, good Mercutio. My business was great, and in such a case as mine a man may strain courtesy.

45 **Mercutio.** That's as much as to say, such a case as yours constrains a man to bow in the hams.

Romeo. Meaning, to curtsy.

---

[5] butcher . . . button—one who can use his sword to cut a button off his opponent's clothes.

[6] of the first . . . cause—ready to fight over anything or nothing.

[7] *passado . . . hay*—fencing moves.

[8] The pox of—may the plague take.

[9] new . . . accent—those who use new slang and foreign words.

[10] roe—fish eggs (that is, looking very thin); also a pun on the first syllable of Romeo.

[11] Petrarch—Italian poet who wrote poems to his beloved, Laura. The other names are also those of romantic heroines.

[12] hildings—good-for-nothings.

[13] French slop—loose trousers of French fashion.

[14] gave . . . counterfeit—gave us the slip; left without being noticed.

[15] Can . . . conceive?—Don't you get it?

Mercutio. Thou hast most kindly hit it.

Romeo. A most courteous exposition.

50 **Mercutio.** Nay, I am the very pink of courtesy.[16]

Romeo. Pink for flower.

Mercutio. Right.

Romeo. Why then is my pump well flowered.

Mercutio. Sure wit, follow me this jest now till thou hast worn out thy
55 pump, that when the single sole of it is worn, the jest may remain,
after the wearing, solely singular.

Romeo. O single-soled jest, solely singular for the singleness!

Mercutio. Come between us, good Benvolio. My wits faints.

Romeo. Switch and spurs,[17] switch and spurs! Or I'll cry a match.

60 **Mercutio.** Nay, if our wits run the wild-goose chase, I am done, for thou
hast more of the wild goose in one of thy wits than, I am sure, I have
in my whole five. Was I with you there for the goose?[18]

Romeo. Thou wast never with me for anything when thou wast not there
for the goose.

65 **Mercutio.** I will bite thee by the ear for that jest.

Romeo. Nay, good goose, bite not.

Mercutio. Thy wit is a very bitter sweeting;[19] it is a most sharp sauce.

Romeo. And is it not, then, well served into a sweet goose?

Mercutio. O, here's a wit of cheveril, that stretches from an inch narrow
70 to an ell broad![20]

Romeo. I stretch it out for that word "broad," which, added to the goose,
proves thee far and wide a broad goose.

Mercutio. Why, is not this better now than groaning for love? Now art
thou sociable, now art thou Romeo; now art thou what thou art, by

---

[16] pink of courtesy—perfection of manners. A *pink* is also a flower, and *pinking* is a kind of decoration used on clothes, such as Romeo's shoe (pump).

[17] Switch and spurs—Keep up the pace (of the wordplay).

[18] Was . . . goose?—Did I score a point in calling you a goose?

[19] sweeting—variety of sweet apple.

[20] here's . . . broad—Your wit is like kid leather, which easily stretches from an inch to forty-five inches.

75 art as well as by nature. For this driveling love is like a great natural[21]
that runs lolling up and down to hide his bauble in a hole.

Benvolio. Stop there, stop there.

Mercutio. Thou desirest me to stop in my tale against the hair.[22]

Benvolio. Thou wouldst else have made thy tale large.

80 **Mercutio.** O, thou art deceived; I would have made it short, for I was
come to the whole depth of my tale and meant indeed to occupy the
argument no longer.

[*Enter* Nurse *and her man* Peter.]

Romeo. Here's goodly gear! A sail, a sail!

Mercutio. Two, two: a shirt and a smock.[23]

85 **Nurse.** Peter!

Peter. Anon!

Nurse. My fan, Peter.

Mercutio. Good Peter, to hide her face, for her fan's the fairer face.

Nurse. God gi' good morrow, gentlemen.

90 **Mercutio.** God gi' good e'en, fair gentlewoman.

Nurse. Is it good e'en?

Mercutio. 'Tis no less, I tell ye, for the **bawdy**[24] hand of the dial is now
upon the prick of noon.

Nurse. Out upon you! What a man are you?

95 **Romeo.** One, gentlewoman, that God hath made for himself to mar.

Nurse. By my troth,[25] it is well said. "For himself to mar," quoth he?
Gentlemen, can any of you tell me where I may find the
young Romeo?

Romeo. I can tell you; but young Romeo will be older when you have

100 found him than he was when you sought him. I am the youngest of
that name, for fault of a worse.

Nurse. You say well.

Mercutio. Yea, is the worst well? Very well took, i' faith, wisely, wisely.

Nurse. If you be he, sir, I desire some confidence[26] with you.

---

[21] natural—idiot.

[22] against the hair—against the grain; against my wish.

[23] shirt . . . smock—man and woman.

[24] **bawdy**—indecent; obscene.

[25] By my troth—in truth.

[26] confidence—Nurse's mistake for "conference."

Benvolio. She will indite[27] him to some supper.

Mercutio. A bawd, a bawd, a bawd! So ho![28]

Romeo. What hast thou found?

Mercutio. No hare, sir, unless a hare, sir, in a lenten pie,[29] that is something stale and hoar ere it be spent.[30]

[*He sings.*]

An old hare hoar,

And an old hare hoar,

Is very good meat in Lent.

But a hare that is hoar

Is too much for a score,[31]

When it hoars ere it be spent.

Romeo, will you come to your father's? We'll to dinner thither.

Romeo. I will follow you.

Mercutio. Farewell, ancient lady. Farewell, [*singing*]

"Lady, lady, lady."

[*Exit* Mercutio *and* Benvolio.]

Nurse. I pray you, sir, what saucy merchant was this that was so full of his ropery?[32]

Romeo. A gentleman, Nurse, that loves to hear himself talk, and will speak more in a minute than he will stand to[33] in a month.

Nurse. An he speak anything against me, I'll take him down, an he were lustier than he is, and twenty such jacks. And if I cannot, I'll find those that shall. Scurvy knave! I am none of his flirt-gills. I am none of his skains-mates. [*To* Peter.] And thou must stand by, too, and suffer every knave to use me at his pleasure!

Peter. I saw no man use you at his pleasure. If I had, my weapon should quickly have been out; I warrant you, I dare draw as soon as another man, if I see occasion in a good quarrel, and the law on my side.

---

[27] indite—Imitating the Nurse, Benvolio jokingly misuses *indite* (write; compose) for "invite."

[28] bawd . . . ho—woman who employs prostitutes, but also a dialect word for *hare*, followed by the cry of a hunter sighting game.

[29] lenten pie—pie that should contain no meat.

[30] hoar ere it be spent—moldy before it's used up.

[31] for a score—to pay good money for.

[32] saucy . . . ropery—rude fellow who was so full of vulgar humor.

[33] stand to—perform; abide by.

Nurse. Now, afore God, I am so vexed that every part about me quivers. Scurvy knave! [*To Romeo.*] Pray you, sir, a word. And as I told you, my young lady bid me inquire you out. What she bid me say, I will keep to myself. But first let me tell ye, if you should lead her in a fool's paradise, as they say, it were a very gross kind of behavior, as they say. For the gentlewoman is young; and therefore, if you should deal double with her, truly it were an ill thing to be offered to any gentlewoman, and very weak dealing.

135

Juliet's nurse (Roberta Maxwell) confers with Romeo (Robert Petkoff) in the Hartford Stage production.

Romeo. Nurse, commend me to thy lady and mistress. I protest
    unto thee—
140

Nurse. Good heart, and i' faith I will tell her as much. Lord, Lord, she
    will be a joyful woman.

Romeo. What wilt thou tell her, Nurse? Thou dost not mark me.[34]

Nurse. I will tell her, sir, that you do protest, which, as I take it, is a
145   gentlemanlike offer.[35]

Romeo. Bid her devise
    Some means to come to shrift this afternoon,
    And there she shall at Friar Laurence' cell
150   Be shrived and married. Here is for thy pains.

[*He offers her money.*]

Nurse. No, truly, sir, not a penny.

Romeo. Go to, I say you shall.

Nurse. This afternoon, sir? Well, she shall be there.

Romeo. And stay, good Nurse, behind the abbey wall.
155   Within this hour my man shall be with thee
    And bring thee cords made like a tackled stair[36]
    Which to the high topgallant[37] of my joy
    Must be my convoy[38] in the secret night.
    Farewell. Be trusty, and I'll quit[39] thy pains.
160   Farewell. Commend me to thy mistress.

[Romeo *starts to leave.*]

Nurse. Now God in heaven bless thee! Hark you, sir.

Romeo. What sayst thou, my dear Nurse?

Nurse. Is your man secret?[40] Did you ne'er hear say,
    "Two may keep counsel, putting one away"?
165 **Romeo.** 'Warrant thee, my man's as true as steel.

---

[34] mark me—listen to me.

[35] protest . . . offer—The Nurse apparently takes Romeo's "protest" as a proposal of marriage.

[36] cords . . . tackled stair—rope ladder.

[37] topgallant—highest mast and sail of a ship.

[38] convoy—means of travel.

[39] quit—reward.

[40] secret—trustworthy.

Nurse. Well, sir, my mistress is the sweetest lady—Lord, Lord! When
'twas a little prating thing[41]—O, there is a nobleman in town, one
Paris, that would fain lay knife aboard; but she, good soul, had as
lief[42] see a toad, a very toad, as see him. I anger her sometimes and
tell her that Paris is the properer man, but I'll warrant you, when I
say so, she looks as pale as any clout in the versal world.[43] Doth not
rosemary and Romeo begin both with a letter?[44]

Romeo. Ay, Nurse, what of that? Both with an R.

Nurse. Ah, mocker! That's the dog's name;[45] R is for
the— No; I know it begins with some other letter; and
she hath the prettiest sententious[46] of it, of you and
rosemary, that it would do you good to hear it.

Romeo. Commend me to thy lady.

Nurse. Ay, a thousand times.

[*Exit* Romeo.]

Peter!

Peter. Anon!

Nurse. Before, and apace.

[*They exit.*]

---

[41] When . . . thing—when she was a little chattering child.

[42] lief—willingly.

[43] clout . . . world—rag in the universal world.

[44] with a letter—with the same letter.

[45] the dog's name— because the letter *R* sounds like the growl of a dog.

[46] sententious—full of meaning. The Nurse misuses it to mean "clever sayings."

Act Two, Scene Five

In a room in the Capulets' house, Juliet impatiently awaits the Nurse and then can barely endure her slowness in delivering Romeo's message. Juliet is overjoyed by the Nurse's message and prepares to meet Romeo as planned.

Enter Juliet.

Juliet. The clock struck nine when I did send the Nurse;
In half an hour she promised to return.
Perchance[1] she cannot meet him. That's not so.
O, she is lame! Love's heralds should be thoughts,

5 Which ten times faster glides than the sun's beams
Driving back shadows over louring[2] hills.
Therefore do nimble-pinioned doves draw Love[3]
And therefore hath the wind-swift Cupid wings.
Now is the sun upon the highmost hill

10 Of this day's journey, and from nine till twelve
Is three long hours, yet she is not come.
Had she affections and warm youthful blood,
She would be as swift in motion as a ball;
My words would bandy[4] her to my sweet love,

15 And his to me.
But old folks, many **feign**[5] as they were dead—
Unwieldy, slow, heavy, and pale as lead.
[*Enter* Nurse *and* Peter.]
O God, she comes!—O honey Nurse, what news?
Hast thou met with him? Send thy man away.

20 **Nurse.** Peter, stay at the gate.
[*Exit* Peter.]

---

[1] Perchance—perhaps.
[2] louring—dark and threatening.
[3] nimble-pinioned . . . Love—Swift-winged doves draw the chariot of the goddess of love.
[4] bandy—toss back and forth.
[5] **feign**—pretend.

Juliet. Now, good sweet Nurse—O Lord, why lookest thou sad?
Though news be sad, yet tell them merrily;
If good, thou shamest the music of sweet news
By playing it to me with so sour a face.

25 **Nurse.** I am aweary. Give me leave awhile.
Fie, how my bones ache! What a jaunce[6] have I had!

Juliet. I would thou hadst my bones and I thy news.
Nay, come, I pray thee, speak. Good, good Nurse, speak.

Nurse. Jesu, what haste! Can you not stay[7] awhile?
30 Do you not see that I am out of breath?

Juliet. How art thou out of breath, when thou hast breath
To say to me that thou art out of breath?
The excuse that thou dost make in this delay
Is longer than the tale thou dost excuse.
35 Is thy news good or bad? Answer to that;
Say either, and I'll stay the circumstance.[8]
Let me be satisfied: is 't good or bad?

Nurse. Well, you have made a simple[9] choice. You know not how to
choose a man. Romeo? No, not he. Though his face be better than
40 any man's, yet his leg excels all men's; and for a hand, and a foot, and
a body, though they be not to be talked on, yet they are past compare.
He is not the flower of courtesy, but, I'll warrant[10] him, as gentle
as a lamb. Go thy ways, wench. Serve God. What, have you dined
at home?

45 **Juliet.** No, no; but all this did I know before.
What says he of our marriage? What of that?

Nurse. Lord, how my head aches! What a head have I!
It beats as it would fall in twenty pieces.
My back o' t'other side—ah, my back, my back!
50 Beshrew[11] your heart for sending me about
To catch my death with jauncing up and down!

---

[6] jaunce—jolting; hard time of it.

[7] stay—wait.

[8] stay the circumstance—wait for the details.

[9] simple—foolish.

[10] warrant—vouch for.

[11] Beshrew—curse.

Juliet. I' faith, I am sorry that thou art not well.

Sweet, sweet, sweet Nurse, tell me, what says my love?

Nurse. Your love says, like an honest gentleman,

55 And a courteous, and a kind, and a handsome,

And, I warrant, a virtuous—Where is your mother?

Juliet. Where is my mother? Why, she is within,

Where should she be? How oddly thou repliest!

"Your love says, like an honest gentleman,

60 'Where is your mother?' "

Nurse.   O God's Lady dear!

Are you so hot? Marry, come up, I trow.

Is this the **poultice**[12] for my aching bones?

Henceforward do your messages yourself.

Juliet. Here's such a coil![13] Come, what says Romeo?

65 **Nurse.** Have you got leave to go to shrift today?

Juliet. I have.

Nurse. Then hie[14] you hence to Friar Laurence' cell;

There stays a husband to make you a Lady Capulet.

Now comes the wanton blood up in your cheeks;

70 They'll be in scarlet straight at any news.

Hie you to church. I must another way,

To fetch a ladder, by the which your love

Must climb a bird's nest soon when it is dark.

I am the drudge, and toil in your delight,

75 But you shall bear the burden soon at night.

Go. I'll to dinner. Hie you to the cell.

Juliet. Hie to high fortune! Honest Nurse, farewell.

[*They exit separately.*]

---

[12] **poultice**—medicinal paste applied to the body.

[13] coil—fuss.

[14] hie—hurry.

Act Two, Scene Six

Outside Friar Laurence's cell, that evening,
Romeo and Juliet meet Friar Laurence and
go in with him to be married.

Enter Friar Laurence *and* Romeo.

Friar Laurence. So smile the heavens upon this holy act
　　That after-hours with sorrow chide us not![1]
Romeo. Amen, amen! But come what sorrow can,
　　It cannot countervail[2] the exchange of joy
5　　That one short minute gives me in her sight.
　　Do thou but close our hands with holy words,
　　Then love-devouring death do what he dare;
　　It is enough I may but call her mine.
Friar Laurence. These violent delights have violent ends
10　　And in their triumph die, like fire and powder,[3]
　　Which, as they kiss, consume. The sweetest honey
　　Is **loathsome**[4] in his own deliciousness,
　　And in the taste confounds[5] the appetite.
　　Therefore love moderately. Long love doth so;
15　　Too swift arrives as tardy as too slow.
　　[*Enter* Juliet.]
　　Here comes the lady. O, so light a foot
　　Will ne'er wear out the everlasting flint.
　　A lover may bestride the gossamers[6]
　　That idles in the wanton summer air,
20　　And yet not fall, so light is vanity.[7]

---

[1] So smile . . . not—May the heavens bless this holy act so that what happens afterward will not bring us sorrow.

[2] countervail—outweigh.

[3] powder—gunpowder.

[4] **loathsome**—hateful, sickening.

[5] confounds—destroys.

[6] gossamers—cobwebs.

[7] so . . . vanity—so insubstantial are the illusions of love.

In the Yale School of Drama production, Friar Lawrence (Stephen De Rosa) marries Romeo (Nathan Hinton) and Juliet (Sanaa Lathan).

Juliet. Good even to my ghostly confessor.
Friar Laurence. Romeo shall thank thee, daughter, for us both.
Juliet. As much to him,[8] else is his thanks too much.
Romeo. Ah, Juliet, if the measure of thy joy
25   Be heaped like mine, and that thy skill be more
        To blazon it,[9] then sweeten with thy breath
        This neighbor air, and let rich music's tongue
        Unfold the imagined happiness that both
        Receive in either by this dear encounter.
30 **Juliet.** Conceit, more rich in matter than in words,
        Brags of his substance, not of ornament.[10]
        They are but beggars that can count their worth.
        But my true love is grown to such excess
        I cannot sum up sum of half my wealth.
35 **Friar Laurence.** Come, come with me, and we will make short work;
        For, by your leaves, you shall not stay alone
        Till Holy Church incorporate two in one.
        [*They exit.*]

---

[8] As . . . him—the same greeting to him.
[9] that . . . blazon it—if you have more skill in proclaiming your love.
[10] Conceit . . . ornament—True understanding comes from the reality of love, not from boasts and outward show.

Act Three, Scene One

On a street in Verona, Benvolio and Mercutio meet Tybalt. When Romeo arrives, Tybalt challenges him to fight but Romeo refuses. Mercutio takes the challenge, and he and Tybalt fight. When Romeo tries to stop them, Tybalt stabs Mercutio. Dying, Mercutio curses both the Montagues and the Capulets.

Romeo fights Tybalt, kills him, and runs off. Prince Escalus appears with the Montague and Capulet households and commands Benvolio to explain what happened. The Prince fines Montague and Capulet heavily and exiles Romeo on threat of death.

Enter Mercutio, Benvolio, *and* Servants.

Benvolio. I pray thee, good Mercutio, let's retire.
The day is hot, the Capels[1] are abroad,
And if we meet we shall not scape a brawl,
For now, these hot days, is the mad blood stirring.

5 **Mercutio.** Thou art like one of these fellows that when he enters the confines of a tavern, claps me his sword upon the table and says, "God send me no need of thee!" and, by the operation of the second cup, draws him on the drawer,[2] when indeed there is no need.

Benvolio. Am I like such a fellow?

10 **Mercutio.** Come, come, thou art as hot a jack in thy mood as any in Italy, and as soon moved to be moody, and as soon moody to be moved.[3]

Benvolio. And what to?

Mercutio. Nay, an there were two such, we should have none shortly, for one would kill the other. Thou! Why, thou wilt quarrel with a man that hath a hair more or a hair less in his beard than thou hast. Thou

15 wilt quarrel with a man for cracking nuts, having no other reason but because thou hast hazel eyes. What eye but such an eye would spy out such a quarrel? Thy head is as full of quarrels as an egg is full

---

[1] Capels—Capulets.

[2] by the operation . . . drawer—by the time the second cup of wine affects him, draws his sword on the waiter.

[3] moved . . . moved—as inclined to get angry as to be angry when crossed.

of meat, and yet thy head hath been beaten as addle[4] as an egg for
quarreling. Thou hast quarreled with a man for coughing in the
street, because he hath wakened thy dog that hath lain asleep in the
sun. Didst thou not fall out with a tailor for wearing his new doublet
before Easter? With another, for tying his new shoes with old ribbon?
And yet thou wilt tutor me from quarreling!

Benvolio. An I were so apt to quarrel as thou art, any man should buy the
fee simple[5] of my life for an hour and a quarter.

Mercutio. The fee simple! O simple!

[*Enter* Tybalt, Petruchio, *and their followers.*]

Benvolio. By my head, here comes the Capulets.

Mercutio. By my heel, I care not.

Tybalt [*to his companions*]. Follow me close, for I will speak to them.—
Gentlemen, good e'en. A word with one of you.

Mercutio. And but one word with one of us? Couple it with something:
make it a word and a blow.

Tybalt. You shall find me apt enough to that, sir, an you will give
me occasion.

Mercutio. Could you not take some occasion without giving?

Tybalt. Mercutio, thou consortest[6] with Romeo.

Mercutio. "Consort"? What, dost thou make us minstrels? An thou make
minstrels of us, look to hear nothing but discords. Here's my fiddlestick;[7] here's that shall make you dance. Zounds, "consort"!

Benvolio. We talk here in the public haunt of men.
Either withdraw unto some private place,
Or reason coldly of your grievances,
Or else depart. Here all eyes gaze on us.

Mercutio. Men's eyes were made to look, and let them gaze.
I will not budge for no man's pleasure, I.

[*Enter* Romeo.]

Tybalt. Well, peace be with you, sir. Here comes my man.

---

[4] addle—confused. An addle egg is rotten.
[5] fee simple—outright possession.
[6] consortest—keep company. *Consort* also means "make music together," the meaning Mercutio chooses to give it.
[7] fiddlestick—Mercutio means his sword.

Mercutio. But I'll be hanged, sir, if he wear your livery.[8]

Marry, go before to field, he'll be your follower,[9]

50   Your Worship in that sense may call him "man."

Tybalt. Romeo, the love I bear thee can afford

No better term than this: thou art a villain.

Romeo. Tybalt, the reason that I have to love thee

Doth much excuse the appertaining rage

55   To such a greeting.[10] Villain am I none.

Therefore, farewell. I see thou knowest me not.

Tybalt. Boy, this shall not excuse the injuries

That thou hast done me. Therefore turn and draw.

Romeo. I do protest I never injured thee,

60   But love thee better than thou canst devise

Till thou shalt know the reason of my love.

And so, good Capulet—which name I tender[11]

As dearly as mine own—be satisfied.

Mercutio. O calm, dishonorable, vile submission!

65   *Alla stoccado*[12] carries it away.

[He draws.]

Tybalt, you ratcatcher, will you walk?

Tybalt. What wouldst thou have with me?

Mercutio. Good king of cats, nothing but one of your nine lives, that

I mean to make bold withal, and, as you shall use me hereafter,

70   dry-beat the rest of the eight.[13] Will you pluck your sword out of his

pilcher by the ears?[14] Make haste, lest mine be about your ears

ere it be out.

Tybalt. I am for you.

[He draws.]

Romeo. Gentle Mercutio, put thy rapier up.

---

[8] livery—Mercutio chooses to interpret Tybalt's "my man" as "servant" and denies that Romeo wears the uniform of Tybalt's servant.

[9] go . . . follower—If you go to a dueling place, he will take up your challenge.

[10] appertaining . . . greeting—rage resulting from such a greeting.

[11] tender—cherish.

[12] *Alla stoccado*—Italian for "at the thrust." Mercutio, calling Romeo dishonorable and vile for not fighting, claims that Tybalt has won the battle.

[13] dry-beat . . . eight—beat you soundly out of your other eight lives.

[14] out . . . ears—out of its sheath by its handle.

75 **Mercutio.** Come, sir, your passado.

[Mercutio *and* Tybalt *fight.*]

Romeo. Draw, Benvolio, beat down their weapons.
Gentlemen, for shame, forbear[15] this outrage!
Tybalt, Mercutio, the prince expressly hath
Forbid this bandying in Verona streets.

80 Hold, Tybalt! Good Mercutio!

[*Under* Romeo's *arm,* Tybalt *stabs* Mercutio.] [*Exit* Tybalt, Petruchio, *and his followers.*]

Mercutio. I am hurt.
A plague o' both your houses! I am sped.[16]
Is he gone, and hath nothing?

Benvolio. What, art thou hurt?

Mercutio. Ay, ay, a scratch, a scratch. Marry, 'tis enough.
Where is my page?—Go, villain, fetch a surgeon.

[*Exit* Page.]

85 **Romeo.** Courage, man, the hurt cannot be much.

Mercutio. No, 'tis not so deep as a well, nor so wide as a church door, but 'tis enough, 'twill serve. Ask for me tomorrow, and you shall find me a grave[17] man. I am peppered,[18] I warrant, for this world. A plague o' both your houses! Zounds, a dog, a rat, a mouse, a cat, to scratch
90 a man to death! A braggart, a rogue, a villain that fights by the book of arithmetic![19] Why the devil came you between us? I was hurt under your arm.

Romeo. I thought all for the best.

Mercutio. Help me into some house, Benvolio,
95 Or I shall faint. A plague o' both your houses!
They have made worm's meat of me. I have it,
And soundly too. Your houses!

---

[15] forbear—stop.

[16] sped—killed.

[17] grave—both "serious" and "in the grave." Although dying, Mercutio can't resist a pun.

[18] peppered—finished off.

[19] by . . . arithmetic—as if by a textbook on fencing.

[*Exit* Mercutio, *supported by* Benvolio, *and all but* Romeo.]

Romeo. This gentleman, the prince's near ally,

My very friend, hath got this mortal hurt

100   In my behalf. My reputation stained

With Tybalt's slander—Tybalt, that an hour

Hath been my cousin! O sweet Juliet,

Thy beauty hath made me effeminate,

And in my temper[20] softened valor's steel.

[*Enter* Benvolio.]

105 **Benvolio.** O Romeo, Romeo, brave Mercutio is dead!

That gallant spirit hath aspired the clouds,[21]

Which too untimely here did scorn the earth.

Romeo. This day's black fate on more days doth depend;[22]

This but begins the woe others must end.

[*Enter* Tybalt.]

110 **Benvolio.** Here comes the furious Tybalt back again.

Romeo. Alive in triumph, and Mercutio slain!

Away to heaven, respective lenity,[23]

And fire-eyed fury be my conduct[24] now! —

Now, Tybalt, take the "villain" back again

115   That late thou gavest me, for Mercutio's soul

Is but a little way above our heads,

Staying for thine to keep him company.

Either thou or I, or both, must go with him.

Tybalt. Thou, wretched boy, that didst consort him here,

120   Shalt with him hence.

Romeo.   This shall determine that.

[*They fight.* Tybalt *falls.*]

Benvolio. Romeo, away, begone!

The citizens are up, and Tybalt slain.

Stand not amazed. The prince will doom thee death

If thou art taken. Hence, begone, away!

---

[20] temper—nature (with a pun on the tempering of steel).

[21] aspired the clouds—risen to heaven.

[22] on . . . depend—hangs over more days to come.

[23] respective lenity—considerate mildness.

[24] conduct—guide.

Romeo (Nathan Hinton) kills Tybalt (Thomas McCarthy) in the Yale School of Drama production.

125 **Romeo.** O, I am Fortune's fool![25]

Benvolio. Why dost thou stay?

[*Exit* Romeo.]

[*Enter* Citizens.]

First Citizen. Which way ran he that killed Mercutio?

Tybalt, that murderer, which way ran he?

Benvolio. There lies that Tybalt.

First Citizen [*to* Tybalt].   Up, Sir, go with me.

130 I charge thee in the prince's name, obey.

---

[25] Fortune's fool—victim of fate.

O, I am Fortune's fool!

[*Enter* Prince *with* Attendants, Lord Montague, Lord Capulet, *their* Wives, *and all.*]

Prince. Where are the vile beginners of this fray?

Benvolio. O noble Prince, I can discover all
    The unlucky manage[26] of this fatal brawl.
    There lies the man, slain by young Romeo,
135   That slew thy kinsman, brave Mercutio.

Lady Capulet. Tybalt, my cousin! O my brother's child!
    O Prince! O cousin! Husband! O, the blood is spilled
    Of my dear kinsman! Prince, as thou art true,
    For blood of ours shed blood of Montague.
140   O cousin, cousin!

Prince. Benvolio, who began this bloody fray?

Benvolio. Tybalt, here slain, whom Romeo's hand did slay.
    Romeo, that spoke him fair, bid him bethink
    How nice[27] the quarrel was, and urged withal
145   Your high displeasure. All this—utterèd
    With gentle breath, calm look, knees humbly bowed—
    Could not take truce with the unruly spleen[28]
    Of Tybalt deaf to peace, but that he tilts[29]
    With piercing steel at bold Mercutio's breast,
150   Who, all as hot, turns deadly point to point,
    And, with a **martial**[30] scorn, with one hand beats
    Cold death aside and with the other sends
    It back to Tybalt, whose dexterity
    Retorts it.[31] Romeo he cries aloud,
155   "Hold, friends! Friends, part!" and swifter than his tongue
    His agile arm beats down their fatal points,
    And twixt them rushes; underneath whose arm

---

[26] I can ... manage—I can explain this unfortunate course of events.

[27] nice—trivial.

[28] take ... spleen—make peace with the uncontrollable rage.

[29] tilts—strikes.

[30] **martial**—warlike.

[31] whose ... it—whose skill returns it.

An envious thrust from Tybalt hit the life
Of stout[32] Mercutio, and then Tybalt fled;
160   But by and by comes back to Romeo,
Who had but newly entertained[33] revenge,
And to 't they go like lightning, for, ere I
Could draw to part them, was stout Tybalt slain,
And, as he fell, did Romeo turn and fly.
165   This is the truth, or let Benvolio die.

Lady Capulet. He is a kinsman to the Montague.
Affection makes him false; he speaks not true.
Some twenty of them fought in this black strife,
And all those twenty could but kill one life.
170   I beg for justice, which thou, Prince, must give.
Romeo slew Tybalt; Romeo must not live.

Prince. Romeo slew him, he slew Mercutio.
Who now the price of his dear blood doth owe?

Montague. Not Romeo, Prince, he was Mercutio's friend.
175   His fault concludes but what the law should end,
The life of Tybalt.

Prince.   And for that offense
Immediately we do exile him hence.
I have an interest in your hate's proceeding;
My blood[34] for your rude brawls doth lie a-bleeding;
180   But I'll amerce[35] you with so strong a fine
That you shall all repent the loss of mine.
I will be deaf to pleading and excuses;
Nor tears nor prayers shall purchase out abuses.
Therefore use none. Let Romeo hence in haste,
185   Else, when he is found, that hour is his last.
Bear hence this body and attend our will.[36]
Mercy but murders, pardoning those that kill.

[*They exit, the* Capulet men *carrying* Tybalt's *body.*]

---

[32] stout—stout-hearted; brave.

[33] entertained—thought about.

[34] My blood—blood of my kinsman.

[35] amerce—punish by a fine.

[36] attend our will—wait for further judgments.

Act Three, Scene Two

In a room in the Capulets' house that evening, the Nurse brings Juliet news of Tybalt's death and Romeo's banishment. Juliet is distressed at Tybalt's death, but she reasons that he would otherwise have killed Romeo. She is far more distressed at Romeo's banishment. The Nurse tells Juliet to go to her room and wait for Romeo there.

Enter Juliet *alone.*

Juliet. Gallop apace, you fiery-footed steeds,
    Towards Phoebus' lodging! Such a wagoner
    As Phaëton would whip you to the west
    And bring in cloudy night immediately.[1]
5   Spread thy close curtain, love-performing night,
    That runaways' eyes may wink, and Romeo
    Leap to these arms, untalked of and unseen.
    Lovers can see to do their amorous rites
    By their own beauties; or, if love be blind,
10   It best agrees with night. Come, civil[2] night,
    Thou sober-suited matron all in black,
    And learn me how to lose a winning match
    Played for a pair of stainless maidenhoods.
    Hood my unmanned blood,[3] bating[4] in my cheeks,
15   With thy black mantle till strange[5] love grown bold
    Think true love acted simple modesty.
    Come, night. Come, Romeo. Come, thou day in night;
    For thou wilt lie upon the wings of night
    Whiter than new snow upon a raven's back.
20   Come, gentle night, come, loving, black-browed night,
    Give me my Romeo, and when I shall die
    Take him and cut him out in little stars,

---

[1] Gallop . . . immediately—Hurry, you horses, to bring the chariot of Phoebus, the sun god, home! A driver such as Phaëthon (Phoebus's son, who was once allowed to drive his father's chariot but lost control) would end the day quickly.

[2] civil—cautious; soberly dressed.

[3] Hood . . . blood—cover my untamed blood.

[4] bating—fluttering.

[5] strange—unfamiliar; shy.

Act Three, Scene Two 89

And he will make the face of heaven so fine
That all the world will be in love with night

25 And pay no worship to the garish sun.
O, I have bought the mansion of a love
But not possessed it, and though I am sold,
Not yet enjoyed. So tedious is this day
As is the night before some festival

30 To an impatient child that hath new robes
And may not wear them. O, here comes my nurse

[*Enter* Nurse, *with the rope ladder.*]

And she brings news, and every tongue that speaks
But Romeo's name speaks heavenly **eloquence**.[5]—
Now, Nurse, what news? What hast thou there? The cords

35 That Romeo bid thee fetch?

Nurse.   Ay, ay, the cords.

[*She throws the ladder down.*]

Juliet. Ay me, what news? Why dost thou wring thy hands?

Nurse. Ah, weraday![6] He's dead, he's dead, he's dead!
We are undone, lady, we are undone!
Alack the day, he's gone, he's killed, he's dead!

40 **Juliet.** Can heaven be so envious?

Nurse.   Romeo can,
Though heaven cannot. O Romeo, Romeo!
Who ever would have thought it? Romeo!

Juliet. What devil art thou that dost torment me thus?
This torture should be roared in dismal hell.

45 Hath Romeo slain himself? Say thou but "Ay,"
And that bare vowel "I" shall poison more
Than the death-darting eye of cockatrice.[7]
I am not I, if there be such an "Ay,"
Or those eyes shut, that makes thee answer "Ay."

50 If he be slain, say "Ay," or if not, "No."
Brief sounds determine of my weal or woe.[8]

---

[6] **eloquence**—graceful and beautiful speech.

[7] weraday—alas.

[8] cockatrice—legendary serpent that could kill with its look.

[9] determine . . . woe—decide my happiness or sorrow.

Nurse. I saw the wound. I saw it with mine eyes—
 God save the mark!—here on his manly breast.
 A piteous corpse, a bloody piteous corpse;
55 Pale, pale as ashes, all bedaubed in blood,
 All in gore-blood.[10] I swoonèd at the sight.
Juliet. O, break, my heart! Poor bankrupt, break at once!
 To prison, eyes; ne'er look on liberty!
 Vile earth, to earth resign;[11] end motion here,
60 And thou and Romeo press one heavy bier![12]
Nurse. O Tybalt, Tybalt, the best friend I had!
 O courteous Tybalt! Honest gentleman!
 That ever I should live to see thee dead!
Juliet. What storm is this that blows so contrary?
65 Is Romeo slaughtered, and is Tybalt dead?
 My dearest cousin, and my dearer lord?
 Then, dreadful trumpet, sound the general doom!
 For who is living, if those two are gone?
Nurse. Tybalt is gone, and Romeo banishèd;
70 Romeo that killed him, he is banishèd.
Juliet. O God! Did Romeo's hand shed Tybalt's blood?
Nurse. It did, it did. Alas the day, it did!
Juliet. O serpent heart, hid with a flowering face!
 Did ever dragon keep so fair a cave?
75 Beautiful tyrant! Fiend angelical!
 Dove-feathered raven! Wolvish-ravening lamb!
 Despisèd substance of divinest show!
 Just opposite to what thou justly seem'st,
 A damnèd saint, an honorable villain!
80 O nature, what hadst thou to do in hell
 When thou didst bower[13] the spirit of a fiend
 In mortal paradise of such sweet flesh?
 Was ever book containing such vile matter

---

[10] gore-blood—clotted blood.

[11] Vile . . . resign—Miserable body, prepare yourself for death.

[12] bier—coffin and its support.

[13] bower—give home to.

So fairly bound? O, that deceit should dwell
85 In such a gorgeous palace!
Nurse.   There's no trust,
No faith, no honesty in men. All perjured,
All forsworn, all naught, all dissemblers.[14]
Ah, where's my man? Give me some aqua vitae.[15]
These griefs, these woes, these sorrows make me old.
90 Shame come to Romeo!
Juliet.   Blistered be thy tongue
For such a wish! He was not born to shame.
Upon his brow shame is ashamed to sit,
For 'tis a throne where honor may be crowned
Sole monarch of the universal earth.
95 O, what a beast was I to chide at him!
Nurse. Will you speak well of him that killed your cousin?
Juliet. Shall I speak ill of him that is my husband?
Ah, poor my lord, what tongue shall smooth thy name
When I, thy three-hours Lady Capulet, have mangled it?
100 But wherefore, villain, didst thou kill my cousin?
That villain cousin would have killed my husband.
Back, foolish tears, back to your native spring!
Your tributary drops belong to woe,
Which you, mistaking, offer up to joy.
105 My husband lives, that Tybalt would have slain,
And Tybalt's dead, that would have slain my husband.
All this is comfort. Wherefore weep I then?
Some word there was, worser than Tybalt's death,
That murdered me. I would forget it fain,[16]
110 But O, it presses to my memory
Like damnèd guilty deeds to sinners' minds:
"Tybalt is dead, and Romeo banishèd."
That "banishèd," that one word "banishèd,"
Hath slain ten thousand Tybalts. Tybalt's death
115 Was woe enough, if it had ended there;

---

[14] dissemblers—liars.

[15] aqua vitae—liquor to restore calmness.

[16] fain—gladly.

In the Hartt School production, Juliet (Hannah Mellow) learns from her nurse (Melissa Roth) that Romeo has been banished for killing Tybalt.

> Or, if sour woe delights in fellowship
> And needly will be ranked with other griefs,
> Why followed not, when she said "Tybalt's dead,"
> "Thy father," or "thy mother," nay, or both,
> Which modern lamentation[17] might have moved?
> But with a rearward[18] following Tybalt's death,
> "Romeo is banishèd"—to speak that word
> Is father, mother, Tybalt, Romeo, Juliet,
> All slain, all dead. "Romeo is banishèd!"

120

---

[17] modern lamentation—ordinary grief.

[18] rearward—guard following behind.

125   There is no end, no limit, measure, bound,

    In that word's death; no words can that woe sound.[19]

    Where is my father and my mother, Nurse?

Nurse. Weeping and wailing over Tybalt's corpse.

    Will you go to them? I will bring you thither.

130 **Juliet.** Wash they his wounds with tears? Mine shall be spent,

    When theirs are dry, for Romeo's banishment.

    Take up those cords. Poor ropes, you are beguiled,[20]

    Both you and I, for Romeo is exiled.

    He made you for a highway to my bed,

135   But I, a maid, die maiden-widowèd.

    Come, cords, come, Nurse. I'll to my wedding bed,

    And death, not Romeo, take my maidenhead!

Nurse [*picking up the ladder*]. Hie to your chamber. I'll find Romeo

    To comfort you. I wot[21] well where he is.

140   Hark you, your Romeo will be here at night.

    I'll to him. He is hid at Laurence' cell.

Juliet. O, find him! Give this ring to my true knight,

[*Giving the* Nurse *a ring.*]

    And bid him come to take his last farewell.

[*They exit separately.*]

---

[19] sound—understand; measure.

[20] beguiled—tricked, deceived.

[21] wot—know.

Act Three, Scene Three

In Friar Laurence's cell, Romeo complains that banishment from Verona—and from Juliet— is worse than death, but Friar Laurence calls him ungrateful. The Nurse comes to tell them of Juliet's despair. Friar Laurence angrily prevents Romeo from killing himself and tells him to go to Juliet, but to leave before daybreak and escape to Mantua.

Enter Friar Laurence.

Friar Laurence. Romeo, come forth; come forth, thou fearful man.
    Affliction is enamored of thy parts,[1]
    And thou art wedded to calamity.
[*Enter* Romeo.]
Romeo. Father, what news? What is the prince's doom?
5   What sorrow craves acquaintance at my hand
    That I yet know not?
Friar Laurence.   Too familiar
    Is my dear son with such sour company.
    I bring thee tidings of the prince's doom.
Romeo. What less than doomsday is the prince's doom?
10 **Friar Laurence.** A gentler judgment vanished[2] from his lips:
    Not body's death, but body's banishment.
Romeo. Ha, banishment? Be merciful, say "death";
    For exile hath more terror in his look,
    Much more than death. Do not say "banishment."
15 **Friar Laurence.** Here from Verona art thou banishèd.
    Be patient, for the world is broad and wide.
Romeo. There is no world without[3] Verona walls
    But purgatory, torture, hell itself.
    Hence "banishèd" is banished from the world,
20   And world's exile is death.[4] Then "banishèd"
    Is death mistermed. Calling death "banishèd,"

---

[1] Affliction . . . parts—Misfortune thrives on the qualities (of despair and self-pity) you are showing.

[2] vanished—came forth.

[3] without—outside.

[4] world's . . . death—Exile from the world that contains Juliet is the same as death.

Thou cutt'st my head off with a golden ax
And smilest upon the stroke that murders me.

Friar Laurence. O deadly sin! O rude unthankfulness!
25   Thy fault our law calls death, but the kind prince,
Taking thy part, hath rushed aside[5] the law
And tamed that black word "death" to "banishment."
This is dear mercy, and thou seest it not.

Romeo. 'Tis torture, and not mercy. Heaven is here
30   Where Juliet lives, and every cat and dog
And little mouse, every unworthy thing,
Live here in heaven and may look on her,
But Romeo may not. More validity,
More honorable state, more courtship lives
35   In carrion flies[6] than Romeo. They may seize
On the white wonder of dear Juliet's hand
And steal immortal blessing from her lips,
Who even in pure and vestal modesty
Still blush, as thinking their own kisses sin;[7]
40   But Romeo may not, he is banishèd.
Flies may do this, but I from this must fly.
They are free men, but I am banishèd.
And sayest thou yet that exile is not death?
Hadst thou no poison mixed, no sharp-ground knife,
45   No sudden mean of death, though ne'er so mean,[8]
But "banishèd" to kill me? "Banishèd"?
O Friar, the damnèd use that word in hell;
Howling attends it. How hast thou the heart,
Being a divine, a ghostly confessor,
50   A sin absolver, and my friend professed,
To mangle me with that word "banishèd"?

Friar Laurence. Thou fond[9] mad man, hear me a little speak.

Romeo. O, thou wilt speak again of banishment.

---

[5] rushed aside—thrust aside.

[6] carrion flies—flies that feed on dead animals.

[7] thinking . . . sin—When Juliet's lips touch each other, it seems a sin to them, so pure and modest is she.

[8] mean . . . mean—Romeo puns on two meanings of *mean*: "method" and "vile."

[9] fond—foolish.

Adversity's sweet milk, philosophy.

Friar Laurence. I'll give thee armor to keep off that word,
55   **Adversity's**[10] sweet milk, philosophy,
     To comfort thee, though thou art banishèd.
Romeo. Yet "banishèd"? Hang up philosophy!
     Unless philosophy can make a Juliet,
     Displant[11] a town, reverse a prince's doom,
60   It helps not, it prevails not. Talk no more.
Friar Laurence. O, then I see that madmen have no ears.
Romeo. How should they, when that wise men have no eyes?
Friar Laurence. Let me dispute with thee of thy estate.[12]
Romeo. Thou canst not speak of that thou dost not feel.
65   Wert thou as young as I, Juliet thy love,
     An hour but married, Tybalt murderèd,
     Doting like me, and like me banishèd,
     Then mightst thou speak, then mightst thou tear thy hair,
     And fall upon the ground, as I do now,
     [*He falls upon the ground.*]
70   Taking the measure of an unmade grave.
     [*Knock within.*]
Friar Laurence. Arise. One knocks. Good Romeo, hide thyself.
Romeo. Not I, unless the breath of heartsick groans,
     Mistlike, infold me from the search of eyes.[13]
     [*Knock.*]
Friar Laurence. Hark, how they knock!—Who's there?—Romeo, arise.
75   Thou wilt be taken.—Stay awhile!—Stand up.
     [*Knock.*]
     Run to my study.—By and by!—God's will,
     What simpleness is this?—I come, I come!
     [*Knock.*]
     Who knocks so hard? Whence come you? What's your will?
     [*Going to the door.*]

---

[10] **Adversity's**—hardship's.

[11] Displant—uproot.

[12] dispute . . . estate—reason with you about your situation.

[13] unless . . . eyes—unless my own grieving breaths will hide me, like a mist, from others' sight.

Julet's nurse (Melissa Roth) and Friar Laurence (Maxwell Williamson) try to comfort Romeo (Keir O'Donnell) in the Hartt School production.

Nurse [*within*]. Let me come in, and you shall know my errand.

80   I come from Lady Juliet.

Friar Laurence.   Welcome, then.

[*He opens the door.*]

[*Enter* Nurse.]

Nurse. O holy Friar, O, tell me, holy Friar,

     Where's my lady's lord, where's Romeo?

Friar Laurence. There on the ground, with his own tears made drunk.

Nurse. O, he is even in my mistress' case,[14]

85   Just in her case! O woeful sympathy!

     Piteous predicament! Even so lies she,

     Blubbering and weeping, weeping and blubbering.—

     Stand up, stand up! Stand, an you be a man.

---

[14] he is . . . case—He is in the same state as Juliet.

	For Juliet's sake, for her sake, rise and stand!
90	Why should you fall into so deep an O?[15]

Romeo. Nurse!

[*He rises.*]

Nurse. Ah sir, ah sir! Death's the end of all.

Romeo. Spakest thou of Juliet? How is it with her?
Doth not she think me an old[16] murderer,
95   Now I have stained the childhood of our joy
With blood removed but little from her own?
Where is she? And how doth she? And what says
My concealed lady[17] to our canceled love?

Nurse. O, she says nothing, Sir, but weeps and weeps,
100   And now falls on her bed, and then starts up,
And "Tybalt" calls, and then on Romeo cries,
And then down falls again.

Romeo.   As if that name,
Shot from the deadly level[18] of a gun,
Did murder her, as that name's cursèd hand
105   Murdered her kinsman.—O, tell me, Friar, tell me,
In what vile part of this anatomy
Doth my name lodge? Tell me, that I may sack
The hateful mansion.[19]

[*He draws his dagger, but is restrained.*]

Friar Laurence. Hold thy desperate hand!
110   Art thou a man? Thy form cries out thou art;
Thy tears are womanish, thy wild acts denote
The unreasonable fury of a beast.
Unseemly woman in a seeming man,
And ill-beseeming[20] beast in seeming both!
115   Thou hast amazed me. By my holy order,
I thought thy disposition better tempered.[21]

---

[15] an O—fit of grieving.

[16] old—hardened.

[17] concealed lady—secret wife.

[18] level—aim.

[19] In what . . . mansion—What part of my hateful body contains my name? Tell me, so that I can destroy that part.

[20] ill-beseeming—unsuitable; inappropriate.

[21] tempered—balanced.

Hast thou slain Tybalt? Wilt thou slay thyself,
And slay thy lady, that in thy life lives,
By doing damnèd hate upon thyself?

120 Why railest thou on[22] thy birth, the heaven, and earth,[23]
Since birth, and heaven, and earth, all three do meet
In thee at once, which thou at once wouldst lose?
Fie, fie, thou shamest thy shape, thy love, thy wit,
Which, like a usurer, abound'st in all,

125 And usest none in that true use indeed[24]
Which should bedeck thy shape, thy love, thy wit.
Thy noble shape is but a form of wax,
Digressing from the valor of a man;
Thy dear love sworn but hollow perjury,

130 Killing that love which thou hast vowed to cherish;[25]
Thy wit, that ornament to shape and love,
Misshapen in the conduct of them both,
Like powder in a skilless soldier's flask[26]
Is set afire by thine own ignorance,

135 And thou dismembered with thine own defense.[27]
What, rouse thee, man! Thy Juliet is alive,
For whose dear sake thou wast but lately dead;
There art thou happy. Tybalt would kill thee,
But thou slewest Tybalt; there art thou happy.

140 The law that threatened death becomes thy friend
And turns it to exile; there art thou happy.
A pack of blessings light upon thy back,
Happiness courts thee in her best array,
But like a mishaved[28] and sullen wench

145 Thou pout'st upon thy fortune and thy love.
Take heed, take heed, for such die miserable.

---

[22] Why railest . . . on—Why do you complain about.

[23] heaven, and earth—soul and body.

[24] Which . . . indeed—who, like a moneylender, have so many capabilities, and yet you put none of your resources to their proper use.

[25] Thy noble . . . cherish—Your noble appearance is only outward show if you turn aside from bravery; the love you swear is only lies if you kill that love by killing yourself.

[26] powder . . . flask—gunpowder in a careless soldier's powderhorn.

[27] dismembered . . . defense—blown up with your own weapon.

[28] mishaved—misbehaved.

Go, get thee to thy love, as was decreed.
Ascend her chamber. Hence and comfort her.
But look thou stay not till the watch be set,[29]

150   For then thou canst not pass to Mantua,
Where thou shalt live till we can find a time
To blaze[30] your marriage, **reconcile**[31] your friends,
Beg pardon of the prince, and call thee back
With twenty hundred thousand times more joy

155   Than thou went'st forth in lamentation.
Go before, Nurse. Commend me to thy lady,
And bid her hasten all the house to bed,
Which heavy sorrow makes them apt unto.[32]
Romeo is coming.

160   **Nurse.** O Lord, I could have stayed here all the night
To hear good counsel. O, what learning is!—
My lord, I'll tell my lady you will come.

Romeo. Do so, and bid my sweet prepare to chide.

Nurse [*giving a ring*]. Here, sir, a ring she bid me give you, sir.

165   Hie you, make haste, for it grows very late. [*Exit* Nurse.]

Romeo. How well my comfort is revived by this!

Friar Laurence. Go hence. Good night. And here stands all your state:[33]
Either be gone before the watch be set,
Or by the break of day disguised from hence.

170   Sojourn[34] in Mantua. I'll find out your man,
And he shall signify from time to time
Every good hap to you that chances here.
Give me thy hand. 'Tis late. Farewell, good night.

Romeo. But that a joy past joy calls out on me,

175   It were a grief so brief to part with thee.
Farewell.

[*They exit separately.*]

---

[29] watch be set—when watchmen take their posts at the gates of Verona.

[30] blaze—announce.

[31] **reconcile**—make peace among.

[32] apt unto—inclined to do.

[33] here . . . state—Your fortune depends on your acting exactly like this.

[34] Sojourn—stay, reside.

Act Three, Scene Four

*In a room in the Capulets' house, that night,
Capulet tells Paris that Juliet is too sad for
company tonight but that he will talk to her*
*about marriage. He and Paris agree to hold
the wedding in three days.*

Enter Lord Capulet, Lady Capulet, *and* Paris.

Capulet. Things have fall'n out, sir, so unluckily,
    That we have had no time to move our daughter.[1]
    Look you, she loved her kinsman Tybalt dearly,
    And so did I. Well, we were born to die.
5   'Tis very late. She'll not come down tonight.
    I promise you, but for your company
    I would have been abed an hour ago.
Paris. These times of woe afford no times to woo.—
    Madam, good night. Commend me to your daughter.
10 **Lady Capulet.** I will, and know her mind early tomorrow.
    Tonight she's mewed up to her heaviness.[2]
Capulet. Sir Paris, I will make a desperate tender[3]
    Of my child's love. I think she will be ruled
    In all respects by me.—Nay, more, I doubt it not.—
15   Lady Capulet, go you to her ere you go to bed.
    Acquaint her here of my son Paris' love,
    And bid her, mark you me, on Wednesday next—
    But soft, what day is this?
Paris.   Monday, my lord.
Capulet. Monday! Ha, ha! Well, Wednesday is too soon;
20   O' Thursday let it be. O' Thursday, tell her,
    She shall be married to this noble earl.—
    Will you be ready? Do you like this haste?

---

[1] move our daughter—talk to Juliet about marrying you.

[2] mewed ... heaviness—shut up in her room with her grief.

[3] desperate tender—rash offer.

We'll keep no great ado[4]—a friend or two;
For hark you, Tybalt being slain so late,
25   It may be thought we held him carelessly,
Being our kinsman, if we revel much.
Therefore we'll have some half a dozen friends,
And there an end. But what say you to Thursday?
Paris. My lord, I would that Thursday were tomorrow.
30   **Capulet.** Well, get you gone. O' Thursday be it, then.
[*To* Lady Capulet.] Go you to Juliet ere you go to bed;
Prepare her, Lady Capulet, against this wedding day.—
Farewell, my lord.—Light to my chamber, ho!—
Afore me, it is so very late
35   That we may call it early by and by.—
Good night.
[*They exit.*]

---

[4] ado—fuss; noisy activity.

Act Three, Scene Five

In Juliet's room, the next morning, Romeo is preparing to leave after having spent the night. After the Nurse warns them of Lady Capulet's approach, Romeo climbs down from the window. When Lady Capulet tells Juliet of her planned marriage, Juliet refuses. When Capulet hears her refusal, he becomes enraged and threatens to disown her. The Nurse advises Juliet to marry Paris, since Romeo is as good as dead to her. Juliet pretends to give in and says she will go to Friar Laurence to make her confession.

Enter Romeo *and* Juliet *aloft at the window.*

Juliet. Wilt thou be gone? It is not yet near day.
    It was the nightingale, and not the lark,[1]
    That pierced the fearful hollow of thine ear;
    Nightly she sings on yond pomegranate tree.
5   Believe me, love, it was the nightingale.

Romeo. It was the lark, the herald of the morn,
    No nightingale. Look, love, what envious streaks
    Do lace the severing clouds in yonder east.
    Night's candles are burnt out, and jocund[2] day
10   Stands tiptoe on the misty mountain tops.
    I must be gone and live, or stay and die.

Juliet. Yond light is not daylight, I know it, I.
    It is some meteor that the sun exhaled
    To be to thee this night a torchbearer
15   And light thee on thy way to Mantua.
    Therefore stay yet. Thou need'st not to be gone.

Romeo. Let me be ta'en; let me be put to death.
    I am content, so thou wilt have it so.
    I'll say yon gray is not the morning's eye;
20   'Tis but the pale reflex of Cynthia's brow.[3]
    Nor that is not the lark whose notes do beat
    The vaulty heaven so high above our heads.

---

[1] nightingale . . . lark—The nightingale's song is associated with night; the lark's song is associated with dawn.
[2] jocund—merry; cheerful.
[3] reflex . . . brow—reflection of the moon (Cynthia).

I have more care to stay than will to go.

Come, death, and welcome! Juliet wills it so.

25   How is 't, my soul? Let's talk. It is not day.

Juliet. It is, it is. Hie hence, begone, away!

It is the lark that sings so out of tune,

Straining harsh discords and unpleasing sharps.

Some say the lark makes sweet division;[4]

30   This doth not so, for she divideth us.

Some say the lark and loathèd toad changed eyes;[5]

O, now I would they had changed voices too,

Since arm from arm that voice doth us affray,

Hunting thee hence with hunt's-up[6] to the day.

35   O, now begone! More light and light it grows.

Romeo. More light and light, more dark and dark our woes!

[*Enter* Nurse *hastily.*]

Nurse. Madam!

Juliet. Nurse?

Nurse. Your lady mother is coming to your chamber.

40   The day is broke; be wary, look about.

[*Exit* Nurse.]

Juliet. Then window, let day in, and let life out.

Romeo. Farewell, farewell! One kiss, and I'll descend.

[*They kiss. He climbs down from the window.*]

Juliet. Art thou gone so? Love, lord, ay, husband, friend!

I must hear from thee every day in the hour,

45   For in a minute there are many days.

O, by this count I shall be much in years

Ere I again behold my Romeo!

Romeo [*from below her window*]. Farewell!

I will omit no opportunity

50   That may convey my greetings, love, to thee.

Juliet. O, think'st thou we shall ever meet again?

Romeo. I doubt it not, and all these woes shall serve

For sweet discourses in our times to come.

---

[4] division—variations on a melody.

[5] lark . . . eyes—reference to an old saying that the lark and toad had exchanged eyes; for the lark's eyes are ordinary and the toad's remarkable.

[6] hunt's-up—wake-up call for hunters.

Juliet (Whitney Sneed) clings to Romeo (Matthew Carter) in the 2000 production of *Romeo and Juliet* at the Chicago Shakespeare Theatre.

Juliet. O God, I have an ill-divining[7] soul!
55   Methinks I see thee, now thou art so low,
        As one dead in the bottom of a tomb.
        Either my eyesight fails or thou lookest pale.
Romeo. And trust me, love, in my eye so do you.
        Dry sorrow drinks our blood.[8] Adieu, adieu!
[*Exit* Romeo.]
60 **Juliet.** O Fortune, Fortune! All men call thee fickle.[9]
        If thou art fickle, what dost thou with him
        That is renowned for faith? Be fickle, Fortune.
        For then, I hope, thou wilt not keep him long,
        But send him back.

---

[7] ill-divining—prophesying evil.
[8] Dry . . . blood—It was believed that sorrow dries up the blood.
[9] fickle—changeable; not constant.

Lady Capulet [*within*].   Ho, daughter, are you up?

65 **Juliet.** Who is 't that calls? It is my lady mother.

Is she not down so late, or up so early?

What unaccustomed cause procures her hither?

[*She goes down from the window.*]

[*Enter* Lady Capulet.]

Lady Capulet. Why, how now, Juliet?

Juliet.   Madam, I am not well.

Lady Capulet. Evermore weeping for your cousin's death?

70 What, wilt thou wash him from his grave with tears?

An if thou couldst, thou couldst not make him live;

Therefore, have done. Some grief shows much of love,

But much of grief shows still some want of wit.

Juliet. Yet let me weep for such a feeling loss.

75 **Lady Capulet.** So shall you feel the loss, but not the friend

Which you weep for.

Juliet.   Feeling so the loss,

I cannot choose but ever weep the friend.

Lady Capulet. Well, girl, thou weep'st not so much for his death

As that the villain lives which slaughtered him.

80 **Juliet.** What villain, madam?

Lady Capulet.   That same villain, Romeo.

Juliet [*aside*]. Villain and he be many miles asunder.—

God pardon him! I do, with all my heart;

And yet no man like he doth grieve my heart.

Lady Capulet. That is because the traitor murderer lives.

85 **Juliet.** Ay, madam, from the reach of these my hands.

Would none but I might venge my cousin's death!

Lady Capulet. We will have vengeance for it, fear thou not.

Then weep no more. I'll send to one in Mantua,

Where that same banished runagate doth live,

90 Shall give him such an unaccustomed dram[10]

That he shall soon keep Tybalt company.

And then, I hope, thou wilt be satisfied.

Juliet. Indeed, I never shall be satisfied

With Romeo till I behold him—dead—

---

[10] dram—drink; dose (of poison).

95   Is my poor heart, so for a kinsman vexed.

Madam, if you could find out but a man

To bear a poison, I would temper[11] it,

That Romeo should, upon receipt thereof,

Soon sleep in quiet. O, how my heart **abhors**[12]

100   To hear him named, and cannot come to him

To wreak the love I bore my cousin

Upon his body that hath slaughtered him!

Lady Capulet. Find thou the means, and I'll find such a man.

But now I'll tell thee joyful tidings, girl.

105 **Juliet.** And joy comes well in such a needy time.

What are they, beseech your ladyship?

Lady Capulet. Well, well, thou hast a careful father, child,

One who, to put thee from thy heaviness,

Hath sorted out a sudden day of joy

110   That thou expects not, nor I looked not for.

Juliet. Madam, in happy time. What day is that?

Lady Capulet. Marry, my child, early next Thursday morn,

The gallant, young, and noble gentleman,

The County Paris, at Saint Peter's Church

115   Shall happily make thee there a joyful bride.

Juliet. Now, by Saint Peter's Church, and Peter too,

He shall not make me there a joyful bride!

I wonder at this haste, that I must wed

Ere he that should be husband comes to woo.

120   I pray you, tell my lord and father, madam,

I will not marry yet, and when I do I swear

It shall be Romeo, whom you know I hate,

Rather than Paris. These are news indeed!

Lady Capulet. Here comes your father. Tell him so yourself,

125   And see how he will take it at your hands.

[*Enter Capulet and Nurse.*]

Capulet. When the sun sets, the earth doth drizzle dew,

But for the sunset of my brother's son

It rains downright.

---

[11] temper—mix, concoct; but also moderate, dilute.

[12] **abhors**—hates, detests.

Thank me no thankings,
nor proud me no prouds.

How now, a conduit,[13] girl? What, still in tears?

130   Evermore showering? In one little body

Thou counterfeits[14] a bark, a sea, a wind;

For still thy eyes, which I may call the sea,

Do ebb and flow with tears; the bark thy body is,

Sailing in this salt flood; the winds, thy sighs,

135   Who, raging with thy tears, and they with them,

Without a sudden calm, will overset

Thy tempest-tossèd body.—How now, Lady Capulet?

Have you delivered to her our decree?

Lady Capulet. Ay, sir, but she will none, she gives you thanks.

140   I would the fool were married to her grave!

Capulet. Soft, take me with you, take me with you, Lady Capulet.

How? Will she none? Doth she not give us thanks?

Is she not proud? Doth she not count her blest,

Unworthy as she is, that we have wrought

145   So worthy a gentleman to be her bridegroom?

Juliet. Not proud you have, but thankful that you have.

Proud can I never be of what I hate,

But thankful even for hate that is meant love.[15]

Capulet. How, how, how, how? Chopped logic? What is this?

150   "Proud," and "I thank you," and "I thank you not,"

And yet "not proud"? Mistress minion,[16] you,

Thank me no thankings, nor proud me no prouds,

But fettle your fine joints[17] 'gainst Thursday next

To go with Paris to Saint Peter's Church,

155   Or I will drag thee on a hurdle[18] thither.

---

[13] conduit—fountain.

[14] counterfeits—imitates.

[15] thankful . . . love—thankful for something hateful that was done for love, with good intentions.

[16] minion—spoiled brat.

[17] fettle . . . joints—get yourself ready.

[18] hurdle—cart to carry criminals to be executed.

Out, you green-sickness carrion! Out, you baggage!
You tallow-face!

Lady Capulet [*to* Capulet].

                   Fie, fie! What, are you mad?

Juliet [*kneeling*]. Good father, I beseech you on my knees,
Hear me with patience but to speak a word.

160 **Capulet.** Hang thee, young baggage, disobedient wretch!
I tell thee what: get thee to church o' Thursday
Or never after look me in the face.
Speak not, reply not; do not answer me!
My fingers itch.[19]— Lady Capulet, we scarce thought us blest

165 That God had lent us but this only child;
But now I see this one is one too much,
And that we have a curse in having her.
Out on her, hilding!

Nurse.   God in heaven bless her!
You are to blame, my lord, to rate[20] her so.

170 **Capulet.** And why, my Lady Wisdom? Hold your tongue,
Good Prudence. Smatter with your gossips,[21] go.

Nurse. I speak no treason.

Capulet.   O, God-i'-good-e'en!

Nurse. May not one speak?

Capulet.   Peace, you mumbling fool!
Utter your gravity o'er a gossip's bowl,[22]

175 For here we need it not.

Lady Capulet.   You are too hot.

Capulet. God's bread, it makes me mad!
Day, night, hour, tide, time, work, play,
Alone, in company, still my care hath been
To have her matched. And having now provided

180 A gentleman of noble parentage,
Of fair demesnes, youthful, and nobly liened,[23]

---

[19] My fingers itch—My hands want to choke or strike you.

[20] rate—scold.

[21] Good Prudence . . . gossips—Wise one, chatter with your friends.

[22] Utter . . . bowl—Go share your wisdom with other foolish old women.

[23] Of fair . . . liened—with fine estates and property, young, and nobly descended.

Stuffed, as they say, with honorable parts,
Proportioned as one's thought would wish a man—
And then to have a wretched puling fool,
A whining mammet, in her fortune's tender,[24]
To answer, "I'll not wed, I cannot love,
I am too young; I pray you, pardon me."
But, an you will not wed, I'll pardon you!
Graze where you will, you shall not house with me.
Look to 't, think on 't. I do not use to jest.
Thursday is near. Lay hand on heart, advise.
An you be mine, I'll give you to my friend;
An you be not, hang, beg, starve, die in the streets,
For, by my soul, I'll ne'er acknowledge thee,
Nor what is mine shall never do thee good.
Trust to 't, bethink you. I'll not be forsworn.

[*Exit* Capulet.]

Juliet. Is there no pity sitting in the clouds
That sees into the bottom of my grief?—
O sweet my mother, cast me not away!
Delay this marriage for a month, a week;
Or, if you do not, make the bridal bed
In that dim monument where Tybalt lies.

Lady Capulet. Talk not to me, for I'll not speak a word.
Do as thou wilt, for I have done with thee.

[*Exit* Lady Capulet.]

Juliet [*rising*]. O God!—O Nurse, how shall this be prevented?
My husband is on earth, my faith in heaven.
How shall that faith return again to earth,
Unless that husband send it me from heaven
By leaving earth? Comfort me, counsel me.—
Alack, alack, that heaven should practice stratagems[25]
Upon so soft a subject as myself!—
What sayst thou? Hast thou not a word of joy?
Some comfort, Nurse.

---

[24] puling ... tender—crying fool, whining doll, when an offer of good fortune is made to her.

[25] practice stratagems—play such tricks.

Nurse. Faith, here it is.
Romeo is banished, and all the world to nothing

215 That he dares ne'er come back to challenge you,[26]
Or if he do, it needs must be by **stealth.**[27]
Then, since the case so stands as now it doth,
I think it best you married with the County.
O, he's a lovely gentleman!

220 Romeo's a dishclout to him. An eagle, madam,
Hath not so green, so quick, so fair an eye
As Paris hath. Beshrew my very heart,
I think you are happy in this second match,
For it excels your first, or, if it did not,

225 Your first is dead—or 'twere as good he were,
As living here and you no use of him.

Juliet. Speak'st thou from thy heart?

Nurse. And from my soul too. Else beshrew them both.

Juliet. Amen!

230 **Nurse.** What?

Juliet. Well, thou hast comforted me marvelous much.
Go in, and tell my lady I am gone,
Having displeased my father, to Laurence' cell
To make confession and to be absolved.

235 **Nurse.** Marry, I will; and this is wisely done.
[*Exit* Nurse.]

Juliet. Ancient damnation![28] O most wicked fiend!
Is it more sin to wish me thus forsworn,
Or to dispraise my lord with that same tongue
Which she hath praised him with above compare

240 So many thousand times? Go, counselor,
Thou and my bosom henceforth shall be twain.[29]
I'll to the Friar to know his remedy.
If all else fail, myself have power to die.
[*She exits.*]

---

[26] all the world . . . you—The odds are that he will not dare to come back to claim you.

[27] **stealth**—sly, secret actions.

[28] Ancient damnation—damned old woman.

[29] Thou . . . twain—I won't tell my secrets to you anymore.

Act Four, Scene One

Outside Friar Laurence's cell, later that morning, Paris tries to make arrangements with Friar Laurence to marry him and Juliet. Juliet, when she is alone with the Friar, claims she is ready to kill herself rather than be forced to marry. Friar Laurence gives her a drug that will make her appear as dead. He tells her that when she is laid in the Capulet tomb, Romeo can come and take her away to Mantua with him. Juliet accepts the Friar's solution eagerly.

Enter Friar Laurence *and* County Paris.

Friar Laurence. On Thursday, sir? The time is very short.

Paris. My father Capulet will have it so,
    And I am nothing slow to slack his haste.[1]

Friar Laurence. You say you do not know the lady's mind?
5   Uneven is the course. I like it not.

Paris. Immoderately she weeps for Tybalt's death,
    And therefore have I little talked of love,
    For Venus smiles not in a house of tears.
    Now, sir, her father counts it dangerous
10   That she do give her sorrow so much sway,
    And in his wisdom hastes our marriage
    To stop the **inundation**[2] of her tears,
    Which, too much minded by herself alone,
    May be put from her by society.
15   Now do you know the reason of this haste.

Friar Laurence [*aside*]. I would I knew not why it should be slowed.—
    Look, sir, here comes the lady toward my cell.

[*Enter* Juliet.]

Paris. Happily met, my lady and my Lady Capulet!

Juliet. That may be, sir, when I may be a Lady Capulet.

20 **Paris.** That "may be" must be, love, on Thursday next.

Juliet. What must be shall be.

Friar Laurence.   That's a certain text.

---

[1] nothing . . . haste—anxious to do nothing that might slow down his plans for a quick marriage.

[2] **inundation**—flood.

Paris. Come you to make confession to this father?

Juliet. To answer that, I should confess to you.

Paris. Do not deny to him that you love me.

25 **Juliet.** I will confess to you that I love him.

Paris. So will you, I am sure, that you love me.

Juliet. If I do so, it will be of more price,[3]
　　　　Being spoke behind your back, than to your face.

Paris. Poor soul, thy face is much abused with tears.

30 **Juliet.** The tears have got small victory by that,
　　　　For it was bad enough before their spite.

Paris. Thou wrong'st it more than tears with that report.

Juliet. That is no slander,[4] sir, which is a truth;
　　　　And what I spake, I spake it to my face.

35 **Paris.** Thy face is mine, and thou hast slandered it.

Juliet. It may be so, for it is not mine own.—
　　　　Are you at leisure, holy Father, now,
　　　　Or shall I come to you at evening Mass?

Friar Laurence. My leisure serves me, **pensive**[5] daughter, now.
40 　　　　My lord, we must entreat the time alone.

Paris. God shield I should disturb devotion!—
　　　　Juliet, on Thursday early will I rouse you.
　　　　Till then, adieu, and keep this holy kiss.

[*Exit* Paris.]

Juliet. O, shut the door! And when thou hast done so,
45 　　　　Come weep with me, past hope, past cure, past help!

Friar Laurence. Ah, Juliet, I already know thy grief;
　　　　It strains me past the compass of my wits.[6]
　　　　I hear thou must, and nothing may prorogue it,
　　　　On Thursday next be married to this county.

50 **Juliet.** Tell me not, Friar, that thou hearest of this,
　　　　Unless thou tell me how I may prevent it.
　　　　If in thy wisdom thou canst give no help,

---

[3] of more price—of greater value.

[4] slander—false statement made with an intent to harm others.

[5] **pensive**—sad.

[6] It strains ... wits—I'm at my wits' end.

Do thou but call my **resolution**[7] wise
And with this knife I'll help it presently.

[*She shows him a knife.*]

55   God joined my heart and Romeo's, thou our hands;
And ere this hand, by thee to Romeo sealed,
Shall be the label to another deed,
Or my true heart with treacherous revolt
Turn to another, this shall slay them both.
60   Therefore, out of thy long-experienced time,
Give me some present counsel, or, behold,
Twixt my extremes and me this bloody knife
Shall play the umpire, arbitrating that
Which the commission of thy years and art
65   Could to no issue of true honor bring.[8]
Be not so long to speak; I long to die
If what thou speak'st speak not of remedy.

Friar Laurence. Hold, daughter. I do spy a kind of hope,
Which craves as desperate an execution
70   As that is desperate which we would prevent.
If, rather than to marry County Paris,
Thou hast the strength of will to slay thyself,
Then is it likely thou wilt undertake
A thing like death to chide away this shame,
75   That cop'st with Death himself to scape from it;[9]
And if thou darest, I'll give thee remedy.

Juliet. O, bid me leap, rather than marry Paris,
From off the battlements of any tower,
Or walk in thievish ways, or bid me lurk
80   Where serpents are. Chain me with roaring bears,
Or hide me nightly in a charnel house,[10]
O'ercovered quite with dead men's rattling bones,
With reeky shanks and yellow chopless skulls;
Or bid me go into a new-made grave

---

[7] **resolution**—determination.

[8] Twixt . . . bring—This knife will provide a solution for me and my troubles that you, with your age and wisdom, cannot.

[9] That cop'st . . . it—that bargains with death to escape it.

[10] charnel house—vault where the bones of the dead are placed.

Friar Lawrence (Stephen De Rosa) describes his plan to Juliet (Sanaa Lathan) in the Yale School of Drama production.

85   And hide me with a dead man in his tomb—
       Things that, to hear them told, have made me tremble—
       And I will do it without fear or doubt,
       To live an unstained Lady Capulet to my sweet love.
Friar Laurence. Hold, then. Go home, be merry, give consent
90   To marry Paris. Wednesday is tomorrow.
       Tomorrow night look that thou lie alone;
       Let not the Nurse be with thee in thy chamber.
       Take thou this vial,[11] being then in bed,
[*He shows her a vial.*]
       And this distilling liquor drink thou off,
95   When presently through all thy veins shall run
       A cold and drowsy humor; for no pulse
       Shall keep his native progress, but surcease; [12]
       No warmth, no breath shall testify thou livest;

---

[11] vial—small bottle.

[12] no pulse . . . surcease—You will seem to have no pulse.

The roses in thy lips and cheeks shall fade

100　To wanny ashes, thy eyes' windows fall

Like death when he shuts up the day of life;

Each part, deprived of supple government,[13]

Shall, stiff and stark and cold, appear like death.

And in this borrowed likeness of shrunk death

105　Thou shalt continue two-and-forty hours,

And then awake as from a pleasant sleep.

Now, when the bridegroom in the morning comes

To rouse thee from thy bed, there art thou dead.

Then, as the manner of our country is,

110　In thy best robes uncovered on the bier

Thou shalt be borne to that same ancient vault

Where all the kindred of the Capulets lie.

In the meantime, against thou shalt awake,

Shall Romeo by my letters know our drift,[14]

115　And hither shall he come; and he and I

Will watch thy waking, and that very night

Shall Romeo bear thee hence to Mantua.

And this shall free thee from this present shame,

If no inconstant toy[15] nor womanish fear

120　Abate thy valor[16] in the acting it.

Juliet [*taking the vial*]. Give me, give me! O, tell not me of fear!

Friar Laurence. Hold, get you gone. Be strong and prosperous

In this resolve. I'll send a friar with speed

To Mantua, with my letters to thy lord.

125　**Juliet.** Love give me strength, and strength shall help afford.

Farewell, dear Father!

[*They exit separately.*]

---

[13] supple government—control of movement.

[14] against . . . drift—In preparation for your awakening, I'll write to Romeo about our plan.

[15] inconstant toy—change of mind.

[16] Abate thy valor—diminish your courage.

Act Four, Scene Two

In a room in the Capulets' house, soon after, Juliet tells her parents she is sorry for disobeying them and promises to marry Paris the next day. Capulet, Lady Capulet, and the Nurse start their hasty preparations.

Enter Lord Capulet, Lady Capulet, Nurse, *and two or three* Servingmen.

Capulet. So many guests invite as here are writ.

[*Exit one or two* Servingmen.]

Sirrah, go hire me twenty cunning cooks.

Servingman. You shall have none ill, sir, for I'll try if they can lick their fingers.

5   **Capulet.** How canst thou try them so?

Servingman. Marry, sir, 'tis an ill cook that cannot lick his own fingers.

Therefore he that cannot lick his fingers goes not with me.

Capulet. Go, begone.

[*Exit* Servingman.]

We shall be much unfurnished for this time.

10   What, is my daughter gone to Friar Laurence?

Nurse. Ay, forsooth.

Capulet. Well, he may chance to do some good on her.

A peevish self-willed harlotry it is.[1]

[*Enter* Juliet.]

Nurse. See where she comes from shrift with merry look.

15   **Capulet.** How now, my headstrong, where have you been gadding?[2]

Juliet. Where I have learned me to repent the sin

Of disobedient opposition

To you and your behests,[3] and am enjoined

By holy Laurence to fall **prostrate**[4] here,

[*Kneeling.*]

---

[1] peevish . . . is—ill-tempered, selfish wench.

[2] gadding—roving about looking for pleasure or excitement.

[3] behests—commands, orders.

[4] **prostrate**—face down; helpless.

'Tis an ill cook that cannot lick his own fingers.

20	To beg your pardon. Pardon, I beseech you!
	Henceforward I am ever ruled by you.

Capulet. Send for the county! Go tell him of this.
I'll have this knot knit up tomorrow morning.

Juliet. I met the youthful lord at Laurence' cell

25 And gave him what becomèd[5] love I might,
Not stepping o'er the bounds of modesty.

Capulet. Why, I am glad on 't. This is well. Stand up.

[Juliet *rises.*]

This is as 't should be. Let me see the county;
Ay, marry, go, I say, and fetch him hither.

30 Now, afore God, this reverend holy friar,
All our whole city is much bound to him.

Juliet. Nurse, will you go with me into my closet[6]
To help me sort such needful ornaments
As you think fit to furnish me tomorrow?

35 **Lady Capulet.** No, not till Thursday. There is time enough.

Capulet. Go, Nurse, go with her. We'll to church tomorrow.

[*Exit* Juliet *and* Nurse.]

Lady Capulet. We shall be short in our provision.
'Tis now near night.

Capulet. Tush, I will stir about,
And all things shall be well, I warrant thee, Lady Capulet.

40 Go thou to Juliet, help to deck up her.[7]
I'll not to bed tonight. Let me alone.
I'll play the huswife Capulet[8] for this once.—What, ho!—
They are all forth. Well, I will walk myself
To County Paris, to prepare up him

45 Against tomorrow. My heart is wondrous light,
Since this same wayward girl is so reclaimed.

[*They exit.*]

---

[5] becomèd—suitable.

[6] closet—private room.

[7] deck up her—clothe and adorn her.

[8] huswife Capulet—housewife.

Act Four, Scene Three

In Juliet's room, that night, Juliet tells Lady Capulet and the Nurse that she is ready for the wedding. Left alone, Juliet voices her fears and then drinks the drug Friar Laurence gave her.

Enter Juliet *and* Nurse.

Juliet. Ay, those attires are best. But, gentle Nurse,
    I pray thee, leave me to myself tonight;
    For I have need of many orisons[1]
    To move the heavens to smile upon my state,
5   Which, well thou knowest, is cross[2] and full of sin.
[*Enter* Lady Capulet.]
Lady Capulet. What, are you busy, ho? Need you my help?
Juliet. No, madam, we have culled such necessaries
    As are behooveful for our state tomorrow.[3]
    So please you, let me now be left alone,
10   And let the Nurse this night sit up with you,
    For I am sure you have your hands full all
    In this so sudden business.
Lady Capulet. Good night.
    Get thee to bed and rest, for thou hast need.
[*Exit* Lady Capulet *and* Nurse.]
15 **Juliet.** Farewell!—God knows when we shall meet again.
    I have a faint cold fear thrills through my veins
    That almost freezes up the heat of life.
    I'll call them back again to comfort me.
    Nurse!—What should she do here?
20   My **dismal**[4] scene I needs must act alone.
    Come, vial.
[*She takes out the vial.*]

---

[1] orisons—prayers.

[2] cross—contrary.

[3] culled . . . state—chosen what is needed for the ceremony.

[4] **dismal**—miserable.

What if this mixture do not work at all?
Shall I be married then tomorrow morning?
No, no, this shall forbid it. Lie thou there.
[*She takes out a dagger and puts it down beside her.*]
25 What if it be a poison, which the friar
Subtly hath ministered to have me dead,
Lest in this marriage he should be dishonored
Because he married me before to Romeo?
I fear it is; and yet methinks it should not,
30 For he hath still been tried a holy man.
How if, when I am laid into the tomb,
I wake before the time that Romeo
Come to redeem me? There's a fearful point!
Shall I not then be stifled in the vault,
35 To whose foul mouth no healthsome air breathes in,
And there die strangled ere my Romeo comes?
Or, if I live, is it not very like
The horrible conceit⁵ of death and night,
Together with the terror of the place—
40 As in a vault, an ancient receptacle,
Where for this many hundred years the bones
Of all my buried ancestors are packed;
Where bloody Tybalt, yet but green in earth,
Lies fest'ring in his shroud;⁶ where, as they say,
45 At some hours in the night spirits resort—
Alack, alack, is it not like that I,
So early waking, what with loathsome smells,
And shrieks like mandrakes torn out of the earth,
That living mortals, hearing them, run mad⁷—
50 O, if I wake, shall I not be **distraught**,⁸
Environèd⁹ with all these hideous fears,
And madly play with my forefathers' joints,

---

⁵ conceit—idea.

⁶ yet but . . . shroud—freshly buried, lies rotting in his burial wrappings.

⁷ shrieks . . . mad—The mandrake, a plant whose root sometimes resembles a human body, was popularly thought to scream when pulled from the earth, a sound that caused madness in humans.

⁸ **distraught**—in a state of great terror or confusion.

⁹ Environèd—surrounded.

In the Yale School of Drama production, Juliet (Sanaa Lathan) prepares to swallow the drug that will make her appear dead.

And pluck the mangled Tybalt from his shroud,
And, in this rage, with some great kinsman's bone

55 As with a club dash out my desp'rate brains?
O, look! Methinks I see my cousin's ghost
Seeking out Romeo, that did spit his body
Upon a rapier's point. Stay, Tybalt, stay!
Romeo, Romeo, Romeo! Here's drink—I drink to thee.
[*She drinks and falls upon her bed, within the curtains.*]

Act Four, Scene Four

In a room in the Capulets' house, very early the next morning, Capulet, Lady Capulet, and the Nurse direct the servants in preparation for the wedding celebration. Hearing Paris arrive, Capulet sends the Nurse to wake Juliet.

Enter Lady Capulet *and* Nurse.

Lady Capulet. Hold, take these keys, and fetch more spices, Nurse.

Nurse. They call for dates and quinces in the pastry.

[*Enter* Lord Capulet.]

Capulet. Come, stir, stir, stir! The second cock hath crowed,
The curfew bell hath rung. 'Tis three o'clock.

5   Look to the baked meats,[1] good Angelica.
Spare not for cost.

Nurse.   Go, you cotquean,[2] go,
Get you to bed. Faith, you'll be sick tomorrow
For this night's watching.

Capulet. No, not a whit. What, I have watched ere now

10   All night for lesser cause, and ne'er been sick.

Lady Capulet. Ay, you have been a mouse-hunt[3] in your time,
But I will watch you from such watching now.

[*Exit* Lady Capulet *and* Nurse.]

Capulet. A jealous hood,[4] a jealous hood!

[*Enter three or four* Servingmen *with spits and logs and baskets.*]
Now, fellow, what is there?

15 **First Servingman.** Things for the cook, sir, but I know not what.

Capulet. Make haste, make haste.

[*Exit* First Servingman.] Sirrah, fetch drier logs.
Call Peter. He will show thee where they are.

---

[1] baked meats—pies and pastries.

[2] cotquean—man who acts like a housewife.

[3] mouse-hunt—chaser of women.

[4] hood—person.

Second Servingman. I have a head, sir, that will find out logs

20   And never trouble Peter for the matter.

Capulet. Mass, and well said. A merry whoreson, ha!

Thou shalt be loggerhead.[5] [*Exit* Servingman.] Good faith, 'tis day.

The County will be here with music straight,

For so he said he would.

[*Music plays within.*]

25   I hear him near.

Nurse!—Wife! What, ho!—What, Nurse, I say!

[*Enter* Nurse.]

Go waken Juliet, go and trim her up.

I'll go and chat with Paris. Hie, make haste,

Make haste. The bridegroom he is come already.

30   Make haste, I say.

[*They all exit.*]

---

[5] loggerhead—stupid fellow; blockhead.

Act Four, Scene Five

In Juliet's bedroom, the Nurse finds Juliet in a deathlike trance. Juliet's parents and Paris all *lament. Friar Laurence comes and begins to arrange Juliet's funeral.*

Juliet *in bed behind curtains. The* Nurse *goes to the bed.*

Nurse. Mistress! What, mistress! Juliet!—Fast, I warrant her,[1] she.—
    Why, lamb, why, lady! Fie, you slugabed!
    Why, love, I say! Madam! Sweetheart! Why, bride!
    What, not a word? You take your pennyworths[2] now.
5   Sleep for a week; for the next night, I warrant,
    The County Paris hath set up his rest[3]
    That you shall rest but little. God forgive me,
    Marry, and amen! How sound is she asleep!
    I needs must wake her.—Madam, madam, madam!
10   Ay, let the County take you in your bed;
    He'll fright you up, i' faith. Will it not be?
[*She opens the bed curtains.*]
    What, dressed, and in your clothes, and down again?
    I must needs wake you. Lady, lady, lady!—
    Alas, alas! Help, help! My lady's dead!—
15   O, weraday, that ever I was born!
    Some aqua vitae, ho!—My lord! My lady!
[*Enter* Lady Capulet.]
Lady Capulet. What noise is here?
Nurse.   O lamentable day!
Lady Capulet. What is the matter?
Nurse.   Look, look! O heavy day!
Lady Capulet. O me, O me! My child, my only life!
20   Revive, look up, or I will die with thee!
    Help, help! Call help.
[*Enter* Lord Capulet.]

---

[1] Fast . . . her—She's fast asleep, I swear.
[2] pennyworths—short naps.
[3] set . . . rest—firmly resolved.

Capulet. For shame, bring Juliet forth. Her lord is come.

Nurse. She's dead, deceased. She's dead, alack the day!

Lady Capulet. Alack the day, she's dead, she's dead, she's dead!

25 **Capulet.** Ha! Let me see her. Out, alas! She's cold.

Her blood is settled, and her joints are stiff;

Life and these lips have long been separated.

Death lies on her like an untimely frost

Upon the sweetest flower of all the field.

30 **Nurse.** O lamentable day!

Lady Capulet. O woeful time!

Capulet. Death, that hath ta'en her hence to make me wail,

Ties up my tongue and will not let me speak.

[*Enter* Friar Laurence *and* Count Paris, *with* Musicians.]

Friar Laurence. Come, is the bride ready to go to church?

Capulet. Ready to go, but never to return.—

35 O son, the night before thy wedding day

Hath Death lain with thy Lady Capulet. There she lies,

Flower as she was, deflowered by him.

Death is my son-in-law, death is my heir;

My daughter he hath wedded. I will die,

40 And leave him all. Life, living, all is death's.

Paris. Have I thought long to see this morning's face,

And doth it give me such a sight as this?

Lady Capulet. Accurst, unhappy, wretched, hateful day!

Most miserable hour that e'er time saw

45 In lasting labor of his pilgrimage!

But one, poor one, one poor and loving child,

But one thing to rejoice and **solace**[4] in,

And cruel death hath catched it from my sight!

Nurse. O woe! O woeful, woeful, woeful day!

50 Most lamentable day, most woeful day

That ever, ever I did yet behold!

O day, O day, O day! O hateful day!

Never was seen so black a day as this.

O woeful day, O woeful day!

---

[4] **solace**—find comfort.

In the Hartford stage production, Juliet (Calista Flockhart) is believed to be dead.

55   **Paris.** Beguiled, divorcèd, wrongèd, spited, slain!
        Most detestable death, by thee beguiled,
        By cruel, cruel thee quite overthrown!
        O love! O life! Not life, but love in death!
    Capulet. Despised, distressèd, hated, martyred, killed!
60   Uncomfortable time, why cam'st thou now
        To murder, murder our solemnity?[5]
        O child! O child! My soul, and not my child!
        Dead art thou! Alack, my child is dead,
        And with my child my joys are burièd.
65   **Friar Laurence.** Peace, ho, for shame! Confusion's cure[6] lives not
        In these confusions. Heaven and yourself
        Had part in this fair maid. Now heaven hath all,

---

[5] murder our solemnity—ruin our joyful celebration.
[6] Confusion's cure—remedy for destruction.

And all the better is it for the maid.
Your part in her you could not keep from death,
70   But heaven keeps his part in eternal life.
The most you sought was her promotion,
For 'twas your heaven she should be advanced;[7]
And weep ye now, seeing she is advanced
Above the clouds, as high as heaven itself?
75   O, in this love, you love your child so ill
That you run mad, seeing that she is well.
She's not well married that lives married long,
But she's best married that dies married young.
Dry up your tears, and stick your rosemary
80   On this fair corpse, and, as the custom is,
And in her best array, bear her to church,
For though fond nature bids us all lament,
Yet nature's tears are reason's merriment.[8]

Capulet. All things that we ordainèd festival
85   Turn from their office to black funeral:
Our instruments to melancholy bells,
Our wedding cheer to a sad burial feast,
Our solemn hymns to sullen dirges[9] change,
Our bridal flowers serve for a buried corpse,
90   And all things change them to the contrary.

Friar Laurence. Sir, go you in, and, madam, go with him,
And go, Sir Paris. Everyone prepare
To follow this fair corpse unto her grave.
The heavens do lour upon you for some ill;[10]
95   Move them no more by crossing their high will.

[*Exit all but* Nurse *and* Musicians.]

First Musician. Faith, we may put up our pipes and be gone.

Nurse. Honest good fellows, ah, put up, put up!
For well you know this is a pitiful case.

[*Exit* Nurse.]

---

[7] The most ... advanced—All you looked for was her social advancement (through marriage) because you believed that was the greatest good.

[8] nature's ... merriment—that which makes human nature mourn is cause for joy to the reason.

[9] dirges—funeral songs.

[10] lour ... ill—frown upon you because of some sin you have committed.

First Musician. Ay, by my troth, the case may be amended.[11]

[*Enter* Peter.]

100   **Peter.** Musicians, O, musicians, "Heart's ease," "Heart's ease." O, an you
        will have me live, play "Heart's ease."

First Musician. Why "Heart's ease"?

Peter. O, musicians, because my heart itself plays "My heart is full."
        O, play me some merry dump[12] to comfort me.

105   **First Musician.** Not a dump we! 'Tis no time to play now.

Peter. You will not, then?

First Musician. No.

Peter. I will then give it you soundly.

First Musician. What will you give us?

110   **Peter.** No money, on my faith, but the gleek, I will give you
        the minstrel.[13]

First Musician. Then will I give you the serving-creature.

Peter. Then will I lay the serving-creature's dagger on your pate.[14]
        I will carry no crotchets.[15] I'll re you, I'll fa you. Do you note me?

115   **First Musician.** An you *re* us and *fa* us, you note us.

Second Musician. Pray you, put up your dagger and put out your wit.

Peter. Then have at you with my wit! I will dry-beat you with an iron
        wit, and put up my iron dagger. Answer me like men:

[*Sings.*]

        When griping griefs the heart doth wound,

120   *And doleful dumps the mind oppress,*
        Then music with her silver sound—
        Why "silver sound"? Why "music with her silver sound"?
        What say you, Simon Catling?

First Musician. Marry, Sir, because silver hath a sweet sound.

125   **Peter.** Pretty! What say you, Hugh Rebeck?

Second Musician. I say "silver sound" because musicians sound
        for silver.

Peter. Pretty too! What say you, James Soundpost?

---

[11] case . . . amended—The situation could be improved, with a pun that an instrument case may be repaired.

[12] dump—mournful tune or dance.

[13] the gleek . . . minstrel—as a joke I will call you a minstrel, or vagabond.

[14] pate—head.

[15] I will . . . crotchets—I will not sing any quarternotes, with a pun that I will not put up with your whims.

Third Musician. Faith, I know not what to say.

130   **Peter.** O, I cry you mercy, you are the singer. I will say for you. It is "music with her silver sound" because musicians have no gold for sounding.

[*Sings.*]

    Then music with her silver sound
    With speedy help doth lend redress.

[*Exit* Peter.]

135   **First Musician.** What a pestilent knave is this same!

Second Musician. Hang him, Jack! Come, we'll in here, tarry for the mourners, and stay dinner.[16]

[*They exit.*]

---

[16] we'll in . . . dinner—We'll go inside, wait for the mourners, and then stay for dinner.

Act Five, Scene One

On a street in Mantua, a day later, Romeo's servant, Balthasar, brings him news of Juliet's death and burial. Romeo sends him to hire horses to return to Verona. Although the sale of poison is illegal in Mantua, Romeo finds a poor apothecary, a seller of drugs. The apothecary is willing, for enough money, to sell Romeo a vial of poison.

Enter Romeo.

    Romeo. If I may trust the flattering truth of sleep,
        My dreams presage[1] some joyful news at hand.
        My bosom's lord sits lightly in his throne,[2]
        And all this day an unaccustomed spirit
5   Lifts me above the ground with cheerful thoughts.
        I dreamt my lady came and found me dead—
        Strange dream, that gives a dead man leave to think!—
        And breathed such life with kisses in my lips
        That I revived and was an emperor.
10   Ah me, how sweet is love itself possessed
        When but love's shadows are so rich in joy![3]
    [*Enter* Romeo's *servant* Balthasar, *booted.*]
        News from Verona!—How now, Balthasar,
        Dost thou not bring me letters from the Friar?
        How doth my lady? Is my father well?
15   How doth my Juliet? That I ask again,
        For nothing can be ill if she be well.
    Balthasar. Then she is well, and nothing can be ill.
        Her body sleeps in Capels' monument,
        And her immortal part with angels lives.
20   I saw her laid low in her kindred's vault,
        And presently took post to tell it you.

---

[1] presage—foretell.

[2] My bosom's . . . throne—My heart is light.

[3] how sweet . . . joy—When dreams of love are so joyful, how much sweeter is love itself?

Romeo (Jay Goede) purchases poison from an apothecary (Jason Novak) in The Shakespeare Theatre's 1994 production of *Romeo and Juliet.*

O, pardon me for bringing these ill news,
Since you did leave it for my office,[4] sir.

Romeo. Is it e'en so?—Then I defy you, stars!—

25   Thou knowest my lodging. Get me ink and paper,
And hire post-horses. I will hence tonight.

Balthasar. I do beseech you, sir, have patience.
Your looks are pale and wild, and do import[5]
Some misadventure.

Romeo.   Tush, thou art deceived.

30   Leave me, and do the thing I bid thee do.
Hast thou no letters to me from the Friar?

Balthasar. No, my good lord.

Romeo.   No matter. Get thee gone,
And hire those horses. I'll be with thee straight.

---

[4] office—duty.

[5] import—suggest.

[*Exit* Balthasar.]

Well, Juliet, I will lie with thee tonight.
35 Let's see for means. O mischief, thou art swift
To enter in the thoughts of desperate men!
I do remember an apothecary—
And hereabouts he dwells—which late I noted
In tattered weeds, with overwhelming brows,
40 Culling of simples.[6] Meager were his looks;
Sharp misery had worn him to the bones;
And in his needy shop a tortoise hung,
An alligator stuffed, and other skins
Of ill-shaped fishes; and about his shelves
45 A beggarly account of empty boxes,
Green earthen pots, bladders, and musty seeds,
Remnants of packthread, and old cakes of roses
Were thinly scattered to make up a show.
Noting this **penury**,[7] to myself I said,
50 "An if a man did need a poison now,
Whose sale is present death in Mantua,[8]
Here lives a caitiff[9] wretch would sell it him."
O, this same thought did but forerun my need,
And this same needy man must sell it me.
55 As I remember, this should be the house.
Being holiday, the beggar's shop is shut.—
What, ho! Apothecary!

[*Enter* Apothecary.]

Apothecary.   Who calls so loud?

Romeo. Come hither, man. I see that thou art poor.
Hold, there is forty ducats. [*He shows gold.*] Let me have
60 A dram of poison, such soon-speeding gear
As will **disperse**[10] itself through all the veins

---

[6] Culling of simples—selecting medicinal herbs.

[7] **penury**—extreme poverty.

[8] Whose . . . Mantua—The sale of poison is punishable by death in Mantua.

[9] caitiff—miserable.

[10] **disperse**—spread out.

That the life-weary taker may fall dead,
And that the trunk[11] may be discharged of breath
As violently as hasty powder fired
65   Doth hurry from the fatal cannon's womb.

Apothecary. Such mortal drugs I have, but Mantua's law
Is death to any he that utters[12] them.

Romeo. Art thou so bare and full of wretchedness,
And fearest to die? Famine is in thy cheeks,
70   Need and oppression starveth in thy eyes,
Contempt and beggary hangs upon thy back.
The world is not thy friend, nor the world's law;
The world affords no law to make thee rich.
Then be not poor, but break it, and take this.

75   **Apothecary.** My poverty, but not my will, consents.

Romeo. I pay thy poverty and not thy will.

Apothecary [*giving him the poison*]. Put this in any liquid thing you will
And drink it off, and if you had the strength
Of twenty men it would dispatch you straight.

80   **Romeo** [*giving him the money*]. There is thy gold—worse poison to
          men's souls,
Doing more murder in this loathsome world
Than these poor compounds that thou mayst not sell.[13]
I sell thee poison; thou hast sold me none.
Farewell. Buy food, and get thyself in flesh.
[*Exit* Apothecary.]

85   Come, cordial[14] and not poison, go with me
To Juliet's grave, for there must I use thee.
[*He exits.*]

---

[11] trunk—body.

[12] utters—sells.

[13] gold . . . sell—Gold does more harm than the poisons you're not supposed to sell.

[14] cordial—stimulating drink.

Act Five, Scene Two

Outside Friar Laurence's cell, the next day, Friar John tells Friar Laurence why he was unable to deliver Laurence's message to Romeo. Friar Laurence calls for a crowbar and heads for Juliet's tomb so that he can be there when she wakes up.

Enter Friar John.

Friar John. Holy Franciscan friar! Brother, ho!
[*Enter* Friar Laurence.]
Friar Laurence. This same should be the voice of Friar John.
    Welcome from Mantua! What says Romeo?
    Or if his mind be writ, give me his letter.
5 **Friar John.** Going to find a barefoot brother out—
    One of our order—to associate[1] me
    Here in this city visiting the sick,
    And finding him, the searchers of the town,
    Suspecting that we both were in a house
10   Where the infectious pestilence[2] did reign,
    Sealed up the doors and would not let us forth,
    So that my speed to Mantua there was stayed.
Friar Laurence. Who bare my letter, then, to Romeo?
Friar John. I could not send it—here it is again—
15   Nor get a messenger to bring it thee,
    So fearful were they of infection.
[*He gives* Friar Laurence *a letter.*]
Friar Laurence. Unhappy fortune! By my brotherhood,
    The letter was not nice but full of charge,
    Of dear import,[3] and the neglecting it
20   May do much danger. Friar John, go hence.

---

[1] associate—accompany.

[2] infectious pestilence—plague, highly contagious disease.

[3] not nice ... import—not trivial but very important.

Get me an iron crow[4] and bring it straight
Unto my cell.

Friar John. Brother, I'll go and bring it thee.

[*Exit* Friar John.]

Friar Laurence. Now must I to the monument alone.
25   Within this three hours will fair Juliet wake.
She will beshrew me much that Romeo
Hath had no notice of these accidents;[5]
But I will write again to Mantua,
And keep her at my cell till Romeo come—
30   Poor living corpse, closed in a dead man's tomb!

[*He exits.*]

---

[4] iron crow—crowbar.

[5] accidents—events.

Act Five, Scene Three

Paris comes to the Capulet tomb to scatter flowers. He hides in the graveyard around the tomb when Romeo enters with Balthasar, carrying tools. Romeo gives Balthasar some money and a letter to deliver to Romeo's father. Balthasar hides nearby. As Romeo begins to pry open the tomb, Paris challenges him. Romeo doesn't want to fight, but Paris attacks, and in the duel that follows, Romeo kills him. Romeo opens the tomb and carries Paris inside. Noting that Juliet still looks beautiful, even in death, Romeo kisses her, drinks his poison, and dies. Out in the graveyard, Friar Laurence meets Balthasar, who tells him that Romeo is inside. When Juliet awakes, she sees the dead Romeo and Paris and kills herself with Romeo's dagger. Watchmen capture Balthasar and Friar Laurence as Prince Escalus arrives with Capulet and Montague. Friar Laurence tells the Prince what has happened, and Balthasar and Paris's page confirm his story. Capulet and Montague at last make their peace.

Enter Paris, *and his* Page *bearing flowers, perfumed water, and a torch.*

Paris. Give me thy torch, boy. Hence, and stand aloof.[1]
    Yet put it out, for I would not be seen.
    Under yond yew trees lay thee all along,[2]
    Holding thy ear close to the hollow ground:
5   So shall no foot upon the churchyard tread,—
    Being loose, unfirm, with digging up of graves,—
    But thou shalt hear it. Whistle then to me
    As signal that thou hearest something approach.
    Give me those flowers. Do as I bid thee. Go.
10 **Page** [*aside*]. I am almost afraid to stand alone
    Here in the churchyard, yet I will adventure.
[*He moves away from* Paris.]
Paris [*strewing flowers and perfumed water*].
    Sweet flower, with flowers thy bridal bed I strew
    O woe! Thy canopy is dust and stones—
    Which with sweet water nightly I will dew,
15   Or wanting that, with tears distilled by moans.

---

[1] aloof—at a distance.
[2] Under . . . along—Go lie under those yew trees.

The obsequies[3] that I for thee will keep
Nightly shall be to strew thy grave and weep.
[*The Page whistles.*]
The boy gives warning something doth approach.
What cursèd foot wanders this way tonight
20   To cross my obsequies and true love's rite?
What, with a torch? Muffle me, night, awhile.
[*He steps aside.*]
[*Enter* Romeo *and* Balthasar, *with a torch, a mattock, and a crowbar.*]
Romeo. Give me that mattock and the wrenching iron.
[*He takes the tools.*]
Hold, take this letter. Early in the morning
See thou deliver it to my lord and father.
[*He gives a letter and takes a torch.*]
25   Give me the light. Upon thy life I charge thee,
Whate'er thou hearest or seest, stand all aloof
And do not interrupt me in my course.
Why I descend into this bed of death
Is partly to behold my lady's face,
30   But chiefly to take thence from her dead finger
A precious ring—a ring that I must use
In dear employment. Therefore hence, begone.
But if thou, jealous, dost return to pry
In what I farther shall intend to do,
35   By heaven, I will tear thee joint by joint
And strew this hungry churchyard with thy limbs.
The time and my intents are savage-wild,
More fierce and more **inexorable**[4] far
Than empty tigers or the roaring sea.
40   **Balthasar.** I will be gone, sir, and not trouble ye.
Romeo. So shalt thou show me friendship. Take thou that.
[*He gives him money.*]
Live, and be prosperous; and farewell, good fellow.
Balthasar [*aside*]. For all this same, I'll hide me hereabout.
His looks I fear, and his intents I doubt.
[*He steps aside.*]

---

[3] obsequies—ceremonies to honor the dead.
[4] **inexorable**—relentless; unyielding.

Romeo. Thou detestable maw, thou womb of death,[5]
45
    Gorged with the dearest morsel of the earth,
    Thus I enforce thy rotten jaws to open,
    And in despite[6] I'll cram thee with more food.
[*He begins to force the tomb open.*]
Paris. This is that banished haughty Montague
50
    That murdered my love's cousin, with which grief
    It is supposèd the fair creature died,
    And here is come to do some villainous shame
    To the dead bodies. I will apprehend him.
[*He comes forward.*]
    Stop thy unhallowed[7] toil, vile Montague!
55
    Can vengeance be pursued further than death?
    Condemnèd villain, I do apprehend thee.
    Obey and go with me, for thou must die.
Romeo. I must indeed, and therefore came I hither.
    Good gentle youth, tempt not a desp'rate man.
60
    Fly hence and leave me. Think upon these gone;
    Let them affright thee. I beseech thee, youth,
    Put not another sin upon my head
    By urging me to fury. O, begone!
    By heaven, I love thee better than myself,
65
    For I come hither armed against myself.
    Stay not, begone. Live, and hereafter say
    A madman's mercy bid thee run away.
Paris. I do defy thy conjuration,[8]
    And apprehend thee for a felon here.
70
Romeo. Wilt thou provoke me? Then have at thee, boy!
    [*They fight.*]
Page. O Lord, they fight! I will go call the watch.
    [*He runs off.*]
Paris. O, I am slain! [*He falls.*] If thou be merciful,
    Open the tomb, lay me with Juliet.
    [*He dies.*]

---

[5] maw . . . of death—belly of death (the tomb).

[6] despite—defiance.

[7] unhallowed—wicked, evil.

[8] conjuration—appeal.

Ah, dear Juliet,
Why art thou yet so fair?

Romeo. In faith, I will.—Let me peruse[9] this face.
75   Mercutio's kinsman, noble County Paris!
What said my man when my betossèd soul
Did not attend him as we rode? I think
He told me Paris should have married Juliet.
Said he not so? Or did I dream it so?
80   Or am I mad, hearing him talk of Juliet,
To think it was so?—O, give me thy hand,
One writ with me in sour misfortune's book.
I'll bury thee in a triumphant grave.

[*He opens the tomb.*]

     A grave? O, no! A lantern,[10] slaughtered youth,
85   For here lies Juliet, and her beauty makes
This vault a feasting presence[11] full of light.
Death, lie thou there, by a dead man **interred**.[12]

[*He lays* Paris *in the tomb.*]

     How oft when men are at the point of death
Have they been merry, which their keepers call
90   A light'ning before death! O, how may I
Call this a light'ning? O my love, my wife!
Death, that hath sucked the honey of thy breath,
Hath had no power yet upon thy beauty.
Thou art not conquered. Beauty's ensign[13] yet
95   Is crimson in thy lips and in thy cheeks,
And death's pale flag is not advancèd there.
Tybalt, liest thou there in thy bloody sheet?
O, what more favor can I do to thee
Than with that hand that cut thy youth in twain

---

[9] peruse—carefully examine.

[10] lantern—tower room with many windows.

[11] feasting presence—splendid reception room.

[12] **interred**—buried.

[13] ensign—banner, flag.

In the Yale School of Drama production, Romeo (Nathan Hinton) believing Juliet (Sanaa Lathan) to be dead, embraces her for the last time.

100 To sunder his that was thine enemy?[14]
Forgive me, cousin!—Ah, dear Juliet,
Why art thou yet so fair? Shall I believe
That unsubstantial death is amorous,
And that the lean abhorrèd monster keeps
105 Thee here in dark to be his paramour?[15]
For fear of that I still will stay with thee
And never from this palace of dim night
Depart again. Here, here will I remain
With worms that are thy chambermaids. O, here
110 Will I set up my everlasting rest
And shake the yoke of inauspicious[16] stars
From this world-wearied flesh. Eyes, look your last!
Arms, take your last embrace! And, lips, O, you
The doors of breath, seal with a righteous kiss
115 A dateless bargain to engrossing death![17]

[14] with . . . enemy—to kill myself with the same hand that killed you.
[15] paramour—lover.
[16] inauspicious—unfavorable, unlucky.
[17] dateless . . . death—everlasting contract with all-absorbing death.

[*He kisses* Juliet.]

> Come, bitter conduct,[18] come, unsavory guide,
> Thou desperate pilot, now at once run on
> The dashing rocks thy seasick weary bark![19]
> Here's to my love. [*He drinks.*] O true apothecary!
120 Thy drugs are quick. Thus with a kiss I die.

[*He dies.*]

[*Enter at the other end of the churchyard* Friar Laurence *with lantern, crowbar, and spade.*]

Friar Laurence. Saint Francis be my speed![20] How oft tonight
> Have my old feet stumbled at graves!—Who's there?

Balthasar. Here's one, a friend, and one that knows you well.

Friar Laurence. Bliss be upon you. Tell me, good my friend,
125 What torch is yond that vainly lends his fight
> To grubs and eyeless skulls? As I discern,
> It burneth in the Capels' monument.

Balthasar. It doth so, holy sir, and there's my master,
> One that you love.

Friar Laurence.   Who is it?

Balthasar.   Romeo.

130 **Friar Laurence.** How long hath he been there?

Balthasar.   Full half an hour.

Friar Laurence. Go with me to the vault.

Balthasar.   I dare not, Sir.
> My master knows not but I am gone hence,
> And fearfully did menace me with death
> If I did stay to look on his intents.

135 **Friar Laurence.** Stay, then, I'll go alone. Fear comes upon me.
> O, much I fear some ill unthrifty[21] thing.

Balthasar. As I did sleep under this yew tree here
> I dreamt my master and another fought,
> And that my master slew him.

Friar Laurence [*moving toward the tomb*].
>   Romeo!—

---

[18] conduct—guide (the poison).

[19] bark—ship (Romeo's body).

[20] be my speed—let me arrive in time.

[21] unthrifty—unfortunate.

Thus with a kiss I die.

140   Alack, alack, what blood is this which stains

The stony entrance of this **sepulcher?**[22]

What mean these masterless and gory swords

To lie discolored by this place of peace?

[_He enters the tomb._]

Romeo! O, pale! Who else? What, Paris too?

145   And steeped in blood? Ah, what an unkind hour

Is guilty of this lamentable chance!

The lady stirs.

[Juliet _wakes._]

Juliet. O comfortable[23] Friar, where is my lord?

I do remember well where I should be,

150   And there I am. Where is my Romeo?

[_A noise within._]

Friar Laurence. I hear some noise.—Lady, come from that nest

Of death, contagion, and unnatural sleep.

A greater power than we can contradict

Hath thwarted our intents. Come, come away.

155   Thy husband in thy bosom there lies dead,

And Paris, too. Come, I'll dispose of thee

Among a sisterhood of holy nuns.

Stay not to question, for the watch is coming.

Come, go, good Juliet.

[_A noise again._]

                 I dare no longer stay.

[_Exit_ Friar Laurence.]

160   **Juliet.** Go, get thee hence, for I will not away.

What's here? A cup, closed in my true love's hand?

Poison, I see, hath been his timeless end.

O churl,[24] drunk all, and left no friendly drop

To help me after? I will kiss thy lips;

---

[22] **sepulcher**—tomb.

[23] comfortable—comforting.

[24] churl—selfish miser.

The anguished Juliet (Tari Signor) reaches toward the dying Romeo (Mark H. Dold) in the 1997 production of *Romeo and Juliet* by the Trinity Repertory Company.

165   Haply some poison yet doth hang on them,
      To make me die with a restorative.
      [*She kisses him.*]
        Thy lips are warm.
      [*Enter* Paris' Page *and* Watchmen *at the other end of the churchyard.*]
      First Watch. Lead, boy. Which way?
      Juliet. Yea, noise? Then I'll be brief. O happy dagger!
      [*She takes* Romeo's *dagger.*]
170   This is thy sheath. There rust, and let me die.
      [*She stabs herself and dies.*]
      Page. This is the place, there where the torch doth burn.
      First Watch. The ground is bloody. Search about the churchyard.
        Go, some of you, whoe'er you find attach.[25]
      [*Some exit.*]

---

[25] whoe'er . . . attach—arrest anyone you find.

Pitiful sight! Here lies the County slain,
175   And Juliet bleeding, warm, and newly dead,
Who here hath lain these two days burièd
Go tell the Prince. Run to the Capulets.
Raise up the Montagues. Some others search.
[*Others exit.*]
We see the ground whereon these woes do lie,
180   But the true ground of all these piteous woes
We cannot without circumstance descry.[26]
[*Enter* Watchmen, *with* Balthasar.]
Second Watch. Here's Romeo's man. We found him in the churchyard.
First Watch. Hold him in safety till the Prince come hither.
[*Enter* Friar Laurence, *and another* Watchman *with tools.*]
Third Watch. Here is a friar, that trembles, sighs, and weeps.
185   We took this mattock and this spade from him
As he was coming from this churchyard's side.
First Watch. A great suspicion. Stay the friar, too.
[*Enter the* Prince *and* attendants.]
Prince. What misadventure is so early up
That calls our person from our morning rest?
[*Enter* Capulet *and* Lady Capulet.]
190   **Capulet.** What should it be that is so shrieked abroad?
Lady Capulet. O, the people in the street cry "Romeo,"
Some "Juliet," and some "Paris," and all run
With open outcry toward our monument.
Prince. What fear is this which startles in our ears?
195   **First Watch.** Sovereign, here lies the County Paris slain,
And Romeo dead, and Juliet, dead before,
Warm and new killed.
Prince. Search, seek, and know how this foul murder comes.
First Watch. Here is a friar, and slaughtered Romeo's man,
200   With instruments upon them fit to open
These dead men's tombs.
Capulet. O heavens! O wife, look how our daughter bleeds!
This dagger hath mista'en, for lo, his house

---

[26] without . . . descry—understand without the details.

Is empty on the back of Montague,

205 And it mis-sheathèd in my daughter's bosom![27]

Lady Capulet. O me! This sight of death is as a bell

That warns my old age to a sepulcher.

[*Enter* Montague.]

Prince. Come, Montague, for thou art early up

To see thy son and heir now early down.

210 **Montague.** Alas, my liege, my wife is dead tonight.

Grief of my son's exile hath stopped her breath.

What further woe conspires against mine age?

Prince. Look, and thou shalt see.

Montague [*seeing* Romeo's *body*].

O thou untaught![28]

What manners is in this,

215 To press before thy father to a grave?

Prince. Seal up the mouth of outrage for a while,

Till we can clear these **ambiguities**[29]

And know their spring, their head,[30] their true descent,

And then will I be general of your woes

220 And lead you even to death. Meantime, forbear,

And let mischance be slave to patience.[31]

Bring forth the parties of suspicion.

Friar Laurence. I am the greatest, able to do least,

Yet most suspected, as the time and place

225 Doth make against me, of this direful murder;

And here I stand, both to impeach and purge[32]

Myself condemnèd and myself excused.

Prince. Then say at once what thou dost know in this.

Friar Laurence. I will be brief, for my short date of breath[33]

230 Is not so long as is a tedious tale.

Romeo, there dead, was husband to that Juliet,

---

[27] This dagger . . . bosom—This dagger has mistakenly sheathed itself in Juliet's chest instead of the sheath (its house) that Romeo wears.

[28] untaught—bad-mannered youth.

[29] **ambiguities**—confusions.

[30] spring . . . head—source.

[31] let mischance . . . patience—bear misfortune patiently.

[32] impeach and purge—accuse and free from blame.

[33] short . . . breath—short time I have to live.

And she, there dead, that Romeo's faithful Lady Capulet.
I married them, and their stol'n marriage day
Was Tybalt's doomsday, whose untimely death
235   Banished the new-made bridegroom from this city,
For whom, and not for Tybalt, Juliet pined.
You, to remove that siege of grief from her,
Betrothed and would have married her perforce
To County Paris. Then comes she to me,
240   And with wild looks bid me devise some means
To rid her from this second marriage,
Or in my cell there would she kill herself.
Then gave I her—so tutored by my art—
A sleeping potion, which so took effect
245   As I intended, for it wrought on her
The form of death. Meantime I writ to Romeo
That he should hither come as this dire night
To help to take her from her borrowed grave,
Being the time the potion's force should cease.
250   But he which bore my letter, Friar John,
Was stayed by accident, and yesternight
Returned my letter back. Then all alone
At the prefixèd hour of her waking
Came I to take her from her kindred's vault,
255   Meaning to keep her closely at my cell
Till I conveniently could send to Romeo.
But when I came, some minute ere the time
Of her awakening, here untimely lay
The noble Paris and true Romeo dead.
260   She wakes, and I entreated her come forth
And bear this work of heaven with patience.
But then a noise did scare me from the tomb,
And she, too desperate, would not go with me,
But, as it seems, did violence on herself.
265   All this I know, and to the marriage
Her nurse is privy;[34] and if aught in this
Miscarried by my fault, let my old life

---

[34] privy—in on the secret.

Be sacrificed some hour before his time
Unto the rigor of severest law.

270 **Prince.** We still have known thee for a holy man.—
Where's Romeo's man? What can he say to this?

Balthasar. I brought my master news of Juliet's death,
And then in post he came from Mantua
To this same place, to this same monument.

275 This letter he early bid me give his father,
[*Showing a letter.*]
And threatened me with death, going in the vault,
If I departed not and left him there.

Prince [*taking the letter*]. Give me the letter. I will look on it.
Where is the County's page, that raised the watch?—

280 Sirrah, what made your master in this place?

Page. He came with flowers to strew his lady's grave,
And bid me stand aloof, and so I did.
Anon comes one with light to ope the tomb,
And by and by my master drew on him,

285 And then I ran away to call the watch.

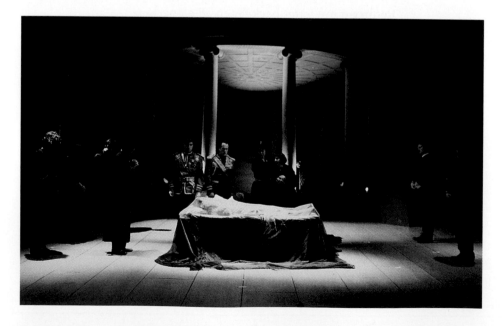

Their feud finally over, the Capulets and Montagues stand around the shrouded bodies of the young lovers at the close of the Commonwealth Shakespeare Company production.

For never was a story of more woe
Than this of Juliet and her Romeo.

Prince. This letter doth make good the friar's words,
Their course of love, the tidings of her death;
And here he writes that he did buy a poison
Of a poor 'pothecary, and therewithal.
290   Came to this vault to die and lie with Juliet.
Where be these enemies? Capulet, Montague,
See what a scourge[35] is laid upon your hate,
That heaven finds means to kill your joys[36] with love.
And I, for winking at your discords,[37] too
295   Have lost a brace[38] of kinsmen. All are punished.
Capulet. O brother Montague, give me thy hand.
This is my daughter's jointure,[39] for no more
Can I demand.
Montague.   But I can give thee more,
For I will raise her statue in pure gold,
300   That whiles Verona by that name is known
There shall no figure at such rate be set
As that of true and faithful Juliet.
Capulet. As rich shall Romeo's[40] by his lady's lie;
Poor sacrifices of our enmity!
305   **Prince.** A glooming peace this morning with it brings;
The sun, for sorrow, will not show his head.
Go hence to have more talk of these sad things.
Some shall be pardoned, and some punishèd;
For never was a story of more woe
310   Than this of Juliet and her Romeo.
[*All exit.*]

---

[35] scourge—punishment.
[36] your joys—your children, your happiness.
[37] winking . . . discords—ignoring your feuds.
[38] brace—pair.
[39] jointure—dowry.
[40] Romeo's—Romeo's statue.

Understanding the Play

Act One

1. In Scene One, what is the relationship between the houses of Montague and Capulet? How serious are their feelings?

2. In Scene Two, what are Capulet's concerns about Juliet's happiness in marriage? Does he seem sincere?

3. In Scene Three, what do you learn of the character of the Nurse and of how she feels toward Juliet and the Capulets?

4. The wordplay between Romeo and Juliet in Scene Five is typical of the wordplay throughout the play. How does it contribute to the mood of the scene?

Act Two

1. Scene Two ends with Romeo and Juliet talking about marriage. Do they seem too hasty to you? Why or why not?

2. In Scene Three, why does Friar Laurence agree to marry Romeo and Juliet? What is your opinion of the judgement he shows here?

3. In Scene Four, what do you learn about the characters of Benvolio and Mercutio?

4. How is humor developed in the exchange between Juliet and the Nurse in Scene Five?

Act Three

1. In Scene One, how do you think Romeo could have prevented the deaths of Mercutio and Tybalt?

2. What actions does the Prince take that will affect the lives of all the characters?

3. In Scene Two, what contradictory reactions does Juliet have to the news that Romeo has killed Tybalt?

4. In Scene Three, how does Friar Laurence take a further hand in events? What is your opinion of his actions?

5. In Scene Five, how does Capulet react when he hears of Juliet's refusal to marry Paris?

Act Four

1. What is Friar Laurence's plan to help Juliet in Scene One?

2. In Scene Two, how does Juliet show herself the "dutiful" daughter? How sincere is she?

3. In Scene Three, what are Juliet's fears before she takes Friar Laurence's drug? In view of those fears, why does she do it?

4. In Scene Five, how does Friar Laurence calm the grief of Capulet, Lady Capulet, and Paris?

Act Five

1. In Scene One, when Romeo learns of Juliet's apparent death, what is his first action? What is his second?

2. In Scene Two, how has Friar Laurence's plan gone wrong? What does he plan to do?

3. In Scene Three, why does Paris challenge Romeo to fight? Why does Romeo accept the challenge?

4. At the end of the play, what does the Prince mean when he says, "All are punished"?

Analyzing the Play

1. One element that makes a tragedy is that the events seem inevitable. What is your opinion of the effect of coincidence or accident on the impact of *Romeo and Juliet* as a tragedy?

2. Many scenes in the play contain irony, either in events that turn out unexpectedly or in events that the audience is aware of but the characters are not. Choose a scene and explain what is ironic in it.

3. There are many scenes of comedy and light-hearted wordplay in *Romeo and Juliet*. In your opinion, how do they contribute to the overall effect of the play?

4. How does the setting—both place and time—influence the actions of the characters and contribute to their fates?

Writing Projects

1. Choose a theme of *Romeo and Juliet* and express it in one carefully worded sentence. In a few paragraphs, explain how the events of the play express and develop that theme.

2. In Act Two, Scene Six, Friar Laurence advises Romeo to "love moderately." How might that advice be applicable to other characters as well? In an essay, explain how the lack of moderation of various characters contributes to the plot of the play.

3. Play the part of a newspaper advice columnist. Write a letter that either Romeo or Juliet might have written you, and add the advice you would give in your column.

4. Both Friar Laurence and the Nurse play a large part in the play. Write a character sketch of either, explaining the kind of person he or she is and why each acts in that way. Include the character's function in the society of Renaissance Verona and whether he or she fulfills it in the play.

Performance Projects

1. In some scenes, the stage is filled with characters from the opposing houses of Montague and Capulet as well as other townspeople. If you were designing a production of *Romeo and Juliet*, how would you help the audience tell the characters apart? Design costumes for two male characters, such as Romeo and Tybalt, or two female characters, such as Lady Montague and Lady Capulet. Use some method such as symbolic colors to differentiate their houses.

2. With a partner, perform Romeo and Juliet's love scene when Romeo is in the orchard and Juliet at her window in Act Two, Scene Two. Consider how you will deliver the light, bantering wordplay in the dialogue so as to reveal the passionate love they are developing for each other.

3. Act One, Scene Five, is a complex scene to stage, involving the movements of several main characters as well as those of the dancing, partying guests. If you were directing the play, how would you stage this scene? Create some director's notes for this scene showing, for example, where Capulet and the Second Capulet sit to watch the festivities, where Romeo is when he first spots Juliet, and where Romeo and Juliet meet and kiss.

4. If you were playing the Nurse, how would you interpret the role? In Act Two, Scene Five, for example, do you think she is sincerely complaining of her aches and pains, or is she teasing Juliet by stringing out her story? Create some actor's notes describing your interpretation of this scene and of the character in general.

A Midsummer Night's Dream

Introduction

A Midsummer Night's Dream *is one of Shakespeare's early comedies. A tragedy ends with the downfall of its main character. Shakespeare's romantic comedies reverse this pattern, ending with a marriage (or promise of marriage). Like tragedy, comedy has conflict; but in comedy this conflict is generally expressed in witty dialogue rather than physical violence. In* **A Midsummer Night's Dream,** *the principal conflict involves two pairs of young lovers. Which boy will get which girl? As one of these young people sadly observes, "The course of true love never did run smooth."*

Lysander and Demetrius compete for the love of Helena (Elizabeth McGovern) in the 1987 New York Shakespeare Festival's production of *A Midsummer Night's Dream.*

▼

Plot

As the play begins, Theseus, duke of Athens, is impatient to marry Hippolyta, queen of the Amazons. At the end of the play, this union is celebrated. Theseus and Hippolyta, as a couple, form the framework of the play, representing mature love, passionate yet sensible.

Much of the play is concerned with four young Athenian lovers. Lysander is in love with Hermia, who returns his passion. But Demetrius, her father's choice, is also in love with Hermia. Helena has been thrown over by Demetrius, but she is still passionately in love with him. During the course of a nightlong wandering in a forest, a misapplied magic charm further scrambles the affections of these young people.

▲

In this scene from a 2001 production of *A Midsummer Night's Dream* at the Hartt School at the University of Hartford, the Athenian tradesmen perform their absurd version of the classical tale of Pyramus and Thisbe.

A second major action in the play is the attempt of six Athenian tradesmen to perform a rustic version of a classical tragedy in honor of the duke's marriage. These men are plagued by their inability to enter into the world of illusion that is acting.

The third element in the plot involves a group of fairies. The King and Queen of the Fairies, Oberon and Titania, have quarreled, but they have come separately to Athens to bless the marriage of Theseus and Hippolyta. Oberon's attempt to punish Titania, with the aid of his mischievous attendant Puck, leads to much of the confusion experienced by the lovers and the tradesmen.

Titania (Janet Zarish) and Oberon (Bradley Whitford) quarrel in midair in this scene from a 1988 production of *A Midsummer Night's Dream* by Connecticut's Hartford Stage theater company. ▶

Settings and Characters

A Midsummer Night's Dream *has two settings: the city of Athens and a great forest outside the city. The city represents order and reason; while the wood is the gateway to imagination, full of illusions and* surprises. *Almost all of the action in the forest takes place at night, under the moonlight—when people question whether what they see and do is madness or sanity. The major characters fall into four groups:*

Athenian Court	Lovers	Fairies	Tradesmen
Theseus, Duke of Athens **Hippolyta,** Queen of the Amazons, engaged to Theseus	**Hermia,** in love with Lysander **Lysander,** in love with Hermia **Demetrius,** formerly in love with Helena; now in love with Hermia **Helena,** in love with Demetrius	**Oberon,** King of the Fairies **Titania,** Queen of the Fairies **Puck,** a mischievous fairy, also known as Robin Goodfellow	**Peter Quince,** a carpenter **Nick Bottom,** a weaver **Francis Flute,** a bellows mender **Tom Snout,** a tinker **Snug,** a joiner **Robin Starveling,** a tailor

Themes

A Midsummer Night's Dream *is a play about love. The play considers the power of love, the fragility of love, and the irrationality of love. Shakespeare has five sets of lovers in the play, each demonstrating a variation on his theme. Theseus and Hippolyta are about to be married and have a stable relationship. Hermia and Lysander represent love beset by obstacles and—when Lysander temporarily discards Hermia for Helena—the fragility of love. Helena and Demetrius represent the irrationality of love: our inability to love those we should and to stop loving those we shouldn't. Titania's infatuation with Bottom shows the transforming power of love. And the reconciliation of Oberon and Titania shows how love brings order and calm to the world.*

A second major theme of the play is imagination. Theseus, like the city he rules, represents reason; but his wife-to-be reminds him that there are other ways to look at things. In the city, the four lovers find only difficulties and strife; but in the forest at night, with their minds open, they are able to find themselves and overcome the obstacles. The tradesmen are characters who cannot imagine anything, which is why their play has such difficulties; but in the forest, Bottom is exposed to the new world—much as a play's audience is exposed to an imagined world. By contrast, the fairies represent the shaping power of imagination, which can turn hate into love, or see beauty in ugliness.

Characters

Theseus, duke of Athens
Hippolyta, queen of the Amazons,
    betrothed to Theseus
Philostrate, master of the revels to
    Theseus
Egeus, father of Hermia
Theseus's **Lords** and **Attendants**

Hermia, daughter of Egeus, in love with
    Lysander
Lysander, in love with Hermia
Demetrius, in love with Hermia and
    favored by Egeus
Helena, in love with Demetrius

Oberon, king of the fairies
Titania, queen of the fairies
Puck, or Robin Goodfellow, in Oberon's
    service

Fairies attending Titania:
    Peaseblossom
    Cobweb
    Mote
    Mustardseed
    Other Fairies

Peter Quince, a carpenter, playing the
    Prologue
Nick Bottom, a weaver, playing Pyramus
Francis Flute, a bellows mender, playing
    Thisbe
Tom Snout, a tinker, playing Wall
Snug, a joiner, playing Lion
Robin Starveling, a tailor, playing
    Moonshine

SCENE: *Athens, and a wood near it*

Act One, Scene One

In his palace, Theseus, duke of Athens, is preparing for his wedding to Hippolyta, queen of the Amazons. Egeus brings his daughter, Hermia, and her two suitors, Demetrius and Lysander, before the duke. Hermia has refused to marry her father's choice, Demetrius, preferring Lysander. Egeus demands that the duke enforce a father's rights under Athenian law. Theseus warns Hermia that she must submit to her father's will, become a nun, or face execution for

disobeying the law. Hermia swears she will never obey. Lysander protests that he is as good a man in every way as Demetrius; and, moreover, that Demetrius has been unfaithful to another woman, Helena. After Theseus takes Demetrius and Egeus off to lecture them, Lysander and Hermia make plans to elope. When Helena enters, pining with love for Demetrius, they tell her their plan. Helena decides to tell Demetrius the plan in the hope of gaining at least his thanks.

Enter Theseus, Hippolyta, *and* Philostrate, *with others.*

Theseus. Now, fair Hippolyta, our nuptial hour
    Draws on apace.[1] Four happy days bring in
    Another moon; but, O, methinks how slow
    This old moon wanes! She lingers my desires,
5   Like to a stepdame or a dowager[2]
    Long withering out a young man's revenue.
Hippolyta. Four days will quickly steep themselves in night;
    Four nights will quickly dream away the time;
    And then the moon, like to a silver bow
10   New bent in heaven, shall behold the night
    Of our solemnities.
Theseus.   Go, Philostrate,
    Stir up the Athenian youth to merriments.
    Awake the pert and nimble spirit of mirth.
    Turn melancholy forth to funerals;
15   The pale companion is not for our pomp.[3]
[*Exit* Philostrate.]
    Hippolyta, I wooed thee with my sword
    And won thy love doing thee injuries;[4]
    But I will wed thee in another key,
    With pomp, with triumph, and with reveling.
[*Enter Egeus and his daughter* Hermia, *and* Lysander *and* Demetrius.]
20 **Egeus.** Happy be Theseus, our renownèd duke!
Theseus. Thanks, good Egeus. What's the news with thee?
Egeus. Full of vexation come I, with complaint
    Against my child, my daughter Hermia.—
    Stand forth, Demetrius.—My noble lord,
25   This man hath my consent to marry her.—
    Stand forth, Lysander.—And, my gracious Duke,
    This man hath bewitched the bosom of my child.—
    Thou, thou, Lysander, thou hast given her rhymes
    And interchanged love tokens with my child.

---

[1] nuptial hour . . . apace—time for our wedding comes swiftly.

[2] stepdame or dowager—stepmother or widow (that is, one who has a right to the son's inheritance).

[3] pale companion . . . pomp—sad-faced fellow is not suitable for our splendid celebrations.

[4] Hippolyta . . . injuries—Theseus had captured Hippolyta during his campaign against the Amazons.

30 Thou hast by moonlight at her window sung
With feigning voice verses of feigning[5] love,
And stol'n the impression of her fantasy[6]
With bracelets of thy hair, rings, gauds, conceits,
Knacks, trifles, nosegays, sweetmeats[7]—messengers
35 Of strong prevailment in unhardened youth.
With cunning hast thou filched[8] my daughter's heart,
Turned her obedience, which is due to me,
To stubborn harshness.—And, my gracious Duke,
Be it so she will not here before Your Grace
40 Consent to marry with Demetrius,
I beg the ancient privilege of Athens:
As she is mine, I may dispose of her,
Which shall be either to this gentleman
Or to her death, according to our law
45 Immediately provided in that case.
Theseus. What say you, Hermia? Be advised, fair maid.
To you your father should be as a god—
One that composed your beauties, yea, and one
To whom you are but as a form in wax
50 By him imprinted, and within his power
To leave the figure or disfigure it.
Demetrius is a worthy gentleman.
Hermia. So is Lysander.
Theseus.   In himself he is;
But in this kind, wanting your father's voice,[9]
55 The other must be held the worthier.
Hermia. I would my father looked but with my eyes.
Theseus. Rather your eyes must with his judgment look.
Hermia. I do entreat Your Grace to pardon me.
I know not by what power I am made bold,
60 Nor how it may concern my modesty
In such a presence here to plead my thoughts;

---

[5] feigning . . . feigning—false . . . pretending.
[6] And stol'n . . . of her fantasy—won her love by putting your image in her imagination.
[7] gauds . . . sweetmeats—toys, baubles, knickknacks, small gifts, flowers, candy.
[8] filched—stolen.
[9] wanting . . . voice—lacking your father's approval.

To live a barren sister all your life,
Chanting faint hymns to the cold fruitless moon.

But I beseech Your Grace that I may know
The worst that may befall me in this case
If I refuse to wed Demetrius.

65   **Theseus.** Either to die the death or to **abjure**[10]
Forever the society of men.
Therefore, fair Hermia, question your desires,
Know of your youth, examine well your blood,
Whether, if you yield not to your father's choice,

70   You can endure the livery[11] of a nun,
For aye to be in shady cloister mewed,
To live a barren sister all your life,
Chanting faint hymns to the cold fruitless moon.[12]
Thrice blessèd they that master so their blood

75   To undergo such maiden pilgrimage;
But earthlier happy is the rose distilled
Than that which, withering on the virgin thorn,
Grows, lives, and dies in single blessedness.[13]

Hermia. So will I grow, so live, so die, my lord,

80   Ere I will yield my virgin patent up
Unto his lordship, whose unwishèd yoke[14]
My soul consents not to give sovereignty.

Theseus. Take time to pause, and by the next new moon—
The sealing day betwixt my love and me

85   For everlasting bond of fellowship—
Upon that day either prepare to die
For disobedience to your father's will,
Or else to wed Demetrius, as he would,

---

[10] **abjure**—renounce under oath.

[11] livery—clothes, usually a uniform.

[12] aye . . . moon—be confined for life as a virgin in the service of Diana, the moon goddess.

[13] earthlier . . . blessedness—those who marry are happier on earth than those who live single. Theseus compares a rose that is used to make perfume (a married woman) to one that lives alone and untouched.

[14] yoke—harness.

Or on Diana's altar to protest[15]

90   For aye **austerity**[16] and single life.

Demetrius. Relent, sweet Hermia, and, Lysander, yield

Thy crazèd title to my certain right.

Lysander. You have her father's love, Demetrius;

Let me have Hermia's. Do you marry him.

95 **Egeus.** Scornful Lysander! True, he hath my love,

And what is mine my love shall render him.

And she is mine, and all my right of her

I do estate unto[17] Demetrius.

Lysander. I am, my lord, as well derived as he,

100   As well possessed; my love is more than his;

My fortunes every way as fairly ranked,

If not with vantage, as Demetrius';

And, which is more than all these boasts can be,

I am beloved of beauteous Hermia.

105   Why should not I then prosecute my right?

Demetrius, I'll avouch it to his head,[18]

Made love to Nedar's daughter, Helena,

And won her soul; and she, sweet lady, dotes,

Devoutly dotes, dotes in **idolatry**[19]

110   Upon this spotted[20] and inconstant man.

Theseus. I must confess that I have heard so much,

And with Demetrius thought to have spoke thereof;

But, being overfull of self-affairs,

My mind did lose it.—But, Demetrius, come,

115   And come, Egeus, you shall go with me;

I have some private schooling for you both.—

For you, fair Hermia, look you arm yourself

To fit your fancies to your father's will,

Or else the law of Athens yields you up,

---

[15] protest—vow.

[16] **austerity**—strict self-discipline.

[17] estate unto—give to.

[18] avouch . . . head—say it to his face.

[19] **idolatry**—blind or excessive devotion to something.

[20] spotted—morally unsound.

120 Which by no means we may **extenuate**,[21]
 To death or to a vow of single life.—
 Come, my Hippolyta. What cheer, my love?—
 Demetrius and Egeus, go along.
 I must employ you in some business
125 Against our nuptial, and confer with you
 Of something nearly that concerns yourselves.

Egeus. With duty and desire we follow you.

[*Exit all but* Lysander *and* Hermia.]

Lysander. How now, my love? Why is your cheek so pale?
 How chance the roses there do fade so fast?

130 **Hermia.** Belike[22] for want of rain, which I could well
 Beteem[23] them from the tempest of my eyes.

Lysander. Ay me! For aught that I could ever read,
 Could ever hear by tale or history,
 The course of true love never did run smooth;
135 But either it was different in blood[24]—

Hermia. O cross! Too high to be enthralled to low.

Lysander. Or else misgrafted in respect of years—

Hermia. O spite! Too old to be engaged to young.

Lysander. Or else it stood upon the choice of friends—

140 **Hermia.** O hell, to choose love by another's eyes!

Lysander. Or if there were a sympathy in choice,
 War, death, or sickness did lay siege to it,
 Making it momentany[25] as a sound,
 Swift as a shadow, short as any dream,
145 Brief as the lightning in the collied[26] night
 That in a spleen[27] unfolds both heaven and earth,

---

[21] **extenuate**—moderate or alleviate.

[22] Belike—probably, perhaps.

[23] Beteem—give, bring forth.

[24] different in blood—unequal in social rank.

[25] momentany—momentary.

[26] collied—black as coal.

[27] in a spleen—in a flash, suddenly.

And ere a man hath power to say "Behold!"
The jaws of darkness do devour it up.
So quick bright things come to confusion.

150 **Hermia.** If then true lovers have been ever crossed,[28]
It stands as an edict[29] in destiny.
Then let us teach our trial patience,
Because it is a customary cross,
As due to love as thoughts, and dreams, and sighs,

155 Wishes and tears, poor fancy's followers.

Lysander. A good persuasion. Therefore, hear me, Hermia:
I have a widow aunt, a dowager
Of great revenue, and she hath no child.
From Athens is her house remote seven leagues;[30]

160 And she respects me as her only son.
There, gentle Hermia, may I marry thee,
And to that place the sharp Athenian law
Cannot pursue us. If thou lovest me, then,
Steal forth thy father's house tomorrow night;

165 And in the wood, a league without the town,
Where I did meet thee once with Helena
To do observance to a morn of May,
There will I stay for thee.

Hermia.   My good Lysander!
I swear to thee, by Cupid's strongest bow,

170 By his best arrow with the golden head,[31]
By the simplicity of Venus' doves,[32]
By that which knitteth souls and prospers loves,
And by that fire which burned the Carthage queen
When the false Trojan under sail was seen,[33]

175 By all the vows that ever men have broke,
In number more than ever women spoke,

---

[28] ever crossed—always frustrated.

[29] edict—an order with the force of law.

[30] seven leagues—twenty-one miles (a league equals three miles).

[31] Cupid's . . . golden head—Cupid, the god of love, used arrows with golden heads to cause love.

[32] simplicity . . . doves—innocence of the doves that were sacred to Venus, the goddess of love.

[33] And by that fire . . . seen—reference to a famous story in Vergil's *Aeneid*. When Dido, queen of Carthage, was abandoned by her lover, the Trojan hero Aeneas, she killed herself; her body was burned on a funeral pyre.

Hermia (Kirsten Potter, right) attempts to comfort Helena (Courtney Peterson) in this scene from a 2001 production of *A Midsummer Night's Dream* by the Seattle Repertory Theatre.

> In that same place thou hast appointed me
> Tomorrow truly will I meet with thee.
> **Lysander.** Keep promise, love. Look, here comes Helena.
> [*Enter* Helena.]
180 **Hermia.** God speed, fair Helena! Whither away?
> **Helena.** Call you me "fair"? That "fair" again unsay.
> Demetrius loves your fair.[34] O happy fair!
> Your eyes are lodestars,[35] and your tongue's sweet air
> More tunable than lark to shepherd's ear
185 When wheat is green, when hawthorn buds appear.
> Sickness is catching. O, were favor[36] so,
> Yours would I catch, fair Hermia, ere I go;
> My ear should catch your voice, my eye your eye,

---

[34] fair—beauty.
[35] lodestars—guiding stars.
[36] favor—appearance (with a pun on "being favored").

My tongue should catch your tongue's sweet melody.

190 Were the world mine, Demetrius being bated,[37]

The rest I'd give to be to you translated.

O, teach me how you look and with what art

You sway the motion of Demetrius' heart.

Hermia. I frown upon him, yet he loves me still.

195 **Helena.** O, that your frowns would teach my smiles such skill!

Hermia. I give him curses, yet he gives me love.

Helena. O, that my prayers could such affection move!

Hermia. The more I hate, the more he follows me.

Helena. The more I love, the more he hateth me.

200 **Hermia.** His folly, Helena, is no fault of mine.

Helena. None, but your beauty. Would that fault were mine!

Hermia. Take comfort. He no more shall see my face.

Lysander and myself will fly this place.

Before the time I did Lysander see

205 Seemed Athens as a paradise to me.

O, then, what graces in my love do dwell,

That he hath turned a heaven unto a hell?

Lysander. Helen, to you our minds we will unfold.

Tomorrow night, when Phoebe[38] doth behold

210 Her silver visage in the watery glass,[39]

Decking with liquid pearl the bladed grass,

A time that lovers' flights doth still conceal,

Through Athens' gates have we devised to steal.

Hermia. And in the wood, where often you and I

215 Upon faint primrose[40] beds were wont[41] to lie,

Emptying our bosoms of their counsel sweet,

There my Lysander and myself shall meet,

And thence from Athens turn away our eyes

To seek new friends and stranger companies.

220 Farewell, sweet playfellow. Pray thou for us,

And good luck grant thee thy Demetrius!

---

[37] bated—excluded.

[38] Phoebe—the moon. Phoebe is another name for Diana.

[39] visage . . . glass—face in a pond or lake that reflects it.

[40] primrose—yellow spring flower.

[41] wont—accustomed.

Keep word, Lysander. We must starve our sight
From lovers' food till morrow deep midnight.

Lysander. I will, my Hermia. [*Exit* Hermia.] Helena, adieu.

225   As you on him, Demetrius dote on you!

[*Exit* Lysander.]

Helena. How happy some o'er other some can be![42]
Through Athens I am thought as fair as she.
But what of that? Demetrius thinks not so;
He will not know what all but he do know.

230   And as he errs, doting on Hermia's eyes,
So I, admiring of his qualities.
Things base and vile, holding no quantity,
Love can transpose to form and dignity.
Love looks not with the eyes, but with the mind,

235   And therefore is winged Cupid painted blind.
Nor hath Love's mind of any judgment taste;[43]
Wings, and no eyes, figure unheedy haste.
And therefore is Love said to be a child,
Because in choice he is so oft beguiled.[44]

240   As waggish boys in game themselves forswear,
So the boy Love is **perjured**[45] everywhere.
For ere Demetrius looked on Hermia's eyne,[46]
He hailed down oaths that he was only mine;
And when this hail some heat from Hermia felt,

245   So he dissolved, and show'rs of oaths did melt.
I will go tell him of fair Hermia's flight.
Then to the wood will he tomorrow night
Pursue her. And for this intelligence
If I have thanks, it is a dear expense.[47]

250   But herein mean I to enrich my pain,
To have his sight thither and back again.

[*She exits*.]

---

[42] How . . . be—How happy some are compared to others.

[43] nor hath . . . taste—Nor does love use reason.

[44] beguiled—cheated; diverted.

[45] **perjured**—guilty of having lied under oath.

[46] eyne—eyes.

[47] dear expense—worthwhile trouble.

Act One, Scene Two

In Quince's house in Athens, six Athenian tradesmen plan to perform a play in honor of the duke's wedding. Their leader, Peter Quince, has written a rustic version of a classical story about two doomed lovers, Pyramus and Thisbe. Nick Bottom, who is to play Pyramus, tries to claim each role. The group agrees to meet the next night in the woods to rehearse in private.

Enter Quince *the carpenter,* Snug *the joiner[1],* Bottom *the weaver,* Flute *the bellows[2] mender,* Snout *the tinker[3], and* Starveling *the tailor.*

Quince. Is all our company here?

Bottom. You were best to call them generally, man by man, according to the scrip.

Quince. Here is the scroll of every man's name which is thought fit, through all Athens, to play in our interlude before the duke and the duchess on his wedding day at night.

Bottom. First, good Peter Quince, say what the play treats on, then read the names of the actors, and so grow to a point.

Quince. Marry,[4] our play is "The most lamentable comedy and most cruel death of Pyramus and Thisbe."

Bottom. A very good piece of work, I assure you, and a merry. Now, good Peter Quince, call forth your actors by the scroll. Masters, spread yourselves.

Quince. Answer as I call you. Nick Bottom, the weaver.

Bottom. Ready. Name what part I am for, and proceed.

Quince. You, Nick Bottom, are set down for Pyramus.

Bottom. What is Pyramus? A lover or a tyrant?

Quince. A lover, that kills himself most gallant for love.

Bottom. That will ask some tears in the true performing of it. If I do it, let the audience look to their eyes. I will move storms; I will condole[5]

---

[1] joiner—cabinetmaker.

[2] bellows—accordion-like device for producing a strong current of air, for example, for stoking fires or for church organs.

[3] tinker—mender of metal housewares.

[4] Marry—indeed (originally a mild oath using the name of the Virgin Mary).

[5] condole—grieve or lament.

in some measure. To the rest—yet my chief humor[6] is for a tyrant.
I could play Ercles[7] rarely, or a part to tear a cat in,[8] to make all split.

> 25

The raging rocks
And shivering shocks
Shall break the locks
Of prison gates;
And Phibbus' car[9]
Shall shine from far
And make and mar

> 30

The foolish Fates.

This was lofty! Now name the rest of the players. This is
Ercles' vein, a tyrant's vein. A lover is more condoling.

Quince. Francis Flute, the bellows mender.

Flute. Here, Peter Quince.

> 35

Quince. Flute, you must take Thisbe on you.

Flute. What is Thisbe? A wandering knight?

Quince. It is the lady that Pyramus must love.

Flute. Nay, faith, let not me play a woman. I have a beard coming.

Quince. That's all one. You shall play it in a mask, and you may speak as

> 40

small as you will.

Bottom. An[10] I may hide my face, let me play Thisbe too. I'll speak in a
monstrous little voice: "Thisbe, Thisbe!" "Ah, Pyramus, my
lover dear! Thy Thisbe dear, and lady dear!"

Quince. No, no, you must play Pyramus, and Flute, you Thisbe.

> 45

Bottom. Well, proceed.

Quince. Robin Starveling, the tailor.

Starveling. Here, Peter Quince.

Quince. Robin Starveling, you must play Thisbe's mother.—Tom Snout,
the tinker.

> 50

Snout. Here, Peter Quince.

Quince. You, Pyramus' father.—Myself, Thisbe's father.—Snug, the joiner,
you, the lion's part. And I hope here is a play fitted.

---

[6] humor—inclination.

[7] Ercles—rustic pronunciation of "Hercules."

[8] part to tear a cat in—traditional description for a stage role full of ranting.

[9] *Phibbus' car*—chariot of Phoebus, the sun god.

[10] An—if.

In a 1999 production of *A Midsummer Night's Dream* by Boston's Huntington Theatre Company, the Athenian tradesmen discuss how to play their parts.

Snug. Have you the lion's part written? Pray you, if it be, give it me, for I am slow of study.

55 **Quince.** You may do it extempore,[11] for it is nothing but roaring.

Bottom. Let me play the lion too. I will roar that I will do any man's heart good to hear me. I will roar that I will make the duke say, "Let him roar again, let him roar again."

Quince. An you should do it too terribly, you would fright the
60 duchess and the ladies, that they would shriek, and that were enough to hang us all.

---

[11] extempore—spoken or carried out without preparation.

I will roar you as gently
as any sucking dove.

All. That would hang us, every mother's son.

Bottom. I grant you, friends, if you should fright the ladies out of their wits, they would have no more discretion but to hang us; but I will aggravate[12] my voice so that I will roar you as gently as any sucking dove; I will roar you an 'twere any nightingale.

Quince. You can play no part but Pyramus, for Pyramus is a sweet-faced man, a proper man as one shall see in a summer's day, a most lovely gentlemanlike man. Therefore you must needs play Pyramus.

Bottom. Well, I will undertake it. What beard were I best to play it in?

Quince. Why, what you will.

Bottom. I will discharge it in either your straw-color beard, your orange-tawny beard, your purple-in-grain[13] beard, or your French-crown-color[14] beard, your perfect yellow.

Quince. Some of your French crowns have no hair at all, and then you will play barefaced. But, masters, here are your parts. [*He distributes parts.*] And I am to entreat you, request you, and desire you to con[15] them by tomorrow night and meet me in the palace wood, a mile without the town, by moonlight. There will we rehearse; for if we meet in the city, we shall be dogged with company, and our devices known. In the meantime I will draw a bill of properties, such as our play wants. I pray you, fail me not.

Bottom. We will meet, and there we may rehearse most obscenely[16] and courageously. Take pains, be perfect. Adieu.

Quince. At the Duke's oak we meet.

Bottom. Enough. Hold, or cut bowstrings.[17]

[*They exit.*]

---

[12] aggravate—make worse. Bottom means to say "moderate," or "mitigate" (soften or tone down).

[13] purple-in-grain—deep scarlet or crimson.

[14] French-crown-color—gold, like a French coin.

[15] con—memorize.

[16] obscenely—offensively. It is Bottom's mistake for "seemly" or "properly."

[17] Hold, or cut bowstrings—Commit yourself or don't show up.

Act Two, Scene One

In the woods outside Athens, two fairies meet: Puck, the mischievous follower of Oberon, the fairy king, and a servant of Titania, the fairy queen. Oberon and Titania have quarreled over a young Indian boy and are avoiding each other, but they have both chosen to spend the night in this forest. They enter from opposite directions and quarrel again. After Titania leaves, Oberon sends Puck to fetch a flower whose juice will make sleepers fall madly in love with the first creature they see on waking. Oberon plans to punish his queen by making her fall in love with some beast. Demetrius enters, pursued by Helena. He is searching for Hermia and trying desperately to make the lovesick Helena leave him. When Puck returns, Oberon tells him to put some of the juice on Demetrius' eyes so that he will fall in love with the ill-treated Helena.

Enter, from opposite sides, a Fairy, *and* Robin Goodfellow (Puck).

Puck. How now, spirit, whither wander you?
Fairy. Over hill, over dale,
    Thorough bush, thorough brier,
    Over park, over pale,[1]
5   Thorough flood, thorough fire,
    I do wander everywhere,
    Swifter than the moon's sphere;
    And I serve the Fairy Queen,
    To dew her orbs[2] upon the green.
10   The cowslips tall her pensioners[3] be.
    In their gold coats spots you see;
    Those be rubies, fairy favors;
    In those freckles live their savors.
    I must go seek some dewdrops here
15   And hang a pearl in every cowslip's ear.
    Farewell, thou lob[4] of spirits; I'll be gone.
    Our queen and all her elves come here anon.[5]

---

[1] pale—fenced-in area.

[2] orbs—fairy rings, circles of rich, thick grass believed to be made by fairies.

[3] cowslips . . . pensioners—Because of their height and bright colors, cowslips are compared to Queen Elizabeth's brightly dressed bodyguards, or pensioners.

[4] lob—awkward or stupid fellow.

[5] anon—soon.

Puck. The king doth keep his revels here tonight.
Take heed the queen come not within his sight.
20   For Oberon is passing fell and wrath,[6]
Because that she, as her attendant hath
A lovely boy, stolen from an Indian king;
She never had so sweet a changeling.[7]
And jealous Oberon would have the child
25   Knight of his train, to trace the forests wild.
But she perforce[8] withholds the lovèd boy,
Crowns him with flowers, and makes him all her joy.
And now they never meet in grove or green,
By fountain clear, or spangled starlight sheen,
30   But they do square,[9] that all their elves for fear
Creep into acorn cups and hide them there.

Fairy. Either I mistake your shape and making quite,
Or else you are that shrewd and knavish sprite[10]
Called Robin Goodfellow. Are not you he
35   That frights the maidens of the villagery,
Skim milk, and sometimes labor in the quern,
And bootless make the breathless huswife churn,[11]
And sometimes make the drink to bear no barm,[12]
Mislead night wanderers, laughing at their harm?
40   Those that "Hobgoblin" call you, and "Sweet Puck,"
You do their work, and they shall have good luck.
Are you not he?

Puck.   Thou speakest aright;
I am that merry wanderer of the night.
I jest to Oberon and make him smile
45   When I a fat and bean-fed horse beguile,
Neighing in likeness of a filly foal;
And sometimes lurk I in a gossip's bowl

---

[6] passing . . . wrath—very fierce and angry.

[7] changeling—child stolen by the fairies.

[8] perforce—by force.

[9] square—argue.

[10] shrewd . . . sprite—mischievous spirit.

[11] skim . . . churn—undo the housewife's work in grinding grain and making butter.

[12] drink . . . barm—beer fail to ferment.

In very likeness of a roasted crab,[13]
And when she drinks, against her lips I bob
50 And on her withered dewlap[14] pour the ale.
The wisest aunt, telling the saddest tale,
Sometimes for three-foot stool mistaketh me;
Then slip I from her bum, down topples she,
And "Tailor" cries, and falls into a cough;
55 And then the whole choir hold their hips and laugh,
And waxen in[15] their mirth, and neeze, and swear
A merrier hour was never wasted there.
But, room, fairy! Here comes Oberon.
Fairy. And here my mistress. Would that he were gone!
[*Enter, from opposite sides,* Oberon, *king of Fairies, with his* Followers,
and Titania, *the queen, with her* Attendants.]
60 **Oberon.** Ill met by moonlight, proud Titania.
Titania. What, jealous Oberon? Fairies, skip hence.
I have forsworn his bed and company.
Oberon. Tarry, rash wanton.[16] Am not I thy lord?
Titania. Then I must be thy lady; but I know
65 When thou hast stolen away from Fairyland
And in the shape of Corin sat all day,
Playing on pipes of corn and versing love
To amorous Phillida.[17] Why art thou here
Come from the farthest step of India,
70 But that, forsooth,[18] the bouncing Amazon,
Your buskined[19] mistress and your warrior love,
To Theseus must be wedded, and you come
To give their bed joy and prosperity.

---

[13] crab—crab apple.

[14] dewlap—fold of loose skin hanging from the neck.

[15] waxen in—add to.

[16] rash wanton—hasty and willful creature.

[17] Corin . . . Phillida—These are traditional names in poetry for a lovesick shepherd and shepherdess.

[18] forsooth—in truth, indeed.

[19] buskined—wearing buskins or half-boots (traditionally worn by hunters and soldiers).

Oberon (Kyle Wrentz) angrily confronts Titania (Katherine Dillingham) in the Hartt School production.

Oberon. How canst thou thus for shame, Titania,

75 Glance at my credit with Hippolyta,

  Knowing I know thy love to Theseus?

  Didst not thou lead him through the glimmering night

  From Perigenia, whom he ravishèd?

  And make him with fair Aegles break his faith,

80 With Ariadne and Antiopa?[20]

Titania. These are the forgeries of jealousy;

  And never, since the middle summer's spring,

  Met we on hill, in dale, forest, or mead,

  By pavèd fountain or by rushy brook,

85 Or in the beachèd margent of the sea,

  To dance our ringlets to the whistling wind,

  But with thy brawls thou hast disturbed our sport.

  Therefore the winds, piping to us in vain,

  As in revenge, have sucked up from the sea

---

[20] From Perigenia ... Antiopa—In myth, Perigenia, Aegles, Ariadne, and Antiopa were all women loved and left by Theseus. Oberon blames Titania for these desertions.

90   Contagious fogs which, falling in the land,
Hath every pelting river made so proud
That they have overborne their continents.
The ox hath therefore stretched his yoke in vain,
The plowman lost his sweat, and the green corn
95   Hath rotted ere his youth attained a beard;
The fold stands empty in the drownèd field,
And crows are fatted with the murrain flock;[21]
The nine-men's morris[22] is filled up with mud,
And the quaint mazes in the wanton green
100   For lack of tread, are undistinguishable.
The human mortals want their winter cheer;
No night is now with hymn or carol blessed.
Therefore the moon, the governess of floods,
Pale in her anger, washes all the air,
105   That rheumatic[23] diseases do abound.
And thorough this distemperature we see
The seasons alter: hoary-headed frosts
Fall in the fresh lap of the crimson rose,
And on old Hiems'[24] thin and icy crown
110   An odorous chaplet[25] of sweet summer buds
Is, as in mockery, set. The spring, the summer,
The childing[26] autumn, angry winter, change
Their wonted liveries,[27] and the mazèd[28] world
By their increase now knows not which is which.
115   And this same progeny of evils comes
From our debate,[29] from our dissension.
We are their parents and original.

---

[21] murrain flock—sheep dead from murrain, an infectious disease.

[22] nine-men's morris—square cut in turf for an outdoor game.

[23] rheumatic—cold- or flu-like.

[24] Hiems'—winter's.

[25] chaplet—wreath or garland for the head.

[26] childing—plentiful, fruitful.

[27] wonted liveries—regular clothes.

[28] mazèd—bewildered.

[29] progeny … debate—evil offspring are produced by our quarrel.

Oberon. Do you amend it, then. It lies in you.

Why should Titania cross her Oberon?

120   I do but beg a little changeling boy

To be my henchman.

Titania.   Set your heart at rest.

The fairy land buys not the child of me.

His mother was a vot'ress of my order,[30]

And in the spicèd Indian air by night

125   Full often hath she gossiped by my side

And sat with me on Neptune's[31] yellow sands,

Marking th' embarkèd traders on the flood,

When we have laughed to see the sails conceive

And grow big-bellied with the wanton[32] wind;

130   Which she, with pretty and with swimming gait,[33]

Following—her womb then rich with my young squire—

Would imitate, and sail upon the land

To fetch me trifles, and return again

As from a voyage, rich with merchandise.

135   But she, being mortal, of that boy did die;

And for her sake do I rear up her boy,

And for her sake I will not part with him.

Oberon. How long within this wood intend you stay?

Titania. Perchance[34] till after Theseus' wedding day.

140   If you will patiently dance in our round

And see our moonlight revels, go with us;

If not, shun me, and I will spare your haunts.

Oberon. Give me that boy, and I will go with thee.

Titania. Not for thy fairy kingdom. Fairies, away!

145   We shall chide[35] downright, if I longer stay.

[*Exit* Titania *and her* Attendants.]

Oberon. Well, go thy way. Thou shalt not from this grove

Till I torment thee for this injury.—

---

[30] vot'ress of my order—woman who vowed to serve me.

[31] Neptune's—the god of the sea.

[32] wanton—playful; immoral.

[33] gait—manner of walking.

[34] Perchance—perhaps, possibly.

[35] chide—scold; quarrel.

My gentle Puck, come hither. Thou rememb'rest
Since once I sat upon a promontory,
150 And heard a mermaid on a dolphin's back
Uttering such dulcet and harmonious breath[36]
That the rude sea grew civil at her song,
And certain stars shot madly from their spheres
To hear the sea-maid's music?

Puck.   I remember.

155 **Oberon.** That very time I saw, but thou couldst not,
Flying between the cold moon and the earth
Cupid, all armed. A certain aim he took
At a fair vestal[37] thronèd by the west,
And loosed his love shaft smartly from his bow
160 As it should pierce a hundred thousand hearts;
But I might see young Cupid's fiery shaft
Quenched in the chaste beams of the watery moon,
And the imperial vot'ress passèd on,
In maiden meditation, fancy-free.
165 Yet marked I where the bolt[38] of Cupid fell:
It fell upon a little western flower,
Before, milk-white, now purple with love's wound,
And maidens call it "love-in-idleness."
Fetch me that flower, the herb I showed thee once.
170 The juice of it on sleeping eyelids laid
Will make or man or woman madly dote
Upon the next live creature that it sees.
Fetch me this herb, and be thou here again
Ere the leviathan[39] can swim a league.

175 **Puck.** I'll put a girdle round about the earth
In forty minutes. [*Exit* Puck.]

Oberon.   Having once this juice,
I'll watch Titania when she is asleep
And drop the liquor of it in her eyes.

---

[36] uttering . . . breath—singing such sweet music.

[37] vestal—virgin; probably an allusion to Queen Elizabeth I (the Virgin Queen). The "imperial vot'ress" of line 163 probably also refers to Elizabeth.

[38] bolt—arrow.

[39] leviathan—sea monster.

The next thing then she, waking, looks upon,
180 Be it on lion, bear, or wolf, or bull,
On meddling monkey, or on busy ape,
She shall pursue it with the soul of love.
And ere I take this charm from off her sight,
As I can take it with another herb,
185 I'll make her render up her page to me.
But who comes here? I am invisible,
And I will overhear their conference.

[*Enter* Demetrius, Helena *following him.*]

Demetrius. I love thee not; therefore pursue me not.
Where is Lysander and fair Hermia?
190 The one I'll slay; the other slayeth me.
Thou toldst me they were stol'n unto this wood;
And here am I, and wood[40] within this wood
Because I cannot meet my Hermia.
Hence, get thee gone, and follow me no more.

195 **Helena.** You draw me, you hardhearted adamant![41]
But yet you draw not iron, for my heart
Is true as steel. Leave you your power to draw,
And I shall have no power to follow you.

Demetrius. Do I entice you? Do I speak you fair?
200 Or rather do I not in plainest truth
Tell you I do not, nor I cannot love you?

Helena. And even for that do I love you the more.
I am your spaniel, and, Demetrius,
The more you beat me I will fawn on you.
205 Use me but as your spaniel: spurn me, strike me,
Neglect me, lose me; only give me leave,
Unworthy as I am, to follow you.
What worser place can I beg in your love—
And yet a place of high respect with me—
210 Than to be usèd as you use your dog?

Demetrius. Tempt not too much the hatred of my spirit,
For I am sick when I do look on thee.

---

[40] wood—insane; also a pun on *wood,* (forest).
[41] adamant—very hard stone; also, a magnet.

Helena. And I am sick when I look not on you.

Demetrius. You do impeach[42] your modesty too much

215   To leave the city and commit yourself

       Into the hands of one that loves you not,

       To trust the opportunity of night

       And the ill counsel of a desert place

       With the rich worth of your virginity.

220 **Helena.** Your virtue is my privilege. For that

       It is not night when I do see your face,

       Therefore I think I am not in the night;

       Nor doth this wood lack worlds of company,

       For you, in my respect, are all the world.

225   Then how can it be said I am alone

       When all the world is here to look on me?

Demetrius. I'll run from thee and hide me in the brakes,[43]

       And leave thee to the mercy of wild beasts.

Helena. The wildest hath not such a heart as you.

230   Run when you will. The story shall be changed:

       Apollo flies and Daphne holds the chase,

       The dove pursues the griffin, the mild hind

       Makes speed to catch the tiger[44]—bootless speed,

       When cowardice pursues and valor flies!

235 **Demetrius.** I will not stay thy questions. Let me go!

       Or if thou follow me, do not believe

       But I shall do thee mischief in the wood.

Helena. Ay, in the temple, in the town, the field,

       You do me mischief. Fie, Demetrius!

240   Your wrongs do set a scandal on my sex.

       We cannot fight for love, as men may do;

       We should be wooed and were not made to woo.

[*Exit* Demetrius.]

       I'll follow thee and make a heaven of hell,

       To die upon the hand I love so well. [*She exits.*]

---

[42] impeach—expose to reproach, discredit.

[43] brakes—bushes.

[44] Apollo . . . tiger—Helena gives three examples of stories that are reversed. The chaste nymph Daphne pursues the god Apollo (in mythology, she fled from him); the dove attacks the griffin, a fierce monster with the head and wings of an eagle and body of a lion; and the female deer chases the tiger.

I know a bank where the wild thyme blows.

245 **Oberon.** Fare thee well, nymph. Ere he do leave this grove
Thou shalt fly him, and he shall seek thy love.
[*Enter* Puck.]
Hast thou the flower there? Welcome, wanderer.
Puck. Ay, there it is.
[*He offers the flower.*]
Oberon.   I pray thee, give it me.
I know a bank where the wild thyme blows,
250 Where oxlips[45] and the nodding violet grows,
Quite overcanopied with luscious woodbine,[46]
With sweet muskroses and with eglantine.[47]
There sleeps Titania sometime of the night,
Lulled in these flowers with dances and delight;
255 And there the snake throws her enameled skin,
Weed[48]wide enough to wrap a fairy in.
And with the juice of this I'll streak her eyes
And make her full of hateful fantasies.
Take thou some of it, and seek through this grove:
[*He gives* Puck *part of the flower.*]
260 A sweet Athenian lady is in love
With a disdainful youth. Anoint[49] his eyes,
But do it when the next thing he espies
May be the lady. Thou shalt know the man
By the Athenian garments he hath on.
265 Effect it with some care, that he may prove
More fond[50] on her than she upon her love;
And look thou meet me ere the first cock crow.
Puck. Fear not, my lord, your servant shall do so.
[*They exit separately.*]

---

[45] oxlips—yellow flowers.
[46] woodbine—climbing vine.
[47] eglantine—sweetbriar. All these flowers have pleasant scents.
[48] Weed—clothing.
[49] Anoint—apply a liquid to.
[50] fond—doting.

Act Two, Scene Two

In another part of the woods, Titania's fairies sing her to sleep. Oberon squeezes the love juice on her eyelids. Lysander and Hermia decide to sleep and wait for daylight. Puck mistakes Lysander for Demetrius and puts the love juice on Lysander's eyelids. Demetrius is finally able to escape Helena because she is worn out. Left alone, Helena sees Lysander and wakes him up. He immediately professes his love for her. She believes that he is making fun of her and flees. Lysander gives chase. Hermia wakes from a nightmare and discovers that Lysander is gone. She runs into the forest to find him.

Enter Titania, *queen of fairies, with her* Attendants.

Titania. Come, now a roundel[1] and a fairy song;
Then, for the third part of a minute, hence—
Some to kill cankers[2] in the muskrose buds,
Some war with reremice[3] for their leathern wings
5   To make my small elves coats, and some keep back
The clamorous owl, that nightly hoots and wonders
At our quaint[4] spirits. Sing me now asleep.
Then to your offices, and let me rest.

[Fairies *sing.*]

First Fairy. *You spotted snakes with double tongue,*
10   *Thorny hedgehogs, be not seen;*
Newts and blindworms, do no wrong;
Come not near our Fairy Queen.

Chorus [*dancing*].
Philomel,[5] with melody
Sing in our sweet lullaby;
15   *Lulla, lulla, lullaby, lulla, lulla, lullaby.*
Never harm
Nor spell nor charm

---

[1] roundel—round dance in which all the dancers hold hands.

[2] cankers—worms that attack the flowers.

[3] reremice—bats.

[4] quaint—dainty; brisk.

[5] *Philomel*—nightingale. In classical myth, Philomel was a woman who was changed into a nightingale.

> *Come our lovely lady nigh.*
> *So good night, with lullaby.*

20 **First Fairy.** *Weaving spiders, come not here;*
> *Hence, you long-legged spinners, hence!*
> *Beetles black, approach not near;*
> *Worm nor snail, do no offense.*

Chorus [*dancing*].
> *Philomel, with melody*
25 > *Sing in our sweet lullaby;*
> *Lulla, lulla, lullaby, lulla, lulla, lullaby.*
> *Never harm*
> *Nor spell nor charm*
> *Come our lovely lady nigh.*
30 > *So good night, with lullaby.*

Titania (Isabell Monk) sits amid her fairy attendants in this 1997 production of *A Midsummer Night's Dream* at the Guthrie Theatre in Minneapolis.

Second Fairy. Hence, away! Now all is well.
  One aloof stand sentinel.[6]
[*Exit* Fairies. Titania *sleeps.*]
[*Enter* Oberon, *and squeezes the flower on* Titania's *eyelids.*]
Oberon. What thou seest when thou dost wake,
  Do it for thy true love take;
35 Love and languish for his sake.
  Be it ounce,[7] or cat, or bear,
  Pard,[8] or boar with bristled hair,
  In thy eye that shall appear
  When thou wak'st, it is thy dear.
40 Wake when some vile thing is near. [*Exit* Oberon.]
[*Enter* Lysander *and* Hermia.]
Lysander. Fair love, you faint with wand'ring in the wood;
  And to speak truth, I have forgot our way.
  We'll rest us, Hermia, if you think it good,
  And tarry[9] for the comfort of the day.
45 **Hermia.** Be it so, Lysander. Find you out a bed,
  For I upon this bank will rest my head.
Lysander. One turf shall serve as pillow for us both;
  One heart, one bed, two bosoms, and one troth.[10]
Hermia. Nay, good Lysander. For my sake, my dear,
50 Lie further off yet. Do not lie so near.
Lysander. O, take the sense, sweet, of my innocence!
  Love takes the meaning in love's conference.
  I mean that my heart unto yours is knit,
  So that but one heart we can make of it;
55 Two bosoms interchainèd with an oath—
  So then two bosoms and a single troth.
  Then by your side no bed-room me deny,
  For lying so, Hermia, I do not lie.

---

[6] aloof stand sentinel—alone stand guard.

[7] ounce—lynx.

[8] Pard—leopard.

[9] tarry—wait.

[10] troth—faithful vow.

Night and silence—Who is here?
Weeds of Athens he doth wear.

Hermia. Lysander riddles very prettily.

60   Now much beshrew[11] my manners and my pride

If Hermia meant to say Lysander lied.

But, gentle friend, for love and courtesy

Lie further off, in human modesty.

Such separation, as may well be said

65   Becomes a virtuous bachelor and a maid,

So far be distant; and, good night, sweet friend.

Thy love ne'er alter till thy sweet life end!

Lysander. Amen, amen, to that fair prayer, say I,

And then end life when I end loyalty!

70   Here is my bed. Sleep give thee all his rest!

Hermia. With half that wish the wisher's eyes be pressed!

[*They sleep.*]

[*Enter* Puck.]

Puck. Through the forest have I gone,

But Athenian found I none

On whose eyes I might approve[12]

75   This flower's force in stirring love.

Night and silence—Who is here?

Weeds of Athens he doth wear.

This is he, my master said,

Despisèd the Athenian maid;

80   And here the maiden, sleeping sound,

On the dank and dirty ground.

Pretty soul, she durst not lie

Near this lack-love, this kill-courtesy.—

Churl,[13] upon thy eyes I throw

85   All the power this charm doth owe.

[*He squeezes the love juice on* Lysander's *eyelids.*]

---

[11] beshrew—curse (but usually, as here, spoken lightly).

[12] approve—demonstrate; test.

[13] Churl—rude person.

Puck (Jeremy Chase) mistakenly applies the love potion to the eyes of the sleeping Lysander (Benjamin McGroarty) in the Hartt School production.

<blockquote>
When thou wak'st, let love forbid
Sleep his seat on thy eyelid.
So awake when I am gone,
For I must now to Oberon. [Exit Puck.]
</blockquote>

[Enter Demetrius and Helena, running.]

90   **Helena.** Stay, though thou kill me, sweet Demetrius!

Demetrius. I charge thee, hence, and do not haunt me thus.

Helena. O, wilt thou darkling[14] leave me? Do not so.

Demetrius. Stay, on thy peril! I alone will go. [Exit Demetrius.]

Helena. O, I am out of breath in this fond chase!

95   The more my prayer, the lesser is my grace.

---

[14] darkling—in the dark.

Happy is Hermia, wheresoe'er she lies,
For she hath blessèd and attractive eyes.
How came her eyes so bright? Not with salt tears.
If so, my eyes are oftener washed than hers.

100 No, no, I am as ugly as a bear,
For beasts that meet me run away for fear.
Therefore no marvel though Demetrius
Do, as a monster, fly my presence thus.
What wicked and dissembling glass[15] of mine

105 Made me compare with Hermia's sphery eyne?[16]
But who is here? Lysander, on the ground?
Dead, or asleep? I see no blood, no wound. —
Lysander, if you live, good sir, awake.

Lysander [*awaking*]. And run through fire I will for thy sweet sake.

110 Transparent Helena! Nature shows art,
That through thy bosom makes me see thy heart.
Where is Demetrius? O, how fit a word
Is that vile name to perish on my sword!

Helena. Do not say so, Lysander; say not so.

115 What though he love your Hermia? Lord, what though?
Yet Hermia still loves you. Then be content.

Lysander. Content with Hermia? No! I do repent
The tedious minutes I with her have spent.
Not Hermia, but Helena I love.

120 Who will not change a raven for a dove?
The will of man is by his reason swayed,
And reason says you are the worthier maid.
Things growing are not ripe until their season;
So I, being young, till now ripe not to reason.

125 And, touching now the point of human skill,
Reason becomes the marshal to my will
And leads me to your eyes, where I o'erlook
Love's stories written in love's richest book.

Helena. Wherefore was I to this keen mockery born?

130 When at your hands did I deserve this scorn?

---

[15] dissembling glass—lying mirror.

[16] sphery eyne—starry eyes.

Is't not enough, is't not enough, young man,
That I did never—no, nor never can—
Deserve a sweet look from Demetrius' eye,
But you must flout my **insufficiency**?[17]
135 Good troth, you do me wrong, good sooth, you do,[18]
In such disdainful manner me to woo.
But fare you well. Perforce I must confess
I thought you lord of more true gentleness.
O, that a lady, of one man refused,
140 Should of another therefore be abused! [*Exit* Helena.]
Lysander. She sees not Hermia.—Hermia, sleep thou there,
And never mayst thou come Lysander near!
For as a surfeit[19] of the sweetest things
The deepest loathing to the stomach brings,
145 Or as the heresies that men do leave
Are hated most of those they did deceive,[20]
So thou, my surfeit and my heresy,
Of all be hated, but the most of me!
And, all my powers, address your love and might
150 To honor Helen and to be her knight! [*Exit* Lysander.]
Hermia [*awaking*]. Help me, Lysander, help me! Do thy best
To pluck this crawling serpent from my breast!
Ay me, for pity! What a dream was here!
Lysander, look how I do quake with fear.
155 Methought a serpent ate my heart away,
And you sat smiling at his cruel prey.
Lysander! What, removed? Lysander, lord!
What, out of hearing? Gone? No sound, no word?
Alack, where are you? Speak, an if you hear;
160 Speak, of all loves! I swoon almost with fear.—
No? Then I well perceive you are not nigh.
Either death, or you, I'll find immediately.
[*Exit* Hermia. *The sleeping* Titania *remains.*]

---

[17] **insufficiency**—lack.

[18] Good troth . . . you do—Truly you do me wrong, really you do.

[19] surfeit—excess.

[20] Or as the heresies . . . did deceive—in the same way a falsehood exposed is hated by those who once believed in it.

Act Three, Scene One

The Athenian tradesmen meet in the woods to rehearse their play. Puck transforms Bottom, giving him the head of a donkey. When Bottom's friends see him, they run away. Bottom thinks they are trying to *frighten him; to prove he is not afraid, he sings. His song awakens Titania, and, under the influence of the love juice, she falls in love with him. She calls her fairies to attend Bottom, and they retire to her bower.*

With Titania *still asleep onstage, enter* Bottom, Quince, Snout, Flute, Snug, *and* Starveling.

Bottom. Are we all met?

Quince. Pat,[1] pat. And here's a marvelous convenient place for our rehearsal. This green plot shall be our stage, this hawthorn brake our tiring-house,[2] and we will do it in action as we will do it before the duke.

5 **Bottom.** Peter Quince?

Quince. What sayest thou, bully[3] Bottom?

Bottom. There are things in this comedy of Pyramus and Thisbe that will never please. First, Pyramus must draw a sword to kill himself, which the ladies cannot abide. How answer you that?

10 **Snout.** By'r lakin, a parlous fear.[4]

Starveling. I believe we must leave the killing out, when all is done.

Bottom. Not a whit. I have a device to make all well. Write me a prologue, and let the prologue seem to say we will do no harm with our swords, and that Pyramus is not killed indeed. And for the more

15 better assurance, tell them that I, Pyramus, am not Pyramus, but Bottom the weaver. This will put them out of fear.

Quince. Well, we will have such a prologue, and it shall be written in eight and six.[5]

Bottom. No, make it two more: let it be written in eight and eight.

20 **Snout.** Will not the ladies be afeard of the lion?

---

[1] Pat—at exactly the right time.

[2] tiring-house—dressing room.

[3] bully—admirable, excellent.

[4] By'r lakin . . . fear—By Our Little Lady (the Virgin Mary), a terrible fear.

[5] eight and six—number of syllables in alternate lines of verse in the poetic form commonly known as ballad meter.

Starveling. I fear it, I promise you.

Bottom. Masters, you ought to consider with yourself, to bring in—God shield us!—a lion among ladies is a most dreadful thing. For there is not a more fearful wildfowl than your lion living, and we ought to look to 't.

Snout. Therefore another prologue must tell he is not a lion.

Bottom. Nay, you must name his name, and half his face must be seen through the lion's neck, and he himself must speak through, saying thus or to the same defect:[6] "Ladies," or "Fair ladies, I would wish you," or "I would request you," or "I would entreat you, not to fear, not to tremble. My life for yours. If you think I come hither as a lion, it were pity of my life. No, I am no such thing. I am a man as other men are." And there indeed let him name his name, and tell them plainly he is Snug the joiner.

Quince. Well, it shall be so. But there is two hard things: that is, to bring the moonlight into a chamber; for, you know, Pyramus and Thisbe meet by moonlight.

Snout. Doth the moon shine that night we play our play?

Bottom. A calendar, a calendar! Look in the almanac. Find out moon-shine, find out moonshine.

[*They consult an almanac.*]

Quince. Yes, it doth shine that night.

Bottom. Why, then, may you leave a casement[7] of the great chamber win-dow where we play open, and the moon may shine in at the casement.

Quince. Ay; or else one must come in with a bush of thorns and a lantern[8] and say he comes to disfigure, or to present, the person of Moonshine. Then there is another thing; we must have a wall in the great chamber, for Pyramus and Thisbe, says the story, did talk through the chink of a wall.

Snout. You can never bring in a wall. What say you, Bottom?

---

[6] defect—Bottom means to say, "effect."

[7] casement—section of a window.

[8] bush . . . lantern—traditional accessories for the man in the moon.

Peter Quince (Jeff Steitzer, right) and his fellow tradesmen rehearse their play in this scene from the Seattle Repertory Theatre production.

50 **Bottom.** Some man or other must present Wall. And let him have some plaster, or some loam, or some roughcast[9] about him, to signify wall; or let him hold his fingers thus, [*Makes a* V *with his first two fingers.*] and through that cranny shall Pyramus and Thisbe whisper.

Quince. If that may be, then all is well. Come, sit down, every mother's 55 son, and rehearse your parts. Pyramus, you begin. When you have spoken your speech, enter into that brake, and so everyone according to his cue.

[*Enter* Puck, *invisible to those onstage.*]

Puck [*aside*]. What hempen homespuns[10] have we swaggering here So near the cradle of the fairy queen? 60 What, a play toward?[11] I'll be an auditor, An actor, too, perhaps, if I see cause.

Quince. Speak, Pyramus.—Thisbe, stand forth.

---

[9] plaster . . . roughcast—All of these are used for plastering walls. Loam is a mixture of clay, sand, and straw. Roughcast is a mixture of lime and gravel.

[10] hempen homespuns—country folk dressed in rough homemade clothes.

[11] toward—beginning.

Bottom [*as Pyramus*]. *Thisbe, the flowers of **odious**[12] savors sweet—*

Quince. Odors, odors.

65   **Bottom** [*as Pyramus*]. *Odors savors sweet;*

      So hath thy breath, my dearest Thisbe dear.—

      But hark, a voice! Stay thou but here awhile,

      And by and by I will to thee appear. [*Exit* Bottom.]

Puck. A stranger Pyramus than e'er played here. [*Exit* Puck.]

70   **Flute.** Must I speak now?

Quince. Ay, marry, must you, for you must understand he goes but to see

      a noise that he heard, and is to come again.

Flute [*as* Thisbe]. *Most radiant Pyramus, most lily-white of hue,*

      Of color like the red rose on triumphant brier,[13]

75   *Most brisky juvenal*[14] *and eke*[15] *most lovely Jew,*

      As true as truest horse that yet would never tire.

      I'll meet thee, Pyramus, at Ninny's tomb.

Quince. "Ninus' tomb," man. Why, you must not

      speak that yet. That you answer to Pyramus. You

80   speak all your part at once, cues and all.—Pyramus,

      enter. Your cue is past; it is "never tire."

Flute. O —*As true as truest horse, that yet would never tire.*

[*Enter* Puck, *and* Bottom *as* Pyramus *with an ass's head.*]

Bottom. *If I were fair, Thisbe, I were only thine.*

Quince. O, monstrous! O, strange! We are haunted.

85   Pray, masters! Fly, masters! Help!

[*Exit* Quince, Snug, Flute, Snout, *and* Starveling.]

Puck. I'll follow you, I'll lead you about a round,

      Thorough bog, thorough bush, thorough brake, thorough brier.

      Sometimes a horse I'll be, sometimes a hound,

      A hog, a headless bear, sometimes a fire;

90   And neigh, and bark, and grunt, and roar, and burn,

      Like horse, hound, hog, bear, fire, at every turn. [*Exit* Puck.]

Bottom. Why do they run away? This is a knavery of them to make

      me afeard.

---

[12] **odious**—hateful (Bottom's mistake for *odors*).

[13] *brier*—wild rose bush. These verses include words that fill out the six-beat lines and words that seem to be attempts to rhyme (e.g., *brier* to rhyme with *tire*).

[14] *brisky juvenal*—ardent youth.

[15] *eke*—also.

Bottom (James McDonell) enters "with an ass's head" in the Hartford Stage production.

[*Enter* Snout.]

Snout. O Bottom, thou art changed! What do I see on thee?

95   **Bottom.** What do you see? You see an ass-head of your own, do you?

[*Exit* Snout.]

[*Enter* Quince.]

Quince. Bless thee, Bottom, bless thee! Thou art translated. [*Exit* Quince.]

Bottom. I see their knavery. This is to make an ass of me, to fright me, if
they could. But I will not stir from this place, do what they can. I will
walk up and down here, and will sing, that they shall hear I am not

100   afraid. [*He sings.*]

    The ouzel[16] *cock so black of hue,*
      With orange-tawny bill,
    The throstle with his note so true,
      The wren with little quill[17]—

105   **Titania** [*waking up*]. What angel wakes me from my flow'ry bed?

---

[16] *ouzel*—blackbird.

[17] *quill*—small piping song.

Bottom [*sings*].

> The finch, the sparrow, and the lark,
> > The plainsong cuckoo gray,
> Whose note full many a man doth mark,
> > And dares not answer "nay"—

110   For indeed, who would set his wit to so foolish a bird? Who
would give a bird the lie,[18] though he cry "cuckoo" never so?

Titania. I pray thee, gentle mortal, sing again.

> Mine ear is much enamored of thy note;
> So is mine eye enthrallèd to thy shape;
115   And thy fair virtue's force perforce doth move me
> On the first view to say, to swear, I love thee.

Bottom. Methinks, mistress, you should have little reason for that.

> And yet, to say the truth, reason and love keep little company
> together nowadays—the more the pity that some honest neighbors
120   will not make them friends. Nay, I can gleek[19] upon occasion.

Titania. Thou art as wise as thou art beautiful.

Bottom. Not so, neither. But if I had wit enough to get out of this wood,

> I have enough to serve mine own turn.

Titania. Out of this wood do not desire to go.

125   Thou shalt remain here, whether thou wilt or no.

> I am a spirit of no common rate.
> The summer still doth tend upon my state,
> And I do love thee. Therefore, go with me.
> I'll give thee fairies to attend on thee,
130   And they shall fetch thee jewels from the deep,
> And sing while thou on pressèd flowers dost sleep.
> And I will purge thy mortal grossness[20] so
> That thou shalt like an airy spirit go.
> Peaseblossom, Cobweb, Mote,[21] and Mustardseed!

[*Enter four* Fairies: Peaseblossom, Cobweb, Mote, *and* Mustardseed.]

---

[18] give a bird the lie—say the bird lies. The cuckoo cry told married men that they were cuckolds; that is, that their wives were unfaithful.

[19] gleek—make a joke.

[20] grossness—body or physical form.

[21] Mote—speck.

135	**Peaseblossom.** Ready.
	Cobweb. And I.
	Mote. And I.
	Mustardseed. And I.
	All. Where shall we go?

Titania. Be kind and courteous to this gentleman.
Hop in his walks and gambol[22] in his eyes;
Feed him with apricocks and dewberries,[23]
With purple grapes, green figs, and mulberries;

140
The honey-bags steal from the humble-bees,
And for night tapers[24] crop their waxen thighs
And light them at the fiery glowworms' eyes,
To have my love to bed and to arise;
And pluck the wings from painted butterflies

145
To fan the moonbeams from his sleeping eyes.
Nod to him, elves, and do him courtesies.

Peaseblossom. Hail, mortal!

Cobweb. Hail!

Mote. Hail!

150
Mustardseed. Hail!

Bottom. I cry your worships mercy, heartily. I beseech your worship's name.

Cobweb. Cobweb.

Bottom. I shall desire you of more acquaintance, good Master Cobweb.
If I cut my finger, I shall make bold with you.[25]—Your name, honest

155
gentleman?

Peaseblossom. Peaseblossom.

Bottom. I pray you, commend me to Mistress Squash,[26] your mother, and
to Master Peascod,[27] your father. Good Master Peaseblossom, I shall
desire you of more acquaintance too.—Your name, I beseech you, sir?

160
Mustardseed. Mustardseed.

---

[22] gambol—leap about playfully, frolic.

[23] dewberries—blackberries.

[24] tapers—candles.

[25] If I cut . . . bold with you—In Shakespeare's time, cobwebs were used to stop bleeding.

[26] Squash—unripe peapod.

[27] Peascod—ripe peapod.

Titania (Katherine Dillingham) admires Bottom (Orin Wolff) in the Hartt School production.

Bottom. Good Master Mustardseed, I know your patience well. That
same cowardly, giantlike ox-beef hath devoured many a gentleman of
your house. I promise you, your kindred hath made my eyes water
ere now. I desire you of more acquaintance, good Master
165   Mustardseed.[28]
Titania. Come wait upon him; lead him to my bower.[29]
The moon, methinks, looks with a watery eye;
And when she weeps, weeps every little flower,
Lamenting some enforcèd chastity.
170   Tie up my lover's tongue; bring him silently.
[*They exit.*]

---

[28] Good Master Mustardseed ... Mustardseed—Mustard is often served with beef.

[29] bower—shady, leafy recess; also, a woman's private chamber.

Act Three, Scene Two

Puck tells Oberon about Titania and Bottom. Hermia enters, pursued by Demetrius. She asks Demetrius to leave her in peace. Resigned, he lies down to sleep. Oberon, realizing Puck's mistake, sends him to find Helena and places the love juice on Demetrius's eyelids. Puck tricks Helena into following him back, with Lysander in pursuit. Their argument wakes Demetrius, who falls in love with Helena. He and Lysander vie for her attention, which only increases her accusations of mockery. Hermia arrives and asks Lysander why he left her alone. He replies that his love for Helena drew him away. When Hermia shows her distress, Helena accuses them all of conspiring against her. The men come to blows. Hermia hangs on to Lysander, who curses her. Hermia threatens Helena, who protests she has never done Hermia wrong. Lysander and Demetrius rush off to fight a duel, and Helena flees Hermia's fury.

Oberon and Puck have watched the whole scene. Oberon orders Puck to keep Demetrius and Lysander apart and, when they fall asleep, to put the antidote to the juice on Lysander's eyelids. Puck leads them apart by imitating their voices. After a long chase, they collapse in separate places, as do Hermia and Helena. Puck applies the antidote to Lysander's eyelids.

Enter Oberon, *king of fairies.*

Oberon. I wonder if Titania be awaked;
    Then, what it was that next came in her eye,
    Which she must dote on in extremity.
[*Enter* Puck.]
    Here comes my messenger. How now, mad spirit?
5   What night-rule now about this haunted grove?
Puck. My mistress with a monster is in love.
    Near to her close and consecrated[1] bower,
    While she was in her dull and sleeping hour,
    A crew of patches, rude mechanicals,[2]
10   That work for bread upon Athenian stalls,
    Were met together to rehearse a play
    Intended for great Theseus' nuptial day.
    The shallowest thickskin of that barren sort,
    Who Pyramus presented in their sport

---

[1] consecrated—sacred.
[2] patches . . . mechanicals—clowns . . . workingmen.

15   Forsook his scene and entered in a brake.
When I did him at this advantage take,
An ass's noll[3] I fixèd on his head.
Anon his Thisbe must be answerèd
And forth my mimic comes. When they him spy,
20   As wild geese that the creeping fowler[4] eye,
Or russet-pated choughs,[5] many in sort,
Rising and cawing at the gun's report,
Sever themselves and madly sweep the sky,
So, at his sight, away his fellows fly,
25   And, at our stamp, here o'er and o'er one falls;
He "Murder!" cries and help from Athens calls.
Their sense thus weak, lost with their fears thus strong,
Made senseless things begin to do them wrong,
For briers and thorns at their apparel snatch;
30   Some sleeves, some hats; from yielders[6] all things catch.
I led them on in this distracted fear
And left sweet Pyramus translated there,
When in that moment, so it came to pass,
Titania waked and straightway loved an ass.
35 **Oberon.** This falls out better than I could devise.
But hast thou yet latched the Athenian's eyes
With the love juice, as I did bid thee do?
Puck. I took him sleeping—that is finished, too—
And the Athenian woman by his side,
40   That, when he waked, of force she must be eyed.
[*Enter* Demetrius *and* Hermia.]
Oberon. Stand close. This is the same Athenian.
Puck. This is the woman, but not this the man.
[*They stand aside.*]
Demetrius. O, why rebuke you him that loves you so?
Lay breath so bitter on your bitter foe.
45 **Hermia.** Now I but chide; but I should use thee worse,
For thou, I fear, hast given me cause to curse.

---

[3] noll—head.

[4] fowler—bird hunter.

[5] choughs—jackdaws.

[6] yielders—those who are afraid.

If thou hast slain Lysander in his sleep,
Being o'er shoes[7] in blood, plunge in the deep,
And kill me too.

50 The sun was not so true unto the day
As he to me. Would he have stolen away
From sleeping Hermia? I'll believe as soon
This whole earth may be bored, and that the moon
May through the center creep, and so displease

55 Her brother's[8] noontide with th' Antipodes.[9]
It cannot be but thou hast murdered him;
So should a murderer look, so dead, so grim.

Demetrius. So should the murdered look, and so should I,
Pierced through the heart with your stern cruelty.

60 Yet you, the murderer, look as bright, as clear
As yonder Venus in her glimmering sphere.

Hermia. What's this to my Lysander? Where is he?
Ah, good Demetrius, wilt thou give him me?

Demetrius. I had rather give his carcass to my hounds.

65 **Hermia.** Out, dog! Out, cur! Thou driv'st me past the bounds
Of maiden's patience. Hast thou slain him, then?
Henceforth be never numbered among men.
O, once tell true! Tell true, even for my sake:
Durst thou[10] have looked upon him, being awake?

70 And hast thou killed him sleeping? O brave touch!
Could not a worm, an adder,[11] do so much?
An adder did it; for with doubler tongue
Than thine, thou serpent, never adder stung.

Demetrius. You spend your passion on a misprised mood.[12]

75 I am not guilty of Lysander's blood,
Nor is he dead, for aught that I can tell.

Hermia. I pray thee, tell me then that he is well.

Demetrius. And if I could, what should I get therefor?

---

[7] Being o'er shoes—having gone this far.

[8] Her brother's—the sun's.

[9] Antipodes—people on the opposite side of the earth.

[10] Durst thou—do you dare.

[11] adder—snake.

[12] misprised mood—mistaken anger.

Oberon, angry at Puck's mistake about the love juice, orders him to go find Helena.

Hermia. A privilege never to see me more.
80   And from thy hated presence part I so.
        See me no more, whether he be dead or no. [*Exit* Hermia.]
Demetrius. There is no following her in this fierce vein.
        Here, therefore, for a while I will remain.
        So sorrow's heaviness doth heavier grow
85   For debt that bankrupt sleep doth sorrow owe,
        Which now in some slight measure it will pay,
        If for his tender here I make some stay.[13]
[*He lies down and sleeps.*]
Oberon [*to* Puck]. What hast thou done? Thou hast mistaken quite
        And laid the love juice on some true-love's sight.
90   Of thy misprision[14] must perforce ensue
        Some true love turned, and not a false turned true.
Puck. Then fate o'errules, that, one man holding troth,
        A million fail, confounding oath on oath.
Oberon. About the wood go swifter than the wind,
95   And Helena of Athens look thou find.
        All fancy-sick she is and pale of cheer

---

[13] For debt . . . stay—Because sleep has lost so much to sorrow, I will lie down to wait for sleep to pay part of its debt.
[14] misprision—mistake.

Lord, what fools these mortals be!

With sighs of love that cost the fresh blood dear.
By some illusion see thou bring her here.
I'll charm his eyes against she do appear.

100   **Puck.** I go, I go, look how I go,
Swifter than arrow from the Tartar's bow.[15] [*Exit* Puck.]

Oberon [*applying love juice to* Demetrius' *eyelids*].
Flower of this purple dye,
Hit with Cupid's archery,
Sink in apple of his eye.

105   When his love he doth espy,
Let her shine as gloriously
As the Venus of the sky.
When thou wak'st if she be by,
Beg of her for remedy.
[*Enter* Puck.]

110   **Puck.** Captain of our fairy band,
Helena is here at hand,
And the youth, mistook by me,
Pleading for a lover's fee.
Shall we their fond pageant see?

115   Lord, what fools these mortals be!

Oberon. Stand aside. The noise they make
Will cause Demetrius to awake.

Puck. Then will two at once woo one;
That must needs be sport alone.

120   And those things do best please me
That befall **preposterously**.[16] [*They stand aside*.]
[*Enter* Lysander *and* Helena.]

Lysander. Why should you think that I should woo in scorn?
Scorn and **derision**[17] never come in tears.
Look when I vow, I weep; and vows so born,

---

[15] Tartar's bow—The Tartars of Central Asia were famous for their archery.
[16] **preposterously**—absurdly.
[17] **derision**—mockery, ridicule.

125	In their nativity[18] all truth appears.
	How can these things in me seem scorn to you,
	Bearing the badge of faith to prove them true?
	Helena. You do advance your cunning more and more.
	When truth kills truth, O, devilish-holy fray!
130	These vows are Hermia's. Will you give her o'er?
	Weigh oath with oath, and you will nothing weigh.
	Your vows to her and me, put in two scales,
	Will even weigh, and both as light as tales.
	Lysander. I had no judgment when to her I swore.
135	**Helena.** Nor none, in my mind, now you give her o'er.
	Lysander. Demetrius loves her, and he loves not you.
	Demetrius [*awaking*]. O Helen, goddess, nymph, perfect, divine!
	To what, my love, shall I compare thine eyne?
	Crystal is muddy. O, how ripe in show
140	Thy lips, those kissing cherries, tempting grow!
	That pure congealèd white, high Taurus' snow,
	Fanned with the eastern wind, turns to a crow
	When thou hold'st up thy hand.[19] O, let me kiss
	This princess of pure white, this seal of bliss!
145	**Helena.** O spite! O hell! I see you all are bent
	To set against me for your merriment.
	If you were civil and knew courtesy,
	You would not do me thus much injury.
	Can you not hate me, as I know you do,
150	But you must join in souls to mock me too?
	If you were men, as men you are in show,
	You would not use a gentle lady so—
	To vow, and swear, and superpraise my parts,
	When, I am sure, you hate me with your hearts.
155	You both are rivals and love Hermia,
	And now both rivals to mock Helena.
	A trim[20] exploit, a manly enterprise,
	To conjure tears up in a poor maid's eyes

---

[18] nativity—birth.

[19] That pure . . . hand—The whiteness of your hand makes snow on a mountain range look black as a crow.

[20] trim—fine (said sarcastically).

Helena (left) is unhinged by her sudden popularity in this scene from a 1997 production of *A Midsummer Night's Dream* by Rhode Island's Trinity Repertory Company.

With your derision! None of noble sort

160 Would so offend a virgin and extort

A poor soul's patience, all to make you sport.

Lysander. You are unkind, Demetrius. Be not so.

For you love Hermia; this you know I know.

And here, with all good will, with all my heart,

165 In Hermia's love I yield you up my part.

And yours of Helena to me bequeath,

Whom I do love, and will do till my death.

Helena. Never did mockers waste more idle breath.

Demetrius. Lysander, keep thy Hermia. I will none.

170 If e'er I loved her, all that love is gone.

My heart to her but as guestwise sojourned,

And now to Helen is it home returned,

There to remain.

Lysander.   Helen, it is not so.

Demetrius. Disparage not the faith thou dost not know,

175   Lest, to thy peril, thou aby it dear.[21]

        Look where thy love comes; yonder is thy dear.

[*Enter* Hermia.]

Hermia [*to* Lysander]. Dark night, that from the eye his function takes,

        The ear more quick of apprehension makes;

        Wherein it doth impair the seeing sense,

180   It pays the hearing double recompense.

        Thou art not by mine eye, Lysander, found;

        Mine ear, I thank it, brought me to thy sound.

        But why unkindly didst thou leave me so?

Lysander. Why should he stay, whom love doth press to go?

185 **Hermia.** What love could press Lysander from my side?

Lysander. Lysander's love, that would not let him bide—

        Fair Helena, who more engilds the night

        Than all yon fiery oes and eyes of light.[22]

        Why seek'st thou me? Could not this make thee know

190   The hate I bear thee made me leave thee so?

Hermia. You speak not as you think. It cannot be.

Helena. Lo, she is one of this confederacy!

        Now I perceive they have conjoined all three

        To fashion this false sport, in spite of me.—

195   Injurious Hermia, most ungrateful maid,

        Have you conspired, have you with these contrived

        To bait me with this foul derision?

        Is all the counsel that we two have shared,

        The sisters' vows, the hours that we have spent

200   When we have chid the hasty-footed time

        For parting us—O, is all forgot?

        All schooldays' friendship, childhood innocence?

        We, Hermia, like two artificial gods

        Have with our needles created both one flower,

205   Both on one sampler,[23] sitting on one cushion,

---

[21] aby it dear—pay dearly for it.

[22] engilds . . . light—covers with gold or light more than all those distant fiery stars.

[23] like . . . sampler—like two skillful gods sewed one flower on one piece of needlework.

Will you rend our ancient love asunder,
To join with men in scorning your poor friend?

Both warbling of one song, both in one key,
As if our hands, our sides, voices, and minds
Had been incorporate.[24] So we grew together,
Like to a double cherry, seeming parted,
210 But yet an union in partition,
Two lovely berries molded on one stem;
So, with two seeming bodies but one heart,
Two of the first, like coats in heraldry,
Due but to one and crownèd with one crest.
215 And will you rend[25] our ancient love asunder,
To join with men in scorning your poor friend?
It is not friendly, 'tis not maidenly.
Our sex, as well as I, may chide you for it,
Though I alone do feel the injury.
220 **Hermia.** I am amazèd at your passionate words.
I scorn you not. It seems that you scorn me.
Helena. Have you not set Lysander, as in scorn,
To follow me and praise my eyes and face?
And made your other love, Demetrius,
225 Who even but now did spurn me with his foot,
To call me goddess, nymph, divine, and rare,
Precious, celestial? Wherefore speaks he this
To her he hates? And wherefore doth Lysander
Deny your love, so rich within his soul,
230 And tender[26] me, forsooth, affection,
But by your setting on, by your consent?
What though I be not so in grace as you,
So hung upon with love, so fortunate,

---

[24] incorporate—united in one body.

[25] rend—tear or split.

[26] tender—offer.

But miserable most, to love unloved?
235　　This you should pity rather than despise.
Hermia. I understand not what you mean by this.
Helena. Ay, do! Persever,[27] counterfeit sad looks,
　　Make mouths upon me when I turn my back,
　　Wink each at other, hold the sweet jest up.
240　　This sport, well carried, shall be chronicled.
　　If you have any pity, grace, or manners,
　　You would not make me such an argument.
　　But fare ye well. 'Tis partly my own fault,
　　Which death, or absence, soon shall remedy.
245　**Lysander.** Stay, gentle Helena; hear my excuse,
　　My love, my life, my soul, fair Helena!
Helena. O excellent!
Hermia [*to* Lysander]. Sweet, do not scorn her so.
Demetrius [*to* Lysander]. If she cannot entreat, I can compel.
Lysander. Thou canst compel no more than she entreat.
250　　Thy threats have no more strength than her weak prayers.
　　Helen, I love thee. By my life, I do!
　　I swear by that which I will lose for thee,
　　To prove him false that says I love thee not.
Demetrius [*to* Helena]. I say I love thee more than he can do.
255　**Lysander.** If thou say so, withdraw, and prove it too.[28]
Demetrius. Quick, come!
Hermia.　　　　　　　Lysander, whereto tends all this?
[*She takes hold of* Lysander.]
Lysander. Away, you Ethiope![29]
[*He tries to break away from* Hermia.]
Demetrius [*to* Lysander].　No, no; he'll
　　Seem to break loose. Take on as you would follow,
　　But yet come not. You are a tame man. Go!
260　**Lysander** [*to* Hermia]. Hang off, thou cat, thou burr! Vile thing, let loose,
　　Or I will shake thee from me like a serpent!

---

[27] Persever—persevere (that is, keep it up).

[28] prove it too—prove your love in a duel.

[29] Ethiope—reference to Hermia's dark hair.

Lysander (Matthew Troyer) scorns Hermia (Kirsten Potter) in this scene
from the Seattle Repertory production.

Hermia. Why are you grown so rude? What change is this,
Sweet love?
Lysander.   Thy love? Out, tawny Tartar, out!
Out, loathèd med'cine! O hated potion, hence!
265 **Hermia.** Do you not jest?
Helena.   Yes, sooth,[30] and so do you.
Lysander. Demetrius, I will keep my word with thee.
Demetrius. I would I had your bond, for I perceive
A weak bond[31] holds you. I'll not trust your word.

---

[30] sooth—truly.
[31] weak bond—that is, Hermia's arms.

Lysander. What, should I hurt her, strike her, kill her dead?

    Although I hate her, I'll not harm her so.

Hermia. What, can you do me greater harm than hate?

    Hate me? Wherefore? O me, what news, my love?

    Am not I Hermia? Are not you Lysander?

    I am as fair now as I was erewhile.

    Since night you loved me; yet since night you left me.

    Why, then, you left me—O the gods forbid!—

    In earnest, shall I say?

Lysander.   Ay, by my life!

    And never did desire to see thee more.

    Therefore be out of hope, of question, of doubt;

    Be certain, nothing truer. 'Tis no jest

    That I do hate thee and love Helena.

[Hermia *turns him loose.*]

Hermia [*to* Helena]. O me! You juggler! You cankerblossom![32]

    You thief of love! What, have you come by night

    And stol'n my love's heart from him?

Helena.   Fine, i' faith!

    Have you no modesty, no maiden shame,

    No touch of bashfulness? What, will you tear

    Impatient answers from my gentle tongue?

    Fie, fie! You counterfeit, you puppet, you!

Hermia. "Puppet"? Why, so! Ay, that way goes the game.

    Now I perceive that she hath made compare

    Between our statures; she hath urged her height,

    And with her personage, her tall personage,

    Her height, forsooth, she hath prevailed with him.

    And are you grown so high in his esteem

    Because I am so dwarfish and so low?

    How low am I, thou painted maypole? Speak!

    How low am I? I am not yet so low

    But that my nails can reach unto thine eyes.

[*She attacks* Helena *but is restrained.*]

---

[32] cankerblossom—cankerworm, worm that attacks flowers.

Helena. I pray you, though you mock me, gentlemen,
300   Let her not hurt me. I was never curst;[33]
    I have no gift at all in shrewishness;
    I am a right maid for my cowardice.
    Let her not strike me. You perhaps may think,
    Because she is something lower than myself,
305   That I can match her.
Hermia.   "Lower"? Hark, again!
Helena. Good Hermia, do not be so bitter with me.
    I evermore did love you, Hermia,
    Did ever keep your counsels, never wronged you,
    Save that, in love unto Demetrius,
310   I told him of your stealth unto this wood.
    He followed you; for love, I followed him.
    But he hath chid me hence and threatened me
    To strike me, spurn me, nay, to kill me too.
    And now, so you will let me quiet go,
315   To Athens will I bear my folly back
    And follow you no further. Let me go.
    You see how simple and how fond I am.
Hermia. Why, get you gone. Who is 't that hinders you?
Helena. A foolish heart, that I leave here behind.
320 **Hermia.** What, with Lysander?
Helena.   With Demetrius.
Lysander. Be not afraid; she shall not harm thee, Helena.
Demetrius. No, sir, she shall not, though you take her part.
Helena. O, when she is angry, she is keen and shrewd.
    She was a vixen when she went to school,
325   And though she be but little, she is fierce.
Hermia. "Little" again? Nothing but "low" and "little"?
    Why will you suffer her to flout me thus?
    Let me come to her.

---

[33] curst—quarrelsome.

Lysander.   Get you gone, you dwarf!
You minimus, of hindering knotgrass made![34]
You bead, you acorn!
Demetrius.   You are too officious
In her behalf that scorns your services.
Let her alone. Speak not of Helena.
Take not her part. For, if thou dost intend
Never so little show of love to her,
Thou shalt aby it.
Lysander.   Now she holds me not.
Now follow, if thou dar'st, to try whose right,
Of thine or mine, is most in Helena. [*Exit* Lysander.]
Demetrius. "Follow"? Nay, I'll go with thee, cheek by jowl.
[*Exit* Demetrius, *following* Lysander.]
Hermia. You, mistress, all this coil is 'long of you.[35]
[Helena *retreats.*]
Nay, go not back.
Helena.   I will not trust you, I,
Nor longer stay in your curst company.
Your hands than mine are quicker for a fray;
My legs are longer, though, to run away. [*Exit* Helena.]
Hermia. I am amazed and know not what to say. [*Exit* Hermia.]
[Oberon *and* Puck *come forward.*]
Oberon. This is thy negligence. Still thou mistak'st,
Or else committ'st thy knaveries willfully.
Puck. Believe me, king of shadows, I mistook.
Did not you tell me I should know the man
By the Athenian garments he had on?
And so far blameless proves my enterprise
That I have 'nointed an Athenian's eyes;
And so far am I glad it so did sort,
As this their jangling I esteem a sport.
Oberon. Thou seest these lovers seek a place to fight.
Hie[36] therefore, Robin, overcast the night;

---

[34] minimus . . . made—midget, made of a weed that stunts growth.
[35] coil is 'long of you—trouble is because of you.
[36] Hie—hurry.

In the Guthrie Theatre production, Helena (Leslie Silva, right) warns Demetrius (Anthony Claravino, right) and Lysander (Joshua Wolf Coleman) about Hermia (Jennifer Abigail Lopez) that "though she be but little, she is fierce."

The starry welkin[37] cover thou anon
With drooping fog as black as Acheron,[38]
And lead these testy rivals so astray
As one come not within another's way.
360   Like to Lysander sometimes frame thy tongue,
Then stir Demetrius up with bitter wrong;
And sometimes rail thou like Demetrius.
And from each other look thou lead them thus,
Till o'er their brows death-counterfeiting sleep
365   With leaden legs and batty wings doth creep.
Then crush this herb into Lysander's eye,
[*He gives the herb to* Puck.]
Whose liquor hath this virtuous property,
To take from thence all error with his might

---

[37] welkin—sky.
[38] Acheron—river in hell in classical mythology.

And make his eyeballs roll with wonted sight.[39]
370 When they next wake, all this derision
Shall seem a dream and fruitless vision,
And back to Athens shall the lovers wend
With league whose date till death shall never end.
Whiles I in this affair do thee employ,
375 I'll to my queen and beg her Indian boy;
And then I will her charmèd eye release
From monster's view, and all things shall be peace.

Puck. My fairy lord, this must be done with haste,
For night's swift dragons[40] cut the clouds full fast,
380 And yonder shines Aurora's harbinger,[41]
At whose approach ghosts, wand'ring here and there,
Troop home to churchyards. Damnèd spirits all,
That in crossways and floods have burial,
Already to their wormy beds are gone.[42]
385 For fear lest day should look their shames upon,
They willfully themselves exile from light
And must for aye[43] consort with black-browed night.

Oberon. But we are spirits of another sort.
I with the Morning's love have oft made sport,
390 And, like a forester, the groves may tread
Even till the eastern gate, all fiery red,
Opening on Neptune with fair blessèd beams,
Turns into yellow gold his salt-green streams.
But notwithstanding, haste! Make no delay.
395 We may effect this business yet ere day. [*Exit* Oberon.]

Puck. Up and down, up and down,
I will lead them up and down.
I am feared in field and town.
Goblin, lead them up and down.
400 Here comes one.

---

[39] wonted sight—normal vision.

[40] dragons—In classical mythology, dragons pulled the moon in a chariot.

[41] Aurora's harbinger—Venus, the morning star, announces the coming of dawn.

[42] That in . . . are gone—Suicides were buried at crossroads, and the drowned have no graves.

[43] aye—forever.

[*Enter* Lysander.]

Lysander. Where art thou, proud Demetrius? Speak thou now.

Puck [*mimicking* Demetrius]. Here, villain, drawn and ready.
    Where art thou?

Lysander. I will be with thee straight.

Puck [*mimicking* Demetrius]   Follow me, then,

405   To plainer ground.

[*Exit* Lysander, *as following the voice.*]

[*Enter* Demetrius.]

Demetrius.   Lysander! Speak again!
    Thou runaway, thou coward, art thou fled?
    Speak! In some bush? Where dost thou hide thy head?

Puck [*mimicking* Lysander]. Thou coward, art thou bragging to the stars,
    Telling the bushes that thou look'st for wars,

410   And wilt not come? Come, recreant!⁴⁴ Come, thou child,
    I'll whip thee with a rod. He is defiled
    That draws a sword on thee.

Demetrius.   Yea, art thou there?

Puck [*mimicking* Lysander]. Follow my voice. We'll try no manhood here.

[*Exit* Puck and Demetrius.]

[Lysander *returns.*]

Lysander. He goes before me and still dares me on.

415   When I come where he calls, then he is gone.
    The villain is much lighter-heeled than I.
    I followed fast, but faster he did fly,
    That fallen am I in dark uneven way,
    And here will rest me. [*He lies down.*] Come, thou gentle day!

420   For if but once thou show me thy gray light,
    I'll find Demetrius and revenge this spite. [*He sleeps.*]

[*Enter* Puck *and* Demetrius.]

Puck [*mimicking* Lysander]. Ho, ho, ho! Coward, why com'st thou not?

Demetrius. Abide me, if thou dar'st; for well I wot
    Thou runn'st before me, shifting every place,

425   And dar'st not stand nor look me in the face.
    Where art thou now?

---

⁴⁴ recreant—coward.

Exhausted by their quarrels, the four lovers lie asleep on the ground in this scene from the Trinity Repertory Company production.

Puck [*mimicking* Lysander].
　　　　　　　　Come hither. I am here.
Demetrius. Nay, then, thou mock'st me. Thou shalt buy this dear,
　　　If ever I thy face by daylight see.
　　　Now go thy way. Faintness constraineth me
430　　　To measure out my length on this cold bed.
　　　By day's approach look to be visited.
[*He lies down and sleeps.*]
[*Enter* Helena.]
Helena. O weary night, O long and tedious night,
　　　Abate[45] thy hours! Shine, comforts, from the east,
　　　That I may back to Athens by daylight
435　　　From these that my poor company detest;

[45] Abate—reduce, lessen.

And sleep, that sometimes shuts up sorrow's eye,
    Steal me awhile from mine own company.
[*She lies down and sleeps.*]
Puck. Yet but three? Come one more;
    Two of both kinds makes up four.
440   Here she comes, curst and sad.
    Cupid is a knavish lad,
    Thus to make poor females mad.
[*Enter* Hermia.]
Hermia. Never so weary, never so in woe,
    Bedabbled with the dew and torn with briers,
445   I can no further crawl, no further go;
    My legs can keep no pace with my desires.
    Here will I rest me till the break of day.
    Heavens shield Lysander, if they mean a fray!
[*She lies down and sleeps.*]
Puck. On the ground
450   Sleep sound.
    I'll apply
    To your eye,
    Gentle lover, remedy.
[*He squeezes the juice on* Lysander's *eyelids.*]
    When thou wak'st,
455   Thou tak'st
    True delight
    In the sight
    Of thy former lady's eye;
    And the country proverb known,
460   That every man should take his own,
    In your waking shall be shown:
    Jack shall have Jill;
    Naught shall go ill;
The man shall have his mare again, and all shall be well.
[*Exit* Puck. *The four sleeping lovers remain.*]

Act Four, Scene One

*In her bower, Titania's fairies fulfill all
Bottom's wishes until he falls asleep in her
arms. Oberon, watching them sleep, tells Puck
that Titania easily parted with the boy they
had argued over. Oberon removes the love
spell from Titania. When she wakes, she is
horrified at Bottom, and peace is restored
between her and Oberon. As dawn breaks,
Puck removes the donkey's head from
Bottom, and Oberon and Titania dance. The
fairies leave. Theseus, Hippolyta, and Egeus
enter the forest with their hunting party.
They wake the sleeping lovers, who think that
everything that happened during the night
was a dream. Theseus insists that Egeus consent
to Lysander and Hermia's marriage. He tells
the two couples to join Hippolyta and him at
the temple where they will all be married.
Bottom wakes and tries to recall his night's
experience, which he thinks was a dream. He
rushes off to Athens to rejoin his friends.*

Enter Titania, *queen of fairies,* Bottom, *and* Fairies. Oberon, *the king, enters
behind them, unseen by those onstage.*

Titania. Come, sit thee down upon this flowery bed,
    While I thy amiable cheeks do coy,[1]
    And stick muskroses in thy sleek smooth head,
    And kiss thy fair large ears, my gentle joy.
[*They recline.*]

5 **Bottom.** Where's Peaseblossom?

Peaseblossom. Ready.

Bottom. Scratch my head, Peaseblossom. Where's Monsieur Cobweb?

Cobweb. Ready.

Bottom. Monsieur Cobweb, good monsieur, get you your weapons in
10   your hand, and kill me a red-hipped humble-bee on the top of a this-
      tle; and, good monsieur, bring me the honey-bag. Do not fret yourself
      too much in the action, monsieur; and, good monsieur, have a care
      the honey-bag break not. I would be loath to have you overflown
      with a honey-bag, signor. [*Exit* Cobweb.] Where's Monsieur
15   Mustardseed?

---

[1] While . . . coy—while I caress your lovable cheeks.

Mustardseed. Ready.

Bottom. Give me your neaf,[2] Monsieur Mustardseed.
Pray you, leave your courtesy, good monsieur.

Mustardseed. What's your will?

20 **Bottom.** Nothing, good monsieur, but to help Cavalery[3] Cobweb to
scratch. I must to the barber's, monsieur, for methinks I am marvelous hairy about the face; and I am such a tender ass, if my hair do
but tickle me I must scratch.

Titania. What, wilt thou hear some music, my sweet love?

25 **Bottom.** I have a reasonable good ear in music. Let's have the tongs and
the bones.[4]

[*Rural music.*]

Titania. Or say, sweet love, what thou desirest to eat.

Bottom. Truly, a peck of provender.[5] I could munch your good dry oats.
Methinks I have a great desire to a bottle[6] of hay. Good hay, sweet

30 hay, hath no fellow.

Titania. I have a venturous fairy that shall seek
The squirrel's hoard, and fetch thee new nuts.

Bottom. I had rather have a handful or two of dried peas. But, I pray
you, let none of your people stir me. I have an exposition[7] of sleep

35 come upon me.

Titania. Sleep thou, and I will wind thee in my arms.
Fairies, begone, and be all ways away.

[*Exit* Fairies.]

So doth the woodbine[8] the sweet honeysuckle
Gently entwist; the female ivy so

40 Enrings the barky fingers of the elm.
O, how I love thee! How I dote on thee!

[*They sleep.*]

[*Enter* Puck.]

---

[2] neaf—fist; hand.

[3] Cavalery—cavalier, a gallant or chivalrous man.

[4] tongs and the bones—simple musical instruments. Tongs were played by hitting pieces of metal; bones were pieces of
bone clicked together.

[5] peck of provender—quarter of a bushel of grain.

[6] bottle—bundle.

[7] exposition—Bottom's mistake for "disposition."

[8] woodbine—climbing vine of the honeysuckle family.

In this scene from the Huntington Theatre Company production, Bottom (Ed Dixon) sits with Titania (Francesca Faridany) and her fairy attendants.

Oberon [*coming forward*]. Welcome, good Robin. Seest thou this sweet sight?
Her dotage[9] now I do begin to pity.
For, meeting her of late behind the wood

45 Seeking sweet favors for this hateful fool,
I did upbraid her and fall out with her.
For she his hairy temples then had rounded
With coronet of fresh and fragrant flowers;
And that same dew, which sometime on the buds

50 Was wont to swell like round and orient pearls,
Stood now within the pretty flowerets' eyes
Like tears that did their own disgrace bewail.
When I had at my pleasure taunted her,

[9] dotage—foolish affection.

What visions have I seen!
Methought I was enamored of an ass.

And she in mild terms begged my patience,
55   I then did ask of her her changeling child,
Which straight she gave me, and her fairy sent
To bear him to my bower in Fairyland.
And, now I have the boy, I will undo
This hateful imperfection of her eyes.
60   And, gentle Puck, take this transformèd scalp
From off the head of this Athenian swain,[10]
That he, awaking when the others do,
May all to Athens back again repair,
And think no more of this night's accidents
65   But as the fierce vexation of a dream.
But first I will release the Fairy queen.
[*He squeezes an herb on her eyes.*]
Be as thou wast wont to be;
See as thou wast wont to see.
Dian's bud o'er Cupid's flower
70   Hath such force and blessèd power.
Now, my Titania, wake you, my sweet queen.

Titania [*awaking*]. My Oberon! What visions have I seen!
Methought I was enamored of an ass.

Oberon. There lies your love.

Titania.   How came these things to pass?
75   O, how mine eyes do loathe his visage now!

Oberon. Silence awhile. Robin, take off this head.—
Titania, music call, and strike more dead
Than common sleep of all these five[11] the sense.

Titania. Music, ho! Music, such as charmeth sleep! [*Music.*]
80   **Puck** [*removing the ass head from* Bottom]. Now, when thou wak'st, with
thine own fool's eyes peep.

---

[10] swain—rustic lover.

[11] these five—four lovers and Bottom.

Titania (Francesca Faridany) and Oberon (John Wojda) are reconciled in this scene from the Huntington Theatre Company production.

Oberon. Sound, music! Come, my queen, take hands with me,
And rock the ground whereon these sleepers be.
[Titania *and* Oberon *dance.*]
Now thou and I are new in **amity,**[12]
85   And will tomorrow midnight solemnly
Dance in Duke Theseus' house triumphantly,
And bless it to all fair prosperity.
There shall the pairs of faithful lovers be
Wedded, with Theseus, all in jollity.
90   **Puck.** Fairy King, attend, and mark:
I do hear the morning lark.

[12] **amity**—friendship.

I never heard

So musical a discord, such sweet thunder.

Oberon. Then, my queen, in silence sad,

    Trip we after night's shade.

    We the globe can compass soon,

95   Swifter than the wandering moon.

Titania. Come, my lord, and in our flight

    Tell me how it came this night

    That I sleeping here was found

    With these mortals on the ground.

[*Exit* Oberon, Titania, *and* Puck.]

[*Hunting horn offstage.*]

[*Enter* Theseus *and his* Followers *and* Attendants, Hippolyta *and* Egeus.]

100 **Theseus.** Go, one of you, find out the forester,

    For now our observation is performed;

    And, since we have the vaward[13] of the day,

    My love shall hear the music of my hounds.

    Uncouple in the western valley; let them go.

105   Dispatch, I say, and find the forester.

[*Exit* Attendant.]

    We will, fair queen, up to the mountain's top

    And mark the musical confusion

    Of hounds and echo in conjunction.

Hippolyta. I was with Hercules and Cadmus[14] once

110   When in a wood of Crete they bayed[15] the bear

    With hounds of Sparta. Never did I hear

    Such gallant chiding; for, besides the groves,

    The skies, the fountains, every region near

    Seemed all one mutual cry. I never heard

115   So musical a **discord**,[16] such sweet thunder.

---

[13] vaward—vanguard, the first part.

[14] Cadmus—founder of Thebes in classical mythology.

[15] bayed—hunted.

[16] **discord**—in music, a combination of notes not in harmony with each other.

Theseus. My hounds are bred out of the Spartan kind,
    So flewed, so sanded;[17] and their heads are hung
    With ears that sweep away the morning dew;
    Crook-kneed, and dewlapped[18] like Thessalian bulls;
120   Slow in pursuit, but matched in mouth like bells,
    Each under each. A cry more tunable
    Was never holloed to, nor cheered with horn,
    In Crete, in Sparta, nor in Thessaly.
    Judge when you hear.—[*He sees the sleepers.*] But soft!
125   What nymphs are these?

Egeus. My lord, this is my daughter here asleep,
    And this Lysander, this Demetrius is;
    This Helena, old Nedar's Helena.
    I wonder of their being here together.

130 **Theseus.** No doubt they rose up early to observe
    The rite of May, and hearing our intent,
    Came here in grace of our solemnity.
    But speak, Egeus. Is not this the day
    That Hermia should give answer of her choice?

135 **Egeus.** It is, my lord.

Theseus. Go bid the huntsmen wake them with their horns.
[*Exit* Attendant.]
[Attendant *shouts within.*[19] *Horns sound. They all start up.*]
    Good morrow, friends. Saint Valentine is past.
    Begin these woodbirds but to couple now?

Lysander. Pardon, my lord. [*The lovers kneel.*]

Theseus.   I pray you all, stand up.
140   I know you two are rival enemies;
    How comes this gentle concord[20] in the world,
    That hatred is so far from jealousy
    To sleep by hate and fear no enmity?

Lysander. My lord, I shall reply amazedly,
145   Half sleep, half waking. But as yet, I swear,

---

[17] So flewed ... sanded—having large folds of flesh around the mouth and a sandy color.
[18] dewlapped—with folds of skin under their necks.
[19] *within*—offstage.
[20] concord—harmony or agreement.

I cannot truly say how I came here.
But, as I think—for truly would I speak,
And now I do bethink me, so it is—
I came with Hermia hither. Our intent
150 Was to be gone from Athens, where we might,
Without the peril of the Athenian law—
Egeus. Enough, enough! My lord; you have enough.
I beg the law, the law, upon his head.
They would have stol'n away.—They would, Demetrius,
155 Thereby to have defeated you and me,
You of your wife and me of my consent,
Of my consent that she should be your wife.
Demetrius. My lord, fair Helen told me of their stealth,
Of this their purpose hither to this wood,
160 And I in fury hither followed them,
Fair Helena in fancy following me.
But, my good lord, I wot not by what power—
But by some power it is—my love to Hermia,
Melted as the snow, seems to me now
165 As the remembrance of an idle gaud
Which in my childhood I did dote upon;
And all the faith, the virtue of my heart,
The object and the pleasure of mine eye,
Is only Helena. To her, my lord,
170 Was I betrothed ere I saw Hermia,
But like a sickness did I loathe this food.
But, as in health, come to my natural taste,
Now I do wish it, love it, long for it,
And will forevermore be true to it.
175 **Theseus.** Fair lovers, you are fortunately met.
Of this discourse we more will hear anon.—
Egeus, I will overbear your will;
For in the temple, by and by, with us
These couples shall eternally be knit.
180 And, for the morning now is something worn,
Our purposed hunting shall be set aside.
Away with us to Athens. Three and three,
We'll hold a feast in great solemnity.
Come, Hippolyta.

[*Exit* Theseus, *his* Followers *and* Attendants, Hippolyta *and* Egeus.]

185 **Demetrius.** These things seem small and undistinguishable,
   Like far-off mountains turnèd into clouds.

Hermia. Methinks I see these things with parted eye,
   When everything seems double.

Helena.   So methinks;
   And I have found Demetrius like a jewel,
190   Mine own, and not mine own.

Demetrius.   Are you sure
   That we are awake? It seems to me
   That yet we sleep, we dream. Do not you think
   The duke was here, and bid us follow him?

Hermia. Yea, and my father.

Helena.   And Hippolyta.

195 **Lysander.** And he did bid us follow to the temple.

Demetrius. Why, then, we are awake. Let's follow him,
   And by the way let us recount our dreams.

[*The lovers exit.*]

Bottom [*awaking*]. When my cue comes, call me, and I will answer. My
   next is "Most fair Pyramus." Heigh-ho! Peter Quince! Flute, the bel-
200   lows mender! Snout, the tinker! Starveling! God's my life! Stolen
   hence and left me asleep! I have had a most rare vision. I have had a
   dream, past the wit of man to say what dream it was. Man is but an
   ass if he go about to expound[21] this dream. Methought I was—there is
   no man can tell what. Methought I was, and methought I had, but
205   man is but a patched fool[22] if he will offer to say what methought I
   had. The eye of man hath not heard, the ear of man hath not seen,
   man's hand is not able to taste, his tongue to conceive, nor his heart
   to report what my dream was. I will get Peter Quince to write a ballad of this dream. It shall be called "Bottom's Dream," because it hath
210   no bottom; and I will sing it in the latter end of a play, before the
   duke. Peradventure,[23] to make it the more gracious, I shall sing it at
   her[24] death. [*He exits.*]

---

[21] go . . . expound—try to explain.

[22] patched fool—clown. He is referring to the patched clothes of jesters.

[23] Peradventure—perhaps.

[24] her—Thisbe's.

Act Four, Scene Two

In a room in Quince's house, the tradesmen are anxiously waiting for Bottom. They are disappointed that they cannot perform their play if he does not return. When Bottom *reappears, they are delighted. He tells them to ready themselves because Theseus has chosen their play to be performed that night.*

Enter Quince, Flute, Snout, *and* Starveling.

Quince. Have you sent to Bottom's house? Is he come home yet?

Starveling. He cannot be heard of. Out of doubt he is transported.[1]

Flute. If he come not, then the play is marred. It goes not forward. Doth it?

Quince. It is not possible. You have not a man in all Athens able to dis-
5   charge Pyramus but he.

Flute. No, he hath simply the best wit of any handicraft man in Athens.

Quince. Yea, and the best person too, and he is a very paramour for a
      sweet voice.

Flute. You must say "paragon." A paramour is, God bless us, a thing of
10   naught.[2]

[*Enter* Snug *the joiner.*]

Snug. Masters, the duke is coming from the temple, and there is two or
      three lords and ladies more married. If our sport had gone forward,
      we had all been made men.

Flute. O sweet bully Bottom! Thus hath he lost sixpence a day during his
15   life. He could not have 'scaped sixpence a day. An the duke had not
      given him sixpence a day for playing Pyramus, I'll be hanged. He
      would have deserved it. Sixpence a day in Pyramus, or nothing.[3]

[*Enter* Bottom.]

Bottom. Where are these lads? Where are these hearts?

Quince. Bottom! O most courageous day! O most happy hour!

---

[1] transported—taken away, possibly by fairies.

[2] thing of naught—disgraceful thing. *Paragon* means "ideal"; *paramour* means "lover."

[3] Thus hath he . . . or nothing—The duke might have rewarded Bottom's great performance with a pension of sixpence a day for life.

And, most dear actors, eat no onions nor garlic, for we are to utter sweet breath.

20 **Bottom.** Masters, I am to discourse wonders. But ask me not what, for if I tell you, I am no true Athenian. I will tell you everything, right as it fell out.

Quince. Let us hear, sweet Bottom.

Bottom. Not a word of me. And that I will tell you is that the duke hath
25 dined. Get your apparel together, good strings to your beards,[4] new ribbons to your pumps.[5] Meet presently at the palace. Every man look o'er his part. For the short and the long is, our play is preferred. In any case, let Thisbe have clean linen, and let not him that plays the lion pare his nails, for they shall hang out for the lion's claws. And,
30 most dear actors, eat no onions nor garlic, for we are to utter sweet breath, and I do not doubt but to hear them say it is a sweet comedy. No more words. Away! Go, away! [*They exit.*]

---

[4] good strings to your beards—tie your fake beards on tight.
[5] ribbons ... pumps—new ribbons for your fancy shoes.

Act Five, Scene One

In the palace, the three sets of newlyweds are celebrating. Theseus calls for entertainment. He chooses the tradesmen's play, countering Philostrate's criticisms by saying that the players must have labored hard and deserve some thanks for their efforts. The play is so ridiculous and so badly acted that the audience laughs at it, even though it is meant to be a tragedy. After the play, Theseus sends everyone to bed as midnight has struck. The fairies appear. During a dance, they bless the house and the newlyweds. As they vanish, Puck asks the audience for its forgiveness and thanks.

Enter Theseus, Hippolyta, *and* Philostrate, Lords, *and* Attendants.

Hippolyta. 'Tis strange, my Theseus, that these lovers speak of.
Theseus. More strange than true. I never may believe
    These antique fables, nor these fairy toys.
    Lovers and madmen have such seething brains,
5   Such shaping fantasies, that apprehend
    More than cool reason ever comprehends.
    The lunatic, the lover, and the poet
    Are of imagination all compact.
    One sees more devils than vast hell can hold;
10   That is the madman. The lover, all as frantic,
    Sees Helen's[1] beauty in a brow of Egypt.[2]
    The poet's eye, in a fine frenzy rolling,
    Doth glance from heaven to earth, from earth to heaven,
    And as imagination bodies forth
15   The forms of things unknown, the poet's pen
    Turns them to shapes and gives to airy nothing
    A local habitation and a name.
    Such tricks hath strong imagination
    That, if it would but apprehend some joy,
20   It comprehends some bringer of that joy.
    Or in the night, imagining some fear,
    How easy is a bush supposed a bear!

---

[1] Helen's—In classical mythology, Helen of Troy was the world's most beautiful woman.
[2] brow of Egypt—gypsy's face.

Hippolyta. But all the story of the night told over,
And all their minds transfigured so together,

25 More witnesseth than fancy's images
And grows to something of great constancy;
But, howsoever, strange and admirable.

[*Enter* Lysander, Demetrius, Hermia, *and* Helena.]

Theseus. Here come the lovers, full of joy and mirth.—
Joy, gentle friends! Joy and fresh days of love

30 Accompany your hearts!

Lysander.   More than to us
Wait in your royal walks, your board, your bed!

Theseus. Come now, what masques,³ what dances shall we have,
To wear away this long age of three hours
Between our after-supper and bedtime?

35 Where is our usual manager of mirth?
What revels are in hand? Is there no play
To ease the anguish of a torturing hour?
Call Philostrate.

Philostrate.   Here, mighty Theseus.

Theseus. Say, what abridgment have you for this evening?

40 What masque? What music? How shall we beguile
The lazy time, if not with some delight?

Philostrate [*giving* Theseus *a paper*].
There is a brief how many sports are ripe.
Make choice of which Your Highness will see first.

Theseus [*reads*]. "The battle with the Centaurs,⁴ to be sung

45 By an Athenian eunuch to the harp."
We'll none of that. That have I told my love,
In glory of my kinsman Hercules.

---

³ masques—royal court performances mixing drama, music, and dance.

⁴ battle . . . Centaurs—The centaur was a creature with the head and torso of a human being and the body and legs of a horse. This probably refers to a famous incident in the life of Hercules.

[*He reads.*] "The riot of the tipsy Bacchanals,
Tearing the Thracian singer in their rage."[5]
50 That is an old device; and it was played
When I from Thebes came last a conqueror.
[*He reads.*] "The thrice three Muses[6] mourning for the death
Of Learning, late deceased in beggary."
That is some satire, keen and critical,
55 Not sorting with[7] a nuptial ceremony.
[*He reads.*] "A tedious brief scene of young Pyramus
And his love Thisbe; very tragical **mirth**?"[8]
"Merry" and "tragical"? "Tedious" and "brief"?
That is, hot ice and wondrous strange snow.
60 How shall we find the concord of this discord?
Philostrate. A play there is, my lord, some ten words long,
Which is as brief as I have known a play;
But by ten words, my lord, it is too long,
Which makes it tedious. For in all the play
65 There is not one word apt, one player fitted.
And tragical, my noble lord, it is.
For Pyramus therein doth kill himself.
Which, when I saw rehearsed, I must confess,
Made mine eyes water; but more merry tears
70 The passion of loud laughter never shed.
Theseus. What are they that do play it?
Philostrate. Hard-handed men that work in Athens here,
Which never labored in their minds till now,
And now have toiled their unbreathed[9] memories
75 With this same play, against your nuptial.
Theseus. And we will hear it.
Philostrate.   No, my noble lord,
It is not for you. I have heard it over,
And it is nothing, nothing in the world.

---

[5] The riot ... rage—This refers to the story of the death of Orpheus, the singer who was torn apart by frenzied female worshippers of Bacchus, the god of wine.

[6] Muses—nine goddesses who were patrons of the arts and learning.

[7] sorting with—appropriate to.

[8] **mirth**—joy.

[9] unbreathed—unused.

Unless you can find sport in their intents,
80   Extremely stretched and conned with cruel pain[10]
        To do you service.

Theseus.   I will hear that play;
        For never anything can be amiss
        When simpleness and duty tender it.
        Go, bring them in—and take your places, ladies.

[Exit Philostrate *to summon the players.]*

85   **Hippolyta.** I love not to see wretchedness o'ercharged,[11]
        And duty in his service perishing.

Theseus. Why, gentle sweet, you shall see no such thing.

Hippolyta. He says they can do nothing in this kind.

Theseus. The kinder we, to give them thanks for nothing.
90   Our sport shall be to take what they mistake;
        And what poor duty cannot do, noble respect
        Takes it in might, not merit.[12]
        Where I have come, great clerks[13] have purposèd
        To greet me with premeditated welcomes;
95   Where I have seen them shiver and look pale,
        Make periods in the midst of sentences,
        Throttle their practiced accent in their fears,
        And in conclusion dumbly have broke off,
        Not paying me a welcome. Trust me, sweet,
100   Out of this silence yet I picked a welcome;
        And in the modesty of fearful duty
        I read as much as from the rattling tongue
        Of saucy and audacious eloquence.[14]
        Love, therefore, and tongue-tied simplicity
105   In least speak most, to my capacity.

[Philostrate returns.]

Philostrate. So please Your Grace, the Prologue is addressed.[15]

---

[10] Extremely stretched . . . cruel pain—overtaxed and memorized with difficulty.

[11] wretchedness o'ercharged—lowly people overburdened.

[12] Takes . . . merit—praises the effort, not its success.

[13] clerks—scholars.

[14] saucy . . . eloquence—rude and bold skill in speaking.

[15] Prologue is addressed—speaker of the prologue is ready.

Theseus. Let him approach. [*A flourish of trumpets.*]

[*Enter the* Prologue (Quince).]

Quince, as Prologue. If we offend, it is with our good will.

That you should think, we come not to offend,

But with good will. To show our simple skill,

That is the true beginning of our end.

Consider, then, we come but in despite.

We do not come, as minding to content you,

Our true intent is. All for your delight

We are not here. That you should here repent you,

The actors are at hand, and, by their show,

You shall know all that you are like to know.

Theseus. This fellow doth not stand upon points.[16]

Lysander. He hath rid his prologue like a rough colt; he knows not

the stop. A good moral, my lord: it is not enough to speak, but to

speak true.

Hippolyta. Indeed, he hath played on his prologue like a child on a

recorder: a sound, but not in government.

Theseus. His speech was like a tangled chain: nothing **impaired**,[17] but all

disordered. Who is next?

[*Enter* Pyramus (Bottom), Thisbe (Flute), Wall (Snout), Moonshine

(Starveling), *and* Lion (Snug).]

Prologue. *Gentles, perchance you wonder at this show;*

But wonder on, till truth make all things plain.

This man is Pyramus, if you would know.

This beauteous lady Thisbe is, certain.

This man with lime and roughcast doth present

Wall, that vile wall which did these lovers sunder;[18]

And through Wall's chink, poor souls, they are content

To whisper. At the which let no man wonder.

This man, with lantern, dog, and bush of thorn,

Presenteth Moonshine; for, if you will know,

By moonshine did these lovers think no scorn

To meet at Ninus' tomb, there, there to woo.

---

[16] stand upon points—Theseus puns that the Prologue is not a stickler for detail and is not careful with punctuation.

[17] **impaired**—damaged.

[18] *sunder*—keep apart.

> This grisly beast, which Lion hight[19] by name,
> The trusty Thisbe coming first by night
> 140   Did scare away, or rather did affright;
> And as she fled, her mantle[20] she did fall,
> Which Lion vile with bloody mouth did stain.
> Anon comes Pyramus, sweet youth and tall,
> And finds his trusty Thisbe's mantle slain;
> 145   Whereat, with blade, with bloody, blameful blade,
> He bravely broached his boiling bloody breast.
> And Thisbe, tarrying in mulberry shade,
> His dagger drew, and died. For all the rest,
> Let Lion, Moonshine, Wall, and lovers twain[21]
> 150   At large discourse, while here they do remain.

[*Exit* Lion, Thisbe, *and* Moonshine.]

Theseus. I wonder if the lion be to speak.

Demetrius. No wonder, my lord. One lion may, when many asses do.

Snout, as Wall. *In this same interlude it doth befall*
> That I, one Snout by name, present a wall;
> 155   And such a wall as I would have you think
> That had in it a crannied hole or chink,
> Through which the lovers, Pyramus and Thisbe,
> Did whisper often, very secretly.
> This loam, this roughcast, and this stone doth show
> 160   That I am that same wall. The truth is so.
> And this the cranny is, right and sinister,[22]
> Through which the fearful lovers are to whisper.

Theseus. Would you desire lime and hair to speak better?

Demetrius. It is the wittiest **partition**[23] that ever I heard discourse,
> 165   my lord.

[Pyramus *comes forward.*]

Theseus. Pyramus draws near the wall. Silence!

Bottom, as Pyramus. *O grim-looked night! O night with hue so black!*
> *O night, which ever art when day is not!*

---

19 *hight*—is called.

20 *mantle*—cape or coat.

21 *twain*—two.

22 *sinister*—left.

23 **partition**—wall.

O night, O night! Alack, alack, alack,

170 *I fear my Thisbe's promise is forgot.*

And thou, O wall, O sweet, O lovely wall,

That stand'st between her father's ground and mine,

Thou wall, O wall, O sweet and lovely wall,

Show me thy chink, to blink through with mine eyne.

[Wall *makes a chink by holding his fingers in the shape of a* V.]

175 *Thanks, courteous wall. Jove*[24] *shield thee well for this.*

But what see I? No Thisbe do I see.

O wicked wall, through whom I see no bliss!

Cursed be thy stones for thus deceiving me!

Theseus. The wall, methinks, being sensible, should curse again.

180 **Bottom, as Pyramus.** No, in truth, sir, he should not. "Deceiving me" is Thisbe's cue. She is to enter now, and I am to spy her through the wall. You shall see, it will fall pat as I told you. Yonder she comes.

[*Enter* Flute (Thisbe).]

Flute, as Thisbe. *O wall, full often hast thou heard my moans*

For parting my fair Pyramus and me.

185 *My cherry lips have often kissed thy stones,*

Thy stones with lime and hair knit up in thee.

Bottom, as Pyramus. *I see a voice. Now will I to the chink,*

To spy an I can hear my Thisbe's face.

Thisbe!

190 **Flute, as Thisbe.** *My love! Thou art my love, I think.*

Bottom, as Pyramus. *Think what thou wilt, I am thy lover's grace,*

And like Limander am I trusty still.

Flute, as Thisbe. *And I like Helen,*[25] *till the Fates me kill.*

Bottom, as Pyramus. *Not Shafalus to Procrus*[26] *was so true.*

195 **Flute, as Thisbe.** *As Shafalus to Procrus, I to you.*

Bottom, as Pyramus. *O, kiss me through the hole of this vile wall!*

Flute, as Thisbe. *I kiss the wall's hole, not your lips at all.*

Bottom, as Pyramus. *Wilt thou at Ninny's tomb meet me straightway?*

Flute, as Thisbe. *'Tide life, 'tide death,*[27] *I come without delay.*

[*Exit* Bottom *and* Flute.]

---

[24] *Jove*—Jupiter, king of the gods.

[25] *Limander . . . Helen*—Bottom's and Flute's mistakes for Leander and Hero, two tragic lovers in classical mythology.

[26] *Shafalus to Procrus*—Bottom's mistake for Cephalus and Procris, another set of tragic lovers.

[27] *'Tide . . . death*—come life or death.

Snout, as Wall. *Thus have I, Wall, my part dischargèd so;*
And, being done, thus Wall away doth go. [*Exit* Snout.]

Theseus. Now is the mural[28] down between the two
neighbors.

Demetrius. No remedy, my lord, when walls are so willful to hear
without warning.

Hippolyta. This is the silliest stuff that ever I heard.

Theseus. The best in this kind are but shadows; and the worst are no
worse, if imagination amend[29] them.

Hippolyta. It must be your imagination then, and not theirs.

Theseus. If we imagine no worse of them than they of themselves,
they may pass for excellent men. Here come two noble beasts in, a
man and a lion.

[*Enter* Lion (Snug) *and* Moonshine (Starveling).]

Snug, as Lion. *You, ladies, you, whose gentle hearts do fear*
The smallest monstrous mouse that creeps on floor,
May now perchance both quake and tremble here,
When lion rough in wildest rage doth roar.
Then know that I, as Snug the joiner, am
A lion fell, nor else no lion's dam;[30]
For, if I should as lion come in strife
Into this place, 'twere pity on my life.

Theseus. A very gentle beast, and of a good conscience.

Demetrius. The very best at a beast, my lord, that e'er I saw.

Lysander. This lion is a very fox for his valor.

Theseus. True; and a goose for his discretion.

Demetrius. Not so, my lord, for his valor cannot carry his discretion,
and the fox carries the goose.

Theseus. His discretion, I am sure, cannot carry his valor, for the goose
carries not the fox. It is well. Leave it to his discretion, and let us
listen to the Moon.

Starveling, as Moonshine. *This lanthorn*[31] *doth the hornèd*[32] *moon present—*

---

[28] mural—wall.

[29] The best . . . amend—The best actors are only likenesses; and the worst are no worse, if helped by the audience's imagination.

[30] I . . . dam—I am only Snug the cabinet maker as a lion, or even as a lioness.

[31] lanthorn—archaic spelling of "lantern."

[32] hornèd—shaped like a horn.

Demetrius. He should have worn the horns on his head.

Theseus. He is no crescent, and his horns are invisible within the circumference.

Starveling, as Moonshine.

> *This lanthorn doth the hornèd moon present;*
> *Myself the man i' the moon do seem to be.*

Theseus. This is the greatest error of all the rest. The man should be put into the lanthorn. How is it else the man i' the moon?

Demetrius. He dares not come there for the candle, for you see it is already in snuff.

Hippolyta. I am aweary of this moon. Would he would change!

Theseus. It appears, by his small light of discretion, that he is in the wane; but yet, in courtesy, in all reason, we must stay the time.

Lysander. Proceed, Moon.

Starveling, as Moonshine. *All that I have to say is to tell you that the lanthorn is the moon, I, the man i' the moon, this thornbush my thornbush, and this dog my dog.*

"This lanthorn does the hornèd moon present," announces Starveling the Tailor (John McAndrew) in a production of *A Midsummer Night's Dream* by the American Repertory Theatre in Portland, Oregon.

Demetrius. Why, all these should be in the lanthorn, for all these are in the moon. But silence! Here comes Thisbe.

[*Enter* Thisbe (Flute).]

Flute, as Thisbe. *This is old Ninny's tomb. Where is my love?*

250 **Snug, as Lion** [*roaring*]. *O!*

Demetrius. Well roared, Lion.

[Thisbe *runs off, dropping her mantle.*]

Theseus. Well run, Thisbe.

Hippolyta. Well shone, Moon. Truly, the moon shines with a good grace.

[*The* Lion *worries Thisbe's mantle.*]

Theseus. Well moused,[33] Lion.

[*Enter* Pyramus (Bottom).]

255 **Demetrius.** And then came Pyramus.

[*Exit* Lion.]

Lysander. And so the lion vanished.

Bottom, as Pyramus. *Sweet Moon, I thank thee for thy sunny beams;*
I thank thee, Moon, for shining now so bright;
For, by thy gracious, golden, glittering gleams,
260 *I trust to take of truest Thisbe sight.*
　　But stay, O spite!
　　But mark, poor knight,
What dreadful dole[34] is here?
　　Eyes, do you see?
265 　　*How can it be?*
O dainty duck! O dear!
　　Thy mantle good—
　　What, stained with blood?
Approach, ye Furies[35] fell!
270 　　*O Fates,[36] come, come,*
　　Cut thread and thrum;[37]
Quail, crush, conclude, and quell!

Theseus. This passion, and the death of a dear friend, would go near to make a man look sad.

275 **Hippolyta.** Beshrew my heart, but I pity the man.

---

[33] *worries . . . moused*—Both words mean "to snake or tear with the teeth" (like a cat with a mouse).

[34] *dole*—sorrow.

[35] *Furies*—avenging goddesses in classical mythology.

[36] *Fates*—three goddesses in classical mythology who spun, measured, and cut the thread of life of every mortal.

[37] *thrum*—loose end of a thread on a loom.

Bottom, as Pyramus. *O, wherefore, Nature, didst thou lions frame?*

Since lion vile hath here deflowered my dear,

Which is—no, no—which was the fairest dame

That lived, that loved, that liked, that looked with cheer.

280   *Come, tears, confound,*

     Out, sword, and wound

The pap[38] *of Pyramus;*

     Ay, that left pap,

     Where heart doth hop. [*He stabs himself.*]

285 *Thus die I, thus, thus, thus.*

     Now am I dead,

     Now am I fled;

My soul is in the sky.

     Tongue, lose thy light;

290   *Moon, take thy flight.* [*Exit* Moonshine.]

Now die, die, die, die, die. [Pyramus *dies.*]

Demetrius. No die, but an ace,[39] for him; for he is but one.

Lysander. Less than an ace, man; for he is dead, he is nothing.

Theseus. With the help of a surgeon he might yet recover, and yet prove

295   an ass.

Hippolyta. How chance Moonshine is gone before Thisbe comes back and

     finds her lover?

Theseus. She will find him by starlight.

[*Enter* Thisbe (Flute).]

     Here she comes; and her passion ends the play.

300 **Hippolyta.** Methinks she should not use a long one for such a

     Pyramus. I hope she will be brief.

Demetrius. A mote will turn the balance, which Pyramus, which Thisbe,

     is the better: he for a man, God warrant us; she for a woman, God

     bless us.

305 **Lysander.** She hath spied him already with those sweet eyes.

Demetrius. And thus she means, videlicet:[40]

Flute, as Thisbe. *Asleep, my love?*

     What, dead, my dove?

     O Pyramus, arise!

---

[38] *pap*—breast.

[39] die . . . ace—one of a pair of dice with one spot on top.

[40] videlicet—namely, to wit.

310   *Speak, speak. Quite dumb?*
                 Dead, dead? A tomb
      Must cover thy sweet eyes.
             These lily lips,
             This cherry nose,
315   *These yellow cowslip cheeks,*
             Are gone, are gone!
             Lovers, make moan.
      His eyes were green as leeks.
             O Sisters Three,[41]
320   *Come, come to me,*
      With hands as pale as milk;
             Lay them in gore,
             Since you have shore[42]
      With shears his thread of silk.
325   *Tongue, not a word!*
             Come, trusty sword,
      Come, blade, my breast imbrue![43]
[*She stabs herself.*]
             And farewell, friends.
             Thus Thisbe ends.
330   *Adieu, adieu, adieu.* [*She dies.*]

Theseus. Moonshine and Lion are left to bury the dead.

Demetrius. Ay, and Wall too.

Bottom [*starting up, as* Flute *does also*]. No, I assure you, the wall is down that parted their fathers. Will it please you to see the epilogue, or to hear a Bergomask dance between two of our company?

[*The other* Players *enter.*]

Theseus. No epilogue, I pray you; for your play needs no excuse. Never excuse. For when the players are all dead, there need none to be blamed. Marry, if he that writ it had played Pyramus and hanged himself in Thisbe's garter, it would have been a fine tragedy; and so it is, truly, and very notably discharged. But, come, your Bergomask. Let your epilogue alone. [*A dance and the* Players *exit.*]

---

[41] *Sisters Three*—the Fates.

[42] *shore*—shorn, cut.

[43] *imbrue*—cover with blood.

The iron tongue of midnight[44] hath told twelve.
Lovers, to bed! 'Tis almost fairy time.
I fear we shall outsleep the coming morn
345   As much as we this night have overwatched.
This palpable-gross[45] play hath well beguiled
The heavy gait[46] of night. Sweet friends, to bed.
A fortnight hold we this solemnity,
In nightly revels and new jollity. [*They exit.*]
[*Enter* Puck, *carrying* a *broom.*]
350   **Puck.** Now the hungry lion roars,
And the wolf behowls the moon,
Whilst the heavy plowman snores,
All with weary task fordone.[47]
Now the wasted brands[48] do glow,
355   Whilst the screech-owl, screeching loud,
Puts the wretch that lies in woe
In remembrance of a shroud.[49]
Now it is the time of night
That the graves, all gaping wide,
360   Every one lets forth his sprite,
In the church-way paths to glide.
And we fairies, that do run
By the triple Hecate's[50] team.
From the presence of the sun,
365   Following darkness like a dream,
Now are frolic. Not a mouse

---

[44] iron tongue of midnight—midnight bell, with its iron clapper.

[45] palpable-gross—obviously unrefined.

[46] gait—slow pace.

[47] fordone—worn out.

[48] wasted brands—burned-out torches.

[49] shroud—cloth used to wrap a body for burial.

[50] triple Hecate's—Hecate had three forms: Luna (the moon) in the sky; Diana on earth; and Proserpina in the underworld.

Puck (Doug Hara) has the last word in this scene from the Huntington Theatre Company production.

Shall disturb this hallowed[51] house.
I am sent with broom before,
To sweep the dust behind the door.

[*Enter* Oberon *and* Titania, *king and queen of fairies, with all their* Followers.]

370   **Oberon.** Through the house give glimmering[52] light,
        By the dead and drowsy fire;
        Every elf and fairy sprite
        Hop as light as bird from brier;
        And this ditty, after me,
375   Sing, and dance it trippingly.

    Titania. First, rehearse your song by rote,
        To each word a warbling note.
        Hand in hand, with fairy grace,
        Will we sing, and bless this place.

[Oberon *leads the* Fairies *in song and dance.*]

380   **Oberon.** Now, until the break of day,
        Through this house each fairy stray.
        To the best bride-bed will we,
        Which by us shall blessèd be;

---

[51] hallowed—sacred, blessed.
[52] glimmering—sparkling or glowing.

And the issue there create

385 Ever shall be fortunate.

So shall all the couples three

Ever true in loving be;

And the blots of Nature's hand

Shall not in their issue[53] stand;

390 Never mole, harelip, nor scar,

Nor mark prodigious,[54] such as are

Despisèd in nativity,

Shall upon their children be.

With this field-dew consecrate,

395 Every fairy take his gait,

And each several chamber bless,

Through this palace, with sweet peace;

And the owner of it blest

Ever shall in safety rest.

400 Trip away. Make no stay.

Meet me all by break of day.

[*Exit all but* Puck.]

Puck [*to the audience*].

If we shadows have offended,

Think but this, and all is mended,

That you have but slumbered here

405 While these visions did appear.

And this weak and idle theme,

No more yielding but a dream,

Gentles, do not reprehend.

If you pardon, we will mend.

410 And, as I am an honest Puck,

If we have unearnèd luck

Now to 'scape the serpent's tongue,

We will make amends ere long;

Else the Puck a liar call.

415 So, good night unto you all

Give your hands, if we be friends,

And Robin shall restore amends. [*He exits.*]

---

[53] issue—children.

[54] prodigious—abnormal.

Understanding the Play

Act One

1. In Scene One, what choices does Theseus offer Hermia?

2. Why does Hermia tell Helena of the elopement plan? Why does Helena decide to tell Demetrius?

3. In Scene Two, why are the tradesmen organizing a play?

4. What kind of person is Bottom? How does Shakespeare make him likeable?

Act Two

1. What is Puck like? How does he differ from the other fairy in Scene One?

2. Why have Titania and Oberon quarreled? Who do you think is in the wrong?

3. Why does Puck mistakenly put the love charm on Lysander's eyelids?

4. What is ironic about Lysander's protestations of love to Helena?

Act Three

1. In Scene One, why do the tradesmen worry about their play?

2. What does Bottom's response to Titania's expressions of love reveal about him?

3. In Scene Two, why is Helena particularly distressed when she believes that Hermia has joined with the men in mocking her?

4. Which insult upsets Hermia the most? What does this indicate about her and about her relationship with Helena?

5. How does Puck feel about the night's doings? How does his reaction differ from that of Oberon?

Act Four

1. In Scene One, to what extent does Bottom seem aware of his transformation? How does he react to his good fortune? How does this affect your view of him?

2. How does Oberon get the boy away from Titania?

3. Why do you think Titania is not angry with Oberon for his tricks?

4. What do the lovers' different responses on awakening convey about them?

5. What does Bottom's dream represent to him? How has it changed his perception of the world?

6. In Scene Two, what do the responses of Bottom's friends to his disappearance and his return suggest about their feelings for him?

Act Five

1. In Scene One, how do Theseus and Hippolyta disagree about the lovers' tale? What does this indicate about their personalities?

2. Why does Theseus insist on seeing the tradesmen's play? Why does Hippolyta disagree with him?

3. How do the courtiers respond to the tradesmen's play? What do their responses convey about them?

4. What is your opinion of the way Theseus treats the tradesmen?

5. What is the dramatic function of Puck's speech at the end of the play? How does it contribute to the overall mood of the play?

Analyzing the Play

1. The conflict in a play is the struggle between opposing forces that gives movement to the dramatic plot. What are the fundamental conflicts in *A Midsummer Night's Dream?*

2. In Act Two, Scene One, Titania describes how nature is out of order because of the discord between her and Oberon. In what other ways is nature out of order during the play? What finally restores normality?

3. Compare and contrast the effects of day and night in the play. What governs the characters during the day? What governs them at night?

4. In his speech at the beginning of Act Five, Theseus analyzes madness, love, and poetry. What does he see as the similarities among these? How is this a commentary on the play as a whole?

5. What is the dramatic function of the "play within the play"? How does it bring the action full circle? What do we learn from seeing it performed?

Writing Projects

1. Write a letter to one of the young lovers counseling him or her to follow either the course of love or the course of reason. First, decide if you want to write as a friend, an older relation, a neutral observer, and so on. Then decide on your advice and maintain a consistent tone as you write the letter.

2. The title of the play indicates that it is a dream, and in his epilogue Puck suggests that if the audience has not enjoyed the play, they should consider it a dream. Write a short essay analyzing the use of dreams within the play. Which characters have dreams? What relationship do these dreams have to the action of the play?

3. Choose one of the young lovers and write an essay comparing and contrasting his or her character before and after the events in the woods. How has the character changed? What brought about this change?

Performance Projects

1. *A Midsummer Night's Dream* is a play dominated by moonlight—the moon is first mentioned in the third line of the play and is even a character in Act Five. Consider how you might light this play on stage. Much of the action takes place in moonlight. How will you indicate that to the audience? How will it be distinct from the action in daylight? Draw up a sequence of lighting instructions, or make a series of sketches of the lighting of the various scenes.

2. With a partner, perform one of the scenes of strife in the play. They are all short and can be learned easily. Choose the character—either Lysander, Hermia, Demetrius, Helena, Titania, Oberon, Theseus, or Hippolyta—closest to your heart and prepare to play the character. You may want to double up with another pair and do one of the longer scenes.

3. There is a great deal of music in *A Midsummer Night's Dream,* such as hunting horns, rustic dance music, songs, and fairy dances. What sort of music do you think would give the right tone to the play? Research music that you think differentiates between the various sets of characters, indicating to the audience the change of scenes and settings.

4. One of the great questions about casting a production of *A Midsummer Night's Dream* is whether to cast the fairies with adult or child actors. If you were directing the play, how would you cast all the roles? Make a list of the characters, and then indicate the age and physical appearance of the actor you want for each role.

Julius Caesar

Introduction

Julius Caesar's lifetime (100 B.C.–44 B.C.) was a critical period in the history of Rome. Rival leaders struggled for power, leading to bloody civil wars. An even more fundamental question remained: Was Rome to be ruled by one man or by the Senate, the representatives of the people? Whoever ruled Rome controlled the huge and ever-growing Roman empire and the vast wealth brought in by trade and taxes. For a time, Caesar had joined two other leaders, Pompey and Crassus, in a triumvirate (three-man rule); but now he had ousted the others from power, and the Senate had named him dictator for life. Caesar was the undisputed ruler of the Roman world. Yet all was not well at home. Some senators feared that Caesar had too much power and that he would abuse it, as others had done before him. The play begins at this point.

Julius Caesar (David McCallum) is attacked by the conspirators in this scene from the 2000 production of *Julius Caesar* at New York's Joseph Papp Public Theater..

▼

Plot

As Caesar passes in triumph through the streets of Rome, a group of senators led by Cassius conspire to murder him. It is important for them to have Brutus on their side, for he is popular and well respected. Because Brutus has already reasoned with himself that Caesar has too much ambition and is likely to misuse his power to the ruin of Rome and its citizens, he agrees to join the conspiracy. Despite warnings, evil omens, and the fears of his wife, Caesar determines to go to the Senate building as usual. There, the conspiring senators crowd around him and stab him to death.

Fearing the citizens' reaction to the assassination, Brutus addresses the crowd, explaining the reasons for the killing. But then Caesar's friend Mark Antony speaks and manages to enrage the citizens to the point of revolt. Brutus and the other conspirators flee Rome, while an unruly mob sets their houses on fire.

◄ Mark Antony (Dmetrius Conley-Williams) gives a funeral oration for the murdered Caesar (Miles Herter) in this scene from the 1999 production of *Julius Caesar* by Boston's Commonwealth Shakespeare Company.

Eighteen months later, an army led by Brutus and Cassius prepares for a last, decisive battle against the army led by Mark Antony and Octavius Caesar. Brutus and Cassius have their own quarrel, but reconcile and agree to cooperate. The battle favors first one side and then the other. Finally Cassius, fearing loss and capture, kills himself. Brutus does the same. Antony mourns Brutus as the one honorable man among the conspirators.

Brutus (Danny Sapani, third from left), and his followers watch the battle of Philippi in this scene from the 1999 production of *Julius Caesar* at London's Globe Theatre.

▼

Settings and Characters

The action of Julius Caesar takes place in various locations in Rome, Italy; in Sardis, (a city in Asia Minor); and on the plains of Philippi in Macedonia. The time is from 44 B.C. to 42 B.C. The major characters of the play fall into two groups: those who support Caesar and the group of conspirators who want to destroy him. Brutus finds himself caught between his friendship with Caesar and his duty to the other Roman senators.

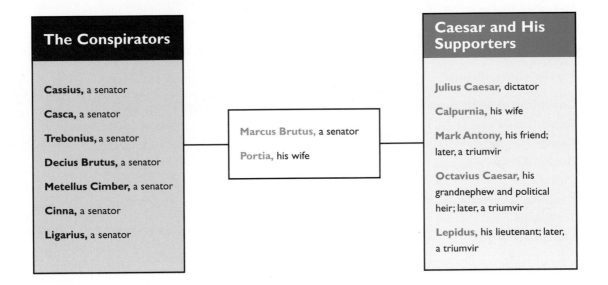

The Conspirators

Cassius, a senator

Casca, a senator

Trebonius, a senator

Decius Brutus, a senator

Metellus Cimber, a senator

Cinna, a senator

Ligarius, a senator

Marcus Brutus, a senator

Portia, his wife

Caesar and His Supporters

Julius Caesar, dictator

Calpurnia, his wife

Mark Antony, his friend; later, a triumvir

Octavius Caesar, his grandnephew and political heir; later, a triumvir

Lepidus, his lieutenant; later, a triumvir

Themes

Julius Caesar is a play about power—who will have it—and about the use and abuse of power. All the main characters have extraordinary abilities but they also have fatal weaknesses. Caesar is a great general and an effective politician; but his pride leads him to his death. Brutus is noble and idealistic, but perhaps not realistic enough; and he also lets his pride in his own rightness bring him down. Antony professes to be Caesar's friend, but he is not above using Caesar's death to stir up civil war.

Ironically, the assassination that Brutus undertakes for Roman liberty brings about a reign of terror and less liberty.

A related theme is that of fate and free will. Time and again, characters ignore warnings from nature and from other characters, only to meet the fates they had been warned against. It is as if, though the leaders of Rome have fallen through their own acts and choices, they have also fulfilled their prearranged destinies.

Characters

Julius Caesar
Calpurnia, wife to Caesar

**Triumvirs after the death
of Julius Caesar:**
Mark Antony,
Octavius Caesar
Lepidus

Marcus Brutus
Portia, wife to Brutus

Conspirators with Brutus:
Caius Cassius
Casca
Decius Brutus
Cinna
Metellus Cimber
Trebonius
Caius Ligarius

Flavius and Marullus,
   tribunes

Cicero, Publius, and
   Popilius Lena, senators
Soothsayer

Artemidorus, a teacher
   of rhetoric

Cinna, a poet
Another Poet

**Friends to Brutus
and Cassius:**
Lucilius
Titinius
Messala
Young Cato
Volumnius
Flavius

Servants to Brutus:
Varro
Claudius
Clitus
Lucius
Strato
Dardanius

Pindarus, servant to Cassius

Ghost of Caesar

Senators, Citizens,
   Guards, Attendants,
   Servants, etc.

SCENE: *Rome; near Sardis; the plains of Philippi.*

Act One, Scene One

On a street in Rome on 15 February, 44 B.C., people are celebrating the Lupercalia, a fertility festival. Excited citizens wait to see Julius Caesar, who has just returned from his triumphant victory over Pompey's sons in Spain. Flavius and Marullus, two tribunes—government officials—try to send the crowd back to their homes and businesses. They scold the citizens for praising Caesar, when so recently they praised Pompey as leader of Rome. The tribunes fear that Caesar's popularity may lead to the end of democracy in Rome.

Enter Flavius, Marullus, *and* Citizens.

Flavius. Hence! Home, you idle creatures, get you home!
    Is this a holiday? What, know you not,
    Being mechanical, you ought not walk
    Upon a laboring day without the sign
5   Of your profession?[1]—Speak, what trade art thou?

Carpenter. Why, sir, a carpenter.

Marullus. Where is thy leather apron and thy rule? What dost thou with
    thy best apparel on?—You, sir, what trade are you?

Cobbler. Truly, sir, in respect of a fine workman, I am but, as you would
10   say, a cobbler.[2]

Marullus. But what trade art thou? Answer me directly.

Cobbler. A trade, sir, that I hope I may use with a safe conscience, which
    is indeed, sir, a mender of bad soles.

Flavius. What trade, thou knave? Thou naughty knave, what trade?

15 **Cobbler.** Nay, I beseech you, sir, be not out[3] with me. Yet if you be out,
    sir, I can mend you.

Flavius. What mean'st thou by that? Mend me, thou saucy fellow?

Cobbler. Why, sir, cobble you.[4]

Flavius. Thou art a cobbler, art thou?

20 **Cobbler.** Truly, sir, all that I live by is with the awl. I meddle with no
    tradesman's matters nor women's matters, but withal[5] I am indeed,
    sir, a surgeon to old shoes. When they are in great danger, I recover
    them. As proper men as ever trod upon neat's leather[6] have gone
    upon my handiwork.

25 **Flavius.** But wherefore art not in thy shop today?
    Why dost thou lead these men about the streets?

---

[1] Being mechanical . . . profession—Being workingmen, you ought not to be on the streets without the clothing and tools of your trade. (Shakespeare refers to an English law of his own time.)

[2] cobbler—In Shakespeare's time, *cobbler* meant a clumsy workman as well as a mender of shoes. That is the reason for Marullus's next question.

[3] out—out of temper, with a pun on having worn-out shoes.

[4] cobble you—mend your shoes.

[5] withal—yet, with a pun on *with all* and *with awl*.

[6] neat's leather—cowhide.

O you hard hearts, you cruel men of Rome!
Knew you not Pompey?

Cobbler. Truly, sir, to wear out their shoes, to get myself into more work. But indeed, sir, we make holiday to see Caesar and to rejoice in his triumph.[7]

30 **Marullus.** Wherefore rejoice? What conquest brings he home?
What tributaries[8] follow him to Rome
To grace in captive bonds his chariot wheels?
You blocks, you stones, you worse than senseless things!
O you hard hearts, you cruel men of Rome!
35 Knew you not Pompey? Many a time and oft
Have you climbed up to walls and battlements,[9]
To towers and windows, yea, to chimney tops,
Your infants in your arms, and there have sat
The livelong day, with patient expectation,
40 To see great Pompey pass the streets of Rome.
And when you saw his chariot but appear,
Have you not made an universal shout,
That Tiber[10] trembled underneath her banks
To hear the replication of your sounds
45 Made in her concave shores?[11]
And do you now put on your best attire?
And do you now cull out[12] a holiday?
And do you now strew flowers in his way
That comes in triumph over Pompey's blood?
50 Be gone!

---

[7] triumph—Caesar's victory over Pompey's sons.

[8] tributaries—conquered rulers bringing tributes of money.

[9] battlements—fortified walls with spaces for shooting.

[10] Tiber—the river Tiber, which runs through Rome.

[11] To hear . . . shores—to hear the echoes of your shouts in her overhanging banks.

[12] cull out—pick out, select.

Run to your houses, fall upon your knees,
Pray to the gods to intermit[13] the plague
That needs must light on this ingratitude.

Flavius. Go, go, good countrymen, and for this fault

55   Assemble all the poor men of your sort;
Draw them to Tiber banks, and weep your tears
Into the channel, till the lowest stream
Do kiss the most exalted shores[14] of all.

[*Exit all the* Citizens.]

See whe'er their basest mettle be not moved.[15]

60   They vanish tongue-tied in their guiltiness.
Go you down that way towards the Capitol;[16]
This way will I. Disrobe the images
If you do find them decked with ceremonies.[17]

Marullus. May we do so?

65   You know it is the Feast of Lupercal.[18]

Flavius. It is no matter. Let no images
Be hung with Caesar's trophies. I'll about
And drive away the vulgar from the streets;
So do you too, where you perceive them thick.

70   These growing feathers plucked from Caesar's wing
Will make him fly an ordinary pitch,[19]
Who else would soar above the view of men
And keep us all in servile fearfulness.

[*They exit.*]

---

[13] intermit—delay.

[14] most exalted shores—highest banks.

[15] See . . . moved—Note how their low natures can be moved.

[16] Capitol—Capitoline Hill, one of the seven hills on which Rome was built. Shakespeare also uses *Capitol* to refer to the meeting-place of the Roman Senate.

[17] Disrobe . . . ceremonies—Take down the crowns that have been placed on Caesar's statues.

[18] Feast of Lupercal—annual Roman fertility festival.

[19] These growing . . . pitch—Falconers sometimes clipped the wings of their hunting birds to keep them from flying at too great a height (pitch). So Caesar, deprived of new followers, will be prevented from reaching greater heights of ambition.

Act One, Scene Two

On a street in Rome, immediately after, Caesar passes through a crowd of citizens on his way to watch a footrace traditionally run on the Lupercalia. A soothsayer calls to Caesar to beware the ides of March (March 15), but Caesar dismisses the warning. Cassius tries to discover Brutus's feelings about Caesar's climb to power. Brutus says he worries that Caesar will abuse his power if the people proclaim him king. Casca reports that during the race, Mark Antony offered Caesar a symbolic crown three times. Caesar refused it, but more reluctantly each time. Cassius and Brutus agree to meet the next day to discuss their concerns further.

Enter Caesar; Antony *(dressed for running the course);* Calpurnia; Portia; Decius; Cicero; Brutus; Cassius; Casca; Citizens *and a* Soothsayer; *after them,* Marullus *and* Flavius.

Caesar. Calpurnia!

Casca.   Peace, ho! Caesar speaks.

Caesar.   Calpurnia!

Calpurnia. Here, my lord.

Caesar. Stand you directly in Antonius' way
      When he doth run his course. Antonius!

5   **Antony.** Caesar, my lord?

Caesar. Forget not, in your speed, Antonius,
      To touch Calpurnia; for our elders say
      The barren, touchèd in this holy chase,
      Shake off their sterile curse.[1]

Antony.   I shall remember.

10   When Caesar says "Do this," it is performed.

Caesar. Set on, and leave no ceremony out. [*Flourish.*][2]

Soothsayer. Caesar!

Caesar. Ha? Who calls?

Casca. Bid every noise be still. Peace yet again!

[*The music ceases.*]

---

[1] The barren . . . curse—The celebrants of Lupercalia raced through certain streets, striking women with goatskin thongs. This was supposed to cure the women of barrenness, failure to produce children.

[2] *Flourish*—sound of trumpets.

Beware the ides of March.

15   **Caesar.** Who is it in the press that calls on me?

        I hear a tongue shriller than all the music

        Cry "Caesar!" Speak! Caesar is turned to hear.

    Soothsayer. Beware the ides of March.[3]

    Caesar.   What man is that?

    Brutus. A soothsayer bids you beware the ides of March.

20   **Caesar.** Set him before me. Let me see his face.

    Cassius. Fellow, come from the throng. [*The* Soothsayer *comes forward.*]

                     Look upon Caesar.

    Caesar. What sayst thou to me now? Speak once again.

    Soothsayer. Beware the ides of March.

    Caesar. He is a dreamer. Let us leave him. Pass.

    [*Trumpet call. Exit all except* Brutus *and* Cassius.]

25   **Cassius.** Will you go see the order of the course?[4]

    Brutus. Not I.

    Cassius. I pray you, do.

    Brutus. I am not gamesome.[5] I do lack some part

        Of that quick spirit that is in Antony.

30   Let me not hinder, Cassius, your desires;

        I'll leave you.

    Cassius. Brutus, I do observe you now of late.

        I have not from your eyes that gentleness

        And show of love as I was wont[6] to have.

35   You bear too stubborn and too strange a hand

        Over your friend that loves you.[7]

    Brutus.   Cassius,

        Be not deceived. If I have veiled my look,

        I turn the trouble of my countenance

        Merely upon myself. Vexèd I am

40   Of late with passions of some difference,[8]

---

[3] ides of March—March 15.

[4] order . . . course—how the race goes.

[5] gamesome—fond of sports.

[6] wont—accustomed.

[7] You bear . . . you—Your behavior to your good friend is rough and aloof.

[8] If I have . . . difference—If I have seemed less friendly, it is because I have been troubled lately with conflicting emotions.

In this scene from a 1991 production of *Julius Caesar* by the Hartford Stage Company, Mark Antony (Tom Hewitt) kneels to Caesar (Donald Buke), who is accompanied by his wife, Calpurnia (Giulia Pagano).

Conceptions only proper to myself,
Which give some soil, perhaps, to my behaviors.
But let not therefore my good friends be grieved—
Among which number, Cassius, be you one—
45   Nor construe any further[9] my neglect
Than that poor Brutus, with himself at war,
Forgets the shows of love to other men.

Cassius. Then, Brutus, I have much mistook your passion,
By means whereof this breast of mine hath buried
50   Thoughts of great value, worthy cogitations.[10]
Tell me, good Brutus, can you see your face?

Brutus. No, Cassius, for the eye sees not itself
But by reflection, by some other things.

Cassius. 'Tis just.
55   And it is very much lamented, Brutus,
That you have no such mirrors as will turn
Your hidden worthiness into your eye,
That you might see your shadow.[11] I have heard
Where many of the best respect in Rome,
60   Except immortal Caesar, speaking of Brutus

---

[9] construe any further—interpret in any other way.

[10] By means . . . cogitations—Because of my misunderstanding (of your behavior), I have kept important thoughts to myself.

[11] shadow—reflection.

And groaning underneath this age's yoke,[12]
Have wished that noble Brutus had his eyes.

Brutus. Into what dangers would you lead me, Cassius,
That you would have me seek into myself
65   For that which is not in me?

Cassius. Therefore, good Brutus, be prepared to hear;
And since you know you cannot see yourself
So well as by reflection, I, your glass,
Will modestly discover to yourself
70   That of yourself which you yet know not of.[13]
And be not jealous on me, gentle Brutus.
Were I a common laughter, or did use
To stale with ordinary oaths my love
To every new protester;[14] if you know
75   That I do fawn on men and hug them hard
And after scandal them, or if you know
That I profess myself in banqueting
To all the rout,[15] then hold me dangerous.

[*Flourish, and shout.*]

Brutus. What means this shouting? I do fear the people
80   Choose Caesar for their king.

Cassius.   Ay, do you fear it?
Then must I think you would not have it so.

Brutus. I would not, Cassius, yet I love him well.
But wherefore do you hold me here so long?
What is it that you would **impart**[16] to me?
85   If it be aught toward the general good,
Set honor in one eye and death i' th' other
And I will look on both indifferently;[17]
For let the gods so speed me as I love
The name of honor more than I fear death.

---

[12] yoke—burden; troubles.

[13] I, your glass . . . of—I will be your mirror and show you things about yourself that you're not aware of.

[14] be not . . . protester—Don't be suspicious of me. If I were a shallow, joking person, or if I made cheap declarations to everyone who claims to be a friend.

[15] fawn . . . rout—am overly friendly to people and embrace them and talk ill of them afterwards, or if I swear friendship to everyone I dine with.

[16] **impart**—tell, reveal.

[17] indifferently—impartially.

90   **Cassius.** I know that virtue to be in you, Brutus,

As well as I do know your outward favor.

Well, honor is the subject of my story.

I cannot tell what you and other men

Think of this life; but, for my single self,

95   I had as lief not be as live to be

In awe of such a thing as I myself.[18]

I was born free as Caesar, so were you.

We both have fed as well, and we can both

Endure the winter's cold as well as he.

100   For once, upon a raw and gusty day,

The troubled Tiber chafing with[19] her shores,

Caesar said to me, "Dar'st thou, Cassius, now

Leap in with me into this angry flood

And swim to yonder point?" Upon the word,

105   Accoutred[20] as I was, I plungèd in

And bade him follow. So indeed he did.

The torrent roared, and we did buffet it

With lusty sinews, throwing it aside

And stemming it with hearts of controversy.[21]

110   But ere we could arrive the point proposed,

Caesar cried, "Help me, Cassius, or I sink!"

Ay, as Aeneas, our great ancestor,

Did from the flames of Troy upon his shoulder

The old Anchises bear,[22] so from the waves of Tiber

115   Did I the tirèd Caesar. And this man

Is now become a god, and Cassius is

A wretched creature and must bend his body

If Caesar carelessly but nod on him.

He had a fever when he was in Spain,

120   And when the fit was on him I did mark

How he did shake. 'Tis true, this god did shake.

---

[18] I had . . . myself—I would just as soon be dead as live in fear of another man like myself.

[19] chafing with—irritating; raging against.

[20] Accoutred—dressed in body armor.

[21] buffet . . . controversy—fought against it with our strong muscles and with hearts full of the spirit of competition.

[22] Aeneas . . . bear—Aeneas, the mythological ancestor of the Romans, carried his father Anchises on his back out of the city of Troy when it was captured and burned by the Greeks.

His coward lips did from their color fly,
And that same eye whose bend doth awe the world
Did lose his luster.[23] I did hear him groan.
125 Ay, and that tongue of his that bade the Romans
Mark him and write his speeches in their books,
"Alas," it cried, "Give me some drink, Titinius,"
As a sick girl! Ye gods, it doth amaze me
A man of such a feeble temper should
130 So get the start of the majestic world
And bear the palm[24] alone. [*Shout. Flourish.*]
Brutus. Another general shout?
I do believe that these applauses are
For some new honors that are heaped on Caesar.
135 **Cassius.** Why, man, he doth bestride the narrow world
Like a Colossus,[25] and we petty men
Walk under his huge legs and peep about
To find ourselves dishonorable graves.
Men at some time are masters of their fates.
140 The fault, dear Brutus, is not in our stars,
But in ourselves, that we are underlings.
"Brutus" and "Caesar." What should be in that "Caesar"?
Why should that name be sounded more than yours?
Write them together, yours is as fair a name.
145 Sound them, it doth become the mouth as well.
Weigh them, it is as heavy. Conjure with 'em,
"Brutus" will start a spirit[26] as soon as "Caesar."
Now, in the names of all the gods at once,
Upon what meat doth this our Caesar feed
150 That he is grown so great? Age, thou art shamed!
Rome, thou hast lost the breed of noble bloods!
When went there by an age since the great flood
But it was famed with more than with one man?
When could they say, till now, that talked of Rome,

---

[23] His coward . . . luster—His lips turned pale, and his eyes, whose glance holds the world in awe, glazed over.

[24] bear the palm—win the symbol of victory.

[25] Colossus—huge statue of the Greek god Apollo at Rhodes. According to legend, it stood with its legs spanning the entrance of the harbor.

[26] start a spirit—call forth a ghost from the spirit world.

155	That her wide walks **encompassed**[27] but one man?
	Now is it Rome indeed, and room enough,
	When there is in it but one only man.
	O, you and I have heard our fathers say
	There was a Brutus once that would have brooked
160	Th' eternal devil to keep his state in Rome
	As easily as a king.[28]

Brutus. That you do love me I am nothing jealous.
What you would work me to, I have some aim.[29]
How I have thought of this and of these times
I shall recount hereafter. For this present,
I would not, so with love I might entreat you,
Be any further moved. What you have said
I will consider; what you have to say
I will with patience hear, and find a time
Both meet[30] to hear and answer such high things.
Till then, my noble friend, chew upon this:
Brutus had rather be a villager
Than to repute himself a son of Rome
Under these hard conditions as this time
Is like to lay upon us.

Cassius. I am glad that my weak words
Have struck but thus much show of fire from Brutus.

[*Enter* Caesar *and his* Followers.]

Brutus. The games are done, and Caesar is returning.

Cassius. As they pass by, pluck Casca by the sleeve,
And he will, after his sour fashion, tell you
What hath proceeded worthy note today.

Brutus. I will do so. But look you, Cassius,
The angry spot doth glow on Caesar's brow,
And all the rest look like a chidden train.[31]
Calpurnia's cheek is pale, and Cicero

---

[27] **encompassed**—contained, included.

[28] There was . . . king—Cassius says that Lucius Junius Brutus (who helped establish the Roman republic about 509 B.C.) would have let the devil rule Rome as soon as he would let a king rule. Marcus Brutus claimed to be his descendant.

[29] That you . . . aim—I don't doubt you love me, and I can guess what you want to persuade me to do.

[30] meet—suitable.

[31] chidden train—group of followers who have been scolded.

Yond Cassius has a lean and hungry look.

        Looks with such ferret[32] and such fiery eyes

        As we have seen him in the Capitol,

        Being crossed in conference by some senators.

Cassius. Casca will tell us what the matter is.

190   **Caesar.** Antonius!

    Antony. Caesar?

    Caesar. Let me have men about me that are fat,

        Sleek-headed men, and such as sleep o' nights.

        Yond Cassius has a lean and hungry look.

195   He thinks too much. Such men are dangerous.

    Antony. Fear him not, Caesar, he's not dangerous.

        He is a noble Roman, and well given.[33]

    Caesar. Would he were fatter! But I fear him not.

        Yet if my name were liable to fear,

200   I do not know the man I should avoid

        So soon as that spare Cassius. He reads much,

        He is a great observer, and he looks

        Quite through the deeds of men. He loves no plays,

        As thou dost, Antony. He hears no music.

205   Seldom he smiles, and smiles in such a sort

        As if he mocked himself and scorned his spirit

        That could be moved to smile at anything.

        Such men as he be never at heart's ease

        Whiles they behold a greater than themselves,

210   And therefore are they very dangerous.

        I rather tell thee what is to be feared

        Than what I fear, for always I am Caesar.

        Come on my right hand, for this ear is deaf,

        And tell me truly what thou think'st of him.

    [*Trumpet call. Exit* Caesar *and his* Followers. Casca *remains with* Brutus *and* Cassius.]

215   **Casca.** You pulled me by the cloak. Would you speak with me?

---

[32] ferret—red, angry (like those of a ferret, or weasel).

[33] well given—thinks well of Caesar.

Brutus. Ay, Casca. Tell us what hath chanced today,
That Caesar looks so sad.[34]

Casca. Why, you were with him, were you not?

Brutus. I should not then ask Casca what had chanced.

220 **Casca.** Why, there was a crown offered him; and, being offered him, he put it
by with the back of his hand, thus, and then the people fell a-shouting.

Brutus. What was the second noise for?

Casca. Why, for that too.

Cassius. They shouted thrice. What was the last cry for?

225 **Casca.** Why, for that too.

Brutus. Was the crown offered him thrice?

Casca. Ay, marry,[35] was't, and he put it by thrice, every time gentler than
other, and at every putting-by mine honest neighbors shouted.

Cassius. Who offered him the crown?

230 **Casca.** Why, Antony.

Brutus. Tell us the manner of it, gentle Casca.

Casca. I can as well be hanged as tell the manner of it. It was mere foolery; I did not mark it. I saw Mark Antony offer him a crown—yet
'twas not a crown neither, 'twas one of these coronets[36]—and, as I told
235 you, he put it by once; but for all that, to my thinking, he would fain
have had it. Then he offered it to him again; then he put it by again;
but to my thinking he was very loath to lay his fingers off it. And
then he offered it the third time. He put it the third time by, and still
as he refused it, the rabblement[37] hooted and clapped their chapped
240 hands, and threw up their sweaty night caps, and uttered such a deal
of stinking breath because Caesar refused the crown that it had
almost choked Caesar, for he **swooned**[38] and fell down at it. And for
mine own part I durst not laugh for fear of opening my lips and
receiving the bad air.

245 **Cassius.** But soft,[39] I pray you. What, did Caesar swoon?

Casca. He fell down in the marketplace, and foamed at
mouth, and was speechless.

---

[34] chanced . . . sad—happened that Caesar looks so serious.

[35] marry—indeed (originally, "by the Virgin Mary").

[36] coronets—garlands or wreaths.

[37] rabblement—common people (a term of contempt).

[38] **swooned**—fainted. In Caesar's case, his faint signals an epileptic seizure.

[39] soft—wait.

Brutus. 'Tis very like. He hath the falling sickness.[40]

Cassius. No, Caesar hath it not, but you and I,

250 And honest Casca, we have the falling sickness.

Casca. I know not what you mean by that, but I am sure Caesar fell
down. If the tag-rag people did not clap him and hiss him, according
as he pleased and displeased them, as they use to do the players in
the theater, I am no true man.

255 **Brutus.** What said he when he came unto himself?

Casca. Marry, before he fell down, when he perceived the common
herd was glad he refused the crown, he plucked me ope his doublet
and offered them his throat to cut.[41] An I had been a man of any
occupation,[42] if I would not have taken him at a word, I would I
260 might go to hell among the rogues. And so he fell. When he came
to himself again, he said if he had done or said anything amiss, he
desired their worships to think it was his infirmity. Three or four
wenches where I stood cried, "Alas, good soul!" and forgave him
with all their hearts. But there's no heed to be taken of them; if Caesar
265 had stabbed their mothers they would have done no less.

Brutus. And after that, he came thus sad away?

Casca. Ay.

Cassius. Did Cicero say anything?

Casca. Ay, he spoke Greek.

270 **Cassius.** To what effect?

Casca. Nay, an I tell you that, I'll ne'er look you i' the face again. But
those that understood him smiled at one another and shook their
heads; but, for mine own part, it was Greek to me. I could tell you
more news too. Marullus and Flavius, for pulling scarves off Caesar's
275 images, are put to silence.[43] Fare you well. There was more foolery
yet, if I could remember it.

Cassius. Will you sup with me tonight, Casca?

Casca. No, I am promised forth.

Cassius. Will you dine with me tomorrow?

280 **Casca.** Ay, if I be alive, and your mind hold, and your dinner worth
the eating.

---

[40] falling sickness—epilepsy. Cassius puns in reply that they have the "falling sickness"—because Caesar is rising.

[41] he plucked . . . cut—He pulled open his jacket and bared his throat to prove his sincerity.

[42] An . . . occupation—if I had been a working man.

[43] put to silence—dismissed from office.

Cassius. Good. I will expect you.

Casca. Do so. Farewell both. [*Exit* Casca.]

Brutus. What a blunt fellow is this grown to be!

285   He was quick mettle[44] when he went to school.

Cassius. So is he now in execution

          Of any bold or noble enterprise,

          However he puts on this tardy form.

          This rudeness is a sauce to his good wit,

290   Which gives men stomach to digest his words

          With better appetite.[45]

Brutus. And so it is. For this time I will leave you.

          Tomorrow, if you please to speak with me,

          I will come home to you; or, if you will,

295   Come home to me, and I will wait for you.

Cassius. I will do so. Till then, think of the world.

[*Exit* Brutus.]

          Well, Brutus, thou art noble. Yet I see

          Thy honorable mettle may be wrought

          From that it is disposed.[46] Therefore it is meet

300   That noble minds keep ever with their likes;

          For who so firm that cannot be seduced?

          Caesar doth bear me hard, but he loves Brutus.

          If I were Brutus now, and he were Cassius,

          He should not humor me. I will this night

305   In several hands[47] in at his windows throw,

          As if they came from several citizens,

          Writings, all tending to the great opinion

          That Rome holds of his name, wherein obscurely

          Caesar's ambition shall be glancèd at.

310   And after this let Caesar seat him sure,[48]

          For we will shake him, or worse days endure.

[*He exits.*]

---

[44] quick mettle—high-spirited.

[45] However . . . appetite—No matter how much he pretends to be slow and simple, his rude manner makes it easier for others to accept what he says.

[46] mettle . . . disposed—temperament (with a pun on *metal*, substance) may be worked or formed into something different from its natural state.

[47] in several hands—in different handwritings.

[48] let Caesar . . . sure—let Caesar be secure in his power (but meant ironically).

Act One, Scene Three

On a street in Rome, late at night on March 14, a storm rages, with thunder and lightning. Casca tells Cicero of evil omens he has seen. Cassius urges Casca to join a group of like-minded senators to prevent Caesar from becoming a tyrant. Cassius gives Cinna messages to deliver to Brutus as if they came from anonymous citizens. Then Cassius and Casca, planning to visit Brutus the next morning, set off to meet the other conspirators.

Thunder and lightning. Enter Cicero *and* Casca *from different directions,* Casca *with his sword in hand.*

Cicero. Good even, Casca. Brought you Caesar home?[1]
Why are you breathless? And why stare you so?

Casca. Are not you moved, when all the sway of earth
Shakes like a thing unfirm?[2] O Cicero,

5   I have seen tempests when the scolding winds
Have rived[3] the knotty oaks, and I have seen
Th' ambitious ocean swell and rage and foam
To be exalted with the threat'ning clouds;
But never till tonight, never till now,

10   Did I go through a tempest dropping fire.
Either there is a civil strife in heaven,
Or else the world, too saucy[4] with the gods,
Incenses[5] them to send destruction.

Cicero. Why, saw you anything more wonderful?

15   **Casca.** A common slave—you know him well by sight—
Held up his left hand, which did flame and burn
Like twenty torches joined, and yet his hand,
Not sensible of fire,[6] remained unscorched.
Besides—I ha' not since put up my sword—

---

[1] Brought . . . home—Did you escort Caesar home?

[2] all the sway . . . unfirm—The established order is disturbed.

[3] rived—split.

[4] saucy—insolent, disrespectful.

[5] **Incenses**—enrages, makes furious.

[6] Not sensible of—not feeling.

	Against the Capitol I met a lion,
20	Against the Capitol I met a lion,
	Who glazed upon me and went surly by
	Without annoying me.[7] And there were drawn
	Upon a heap[8] a hundred ghastly women,
	Transformèd with their fear, who swore they saw
25	Men all in fire walk up and down the streets.
	And yesterday the bird of night[9] did sit
	Even at noonday upon the marketplace,
	Hooting and shrieking. When these prodigies
	Do so conjointly meet,[10] let not men say,
30	"These are their reasons, they are natural,"
	For I believe they are **portentous**[11] things
	Unto the climate that they point upon.

Cicero. Indeed, it is a strange-disposèd time.
    But men may construe things after their fashion,
35   Clean from the purpose of the things themselves.
    Comes Caesar to the Capitol tomorrow?

Casca. He doth; for he did bid Antonius
    Send word to you he would be there tomorrow.

Cicero. Good night then, Casca. This disturbèd sky
40   Is not to walk in.

Casca.   Farewell, Cicero. [*Exit* Cicero.]
[*Enter* Cassius.]

Cassius. Who's there?

Casca.   A Roman.

Cassius.   Casca, by your voice.

Casca. Your ear is good. Cassius, what night is this!

Cassius. A very pleasing night to honest men.

Casca. Who ever knew the heavens menace so?

45 **Cassius.** Those that have known the earth so full of faults.
    For my part, I have walked about the streets,
    Submitting me unto the perilous night,
    And thus unbracèd, Casca, as you see,

---

[7] glazed . . . annoying me—stared at me and passed angrily, but without harming me.

[8] drawn . . . heap—huddled together.

[9] bird of night—owl, an evil omen.

[10] prodigies . . . meet—wonders all come together.

[11] **portentous**—ominous, full of terrible meaning.

Have bared my bosom to the thunder-stone;[12]
50 And when the cross blue lightning seemed to open
The breast of heaven, I did present myself
Even in the aim and very flash of it.

Casca. But wherefore did you so much tempt the heavens?
It is the part of men to fear and tremble
55 When the most mighty gods by tokens send
Such dreadful heralds to astonish us.[13]

Cassius. You are dull, Casca, and those sparks of life
That should be in a Roman you do want,
Or else you use not. You look pale, and gaze,
60 And put on fear, and cast yourself in wonder,
To see the strange impatience of the heavens.
But if you would consider the true cause
Why all these fires, why all these gliding ghosts,
Why birds and beasts, from quality and kind,
65 Why old men, fools, and children calculate,
Why all these things change from their ordinance,
Their natures, and preformèd faculties,
To monstrous quality[14]—why, you shall find
That heaven hath **infused**[15] them with these spirits
70 To make them instruments of fear and warning
Unto some monstrous state.
Now could I, Casca, name to thee a man
Most like this dreadful night,
That thunders, lightens, opens graves, and roars
75 As doth the lion in the Capitol—
A man no mightier than thyself or me
In personal action, yet prodigious grown
And fearful,[16] as these strange eruptions are.

---

[12] Submitting . . . thunder-stone—surrendering myself to the dangerous night, and with my robe opened have exposed my chest to lightning bolts.

[13] heralds to astonish us—messages to terrify us.

[14] Why birds . . . quality—Why birds and animals change their nature; old men, children, and fools predict the future; and all these change from their natural states to something unnatural and horrible.

[15] **infused**—filled, poured into.

[16] prodigious . . . fearful—becoming huge and threatening and causing fear; ominous.

The conspirators gather by night in this scene from the Hartford Stage production.

Casca. 'Tis Caesar that you mean, is it not, Cassius?
80 Cassius. Let it be who it is. For Romans now
Have thews and limbs like to their ancestors;
But, woe the while, our fathers' minds are dead,[17]
And we are governed with our mothers' spirits.
Our yoke and sufferance show us womanish.
85 Casca. Indeed, they say the senators tomorrow
Mean to establish Caesar as a king,

[17] Romans . . . dead—Romans today have the bodies and muscles of their ancestors but, alas for the times, not their spirits.

And he shall wear his crown by sea and land
In every place save here in Italy.
Cassius. I know where I will wear this dagger then;

90   Cassius from bondage will deliver Cassius.
Therein, ye gods, you make the weak most strong;
Therein, ye gods, you tyrants do defeat.[18]
Nor stony tower, nor walls of beaten brass,
Nor airless dungeon, nor strong links of iron,

95   Can be retentive to the strength of spirit;
But life, being weary of these worldly bars,
Never lacks power to dismiss itself.
If I know this, know all the world besides,
That part of tyranny that I do bear

100   I can shake off at pleasure.

[_Thunder sounds again._]

Casca.   So can I.
So every bondman in his own hand bears
The power to cancel his captivity.

Cassius. And why should Caesar be a tyrant then?
Poor man, I know he would not be a wolf

105   But that he sees the Romans are but sheep;
He were no lion, were not Romans hinds.[19]
Those that with haste will make a mighty fire
Begin it with weak straws. What trash is Rome,
What rubbish and what offal, when it serves

110   For the base matter to illuminate
So vile a thing as Caesar![20] But, O grief,
Where hast thou led me? I perhaps speak this
Before a willing bondman. Then I know

---

[18] Therein . . . defeat—Cassius means that the ability to commit suicide makes weak men strong and defeats tyrants.

[19] He were . . . hinds—He would not behave like a lion if the Romans didn't behave like female deer or menial servants.

[20] What trash . . . Caesar—What good is Rome when it serves only as cheap fuel for a fire to cast a glow upon so degraded a man as Caesar?

My answer must be made. But I am armed,
115   And dangers are to me indifferent.

Casca. You speak to Casca, and to such a man
    That is no fleering[21] telltale. Hold, my hand.
    Be factious for redress of all these griefs,
    And I will set this foot of mine as far
120   As who goes farthest.[22]

[They shake hands.]

Cassius.   There's a bargain made.
    Now know you, Casca, I have moved already
    Some certain of the noblest-minded Romans
    To undergo with me an enterprise
    Of honorable-dangerous consequence;
125   And I do know, by this, they stay for me
    In Pompey's porch.[23] For now, this fearful night,
    There is no stir or walking in the streets,
    And the complexion of the element
    In favor's like[24] the work we have in hand,
130   Most bloody, fiery, and most terrible.

[Enter Cinna.]

Casca. Stand close awhile, for here comes one in haste.

Cassius. 'Tis Cinna; I do know him by his **gait**.[25]
    He is a friend.—Cinna, where haste you so?

Cinna. To find out you. Who's that? Metellus Cimber?

135 **Cassius.** No, it is Casca, one incorporate
    To our attempts.[26] Am I not stayed for, Cinna?

Cinna. I am glad on 't. What a fearful night is this!
    There's two or three of us have seen strange sights.

Cassius. Am I not stayed for? Tell me.

Cinna.   Yes, you are.
140   O Cassius, if you could
    But win the noble Brutus to our party—

---

[21] fleering—fawning; scornful.

[22] Be factious . . . farthest—Work actively to improve all these troubles, and I will go as far as anyone else.

[23] Pompey's porch—passage with pillars attached to Pompey's great theater.

[24] In favor's like—in appearance is like.

[25] **gait**—footstep.

[26] one . . . attempts—one who knows of our plans and who will join us.

Cassius. Be you content. Good Cinna, take this paper,

[*Giving him papers.*]

And look you lay it in the praetor's chair,[27]

Where Brutus may but find it. And throw this

145   In at his window. Set this up with wax

Upon old Brutus' statue.[28] All this done,

Repair[29] to Pompey's porch, where you shall find us.

Is Decius Brutus and Trebonius there?

Cinna. All but Metellus Cimber, and he's gone

150   To seek you at your house. Well, I will hie,[30]

And so bestow these papers as you bade me.

Cassius. That done, repair to Pompey's theater. [*Exit Cinna.*]

Come, Casca, you and I will yet ere day

See Brutus at his house. Three parts of him

155   Is ours already, and the man entire

Upon the next encounter yields him ours.

Casca. O, he sits high in all the people's hearts;

And that which would appear offense in us,

His countenance, like richest alchemy,

160   Will change to virtue and to worthiness.[31]

Cassius. Him and his worth, and our great need of him,

You have right well conceited.[32] Let us go,

For it is after midnight, and ere day

We will awake him and be sure of him. [*They exit.*]

---

[27] praetor's chair—official's chair in which Brutus would sit.

[28] old Brutus' statue—statue of Lucius Janius Brutus, Brutus's ancestor.

[29] Repair—proceed; go on.

[30] hie—go quickly.

[31] His countenance ... worthiness—His approval, like the chemical change of base metal to gold, will make our deeds seem worthy.

[32] conceited—understood and expressed.

Act Two, Scene One

In his orchard a few hours before dawn on March 15, Brutus debates with himself whether to continue to live under Caesar's tyranny or to kill him. Reading an anonymous letter from Cassius, Brutus vows to do his part to stop Caesar. Soon after, Cassius and the other conspirators come to persuade Brutus to join them. Together they all agree to kill Caesar that day but to spare Mark Antony. Brutus's wife, Portia, worries about her husband being up so late and refuses to accept his explanation that he is ill. Brutus promises to tell her what is troubling him.

Enter Brutus.

Brutus. What, Lucius, ho!—
    I cannot by the progress of the stars
    Give guess how near to day.[1]—Lucius, I say!—
    I would it were my fault to sleep so soundly.—
5   When, Lucius, when? Awake, I say! What, Lucius!
[*Enter* Lucius.]
Lucius. Called you, my lord?
Brutus. Get me a taper[2] in my study, Lucius.
    When it is lighted, come and call me here.
Lucius. I will, my lord. [*Exit* Lucius.]
10 **Brutus.** It must be by his death. And for my part
    I know no personal cause to spurn at him,
    But for the general.[3] He would be crowned.
    How that might change his nature, there's the question.
    It is the bright day that brings forth the adder,
15   And that craves wary walking.[4] Crown him that,[5]
    And then I grant we put a sting in him
    That at his will he may do danger with.
    Th' abuse of greatness is when it disjoins

---

[1] I cannot . . . day—I can't tell from looking at the sky how soon dawn is.

[2] taper—candle.

[3] I know . . . general—I have no personal cause to attack him, only for the general good.

[4] It . . . walking—Sunshine brings out the poisonous snake and makes it necessary to walk carefully.

[5] that—king.

Remorse from power.⁶ And to speak truth of Caesar,

20   I have not known when his affections swayed⁷

More than his reason. But 'tis a common proof

That lowliness is young ambition's ladder,

Whereto the climber upward turns his face;

But when he once attains the upmost round

25   He then unto the ladder turns his back,

Looks in the clouds, scorning the base degrees⁸

By which he did ascend. So Caesar may.

Then, lest he may, prevent. And since the quarrel

Will bear no color for the thing he is,

30   Fashion it thus: that what he is, augmented,

Would run to these and these extremities.

And therefore think him as a serpent's egg

Which, hatched, would, as his kind, grow mischievous;

And kill him in the shell.⁹

   [*Enter* Lucius.]

35 **Lucius.** The taper burneth in your closet,¹⁰ sir.

Searching the window for a flint,¹¹ I found

This paper, thus sealed up, and I am sure

It did not lie there when I went to bed.

  [*Gives him the letter.*]

  Brutus. Get you to bed again. It is not day.

40   Is not tomorrow, boy, the ides of March?

  Lucius. I know not, sir.

  Brutus. Look in the calendar and bring me word.

  Lucius. I will, sir. [*Exit* Lucius.]

  Brutus. The exhalations¹² whizzing in the air

45   Give so much light that I may read by them.

  [*Opens the letter and reads.*]

---

⁶ disjoins . . . power—separates mercy from power.

⁷ affections swayed—emotions ruled.

⁸ 'tis . . . ascend—It's a common experience that an ambitious person pretends to be humble in order to climb the social ladder, when he reaches the top, he despises the people that helped him get there.

⁹ lest . . . shell—Rather than let Caesar do that, we must prevent it. And since his behavior so far will not justify killing him, we must shape our argument in this way: if the kind of person he is now were allowed to develop and grow, he would reach extremes of tyranny. So we must treat him as a serpent's egg and kill him before he hatches.

¹⁰ closet—private room.

¹¹ flint—rock used to strike a spark against steel to light a flame.

¹² exhalations—meteors.

"Brutus, thou sleep'st. Awake, and see thyself!
Shall Rome, et cetera? Speak, strike, **redress**!"[13]
"Brutus, thou sleep'st. Awake!"
Such instigations have been often dropped
50 Where I have took them up.
"Shall Rome, et cetera?" Thus must I piece it out:[14]
Shall Rome stand under one man's awe? What, Rome?
My ancestors did from the streets of Rome
The Tarquin drive, when he was called a king.[15]
55 "Speak, strike, redress!" Am I **entreated**[16]
To speak and strike? O Rome, I make thee promise,
If the redress will follow, thou receivest
Thy full petition at the hand of Brutus.[17]

[*Enter* Lucius.]

Lucius. Sir, March is wasted fifteen days.

[*Knock within.*[18]]

60 Brutus. 'Tis good. Go to the gate; somebody knocks.

[*Exit* Lucius.]

Since Cassius first did whet[19] me against Caesar,
I have not slept.
Between the acting of a dreadful thing
And the first motion, all the interim is
65 Like a phantasma[20] or a hideous dream.
The genius and the mortal instruments
Are then in council; and the state of man,
Like to a little kingdom, suffers then
The nature of an insurrection.[21]

[*Enter* Lucius.]

---

[13] **redress**—right a wrong.

[14] piece it out—guess at its meaning.

[15] My ancestors . . . king—Brutus refers to his ancestors, including Lucius Junius Brutus, who drove out Rome's last king. After that, rule by the Senate was established.

[16] **entreated**—begged.

[17] If . . . Brutus—If a remedy for our troubles will result from my action, you will get what you need from Brutus.

[18] within—offstage.

[19] whet—incite.

[20] the interim . . . phantasma—The time between is like a hallucination.

[21] the genius . . . insurrection—The soul and body debate the subject, and the man himself feels like a kingdom undergoing civil war.

In this scene from the Hartford Stage production, the other conspirators discuss the plot with Brutus (Justin Deas, second from right).

70   **Lucius.** Sir, 'tis your brother Cassius at the door,
Who doth desire to see you.

Brutus.   Is he alone?

Lucius. No, sir. There are more with him.

Brutus.   Do you know them?

Lucius. No, sir. Their hats are plucked about their ears,
And half their faces buried in their cloaks,

75   That by no means I may discover them
By any mark of favor.[21]

Brutus. Let 'em enter. [*Exit* Lucius.]
They are the **faction**.[22] O conspiracy,
Sham'st thou to show thy dang'rous brow by night,

80   When evils are most free? O, then by day
Where wilt thou find a cavern dark enough
To mask thy monstrous **visage?**[23] Seek none, conspiracy!
Hide it in smiles and affability;
For if thou put thy native semblance on,

---

[21] by no means ... favor—I can't tell who they are from their looks.

[22] **faction**—group of people inside a political party working for a common cause.

[23] **visage**—face.

85   Not Erebus itself were dim enough
        To hide thee from prevention.[24]

[*Enter the conspirators,* Cassius, Casca, Decius, Cinna, Metellus Cimber,
and Trebonius.]

Cassius. I think we are too bold upon your rest.
        Good morrow, Brutus. Do we trouble you?

Brutus. I have been up this hour, awake all night.
90   Know I these men that come along with you?

Cassius. Yes, every man of them, and no man here
        But honors you; and every one doth wish
        You had but that opinion of yourself
        Which every noble Roman bears of you.
95   This is Trebonius.

Brutus.   He is welcome hither.

Cassius. This, Decius Brutus.

Brutus.   He is welcome too.

Cassius. This, Casca; this, Cinna; and this, Metellus Cimber.

Brutus. They are all welcome.
        What watchful cares do interpose themselves
100   Betwixt your eyes and night?[25]

Cassius. Shall I entreat a word?

[Brutus *and* Cassius *whisper.*]

Decius. Here lies the east. Doth not the day break here?

Casca. No.

Cinna. O, pardon, sir, it doth; and yon gray lines
105   That fret the clouds are messengers of day.

Casca. You shall confess that you are both deceived.
        Here, as I point my sword, the sun arises,
        Which is a great way growing on the south,
        Weighing the youthful season of the year.
110   Some two months hence, up higher toward the north
        He first presents his fire; and the high east
        Stands, as the Capitol, directly here.[26]

---

[24] Hide . . . prevention—Hide your terrible face in smiles and pleasantness, for if you look as you feel, even Erebus, the gateway to Hell, wouldn't be dark enough to keep you from being found out.

[25] What watchful . . . night—What troubles keep you awake at night?

[26] Which is . . . here—from a southerly direction, since it is still early in the year. In two months, the sun will rise further north; and due east is in this direction toward the Capitoline Hill.

Brutus [*coming forward*]. Give me your hands all over, one by one.

Cassius. And let us swear our resolution.

115   **Brutus.** No, not an oath. If not the face of men,

     The sufferance of our souls, the time's abuse—

     If these be motives weak, break off betimes,

     And every man hence to his idle bed;

     So let high-sighted tyranny range on

120   Till each man drop by lottery.[27] But if these,

     As I am sure they do, bear fire enough

     To kindle cowards and to steel with valor[28]

     The melting spirits of women, then, countrymen,

     What need we any spur but our own cause

125   To prick us to redress?[29] What other bond

     Than secret Romans that have spoke the word

     And will not palter?[30] And what other oath

     Than honesty to honesty engaged

     That this shall be, or we will fall for it?

130   Swear priests and cowards and men cautelous,

     Old feeble carrions, and such suffering souls

     That welcome wrongs; unto bad causes swear

     Such creatures as men doubt.[31] But do not stain

     The even virtue of our enterprise,

135   Nor th' insuppressive mettle of our spirits,

     To think that or our cause or our performance

     Did need an oath, when every drop of blood

     That every Roman bears—and nobly bears—

     Is guilty of a several bastardy[32]

140   If he do break the smallest particle

     Of any promise that hath passed from him.

---

[27] If not . . . lottery—If the misery in men's faces, our suffering souls, and the corruptions of the present day aren't strong enough to hold us together, then let's all go back to bed and let tyranny rule until we die off one by one.

[28] steel with valor—make strong with courage.

[29] What need . . . redress—What do we need but our own cause to drive us to make things right?

[30] palter—go back on our word.

[31] Swear . . . doubt—Make priests, cowards, and deceitful people swear oaths, or dying old men and weak people who submit to tyranny, the oaths of people that no one trusts damage a cause.

[32] guilty . . . bastardy—guilty of an act that shows his blood is not truly Roman.

Cassius. But what of Cicero? Shall we sound him?[33]
    I think he will stand very strong with us.

Casca. Let us not leave him out.

Cinna.   No, by no means.

145   **Metellus.** O, let us have him, for his silver hairs
    Will purchase us a good opinion[34]
    And buy men's voices to commend our deeds.
    It shall be said his judgment ruled our hands.
    Our youths and wildness shall no whit appear,
150   But all be buried in his gravity.[35]

Brutus. O, name him not. Let us not break with[36] him,
    For he will never follow anything
    That other men begin.

Cassius. Then leave him out.

155   **Casca.** Indeed he is not fit.

Decius. Shall no man else be touched but only Caesar?

Cassius. Decius, well urged. I think it is not meet[37]
    Mark Antony, so well beloved of Caesar,
    Should outlive Caesar. We shall find of him
160   A shrewd contriver; and you know his means,
    If he improve them, may well stretch so far
    As to annoy us all.[38] Which to prevent,
    Let Antony and Caesar fall together.

Brutus. Our course will seem too bloody, Caius Cassius,
165   To cut the head off and then hack the limbs,
    Like wrath in death and envy[39] afterwards;
    For Antony is but a limb of Caesar.
    Let's be sacrificers, but not butchers, Caius.
    We all stand up against the spirit of Caesar,
170   And in the spirit of men there is no blood.
    O, that we then could come by Caesar's spirit

---

[33] sound him—sound him out; get his opinion.

[34] his silver . . . opinion—His age will win us popular support.

[35] buried . . . gravity—influenced by his sound judgment.

[36] break with—confide in.

[37] meet—proper.

[38] his means . . . all—His power, if he makes good use of it, could mean trouble for us.

[39] envy—malice.

Let's carve him as a dish fit for the gods,
Not hew him as a carcass fit for hounds.

And not dismember Caesar![40] But, alas,
Caesar must bleed for it. And, gentle friends,
Let's kill him boldly, but not wrathfully;
175 Let's carve him as a dish fit for the gods,
Not hew him as a carcass fit for hounds.
And let our hearts, as subtle masters do,
Stir up their servants to an act of rage
And after seem to chide 'em.[41] This shall make
180 Our purpose necessary, and not envious;
Which so appearing to the common eyes,
We shall be called purgers,[42] not murderers.
And for Mark Antony, think not of him;
For he can do no more than Caesar's arm
185 When Caesar's head is off.

Cassius.   Yet I fear him,
For in the engrafted[43] love he bears to Caesar—

Brutus. Alas, good Cassius, do not think of him.
If he love Caesar, all that he can do
Is to himself—take thought and die for Caesar.
190 And that were much he should,[44] for he is given
To sports, to wildness, and much company.

Trebonius. There is no fear in him. Let him not die,
For he will live, and laugh at this hereafter.

[*Clock strikes.*]

Brutus. Peace! Count the clock.

Cassius.   The clock hath stricken three.

195 **Trebonius.** 'Tis time to part.

Cassius.   But it is doubtful yet
Whether Caesar will come forth today or no;

---

[40] come by . . . Caesar—take Caesar's soul without destroying his body.

[41] And . . . 'em—Let our hearts stir our hands to be violent, and then seem to rebuke them.

[42] purgers—healers.

[43] engrafted—firmly established.

[44] much he should—more than he is likely to do.

For he is superstitious grown of late,
Quite from the main opinion he held once
Of fantasy, of dreams, and ceremonies.
200 It may be these apparent prodigies,
The unaccustomed terror of this night,
And the persuasion of his augurers[45]
May hold him from the Capitol today.
Decius. Never fear that. If he be so resolved,
205 I can o'ersway him; for he loves to hear
That unicorns may be betrayed with trees,
And bears with glasses, elephants with holes,
Lions with toils, and men with flatterers;
But when I tell him he hates flatterers,
210 He says he does, being then most flattered.[46]
Let me work;
For I can give his humor the true bent,
And I will bring him to the Capitol.
Cassius. Nay, we will all of us be there to fetch him.
215 **Brutus.** By the eighth hour. Is that the uttermost?
Cinna. Be that the uttermost, and fail not then.
Metellus. Caius Ligarius doth bear Caesar hard,
Who rated[47] him for speaking well of Pompey.
I wonder none of you have thought of him.
220 **Brutus.** Now, good Metellus, go along by him.
He loves me well, and I have given him reasons;
Send him but hither, and I'll fashion him.[48]
Cassius. The morning comes upon 's. We'll leave you, Brutus.
And, friends, **disperse**[49] yourselves; but all remember
225 What you have said, and show yourselves true Romans.
Brutus. Good gentlemen, look fresh and merrily;
Let not our looks put on our purposes,
But bear it as our Roman actors do,

---

[45] apparent prodigies ... augurers—these strange events and the interpretations of his fortune tellers.

[46] That unicorns ... flattered—Decius tells of ways to trap wily or dangerous animals. Caesar can also be trapped by the flattery of telling him that he can't be touched by flattery.

[47] rated—criticized.

[48] fashion him—bring him to our side.

[49] **disperse**—go in different directions.

With untired spirits and formal constancy.
230 And so good morrow to you every one.

[*Exit all except* Brutus.]

Boy! Lucius!—Fast asleep? It is no matter.
Enjoy the honey-heavy dew of slumber.
Thou hast no figures nor no fantasies
Which busy care draws in the brains of men;
235 Therefore thou sleep'st so sound.

[*Enter* Portia.]

Portia.   Brutus, my lord!

Brutus. Portia, what mean you? Wherefore rise you now?
It is not for your health thus to commit
Your weak condition to the raw cold morning.

Portia. Nor for yours neither. You've ungently, Brutus,
240 Stole from my bed. And yesternight, at supper,
You suddenly arose, and walked about
Musing and sighing, with your arms across,
And when I asked you what the matter was,
You stared upon me with ungentle looks.
245 I urged you further; then you scratched your head
And too impatiently stamped with your foot.
Yet I insisted, yet you answered not,

In the Commonwealth
Shakespeare Company production,
Portia (Paula Plum) asks Brutus
(Will Lyman) the cause of the
change in his behavior toward her.

But with an angry wafter[50] of your hand
Gave sign for me to leave you. So I did,
Fearing to strengthen that impatience
Which seemed too much enkindled, and withal
Hoping it was but an effect of humor,[51]
Which sometimes hath his hour with every man.
It will not let you eat, nor talk, nor sleep,
And could it work so much upon your shape
As it hath much prevailed on your condition,
I should not know you Brutus.[52] Dear my lord,
Make me acquainted with your cause of grief.

Brutus. I am not well in health, and that is all.

Portia. Brutus is wise, and were he not in health
He would embrace the means[53] to come by it.

Brutus. Why, so I do. Good Portia, go to bed.

Portia. Is Brutus sick? And is it physical
To walk unbracèd[54] and suck up the humors
Of the dank morning? What, is Brutus sick,
And will he steal out of his wholesome bed
To dare the vile contagion of the night,
And tempt the rheumy and unpurgèd air
To add unto his sickness? No, my Brutus,
You have some sick offense within your mind,
Which by the right and virtue of my place
I ought to know of. [*She kneels.*] And upon my knees
I charm[55] you, by my once-commended beauty,
By all your vows of love, and that great vow
Which did incorporate and make us one,
That you unfold to me, your self, your half,
Why you are heavy, and what men tonight
Have had resort to[56] you; for here have been

---

[50] wafter—wave.

[51] effect of humor—sign of a temporary bad temper.

[52] could it . . . Brutus—If it changed your appearance as much as it has changed your behavior, I wouldn't recognize you.

[53] embrace the means—take action.

[54] physical . . . unbracèd—healthy to walk with your robe open.

[55] charm—beg.

[56] had resort to—visited.

Some six or seven, who did hide their faces
280   Even from darkness.

Brutus.   Kneel not, gentle Portia.

[*He raises her.*]

Portia. I should not need if you were gentle Brutus.
     Within the bond of marriage, tell me, Brutus,
     Is it excepted I should know no secrets
     That **appertain**[57] to you? Am I your self
285   But, as it were, in sort or limitation,
     To keep with you at meals, comfort your bed,
     And talk to you sometimes? Dwell I but in the suburbs
     Of your good pleasure? If it be no more,
     Portia is Brutus's harlot, not his wife.

290 **Brutus.** You are my true and honorable wife,
     As dear to me as are the ruddy drops
     That visit my sad heart.[58]

Portia. If this were true, then should I know this secret.
     I grant I am a woman, but withal
295   A woman that Lord Brutus took to wife.
     I grant I am a woman, but withal
     A woman well reputed, Cato's daughter.[59]
     Think you I am no stronger than my sex,
     Being so fathered and so husbanded?
300   Tell me your counsels, I will not disclose 'em.
     I have made strong proof of my constancy,
     Giving myself a voluntary wound
     Here, in the thigh. Can I bear that with patience,
     And not my husband's secrets?

Brutus.   O ye gods,
305   Render me worthy of this noble wife!

[*Knock within.*]

     Hark, hark, one knocks. Portia, go in a while,
     And by and by thy bosom shall partake
     The secrets of my heart.
     All my engagements I will construe to thee,

---

[57] **appertain**—relate.
[58] the ruddy . . . heart—my blood.
[59] Cato's daughter—Portia's father, Cato the Younger, was famous for his integrity.

310   All the charactery of my sad brows.[60]

       Leave me with haste. [*Exit* Portia.] Lucius, who's that knocks?

[*Enter* Lucius *and* Caius Ligarius *wearing a kerchief.*[61]]

Lucius. Here is a sick man that would speak with you.

Brutus. Caius Ligarius, that Metellus spake of.

       Boy, stand aside. [*Exit* Lucius.] Caius Ligarius, how?

315 **Caius.** Vouchsafe good morrow from a feeble tongue.

Brutus. O, what a time have you chose out, brave Caius,

       To wear a kerchief! Would you were not sick!

Caius. I am not sick, if Brutus have in hand

       Any **exploit**[62] worthy the name of honor.

320 **Brutus.** Such an exploit have I in hand, Ligarius,

       Had you a healthful ear to hear of it.

Caius. By all the gods that Romans bow before,

       I here discard my sickness! Soul of Rome!

[*He throws off his kerchief.*]

       Brave son, derived from honorable loins!

325   Thou, like an exorcist, hast conjured up

       My mortifièd spirit.[63] Now bid me run,

       And I will strive with things impossible,

       Yea, get the better of them. What's to do?

Brutus. A piece of work that will make sick men whole.

330 **Caius.** But are not some whole that we must make sick?

Brutus. That must we also. What it is, my Caius,

       I shall unfold to thee as we are going

       To whom it must be done.

Caius.   Set on your foot,

       And with a heart new-fired I follow you

335   To do I know not what; but it **sufficeth**[64]

       That Brutus leads me on.

[*Thunder.*]

Brutus.   Follow me, then.

[*They exit.*]

---

[60] And by . . . brows—Soon you shall hear my secrets. I will explain to you all the plans that you have seen reflected in my serious looks.

[61] *kerchief*—head covering worn because he is ill.

[62] **exploit**—deed.

[63] Thou . . . spirit—Like one who calls spirits from the dead, you have raised my deadened spirit.

[64] it sufficeth—It is enough.

Act Two, Scene Two

In Caesar's house, about 8 o'clock on the morning of March 15, Calpurnia begs Caesar not to go to the Senate because of the bad omens. Caesar agrees to stay home, but changes his mind when Decius convinces him that he would appear ridiculous if he stayed because of his wife's superstitions. The rest of the conspirators arrive to escort Caesar to the Capitol, and Mark Antony joins Caesar's group.

Thunder and lightning. Enter Caesar, *in his dressing gown.*

Caesar. Nor heaven nor earth have been at peace tonight.
Thrice hath Calpurnia in her sleep cried out,
"Help, ho, they murder Caesar!"—Who's within?

[*Enter a* Servant.]

Servant. My lord?

5   **Caesar.** Go bid the priests do present sacrifice
And bring me their opinions of success.[1]

Servant. I will, my lord.

[*Exit* Servant.]

[*Enter* Calpurnia.]

Calpurnia. What mean you, Caesar? Think you to walk forth?
You shall not stir out of your house today.

10   **Caesar.** Caesar shall forth. The things that threatened me
Ne'er looked but on my back. When they shall see
The face of Caesar, they are vanishèd.[2]

Calpurnia. Caesar, I never stood on ceremonies,[3]
Yet now they fright me. There is one within,[4]

15   Besides the things that we have heard and seen,
Recounts most horrid sights seen by the watch.
A lioness hath whelpèd in the streets,

---

[1] Go bid . . . success—Roman priests would kill an animal as a sacrifice to the gods. Then they would cut the animal open and examine its internal organs for signs of future events.

[2] The things . . . vanishèd—When I turn to face the things that threaten me, they disappear.

[3] stood on ceremonies—believed in omens.

[4] one within—person inside the house.

Cowards die many times before their deaths; The valiant never taste of death but once.

And graves have yawned and yielded up their dead.
Fierce fiery warriors fight upon the clouds
20   In ranks and squadrons and right form of war,
Which drizzled blood upon the Capitol.
The noise of battle hurtled in the air,
Horses did neigh, and dying men did groan,
And ghosts did shriek and squeal about the streets.
25   O Caesar, these things are beyond all use,[5]
And I do fear them.

Caesar.   What can be avoided
Whose end is purposed by the mighty gods?
Yet Caesar shall go forth; for these predictions
Are to the world in general as to Caesar.[6]

30 **Calpurnia.** When beggars die, there are no comets seen;
The heavens themselves blaze forth the death of princes.

Caesar. Cowards die many times before their deaths;
The **valiant**[7] never taste of death but once.
Of all the wonders that I yet have heard,
35   It seems to me most strange that men should fear,
Seeing that death, a necessary end,
Will come when it will come.

[*Enter a* Servant.]
                      What say the augurers?[8]

Servant. They would not have you to stir forth today.
Plucking the entrails of an offering forth,[9]
40   They could not find a heart within the beast.

---

[5] beyond all use—outside of normal experience.

[6] Are to . . . Caesar—apply as much to the world in general as they do to Caesar.

[7] **valiant**—brave.

[8] augurers—priests.

[9] Plucking . . . forth—examining the internal organs of a slaughtered animal.

Calpurnia (Giula Pagano) shares her fears with Caesar (Donald Buka) in this scene from the Hartford Stage production.

Caesar. The gods do this in shame of cowardice.
Caesar should be a beast without a heart
If he should stay at home today for fear.
No, Caesar shall not. Danger knows full well
45   That Caesar is more dangerous than he.
We are two lions littered in one day,[10]
And I the elder and more terrible;
And Caesar shall go forth.

---

[10] littered . . . day—born at the same time.

Calpurnia.   Alas, my lord,
     Your wisdom is consumed in confidence.
50   Do not go forth today! Call it my fear
     That keeps you in the house, and not your own.
     We'll send Mark Antony to the Senate House,
     And he shall say you are not well today.
     Let me, upon my knee, **prevail**[11] in this. [*She kneels.*]
55   **Caesar.** Mark Antony shall say I am not well,
     And for thy humor I will stay at home.
[*He raises her.*]
[*Enter Decius.*]
     Here's Decius Brutus. He shall tell them so.
Decius. Caesar, all hail! Good morrow, worthy Caesar.
     I come to fetch you to the Senate House.
60   **Caesar.** And you are come in very happy time
     To bear my greeting to the senators
     And tell them that I will not come today.
     Cannot is false, and that I dare not, falser.
     I will not come today. Tell them so, Decius.
65   **Calpurnia.** Say he is sick.
Caesar.   Shall Caesar send a lie?
     Have I in conquest stretched mine arm so far
     To be afeard to tell graybeards the truth?[12]
     Decius, go tell them Caesar will not come.
Decius. Most mighty Caesar, let me know some cause,
70   Lest I be laughed at when I tell them so.
Caesar. The cause is in my will: I will not come.
     That is enough to satisfy the Senate.
     But for your private satisfaction,
     Because I love you, I will let you know.
75   Calpurnia here, my wife, stays me at home.
     She dreamt tonight she saw my statue,
     Which like a fountain with an hundred spouts

---

[11] **prevail**—win out; have the last word.

[12] Have I . . . truth—Have I won so many victories in battle to be afraid now to tell the truth to old men?

Did run pure blood; and many lusty[13] Romans
Came smiling and did bathe their hands in it.
80 And these does she apply for warnings and portents
Of evils imminent,[14] and on her knee
Hath begged that I will stay at home today.
Decius. This dream is all amiss[15] interpreted;
It was a vision fair and fortunate.
85 Your statue spouting blood in many pipes,
In which so many smiling Romans bathed,
Signifies that from you great Rome shall suck
Reviving blood, and that great men shall press
For tinctures, stains, relics, and cognizance.[16]
90 This by Calpurnia's dream is signified.
Caesar. And this way have you well expounded[17] it.
Decius. I have, when you have heard what I can say;
And know it now. The Senate have concluded
To give this day a crown to mighty Caesar.
95 If you shall send them word you will not come,
Their minds may change. Besides, it were a mock
Apt to be rendered[18] for someone to say
"Break up the Senate till another time
When Caesar's wife shall meet with better dreams."
100 If Caesar hide himself, shall they not whisper
"Lo, Caesar is afraid"?
Pardon me, Caesar, for my dear dear love
To your proceeding bids me tell you this;
And reason to my love is liable.[19]
105 **Caesar.** How foolish do your fears seem now, Calpurnia!
I am ashamèd I did yield to them.
Give me my robe, for I will go.

---

[13] lusty—lively.

[14] portents . . . imminent—omens of evils about to happen.

[15] amiss—wrongly.

[16] tinctures . . . cognizance—*Tinctures* and *stains* are cloths dipped in the blood of martyrs; *cognizance* refers to the heraldic emblems worn by a nobleman's followers.

[17] expounded—explained.

[18] it were . . . rendered—It's likely that someone will make a sarcastic comment.

[19] my dear . . . liable—my sincere interest in your career makes me tell you; my feeling for you is so strong that it rules my judgment.

[*Enter* Brutus, Caius Ligarius, Metellus, Casca, Trebonius, Cinna, *and* Publius.]

And look where Publius is come to fetch me.

Publius. Good morrow, Caesar.

Caesar.   Welcome, Publius.

110   What, Brutus, are you stirred so early too?

Good morrow, Casca. Caius Ligarius,

Caesar was ne'er so much your enemy

As that same ague[20] which hath made you lean.

What is 't o'clock?

115   **Brutus.** Caesar, 'tis strucken eight.

Caesar. I thank you for your pains and courtesy.

[*Enter* Antony.]

See, Antony, that revels long o' nights,

Is notwithstanding up.[21] Good morrow, Antony.

Antony. So to most noble Caesar.

120   **Caesar** [*to a* Servant]. Bid them prepare within.

[*Exit* Servant.]

I am to blame to be thus waited for.

Now, Cinna. Now, Metellus. What, Trebonius,

I have an hour's talk in store for you;

Remember that you call on me today.

125   Be near me, that I may remember you.

Trebonius. Caesar, I will. [*Aside.*[22]] And so near will I be

That your best friends shall wish I had been further.

Caesar. Good friends, go in and taste some wine with me,

And we, like friends, will straightway go together.

130   **Brutus** [*aside*]. That every like is not the same, O Caesar,

The heart of Brutus yearns to think upon![23]

[*They exit.*]

---

[20] ague—fever; sickness.

[21] Antony . . . up—Antony hasn't let his late-night parties keep him from rising early.

[22] *Aside*—so that the audience can hear, but the other characters are not supposed to be able to hear.

[23] That every . . . upon—The fact that we behave like friends doesn't mean we are friends. My heart is sad to think of it.

Act Two, Scene Three

*On a street in Rome, close to Brutus's house,
Artemidorus reads a letter he has written to
warn Caesar of the conspiracy.*

Enter Artemidorus, *reading a paper.*

Artemidorus. *Caesar, beware of Brutus; take heed of Cassius; come not near
Casca; have an eye to Cinna; trust not Trebonius; mark well Metellus
Cimber; Decius Brutus loves thee not; thou hast wronged Caius Ligarius.
There is but one mind in all these men, and it is bent[1] against Caesar. If thou*

5   *beest not immortal,[2] look about you. Security gives way to conspiracy. The
mighty gods defend thee! Thy lover,*

                                Artemidorus.

Here will I stand till Caesar pass along,
And as a suitor[3] will I give him this.

10   My heart laments that virtue cannot live
Out of the teeth of emulation.[4]
If thou read this, O Caesar, thou mayest live;
If not, the Fates[5] with traitors do contrive.

[*He exits.*]

---

[1] bent—directed.

[2] immortal—able to live forever.

[3] as a suitor—as if I had a request for him.

[4] My heart . . . emulation—My heart is sad that Caesar's greatness can't escape jealousy.

[5] Fates—classical mythology, three goddesses who govern human destiny.

Act Two, Scene Four

On the street in front of Brutus's house, about 9 o'clock the same morning, Portia, who is anxious about her husband, sends the servant boy Lucius to find out what is happening at the Senate House. The Soothsayer arrives and tells Portia he plans to warn Caesar again.

Enter Portia *and* Lucius.

Portia. I prithee,[1] boy, run to the Senate House.
     Stay not to answer me, but get thee gone.—
     Why dost thou stay?

Lucius.   To know my errand, madam.

Portia. I would have had thee there and here again

5   Ere I can tell thee what thou shouldst do there.
     [*Aside.*] O constancy, be strong upon my side;
     Set a huge mountain 'tween my heart and tongue!
     I have a man's mind, but a woman's might.
     How hard it is for women to keep counsel![2]—

10   Art thou here yet?

Lucius.   Madam, what should I do?
     Run to the Capitol, and nothing else?
     And so return to you, and nothing else?

Portia. Yes, bring me word, boy, if thy lord look well,
     For he went sickly forth, and take good note

15   What Caesar doth, what suitors press to him.
     Hark, boy, what noise is that?

Lucius. I hear none, madam.

Portia.   Prithee, listen well.
     I heard a bustling rumor, like a fray,[3]

20   And the wind brings it from the Capitol.

Lucius. Sooth,[4] madam, I hear nothing.

---

[1] prithee—beg you.

[2] keep counsel—keep a secret.

[3] bustling . . . fray—confused sound like a battle.

[4] Sooth—in truth.

[*Enter the* Soothsayer.]

Portia. Come hither, fellow. Which way hast thou been?

Soothsayer. At mine own house, good lady.

Portia. What is 't o'clock?

Soothsayer. About the ninth hour, lady.

25 **Portia.** Is Caesar yet gone to the Capitol?

Portia (Lisa C. Arrindell, left) speaks to the Soothsayer (Tamu Gray) in this scene from the 1992 production of *Julius Caesar* by the Seattle Repertory Theatre Company.

Soothsayer. Madam, not yet. I go to take my stand,
    To see him pass on to the Capitol.
Portia. Thou hast some suit[5] to Caesar, hast thou not?
Soothsayer. That I have, lady, if it will please Caesar
30   To be so good to Caesar as to hear me:
    I shall beseech him to befriend himself.
Portia. Why, know'st thou any harms intended towards him?
Soothsayer. None that I know will be, much that I fear may chance.[6]
    Good morrow to you. Here the street is narrow.
35   The throng that follows Caesar at the heels,
    Of senators, of praetors, common suitors,
    Will crowd a feeble man almost to death.
    I'll get me to a place more void,[7] and there
    Speak to great Caesar as he comes along. [*Exit* Soothsayer.]
40 **Portia.** I must go in. Ay me, how weak a thing
    The heart of woman is! O Brutus,
    The heavens speed thee in thine enterprise![8]
    Sure, the boy heard me.—Brutus hath a suit
    That Caesar will not grant.—O I grow faint.
45   Run, Lucius, and commend me to my lord;[9]
    Say I am merry. Come to me again
    And bring me word what he doth say to thee.
    [*They exit separately.*]

---

[5] suit—request.

[6] None . . . chance—I don't know of any specific danger, but I fear that some may come about.

[7] place more void—emptier spot.

[8] speed . . . enterprise—help you in what you're about to do.

[9] commend . . . lord—Give my husband my good wishes.

Act Three, Scene One

At the Senate House, soon after, a crowd awaits Caesar's arrival. Caesar accepts Artemidorus's letter but refuses to look at it. Metellus Cimber petitions Caesar to cancel his brother's banishment, but Caesar remains firm. As Caesar walks into the Senate House, the conspirators surround him and stab him to death. Quickly sending out word that all other citizens are safe, Brutus persuades them to let Mark Antony live and speak at Caesar's funeral. Mark Antony pretends to go along with the conspirators, but left alone with Caesar's body, he vows revenge. Antony tells a servant to warn Octavius Caesar not to return to Rome yet.

Flourish. Enter Caesar, Brutus, Cassius, Casca, Decius, Metellus Cimber, Trebonius, Cinna, Antony, Lepidus, Artemidorus, Publius, Popilius Lena, *and the* Soothsayer; *other following.*

Caesar [*to the* Soothsayer]. The ides of March are come.

Soothsayer. Ay, Caesar, but not gone.

Artemidorus. Hail, Caesar! Read this schedule.[1]

Decius. Trebonius doth desire you to o'er-read,

5   At your best leisure, this his humble suit.

Artemidorus. O Caesar, read mine first, for mine's a suit

    That touches Caesar nearer. Read it, great Caesar.

Caesar. What touches us ourself shall be last served.[2]

Artemidorus. Delay not, Caesar, read it instantly.

10 **Caesar.** What, is the fellow mad?

Publius.   Sirrah, give place.[3]

Cassius. What, urge you your petitions in the street?

    Come to the Capitol.

[Caesar *goes to the Capitol and takes his place, the rest following.*]

Popilius [*to* Cassius]. I wish your enterprise today may thrive.

Cassius. What enterprise, Popilius?

15 **Popilius** [*to* Cassius]. Fare you well.

[*He advances to* Caesar.]

---

[1] schedule—document, scroll.

[2] What . . . served—I will deal with personal matters only after I have dealt with the public ones.

[3] Sirrah, give place—Fellow, get out of the way. *Sirrah* was usually used with servants or inferiors.

Brutus. What said Popilius Lena?

Cassius. He wished our enterprise today may thrive.

    I fear our purpose is discoverèd.

Brutus. Look how he makes to Caesar. Mark him.

[Popilius *speaks apart to* Caesar.]

20 **Cassius.** Casca, be sudden, for we fear prevention.[4]

    Brutus, what shall be done? If this be known,

    Cassius or Caesar never shall turn back,

    For I will slay myself.

Brutus.   Cassius, be constant.

    Popilius Lena speaks not of our purposes;

25   For look, he smiles, and Caesar doth not change.[5]

Cassius. Trebonius knows his time, for look you, Brutus,

    He draws Mark Antony out of the way.

[*Exit* Trebonius *with* Antony.]

Decius. Where is Metellus Cimber? Let him go

    And presently prefer[6] his suit to Caesar.

30 **Brutus.** He is addressed. Press near and second him.[7]

Cinna. Casca, you are the first that rears your hand.

[*They press near* Caesar.]

Caesar. Are we all ready? What is now amiss

    That Caesar and his Senate must redress?

Metellus [*kneeling*]. Most high, most mighty, and most puissant[8] Caesar,

35   Metellus Cimber throws before thy seat

    An humble heart—

Caesar.   I must prevent thee, Cimber.

    These couchings and these lowly courtesies

    Might fire the blood of ordinary men,

    And turn preordinance and first decree

40   Into the law of children. Be not fond

---

[4] sudden . . . prevention—quick, for someone may try to stop us.

[5] change—change his expression.

[6] prefer—present.

[7] He is . . . him—He's ready. Get near and back up his request.

[8] puissant—powerful.

To think that Caesar bears such rebel blood
That will be thawed from the true quality
With that which melteth fools—I mean, sweet words,
Low-crookèd curtsies, and base spaniel fawning.[9]
45   Thy brother by decree is banishèd.
If thou dost bend and pray and fawn for him,
I spurn thee like a cur out of my way.
Know, Caesar doth not wrong, nor without cause
Will he be satisfied.
50 **Metellus.** Is there no voice more worthy than my own
To sound more sweetly in great Caesar's ear
For the repealing of my banished brother?
Brutus [*kneeling*]. I kiss thy hand, but not in flattery, Caesar,
Desiring thee that Publius Cimber may
55   Have an immediate freedom of repeal.[10]
Caesar. What, Brutus?
Cassius [*kneeling*]. Pardon, Caesar! Caesar, pardon!
As low as to thy foot doth Cassius fall,
To beg enfranchisement[11] for Publius Cimber.
60 **Caesar.** I could be well moved, if I were as you;
If I could pray to move, prayers would move me.
But I am constant as the Northern Star,
Of whose true-fixed and resting quality
There is no fellow in the firmament.
65   The skies are painted with unnumbered sparks;
They are all fire and every one doth shine;
But there's but one in all doth hold his place.
So in the world: 'tis furnished well with men,
And men are flesh and blood, and apprehensive;
70   Yet in the number I do know but one
That unassailable holds on his rank,
Unshaked of motion.[12] And that I am he,

---

[9] These couchings . . . fawning—This bowing and scraping might influence ordinary men and turn the laws of the country into the rules of a children's game, that is, easily changed. But don't be so foolish as to think that I can be swayed by the flattery and doglike, cringing behavior that would sway fools.

[10] freedom of repeal—permission to return.

[11] enfranchisement—freedom; liberation from political subjection.

[12] If . . . motion—If I were capable of pleading like you, pleas might move me, but I remain as fixed as the North Star, unique among all the stars in the sky because it remains in one place. In the same way among the men of the world, I do not move.

Brutus (Rick Tutor, left) stands waiting, as Casca (Kenneth Smaltz) stabs Caesar (John Aylward) in this scene from the Seattle Repertory Theatre production.

Let me a little show it even in this—
That I was constant Cimber should be banished,
75 And constant do remain to keep him so.
Cinna [*kneeling*]. O Caesar—
Caesar.   Hence! Wilt thou lift up Olympus?[13]
Decius [*kneeling*]. Great Caesar—
Caesar.   Doth not Brutus bootless[14] kneel?
Casca. Speak, hands, for me!
[*They stab* Caesar; Casca *first*, Brutus *last*.]
Caesar. Et tu, Brutè?[15] Then fall, Caesar! [*Dies.*]
80 **Cinna.** Liberty! Freedom! Tyranny is dead!
Run hence, proclaim, cry it about the streets.

---

[13] Olympus—Mount Olympus, home of the gods in classical mythology.
[14] bootless—uselessly.
[15] Et tu, Brutè—Latin for "And you, too, Brutus?"

Cassius. Some to the common pulpits,[16] and cry out

    "Liberty, freedom, and enfranchisement!"

Brutus. People and senators, be not affrighted.

85   Fly not; stand still. Ambition's debt is paid.

Casca. Go to the pulpit, Brutus.

Decius.   And Cassius too.

Brutus. Where's Publius?

Cinna. Here, quite confounded with this mutiny.[17]

Metellus. Stand fast together, lest some friend of Caesar's

90   Should chance—

Brutus. Talk not of standing. Publius, good cheer.

    There is no harm intended to your person,

    Nor to no Roman else. So tell them, Publius.

Cassius. And leave us, Publius, lest that the people,

95   Rushing on us, should do your age some mischief.

Brutus. Do so, and let no man abide[18] this deed

    But we the doers.

[*Exit all but the conspirators.*]

[*Enter* Trebonius.]

Cassius. Where is Antony?

Trebonius.   Fled to his house amazed.

    Men, wives, and children stare, cry out, and run

100   As it were doomsday.

Brutus.   Fates, we will know your pleasures.

    That we shall die, we know; 'tis but the time,

    And drawing days out, that men stand upon.[19]

Casca. Why, he that cuts off twenty years of life

    Cuts off so many years of fearing death.

105 **Brutus.** Grant that, and then is death a benefit.

    So are we Caesar's friends, that have abridged

    His time of fearing death. Stoop, Romans, stoop,

---

[16] common pulpits—platforms for public speakers.

[17] confounded . . . mutiny—amazed at this uprising.

[18] abide—suffer for.

[19] drawing . . . upon—prolonging their lives that men are concerned about.

And let us bathe our hands in Caesar's blood
Up to the elbows, and besmear our swords.
110   Then walk we forth, even to the marketplace,
And, waving our red weapons o'er our heads,
Let's all cry "Peace, freedom, and liberty!"

Cassius. Stoop, then, and wash.

[*They bathe their hands and weapons in Caesar's blood.*]

                                 How many ages hence
Shall this our lofty scene be acted over
115   In states unborn and accents yet unknown![20]

Brutus. How many times shall Caesar bleed in sport,
That now on Pompey's basis[21] lies along
No worthier than the dust!

Cassius.   So oft as that shall be,
So often shall the knot of us be called
120   The men that gave their country liberty.

Decius. What, shall we forth?

Cassius.   Ay, every man away.
Brutus shall lead, and we will grace[22] his heels
With the most boldest and best hearts of Rome.

[*Enter a* Servant.]

Brutus. Soft, who comes here? A friend of Antony's.

125   **Servant** [*kneeling*]. Thus, Brutus, did my master bid me kneel;
Thus did Mark Antony bid me fall down,
And, being prostrate,[23] thus he bade me say:
"Brutus is noble, wise, valiant, and honest;
Caesar was mighty, bold, royal, and loving.
130   Say I love Brutus and I honor him;
Say I feared Caesar, honored him, and loved him.
If Brutus will vouchsafe[24] that Antony
May safely come to him and be resolved
How Caesar hath deserved to lie in death,

---

[20] How many . . . unknown—How many years in the future will this deed be repeated in countries and in languages that don't exist yet!

[21] Pompey's basis—base of Pompey's statue.

[22] grace—follow him with honor.

[23] prostrate—at full length.

[24] vouchsafe—promise.

135   Mark Antony shall not love Caesar dead

    So well as Brutus living, but will follow

    The fortunes and affairs of noble Brutus

    Thorough the hazards of this untrod state[25]

    With all true faith." So says my master Antony.

140 **Brutus.** Thy master is a wise and valiant Roman;

    I never thought him worse.

    Tell him, so please him come unto this place,

    He shall be satisfied and, by my honor,

    Depart untouched.

    Servant.   I'll fetch him presently.

    [*Exit* Servant.]

145 **Brutus.** I know that we shall have him well to friend.

    Cassius. I wish we may. But yet have I a mind

    That fears him much, and my misgiving still

    Falls shrewdly to the purpose.[26]

    [*Enter* Antony.]

    Brutus. But here comes Antony.—Welcome, Mark Antony.

150 **Antony.** O mighty Caesar! Dost thou lie so low?

    Are all thy conquests, glories, triumphs, spoils,

    Shrunk to this little measure? Fare thee well.—

    I know not, gentlemen, what you intend,

    Who else must be let blood, who else is rank;[27]

155   If I myself, there is no hour so fit

    As Caesar's death's hour, nor no instrument

    Of half that worth as those your swords, made rich

    With the most noble blood of all this world.

    I do beseech ye, if you bear me hard,

160   Now, whilst your purpled hands do reek and smoke,

    Fulfill your pleasure. Live a thousand years,

    I shall not find myself so apt to die;

---

[25] untrod state—new and uncertain state of affairs.

[26] my misgiving . . . purpose—My doubts about such things are usually accurate.

[27] rank—diseased, or too powerful (so that he must be "cured" by death).

No place will please me so, no means of death,

As here by Caesar, and by you cut off,

165   The choice and master spirits of this age.

Brutus. O Antony! Beg not your death of us.

Though now we must appear bloody and cruel,

As by our hands and this our present act

You see we do, yet see you but our hands

170   And this the bleeding business they have done.

Our hearts you see not. They are pitiful;

And pity to the general wrong of Rome—

As fire drives out fire, so pity pity[28]—

Hath done this deed on Caesar. For your part,

175   To you our swords have leaden points, Mark Antony.

Our arms in strength of malice, and our hearts

Of brothers' temper, do receive you in

With all kind love, good thoughts, and reverence.

Cassius. Your voice shall be as strong as any man's

180   In the disposing of new dignities.[29]

Brutus. Only be patient till we have **appeased**[30]

The multitude, beside themselves with fear,

And then we will deliver you the cause

Why I, that did love Caesar when I struck him,

185   Have thus proceeded.

Antony.   I doubt not of your wisdom.

Let each man render me his bloody hand.

[*He shakes hands with the conspirators.*]

First, Marcus Brutus, will I shake with you;

Next, Caius Cassius, do I take your hand;

Now, Decius Brutus, yours; now yours, Metellus;

190   Yours, Cinna; and, my valiant Casca, yours;

Though last, not least in love, yours, good Trebonius.

Gentlemen all—alas, what shall I say?

My credit now stands on such slippery ground

That one of two bad ways you must conceit me,[31]

---

[28] As fire ... pity—As one fire consumes another, our pity for Rome became greater than our pity for Caesar.

[29] Your voice ... dignities—You will have an equal vote in giving out honors from the new government.

[30] **appeased**—calmed; pacified by satisfying demands.

[31] My credit ... conceit me—My reputation must seem so questionable that you must think of me in one of two unfavorable ways.

Revealing varying emotions about their deed, the conspirators surround Caesar's body in the Commonwealth Shakespeare Company production.

195   Either a coward or a flatterer. [*He speaks to Caesar's corpse.*]
           That I did love thee, Caesar, O, 'tis true!
           If then thy spirit look upon us now,
           Shall it not grieve thee dearer than thy death
           To see thy Antony making his peace,
200   Shaking the bloody fingers of thy foes,
           Most noble! in the presence of thy corpse?
           Had I as many eyes as thou hast wounds,
           Weeping as fast as they stream forth thy blood,
           It would become me better than to close
205   In terms of friendship with thine enemies.
           Pardon me, Julius! Here wast thou bayed, brave hart,
           Here didst thou fall, and here thy hunters stand,

Signed in thy spoil and crimsoned in thy lethe.[32]
O world, thou wast the forest to this hart,
210 And this indeed, O world, the heart of thee![33]
How like a deer, strucken by many princes,
Dost thou here lie!

Cassius. Mark Antony—

Antony.   Pardon me, Caius Cassius.
The enemies of Caesar shall say this;
215 Then, in a friend, it is cold modesty.[34]

Cassius. I blame you not for praising Caesar so,
But what compact mean you to have with us?
Will you be pricked in number of our friends,
Or shall we on, and not depend on you?[35]

220 **Antony.** Therefore I took your hands, but was indeed
Swayed from the point by looking down on Caesar.
Friends am I with you all, and love you all,
Upon this hope, that you shall give me reasons
Why and wherein Caesar was dangerous.

225 **Brutus.** Or else were this a savage spectacle.
Our reasons are so full of good regard[36]
That were you, Antony, the son of Caesar,
You should be satisfied.

Antony.   That's all I seek,
And am moreover suitor that I may
230 Produce his body to the marketplace,
And in the pulpit, as becomes a friend,
Speak in the order of his funeral.

Brutus. You shall, Mark Antony.

Cassius.   Brutus, a word with you.
[*Aside to* Brutus.]
You know not what you do. Do not consent
235 That Antony speak in his funeral.

---

[32] lethe—stream of death (that is, Caesar's life-blood). Lethe was a river in the underworld.

[33] Here wast . . . of thee—Here you were hunted like a deer, here you fell, and here your hunters stand, marked with your blood and red with your death. Oh world, you were this deer's forest, and (with a pun on *hart*, deer) he was the world's heart.

[34] cold modesty—sober moderation.

[35] But what . . . on you—But what agreement do you intend to have with us? Will you be marked down ("pricked") on a list of our friends, or shall we continue without you?

[36] regard—consideration.

O, pardon me, thou bleeding piece of earth, That I am meek and gentle with these butchers!

Know you how much the people may be moved
By that which he will utter?

Brutus [*aside to* Cassius].   By your pardon:
I will myself into the pulpit first
And show the reason of our Caesar's death.

240   What Antony shall speak, I will protest[37]
He speaks by leave and by permission,
And that we are contented Caesar shall
Have all true rites and lawful ceremonies.
It shall advantage more than do us wrong.

245   **Cassius** [*aside to* Brutus]. I know not what may fall. I like it not.

Brutus. Mark Antony, here, take you Caesar's body.
You shall not in your funeral speech blame us,
But speak all good you can devise of Caesar,
And say you do 't by our permission.

250   Else shall you not have any hand at all
About his funeral. And you shall speak
In the same pulpit whereto I am going,
After my speech is ended.

Antony.   Be it so.
I do desire no more.

255   **Brutus.** Prepare the body then, and follow us.

[*Exit all but* Antony.]

Antony. O, pardon me, thou bleeding piece of earth,
That I am meek and gentle with these butchers!
Thou art the ruins of the noblest man
That ever livèd in the tide of times.[38]

260   Woe to the hand that shed this costly blood!
Over thy wounds now do I prophesy—
Which, like dumb mouths, do ope their ruby lips

---

[37] protest—explain.

[38] in the tide of times—in all history.

The grief-stricken Antony (Tom Hewitt) holds the dead Caesar in his arms in this scene from the Hartford Stage Company production.

<blockquote>

To beg the voice and utterance of my tongue—
A curse shall light upon the limbs of men;

265   Domestic fury and fierce civil strife
Shall cumber all the parts of Italy;
Blood and destruction shall be so in use
And dreadful objects so familiar
That mothers shall but smile when they behold

270   Their infants quartered with the hands of war,
All pity choked with custom of fell deeds;[39]
And Caesar's spirit, ranging for revenge,

</blockquote>

[39] Domestic fury . . . deeds—Italy will be torn by civil war. People will become so accustomed to horrible sights that mothers will simply smile when they see their children cut into pieces. Pity will disappear among so much cruelty.

Cry "Havoc!" and let slip the dogs of war.

    With Ate[40] by his side come hot from hell,
    Shall in these confines with a monarch's voice
275 Cry "Havoc!"[41] and let slip the dogs of war,
    That this foul deed shall smell above the earth
    With carrion men, groaning for burial.
  [*Enter Octavius's Servant.*]
    You serve Octavius Caesar, do you not?
  Servant. I do, Mark Antony.
280 **Antony.** Caesar did write for him to come to Rome.
  Servant. He did receive his letters, and is coming,
    And bid me say to you by word of mouth— [*Seeing the body.*]
    O Caesar—
  Antony. Thy heart is big. Get thee apart and weep.
285 Passion, I see, is catching, for mine eyes,
    Seeing those beads of sorrow stand in thine,
    Began to water. Is thy master coming?
  Servant. He lies tonight within seven leagues of Rome.[42]
  Antony. Post back with speed and tell him what hath chanced.
290 Here is a mourning Rome, a dangerous Rome,
    No Rome of safety for Octavius yet;
    Hie hence and tell him so. Yet stay awhile;
    Thou shalt not back till I have borne this corpse
    Into the marketplace. There shall I try,
295 In my oration, how the people take
    The cruel issue of these bloody men,
    According to the which thou shalt discourse
    To young Octavius of the state of things.[43]
    Lend me your hand.
  [*They exit with* Caesar's *body.*]

---

[40] Ate—goddess of revenge.

[41] Cry "Havoc"—Give the word for mass slaughter and destruction.

[42] He lies . . . Rome—Octavius will camp tonight less than 21 miles from Rome. A league is 3 miles.

[43] There shall I . . . things—In my funeral speech, I will test how the people react to the cruel deeds of these murderers, and then you can report the state of things to Octavius.

Act Three, Scene Two

Soon after, at the public speaking platform in the Roman Forum, Brutus tells the unruly crowd why Caesar had to be killed for the good of Rome. Then he introduces Mark Antony, who says he will not speak against Brutus or the other conspirators because they are honorable men. Antony then reminds the people of all the good that Caesar did and stirs them up to find and kill Caesar's assassins. He rekindles the crowd's anger by showing them Caesar's bloody corpse and then reads the dead man's will, in which he left money and land to the citizens of Rome. The enraged crowd sets out to burn the conspirators' houses. A servant tells Antony that Octavius has arrived in Rome and that Brutus and Cassius have left the city.

Enter a crowd. Enter Brutus *and* Cassius.

Citizens. We will be satisfied! Let us be satisfied!

Brutus. Then follow me, and give me audience, friends.
Cassius, go you into the other street
And part the numbers.[1]

5   Those that will hear me speak, let 'em stay here;
Those that will follow Cassius, go with him;
And public reasons shall be renderèd[2]
Of Caesar's death.

First Citizen.   I will hear Brutus speak.

Second Citizen. I will hear Cassius, and compare their reasons

10   When severally we hear them renderèd.

[*Exit* Cassius, *with some of the* Citizens.]

Third Citizen. The noble Brutus is ascended. Silence!

Brutus. Be patient till the last.
Romans, countrymen, and lovers,[3] hear me for my cause, and be
silent that you may hear. Believe me for mine honor, and have respect

15   to mine honor, that you may believe. Censure[4] me in your wisdom,
and awake your senses, that you may the better judge. If there be any
in this assembly, any dear friend of Caesar's, to him I say that Brutus'

---

[1] part the numbers—divide the crowd.

[2] renderèd—given.

[3] lovers—dear friends.

[4] Censure—judge.

Not that I loved Caesar less,
but that I loved Rome more.

love to Caesar was no less than his. If then that friend demand why Brutus rose against Caesar, this is my answer: Not that I loved Caesar

20 less, but that I loved Rome more. Had you rather Caesar were living and die all slaves, than that Caesar were dead, to live all free men? As Caesar loved me, I weep for him; as he was fortunate, I rejoice at it; as he was valiant, I honor him; but, as he was ambitious, I slew him. There is tears for his love; joy for his fortune; honor for his valor;

25 and death for his ambition. Who is here so base that would be a bondman?[5] If any, speak, for him have I offended. Who is here so rude[6] that would not be a Roman? If any, speak, for him have I offended. Who is here so vile that will not love his country? If any, speak, for him have I offended. I pause for a reply.

30 **All.** None, Brutus, none!

Brutus. Then none have I offended. I have done no more to Caesar than you shall do to Brutus. The question of his death is enrolled in the Capitol, his glory not extenuated wherein he was worthy, nor his offenses enforced for which he suffered death.[7]

[*Enter* Mark Antony *and others with* Caesar's *body.*]

35 Here comes his body, mourned by Mark Antony, who, though he had no hand in his death, shall receive the benefit of his dying, a place in the commonwealth, as which of you shall not? With this I depart, that, as I slew my best lover for the good of Rome, I have the same dagger for myself when it shall please my country to need my death.

40 **All.** Live, Brutus, live, live! [Brutus *comes down.*]

First Citizen. Bring him with triumph home unto his house.

Second Citizen. Give him a statue with his ancestors.

Third Citizen. Let him be Caesar.

Fourth Citizen.   Caesar's better parts

Shall be crowned in Brutus.

---

[5] Who . . . bondman—Which of you is so low that you would prefer to be a slave?

[6] rude—uncivilized.

[7] The question . . . death—The reasons for his death are on record in the Capitol. We have not belittled his accomplishments or exaggerated the failings for which he was killed.

Friends, Romans, countrymen, lend me your ears. I come to bury Caesar, not to praise him.

45 **First Citizen.** We'll bring him to his house with shouts and clamors.

Brutus. My countrymen—

Second Citizen. Peace, silence! Brutus speaks.

First Citizen. Peace, ho!

Brutus. Good countrymen, let me depart alone,

50   And, for my sake, stay here with Antony.

    Do grace to Caesar's corpse, and grace his speech[8]

    Tending to Caesar's glories, which Mark Antony,

    By our permission, is allowed to make.

    I do entreat you, not a man depart,

55   Save[9] I alone, till Antony have spoke. [*Exit Brutus.*]

First Citizen. Stay, ho, and let us hear Mark Antony.

Third Citizen. Let him go up into the public chair.

    We'll hear him. Noble Antony, go up.

Antony. For Brutus' sake I am beholding[10] to you.

[*He goes into the pulpit.*]

60 **Fourth Citizen.** What does he say of Brutus?

Third Citizen.   He says, for Brutus' sake

    He finds himself beholding to us all.

Fourth Citizen. 'Twere best he speak no harm of Brutus here.

First Citizen. This Caesar was a tyrant.

Third Citizen.   Nay, that's certain.

    We are blest that Rome is rid of him.

65 **Second Citizen.** Peace! Let us hear what Antony can say.

Antony. You gentle Romans—

All.   Peace, ho! Let us hear him.

Antony. Friends, Romans, countrymen, lend me your ears.

    I come to bury Caesar, not to praise him.

    The evil that men do lives after them;

---

[8] Do grace . . . speech—Show respect to dead Caesar and listen respectfully to Antony's speech.

[9] Save—except.

[10] beholding—indebted; owing thanks.

70 The good is oft interrèd[11] with their bones.
So let it be with Caesar. The noble Brutus
Hath told you Caesar was ambitious.
If it were so, it was a **grievous**[12] fault,
And grievously hath Caesar answered[13] it.
75 Here, under leave of Brutus and the rest—
For Brutus is an honorable man,
So are they all, all honorable men—
Come I to speak in Caesar's funeral.
He was my friend, faithful and just to me;
80 But Brutus says he was ambitious,
And Brutus is an honorable man.
He hath brought many captives home to Rome,
Whose ransoms did the general coffers[14] fill.
Did this in Caesar seem ambitious?
85 When that the poor have cried, Caesar hath wept;
Ambition should be made of sterner stuff.
Yet Brutus says he was ambitious,
And Brutus is an honorable man.
You all did see that on the Lupercal
90 I thrice presented him a kingly crown,
Which he did thrice refuse. Was this ambition?
Yet Brutus says he was ambitious,
And sure he is an honorable man.
I speak not to disprove what Brutus spoke,
95 But here I am to speak what I do know.
You all did love him once, not without cause.
What cause withholds you then to mourn for him?
O judgment! Thou art fled to brutish beasts,
And men have lost their reason! Bear with me;
100 My heart is in the coffin there with Caesar,
And I must pause till it come back to me.
First Citizen. Methinks there is much reason in his sayings.

---

[11] interrèd—buried.

[12] **grievous**—very serious.

[13] answered—paid for.

[14] general coffers—Roman government's treasury.

Second Citizen. If thou consider rightly of the matter,
Caesar has had great wrong.
Third Citizen.   Has he, masters?
105   I fear there will a worse come in his place.
Fourth Citizen. Marked ye his words? He would not take the crown,
Therefore 'tis certain he was not ambitious.
First Citizen. If it be found so, some will dear abide it.[15]
Second Citizen. Poor soul, his eyes are red as fire with weeping.
110   **Third Citizen.** There's not a nobler man in Rome than Antony.
Fourth Citizen. Now mark him. He begins again to speak.
Antony. But yesterday the word of Caesar might
Have stood against the world. Now lies he there,
And none so poor to do him reverence.[16]
115   O masters! If I were disposed to stir
Your hearts and minds to mutiny and rage,
I should do Brutus wrong, and Cassius wrong,
Who, you all know, are honorable men.
I will not do them wrong; I rather choose
120   To wrong the dead, to wrong myself and you.
Than I will wrong such honorable men.
But here's a parchment[17] with the seal of Caesar
I found it in his closet; 'tis his will.
[*He shows the will.*]
Let but the commons hear this testament—
125   Which, pardon me, I do not mean to read—
And they would go and kiss dead Caesar's wounds
And dip their napkins[18] in his sacred blood,
Yea, beg a hair of him for memory,
And dying, mention it within their wills,
130   Bequeathing it as a rich legacy
Unto their issue.[19]
Fourth Citizen. We'll hear the will! Read it, Mark Antony.
All. The will, the will! We will hear Caesar's will.

---

[15] dear abide it—suffer the consequences.

[16] none . . . reverence—Nobody is below Caesar in fortune now.

[17] parchment—document.

[18] napkins—handkerchiefs.

[19] issue—children; descendants.

Delivering Caesar's funeral oration, Antony (Tom Hewitt) draws aside the dead man's cloak to reveal his wounds in the Hartford Stage Company production.

Antony. Have patience, gentle friends: I must not read it.

135   It is not meet[20] you know how Caesar loved you.

You are not wood, you are not stones, but men.

And being men, hearing the will of Caesar,

It will inflame you, it will make you mad.

'Tis good you know not that you are his heirs,

140   For if you should, O, what would come of it?

Fourth Citizen. Read the will! We'll hear it, Antony.

You shall read us the will, Caesar's will.

---

[20] meet—fitting, proper.

Antony. Will you be patient? Will you stay awhile?

I have o'ershot myself[21] to tell you of it.

145   I fear I wrong the honorable men

Whose daggers have stabbed Caesar. I do fear it.

Fourth Citizen. They were traitors. "Honorable men"!

All. The will! The testament!

Second Citizen. They were villains, murderers! The will! Read the will!

150   **Antony.** You will **compel**[22] me then to read the will?

Then make a ring about the corpse of Caesar

And let me show you him that made the will.

Shall I descend? And will you give me leave?[23]

All. Come down.

155   **Second Citizen.** Descend.

Third Citizen. You shall have leave.

[Antony *comes down. They gather around* Caesar's *body.*]

Fourth Citizen. A ring! Stand round.

First Citizen. Stand from the hearse.[24] Stand from the body.

Second Citizen. Room for Antony, most noble Antony!

160   **Antony.** Nay, press not so upon me. Stand far off.

All. Stand back! Room! Bear back!

Antony. If you have tears, prepare to shed them now.

You all do know this mantle.[25] I remember

The first time ever Caesar put it on;

165   'Twas on a summer's evening in his tent,

That day he overcame the Nervii.[26]

Look, in this place ran Cassius' dagger through.

See what a rent the envious[27] Casca made.

Through this the well-belovèd Brutus stabbed,

170   And as he plucked his cursèd steel away,

Mark how the blood of Caesar followed it,

As rushing out of doors to be resolved

---

[21] o'ershot myself—done more than I should have.

[22] **compel**—force; require.

[23] Shall . . . leave—Will you give me permission to come down?

[24] Stand . . . hearse—Stand back from the bier (support for a dead body).

[25] mantle—Caesar's toga or cloak.

[26] Nervii—fierce Celtic tribe that Caesar defeated thirteen years earlier.

[27] rent . . . envious—tear . . . spiteful.

If Brutus so unkindly knocked or no;[28]
For Brutus, as you know, was Caesar's angel.
175 Judge, O you gods, how dearly Caesar loved him!
This was the most unkindest cut of all;
For when the noble Caesar saw him stab,
Ingratitude, more strong than traitors' arms,
Quite vanquished him. Then burst his mighty heart,
180 And in his mantle muffling up his face,
Even at the base of Pompey's statue,
Which all the while ran blood, great Caesar fell.
O, what a fall was there, my countrymen!
Then I, and you, and all of us fell down,
185 Whilst bloody treason flourished over us.
O, now you weep, and I perceive you feel
The dint[29] of pity. These are gracious drops.
Kind souls, what weep you when you but behold
Our Caesar's vesture wounded? Look you here!
190 Here is himself,[30] marred as you see with traitors.

[_He lifts_ Caesar's _mantle._]

First Citizen. O piteous spectacle!
Second Citizen. O noble Caesar!
Third Citizen. O woeful day!
Fourth Citizen. O traitors, villains!
195 **First Citizen.** O most bloody sight!
Second Citizen. We will be revenged.
All. Revenge! About! Seek! Burn! Fire! Kill! Slay! Let not a traitor live!
Antony. Stay, countrymen.
First Citizen. Peace there! Hear the noble Antony.
200 **Second Citizen.** We'll hear him, we'll follow him, we'll die
with him!
Antony. Good friends, sweet friends, let me not stir you up

---

[28] As rushing ... or no—Antony means that Caesar's blood rushed out of that opening to find out if it was really Brutus who cruelly made the wound.

[29] dint—impression; force.

[30] weep you ... himself—Do you cry when you look only at his wounded clothing? Look at his body!

To such a sudden flood of mutiny.
They that have done this deed are honorable.
205 What private griefs they have, alas, I know not,
That made them do it. They are wise and honorable,
And will, no doubt, with reasons answer you.
I come not, friends, to steal away your hearts.
I am no orator, as Brutus is,
210 But, as you know me all, a plain blunt man
That love my friend, and that they know full well
That gave me public leave to speak of him.
For I have neither wit, nor words, nor worth,
Action, nor utterance, nor the power of speech
215 To stir men's blood. I only speak right on.
I tell you that which you yourselves do know,
Show you sweet Caesar's wounds, poor poor dumb mouths,
And bid them speak for me. But were I Brutus,
And Brutus Antony, there were an Antony
220 Would ruffle up your spirits and put a tongue
In every wound of Caesar that should move
The stones of Rome to rise and mutiny.[31]

All. We'll mutiny!

First Citizen. We'll burn the house of Brutus!

225 **Third Citizen.** Away, then! Come, seek the conspirators.

Antony. Yet hear me, countrymen. Yet hear me speak.

All. Peace, ho! Hear Antony, most noble Antony!

Antony. Why, friends, you go to do you know not what.
Wherein hath Caesar thus deserved your loves?
230 Alas, you know not. I must tell you then:
You have forgot the will I told you of.

All. Most true. The will! Let's stay and hear the will.

Antony. Here is the will, and under Caesar's seal.
To every Roman citizen he gives,
235 To every several man, seventy-five drachmas.[32]

Second Citizen. Most noble Caesar! We'll revenge his death.

Third Citizen. O royal Caesar!

---

[31] But were . . . mutiny—But if I were Brutus, and he were me, then you would have an Antony capable of stirring your emotions and giving such a voice to Caesar's wounds that the very stones of the city would rebel.

[32] several man . . . drachmas—individual man, seventy-five silver coins (worth quite a lot to the poor).

Antony. Hear me with patience.

All. Peace, ho!

240 **Antony.** Moreover, he hath left you all his walks,
His private arbors, and new-planted orchards,
On this side Tiber;[33] he hath left them you,
And to your heirs forever—common pleasures,
To walk abroad and recreate yourselves.

245 Here was a Caesar! When comes such another?

First Citizen. Never, never! Come, away, away!
We'll burn his body in the holy place
And with the brands[34] fire the traitors' houses.
Take up the body.

250 **Second Citizen.** Go fetch fire!

Third Citizen. Pluck down benches!

Fourth Citizen. Pluck down forms, windows, anything!

[Exit Citizens with the body.]

Antony. Now let it work. Mischief, thou art afoot.
Take thou what course thou wilt.

[Enter Octavius's Servant.]

255 How now, fellow?

Servant. Sir, Octavius is already come to Rome.

Antony. Where is he?

Servant. He and Lepidus are at Caesar's house.

Antony. And thither will I straight[35] to visit him.

260 He comes upon a wish.[36] Fortune is merry,
And in this mood will give us anything.

Servant. I heard him say Brutus and Cassius
Are rid[37] like madmen through the gates of Rome.

Antony. Belike they had some notice of[38] the people,

265 How I had moved them. Bring me to Octavius.

[They exit.]

---

[33] His private ... Tiber—his private gardens on this side of the river Tiber.

[34] brands—pieces of burning wood.

[35] straight—at once.

[36] upon a wish—just when wanted.

[37] Are rid—have ridden.

[38] Belike ... of—probably they had news about.

Act Three, Scene Three

On a street in Rome, the mob confuses Cinna the poet with Cinna the conspirator, and *attacks him. The mob then rushes out after the conspirators.*

Enter Cinna the Poet *followed by several* Citizens, *some carrying torches.*

Cinna. I dreamt tonight that I did feast with Caesar,
    And things unluckily charge my fantasy.[1]
    I have no will to wander forth of doors,
    Yet something leads me forth.

5 **First Citizen.** What is your name?

Second Citizen. Whither are you going?

Third Citizen. Where do you dwell?

Fourth Citizen. Are you a married man or a
    bachelor?

10 **Second Citizen.** Answer every man directly.

First Citizen. Ay, and briefly.

Fourth Citizen. Ay, and wisely.

Third Citizen. Ay, and truly, you were best.

Cinna. What is my name? Whither am I going? Where

15   do I dwell? Am I a married man or a bachelor? Then
    to answer every man directly and briefly, wisely and
    truly: wisely I say, I am a bachelor.

Second Citizen. That's as much as to say they are fools that marry.
    You'll bear me a bang for that,[2] I fear. Proceed directly.

20 **Cinna.** Directly, I am going to Caesar's funeral.

First Citizen. As a friend or an enemy?

Cinna. As a friend.

Second Citizen. That matter is answered directly.

Fourth Citizen. For your dwelling—briefly.

25 **Cinna.** Briefly, I dwell by the Capitol.

Third Citizen. Your name, sir, truly.

---

[1] things . . . fantasy—Recent events have caused me to imagine awful things.

[2] You'll . . . that—I'll beat you for saying that.

Tear him for his bad verses,
tear him for his bad verses!

Cinna. Truly, my name is Cinna.

First Citizen. Tear him to pieces! He's a conspirator!

Cinna. I am Cinna the poet, I am Cinna the poet!

30 **Fourth Citizen.** Tear him for his bad verses, tear him for his bad verses!

Cinna. I am not Cinna the conspirator.

Fourth Citizen. It is no matter, his name's Cinna. Pluck but his name out of his heart, and turn him going.[3]

Third Citizen. Tear him, tear him! [_They attack_ Cinna.] Come, brands, ho,
35 firebrands! To Brutus', to Cassius'; burn all! Some to Decius' house, and some to Casca's; some to Ligarius'. Away, go!

[Citizens _exit, dragging off_ Cinna.]

---

[3] Pluck . . . going—Tear his name out of his heart and send him away.

Act Four, Scene One

Eighteen months later, Mark Antony, Octavius, and Lepidus rule Rome as the Second Triumvirate. In Antony's house in Rome, they plan the deaths of their enemies.

When Lepidus goes to get Caesar's will, Antony and Octavius discuss getting rid of him, but they decide that first they must deal with the armies of Brutus and Cassius.

Antony, Octavius, and Lepidus *are seated at a table, studying a list.*

Antony. These many, then, shall die. Their names are pricked.
Octavius. Your brother too must die. Consent you, Lepidus?
Lepidus. I do consent—
Octavius.   Prick him down, Antony.
Lepidus. Upon condition Publius shall not live,

5   Who is your sister's son, Mark Antony.
Antony. He shall not live. Look, with a spot I damn him.[1]
          But Lepidus, go you to Caesar's house.
          Fetch the will hither, and we shall determine
          How to cut off some charge in legacies.[2]

10   **Lepidus.** What, shall I find you here?
Octavius. Or here or at the Capitol. [*Exit* Lepidus.]
Antony. This is a slight, unmeritable[3] man,
          Meet to be sent on errands. Is it fit,
          The threefold world divided, he should stand

15   One of the three to share it?[4]
Octavius.   So you thought him,
          And took his voice who should be pricked to die
          In our black sentence and proscription.[5]
Antony. Octavius, I have seen more days than you;
          And though we lay these honors on this man

---

[1] with . . . damn him—With a mark on the list, I condemn him.

[2] How to . . . legacies—how to alter the will so as to cut down the amounts of money people get.

[3] unmeritable—not deserving (respect or honor).

[4] Is it . . . share it—Is it right that he should be one of the three men in control of Rome's lands in Europe, Asia, and Africa?

[5] black . . . proscription—death sentence and decrees making men outlaws and confiscating their properties.

In this scene from the Hartford Stage production, Octavius (Sheridan Crist, standing) and Antony (Tom Hewitt) decide which Romans must die.

20   To ease ourselves of divers slanderous loads,[6]
     He shall but bear them as the ass bears gold,
     To groan and sweat under the business,
     Either led or driven, as we point the way;
     And having brought our treasure where we will,
25   Then take we down his load, and turn him off,
     Like to the empty ass, to shake his ears
     And graze in commons.[7]

---

[6] divers slanderous loads—various troublesome accusations.

[7] and turn . . . commons—drive him away, like a donkey without a load, to eat grass in the public pasture.

Octavius.   You may do your will;
But he's a tried and valiant soldier.

Antony. So is my horse, Octavius, and for that

30   I do appoint him store of provender.[8]
It is a creature that I teach to fight,
To wind,[9] to stop, to run directly on,
His corporal motion[10] governed by my spirit.
And in some taste is Lepidus but so.

35   He must be taught, and trained, and bid go forth—
A barren-spirited fellow, one that feeds
On objects, arts, and imitations,
Which, out of use and staled by other men,
Begin his fashion.[11] Do not talk of him

40   But as a property. And now, Octavius,
Listen great things. Brutus and Cassius
Are levying powers. We must straight make head.[12]
Therefore let our alliance be combined,
Our best friends made, our means stretched;

45   And let us presently go sit in council
How covert matters may be best disclosed
And open perils surest answerèd.[13]

Octavius. Let us do so, for we are at the stake
And bayed about with many enemies;[14]

50   And some that smile have in their hearts, I fear,
Millions of mischiefs. [*They exit.*]

---

[8] provender—food.

[9] wind—turn.

[10] corporal motion—body movements.

[11] On objects . . . fashion—on curiosities and fads, which, overused and rejected by others, he considers the height of fashion.

[12] levying . . . head—gathering armies. We must immediately gather troops.

[13] How covert . . . answerèd—how we can best discover hidden dangers and encounter open dangers.

[14] we are . . . enemies—We are like a bear in the sport of bearbaiting, tied to a stake and surrounded by enemies like barking dogs.

Act Four, Scene Two

In front of Brutus's tent at the military camp at Sardis, several months later, Brutus tells Lucilius that he is not pleased with Cassius's actions. He and Lucilius are suspicious because Cassius appears to be cold and distant. After Cassius arrives, he accuses Brutus of wronging him; but Brutus insists that they talk privately. They go into Brutus's tent to discuss their disagreements.

Drum. Enter Brutus, Lucilius, *and the army.* Titinius *and* Pindarus *meet them.*

Brutus. Stand, ho!

Lucilius. Give the word, ho, and stand!

Brutus. What now, Lucilius, is Cassius near?

Lucilius. He is at hand, and Pindarus is come
    To do you salutation[1] from his master.

5   **Brutus.** He greets me well. Your master, Pindarus,
    In his own change, or by ill officers,
    Hath given me some worthy cause to wish
    Things done, undone; but if he be at hand
    I shall be satisfied.[2]

10   **Pindarus.**   I do not doubt
    But that my noble master will appear
    Such as he is, full of regard and honor.

Brutus. He is not doubted.—A word, Lucilius.

[Brutus *and* Lucilius *speak apart.*]
    How he received you let me be resolved.[3]

Lucilius. With courtesy and with respect enough,

15   But not with such familiar instances[4]
    Nor with such free and friendly conference
    As he hath used of old.

---

[1] do you salutation—give you greetings.

[2] Your master . . . satisfied—Cassius, either through some change in his own character or because of bad subordinates, has done things that I very much wish he had not. But if he is coming soon, I can have things explained to my satisfaction.

[3] How . . . resolved—How did he treat you when you met?

[4] familiar instances—proofs of friendship.

Brutus (John C. Vennema, right) and Cassius (Richard Howard) stand in front of their soldiers in this scene from the 1999 production of *Julius Caesar* by the Guthrie Theatre in Minneapolis.

	Brutus.	Thou hast described
		A hot friend cooling. Ever note, Lucilius:
20		When love begins to sicken and decay
		It useth an enforcèd ceremony.[5]
		There are no tricks in plain and simple faith.
		But hollow men, like horses hot at hand,
		Make gallant show and promise of their mettle;

[*Low march within.*]

25	But when they should endure the bloody spur,
	They fall their crests and like deceitful jades
	Sink in the trial.[6] Comes his army on?

---

[5] enforcèd ceremony—stiff politeness.

[6] But hollow . . . trial—But insincere men, like horses too spirited at the beginning, look brave, but when they should be spurred to action, they bow their heads and fall in battle.

Lucilius. They mean this night in Sardis to be quartered.

    The greater part, the horse in general,[7]

30   Are come with Cassius.

[*Enter* Cassius *and his army.*]

Brutus.   Hark, he is arrived.

    March gently on to meet him.

Cassius. Stand, ho!

Brutus. Stand, ho! Speak the word along.

First Soldier. Stand!

35 **Second Soldier.** Stand!

Third Soldier. Stand!

Cassius. Most noble brother, you have done me wrong.

Brutus. Judge me, you gods! Wrong I mine enemies?

    And if not so, how should I wrong a brother?

40 **Cassius.** Brutus, this sober form[8] of yours hides wrongs;

    And when you do them—

Brutus.   Cassius, be content;[9]

    Speak your griefs softly. I do know you well.

    Before the eyes of both our armies here,

    Which should perceive nothing but love from us,

45   Let us not wrangle. Bid them move away.

    Then in my tent, Cassius, enlarge your griefs,[10]

    And I will give you audience.

Cassius.   Pindarus,

    Bid our commanders lead their charges off

    A little from this ground.

50 **Brutus.** Lucius, do you the like, and let no man

    Come to our tent till we have done our conference.

    Let Lucilius and Titinius guard our door.

[Brutus *and* Cassius *go into* Brutus's *tent.*]

[*All exit but* Lucilius *and* Titinius *who stand guard at the door.*]

---

[7] horse in general—all the cavalry.

[8] sober form—serious manner.

[9] be content—keep calm.

[10] enlarge your griefs—speak your complaints freely.

Act Four, Scene Three

Inside Brutus's tent, Brutus and Cassius argue bitterly. Brutus accuses Cassius of corruption and greed. After Cassius offers to let Brutus kill him, they become friendlier. Brutus tells Cassius that Portia is dead. Soon after, Messala and Titinius arrive to discuss military strategy. Messala tells about the killings in Rome and that Anthony and Octavius are approaching with their armies. When all but Brutus are asleep, Caesar's ghost appears and warns Brutus that they will meet at Philippi.

Enter Cassius *and* Brutus, *arguing.*

Cassius. That you have wronged me doth appear in this:
    You have condemned and noted[1] Lucius Pella
    For taking bribes here of the Sardians,
    Wherein my letters, praying on his side,
5   Because I knew the man, was slighted off.[2]
Brutus. You wronged yourself to write in such a case.
Cassius. In such a time as this it is not meet
    That every nice offense should bear his comment.[3]
Brutus. Let me tell you, Cassius, you yourself
10   Are much condemned to have an itching palm,
    To sell and mart your offices for gold[4]
    To undeservers.
Cassius.   I an itching palm?
    You know that you are Brutus that speaks this,
    Or, by the gods, this speech were else your last.
15 **Brutus.** The name of Cassius honors this corruption,
    And chastisement doth therefore hide his head.[5]
Cassius. Chastisement?

---

[1] noted—publicly shamed.

[2] letters . . . slighted off—You ignored my letters that appealed on his behalf.

[3] every nice . . . comment—Every trivial offense should be criticized.

[4] to have . . . gold—to be looking for bribes, to sell and market your favors for gold.

[5] The name . . . head—Because Cassius's name is linked to the bribery, no one dares talk about punishment for those who accept the bribes.

You yourself are much condemned to have an itching palm.

Brutus. Remember March, the ides of March remember.
Did not great Julius bleed for justice's sake?

20   What villain touched his body that did stab
And not for justice?[6] What, shall one of us,
That struck the foremost man of all this world
But for supporting robbers, shall we now
Contaminate our fingers with base bribes,

25   And sell the mighty space of our large honors
For so much trash as may be graspèd thus?
I had rather be a dog and bay[7] the moon
Than such a Roman.

Cassius.   Brutus, bait not me.[8]
I'll not endure it. You forget yourself

30   To hedge me in. I am a soldier, I,
Older in practice, abler than yourself
To make conditions.[9]

Brutus. Go to! You are not, Cassius.

Cassius. I am.

35   **Brutus.** I say you are not.

Cassius. Urge me no more; I shall forget myself.
Have mind upon your health. Tempt me no farther.

Brutus. Away, slight man!

Cassius. Is't possible?

Brutus.   Hear me, for I will speak.

40   Must I give way and room to your rash choler?[10]
Shall I be frighted when a madman stares?

Cassius. O ye gods, ye gods! Must I endure all this?

---

[6] What villain . . . justice—Which of us was criminal enough to stab Caesar for a cause other than justice?

[7] bay—howl at.

[8] bait not me—Don't try to provoke me.

[9] make conditions—manage affairs; make decisions.

[10] Must I . . . choler—Must I give in and accept your angry temper?

Brutus. All this? Ay, more. Fret till your proud heart break.

Go show your slaves how choleric you are

45   And make your bondmen tremble. Must I budge?

Must I observe[11] you? Must I stand and crouch

Under your testy humor? By the gods,

You shall digest the venom of your spleen

Though it do split you; for, from this day forth,

50   I'll use you for my mirth, yea, for my laughter,

When you are waspish.[12]

Cassius.   Is it come to this?

Brutus. You say you are a better soldier.

Let it appear so; make your vaunting[13] true,

And it shall please me well. For mine own part,

55   I shall be glad to learn of noble men.

Cassius. You wrong me every way! You wrong me, Brutus.

I said an elder soldier, not a better.

Did I say "better"?

Brutus.   If you did, I care not.

Cassius. When Caesar lived, he durst not thus have moved me.

60   **Brutus.** Peace, peace! You durst not so have tempted him.

Cassius. I durst not?

Brutus. No.

Cassius. What, durst not tempt him?

Brutus.   For your life you durst not.

Cassius. Do not presume too much upon my love.

65   I may do that I shall be sorry for.

Brutus. You have done that you should be sorry for.

There is no terror, Cassius, in your threats,

For I am armed so strong in honesty

That they pass by me as the idle wind,

70   Which I respect not. I did send to you

For certain sums of gold, which you denied me;

For I can raise no money by vile means.

By heaven, I had rather coin my heart

---

[11] observe—defer to.

[12] You shall . . . waspish—You shall swallow your anger, even if it splits you. From now on, I'll laugh at you when you are hotheaded.

[13] vaunting—bragging.

Brutus (Martin Sheen, left) accuses Cassius (Edward Herrman) of greed
in the 1988 New York Shakespeare Festival production of *Julius Caesar*.

	And drop my blood for drachmas than to wring
75	From the hard hands of peasants their vile trash
	By any indirection.[14] I did send
	To you for gold to pay my legions,
	Which you denied me. Was that done like Cassius?
	Should I have answered Caius Cassius so?
80	When Marcus Brutus grows so covetous
	To lock such rascal counters[15] from his friends,
	Be ready, gods, with all your thunderbolts;
	Dash him to pieces!

[14] For I can ... indirection—I cannot raise money by dishonest methods. I would rather make coins out of my heart and blood than steal money from peasants by lying to them.

[15] To lock ... counters—to hold back such insignificant amounts of money.

A friend should bear his friend's infirmities,
But Brutus makes mine greater than they are.

Cassius.   I denied you not.

Brutus. You did.

Cassius.   I did not. He was but a fool

85 That brought my answer back. Brutus hath rived[16] my heart.

A friend should bear his friend's infirmities,

But Brutus makes mine greater than they are.

Brutus. I do not, till you practice them on me.

Cassius. You love me not.

Brutus.   I do not like your faults.

90 **Cassius.** A friendly eye could never see such faults.

Brutus. A flatterer's would not, though they do appear

As huge as high Olympus.

Cassius. Come, Antony, and young Octavius, come,

Revenge yourselves alone on Cassius;

95 For Cassius is aweary of the world,

Hated by one he loves, braved[17] by his brother,

Checked like a bondman, all his faults observed,

Set in a notebook, learned and conned by rote[18]

To cast into my teeth. O, I could weep

100 My spirit from mine eyes! There is my dagger,

[*Offering his unsheathed dagger.*]

And here my naked breast; within, a heart

Dearer than Pluto's mine,[19] richer than gold.

If that thou be'st a Roman, take it forth.

I, that denied thee gold, will give my heart.

105 Strike, as thou didst at Caesar; for I know,

When thou didst hate him worst, thou loved'st him better

Than ever thou loved'st Cassius.

---

[16] rived—split.

[17] braved—defied.

[18] conned by rote—memorized.

[19] Dearer . . . mine—richer than underground mines. Pluto was god of the underworld; Plutus was the god of wealth. Both seemed to be meant.

Brutus. Sheathe your dagger.
Be angry when you will, it shall have scope;
Do what you will, dishonor shall be humor.[20]
110 O Cassius, you are yokèd with a lamb
That carries anger as the flint bears fire,
Who, much enforced, shows a hasty spark
And straight is cold again.[21]

Cassius. Hath Cassius lived
To be but mirth and laughter to his Brutus
115 When grief and blood ill-tempered vexeth him?

Brutus.
When I spoke that, I was ill-tempered too.

Cassius. Do you confess so much? Give me your hand.

Brutus. And my heart too. [*They embrace.*]

Cassius. O Brutus!

Brutus. What's the matter?

Cassius. Have not you love enough to bear with me,
120 When that rash humor which my mother gave me
Makes me forgetful?

Brutus. Yes, Cassius, and from henceforth,
When you are over-earnest with your Brutus,
He'll think your mother chides, and leave you so.

[*Enter a* Poet, *followed by* Lucilius *and* Titinius, *who have been standing
guard at the door.*]

Poet. Let me go in to see the generals!
125 There is some grudge between 'em; 'tis not meet
They be alone.

Lucilius. You shall not come to them.

Poet. Nothing but death shall stay me.

Cassius. How now? What's the matter?

Poet. For shame, you generals! What do you mean?
130 Love and be friends, as two such men should be;
For I have seen more years, I'm sure, than ye.

Cassius. Ha, ha, how vilely doth this cynic[22] rhyme!

---

[20] scope . . . humor—freedom of expression. Do what you want, insults shall be taken as coming from a bad mood.

[21] you are . . . again—You are partnered with a mild man (Brutus himself), to whom anger is like fire to a flint. When the flint is struck against steel, it creates a spark but then cools immediately.

[22] cynic—rude fellow.

Brutus. Get you hence, sirrah. Saucy fellow, hence!

Cassius. Bear with him, Brutus. 'Tis his fashion.

135 **Brutus.** I'll know his humor when he knows his time.²³
    What should the wars do with these jigging fools?
    Companion, hence!

Cassius.   Away, away, begone! [*Exit* Poet.]

Brutus. Lucilius and Titinius, bid the commanders
    Prepare to lodge their companies tonight.

140 **Cassius.** And come yourselves, and bring Messala with you
    Immediately to us. [*Exit* Lucilius *and* Titinius.]

Brutus [*to* Lucius *within*]. Lucius, a bowl of wine.

Cassius. I did not think you could have been so angry.

Brutus. O Cassius, I am sick of many griefs.

145 **Cassius.** Of your philosophy you make no use
    If you give place to accidental evils.²⁴

Brutus. No man bears sorrow better. Portia is dead.

Cassius. Ha? Portia?

Brutus. She is dead.

150 **Cassius.** How scaped I killing when I crossed you so?²⁵
    O insupportable and touching loss!
    Upon what sickness?

Brutus.   Impatient of my absence,
    And grief that young Octavius with Mark Antony
    Have made themselves so strong—for with her death

155   That tidings came—with this she fell distract
    And, her attendants absent, swallowed fire.²⁶

Cassius. And died so?

Brutus.   Even so.

Cassius.   O ye immortal gods!

[*Enter* Lucius *with wine and tapers.*]

Brutus. Speak no more of her.—Give me a bowl of wine.—
    In this I bury all unkindness, Cassius.

[*He drinks.*]

---

²³ I'll know . . . time—I'll indulge his odd behavior when he knows the proper time for it.

²⁴ If you . . . evils—if you let chance misfortunes affect you. (Brutus seems not to act as a stoic philosopher should.)

²⁵ How scaped . . . so—How did I escape being killed when I angered you so badly?

²⁶ Impatient . . . fire—She was worried about my long absence and about Octavius and Anthony's having gained so much power. She became depressed, and when her servants were not around, she swallowed a hot coal.

160   **Cassius.** My heart is thirsty for that noble pledge.
         Fill, Lucius, till the wine o'erswell the cup;
         I cannot drink too much of Brutus' love.
    [*He drinks. Exit* Lucius.]
    [*Enter* Titinius *and* Messala.]
    Brutus. Come in, Titinius. Welcome, good Messala.
         Now sit we close about this taper here
         And call in question our necessities.[27]

165   [*They sit.*]
    Cassius. Portia, art thou gone?
    Brutus.   No more, I pray you.
         Messala, I have here receivèd letters
         That young Octavius and Mark Antony
         Come down upon us with a mighty power,
         Bending their expedition toward Philippi.

170   [*He shows letters.*]
    Messala. Myself have letters of the selfsame tenure.[28]
    Brutus. With what addition?
    Messala. That by proscription and bills of outlawry[29]
         Octavius, Antony, and Lepidus
         Have put to death an hundred senators.

175   **Brutus.** Therein our letters do not well agree;
         Mine speak of seventy senators that died
         By their proscriptions, Cicero being one.
    Cassius. Cicero one?
    Messala.   Cicero is dead,
180   And by that order of proscription.
         Had you your letters from your wife, my lord?
    Brutus. No, Messala.
    Messala. Nor nothing in your letters writ of her?[30]
    Brutus. Nothing, Messala.
    Messala.   That, methinks, is strange.

---

[27] call in . . . necessities—discuss what we must do.

[28] selfsame tenure—same meaning.

[29] proscription . . . outlawry—official statements that declare certain acts to be criminal.

[30] nothing . . . her—nothing written about her in the letters you've received.

185   **Brutus.** Why ask you? Hear you aught of her in yours?

         Messala. No, my lord.

         Brutus. Now, as you are a Roman, tell me true.

         Messala. Then like a Roman bear the truth I tell,

             For certain she is dead, and by strange manner.

190   **Brutus.** Why, farewell, Portia. We must die, Messala.

             With meditating that she must die once,[31]

             I have the patience to endure it now.

         Messala. Even so great men great losses should endure.

         Cassius. I have as much of this in art as you,

195   But yet my nature could not bear it so.

         Brutus. Well, to our work alive. What do you think

             Of marching to Philippi presently?

         Cassius. I do not think it good.

         Brutus.   Your reason?

         Cassius.   This it is:

             'Tis better that the enemy seek us.

200   So shall he waste his means, weary his soldiers,

             Doing himself offense,[32] whilst we, lying still,

             Are full of rest, defense, and nimbleness.

         Brutus. Good reasons must of force give place to better.

             The people twixt Philippi and this ground

205   Do stand but in a forced affection,

             For they have grudged us contribution.

             The enemy, marching along by them,

             By them shall make a fuller number up,

             Come on refreshed, new-added, and encouraged;

210   From which advantage shall we cut him off

             If at Philippi we do face him there,

             These people at our back.[33]

---

[31] With . . . once—by thinking about the fact that she must die sooner or later. Some editors think this was the original version of Portia's death and that Shakespeare later deleted it and wrote the version with Brutus and Cassius, preferring to show Brutus's humanity rather than his stoicism. The printer then set both by mistake.

[32] offense—harm.

[33] The people . . . back—The people between here and Philippi are friendly only because they have to be. They have given us aid grudgingly. If the enemy marches through, they may find willing recruits to increase their armies. But if we move to Philippi, we'll eliminate this advantage by keeping these unfriendly people behind us.

Brutus (John C. Vennema) is haunted by the ghost of Caesar (Edwin C. Owens) in this scene from the Guthrie Theatre production.

Cassius.   Hear me, good brother—

Brutus. Under your pardon. You must note besides

That we have tried the utmost[34] of our friends;

215   Our legions are brimful, our cause is ripe.

The enemy increaseth every day;

We, at the height, are ready to decline.

There is a tide in the affairs of men

Which, taken at the flood, leads on to fortune;

220   Omitted, all the voyage of their life

Is bound in shallows and in miseries.[35]

On such a full sea are we now afloat,

And we must take the current when it serves

Or lose our ventures.

Cassius.   Then, with your will, go on.

225   We'll along ourselves and meet them at Philippi.

Brutus. The deep of night is crept upon our talk,

And nature must obey necessity,

Which we will niggard[36] with a little rest.

There is no more to say?

Cassius.   No more. Good night.

230   Early tomorrow will we rise and hence.

Brutus. Lucius! [*Enter* Lucius.] My gown. [*Exit* Lucius.]

Farewell, good Messala.

Good night, Titinius. Noble, noble Cassius,

Good night, and good repose.[37]

Cassius.   O my dear brother!

235   This was an ill beginning of the night.

---

[34] tried the utmost—received everything we can expect.

[35] There is ... miseries—There is a time when action leads to success, the way a ship must sail at high tide or else be stuck in shallow water.

[36] niggard—stint.

[37] repose—rest.

Never come such division 'tween our souls!

Let it not, Brutus.

[*Enter* Lucius *with the dressing gown.*]

Brutus. Everything is well.

Cassius. Good night, my lord.

240 **Brutus.** Good night, good brother.

Titinius, Messala. Good night, Lord Brutus.

Brutus. Farewell, everyone.

[*Exit all but* Brutus *and* Lucius.]

Give me the gown. Where is thy instrument?

Lucius. Here in the tent.

Brutus. What, thou speak'st drowsily?

245 Poor knave, I blame thee not; thou art o'erwatched.[38]

Call Claudius and some other of my men;

I'll have them sleep on cushions in my tent.

Lucius. Varro and Claudius!

[*Enter* Varro *and* Claudius.]

Varro. Calls my lord?

250 **Brutus.** I pray you, sirs, lie in my tent and sleep.

It may be I shall raise you by and by

On business to my brother Cassius.

Varro. So please you, we will stand and watch your pleasure.

Brutus. I will not have it so. Lie down, good sirs.

255 It may be I shall otherwise bethink me.[39]

[Varro *and* Claudius *lie down.*]

Look, Lucius, here's the book I sought for so;

I put it in the pocket of my gown.

Lucius. I was sure your lordship did not give it me.

Brutus. Bear with me, good boy, I am much forgetful.

260 Canst thou hold up thy heavy eyes awhile

And touch thy instrument a strain or two?[40]

Lucius. Ay, my lord, an't please you.

---

[38] Poor knave . . . o'erwatched—Poor boy, I don't blame you; you are tired from lack of sleep.

[39] It may be . . . me—I may change my mind.

[40] touch . . . two—play a melody or two on your instrument.

Brutus.   It does, my boy.
  I trouble thee too much, but thou art willing.

Lucius. It is my duty, sir.

265 **Brutus.** I should not urge thy duty past thy might;
  I know young bloods look for a time of rest.

Lucius. I have slept, my lord, already.

Brutus. It was well done, and thou shalt sleep again;
  I will not hold thee long. If I do live,
270   I will be good to thee.

[*Music, and a song.* Lucius *falls asleep.*]
  This is a sleepy tune. O murderous slumber,
  Layest thou thy leaden mace[41] upon my boy,
  That plays thee music? Gentle knave, good night;
  I will not do thee so much wrong to wake thee.
275   If thou dost nod, thou break'st thy instrument;
  I'll take it from thee. And, good boy, good night.

[*He removes* Lucius's *instrument, and begins to read.*]
  Let me see, let me see; is not the leaf turned down
  Where I left reading? Here it is, I think.

[*Enter the* Ghost of Caesar.]
  How ill this taper burns! Ha! Who comes here?
280   I think it is the weakness of mine eyes
  That shapes this monstrous apparition.
  It comes upon me.—Art thou any thing?
  Art thou some god, some angel, or some devil,
  That mak'st my blood cold and my hair to stare?[42]
285   Speak to me what thou art.

Ghost. Thy evil spirit, Brutus.

Brutus.   Why com'st thou?

Ghost. To tell thee thou shalt see me at Philippi.

Brutus. Well, then I shall see thee again?

Ghost. Ay, at Philippi.

---

[41] leaden mace—heavy staff of office used by a sheriff to touch the shoulder of someone being placed under arrest.

[42] stare—stand on end.

	Brutus. Why, I will see thee at Philippi, then. [Ghost *exits*.]
290	Now I have taken heart, thou vanishest.
	Ill spirit, I would hold more talk with thee.—
	Boy, Lucius! Varro! Claudius! Sirs, awake!
	Claudius!
295	Lucius. The strings, my lord, are false.[43]
	Brutus. He thinks he still is at his instrument.
	Lucius, awake!
	Lucius. My lord?
	Brutus. Didst thou dream, Lucius, that thou so criedst out?
300	Lucius. My lord, I do not know that I did cry.
	Brutus. Yes, that thou didst. Didst thou see anything?
	Lucius. Nothing, my lord.
	Brutus. Sleep again, Lucius. Sirrah Claudius!
	[*To* Varro.] Fellow thou, awake!
	Varro. My lord?
	Claudius. My lord?
	[*They get up.*]
305	Brutus. Why did you so cry out, sirs, in your sleep?
	Varro, Claudius. Did we, my lord?
	Brutus. Ay. Saw you anything?
	Varro. No, my lord, I saw nothing.
	Claudius. Nor I, my lord.
	Brutus. Go and commend me to my brother Cassius.
	Bid him set on his powers betimes before,[44]
310	And we will follow.
	Varro, Claudius. It shall be done, my lord.
	[*They exit.*]

---

[43] false—out of tune.

[44] Bid . . . before—Tell him to get his army moving early in the morning.

Act Five, Scene One

On the plains of Philippi in Macedonia, some days later, the army of Mark Antony and Octavius meets the forces of Brutus and Cassius. The four leaders exchange insults and taunts. Cassius tells Messala about his fears. Then Brutus and Cassius say goodbye in case they are killed in battle.

Enter Octavius, Mark Antony, *and their army.*

Octavius. Now, Antony, our hopes are answerèd.
　　　You said the enemy would not come down,
　　　But keep the hills and upper regions.
　　　It proves not so. Their battles are at hand;
5　　They mean to warn us[1] at Philippi here,
　　　Answering before we do demand of them.
Antony. Tut, I am in their bosoms, and I know
　　　Wherefore they do it.[2] They could be content
　　　To visit other places, and come down
10　　With fearful bravery, thinking by this face
　　　To fasten in our thoughts that they have courage;
　　　But 'tis not so.[3]
[*Enter a* Messenger.]
Messenger. Prepare you, generals.
　　　The enemy comes on in gallant show.
15　　Their bloody sign of battle[4] is hung out,
　　　And something to be done immediately.
Antony. Octavius, lead your battle softly on
　　　Upon the left hand of the even field.
Octavius. Upon the right hand, I. Keep thou the left.
20　**Antony.** Why do you cross me in this exigent?[5]

---

[1] battles . . . warn us—forces are near; they intend to challenge us.

[2] I am . . . do it—I know their secrets, and I know why they do it.

[3] thinking . . . not so—thinking they will convince us with this show that they have courage when they don't.

[4] bloody sign of battle—red battle flag.

[5] exigent—critical moment.

Octavius. I do not cross you, but I will do so.

[*March.*]

[*Drum. Enter* Brutus, Cassius, *and their army;* Lucilius, Titinius, Messala, *and others.*]

Brutus. They stand and would have parley.[6]

Cassius. Stand fast, Titinius. We must out and talk.

Octavius. Mark Antony, shall we give sign of battle?

25 **Antony.** No, Caesar, we will answer on their charge.

    Make forth.[7] The generals would have some words.

Octavius [*to his officers*]. Stir not until the signal.

[Brutus, Cassius, Octavius, *and* Antony *meet.*]

Brutus. Words before blows. Is it so, countrymen?

Octavius. Not that we love words better, as you do.

30 **Brutus.** Good words are better than bad strokes, Octavius.

Antony. In your bad strokes, Brutus, you give good words.

    Witness the hole you made in Caesar's heart,

    Crying "Long live! Hail, Caesar!"

Cassius.   Antony,

    The posture of your blows are yet unknown;

35   But for your words, they rob the Hybla bees,

    And leave them honeyless.[8]

Antony. Not stingless too?

Brutus. O, yes, and soundless too.

    For you have stolen their buzzing, Antony,

40   And very wisely threat before you sting.

Antony. Villains! You did not so when your vile daggers

    Hacked one another in the sides of Caesar.

    You showed your teeth like apes, and fawned like hounds,

    And bowed like bondmen, kissing Caesar's feet,

45   Whilst damned Casca, like a cur, behind,

    Struck Caesar on the neck.[9] O you flatterers!

---

[6] parley—conference.

[7] answer . . . Make forth—respond when they attack. Go forward.

[8] The posture . . . honeyless—We don't know yet how effective you'll be as a soldier, but your words are sweeter than the famous honey from Hybla, in Sicily.

[9] You showed . . . neck—You acted like loving pets and slaves to Caesar's face, while Casca, like a dog, struck Caesar in the back.

In the Hartford Stage Company production, Antony (Tom Hewitt, left) and Octavius (Sheridan Crist) prepare to lead their army into battle.

Cassius. Flatterers? Now, Brutus, thank yourself!
    This tongue had not offended so today
    If Cassius might have ruled.[10]
50   **Octavius.** Come, come, the cause. If arguing make us sweat,
    The proof of it will turn to redder drops.[11]
    Look, [*He draws his sword.*]
    I draw a sword against conspirators.
    When think you that the sword goes up again?

---

[10] This tongue . . . ruled—Antony wouldn't be insulting us if you had let me have my way (and killed Antony when we killed Caesar).

[11] Come . . . drops—Let's get to the business at hand. We will settle this argument by shedding blood in battle.

The storm is up,
and all is on the hazard.

55   Never, till Caesar's three-and-thirty wounds
Be well avenged, or till another Caesar
Have added slaughter to the sword of traitors.[12]
Brutus. Caesar, thou canst not die by traitors' hands,
Unless thou bring'st them with thee.[13]
60   **Octavius.** So I hope.
I was not born to die on Brutus' sword.
Brutus. O, if thou wert the noblest of thy strain,
Young man, thou couldst not die more honorable.
Cassius. A peevish schoolboy, worthless of such honor,
65   Joined with a masker and a reveler!
Antony. Old Cassius still!
Octavius.   Come, Antony, away!—
Defiance, traitors, hurl we in your teeth.
If you dare fight today, come to the field;
If not, when you have stomachs.[14]
[*Exit* Octavius, Antony, *and army.*]
70   **Cassius.** Why, now blow wind, swell billow, and swim bark!
The storm is up, and all is on the hazard.[15]
Brutus. Ho, Lucilius! Hark, a word with you.
Lucilius [*steps forward*]. My lord?
[Brutus *and* Lucilius *speak apart.*]
Cassius. Messala!
75   **Messala** [*steps forward*]. What says my general?
Cassius.   Messala,
This is my birthday; as this very day
Was Cassius born. Give me thy hand, Messala.
Be thou my witness that against my will,

---

[12] till another . . . traitors—until a second Caesar (Octavius himself) has also been killed by the traitors.

[13] Caesar . . . with thee—Octavius, the only way you'll die by a traitor's hands is if you kill yourself.

[14] stomachs—enough nerve; courage.

[15] on the hazard—at stake.

As Pompey was, am I compelled to set
80 Upon one battle all our liberties.
You know that I held Epicurus[16] strong
And his opinion. Now I change my mind
And partly credit things that do presage.[17]
Coming from Sardis, on our former ensign
85 Two mighty eagles fell, and there they perched,
Gorging and feeding from our soldiers' hands,
Who to Philippi here consorted us.[18]
This morning are they fled away and gone,
And in their steads do ravens, crows, and kites
90 Fly o'er our heads and downward look on us
As we were sickly prey. Their shadows seem
A canopy most fatal, under which
Our army lies, ready to give up the ghost.

Messala. Believe not so.

Cassius.   I but believe it partly,
95 For I am fresh of spirit and resolved
To meet all perils very constantly.[19]

Brutus. Even so, Lucilius. [*He rejoins* Cassius.]

Cassius.   Now, most noble Brutus,
The gods today stand friendly, that we may,
Lovers in peace, lead on our days to age!
100 But since the affairs of men rest still incertain,
Let's reason with the worst that may befall.
If we do lose this battle, then is this
The very last time we shall speak together.
What are you then determinèd to do?

105 **Brutus.** Even by the rule of that philosophy
By which I did blame Cato[20] for the death
Which he did give himself—I know not how,

---

[16] Epicurus—Epicurus was a Greek philosopher who did not believe in omens or fortunetelling.

[17] presage—tell the future.

[18] Two mighty . . . us—Two eagles perched on the foremost flag and fed from the hands of the soldiers who came with us.

[19] constantly—boldly.

[20] Cato—Brutus' father-in-law, who killed himself to avoid submitting to Caesar.

But I do find it cowardly and vile,
For fear of what might fall, so to prevent

110   The time of life[21]—arming myself with patience
To stay the providence of some high powers
That govern us below.

Cassius.   Then, if we lose this battle,
You are contented to be led in triumph[22]
Through the streets of Rome?

115   **Brutus.** No, Cassius, no. Think not, thou noble Roman,
That ever Brutus will go bound to Rome;
He bears too great a mind. But this same day
Must end that work the ides of March begun.
And whether we shall meet again I know not;

120   Therefore our everlasting farewell take.
Forever, and forever, farewell, Cassius!
If we do meet again, why, we shall smile;
If not, why then this parting was well made.

Cassius. Forever, and forever, farewell, Brutus!

125   If we do meet again, we'll smile indeed.
If not, 'tis true this parting was well made.

Brutus. Why then, lead on. O, that a man might know
The end of this day's business ere it come!
But it sufficeth that the day will end,

130   And then the end is known.—Come, ho, away!

[*All exit.*]

---

[21] prevent . . . life—to cut your life short.

[22] led in triumph—led as a captive in the victor's procession.

Act Five, Scene Two

***On the battlefield, later that day, Brutus,
because he thinks Octavius is faltering, sends
Messala with a message to Cassius to attack
at once.***

Alarum.[1] Enter Brutus *and* Messala.

Brutus. Ride, ride, Messala, ride, and give these bills
    Unto the legions on the other side.[2]
[*He hands him written orders.*]
[*Loud alarum.*]
    Let them set on at once; for I perceive
    But cold demeanor in Octavio's wing,
5   And sudden push gives them the overthrow.[3]
    Ride, ride, Messala! Let them all come down.
[*They exit separately.*]

---

[1] Alarum—sounds of battle, such as trumpet calls and shouts.

[2] give . . . side—give these orders to our soldiers on the other side of the field.

[3] I perceive . . . overthrow—I sense a lack of courage in Octavius' army, and if we rush them, we can overthrow them.

Act Five, Scene Three

On another part of the battlefield, soon after, Cassius sends Titinius to find out whether the soldiers he sees are friends or enemies. Pindarus reports that Titinius has been captured. Cassius frees Pindarus from slavery on condition that he help Cassius commit suicide.

Cassius dies on the sword he had used to kill Caesar. When Titinius finds Cassius's body, he kills himself with Cassius's sword. Brutus comes from a victory over Octavius's army. He mourns the two who have died, but anticipates a second battle.

Alarums. Enter Cassius *and* Titinius.

Cassius. O, look, Titinius, look, the villains fly!
Myself have to mine own turned enemy.
This ensign here of mine was turning back;
I slew the coward and did take it from him.[1]

5 **Titinius.** O Cassius, Brutus gave the word too early,
Who, having some advantage on Octavius,
Took it too eagerly. His soldiers fell to spoil,[2]
Whilst we by Antony are all enclosed.

[*Enter* Pindarus.]

Pindarus. Fly further off, my lord, fly further off!
10 Mark Antony is in your tents, my lord.
Fly, therefore, noble Cassius, fly far off.

Cassius. This hill is far enough. Look, look, Titinius:
Are those my tents where I perceive the fire?

Titinius. They are, my lord.

Cassius. Titinius, if thou lovest me,
15 Mount thou my horse, and hide thy spurs in him
Till he have brought thee up to yonder troops
And here again, that I may rest assured
Whether yond troops are friend or enemy.

Titinius. I will be here again even with a thought.[3] [*Exit* Titinius.]

---

[1] villains . . . from him—My cowardly soldiers are running away. I have become an enemy to my own men. My flag-bearer was running away, so I killed him and took the flag from him.

[2] fell to spoil—started looting (instead of fighting).

[3] even . . . thought—as fast as you can think of it.

20   **Cassius.** Go, Pindarus, get higher on that hill.

         My sight was ever thick.[4] Regard Titinius,

         And tell me what thou not'st about the field.

[Pindarus *goes up.*]

         This day I breathèd first. Time is come round,

         And where I did begin, there shall I end.

25   My life is run his compass.[5]—Sirrah, what news?

Pindarus [*above*]. O my lord!

Cassius. What news?

Pindarus [*above*]. Titinius is enclosèd round about

         With horsemen, that make to him on the spur,

30   Yet he spurs on. Now they are almost on him.

         Now, Titinius! Now some light.[6] O, he

         Lights too. He's ta'en. [*Shout.*] And hark! They shout for joy.

Cassius. Come down, behold no more.

         O coward that I am, to live so long

35   To see my best friend ta'en before my face!

[*Enter* Pindarus *from above.*]

         Come hither, sirrah.

         In Parthia did I take thee prisoner,

         And then I swore thee, saving of thy life,

         That whatsoever I did bid thee do

40   Thou shouldst attempt it. Come now, keep thine oath;

         Now be a freeman, and with this good sword,

         That ran through Caesar's bowels, search this bosom.

         Stand not to answer.[7] Here, take thou the hilts,

         And when my face is covered, as 'tis now,

45   Guide thou the sword. [Pindarus *does so.*]

---

[4] my . . . thick—I have always been nearsighted.

[5] This day . . . compass—Today is my birthday. I shall end where I began. My life has come full circle.

[6] light—alight, dismount.

[7] In Parthia . . . answer—I captured you in Parthia (now northern Iran) and saved your life by making you my slave. You swore to do whatever I asked. Keep your word now. Become a free man by killing me with this sword that killed Caesar. Don't argue.

Brutus (Will Lyman) finds the dead Cassius (Jeremiah Kissel) in this
scene from the Commonwealth Shakespeare Company production.

      Caesar, thou art revenged,
      Even with the sword that killed thee. [*He dies.*]
Pindarus. So, I am free, yet would not so have been,
      Durst I have done my will.[8] O Cassius!
50   Far from this country Pindarus shall run,
      Where never Roman shall take note of him. [*Exit* Pindarus.]
[*Enter* Titinius, *wearing a garland of laurel, and* Messala.]
Messala. It is but change,[9] Titinius; for Octavius
      Is overthrown by noble Brutus' power,
      As Cassius' legions are by Antony.
55   **Titinius.** These tidings will well comfort Cassius.
Messala. Where did you leave him?
Titinius.   All disconsolate,
      With Pindarus his bondman, on this hill.

---

[8] So . . . will—I am free, but I wouldn't be if I had done what I wanted (and refused to kill Cassius).
[9] change—even exchange.

Messala. Is not that he that lies upon the ground?

Titinius. He lies not like the living. O my heart!

60 Messala. Is not that he?

Titinius.   No, this was he, Messala,
    But Cassius is no more. O setting sun,
    As in thy red rays thou dost sink to night,
    So in his red blood Cassius' day is set.
    The sun of Rome is set. Our day is gone;
65   Clouds, dews, and dangers come; our deeds are done.
    Mistrust of my success[10] hath done this deed.

Messala. Mistrust of good success hath done this deed.
    O hateful Error, Melancholy's child,
    Why dost thou show to the apt thoughts of men
70   The things that are not? O Error, soon conceived,
    Thou never com'st unto a happy birth,
    But killst the mother that engendered thee.[11]

Titinius. What, Pindarus! Where art thou, Pindarus?

Messala. Seek him, Titinius, whilst I go to meet
75   The noble Brutus, thrusting this report
    Into his ears. I may say "thrusting" it,
    For piercing steel and darts envenomèd[12]
    Shall be as welcome to the ears of Brutus
    As tidings of this sight.

Titinius.   Hie you, Messala,
80   And I will seek for Pindarus the while.

[*Exit* Messala.]

    Why didst thou send me forth, brave Cassius?
    Did I not meet thy friends? And did not they
    Put on my brows this wreath of victory
    And bid me give it thee? Didst thou not hear their shouts?
85   Alas, thou hast **misconstrued**[13] everything.
    But, hold thee, take this garland on thy brow.

[*He places the garland on* Cassius's *head.*]

---

[10] Mistrust . . . success—Cassius's lack of confidence in my success.

[11] O hateful . . . thee—Why are melancholy (depressed) people so easily impressed by mistaken thoughts? A mistake is easily made, but kills the melancholy person who conceived it.

[12] envenomèd—poisoned.

[13] **misconstrued**—misunderstood.

Thy Brutus bid me give it thee, and I
Will do his bidding. Brutus, come apace
And see how I regarded Caius Cassius.

90 By your leave, gods! This is a Roman's part.[14]
Come, Cassius' sword, and find Titinius's heart.

[*He stabs himself and dies.*]

[*Enter* Brutus, Messala, *young* Cato, Strato, Volumnius, *and* Lucilius.]

Brutus. Where, where, Messala, doth his body lie?

Messala. Lo, yonder, and Titinius mourning it.

Brutus. Titinius's face is upward.

Cato. He is slain.

95 **Brutus.** O Julius Caesar, thou art mighty yet!
Thy spirit walks abroad and turns our swords
In our own proper entrails.

[*Low alarums.*]

Cato. Brave Titinius!
Look whe'er he have not crowned dead Cassius.

Brutus. Are yet two Romans living such as these?

100 The last of all the Romans, fare thee well!
It is impossible that ever Rome
Should breed thy fellow.[15] Friends, I owe more tears
To this dead man than you shall see me pay.—
I shall find time, Cassius, I shall find time.—

105 Come, therefore, and to Thasos[16] send his body.
His funerals shall not be in our camp,
Lest it discomfort us.[17] Lucilius, come,
And come, young Cato, let us to the field.
Labeo and Flavius set our battles on.

110 'Tis three o'clock, and, Romans, yet ere night
We shall try fortune in a second fight.

[*They exit with the bodies.*]

---

[14] This ... part—This (killing myself) is the proper thing for a brave Roman to do.

[15] fellow—equal.

[16] Thasos—island near Philippi.

[17] Lest ... us—because Cassius's funeral rites might discourage our soldiers.

Act Five, Scene Four

In another part of the battlefield, soon after, young Cato is killed. Lucilius is captured and says he is Brutus. Then he tells Antony that Brutus will never be taken alive.

Alarum. Enter Brutus, Messala, Cato, Lucilius, *and* Flavius.

Brutus. Yet, countrymen, O, yet hold up your heads!
[*Exit* Brutus, *followed by* Messala *and* Flavius.]
Cato. What bastard doth not?[1] Who will go with me?
    I will proclaim my name about the field:
    I am the son of Marcus Cato,[2] ho!
5   A foe to tyrants, and my country's friend.
    I am the son of Marcus Cato, ho!
[*Enter* Soldiers, *and they fight.*]
Lucilius. And I am Brutus, Marcus Brutus I!
    Brutus, my country's friend! Know me for Brutus!
[*Young* Cato *is slain by* Antony's *men.*]
    O young and noble Cato, art thou down?
10   Why, now thou diest as bravely as Titinius,
    And mayst be honored, being Cato's son.
First Soldier [*capturing* Lucilius]. Yield,[3] or thou diest.
Lucilius [*offering money*]. Only I yield to die.
    There is so much that thou wilt kill me straight;
15   Kill Brutus, and be honored in his death.[4]
First Soldier. We must not. A noble prisoner!
Second Soldier. Room, ho! Tell Antony, Brutus is ta'en.
[*Enter* Antony.]
First Soldier. I'll tell the news. Here comes the general—
    Brutus is ta'en, Brutus is ta'en, my lord.

---

[1] What . . . not—Who is so low that he would not do so?

[2] Marcus Cato—Portia's father, a highly respected Roman.

[3] Yield—surrender.

[4] There . . . death—This money is for you, if you will kill me immediately. If you kill Brutus, you will win honor for it. (Lucilius pretends to be Brutus and fools the soldiers.)

Antony. Where is he?

Lucilius. Safe, Antony, Brutus is safe enough.
I dare assure thee that no enemy
Shall ever take alive the noble Brutus.
The gods defend him from so great a shame!
When you do find him, or alive or dead,
He will be found like Brutus, like himself.

Antony [*to* First Soldier]. This is not Brutus, friend, but, I assure you,
A prize no less in worth. Keep this man safe;
Give him all kindness. I had rather have
Such men my friends than enemies.—Go on,
And see whe'er Brutus be alive or dead;
And bring us word unto Octavius' tent
How everything is chanced.[5]

[*They exit separately, some bearing* Cato's *body.*]

---

[5] is chanced—turns out.

Act Five, Scene Five

In another part of the battlefield, soon after, Brutus and his men attempt to rest, but fighting breaks out again. Facing defeat, Brutus urges the others to escape. He asks three men in turn to kill him. Each refuses. Finally Strato agrees to hold the sword and Brutus kills himself on it. The victorious Antony and Octavius promise honorable burial rites for Brutus.

Enter Brutus, Dardanius, Clitus, Strato, *and* Volumnius.

Brutus. Come, poor remains of friends, rest on this rock.
[*He sits.*]
Clitus. Statilius showed the torchlight, but, my lord,
    He came not back. He is or ta'en or slain.[1]
Brutus. Sit thee down, Clitus. Slaying is the word.

5   It is a deed in fashion. Hark thee, Clitus.
[*He whispers.*]
Clitus. What, I, my lord? No, not for all the world.
Brutus. Peace then. No words.
Clitus.   I'll rather kill myself.
Brutus. Hark thee, Dardanius. [*He whispers.*]
Dardanius.   Shall I do such a deed?
[Dardanius *and* Clitus *move away from* Brutus.]
Clitus. O Dardanius!

10   **Dardanius.** O Clitus!
Clitus. What ill request did Brutus make to thee?
Dardanius. To kill him, Clitus. Look, he meditates.
Clitus. Now is that noble vessel full of grief,
    That it runs over even at his eyes.

15   **Brutus.** Come hither, good Volumnius. List[2] a word.
Volumnius. What says my lord?
Brutus.   Why, this, Volumnius:
    The ghost of Caesar hath appeared to me
    Two several times by night; at Sardis once,

---

[1] Statilius . . . slain—Statilius signaled with his torch that all was well at our camp, but since he hasn't come back, he must have been either captured or killed.

[2] List—listen to.

And this last night here in Philippi fields.
20   I know my hour is come.
Volumnius.   Not so, my lord.
Brutus. Nay, I am sure it is, Volumnius.
          Thou seest the world, Volumnius, how it goes;
          Our enemies have beat us to the pit.[3]
[Low alarums.]
          It is more worthy to leap in ourselves
25   Than tarry till they push us.[4] Good Volumnius,
          Thou know'st that we two went to school together.
          Even for that, our love of old, I prithee,
          Hold thou my sword-hilts whilst I run on it.
Volumnius. That's not an office for a friend, my lord.
[Alarums still.]
30 **Clitus.** Fly, fly, my lord! There is no tarrying here.
Brutus. Farewell to you, and you, and you, Volumnius.
          Strato, thou hast been all this while asleep;
          Farewell to thee too, Strato. Countrymen,
          My heart doth joy that yet in all my life
35   I found no man but he was true to me.
          I shall have glory by this losing day
          More than Octavius and Mark Antony
          By this vile conquest shall attain unto.[5]
          So fare you well at once, for Brutus' tongue
40   Hath almost ended his life's history.
          Night hangs upon mine eyes; my bones would rest,
          That have but labored to attain this hour.
[Alarums. Cry within, "Fly, fly, fly!"]
Clitus. Fly, my lord, fly!
Brutus.   Hence, I will follow.
[Exit Clitus, Dardanius, and Volumnius.]
          I prithee, Strato, stay thou by thy lord.
45   Thou art a fellow of a good respect;
          Thy life hath had some smatch[6] of honor in it.

---

[3] the pit—trap for hunted animals; also, a grave.

[4] It is . . . us—It is more honorable to kill ourselves than to wait until they kill us.

[5] attain unto—win; achieve.

[6] smatch—touch, small amount.

Brutus (Justin Deas, right) prepares to commit suicide at the close of the Hartford Stage Company production.

Hold then my sword, and turn away thy face,
While I do run upon it. Wilt thou, Strato?

Strato. Give me your hand first. Fare you well, my lord.

50 **Brutus.** Farewell, good Strato. [*He runs on his sword.*]

Caesar, now be still.

I killed not thee with half so good a will.

[*Dies.*]

[*Alarum. Retreat. Enter* Antony *and* Octavius *with* Messala *and* Lucilius *as prisoners. The army follows.*]

Octavius. What man is that?

Messala. My master's man. Strato, where is thy master?

55 **Strato.** Free from the bondage you are in, Messala.

The conquerors can but make a fire of him,

For Brutus only overcame himself,[7]

And no man else hath honor by his death.

---

[7] Brutus . . . himself—only Brutus conquered Brutus.

This was the noblest Roman of them all.

Lucilius. So Brutus should be found. I thank thee, Brutus,
60   That thou hast proved Lucilius' saying true.[8]
Octavius. All that served Brutus, I will entertain them.[9]
  Fellow, wilt thou bestow thy time with[10] me?
Strato. Ay, if Messala will prefer[11] me to you.
Octavius. Do so, good Messala.
65 **Messala.** How died my master, Strato?
Strato. I held the sword, and he did run on it.
Messala. Octavius, then take him to follow thee,
  That did the latest service to my master.
Antony. This was the noblest Roman of them all.
70   All the conspirators save only he
  Did that they did in envy of great Caesar;
  He only in a general honest thought
  And common good to all made one of them.
  His life was gentle, and the elements
75   So mixed in him[12] that Nature might stand up
  And say to all the world, "This was a man!"
Octavius. According to his virtue let us use him,[13]
  With all respect and rites of burial.
  Within my tent his bones tonight shall lie,
80   Most like a soldier, ordered honorably.
  So call the field[14] to rest, and let's away
  To part[15] the glories of this happy day.
  [*All exit with* Brutus's *body.*]

---

[8] proved . . . true—proved me correct in saying that you would never be taken alive.

[9] All . . . them—All Brutus's men can join my army.

[10] bestow thy time with—join.

[11] prefer—recommend.

[12] He only . . . him—He only had an honorable concern for the good of the commonwealth. His life was noble, and his qualities so balanced.

[13] According . . . him—Let us treat him as he deserves.

[14] field—armies.

[15] part—divide up.

Understanding the Play

Act One

1. In Scene One, what political conflicts are established immediately?

2. In Scene Two, how is Julius Caesar characterized by what he says and does, by what other characters report him saying and doing, and by others' opinions of him?

3. In Scene Three, what extraordinary things are happening in nature? What do the characters make of them?

4. Why do Cinna, Cassius, and Casca want Brutus to join their cause? How do they plan to win him over?

Act Two

1. In Scene One, what conclusions does Brutus come to on his own?

2. How does Portia try to persuade Brutus to confide in her? How well does she succeed?

3. In Scene Two, what is Calpurnia worried about?

4. What finally changes Caesar's mind and persuades him to go to the Senate?

Act Three

1. In Scene One, at what point does Caesar stop trying to avoid the conspirators' knives? Why?

2. What arrangement does Mark Antony make with the conspirators? What are his real plans?

3. In Scene Two, how does Brutus explain Caesar's assassination to the crowd?

4. In his funeral oration, how does Mark Antony manage to work the crowd up into a riotous frenzy?

5. How does Scene Three demonstrate the current state of affairs in Rome?

Act Four

1. In Scene One, how do Antony, Octavius, and Lepidus seem to be performing as the new leaders of Rome?

2. What indication is given in Scene Two that the relationship between Brutus and Cassius is troubled?

3. In Scene Three, what is the basis of the argument between Brutus and Cassius? How do they become reconciled?

4. What does the reaction of Brutus to Portia's death suggest about him?

5. What seems to be foreshadowed by the appearance of Caesar's ghost?

Act Five

1. What seems to be the purpose of the meeting between Brutus, Cassius, Antony, and Octavius in Scene One?

2. How does Brutus answer Cassius's question about what he will do if they lose the battle?

3. In Scene Two, what tactical decision does Brutus make? What results from this decision in Scene Three?

4. What misunderstanding results in Cassius's death?

5. Why does Brutus kill himself in Scene Five?

6. How does Mark Antony distinguish Brutus from the other conspirators?

Analyzing the Play

1. What do Brutus and the others hope to accomplish with Caesar's assassination? What really happens?

2. How do the members of the crowd act as a single character in Act One, Scenes One and Two, and in Act Three, Scenes One, Two, and Three?

3. In Act Five, Scene Three, Titinius says, "This is a Roman's part" before killing himself. What does he mean? Whose deaths are explained by this philosophy?

4. In your opinion, which character would have made the best leader of Rome, if he had no opposition? Why?

5. Some readers have thought that Brutus is the real tragic hero of *Julius Caesar*. What evidence is there to support this view? What do you think?

Writing Projects

1. Write a character sketch of Brutus. Include his strengths and weaknesses and explain how they are revealed through his speeches and actions.

2. Write an essay discussing the uses and abuses of power in *Julius Caesar*. How Is power gained or lost? In which cases is power used for good? for bad? What effect does power have on those in authority? on those being ruled?

3. Write a news story for a radio or television news program covering Caesar's assassination in the Senate. Be sure to include the five W's of journalism: who, what, where, when, and why.

4. Artemidorus tries to warn Caesar about the conspiracy, but he picks a bad time and place. Imagine yourself as one of the characters in the play or another character you create. Write a scene in which you warn Caesar.

5. Suppose you were a journalist in Caesar's day and yet had the freedom of speech we enjoy today. Write a newspaper editorial giving your opinions on Julius Caesar as ruler of Rome and your reasons for them.

Performance Projects

1. In Shakespeare's day, *Julius Caesar* was staged against the unchanging background of the Globe playhouse. Since then, it has been staged with completely realistic sets, with almost bare stages, and with many other designs in between. Design a stage setting for *Julius Caesar* and prepare a brief rationale explaining how your setting would accommodate the various places and actions of the play.

2. Mark Antony's funeral oration is one of the most famous speeches in theater. Rehearse this speech out loud, planning carefully for pauses and inflections, particularly on the words "honorable man." Present the speech for an audience of your classmates.

3. Women don't have much to do in *Julius Caesar*, but Portia's speech to Brutus in Act Two, Scene One, offers an opportunity for thoughtful interpretation and a range of emotions. Rehearse the speech out loud and present it for an audience of your classmates.

4. The staging of Caesar's assassination in Act Three, Scene One, requires careful planning, for there are many people onstage, and yet the main actions must be clear. Draw up a stage plan and, using symbols for characters, plan the movements of all the characters up to Caesar's death.

Great Shakespearean Characters

Shakespeare filled his plays with vivid, memorable characters. Many of them, such as Richard III, Cleopatra, and Macbeth, were historical figures; but Shakespeare's version of them is what endures. His invented people serve as models to which we compare our real-life experience of human nature: young lovers remind us of Romeo and Juliet; someone full of self-doubt recalls Hamlet. Here are some of Shakespeare's best-known characters.

▲
Shakespeare often used clowns to comment on the folly of other characters in his plays. Here, Gregory Hines plays the jester Feste in a 1989 production of *Twelfth Night* at the New York Shakespeare Festival.

Shakespeare's Shylock is a Jewish moneylender determined to revenge himself on the Christians that have mistreated him. In another playwright's hands, he would have been simply a villain; Shakespeare turned him into a tragic figure. Here, Shylock (Dustin Hoffman) argues points of law with Portia (Geraldine James), a young woman disguised as a man, in a 1989 Broadway production of *The Merchant of Venice.*

▲
Queen Elizabeth so enjoyed Shakespeare's great comic character Sir John Falstaff in the two *Henry IV* plays that she commanded him to write another play showing Sir John in love, which Shakespeare did in *The Merry Wives of Windsor.* This painting shows the English actor Ralph Richardson (1902–1983) in the role of Falstaff.

 The historical Richard III was an ambitious, but effective ruler during his short reign. He may have had some slight physical deformity. Shakespeare's version of Richard as a hunchback and a monster is what everyone remembers. Here, Denzel Washington played him in a 1990 production of *Richard III* at the New York Shakespeare Festival.

The real hero of Shakespeare's *Julius Caesar* is Brutus, who even his enemy Mark Antony praises as "the noblest Roman of them all." James Mason played Brutus in the 1952 film version of *Julius Caesar.*
▼

▲
The quick-witted Rosalind, heroine of the comedy *As You Like It,* is one of Shakespeare's most attractive characters. Gwyneth Paltrow played her in a 1999 production at the Williamstown Theatre Festival.

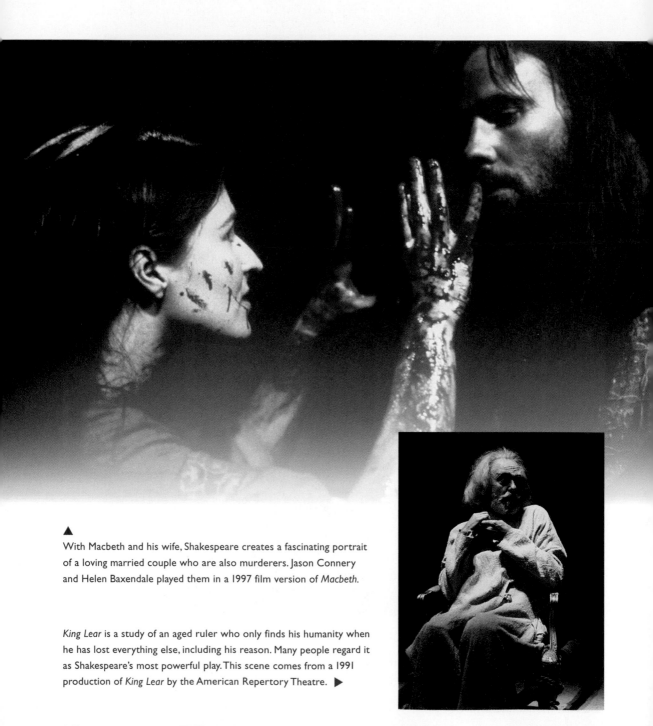

▲

With Macbeth and his wife, Shakespeare creates a fascinating portrait of a loving married couple who are also murderers. Jason Connery and Helen Baxendale played them in a 1997 film version of *Macbeth*.

King Lear is a study of an aged ruler who only finds his humanity when he has lost everything else, including his reason. Many people regard it as Shakespeare's most powerful play. This scene comes from a 1991 production of *King Lear* by the American Repertory Theatre. ▶

Although he is a spoilsport whom the other characters detest, audiences have always enjoyed Malvolio, the self-important steward in Shakespeare's comedy *Twelfth Night*. Seth McClellan played him in a 2000 production of the play at the Hartt School at the University of Hartford. ▶

Among Shakespeare's most popular characters are Beatrice and Benedick, lovers who quarrel their way through a screwball romance in *Much Ado About Nothing*. In this 1999 production at the Long Wharf Theatre, Michael Genet plays Benedick and Caroline Clay plays Beatrice.
▼

◀ The mysterious motives of Iago, Shakespeare's villain in *Othello,* fascinate audiences, who find him at least as interesting as the hero he destroys. Jose Ferrer played Iago and Paul Robeson played Othello in a 1942 Broadway production of Shakespeare's tragedy.

▲
Claire Danes and Leonardo DiCaprio played Shakespeare's immortal lovers in a 1996 film version of *Romeo and Juliet.*

Shakespeare's most famous character is Hamlet, who has become a kind of modern everyman figure. Mark Rylance played him in a 2000 production at London's Globe Theatre.

Prospero, the magician who abandons magic in Shakespeare's final play, *The Tempest,* has often been viewed as a symbol of the playwright himself, bidding farewell to his art. Arnold Moss played Prospero and Vera Zorina played Ariel, the spirit who serves him, in a 1945 Broadway production.

▲
Shakespeare gave Caliban, a half-human monster in *The Tempest,* some of the most beautiful and moving lines in the play. Jack Willis played Caliban in a 1995 production at the American Repertory Theatre.

◄ "Age cannot wither her," says another character of Shakespeare's Cleopatra, "or custom stale her infinite variety." Vanessa Redgrave played Cleopatra in a 1996 production of *Antony and Cleopatra* at Houston's Alley Theatre.

Twelfth Night, or What You Will

Introduction

Twelfth Night is the Christian feast of the Epiphany on January 6, the twelfth day after Christmas. For Christians, this marks the day when the three Magi, or "wise men" from the East, brought gifts to the infant Jesus at Bethlehem. Twelfth Night also traditionally marks the end of the Christmas season. In giving this title to his play, Shakespeare was not so much alluding to the feast itself as invoking the mood of the entire holiday season. During the Middle Ages and Renaissance, the 12 days after Christmas were a festive period, when authority was laughed at and pranks and jokes were the rule. It was a time for dressing up, for going out, and for being merry. The festive tone of this season is the tone of the play, and the play's subtitle, **What You Will,** *expresses this light-hearted spirit of freedom.*

In the 1996 film version of *Twelfth Night*, the love triangle features (left to right) Imogen Stubbs as Viola, Helena Bonham Carter as Olivia, and Toby Stephens as Orsino.

▼

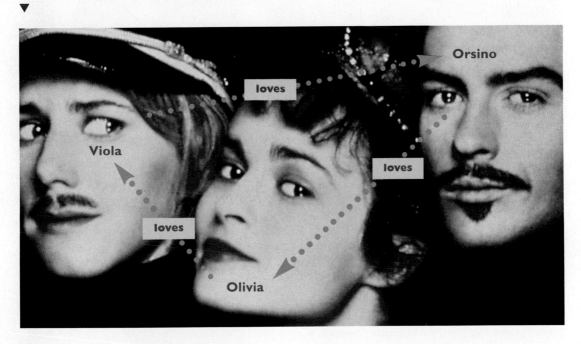

Plot

At the center of the action of Twelfth Night *is a love triangle. Orsino, a romantic duke, is madly in love with Olivia, a grief-stricken countess. Obsessed with her mourning, Olivia rejects Orsino, but then falls in love with Viola, a young woman pretending to be a man. Viola, in turn, is in love with her master, Orsino, but can't do anything about it because of her disguise.*

The second major action in the play is the downfall of Olivia's steward Malvolio. The other members of her household hate him for his petty tyranny, and they revenge themselves with a cruel practical joke. They trick him into believing that Olivia is in love with him and that she demands that he perform a variety of absurd actions as proof of his love.

◄ Malvolio (Dean Nolen) dresses up in the hope of pleasing Countess Olivia in a 1999 production of *Twelfth Night* at the Yale Repertory Theatre.

The third major action of Twelfth Night *involves mistaken identity. Viola and her brother Sebastian are twins. They both survive a shipwreck, but each believes the other has drowned. For security, Viola disguises herself as a boy, exactly imitating her brother in her disguise. When Sebastian reappears, much confusion results.*

In this 1966 Royal Shakespeare Company production at Stratford, England, the twins Viola and Sebastian were played by Diana Rigg (right) and Christopher Bidmead. ▶

Settings and Characters

The action of Twelfth Night takes place in three principal settings: the coast of Illyria, an ancient country in the Balkan Peninsula on the Adriatic Sea; the court of Illyria's ruler, Duke Orsino; and the estate of an Illyrian noblewoman, Countess Olivia. The characters fall into three corresponding groups:

Seacoast	Orsino's court	Olivia's household
Viola, a lady of Messaline shipwrecked on the coast of Illyria; twin sister of Sebastian; later disguised as a boy, Cesario	**Orsino**, duke of Illyria **Cesario**, Viola disguised as a boy **Curio and Valentine**, courtiers	**Olivia**, an Illyrian countess in mourning for her dead brother **Toby Belch**, Olivia's kinsman **Andrew Aguecheek**, Sir Toby's companion
Sebastian, twin brother of Viola		**Malvolio**, a steward
Captain, rescuer of Viola		**Maria**, a lady-in-waiting
Antonio, rescuer and companion of Sebastian; enemy of Orsino		**Fabian**, a servant
		Feste, Olivia's jester

Themes

Twelfth Night is a play about love and the crazy things people do for love. The wildly romantic Orsino is in love with the idea of being in love. Olivia, mourning her dead brother, is in love with her grief. Olivia's ambitious steward Malvolio, who is in love with himself, is easily tricked into believing Olivia loves him too.

Twelfth Night is also a play about disguise and the dangers of pretending to be someone you're not. To protect herself, Viola disguises herself as a man and becomes Orsino's page. She promptly falls in love with him, but is tripped up by her disguise.

Orsino thinks she's a man. Malvolio also learns the danger of pretending when he dresses up absurdly and presents himself as Olivia's lover. She thinks he's gone mad.

One of Shakespeare's most high-spirited comedies, Twelfth Night is also a play about the joy of life. Expressed in some of his most beautiful songs, there is bittersweet advice on how to live life to the fullest:

> In delay there lies no plenty,
> Then come kiss me, sweet and twenty.
> Youth's a stuff will not endure.

Characters

Orsino, duke of Illyria
Valentine, gentleman serving Orsino
Curio, gentleman serving Orsino
Viola, a shipwrecked lady, later disguised
    as Cesario
Sebastian, twin brother of Viola
Antonio, a sea captain, friend to Sebastian
Captain of the shipwrecked vessel

Olivia, a countess of Illyria
Maria, gentlewoman in Olivia's household
Sir Toby Belch, Olivia's uncle

Sir Andrew Aguecheek, Sir Toby's
    companion
Malvolio, steward in Olivia's household
Fabian, gentleman in Olivia's household
Feste, a clown, also called Fool,
    Olivia's jester
Priest
First Officer
Second Officer

Lords, Sailors, Musicians, and other
    Attendants

SCENE: *A city in Illyria and the seacoast near it.*

Act One, Scene One

The play opens in Duke Orsino's palace. As Orsino enters, he calls for music, hoping that too much of it will cure him of love. Curio tries to interest his master in hunting, but Orsino is completely absorbed with his love for Countess Olivia. She is in mourning for her brother's death, and when Valentine returns after attempting to deliver Orsino's messages of love, he tells the duke that Olivia has vowed to keep herself veiled for seven years and weep daily for her brother. Orsino wonders what the effect of falling in love would be on Olivia if she is so affected by the death of merely a brother.

Enter Orsino, *duke of Illyria,* Curio, *other* Lords, *and* Musicians.

    Orsino. If music be the food of love, play on;
        Give me excess of it, that, **surfeiting,**[1]
        The appetite may sicken and so die.

---

[1] **surfeiting**—having more than enough.

If music be the food of love, play on.

That strain again! It had a dying fall;[2]

5 O, it came o'er my ear like the sweet sound

That breathes upon a bank of violets,

Stealing and giving odor. Enough, no more.

'Tis not so sweet now as it was before.

O spirit of love, how quick and fresh art thou,

10 That, notwithstanding thy capacity

Receiveth as the sea, naught enters there,

Of what validity and pitch soe'er,

But falls into abatement and low price

Even in a minute![3] So full of shapes is fancy

15 That it alone is high fantastical.[4]

Curio. Will you go hunt, my lord?

Orsino.   What, Curio?

Curio.   The hart.[5]

Orsino. Why, so I do, the noblest that I have.

O, when mine eyes did see Olivia first,

Methought she purged the air of pestilence.

20 That instant was I turned into a hart,

And my desires, like fell and cruel hounds,

E'er since pursue me.[6]

[*Enter* Valentine.]

                              How now, what news from her?

Valentine. So please my lord, I might not be admitted,

But from her handmaid do return this answer:

25 The element itself, till seven years' heat,[7]

Shall not behold her face at ample view;

---

[2] strain ... fall—passage of music once more. It had a fading sound.

[3] O spirit ... minute—Love is as hungry as the sea; but it soon tires of everything it desires, no matter how precious.

[4] So full ... fantastical—Love (fancy) is so full of fantasies that it surpasses everything else in imaginative power.

[5] hart—female deer: Orsino then puns on *hart* and *heart* ("the noblest that I have").

[6] That instant ... pursue me—Orsino alludes to the myth of Actaeon, a hunter who saw the goddess Diana bathing. She turned him into a deer and he was killed by his own hounds. *Fell* means "fierce."

[7] element ... heat—even the sky, until seven summers have passed.

But like a cloistress[8] she will veilèd walk,
And water once a day her chamber round
With eye-offending brine[9]—all this to season

30   A brother's dead love, which she would keep fresh
And lasting in her sad remembrance.

Orsino. O, she that hath a heart of that fine frame
To pay this debt of love but to a brother,
How will she love, when the rich golden shaft

35   Hath killed the flock of all affections else[10]
That live in her, when liver, brain, and heart,
These sovereign thrones, are all supplied, and filled
Her sweet perfections, with one self king![11]
Away before me to sweet beds of flowers.

40   Love thoughts lie rich when canopied with bowers.[12]

[*They exit.*]

---

[8] cloistress—nun.

[9] brine—salt water; here, tears.

[10] when . . . else—when Cupid's golden arrows have killed all emotions except love.

[11] when . . . king—when one and the same lord is the focus of all her passion (liver), thought (brain), and feeling (heart).

[12] canopied with bowers—shaded with leaves.

Act One, Scene Two

*On the coast of Illyria, the captain of a
wrecked ship attempts to comfort Viola,
a young woman who fears that her twin
brother, Sebastian, has drowned. The captain
describes the love of Duke Orsino for
Countess Olivia. Alone in the world and
unsure of her place in society, Viola wishes
that she could join Olivia's household; but
the captain tells her it is closed to outsiders
because of the countess's mourning. Viola
then resolves to disguise herself as a man and
become one of Orsino's followers. The captain
agrees to help her in her disguise, and she
promises to reward him.*

Enter Viola, *a* Captain, *and* Sailors.

Viola. What country, friends, is this?

Captain. This is Illyria, lady.

Viola. And what should I do in Illyria?

My brother he is in Elysium.[1]

5   Perchance he is not drowned.—What think you, sailors?

Captain. It is perchance that you yourself were saved.

Viola. O, my poor brother! And so perchance may he be.

Captain. True, madam. And to comfort you with chance,

Assure yourself, after our ship did split,

10   When you and those poor number saved with you

Hung on our driving[2] boat, I saw your brother,

Most **provident**[3] in peril, bind himself,

Courage and hope both teaching him the practice,

To a strong mast that lived upon the sea;

15   Where, like Arion[4] on the dolphin's back,

I saw him hold acquaintance with the waves

So long as I could see.

Viola. For saying so, there's gold. [*She gives him money.*]

Mine own escape unfoldeth to my hope,

---

[1] Elysium—in classical mythology, the place where the good go after death.

[2] driving—drifting.

[3] **provident**—acting with foresight.

[4] Arion—Greek poet-musician who was saved from drowning by a dolphin that had been enchanted by his music.

20

Whereto thy speech serves for authority,
The like of him. Know'st thou this country?

Captain. Ay, madam, well, for I was bred and born
Not three hours' travel from this very place.

Viola. Who governs here?

25

Captain. A noble duke, in nature as in name.

Viola. What is his name?

Captain. Orsino.

Viola. Orsino! I have heard my father name him.
He was a bachelor then.

30

Captain. And so is now, or was so very late;
For but a month ago I went from hence,
And then 'twas fresh in murmur—as, you know,
What great ones do the less will prattle of—
That he did seek the love of fair Olivia.

35

Viola. What's she?

Captain. A virtuous maid, the daughter of a count
That died some twelvemonth since, then leaving her
In the protection of his son, her brother,
Who shortly also died, for whose dear love,

40

They say, she hath **abjured**[5] the sight
And company of men.

Viola.   O, that I served that lady,
And might not be delivered to the world
Till I had made mine own occasion mellow,
What my estate is![6]

Captain.   That were hard to compass,

45

Because she will admit no kind of suit,[7]
No, not the duke's.

Viola. There is a fair behavior in thee, captain,
And though that nature with a beauteous wall
Doth oft close in pollution, yet of thee

50

I will believe thou hast a mind that suits
With this thy fair and outward character.

---

[5] **abjured**—given up; abstained from.

[6] **not be delivered . . . estate is**—not reveal my position to the world until I was ready.

[7] **That were . . . suit**—That would be difficult to bring about, because she will not accept requests of any kind.

After surviving a shipwreck, Viola (Sanaa Lathan) is comforted by the Captain (Michael Strickland) in a 1995 production of *Twelfth Night* by the Yale School of Drama.

I prithee,[8] and I'll pay thee bounteously,
Conceal me what I am, and be my aid
For such disguise as haply shall become
The form of my intent. I'll serve this duke.
55   Thou shalt present me as an eunuch[9] to him.
It may be worth thy pains, for I can sing
And speak to him in many sorts of music
That will allow me very worth his service.
60   What else may hap, to time I will commit;
Only shape thou thy silence to my wit.
Captain. Be you his eunuch, and your mute[10] I'll be;
When my tongue blabs, then let mine eyes not see.
Viola. I thank thee. Lead me on.
[*They exit.*]

---

[8] prithee—pray thee, that is, please.
[9] eunuch—boy singer.
[10] mute—silent servant.

Act One, Scene Three

In a room in Olivia's house, her lady-in-waiting, Maria, is scolding Olivia's uncle, Sir Toby Belch, for his all-night drinking. Sir Toby ignores her complaints and defends his companion, Sir Andrew Aguecheek, whom he brought to Olivia's house as a potential husband for her. Maria says that Sir Andrew is a spendthrift and a fool. Sir Andrew then enters and says he is thinking of leaving Illyria, as Olivia is not to be seen or wooed. Sir Toby, alarmed at the thought of losing the money that Sir Andrew has been supplying, convinces him that Olivia will never marry Orsino, leaving the door open for Sir Andrew, who agrees to stay. They both dance around the stage.

A room in Olivia's house. Enter Sir Toby Belch *and* Maria.

Toby. What a plague means my niece to take the death of her brother thus? I am sure care's an enemy to life.

Maria. By my troth,[1] Sir Toby, you must come in earlier o' nights. Your cousin, my lady, takes great exceptions to your ill hours.

5 **Toby.** Why, let her except before excepted.[2]

Maria. Ay, but you must confine yourself within the modest limits of order.

Toby. Confine? I'll confine myself no finer than I am. These clothes are good enough to drink in, and so be these boots too. An[3] they be not,

10 let them hang themselves in their own straps!

Maria. That quaffing and drinking will undo you. I heard my lady talk of it yesterday, and of a foolish knight that you brought in one night here to be her wooer.

Toby. Who, Sir Andrew Aguecheek?

15 **Maria.** Ay, he.

Toby. He's as tall a man as any's in Illyria.

Maria. What's that to th' purpose?

Toby. Why, he has three thousand ducats a year.[4]

---

[1] By my troth—in truth (a mild oath).

[2] except before excepted—pun on the legal phrase *exceptis excipiendis* meaning "with exceptions said before." Sir Toby is saying that she has complained before and he doesn't care.

[3] An—if.

[4] has ... ducats a year—income of 3,000 gold coins a year.

Maria. Ay' but he'll have but a year in all these ducats. He's a very fool
and a **prodigal**.[5]

Toby. Fie,[6] that you'll say so! He plays o' the viol-de-gamboys,[7] and
speaks three or four languages word for word without book, and
hath all the good gifts of nature.

Maria. He hath indeed, almost natural,[8] for, besides that he's a fool, he's a
great quarreler, and, but that he hath the gift of a coward to allay the
gust he hath in quarreling, 'tis thought among the prudent he would
quickly have the gift of a grave.

Toby. By this hand, they are scoundrels and substractors[9] that say so of
him. Who are they?

Maria. They that add, moreover, he's drunk nightly in your company.

Toby. With drinking healths to my niece. I'll drink to her as long as there
is a passage in my throat and drink in Illyria. He's a coward and a
coistrel[10] that will not drink to my niece till his brains turn o' th' toe
like a parish top. What, wench? *Castiliano vulgo!*[11] For here comes Sir
Andrew Agueface.[12]

[*Enter Sir Andrew Aguecheek.*]

Andrew. Sir Toby Belch! How now, Sir Toby Belch?

Toby. Sweet Sir Andrew!

Andrew [*to* Maria]. Bless you, fair shrew.[13]

Maria. And you too, sir.

Toby. Accost,[14] Sir Andrew, accost.

Andrew. What's that?

Toby. My niece's chambermaid.

Andrew. Good Mistress Accost, I desire better acquaintance.

Maria. My name is Mary, Sir.

Andrew. Good Mistress Mary Accost.

---

[5] **prodigal**—spendthrift.

[6] Fie—Shame on you.

[7] viol-de-gamboys—viola da gamba, a stringed instrument like a cello.

[8] almost natural—almost like a "natural" or half-wit.

[9] substractors—detractors, sneerers.

[10] coistrel—horse groom, that is, lowlife fellow.

[11] *Castiliano vulgo*—Meaning is uncertain; perhaps a suggestion to Maria to act with the proverbial decorum
of the Castilians of Spain.

[12] Agueface—pale and thin-faced, like someone suffering from a fever or ague.

[13] shrew—that is, tiny creature. (Maria is very small, and there are references to her size throughout the play.)

[14] Accost—greet, address. (Sir Andrew mistakenly believes Accost is Maria's surname.)

Toby. You mistake, knight. "Accost" is front her, board her, woo her, **assail**[15] her.

Andrew. By my troth, I would not undertake her in this company. Is that the meaning of "accost"?

50   **Maria.** Fare you well, gentlemen.

Toby. An thou let part so,[16] Sir Andrew, would thou mightst never draw sword again.

Andrew. An you part so, mistress, I would I might never draw sword again. Fair lady, do you think you have fools in hand?

55   **Maria.** Sir, I have not you by the hand.

Andrew. Marry,[17] but you shall have, and here's my hand.

Maria. Now, sir, thought is free. I pray you bring your hand to the buttery-bar,[18] and let it drink.

Andrew. Wherefore, sweetheart? What's your metaphor?

60   **Maria.** It's dry, sir.

Andrew. Why, I think so. I am not such an ass but I can keep my hand dry. But what's your jest?

Maria. A dry jest, sir.

Andrew. Are you full of them?

65   **Maria.** Ay, sir, I have them at my fingers' ends. Marry, now I let go your hand, I am barren.

[*Exit* Maria.]

Toby. O knight, thou lack'st a cup of canary![19] When did I see thee so put down?

Andrew. Never in your life, I think, unless you see canary put me down.
70   Methinks sometimes I have no more wit than a Christian or an ordinary man has. But I am a great eater of beef, and I believe that does harm to my wit.

Toby. No question.

Andrew. An I thought that, I'd forswear it. I'll ride home tomorrow,
75   Sir Toby.

Toby. *Pourquoi*,[20] my dear knight?

---

[15] **assail**—attack.

[16] An ... so—if you let her leave this way.

[17] Marry—indeed (originally, "by the Virgin Mary").

[18] buttery-bar—entrance to the room where wine was stored and drinks dispensed.

[19] canary—sweet wine.

[20] *Pourquoi*—French for "Why?"

Sir Andrew (Richard S. Iglewski) offers his hand to Maria (Sally Wingert) in the 2000 production of *Twelfth Night* at Minneapolis's Guthrie Theatre.

Andrew. What is *"pourquoi"*? Do, or not do? I would
I had bestowed that time in the tongues that I
have in fencing, dancing, and bearbaiting. O, had I
80   but followed the arts!

Toby. Then hadst thou had an excellent head of hair.

Andrew. Why, would that have mended my hair?

Toby. Past question, for thou seest it will not curl by nature.

Andrew. But it becomes me well enough, does 't not?

85 **Toby.** Excellent. It hangs like flax on a distaff;[21] and I hope to see a
huswife take thee between her legs and spin it off.

Andrew. Faith, I'll home tomorrow, Sir Toby. Your niece will not be seen,
or if she be, it's four to one she'll none of me. The count himself here
hard by[22] woos her.

90 **Toby.** She'll none o' the count. She'll not match above her degree,[23]
neither in estate, years, nor wit. I have heard her swear 't. Tut,
there's life in 't, man.

---

[21] flax on a distaff—fiber on a staff used for spinning linen thread.

[22] count . . . hard by—Duke Orsino that lives near here.

[23] She'll . . . degree—She won't have anything to do with Duke Orsino. She won't marry above her social position.

Andrew. I'll stay a month longer. I am a fellow o' th' strangest mind i' the world; I delight in masques[24] and revels sometimes altogether.

95   **Toby.** Art thou good at these kickshawses,[25] knight?

Andrew. As any man in Illyria, whatsoever he be, under the degree of my betters, and yet I will not compare with an old[26] man.

Toby. What is thy excellence in a galliard,[27] knight?

100   **Andrew.** Faith, I can cut a caper.[28]

Toby. And I can cut the mutton to't.

Andrew. And I think I have the back-trick simply as strong as any man in Illyria.

Toby. Wherefore are these things hid? Wherefore have these gifts a
105   curtain before 'em? Are they like to take dust, like Mistress Mall's picture?[29] Why dost thou not go to church in a galliard and come home in a coranto? My very walk should be a jig; I would not so much as make water but in a sink-a-pace.[30] What dost thou mean? Is it a world to hide virtues in? I did think, by the excellent
110   constitution of thy leg, it was formed under the star of a galliard.

Andrew. Ay, 'tis strong, and it does indifferent well in a dun-colored stock.[31] Shall we set about some revels?

Toby. What shall we do else? Were we not born under Taurus?[32]

Andrew. Taurus? That's sides and heart.

115   **Toby.** No, sir, it is legs and thighs. Let me see thee caper.

[Sir Andrew *dances.*]

Ha, higher! Ha, ha, excellent!

[*They exit.*]

---

[24] masques—theatrical entertainments with music and dancing.

[25] kickshawses—elegant trifles.

[26] old—experienced.

[27] galliard—lively dance.

[28] cut a caper—execute a leap. Sir Toby makes a pun on the capers served as a relish with meat dishes.

[29] Mistress Mall's picture—Portraits were often protected from fading by curtains.

[30] coranto . . . jig . . . sink-a-pace—lively dances.

[31] dun-colored stock—brown stocking.

[32] Taurus—sign of the Zodiac. Toby is correct; Taurus governed legs and thighs in medical astrology. Leo governed sides and heart.

Act One, Scene Four

In Orsino's palace, Valentine comments on how Cesario—Viola in disguise—has become the duke's closest friend in just a few days. Orsino sends Viola to Olivia to woo her for him. He thinks that Cesario's youth will please Olivia so much that she will listen. As Viola leaves, she comments to herself about the irony of her task: she is in love with Orsino and now must woo another woman for him.

Enter Valentine, *and* Viola *in man's attire.*

Valentine. If the duke continue these favors towards you, Cesario, you
are like to be much advanced. He hath known you but three days,
and already you are no stranger.

Viola. You either fear his humor or my **negligence**,[1] that you call in ques-
5   tion the continuance of his love. Is he inconstant, sir, in his favors?

Valentine. No, believe me.

[*Enter* Duke Orsino, Curio, *and* Attendants.]

Viola. I thank you. Here comes the count.

Orsino. Who saw Cesario, ho?

Viola. On your attendance, my lord, here.

10   **Orsino.** Stand you awhile aloof. [*The others stand aside.*] Cesario,
Thou know'st no less but all. I have unclasped
To thee the book even of my secret soul.
Therefore, good youth, address thy gait unto[2] her;
Be not denied access, stand at her doors,
15   And tell them, there thy fixèd foot shall grow
Till thou have audience.

Viola.   Sure, my noble lord,
If she be so abandoned to her sorrow
As it is spoke, she never will admit me.

Orsino. Be clamorous and leap all civil bounds[3]
20   Rather than make unprofited return.

Viola. Say I do speak with her, my lord, what then?

---

[1] **negligence**—failure to act with care or concern.

[2] address ... unto—go to.

[3] Be ... bounds—Be insistent and go beyond the limits of courtesy.

Orsino. O, then unfold the passion of my love;
Surprise her with discourse of my dear faith.[4]
It shall become thee well to act my woes.

25 She will attend it better in thy youth
Than in a nuncio's of more grave aspect.[5]

Viola. I think not so, my lord.

Orsino.   Dear lad, believe it;
For they shall yet belie[6] thy happy years
That say thou art a man. Diana's[7] lip

30 Is not more smooth and rubious;[8] thy small pipe[9]
Is as the maiden's organ, shrill and sound,
And all is semblative[10] a woman's part.
I know thy constellation[11] is right apt
For this affair.—Some four or five attend him.

35 All, if you will, for I myself am best
When least in company.—[*To Viola.*] Prosper well in this,
And thou shalt live as freely as thy lord,
To call his fortunes thine.

Viola.   I'll do my best
To woo your lady. [*Aside.*] Yet a barful strife![12]

40 Whoe'er I woo, myself would be his wife.
[*They exit.*]

---

[4] surprise . . . faith—overwhelm her with your speech about my loving feeling for her.

[5] nuncio's . . . aspect—older messenger's.

[6] yet belie—still misrepresent.

[7] Diana's—of the Roman virgin goddess. Here she personifies youth and beauty.

[8] rubious—ruby red.

[9] pipe—voice, throat.

[10] semblative—resembling.

[11] constellation—astrological sign; Orsino means Cesario's nature, determined by the position of the stars at his birth.

[12] barful strife—conflict with many obstacles.

Act One, Scene Five

In Olivia's house, the jester Feste returns after an absence. He and Maria exchange quips. Although Olivia is angry with him, he amuses her and saves himself from punishment. Olivia tells Malvolio, her steward, that he must learn to be lighthearted. Sir Toby stumbles in drunk, and Olivia tells Feste to take him away. Malvolio describes a visitor—Viola disguised as Cesario—as a very boyish, though handsome, young man who refuses to leave without speaking to Olivia. Intrigued, Olivia decides to see him. Viola charms Olivia into giving her a private audience and taking off her veil. Viola praises Olivia's beauty, insisting that she has no right to deny the world a copy by not having children. Viola then declares Orsino's great passion. Olivia wishes Orsino would believe that she can never love him. Viola counters that his love is too great. If she loved Olivia as Orsino did, she says, nothing would turn her aside. Olivia, though impressed by this speech, insists that Viola tell Orsino she cannot love him. Left alone, Olivia notes her deep attraction to Cesario. She sends Malvolio to deliver a ring to Cesario and to tell him to visit again tomorrow. As Olivia muses on love, she decides she must accept her fate.

Enter Maria *and* Feste, *the clown.*

Maria. Nay, either tell me where thou hast been, or I will not open my
    lips so wide as a bristle may enter in way of thy excuse. My lady will
    hang thee for thy absence.

Feste. Let her hang me. He that is well hanged in this world needs to fear
5   no colors.[1]

Maria. Make that good.

Feste. He shall see none to fear.

Maria. A good Lenten[2] answer. I can tell thee where that saying was born,
    of "I fear no colors."

10 **Feste.** Where, good Mistress Mary?

Maria. In the wars, and that may you be bold to say in your foolery.

Feste. Well, God give them wisdom that have it, and
    those that are Fools, let them use their talents.

Maria. Yet you will be hanged for being so long absent. Or to be turned
15   away, is not that as good as a hanging to you?

---

[1] fear no colors—fear nothing (a proverb).

[2] Lenten—meager.

Feste. Many a good hanging prevents a bad marriage, and for turning away, let summer bear it out.

Maria. You are resolute, then?

Feste. Not so, neither, but I am resolved on two points.

20 **Maria.** That if one break, the other will hold, or, if both break, your gaskins³ fall.

Feste. Apt, in good faith, very apt. Well, go thy way. If Sir Toby would leave drinking, thou wert as witty a piece of Eve's flesh as any in Illyria.

25 **Maria.** Peace, you rogue, no more o' that. Here comes my lady. Make your excuse wisely, you were best.

[*Exit* Maria.]

[*Enter* Lady Olivia *with* Malvolio *and* Attendants.]

Feste [*aside*]. Wit, an 't be thy will, put me into good fooling! Those wits that think they have thee do very oft prove fools, and I that am sure I lack thee may pass for a wise man. For what says Quinapalus?⁴

30 "Better a witty fool than a foolish wit." — God bless thee, lady!

Olivia [*to* Attendants]. Take the fool away.

Feste. Do you not hear, fellows? Take away the lady.

Olivia. Go to, you're a dry fool. I'll no more of you. Besides, you grow dishonest.

35 **Feste.** Two faults, madonna, that drink and good counsel will amend. For give the dry fool drink, then is the fool not dry. Bid the dishonest man mend himself; if he mend, he is no longer dishonest; if he cannot, let the botcher⁵ mend him. Anything that's mended is but patched; virtue that transgresses is but patched with sin, and sin that amends

40 is but patched with virtue. If that this simple **syllogism**⁶ will serve, so; if it will not, what remedy? As there is no true cuckold but calamity, so beauty's a flower.⁷ The lady bade take away the fool. Therefore I say again, take her away.

Olivia. Sir, I bade them take away you.

---

³ gaskins—breeches or hose. Maria is punning on *points* meaning "laces supporting breeches or hose."

⁴ Quinapalus—Feste's invented authority.

⁵ botcher—cobbler or tailor.

⁶ **syllogism**—form of argument consisting of two propositions and a conclusion drawn from them.

⁷ As there is . . . a flower—Olivia has wedded calamity by taking her vow and will prove a fool, as women are proverbially unfaithful and beauty must fade like a flower.

In the 2000 production of *Twelfth Night* by Shakespeare and Company, the mournful Olivia (Christianna Nelson) enters accompanied by her steward, Malvolio (Michael Hammond).

45 **Feste.** Misprision[8] in the highest degree! Lady, *cucullus non facit monachum;*[9] that's as much to say as I wear not motley[10] in my brain. Good madonna, give me leave to prove you a fool.

Olivia. Can you do it?

Feste. Dexteriously,[11] good madonna.

50 **Olivia.** Make your proof.

Feste. I must catechize[12] you for it, madonna. Good my mouse of virtue, answer me.

Olivia. Well, sir, for want of other idleness, I'll bide your proof.

Feste. Good madonna, why mourn'st thou?

55 **Olivia.** Good fool, for my brother's death.

---

[8] Misprision—mistaking one thing for another.

[9] *cucullus non facit monachum*—Latin for "the cowl does not make the monk" (a proverb).

[10] motley—brightly colored, diamond-shaped patchwork clothes worn by professional fools.

[11] Dexteriously—dexterously, skillfully.

[12] catechize—question formally.

Feste. I think his soul is in hell, madonna.

Olivia. I know his soul is in heaven, fool.

Feste. The more fool, madonna, to mourn for your brother's soul,
being in heaven. Take away the fool, gentlemen.

60 **Olivia.** What think you of this fool, Malvolio? Doth he not mend?

Malvolio. Yes, and shall do till the pangs of death shake him. Infirmity,
that decays the wise, doth ever make the better fool.

Feste. God send you, sir, a speedy infirmity, for the better increasing
your folly! Sir Toby will be sworn that I am no fox, but he will not

65 pass his word for twopence[13] that you are no fool.

Olivia. How say you to that, Malvolio?

Malvolio. I marvel your ladyship takes delight in such a barren rascal.
I saw him put down the other day with an ordinary fool that has no
more brain than a stone. Look you now, he's out of his guard already.

70 Unless you laugh and minister occasion to him,[14] he is gagged. I
protest I take these wise men that crow so at these set kind of fools
no better than the fools' zanies.[15]

Olivia. O, you are sick of self-love, Malvolio, and taste with a distempered appetite. To be generous, guiltless, and of free disposition is

75 to take those things for bird-bolts[16] that you deem cannon bullets.
There is no slander in an allowed fool, though he do nothing but
rail;[17] nor no railing in a known discreet man, though he do nothing
but reprove.

Feste. Now Mercury endue thee with leasing,[18] for thou speak'st well

80 of fools!

[*Enter* Maria.]

Maria. Madam, there is at the gate a young gentleman much desires to
speak with you.

Olivia. From the Count Orsino, is it?

---

[13] pass . . . twopence—bet two pennies.

[14] minister . . . him—give him opportunity.

[15] zanies—stooges.

[16] bird-bolts—blunt arrows.

[17] rail—complain bitterly.

[18] Mercury . . . leasing—Roman god of guile and deception give you the gift of lying.

Maria. I know not, madam. 'Tis a fair young man, and well attended.

85 **Olivia.** Who of my people hold him in delay?

Maria. Sir Toby, madam, your kinsman.

Olivia. Fetch him off, I pray you. He speaks nothing but madman. Fie on him! [*Exit* Maria.] Go you, Malvolio. If it be a suit from the count, I am sick, or not at home; what you will, to dismiss it. [*Exit* Malvolio.]

90 Now you see, sir, how your fooling grows old, and people dislike it.

Feste. Thou hast spoke for us, madonna, as if thy eldest son should be a fool; whose skull Jove[19] cram with brains, for—here he comes— one of thy kin has a most weak *pia mater.*[20]

[*Enter* Sir Toby.]

Olivia. By mine honor, half drunk.—What is he at the gate, cousin?

95 **Toby.** A gentleman.

Olivia. A gentleman? What gentleman?

Toby. 'Tis a gentleman here—[*He belches.*] A plague o' these pickle-herring! [*To* Feste.] How now, sot?[21]

Feste. Good Toby.

100 **Olivia.** Cousin, cousin, how have you come so early by this lethargy?[22]

Toby. Lechery? I defy lechery. There's one at the gate.

Olivia. Ay, marry, what is he?

Toby. Let him be the devil an he will, I care not. Give me faith, say I. Well, it's all one. [*Exit* Sir Toby.]

105 **Olivia.** What's a drunken man like, fool?

Feste. Like a drowned man, a fool, and a madman. One draft above heat makes him a fool, the second mads him, and a third drowns him.

Olivia. Go thou and seek the crowner, and let him sit o' my coz;[23] for he's in the third degree of drink, he's drowned. Go, look after him.

110 **Feste.** He is but mad yet, madonna; and the fool shall look to the madman. [*Exit* Feste.]

[*Enter* Malvolio.]

Malvolio. Madam, yond young fellow swears he will speak with you. I told him you were sick; he takes on him to understand so much, and

---

[19] Jove—king of the Roman gods.

[20] *pia mater*—brain.

[21] sot—fool or drunkard.

[22] lethargy—stupor. Sir Toby mishears it as "lechery" (lewdness).

[23] crowner . . . my coz—Let the coroner hold an inquest on my kinsman.

therefore comes to speak with you. I told him you were asleep; he seems
to have a foreknowledge of that too, and therefore comes to speak with
you. What is to be said to him, lady? He's fortified against any denial.

Olivia. Tell him he shall not speak with me.

Malvolio. He's been told so, and he says he'll stand at your door like a
sheriff's post and be the supporter to a bench, but he'll speak with you.

Olivia. What kind o' man is he?

Malvolio. Why, of mankind.

Olivia. What manner of man?

Malvolio. Of very ill manner. He'll speak with you, will you or no.

Olivia. Of what personage and years is he?

Malvolio. Not yet old enough for a man, nor young enough for a boy—
as a squash is before 'tis a peascod, or a codling when 'tis almost an
apple. 'Tis with him in standing water between boy and man. He is
very well-favored, and he speaks very shrewishly.[24] One would think
his mother's milk were scarce out of him.

Olivia. Let him approach. Call in my gentlewoman.

Malvolio. Gentlewoman, my lady calls. [*Exit* Malvolio.]

[*Enter* Maria.]

Olivia. Give me my veil. Come, throw it o'er my face.
We'll once more hear Orsino's embassy. [Olivia *veils.*]

[*Enter* Viola.]

Viola. The honorable lady of the house, which is she?

Olivia. Speak to me. I shall answer for her. Your will?

Viola. Most radiant, exquisite, and unmatchable beauty—I pray you,
tell me if this be the lady of the house, for I never saw her. I would
be loath to cast away my speech, for, besides that it is excellently
well penned, I have taken great pains to con[25] it. Good beauties,
let me sustain no scorn. I am very comptible, even to the least
sinister usage.[26]

Olivia. Whence came you, sir?

Viola. I can say little more than I have studied, and that question's out
of my part. Good gentle one, give me modest assurance if you be the
lady of the house, that I may proceed in my speech.

---

[24] shrewishly—like a woman; sharply.

[25] con—memorize.

[26] comptible . . . usage—sensitive to the smallest slight.

Olivia. Are you a comedian?[27]

Viola. No, my profound heart. And yet, by the very fangs of malice,
I swear I am not that I play. Are you the lady of the house?

Olivia. If I do not usurp myself, I am.

150 **Viola.** Most certain, if you are she, you do usurp yourself, for what is
yours to bestow is not yours to reserve. But this is from my commission. I will on with my speech in your praise and then show you the
heart of my message.

Olivia. Come to what is important in 't. I forgive you the praise.

155 **Viola.** Alas, I took great pains to study it, and 'tis poetical.

Olivia. It is the more like to be **feigned**.[28] I pray you, keep it in.[29] I heard
you were saucy at my gates and allowed your approach rather to
wonder at you than to hear you. If you be but mad, begone; if you
have reason, be brief. 'Tis not that time of moon[30] with me to make

160 one in so skipping a dialogue.[31]

Maria. Will you hoist sail, sir? Here lies your way.

Viola. No, good swabber,[32] I am to hull[33] here a little longer.—Some
mollification for your giant,[34] sweet lady. Tell me your mind; I am
a messenger.

165 **Olivia.** Sure you have some hideous matter to deliver, when the courtesy
of it is so fearful. Speak your office.

Viola. It alone concerns your ear. I bring no overture of war, no taxation
of homage.[35] I hold the olive in my hand. My words are as full of
peace as matter.

170 **Olivia.** Yet you began rudely. What are you? What would you?

Viola. The rudeness that hath appeared in me have I learned from my
entertainment. What I am and what I would are as secret as
maidenhead[36]—to your ears, divinity; to any other's, profanation.[37]

---

[27] comedian—actor.

[28] **feigned**—false, pretended.

[29] keep it in—do not speak it.

[30] time of moon—Certain phases of the moon were supposed to have a bad influence, particularly on lunatics.

[31] make . . . dialogue—take part in such a flighty conversation.

[32] swabber—sailor who cleans the ship's deck.

[33] hull—drift with sails furled.

[34] giant—Maria is very small.

[35] taxation of homage—demand for tribute.

[36] maidenhead—virginity.

[37] profanation—sacrilege.

Olivia. Give us the place alone. We will hear this divinity.

175 [*Exit* Maria *and* Attendants.] Now, sir, what is your text?

Viola. Most sweet lady—

Olivia. A comfortable doctrine, and much may be said of it. Where lies
    your text?

Viola. In Orsino's bosom.

180 **Olivia.** In his bosom? In what chapter of his bosom?

Viola. To answer by the method, in the first of his heart.

Olivia. O, have read it. It is heresy.[36] Have you no more to say?

Viola. Good madam, let me see your face.

Olivia. Have you any commission from your lord to negotiate with my

185   face? You are now out of your text. But we will draw the curtain and
    show you the picture. [*She removes her veil.*] Look you, sir, such a one
    I was this present. Is 't not well done?

Viola. Excellently done, if God did all.

Olivia. 'Tis in grain, sir; 'twill endure wind and weather.

190 **Viola.** 'Tis beauty truly blent, whose red and white
    Nature's own sweet and cunning hand laid on.
    Lady, you are the cruel'st she alive
    If you will lead these graces to the grave
    And leave the world no copy.

195 **Olivia.** O, sir, I will not be so hardhearted. I will give out divers schedules
    of my beauty. It shall be inventoried and every particle and utensil
    labeled to my will: as, *item*, two lips, indifferent red; *item*, two eyes,
    with lids to them; *item*, one neck, one chin, and so forth. Were you
    sent hither to praise me?

200 **Viola.** I see you what you are. You are too proud.
    But, if you were the devil, you are fair.
    My lord and master loves you. O, such love
    Could be but **recompensed**,[37] though you were crowned
    The nonpareil[38] of beauty!

Olivia.   How does he love me?

205 **Viola.** With adorations, fertile[39] tears,
    With groans that thunder love, with sighs of fire.

---

[36] heresy—religious doctrine that has been outlawed by the church.

[37] **recompensed**—repaid.

[38] nonpareil—one who has no equal.

[39] fertile—abundant, ever-flowing.

Olivia (Kathryn Meisle) finds herself attracted to the disguised
Viola (Opal Alladin) in the Guthrie Theatre production.

Olivia. Your lord does know my mind. I cannot love him.
  Yet I suppose him virtuous, know him noble,
  Of great estate, of fresh and stainless youth,
  In voices well divulged,[40] free, learned, and valiant,
  And in dimension and the shape of nature
  A gracious person. But yet I cannot love him.
  He might have took his answer long ago.

210

---

[40] In . . . divulged—well-reputed by general opinion.

Viola. If I did love you in my master's flame,
215   With such a suff'ring, such a deadly life,
    In your denial I would find no sense;
    I would not understand it.
Olivia.   Why, what would you?
Viola. Make me a willow cabin at your gate
    And call upon my soul within the house;
220   Write loyal cantons of contemnèd love[41]
    And sing them loud even in the dead of night;
    Hallow your name to the reverberate[42] hills,
    And make the babbling gossip of the air
    Cry out "Olivia!" O, you should not rest
225   Between the elements of air and earth
    But you should pity me!
Olivia.   You might do much.
    What is your parentage?
Viola. Above my fortunes, yet my state is well.
    I am a gentleman.
Olivia.   Get you to your lord.
230   I cannot love him. Let him send no more—
    Unless, perchance,[43] you come to me again
    To tell me how he takes it. Fare you well.
    I thank you for your pains. Spend this for me.
    [*She offers a purse.*]
Viola. I am no fee'd post,[44] lady. Keep your purse.
235   My master, not myself, lacks recompense.
    Love make his heart of flint that you shall love,[45]
    And let your fervor, like my master's be
    Placed in contempt! Farewell, fair cruelty. [*Exit* Viola.]
Olivia. "What is your parentage?"
240   "Above my fortunes, yet my state is well.
    I am a gentleman." I'll be sworn thou art!

---

[41] cantons . . . love—songs of rejected love.

[42] reverberate—resounding, echoing.

[43] perchance—perhaps.

[44] fee'd post—paid messenger.

[45] Love make . . . love—May Cupid turn the heart of the man you will love into hard stone.

Farewell, fair cruelty.

Thy tongue, thy face, thy limbs, actions, and spirit
Do give thee fivefold blazon.[45] Not too fast! Soft, soft!
Unless the master were the man. How now?

245 Even so quickly may one catch the plague?
Methinks I feel this youth's perfections
With an invisible and subtle stealth
To creep in at mine eyes. Well, let it be.
What ho, Malvolio!

[*Enter* Malvolio.]

250 **Malvolio.** Here, madam, at your service.

Olivia. Run after that same peevish[46] messenger,
The county's[47] man. He left this ring behind him,
Would I or not. Tell him I'll none of it.
Desire him not to flatter with his lord,

255 Nor hold him up with hopes. I am not for him.
If that the youth will come this way tomorrow,
I'll give him reasons for 't. Hie[48] thee, Malvolio.

Malvolio. Madam, I will.

[*Exit* Malvolio.]

260 **Olivia.** I do I know not what, and fear to find
Mine eye too great a flatterer for my mind.
Fate, show thy force. Ourselves we do not owe.
What is decreed must be, and be this so.

[*She exits.*]

---

[45] give . . . blazon—proclaim your rank five times.

[46] peevish—cross and fretful.

[47] county's—count's.

[48] Hie—Hurry.

Act Two, Scene One

Sebastian, Viola's twin brother, is lost in Illyria. He believes his sister has drowned and tells Antonio, who saved him from the shipwreck, about her. Sebastian plans to make his way to Orsino's court. Antonio, who loves Sebastian, decides to follow him there at the risk of danger to himself because he has been Orsino's enemy.

Enter Antonio *and* Sebastian.

Antonio. Will you stay no longer? Nor will you not that I go with you?[1]

Sebastian. By your patience, no. My stars shine darkly over me. The malignancy of my fate might perhaps distemper yours.[2] Therefore I shall crave of you your leave that I may bear my evils alone. It were a
5 bad recompense for your love to lay any of them on you.

Antonio. Let me yet know of you whither you are bound.

Sebastian. No, sooth,[3] sir; my determinate voyage is mere extravagancy.[4] But I perceive in you so excellent a touch of modesty that you will not extort from me what I am willing to keep in. Therefore it charges me
10 in manners the rather to express myself. You must know of me then, Antonio, my name is Sebastian, which I called Roderigo. My father was that Sebastian of Messaline whom I know you have heard of. He left behind him myself and a sister, both born in an hour. If the heavens had been pleased, would we had so ended! But you, sir,
15 altered that, for some hour before you took me from the breach of the sea was my sister drowned.

Antonio. Alas the day!

Sebastian. A lady, sir, though it was said she much resembled me, was yet of many accounted beautiful. But though I could not with such
20 estimable wonder[5] over-far believe that, yet thus far I will boldly

---

[1] Nor will . . . with you?—And do you not want me to go with you?

[2] malignancy . . . yours—evil influence of my destiny might upset yours.

[3] sooth—truly.

[4] my . . . extravagancy—My journey is just aimless wandering.

[5] estimable wonder—admiring judgment.

publish her: she bore a mind that envy could not but call fair. She is
drowned already, sir, with salt water, though I seem to drown her
remembrance again with more.

Antonio. Pardon me, sir, your bad entertainment.[6]

25 **Sebastian.** O good Antonio, forgive me your trouble.

Antonio. If you will not murder me for my love,[7] let me be your servant.

Sebastian. If you will not undo what you have done, that is, kill him
whom you have recovered, desire it not. Fare ye well at once. My
bosom is full of kindness, and I am yet so near the manners of my
30 mother[8] that upon the least occasion more mine eyes will tell tales
of me. I am bound to the Count Orsino's court. Farewell.

[*Exit* Sebastian.]

Antonio. The gentleness of all the gods go with thee!

    I have many enemies in Orsino's court,

    Else would I very shortly see thee there.

35   But come what may, I do adore thee so

    That danger shall seem sport, and I will go.

[*He exits.*]

---

[6] entertainment—hospitality.

[7] murder . . . love—be the cause of my death because I care for you.

[8] so near . . . mother—so close to behaving like a woman, that is, crying.

Act Two, Scene Two

Outside Olivia's house, Malvolio insists on giving Viola the ring and tells her she should return tomorrow and report on Orsino's reaction to his rejection. Holding the ring, Viola realizes that Olivia has fallen in love with her as Cesario. She sadly reflects that Orsino is in love with Olivia, who is in love with Viola (as Cesario), who is in love with Orsino. She says that only time can resolve this tangle.

Enter Viola *and* Malvolio, *from different directions.*

Malvolio. Were not you even now with the Countess Olivia?

Viola. Even now, sir. On a moderate pace I have since arrived but hither.[1]

Malvolio. She returns this ring to you, sir. You might have saved me my
    pains, to have taken it away yourself. She adds, moreover, that you
5   should put your lord into a desperate assurance she will none of him.
    And one thing more: that you be never so hardy[2] to come again in his
    affairs, unless it be to report your lord's taking of this. Receive it so.

Viola. She took the ring of me. I'll none of it.

Malvolio. Come, sir, you peevishly threw it to her, and her will is it
10   should be so returned. [*He throws down the ring.*] If it be worth
    stooping for, there it lies, in your eye;[3] if not, be it his that finds it.
[*Exit* Malvolio.]

Viola [*picking up the ring*]. I left no ring with her. What means this lady?
    Fortune forbid my outside have not charmed her!
    She made good view of me, indeed so much
15   That sure methought her eyes had lost her tongue,
    For she did speak in starts, distractedly.
    She loves me, sure! The cunning of her passion
    Invites me in this **churlish**[4] messenger.
    None of my lord's ring? Why, he sent her none.

---

[1] arrived but hither—only reached here.

[2] hardy—bold.

[3] in your eye—in plain view.

[4] **churlish**—rude.

Disguise, I see thou art a wickedness.

20	I am the man. If it be so—as tis—
	Poor lady, she were better love a dream.
	Disguise, I see thou art a wickedness
	Wherein the pregnant enemy[5] does much.
	How easy is it for the proper false
25	In women's waxen hearts to set their forms![6]
	Alas, our frailty is the cause, not we,
	For such as we are made of, such we be.
	How will this fadge?[7] My master loves her dearly,
	And I, poor monster,[8] fond as much on him;
30	And she, mistaken, seems to dote on me.
	What will become of this? As I am man,
	My state is desperate for my master's love;
	As I am woman—now, alas the day!—
	What thriftless sighs shall poor Olivia breathe!
35	O Time, thou must untangle this, not I;
	It is too hard a knot for me t' untie.

[Viola *exits*.]

---

[5] pregnant enemy—resourceful devil, who is always ready.

[6] proper false . . . forms—handsome men with untrue hearts to imprint themselves in women's impressionable hearts.

[7] fadge—work out, come off.

[8] monster—being both man and woman.

Act Two, Scene Three

In Olivia's house, Sir Toby and Sir Andrew are up late carousing with Feste. Maria warns that Olivia will send Malvolio to throw them out. Malvolio arrives and orders them to behave. He tells Sir Toby that he must reform or leave Olivia's house. The company mocks Malvolio, and after he leaves Maria suggests that they make sport of him and his great self-regard. She will trap Malvolio with a forged letter, which will appear to be from Olivia, professing her love for him.

Enter Sir Toby *and* Sir Andrew.

Toby. Approach, Sir Andrew. Not to be abed after midnight is to be up betimes,[1] and *diluculo surgere,*[2] thou know'st—

Andrew. Nay, by my troth, I know not, but I know to be up late is to be up late.

5 **Toby.** A false conclusion. I hate it as an unfilled can.[3] To be up after midnight and to go to bed then, is early; so that to go to bed after midnight is to go to bed betimes. Does not our lives consist of the four elements?[4]

Andrew. Faith, so they say, but I think it rather consists of eating
10 and drinking.

Toby. Thou'rt a scholar. Let us therefore eat and drink. Marian, I say, a stoup[5] of wine!

[*Enter* Feste.]

Andrew. Here comes the fool, i' faith.

Feste. How now, my hearts! Did you never see the picture of
15 "We three"?[6]

Toby. Welcome, ass. Now let's have a catch.[7]

---

[1] betimes—early.

[2] *diluculo surgere*—Latin for "To rise early," the beginning of a proverb that concludes, "is very healthy."

[3] can—drinking cup.

[4] four elements—Earth, fire, air, and water were supposed to make up all created things.

[5] stoup—large drinking cup; tankard.

[6] picture of "We three"—picture of two fools with asses' heads. The implication is that the viewer is the third fool.

[7] catch—round or short song.

Andrew. By my troth, the fool has an excellent breast.[8] I had rather than forty shillings[9] I had such a leg, and so sweet a breath to sing, as the fool has. [*To Feste.*] In sooth, thou wast in very gracious fooling last night, when thou spok'st of Pigrogromitus, of the Vapians passing the equinoctial of Queubus.[10] 'Twas very good, i' faith. I sent thee sixpence for thy leman.[11] Hadst it?

Feste. I did impeticos thy gratillity;[12] for Malvolio's nose is no whipstock.[13] My lady has a white hand, and the Myrmidons[14] are no bottle-ale houses.[15]

Andrew. Excellent! Why, this is the best fooling, when all is done. Now, a song.

Toby. Come on, there is sixpence for you. [*He gives money.*] Let's have a song.

Andrew. There's a testril[16] of me too. [*He gives money.*] If one knight give a—

Feste. Would you have a love song, or a song of good life?

Toby. A love song, a love song.

Andrew. Ay, ay, I care not for good life.

Feste [*sings*]. *O mistress mine, where are you roaming?*
O, stay and hear, your true love's coming,
   That can sing both high and low.
Trip no further, pretty sweeting.
Journeys end in lovers' meeting,
   Every wise man's son doth know.

Andrew. Excellent good, i' faith.

Toby. Good, good.

Feste [*sings*]. *What is love? 'Tis not hereafter;*
Present mirth hath present laughter;

---

[8] breast—singing voice, breath.

[9] shillings—coins worth twelve pence apiece.

[10] Pigrogromitus . . . Queubus—Feste's mock scholarship.

[11] leman—sweetheart.

[12] impeticos thy gratillity—mocking way of saying, "I accepted your tip."

[13] Malvolio's . . . whipstock—that is, Malvolio puts his nose into everything.

[14] Myrmidons—tavern named after the warriors who followed Achilles in Greek mythology.

[15] bottle-ale houses—low-class taverns.

[16] testril—sixpence.

> *What's to come is still unsure.*
> 45 *In delay there lies no plenty.*
> *Then come kiss me, sweet and twenty.*
> *Youth's a stuff will not endure.*

Andrew. A **mellifluous**[17] voice, as I am true knight.

Toby. A contagious breath.[18]

50 **Andrew.** Very sweet and contagious, i' faith.

Toby. To hear by the nose, it is dulcet in contagion.[19] But shall we make the welkin[20] dance indeed? Shall we rouse the night owl in a catch that will draw three souls out of one weaver?[21] Shall we do that?

Andrew. An you love me, let's do 't. I am dog at a catch.[22]

55 **Feste.** By 'r Lady, sir, and some dogs will catch well.

Andrew. Most certain. Let our catch be "Thou Knave."[23]

Feste. "Hold thy peace, thou knave," knight? I shall be **constrained**[24] in 't to call thee "knave," knight.

Andrew. 'Tis not the first time I have constrained one to call me "knave."
60 Begin, fool. It begins, "Hold thy peace."

Feste. I shall never begin if I hold my peace.

Andrew. Good, i' faith. Come, begin. [*They sing the catch.*]
[*Enter Maria.*]

Maria. What a caterwauling[25] do you keep here! If my lady have not called up her steward Malvolio and bid him turn you out of doors,
65 never trust me.

---

[17] **mellifluous**—sweet, smooth.

[18] contagious breath—catchy song, but punning on "foul breath."

[19] To hear . . . dulcet in contagion—If we heard with our noses, we could call the song sweet carried by a strong bad smell.

[20] welkin—heavens.

[21] three souls out of one weaver—It was conventional wisdom that music could draw forth the soul from the body. Weavers were supposed to be given to singing psalms.

[22] dog at a catch—expert singer.

[23] "Thou Knave"—song that runs, "Hold thy peace, thou knave, and I prithee hold thy peace," each singer in turn is calling another *knave*, which means "servant" or "villain."

[24] **constrained**—forced, obliged.

[25] caterwauling—wailing like a cat.

Maria (Jeannie Carson) is made uneasy by the drunken reveling of Sir Toby (John Aylward) in this scene from the 1991 production of *Twelfth Night* by the Seattle Repertory Theatre.

Toby. My lady's a Cataian,[26] we are politicians, Malvolio's a Peg-o'-Ramsey,[27] and [*Sings.*] *Three merry men be we.* Am not I consanguineous?[28] Am I not of her blood? Tillyvally![29] "Lady!" [*Sings.*] *There dwelt a man in Babylon, lady, lady.*

70   **Feste.** Beshrew me, the knight's in admirable fooling.

Andrew. Ay, he does well enough if he be disposed, and so do I too. He does it with a better grace, but I do it more natural.

Toby [*sings*]. *O' the twelfth day of December*—

Maria. For the love o' God, peace!

[*Enter* Malvolio.]

---

[26] Cataian—Cathayan or Chinese, slang for someone not to be trusted.

[27] Peg-o'-Ramsey—contemptuous character from a popular song.

[28] consanguineous—related by blood.

[29] Tillyvally—Nonsense.

75   **Malvolio.** My masters, are you mad? Or what are you? Have you no wit, manners, nor honesty but to gabble like tinkers[30] at this time of night? Do ye make an alehouse of my lady's house, that ye squeak out your coziers'[31] catches without any **mitigation**[32] or remorse of voice? Is there no respect of place, persons, nor time in you?

80   **Toby.** We did keep time, sir, in our catches. Sneck up![33]

     Malvolio. Sir Toby, I must be round[34] with you. My lady bade me tell you that, though she harbors you as her kinsman, she's nothing allied to your disorders. If you can separate yourself and your misdemeanors, you are welcome to the house; if not, an it would please you to take

85   leave of her, she is very willing to bid you farewell.

     Toby [*sings*]. *Farewell, dear heart, since I must needs be gone.*

     Maria. Nay, good Sir Toby.

     Feste [*sings*]. *His eyes do show his days are almost done.*

     Malvolio. Is 't even so?

90   **Toby** [*sings*]. *But I will never die.*

     Feste. Sir Toby, there you lie.

     Malvolio. This is much credit to you.

     Toby [*sings*]. *Shall I bid him go?*

     Feste [*sings*]. *What an if you do?*

95   **Toby** [*sings*]. *Shall I bid him go, and spare not?*

     Feste [*sings*]. *O, no, no, no, no, you dare not.*

     Toby. Out o' tune, sir? You lie. Art any more than a steward? Dost thou think, because thou art virtuous, there shall be no more cakes and ale?

---

[30] gabble like tinkers—babble like wandering menders of utensils, famed for their drinking.

[31] coziers'—cobblers'.

[32] **mitigation**—moderation; lessening.

[33] Sneck up—Shut up.

[34] round—plainspoken.

Feste. Yes, by Saint Anne, and ginger[35] shall be hot i' the mouth, too.

Toby. Thou'rt i' the right.—Go, sir, rub your chain with crumbs.[36]—A stoup of wine, Maria!

Malvolio. Mistress Mary, if you prized my lady's favor at anything more than contempt, you would not give means for this uncivil rule. She shall know of it, by this hand.

[*Exit* Malvolio.]

Maria. Go shake your ears!

Andrew. 'Twere as good a deed as to drink when a man's a-hungry, to challenge him the field,[37] and then to break promise with him and make a fool of him.

Toby. Do't, knight. I'll write thee a challenge, or I'll deliver thy indignation to him by word of mouth.

Maria. Sweet Sir Toby, be patient for tonight. Since the youth of the count's was today with my lady, she is much out of quiet. For Monsieur Malvolio, let me alone with him. If I do not gull him into an ayword and make him a common recreation,[38] do not think I have wit enough to lie straight in my bed. I know I can do it.

Toby. Possess[39] us, possess us. Tell us something of him.

Maria. Marry, sir, sometimes he is a kind of puritan.[40]

Andrew. O, if I thought that, I'd beat him like a dog.

Toby. What, for being a puritan? Thy exquisite reason, dear knight?

Andrew. I have no exquisite reason for 't, but I have reason good enough.

Maria. The devil a puritan that he is, or anything constantly, but a time-pleaser;[41] an affectioned ass, that cons state without book and utters it by great swaths; the best persuaded of himself,[42] so crammed, as he thinks, with excellencies, that it is his grounds of faith that all that look on him love him; and on that vice in him will my revenge find notable cause to work.

---

[35] ginger—common addition to ale.

[36] Go, sir . . . crumbs—Go and polish your steward's chain. (He is reminding Malvolio of his position as a servant.)

[37] to challenge him the field—to challenge him to a duel.

[38] gull him . . . recreation—fool him into being a byword for a dupe and make him a laughingstock.

[39] Possess—tell.

[40] puritan—one who professes to be extremely precise in morals.

[41] time-pleaser—self-seeking flatterer.

[42] cons state . . . of himself—commits to memory the speeches and behavior of the great and repeats them to others; having only the highest opinion of himself.

Maria (Greer Goodman) describes her plan to trick Malvolio to Sir Andrew (far left, Trevor Anthony), Sir Toby (James Hallet), and Feste (Stephan De Rosa, lying down) in the Yale School of Drama production.

Toby. What wilt thou do?

Maria. I will drop in his way some obscure epistles[43] of love, wherein by
130   the color of his beard, the shape of his leg, the manner of his gait,
          the expressure of his eye, forehead, and complexion, he shall find
          himself most feelingly personated.[44] I can write very like my lady
          your niece; on a forgotten matter we can hardly make distinction of
          our hands.[45]

135   **Toby.** Excellent! I smell a device.

      Andrew. I have't in my nose too.

---

[43] obscure epistles—puzzling letters.

[44] feelingly personated—exactly represented.

[45] on a forgotten matter ... hands—on an old and unremembered letter, we can barely distinguish her handwriting from mine.

My purpose is indeed
a horse of that color.

Toby. He shall think, by the letters that thou wilt drop, that they come
from my niece, and that she's in love with him.

Maria. My purpose is indeed a horse of that color.

140 **Andrew.** And your horse now would make him an ass.

Maria. Ass, I doubt not.

Andrew. O, 'twill be admirable!

Maria. Sport royal, I warrant you. I know my physic[46] will work with
him. I will plant you two, and let the fool make a third, where he
145 shall find the letter. Observe his construction of it. For this night, to
bed and dream on the event. Farewell.

Toby. Good night, Penthesilea.[47]

[*Exit* Maria.]

Andrew. Before me,[48] she's a good wench.

Toby. She's a beagle[49] true-bred and one that adores me. What o' that?

150 **Andrew.** I was adored once, too.

Toby. Let's to bed, knight. Thou hadst need send for more money.

Andrew. If I cannot recover your niece, I am a foul way out.[50]

Toby. Send for money, knight. If thou hast her not i' the end, call
me "Cut."[51]

155 **Andrew.** If I do not, never trust me, take it how you will.

Toby. Come, come, I'll go burn some sack.[52] 'Tis too late to go to
bed now. Come, knight; come, knight.

[*They exit.*]

---

[46] physic—medicine.

[47] Penthesilea—queen of the Amazons (a joking reference to Maria's small size).

[48] Before me—by my soul.

[49] beagle—small and intelligent hunting dog.

[50] If I . . . out—If I can't marry your niece, I have spent a lot of money for nothing.

[51] Cut—horse with a docked tail.

[52] burn some sack—warm some wine.

Act Two, Scene Four

At Orsino's palace, the duke calls for music and asks the disguised Viola if she has ever been in love. Viola says that she has, with someone very like the duke. Feste sings a sad song, and Orsino sends Viola to try to woo Olivia again. Viola tries to convince the duke that he should respect Olivia's wishes, as he would want a woman who loved him hopelessly to respect his. The duke says that no woman could love as much as he does. Viola denies this and tells her own story as though it were the sad tale of her sister.

Enter Duke Orsino, Viola, Curio, *and other* Attendants.

Orsino. Give me some music. [*Music plays.*] Now, good morrow, friends.—
    Now, good Cesario, but that piece of song,
    That old and antique song we heard last night.
    Methought it did relieve my passion much,
5   More than light airs and recollected terms
    Of these most brisk and giddy-pacèd times.
    Come, but one verse.
Curio. He is not here, so please your lordship, that should sing it.
Orsino. Who was it?
10 **Curio.** Feste the jester, my lord, a fool that the Lady Olivia's father took
    much delight in. He is about the house.
Orsino. Seek him out, and play the tune the while.
[*Exit* Curio. *Music continues.*]
[*To* Viola.] Come hither, boy. If ever thou shalt love,
    In the sweet pangs of it remember me;
15   For such as I am, all true lovers are,
    Unstaid and skittish in all motions else
    Save in the constant image of the creature
    That is beloved. How dost thou like this tune?
Viola. It gives a very echo to the seat
20   Where Love is throned.[1]

---

[1] echo . . . throned—exactly expresses what the heart feels.

For women are as roses, whose fair flower
Being once displayed, doth fall that very hour.

Orsino. Thou dost speak masterly.
My life upon 't, young though thou art, thine eye
Hath stayed upon some favor[2] that it loves.
Hath it not, boy?

Viola. A little, by your favor.[3]

Orsino. What kind of woman is 't?

Viola. Of your complexion.

25 **Orsino.** She is not worth thee, then. What years, i' faith?

Viola. About your years, my lord.

Orsino. Too old, by heaven. Let still the woman take
An elder than herself. So wears she to him;
So sways she level in her husband's heart.
30 For, boy, however we do praise ourselves,
Our fancies are more giddy and unfirm,
More longing, wavering, sooner lost and worn,
Than women's are.

Viola. I think it well, my lord.

Orsino. Then let thy love be younger than thyself,
35 Or thy affection cannot hold the bent;[4]
For women are as roses, whose fair flower
Being once displayed, doth fall that very hour.

Viola. And so they are. Alas, that they are so,
To die even when they to perfection grow!

[*Enter* Curio *and* Feste.]

40 **Orsino.** O fellow, come, the song we had last night.—
Mark it, Cesario, it is old and plain;
The spinsters[5] and the knitters in the sun,

---

[2] stayed upon some favor—rested on a pretty face.

[3] by your favor—if you please (punning on Orsino's use of *favor*; in other words, "with your face").

[4] hold the bent—maintain its intensity.

[5] spinsters—spinning women.

Orsino (Keith Davis) and the disguised Viola (Joey Parsons) listen while Feste (Daniel Cooney, right) sings in the Yale Repertory Theatre production.

And the free maids that weave their thread with bones,[6]
Do use to chant it. It is silly sooth,[7]
45   And dallies with the innocence of love,
Like the old age.[8]

Feste. Are you ready, sir?

Orsino. Ay, prithee, sing.

---

[6] bones—spools for thread were made out of bone.

[7] silly sooth—simple wisdom.

[8] old age—golden age; good old days.

[*Music.*]
Feste [*sings*].

> Come away, come away, death,
>> And in sad cypress let me be laid.
> Fly away, fly away, breath,
>> I am slain by a fair cruel maid.
> My shroud of white, stuck all with yew,[9]
>> O, prepare it!
> My part of death, no one so true
>> Did share it.
>
> Not a flower, not a flower sweet
>> On my black coffin let there be strown;
> Not a friend, not a friend greet
>> My poor corpse, where my bones shall be thrown.
> A thousand thousand sighs to save,
>> Lay me, O, where
> Sad true lover never find my grave,
>> To weep there!

Orsino [*giving money*]. There's for thy pains.

Feste. No pains, sir. I take pleasure in singing, sir.

Orsino. I'll pay thy pleasure, then.

Feste. Truly, sir, and pleasure will be paid, one time or another.

Orsino. Give me now leave to leave thee.

Feste. Now, the melancholy god protect thee, and the tailor make thy doublet of changeable taffeta,[10] for thy mind is a very opal.[11] I would have men of such constancy put to sea, that their business might be everything and their intent everywhere, for that's it that always makes a good voyage of nothing.[12] Farewell.

[*Exit* Feste.]

---

[9] *cypress . . . yew*—trees emblematic of mourning.

[10] doublet . . . taffeta—jacket of shot silk whose color changes in the light.

[11] opal—gemstone that changes color in the light.

[12] I would have . . . voyage of nothing—Men so changeable should sail away, to exercise their inconstancy on the ever-changing sea. Such men arrive at no destination and bring nothing home.

75 **Orsino.** Let all the rest give place.
[Curio *and* Attendants *withdraw.*]

                                           Once more, Cesario,
     Get thee to yond same sovereign cruelty.
     Tell her, my love, more noble than the world,
     Prizes not quantity of dirty lands.[13]
     The parts that fortune hath bestowed upon her,
80   Tell her, I hold as giddily as fortune;[14]
     But 'tis that miracle and queen of gems
     That nature pranks[15] her in attracts my soul.
Viola. But if she cannot love you, sir?
Orsino. I cannot be so answered.
Viola.   Sooth, but you must.
85   Say that some lady, as perhaps there is,
     Hath for your love as great a pang of heart
     As you have for Olivia. You cannot love her;
     You tell her so. Must she not then be answered?
Orsino. There is no woman's sides
90   Can bide the beating of so strong a passion
     As love doth give my heart; no woman's heart
     So big, to hold so much. They lack retention.
     Alas, their love may be called appetite,
     No motion of the liver, but the palate,
95   That suffer surfeit, cloyment, and revolt;[16]
     But mine is all as hungry as the sea,
     And can digest as much. Make no compare
     Between that love a woman can bear me
     And that I owe Olivia.
Viola.   Ay, but I know—
100 **Orsino.** What dost thou know?

---

[13] Prizes . . . dirty lands—Doesn't care about the value of her property.

[14] giddily as fortune—Fortune is known to be fickle.

[15] pranks—dresses.

[16] may be called . . . and revolt—lacks depth, and isn't really passionate, but is only a sensual feeling that can be easily overfed to revulsion.

Viola. Too well what love women to men may owe.
In faith, they are as true of heart as we.
My father had a daughter loved a man
As it might be, perhaps, were I a woman,
105　　 I should your lordship.
Orsino. 　　　　　　　And what's her history?
Viola. A blank, my lord. She never told her love,
But let concealment, like a worm i' the bud,
Feed on her damask[17] cheek. She pined in thought,
And with a green and yellow melancholy
110　　 She sat like Patience on a monument,
Smiling at grief. Was not this love indeed?
We men may say more, swear more, but indeed
Our shows are more than will;[18] for still we prove
Much in our vows, but little in our love.
115　　 **Orsino.** But died thy sister of her love, my boy?
Viola. I am all the daughters of my father's house,
And all the brothers, too—and yet I know not.
Sir, shall I to this lady?
Orsino. 　　　　　　Ay, that's the theme.
To her in haste; give her this jewel. Say
120　　 My love can give no place, bide no denay.[19]
[*He gives her a jewel, and they exit separately.*]

---

[17] damask—pink and white, like a rose.
[18] Our shows ... will—displays of passion are greater than our desire.
[19] give ... no denay—yield no ground and endure no denial.

Act Two, Scene Five

In Olivia's garden, Maria tells Sir Toby, Sir Andrew, and Fabian to hide and watch Malvolio discover the forged letter. Malvolio wonders aloud if Olivia is in love with him. He imagines being her husband and using his new authority to punish Sir Toby. The hidden watchers react violently to Malvolio's fantasies but restrain themselves from disturbing him. He finds the letter that Maria wrote and *identifies the handwriting as Olivia's. He tries to read the letter's puzzling statements as signs of Olivia's love for him. The letter suggests that Malvolio become haughty with the entire household, wear yellow stockings with crossed garters, and smile all the time. He rushes off to obey these instructions, while the tricksters laugh uproariously.*

Enter Sir Toby, Sir Andrew, *and* Fabian.

Toby. Come thy ways, Signior Fabian.

Fabian. Nay, I'll come. If I lose a scruple[1] of this sport, let me be boiled to death with melancholy.

Toby. Wouldst thou not be glad to have the niggardly rascally sheep-
5 biter[2] come by some notable shame?

Fabian. I would exult, man. You know he brought me out o' favor with my lady about a bearbaiting[3] here.

Toby. To anger him we'll have the bear again, and we will fool him black and blue.[4] Shall we not, Sir Andrew?

10 **Andrew.** An we do not, it is pity of our lives.

[*Enter* Maria *with a letter.*]

Toby. Here comes the little villain.—How now, my metal of India![5]

Maria. Get ye all three into the boxtree. Malvolio's coming down this walk. He has been yonder i' the sun practicing behavior to his own shadow this half hour. Observe him, for the love of mockery, for I know this
15 letter will make a contemplative idiot of him. Close, in the name of

---

[1] scruple—tiniest part.

[2] niggardly . . . sheep-biter—stingy, malicious sneak. A "sheep-biter" was literally a dog that attacked sheep.

[3] bearbaiting—"sport" of setting dogs to fight a chained bear. It was a common Elizabethan entertainment.

[4] fool him black and blue—mock him until he is bruised.

[5] metal of India—gold, meaning "my golden girl."

jesting! [*The others hide.*] Lie thou there [*throwing down a letter*], for here comes the trout that must be caught with tickling.[6]

[*Exit* Maria.]

[*Enter* Malvolio.]

Malvolio. 'Tis but fortune, all is fortune. Maria once told me she did affect me,[7] and I have heard herself come thus near, that should she fancy, it

20   should be one of my complexion.[8] Besides, she uses me with a more exalted respect than anyone else that follows her.[9] What should I think on 't?

Toby [*aside*]. Here's an overweening[10] rogue!

Fabian [*aside*]. O, peace! Contemplation makes a rare turkeycock of him.

25   How he jets under his advanced plumes![11]

Andrew [*aside*]. 'Slight,[12] I could so beat the rogue!

Toby [*aside*]. Peace, I say.

Malvolio. To be Count Malvolio.

Toby [*aside*]. Ah, rogue!

30   **Andrew** [*aside*]. Pistol him, pistol him.

Toby [*aside*]. Peace, peace!

Malvolio. There is example for 't. The lady of the Strachy married the yeoman of the wardrobe.[13]

Andrew [*aside*]. Fie on him, Jezebel![14]

35   **Fabian** [*aside*]. O, peace! Now he's deeply in. Look how imagination blows him.

Malvolio. Having been three months married to her, sitting in my state—

Toby [*aside*]. O, for a stone-bow,[15] to hit him in the eye!

Malvolio. Calling my officers about me, in my branched[16] velvet gown;

40   having come from a daybed, where I have left Olivia sleeping—

Toby [*aside*]. Fire and brimstone!

---

[6] tickling—flattery.

[7] she did affect me—Olivia was fond of me.

[8] complexion—nature, appearance.

[9] follows her—is in her service.

[10] overweening—arrogant, presumptuous.

[11] jets . . . plumes—struts about like a turkeycock with its feathers spread.

[12] 'Slight—by God's light (a strong oath).

[13] lady . . . wardrobe—unidentified noblewoman who married the servant in charge of clothing and linen.

[14] Jezebel—cruel and arrogant wife of Ahab in the Bible.

[15] stone-bow—crossbow that shoots pebbles.

[16] branched—printed with the pattern of leaves or flowers.

Fabian [*aside*]. O, peace, peace!

Malvolio. And then to have the humor of state; and after a demure travel of regard,[16] telling them I know my place, as I would they should do
45   theirs, to ask for my kinsman Toby.

Toby [*aside*]. Bolts and shackles!

Fabian [*aside*]. O, peace, peace, peace! Now, now.

Malvolio. Seven of my people, with an obedient start, make out for him. I frown the while, and perchance wind up my watch, or play with
50   my[17]—some rich jewel. Toby approaches; curtsies there to me—

Toby [*aside*]. Shall this fellow live?

Fabian [*aside*]. Though our silence be drawn from us with cars,[18] yet peace.

Malvolio. I extend my hand to him thus, quenching my familiar smile
55   with an austere regard of control[19]—

Toby. And does not Toby take[20] you a blow o' the lips then?

Malvolio. Saying, "Cousin Toby, my fortunes, having cast me on your niece, give me this **prerogative**[21] of speech—"

Toby [*aside*]. What, what?

60   **Malvolio.** "You must amend your drunkenness."

Toby [*aside*]. Out, scab!

Fabian [*aside*]. Nay, patience, or we break the sinews of our plot.

Malvolio. "Besides, you waste the treasure of your time with a foolish knight—"

65   **Andrew** [*aside*]. That's me, I warrant you.

Malvolio. "One Sir Andrew."

Andrew [*aside*]. I knew 'twas I, for many do call me fool.

Malvolio [*seeing the letter*]. What employment have we here?

Fabian [*aside*]. Now is the woodcock near the gin.[22]

70   **Toby** [*aside*]. O, peace, and the spirit of humors intimate[23] reading aloud to him!

---

[16] have the humor . . . of regard—adopt the manner of the great; and having looked each over.

[17] play with my—Malvolio almost says "steward's chain," but catches himself.

[18] with cars—with chariots, that is, by force.

[19] austere regard of control—look of stern authority.

[20] take—give.

[21] **prerogative**—right, privilege.

[22] woodcock near the gin—stupid bird close to a trap.

[23] spirit . . . intimate—whim suggest.

In the Seattle Repertory Theatre production, Malvolio (William Duff-Griffin) reads Maria's forged letter as the other conspirators hide behind a shrub and listen.

Malvolio. By my life, this is my lady's hand. These be her very *c*'s, her *u*'s, and her *t*'s; and thus makes she her great *P*'s. It is in contempt of question[24] her hand.

75 **Andrew** [*aside*]. Her *c*'s, her *u*'s, and her *t*'s. Why that?

Malvolio [*reads*]. *To the unknown beloved, this, and my good wishes.*— Her very phrases! By your leave, wax. Soft! And the impressure her Lucrece, with which she uses to seal.[25] 'Tis my lady. To whom should this be? [*He opens the letter.*]

80 **Fabian** [*aside*]. This wins him, liver and all.

Malvolio [*reads*]. *Jove knows I love,*
　　But who?
　Lips, do not move;
　　No man must know.

85 "No man must know." What follows? The numbers altered![26] "No man must know." If this should be thee, Malvolio?

Toby [*aside*]. Marry, hang thee, brock![27]

---

[24] in contempt of question—beyond dispute.

[25] impressure . . . seal—image of Lucretia stamped on the wax that Olivia uses to seal her letters.

[26] numbers altered—poetic meter changed.

[27] brock—badger; a term of contempt.

Malvolio [*reads*]. *I may command where I adore,*
    But silence, like a Lucrece knife,
90   *With bloodless stroke my heart doth gore;*
    M.O.A.I. doth sway my life.

Fabian [*aside*]. A fustian[28] riddle!

Toby [*aside*]. Excellent wench, say I.

Malvolio. "M.O.A.I. doth sway my life." Nay, but first, let me see, let me
95   see, let me see.

Fabian [*aside*]. What dish o' poison has she dressed him!

Toby [*aside*]. And with what wing the staniel[29] checks at it!

Malvolio. "I may command where I adore." Why, she may command me;
    I serve her, she is my lady. Why, this is evident to any formal
100   capacity.[30] There is no obstruction in this. And the end—what should
    that alphabetical position portend? If I could make that resemble
    something in me! Softly! M.O.A.I.—

Toby [*aside*]. O, ay, make up that.[31] He is now at a cold scent.

Fabian [*aside*]. Sowter will cry upon 't for all this, though it be as rank as
105   a fox.[32]

Malvolio. "M"—Malvolio. "M!" Why, that begins my name!

Fabian [*aside*]. Did not I say he would work it out? The cur is excellent
    at faults.[33]

Malvolio. "M"—But then there is no consonancy in the sequel that suffers
110   under probation. "A" should follow, but "O" does.

Fabian [*aside*]. And "O" shall end, I hope.

Toby [*aside*]. Ay, or I'll cudgel him, and make him cry "O!"[34]

Malvolio. And then "I" comes behind.

Fabian [*aside*]. Ay, an you had any eye behind you, you might see more
115   detraction at your heels than fortunes before you.

Malvolio. "M.O.A.I." This simulation is not as the former. And yet, to
    crush this a little, it would bow to me, for every one of these letters
    are in my name. Soft! Here follows prose.

---

[28] fustian—silly.

[29] staniel—inferior breed of hawk.

[30] formal capacity—normal understanding.

[31] make up that—work it out.

[32] Sowter . . . as a fox—Hounds will bark loudly upon finding the scent, even if it is obvious to all.

[33] at faults—following a lost scent.

[34] And "O" shall . . . cry "O!"—Fabian puns on the last letter of Malvolio's name and a hangman's noose, and Sir Toby adds a pun on a cry from being struck a blow.

Some are born great, some achieve greatness, and some have greatness thrust upon 'em.

[He reads.] *If this fall into thy hand, revolve.*[35] *In my stars I am above thee, but be not afraid of greatness. Some are born great, some achieve greatness, and some have greatness thrust upon 'em. Thy Fates open their hands. Let thy blood and spirit embrace them. And, to inure*[36] *thyself to what thou art like to be, cast thy humble slough*[37] *and appear fresh. Be opposite with a kinsman, surly with servants. Let thy tongue tang*[38] *arguments of state. Put thyself into the trick of singularity. She thus advises thee that sighs for thee. Remember who commended thy yellow stockings and wished to see thee ever cross-gartered.*[39] *I say, remember. Go to, thou art made, if thou desir'st to be so. If not, let me see thee a steward still, the fellow of servants, and not worthy to touch Fortune's fingers. Farewell. She that would alter services*[40] *with thee,*

The Fortunate-Unhappy.

Daylight and champain discovers[41] not more! This is open. I will be proud, I will read politic authors,[42] I will baffle Sir Toby, I will wash off gross[43] acquaintance, I will be point-devise the very man.[44] I do not now fool myself, to let imagination jade me; for every reason excites to this, that my lady loves me. She did commend my yellow stockings of late, she did praise my leg being cross-gartered, and in this she manifests herself to my love and, with a kind of injunction, drives me to these habits of her liking. I thank my stars, I am happy. ·I will be strange, stout,[45] in yellow stockings and cross-gartered, even with the swiftness of putting on. Jove and my stars be praised! Here

---

[35] *revolve*—consider.

[36] *inure*—accustom.

[37] *cast . . . slough*—abandon your humble manner (like a snake discarding its skin).

[38] *tang*—sound loud with.

[39] *cross-gartered*—wearing garters crossed at the back so that in front they pass both above and below the knee.

[40] *alter services*—exchange duties; that is, make you master and become your servant.

[41] champain discovers—open country reveals.

[42] politic authors—writers on political science.

[43] gross—base, common.

[44] point-devise . . . man—correct in every detail to the man described in the letter.

[45] strange, stout—exceptional and haughty.

140 is yet a postscript. [*He reads.*] *Thou canst not choose but know who I am. If thou entertain'st my love, let it appear in thy smiling; thy smiles become thee well. Therefore in my presence still smile, dear my sweet, I prithee.* Jove, I thank thee. I will smile. I will do everything that thou wilt have me. [*Exit* Malvolio.]

145 **Fabian.** I will not give my part of this sport for a pension of thousands to be paid from the Sophy.[46]

Toby. I could marry this wench for this device.

Andrew. So could I too.

Toby. And ask no other dowry with her but such another jest.

150 **Andrew.** Nor I neither.

[*Enter* Maria.]

Fabian. Here comes my noble gull-catcher.[47]

Toby. Wilt thou set thy foot o' my neck?

Andrew. Or o' mine either?

Toby. Shall I play my freedom at tray-trip,[48] and become thy bondslave?

155 **Andrew.** I' faith, or I either?

Toby. Why, thou hast put him in such a dream that when the image of it leaves him he must run mad.

Maria. Nay, but say true, does it work upon him?

Toby. Like aqua vitae[49] with a midwife.

160 **Maria.** If you will then see the fruits of the sport, mark his first approach before my lady. He will come to her in yellow stockings, and 'tis a color she **abhors**,[50] and cross-gartered, a fashion she detests; and he will smile upon her, which will now be so unsuitable to her disposition, being addicted to a melancholy as she is, that it cannot but turn

165 him into a notable contempt.[51] If you will see it, follow me.

Toby. To the gates of Tartar,[52] thou most excellent devil of wit!

Andrew. I'll make one too.[53]

[*They exit.*]

---

[46] Sophy—Shah of Persia.

[47] gull-catcher—one who tricks fools.

[48] tray-trip—game of dice.

[49] aqua vitae—strong drink, usually brandy.

[50] **abhors**—feels disgust or hatred for.

[51] notable contempt—famous object of ridicule.

[52] Tartar—Hell.

[53] I'll make one too—I'll come along.

Act Three, Scene One

In front of Olivia's house, Viola, as Cesario, trades jests with Feste before sending him to announce her arrival. Olivia takes Viola into the garden for a private talk. When Viola begins to speak of Orsino's love, Olivia declares that she is in love with Cesario. Viola rejects this suit and tells Olivia that Cesario has never loved a woman and never shall. As Viola leaves, Olivia asks her to return again.

Enter Viola, *and* Feste, *playing his pipe and tabor.*[1]

Viola. Save thee,[2] friend, and thy music. Dost thou live by thy tabor?

Feste. No, sir, I live by the church.

Viola. Art thou a churchman?

Feste. No such matter, sir. I do live by the church, for I do live at my
5   house, and my house doth stand by the church.

Viola. So thou mayst say the king lies by a beggar if a beggar dwell
near him, or the church stands by thy tabor if thy tabor stand by
the church.

Feste. You have said, sir. To see this age! A sentence is but a chev'ril[3]
10   glove to a good wit. How quickly the wrong side may be turned
outward!

Viola. Nay, that's certain. They that dally nicely with words may quickly
make them wanton.[4]

Feste. I would therefore my sister had had no name, sir.

15 **Viola.** Why, man?

Feste. Why, sir, her name's a word, and to dally with that word might
make my sister wanton. But indeed, words are very rascals since
bonds disgraced them.[5]

Viola. Thy reason, man?

---

[1] *tabor*—small drum.

[2] Save thee—God save thee.

[3] chev'ril—kidskin, very soft material.

[4] wanton—changeable, ambiguous; also unchaste.

[5] bonds disgraced them—Sworn statements were required for a man's word.

20   **Feste.** Troth, sir, I can yield you none without words, and words are grown so false I am loath to prove reason with them.

    Viola. I warrant thou art a merry fellow and car'st for nothing.

    Feste. Not so, sir, I do care for something. But in my conscience, sir, I do not care for you. If that be to care for nothing, sir, I would it would
25   make you invisible.

    Viola. Art not thou the Lady Olivia's fool?

    Feste. No indeed, sir. The Lady Olivia has no folly. She will keep no fool, sir, till she be married, and fools are as like husbands as pilchers are to herrings[6]—the husband's the bigger. I am indeed not her fool but
30   her corrupter of words.

    Viola. I saw thee late at the Count Orsino's.

    Feste. Foolery, sir, does walk about the orb[7] like the sun; it shines everywhere. I would be sorry, sir, but the fool should be as oft with your master as with my mistress. I think I saw Your Wisdom[8] there.

35   **Viola.** Nay, an thou pass upon me, I'll no more with thee. Hold, there's expenses for thee. [*She gives him a coin.*]

    Feste. Now Jove, in his next commodity[9] of hair, send thee a beard!

    Viola. By my troth, I'll tell thee, I am almost sick for one—[*aside*] though I would not have it grow on my chin.—Is thy lady within?

40   **Feste.** Would not a pair of these have bred,[10] sir?

    Viola. Yes, being kept together and put to use.

    Feste. I would play Lord Pandarus of Phrygia,[11] sir, to bring a Cressida to this Troilus.

    Viola. I understand you, sir. 'Tis well begged. [*She gives him another coin.*]

45   **Feste.** The matter, I hope, is not great, sir, begging but a beggar; Cressida was a beggar. My lady is within, sir. I will conster[12] to them whence you come. Who you are and what you would are out of my welkin— I might say "element," but the word is overworn. [*Exit Feste.*]

---

[6] pilchers are to herrings—Pilchers (or pilchards) are smaller but in the same family of fish as herrings.

[7] orb—earth.

[8] Your Wisdom—mocking title.

[9] commodity—supply.

[10] Would . . . bred—that is, please give me another coin (to make a pair).

[11] Lord Pandarus of Phrygia—go-between in the love story of Troilus and Cressida.

[12] conster—explain.

Viola. This fellow is wise enough to play the fool,

50   And to do that well craves a kind of wit.

He must observe their mood on whom he jests,

The quality of persons, and the time,

And, like the haggard,[13] check at every feather

That comes before his eye. This is a practice

55   As full of labor as a wise man's art;

For folly that he wisely shows is fit,

But wise men, folly-fall'n,[14] quite taint their wit.

[*Enter* Sir Toby *and* Sir Andrew.]

Toby. Save you, gentleman.

Viola. And you, sir.

60 **Andrew.** *Dieu vous garde, monsieur.*

Viola. *Et vous aussi; votre serviteur!*[15]

Andrew. I hope, sir, you are, and I am yours.

Toby. Will you encounter the house? My niece is desirous you should

enter, if your trade be to her.

65 **Viola.** I am bound to your niece, sir; I mean, she is the list[16] of

my voyage.

Toby. Taste[17] your legs, sir. Put them to motion.

Viola. My legs do better understand me, sir, than I understand what you

mean by bidding me taste my legs.

70 **Toby.** I mean, to go, sir, to enter.

Viola. I will answer you with gait and entrance.—But we are prevented.

[*Enter* Olivia *and gentlewoman* Maria.]

Most excellent accomplished lady, the heavens rain odors on you!

Andrew. That youth's a rare courtier. "Rain odors," well.

Viola. My matter hath no voice, lady, but to your own most pregnant

75   and vouchsafed[18] ear.

Andrew. "Odors," "pregnant," and "vouchsafed." I'll get 'em all three

all ready.[19]

---

[13] haggard—mature hawk, difficult to train.

[14] folly-fall'n—lapsed into folly.

[15] *Dieu vous garde ... votre serviteur!*—French for "God keep you, sir" and "And you too. Your servant!"

[16] list—limit.

[17] Taste—try.

[18] pregnant and vouchsafed—receptive and attentive.

[19] I'll ... ready—I will remember them for future use.

Olivia. Let the garden door be shut, and leave me to my hearing.
[*Exit* Sir Toby, Sir Andrew, *and* Maria.] Give me your hand, sir.

80 **Viola.** My duty, madam, and most humble service.

Olivia. What is your name?

Viola. Cesario is your servant's name, fair princess.

Olivia. My servant, sir? 'Twas never merry world
　　　Since lowly feigning was called[20] compliment.

85 　　　You're servant to the Count Orsino, youth.

Viola. And he is yours, and his must needs be yours;
　　　Your servant's servant is your servant, madam.

Olivia. For him, I think not on him. For his thoughts,
　　　Would they were blanks, rather than filled with me!

90 **Viola.** Madam, I come to whet your gentle thoughts
　　　On his behalf.

Olivia. 　　　　　O, by your leave, I pray you.
　　　I bade you never speak again of him.
　　　But, would you undertake another suit,
　　　I had rather hear you to solicit that

95 　　　Than music from the spheres.[21]

Viola. 　　　　　　　　　　　Dear lady—

Olivia. Give me leave, beseech you. I did send,
　　　After the last enchantment you did here,
　　　A ring in chase of you. So did I abuse
　　　Myself, my servant, and, I fear me, you.

100 　　　Under your hard construction[22] must I sit,
　　　To force that on you in a shameful cunning
　　　Which you knew none of yours. What might you think?
　　　Have you not set mine honor at the stake
　　　And baited it[23] with all th' unmuzzled thoughts

105 　　　That tyrannous heart can think? To one of your receiving
　　　Enough is shown. A cypress,[24] not a bosom,
　　　Hides my heart. So, let me hear you speak.

---

[20] lowly . . . called—pretended humility began to be considered as.

[21] music . . . spheres—reference to the belief that the motion of the planets produced ravishing music inaudible to human ears.

[22] hard construction—harsh interpretation.

[23] set . . . baited—tied my honor to a stake (like a bear in the sport of bearbaiting) and attacked it (as the bear was with savage dogs).

[24] cypress—nearly transparent black material used for mourning.

Olivia (Christianna Nelson) woos the disguised Viola (Kristin Wold) in the Shakespeare and Company production.

Viola. I pity you.

Olivia.   That's a degree to love.

Viola. No, not a grize;[25] for 'tis a vulgar proof

110   That very oft we pity enemies.

Olivia. Why then, methinks 'tis time to smile again.

O world, how apt the poor are to be proud!

If one should be a prey, how much the better

To fall before the lion than the wolf! [*Clock strikes.*]

115   The clock upbraids me with the waste of time.

Be not afraid, good youth, I will not have you.

And yet, when wit and youth is come to harvest

Your wife is like to reap a proper man.

There lies your way, due west.

---

[25] grize—step.

Viola.   Then westward ho!
120   Grace and good disposition attend your ladyship.
          You'll nothing, madam, to my lord by me?
Olivia. Stay.
          I prithee, tell me what thou think'st of me.
Viola. That you do think you are not what you are.
125   **Olivia.** If I think so, I think the same of you.
      Viola. Then think you right. I am not what I am.
      Olivia. I would you were as I would have you be!
      Viola. Would it be better, madam, than I am?
          I wish it might, for now I am your fool.
130   **Olivia** [*aside*]. O, what a deal of scorn looks beautiful
          In the contempt and anger of his lip!
          A murd'rous guilt shows not itself more soon
          Than love that would seem hid. Love's night is noon.[26]—
          Cesario, by the roses of the spring,
135   By maidhood, honor, truth, and everything,
          I love thee so that, maugre[27] all thy pride,
          Nor wit nor reason can my passion hide.
          Do not extort thy reasons from this clause,
          For that I woo, thou therefore hast no cause.
140   But rather reason thus with reason fetter:[28]
          Love sought is good, but given unsought is better.
      Viola. By innocence I swear, and by my youth,
          I have one heart, one bosom, and one truth,
          And that no woman has, nor never none
145   Shall mistress be of it, save I alone.
          And so adieu, good madam. Nevermore
          Will I my master's tears to you **deplore**.[29]
Olivia. Yet come again, for thou perhaps mayst move
          That heart, which now abhors, to like his love.
[*They exit in different directions.*]

---

[26] Love's . . . noon—Love cannot be hidden.

[27] maugre—in spite of.

[28] Do not extort . . . fetter—Don't think that because I woo you, you have no reason to woo me. But bind reason with the strong reason that follows.

[29] **deplore**—lament.

Act Three, Scene Two

In Olivia's house, Sir Andrew is preparing to leave because he has seen that Olivia prefers Cesario. Sir Toby and Fabian take pains to convince him that Olivia was only trying to make him jealous. Having missed his chance, *they say, he must now challenge Cesario to a duel to impress Olivia. He goes off to write his challenge. Maria hurries the rest off to see Malvolio, who has adopted the costume and attitudes suggested by the letter.*

Enter Sir Toby, Sir Andrew, *and* Fabian.

Andrew. No, faith, I'll not stay a jot longer.

Toby. Thy reason, dear venom, give thy reason.

Fabian. You must needs yield your reason, Sir Andrew.

Andrew. Marry, I saw your niece do more favors to the count's serving-
5   man than ever she bestowed upon me. I saw 't i' the orchard.

Toby. Did she see thee the while, old boy? Tell me that.

Andrew. As plain as I see you now.

Fabian. This was a great argument of love in her toward you.

Andrew. 'Slight, will you make an ass o' me?

10   **Fabian.** I will prove it legitimate, sir, upon the oaths of judgment
        and reason.

Toby. And they have been grand-jurymen since before Noah was a sailor.

Fabian. She did show favor to the youth in your sight only to **exasperate**[1]
        you, to awake your dormouse valor,[2] to put fire in your heart and
15   brimstone in your liver. You should then have accosted her, and with
        some excellent jests, fire-new from the mint, you should have banged
        the youth into dumbness. This was looked for at your hand, and this
        was balked.[3] The double gilt[4] of this opportunity you let time wash
        off, and you are now sailed into the north of my lady's opinion,
20   where you will hang like an icicle on a Dutchman's beard unless you
        do redeem it by some laudable attempt either of valor or policy.[5]

---

[1] **exasperate**—provoke.
[2] dormouse valor—sleeping bravery.
[3] balked—neglected.
[4] gilt—gold plating.
[5] policy—statesmanlike wisdom. Andrew then uses it to mean "political cunning."

Andrew. An 't be any way, it must be with valor, for policy I hate. I had
    as lief be a Brownist[6] as a politician.

Toby. Why, then, build me thy fortunes upon the basis of valor. Challenge
25   me the count's youth to fight with him. Hurt him in eleven places.
    My niece shall take note of it, and assure thyself, there is no love-
    broker in the world can more prevail in man's commendation with
    woman than report of valor.

Fabian. There is no way but this, Sir Andrew.

30 **Andrew.** Will either of you bear me a challenge to him?

Toby. Go, write it in a martial hand. Be curst[7] and brief; it is no matter
    how witty, so it be eloquent and full of invention. Taunt him with the
    license of ink.[8] If thou "thou"-est[9] him some thrice, it shall not be
    amiss, and as many lies as will lie in thy sheet of paper, although the
35   sheet were big enough for the bed of Ware[10] in England, set 'em
    down. Go, about it. Let there be gall[11] enough in thy ink, though thou
    write with a goose-pen,[12] no matter. About it.

Andrew. Where shall I find you?

Toby. We'll call thee at the cubiculo.[13] Go.

[*Exit* Sir Andrew.]

40 **Fabian.** This is a dear manikin[14] to you, Sir Toby.

Toby. I have been dear to him, lad, some two thousand strong or so.[15]

Fabian. We shall have a rare letter from him. But you'll not deliver 't?

Toby. Never trust me, then. And by all means stir on the youth to an
    answer. I think oxen and wainropes cannot hale them together.[16] For
45   Andrew, if he were opened and you find so much blood in his liver as
    will clog the foot of a flea, I'll eat the rest of th' anatomy.

---

[6] Brownist—follower of Robert Browne, who founded the Congregationalist sect in the reign of Elizabeth I.

[7] curst—bad-tempered, insulting.

[8] license of ink—freedom afforded by writing rather speaking to a person.

[9] "thou"-est—use the form of address applied to friends or social inferiors.

[10] bed of Ware—famous 10-foot-wide bed that could hold 12 people.

[11] gall—bitterness, but also a pun on one of the ingredients in ink.

[12] goose-pen—pen made with a goose quill; punning on pen used by a goose (fool).

[13] cubiculo—little room.

[14] manikin—puppet.

[15] I have ... or so—I have cost him much money.

[16] wainropes ... together—wagon ropes cannot haul them together.

Fabian. And his opposite, the youth, bears in his visage no great
presage[17] of cruelty.

[*Enter Maria.*]

Toby. Look where the youngest wren of nine[18] comes.

50 **Maria.** If you desire the spleen,[19] and will laugh yourselves into stitches,
follow me. Yond gull[20] Malvolio is turned heathen, a very renegado;[21]
for there is no Christian that means to be saved by believing rightly
can ever believe such impossible passages of grossness.[22] He's in
yellow stockings.

55 **Toby.** And cross-gartered?

Maria. Most villainously, like a pedant that keeps a school i' the church.
I have dogged him like his murderer. He does obey every point of the
letter that I dropped to betray him. He does smile his face into more
lines than is in the new map with the augmentation of the Indies.[23]

60 You have not seen such a thing as 'tis. I can hardly forbear hurling
things at him. I know my lady will strike him. If she do, he'll smile
and take 't for a great favor.

Toby. Come, bring us, bring us where he is.

[*They all exit.*]

---

[17] presage—indication.

[18] youngest wren of nine—very smallest, another joke on Maria's height.

[19] desire the spleen—want to laugh until it hurts.

[20] gull—fool, dupe.

[21] renegado—renegade, one who has renounced his religion.

[22] passages of grossness—exaggerated misinformation.

[23] new map . . . Indies—reference to a new map of the world printed in 1600, which showed North America (still called the "Indies") as much larger than before.

Act Three, Scene Three

On a street in an Illyrian city, Antonio explains to Sebastian why he has followed him. Antonio then explains why he himself must avoid being seen by Orsino's men. He gives his purse to Sebastian and sends him to see the city. Antonio goes to arrange quiet lodgings for them.

Enter Sebastian *and* Antonio.

Sebastian. I would not by my will have troubled you,
    But since you make your pleasure of your pains,
    I will no further chide[1] you.

Antonio. I could not stay behind you. My desire,
5   More sharp than filèd steel, did spur me forth,
    And not all love to see you—though so much
    As might have drawn one to a longer voyage—
    But jealousy what might befall your travel,
    Being skilless in these parts, which to a stranger,
10   Unguided and unfriended, often prove
    Rough and unhospitable. My willing love,
    The rather by these arguments of fear,
    Set forth in your pursuit.

Sebastian.   My kind Antonio,
    I can no other answer make but thanks,
15   And thanks, and ever thanks. Often good turns
    Are shuffled off with such uncurrent pay.[2]
    But were my worth, as is my conscience, firm,
    You should find better dealing. What's to do?
    Shall we go see the relics[3] of this town?
20 **Antonio.** Tomorrow, sir. Best first go see your lodging.
Sebastian. I am not weary, and 'tis long to night.
    I pray you, let us satisfy our eyes

---

[1] chide—reproach, blame.
[2] shuffled . . . pay—rewarded with worthless words.
[3] relics—ancient monuments.

With the memorials and the things of fame
That do renown this city.

Antonio.   Would you'd pardon me.
25   I do not without danger walk these streets.
Once in a sea fight 'gainst the count his galleys[4]
I did some service, of such note indeed
That were I ta'en here it would scarce be answered.

Sebastian. Belike[5] you slew great number of his people?

30   **Antonio.** Th' offense is not of such a bloody nature,
Albeit the quality of the time and quarrel
Might well have given us bloody argument.
It might have since been answered in repaying
What we took from them, which, for traffic's[6] sake
35   Most of our city did. Only myself stood out,
For which, if I be lapsèd[7] in this place,
I shall pay dear.

Sebastian.   Do not then walk too open.

Antonio. It doth not fit me. Hold, sir, here's my purse.
In the south suburbs, at the Elephant,
40   Is best to lodge. I will bespeak our diet,[8]
Whiles you beguile the time and feed your knowledge
With viewing of the town. There shall you have me.

Sebastian. Why I your purse?

Antonio. Haply your eye shall light upon some toy
45   You have desire to purchase, and your store
I think, is not for idle markets, sir.

Sebastian. I'll be your purse-bearer and leave you
For an hour.

Antonio.   To th' Elephant.

Sebastian.   I do remember.

[*They exit in different directions.*]

---

[4] count his galleys—Count Orsino's ships.

[5] Belike—perhaps.

[6] traffic's—trade's.

[7] lapsèd—caught; arrested.

[8] bespeak our diet—order our dinner.

Act Three, Scene Four

*In Olivia's house, when Malvolio appears
before her dressed ridiculously and smiling like
a fool, she thinks that he has gone mad.
Cesario is announced, and Olivia instructs
Maria to arrange for care for Malvolio. Sir
Toby and Fabian pretend to Malvolio that he
is possessed by a devil, but Malvolio dismisses
them and storms off. Sir Toby promises to
deliver Sir Andrew's challenge letter to
Cesario. Sir Toby plans to convince both Sir
Andrew and Cesario of the great fighting abil-
ity of the other so the two will be terrified.
Viola again asks Olivia to love Orsino. After
Olivia leaves, Sir Toby and Fabian deliver Sir
Andrew's challenge to Viola, who wants no
part in a duel. Sir Toby then goes to tell Sir
Andrew that Cesario is a deadly fighter. Now
both Sir Andrew and Viola are terrified to
fight. As they prepare to face each other,
Antonio enters. He thinks Viola is Sebastian,
and steps between her and Sir Andrew.
Antonio and Sir Toby draw their swords, but
Orsino's soldiers arrest Antonio. He asks Viola
to return his money, but she is mystified.
Antonio thinks that Sebastian has betrayed
him. Because Antonio mistook her for
Sebastian, Viola hopes her brother may be
alive. As she leaves, Sir Toby and Fabian goad
Sir Andrew into chasing her.*

Enter Olivia *and* Maria.

Olivia [*aside*]. I have sent after him. He says he'll come.
How shall I feast him? What bestow of him?
For youth is bought more oft than begged or borrowed.
I speak too loud.—

5   Where's Malvolio? He is sad and civil,[1]
And suits well for a servant with my fortunes.
Where is Malvolio?

Maria. He's coming, madam, but in very strange manner. He is sure
possessed, madam.

10   **Olivia.** Why, what's the matter? Does he rave?

Maria. No, madam, he does nothing but smile. Your ladyship were best
to have some guard about you if he come, for sure the man is tainted
in 's wits.

Olivia. Go call him hither. [*Exit* Maria.]

15   I am as mad as he,

---

[1] sad and civil—serious and polite.

If sad and merry madness equal be.

[*Enter* Maria *with* Malvolio, *cross-gartered and in yellow stockings.*]

How now, Malvolio?

Malvolio. Sweet lady, ho, ho!

Olivia. Smil'st thou? I sent for thee upon a sad occasion.

20 **Malvolio.** Sad, lady? I could be sad. This does make some obstruction in the blood, this cross-gartering, but what of that? If it please the eye of one, it is with me as the very true sonnet[2] is, "Please one, and please all."

Olivia. Why, how dost thou, man? What is the matter with thee?

25 **Malvolio.** Not black in my mind, though yellow in my legs. It did come to his hands, and commands shall be executed. I think we do know the sweet Roman hand.[3]

Olivia. Wilt thou go to bed, Malvolio?

Malvolio. To bed! "Ay, sweetheart, and I'll come to thee."[4]

30 **Olivia.** God comfort thee! Why dost thou smile so and kiss thy hand so oft?

Maria. How do you, Malvolio?

Malvolio. At your request? Yes, nightingales answer daws.[5]

Maria. Why appear you with this ridiculous boldness before my lady?

35 **Malvolio.** "Be not afraid of greatness." 'Twas well writ.

Olivia. What mean'st thou by that, Malvolio?

Malvolio. "Some are born great—"

Olivia. Ha?

Malvolio. "Some achieve greatness—"

40 **Olivia.** What sayst thou?

Malvolio. "And some have greatness thrust upon them."

Olivia. Heaven restore thee!

Malvolio. "Remember who commended thy yellow stockings—"

Olivia. Thy yellow stockings?

45 **Malvolio.** "And wished to see thee cross-gartered."

Olivia. Cross-gartered?

---

[2] sonnet—song ("Please me, and please all" is the refrain of a ballad about women's wishes).

[3] Roman hand—Italian script, which was fashionable.

[4] "Ay . . . thee."—line from a popular song.

[5] nightingales answer daws—Superiors can listen to an inferior.

Malvolio. "Go to, thou art made, if thou desir'st to be so—"
Olivia. Am I made?
Malvolio. "If not, let me see thee a servant still."
50 **Olivia.** Why, this is very midsummer madness.
[*Enter* Servant.]
Servant. Madam, the young gentleman of the Count Orsino's is returned. I could hardly entreat him back. He attends your ladyship's pleasure.
Olivia. I'll come to him. [*Exit* Servant.] Good Maria, let this fellow be looked to. Where's my cousin Toby? Let some of my people have a
55 special care of him. I would not have him miscarry⁶ for the half of my dowry.
[*Exit* Olivia *and* Maria *in different directions.*]
Malvolio. O ho, do you come near me now? No worse man than Sir Toby to look to me! This concurs directly with the letter. She sends him on purpose that I may appear stubborn to him, for she incites me to that
60 in the letter. "Cast thy humble slough," says she. "Be opposite with a kinsman, surly with servants; let thy tongue tang with arguments of state; put thyself into the trick of singularity," and consequently sets down the manner how: as, a sad face, a reverend carriage, a slow tongue, in the habit of some sir of note, and so forth. I have limed⁷
65 her, but it is Jove's doing, and Jove make me thankful! And when she went away now, "Let this fellow be looked to." "Fellow!" Not "Malvolio," nor after my degree, but "fellow." Why, everything adheres together, that no dram of a scruple, no scruple of a scruple,⁸ no obstacle, no incredulous or unsafe⁹ circumstance—what can be
70 said? Nothing that can be can come between me and the full prospect of my hopes. Well, Jove, not I, is the doer of this, and he is to be thanked.
[*Enter* Toby, Fabian, *and* Maria.]

---

⁶ miscarry—come to harm.
⁷ limed—caught, as with birdlime.
⁸ dram . . . scruple—small amount of doubt, not even a small part of a small part.
⁹ incredulous or unsafe—incredible or unreliable.

Malvolio (John Bland) woos Olivia (Mercedes Herrero) in the Yale Repertory Theatre production.

Toby. Which way is he, in the name of sanctity? If all the devils of hell be
drawn in little, and Legion himself possessed him,[10] yet I'll speak to him.

75 **Fabian.** Here he is, here he is. —How is 't with you, sir? How is 't with
you, man?

Malvolio. Go off. I discard you. Let me enjoy my private.[11] Go off.

Maria [*to* Toby]. Lo, how hollow the fiend speaks within him! Did not I
tell you? Sir Toby, my lady prays you to have a care of him.

80 **Malvolio.** Aha, does she so?

Toby [*to* Fabian *and* Maria]. Go to, go to! Peace, peace, we must deal gently
with him. Let me alone.—How do you, Malvolio? How is 't with you?
What, man, defy the devil! Consider, he's an enemy to mankind.

---

[10] drawn . . . possessed him—brought together into the smallest space, and all devils have possessed him.

[11] private—privacy.

If this were played upon a stage now, I could condemn it as an improbable fiction.

Malvolio. Do you know what you say?

85   **Maria** [*to* Toby]. La you, an you speak ill of the devil, how he takes it at heart! Pray God he be not bewitched!

Fabian. Carry his water to th' wisewoman.[12]

Maria. Marry, and it shall be done tomorrow morning if I live. My lady would not lose him for more than I'll say.

90   **Malvolio.** How now, mistress?

Maria. O Lord!

Toby. Prithee, hold thy peace. This is not the way. Do you not see you move[13] him? Let me alone with him.

Fabian. No way but gentleness, gently, gently. The fiend is rough, and

95   will not be roughly used.

Toby [*to* Malvolio]. Why, how now, my bawcock![14] How dost thou, chuck?[15]

Malvolio. Sir!

Toby. Ay, biddy,[16] come with me. What, man, 'tis not for gravity to play at

100   cherry-pit[17] with Satan. Hang him, foul collier![18]

Maria. Get him to say his prayers, good Sir Toby, get him to pray.

Malvolio. My prayers, minx?

Maria. No, I warrant you, he will not hear of godliness.

Malvolio. Go hang yourselves all! You are idle, shallow things. I am not of

105   your element. You shall know more hereafter.

[*Exit* Malvolio.]

Toby. Is 't possible?

Fabian. If this were played upon a stage now, I could condemn it as an improbable fiction.

---

[12] water . . . wisewoman—urine to the healer (to be examined).

[13] move—excite, rouse.

[14] bawcock—fine fellow (from French, *beau coq*, "fine bird").

[15] chuck—chick, a term of endearment.

[16] biddy—common name for a hen (very insulting to Malvolio).

[17] gravity . . . cherry-pit—a serious man to play a child's game. Cherry-pit is a game in which cherry pits are tossed into a hole.

[18] foul collier—filthy coal miner; appropriate to Satan, who is pictured as black.

Toby. His very genius hath taken the infection of the device, man.

110 **Maria.** Nay, pursue him now, lest the device take air and taint.[19]

Fabian. Why, we shall make him mad indeed.

Maria. The house will be the quieter.

Toby. Come, we'll have him in a dark room and bound. My niece is already in the belief that he's mad. We may carry it thus, for our

115 pleasure and his penance, till our very pastime, tired out of breath, prompt us to have mercy on him, at which time we will bring the device to the bar[20] and crown thee for a finder of madmen. But see, but see!

[*Enter* Andrew *with a letter.*]

Fabian. More matter for a May morning.[21]

120 **Andrew.** Here's the challenge. Read it. I warrant there's vinegar and pepper in 't.

Fabian. Is 't so saucy?

Andrew. Ay, is 't, I warrant him. Do but read.

Toby. Give me. [*He reads.*] *Youth, whatsoever thou art, thou art but a*

125 *scurvy[22] fellow.*

Fabian. Good, and valiant.

Toby [*reads*]. *Wonder not, nor admire not in thy mind, why I do call thee so, for I will show thee no reason for 't.*

Fabian. A good note, that keeps you from the blow of the law.

130 **Toby** [*reads*]. *Thou com'st to the Lady Olivia, and in my sight she uses thee kindly. But thou liest in thy throat, that is not the matter I challenge thee for.*

Fabian. Very brief, and to exceeding good sense—less.

Toby [*reads*]. *I will waylay thee going home, where if it be thy chance to kill me—*

135 **Fabian.** Good.

Toby [*reads*]. *Thou kill'st me like a rogue and a villain.*

Fabian. Still you keep o' the windy side[23] of the law. Good.

Toby [*reads*]. *Fare thee well, and God have mercy upon one of our souls! He may have mercy upon mine, but my hope is better, and so look to thyself. Thy*

---

[19] device . . . taint—become known and be spoiled.

[20] bar—place of judgment.

[21] matter . . . morning—material for a May-day comedy.

[22] *scurvy*—mean, contemptible.

[23] windy side—safe side.

140 *friend, as thou usest him, and thy sworn enemy, Andrew Aguecheek.*
If this letter move him not, his legs cannot. I'll give 't him.

Maria. You may have very fit occasion for 't. He is now in some commerce with my lady, and will by and by depart.

Toby. Go, Sir Andrew. Scout me for him at the corner of the orchard like
145 a bum-baily[24] So soon as ever thou seest him, draw, and as thou draw'st swear horrible, for it comes to pass oft that a terrible oath, with a swaggering accent sharply twanged off, gives manhood more approbation[25] than ever proof itself would have earned him. Away!

Andrew. Nay, let me alone for swearing.[26]

[*Exit* Andrew.]

150 **Toby.** Now will not I deliver his letter, for the behavior of the young gentleman gives him out to be of good capacity and breeding; his employment between his lord and my niece confirms no less. Therefore this letter, being so excellently ignorant, will breed no terror in the youth. He will find it comes from a clodpoll.[27] But, sir, I will
155 deliver his challenge by word of mouth, set upon Aguecheek a notable report of valor, and drive the gentleman—as I know his youth will aptly receive it—into a most hideous opinion of his rage, skill, fury, and **impetuosity**.[28] This will so fright them both that they will kill one another by the look, like cockatrices.[29]

[*Enter* Olivia *and* Viola.]

160 **Fabian.** Here he comes with your niece. Give them way till he take leave, and presently[30] after him.

Toby. I will meditate the while upon some horrid message for a challenge.

[*Exit* Toby, Fabian, *and* Maria.]

Olivia. I have said too much unto a heart of stone
And laid mine honor too unchary[31] on 't.

---

[24] bum-baily—officer of the law who arrested people for debt.

[25] approbation—reputation (for courage).

[26] let me alone for swearing—have no fears about my ability to swear.

[27] clodpoll—blockhead.

[28] **impetuosity**—rashness, impulsiveness.

[29] cockatrices—mythological creatures able to kill with a glance.

[30] presently—immediately.

[31] laid . . . unchary—risked good name too carelessly.

165	There's something in me that reproves[32] my fault,
	But such a headstrong potent fault it is
	That it but mocks reproof.

Viola. With the same 'havior[33] that your passion bears

Goes on my master's griefs.

170 **Olivia** [*giving a locket*]. Here, wear this jewel for me. 'Tis my picture.

Refuse it not; it hath no tongue to vex you.

And I beseech you come again tomorrow.

What shall you ask of me that I'll deny,

That honor, saved, may upon asking give?[34]

175 **Viola.** Nothing but this: your true love for my master.

Olivia. How with mine honor may I give him that

Which I have given to you?

Viola.   I will acquit you.

Olivia. Well, come again tomorrow. Fare thee well.

A fiend like thee might bear my soul to hell. [*Exit* Olivia.]

[*Enter* Toby *and* Fabian.]

180 **Toby.** Gentleman, God save thee.

Viola. And you, sir.

Toby. That defense thou hast, betake thee to 't. Of what nature the wrongs

are thou hast done him, I know not, but thy intercepter, full of

despite,[35] bloody as the hunter, attends thee at the orchard end.

185 Dismount thy tuck, be yare in thy preparation,[36] for thy assailant is

quick, skillful, and deadly.

Viola. You mistake sir. I am sure no man hath any quarrel to me. My

remembrance is very free and clear from any image of offense done

to any man.

190 **Toby.** You'll find it otherwise, I assure you. Therefore, if you hold your

life at any price, betake you to your guard, for your opposite hath in

him what youth, strength, skill, and wrath can furnish man withal.

Viola. I pray you, sir, what is he?

---

[32] reproves—shows disapproval of.

[33] 'havior—behavior.

[34] That honor, saved, may upon asking give—that can be granted without dishonor.

[35] intercepter . . . despite—ambusher, full of anger.

[36] Dismount . . . thy preparation—Draw your sword and be ready quickly.

Toby. He is knight, dubbed with unhatched rapier[37] and on carpet
consideration,[38] but he is a devil in private brawl. Souls and bodies
hath he divorced three, and his incensement at this moment is so
implacable[39] that satisfaction can be none but by pangs of death
and sepulcher.[40] Hob, nob is his word; give 't or take 't.[41]

Viola. I will return again into the house and desire some conduct of the
lady. I am no fighter. I have heard of some kind of men that put quarrels purposely on others to taste their valor. Belike this is a man of
that quirk.[42]

Toby. Sir, no. His indignation derives itself out of a very competent
injury.[43] Therefore, get you on and give him his desire. Back you shall
not to the house unless you undertake that with me which with as
much safety you might answer him. Therefore on, or strip your
sword stark naked, for meddle you must, that's certain, or forswear
to wear iron about you.[44]

Viola. This is as uncivil as strange. I beseech you, do me this courteous
office, as to know of the knight what my offense to him is. It is something of my negligence, nothing of my purpose.

Toby. I will do so—Signor Fabian, stay you by this gentleman till my
return.

[*Exit* Sir Toby.]

Viola. Pray you, sir, do you know of this matter?

Fabian. I know the knight is incensed against you, even to a mortal
arbitrament,[45] but nothing of the circumstance more.

Viola. I beseech you, what manner of man is he?

Fabian. Nothing of that wonderful promise, to read him by his form, as
you are like to find him in the proof of his valor. He is, indeed, sir, the
most skillful, bloody, and fatal opposite that you could possibly have

---

[37] unhatched rapier—sword never used in battle.

[38] on carpet consideration—that is, knighted because of connections at court, not valor in battle.

[39] **implacable**—impossible to calm or appease.

[40] sepulcher—tomb.

[41] Hob, nob . . . give 't or take 't—The challenger wants to fight to the death.

[42] quirk—humor.

[43] competent injury—wrong that demands satisfaction.

[44] forswear . . . you—give up your right to wear a sword.

[45] mortal arbitrament—duel to the death.

found in any part of Illyria. Will you walk towards him? I will make your peace with him if I can.

Viola. I shall be much bound to you for 't. I am one that had rather go with Sir Priest than Sir Knight. I care not who knows so much of
225   my mettle.[46]

[*Exit* Fabian *and* Viola.]

[*Enter* Sir Toby *and* Sir Andrew.]

Toby. Why, man, he's a very devil; I have not seen such a firago.[47] I had a pass with him, rapier, scabbard, and all, and he gives me the stuck-in[48] with such a mortal motion that it is **inevitable**;[49] and on the answer, he pays you as surely as your feet hits the ground they
230   step on. They say he has been fencer to the Sophy.

Andrew. Pox on 't, I'll not meddle with him.

Toby. Ay, but he will not now be pacified. Fabian can scarce hold him yonder.

Andrew. Plague on 't! An I thought he had been valiant and so cunning
235   in fence, I'd have seen him damned ere I'd have challenged him. Let him let the matter slip and I'll give him my horse, gray Capilet.

Toby. I'll make the motion. Stand here, make a good show on 't. This shall end without the perdition of souls.[50] [*Aside.*] Marry, I'll ride your horse as well as I ride you.

[*Enter* Fabian *and* Viola.]

240   [*Aside to* Fabian.] I have his horse to take up the quarrel. I have persuaded him the youth's a devil.

Fabian. He is as horribly conceited of him,[51] and pants and looks pale as if a bear were at his heels.

Toby [*to* Viola]. There's no remedy, sir, he will fight with you for 's oath's
245   sake. Marry, he hath better bethought him of his quarrel, and he finds that now scarce to be worth talking of. Therefore, draw for the supportance of his vow. He protests he will not hurt you.

---

[46] mettle—temperament.

[47] firago—virago, a violent, ill-tempered woman.

[48] stuck-in—thrust.

[49] **inevitable**—unavoidable.

[50] perdition of souls—loss of lives.

[51] He . . . him—Cesario has as horrible an image of him.

A terrified Viola (Marin Ireland) crosses swords with the equally frightened Sir Andrew (Wil Fisher) in the 2000 production of *Twelfth Night* at the Hartt School of the University of Hartford.

Viola [*aside*]. Pray God defend me! A little thing would make me tell them
    how much I lack of a man.

250   **Fabian.** Give ground, if you see him furious.

Toby [*crossing to* Sir Andrew]. Come, Sir Andrew, there's no remedy.
    The gentleman will, for his honor's sake, have one bout with you.
    He cannot by the *duello*[52] avoid it. But he has promised me, as he is a
    gentleman and a soldier, he will not hurt you. Come on, to 't.

---

[52] *duello*—code of dueling.

255   **Andrew.** Pray God he keep his oath!

[*Enter* Antonio.]

Viola [*drawing her sword*]. I do assure you, 'tis against my will.

[*Enter* Antonio.]

Antonio [*drawing, to* Sir Andrew].
        Put up your sword. If this young gentleman
        Have done offense, I take the fault on me;
        If you offend him, I for him defy you.

260 **Toby.** You, sir? Why, what are you?

Antonio. One, sir, that for his love dares yet do more
        Than you have heard him brag to you he will.

Toby [*drawing his sword*]. Nay, if you be an undertaker,[53] I am for you.

[*Enter two* Officers.]

Fabian. O good Sir Toby, hold! Here come the officers.

265 **Toby** [*to* Antonio]. I'll be with you anon.

Viola [*to* Sir Andrew]. Pray, sir, put your sword up, if you please.

Andrew. Marry, will I, sir. And for that I promised you, I'll be as good as
        my word. He will bear you easily, and reins well.

First Officer. This is the man. Do thy office.

270 **Second Officer.** Antonio, I arrest thee at the suit
        Of Count Orsino.

Antonio.   You do mistake me, sir.

First Officer. No, sir, no jot. I know your favor well,
        Though now you have no sea-cap on your head.—
        Take him away. He knows I know him well.

275 **Antonio.** I must obey. [*To* Viola.] This comes with seeking you.
        But there's no remedy; I shall answer it.
        What will you do, now my necessity
        Makes me to ask you for my purse? It grieves me
        Much more for what I cannot do for you
280   Than what befalls myself. You stand amazed,
        But be of comfort.

Second Officer. Come, sir, away.

Antonio [*to* Viola]. I must entreat of you some of that money.

Viola. What money, sir?

285   For the fair kindness you have showed me here,

---

[53] undertaker—one who takes up a challenge in place of another.

And part being prompted by your present trouble,
Out of my lean and low ability
I'll lend you something. My having is not much.
I'll make division of my present with you.

290   Hold, there's half my coffer.[54] [*She offers him money.*]

Antonio. Will you deny me now?
Is 't possible that my deserts to you
Can lack persuasion?[55] Do not tempt my misery,
Lest that it make me so unsound a man

295   As to **upbraid**[56] you with those kindnesses
That I have done for you.

Viola.   I know of none,
Nor know I you by voice or any feature.
I hate ingratitude more in a man
Than lying, vainness, babbling drunkenness,

300   Or any taint of vice whose strong corruption
Inhabits our frail blood—

Antonio. O heavens themselves!

Second Officer. Come, sir, I pray you, go.

Antonio. Let me speak a little. This youth that you see here

305   I snatched one half out of the jaws of death,
Relieved him with such sanctity of love,
And to his image,[57] which methought did promise
Most venerable worth, did I devotion.

First Officer. What's that to us? The time goes by. Away!

310 **Antonio.** But, O, how vile an idol proves this god!
Thou hast, Sebastian, done good feature shame.[58]
In nature there's no blemish but the mind;
None can be called deformed but the unkind.
Virtue is beauty, but the beauteous evil

315   Are empty trunks o'erflourished by the devil.

First Officer. The man grows mad. Away with him!
Come, come, sir.

---

[54] coffer—store of wealth (literally, strong box).

[55] my deserts ... persuasion—that my services to you can fail to persuade you.

[56] **upbraid**—find fault, blame.

[57] his image—what he appeared to be.

[58] done ... shame—disgraced your good looks.

A coward, a most devout coward, religious in it.

Antonio. Lead me on.

[*Exit* Antonio *and* Officers.]

Viola [*aside*]. Methinks his words do from such passion fly

320   That he believes himself. So do not I.

     Prove true, imagination, O, prove true,

     That I, dear brother, be now ta'en for you!

Toby. Come hither, knight. Come hither, Fabian.

     We'll whisper o'er a couplet or two of most sage saws.[59]

[Sir Toby, Fabian, *and* Sir Andrew *gather apart from* Viola.]

325 **Viola.** He named Sebastian. I my brother know

     Yet living in my glass.[60] Even such and so

     In favor was my brother, and he went

     Still in this fashion, color, ornament,

     For him I imitate. O, if it prove,

330   Tempests are kind, and salt waves fresh in love!

[*Exit* Viola.]

Toby. A very dishonest paltry[61] boy, and more a coward than a hare.

     His dishonesty appears in leaving his friend here in necessity and

     denying him; and for his cowardship, ask Fabian.

Fabian. A coward, a most devout coward, religious in it.

335 **Andrew.** 'Slid,[62] I'll after him again and beat him.

Toby. Do, cuff him soundly, but never draw thy sword.

Andrew. An I do not—

[*Exit* Andrew.]

Fabian. Come, let's see the event.

Toby. I dare lay any money 'twill be nothing yet.

[*They exit.*]

---

[59] saws—sayings, maxims.

[60] I my brother . . . my glass—I see my brother alive every time I look in a mirror.

[61] dishonest paltry—dishonorable, worthless.

[62] 'Slid—by God's eyelid (an oath).

Act Four, Scene One

In front of Olivia's house, Feste mistakes Sebastian for Cesario and tries to bring him to Olivia. When Sir Toby, Sir Andrew, and Fabian attack Sebastian, he skillfully fights Sir Andrew and is about to duel with Sir Toby when Feste brings Olivia to stop them. Sir Toby, Sir Andrew, and Fabian run away, and Olivia declares her love to the bewildered Sebastian.

Enter Sebastian *and* Feste.

Feste. Will you make me believe that I am not sent for you?

Sebastian. Go to, go to, thou art a foolish fellow. Let me be clear of thee.

Feste. Well held out, i' faith! No, I do not know you, nor I am not sent to
you by my lady to bid you come speak with her, nor your name is not

5 Master Cesario, nor this is not my nose, neither. Nothing that is so is so.

Sebastian. I prithee, vent thy folly somewhere else. Thou know'st not me.

Feste. Vent my folly! He has heard that word of some great man, and
now applies it to a fool. Vent my folly! I am afraid this great lubber,
the world, will prove a cockney.[1] I prithee now, ungird thy strange-

10 ness and tell me what I shall vent to my lady. Shall I vent to her that
thou art coming?

Sebastian. I prithee, foolish Greek,[2] depart from me. There's money
for thee. [*He gives* Feste *money.*] If you tarry longer, I shall give
worse payment.

15 **Feste.** By my troth, thou hast an open hand. These wise men that give
fools money get themselves a good report—after fourteen years'
purchase.[3]

[*Enter* Andrew, Toby, *and* Fabian.]

Andrew. Now, sir, have I met you again? There's for you!

[*He strikes* Sebastian.]

Sebastian. Why, there's for thee, and there, and there!—

20 [*He beats* Sir Andrew *with the hilt of his dagger.*] Are all the people mad?

Toby. Hold, sir, or I'll throw your dagger o'er the house.

---

[1] lubber . . . cockney—lout will prove to be a sissy.

[2] Greek—jester.

[3] after fourteen years' purchase—at a high price.

Feste. This will I tell my lady straight.[4] I would not be in some of your coats for twopence. [*Exit* Feste.]

Toby. Come on, sir, hold! [*He grips Sebastian.*]

25 **Andrew.** Nay, let him alone. I'll go another way to work with him. I'll have an action of battery[5] against him, if there be any law in Illyria. Though I struck him first, yet it's no matter for that.

Sebastian [*to* Toby]. Let go thy hand!

Toby. Come, sir, I will not let you go. Come, my young soldier, put up

30 your iron. You are well fleshed.[6] Come on.

Sebastian. I will be free from thee. [*He breaks free and draws his sword.*] What wouldst thou now?
If thou dar'st tempt me further, draw thy sword.

Toby. What, what? Nay, then, I must have an ounce or two of this mala-

35 pert[7] blood from you. [*He draws.*]

[*Enter* Olivia.]

Olivia. Hold, Toby! On thy life I charge thee, hold!

Toby. Madam—

Olivia. Will it be ever thus? Ungracious wretch,
Fit for the mountains and the barbarous caves,

40 Where manners ne'er were preached! Out of my sight!—
Be not offended, dear Cesario.—
Rudesby,[8] begone!

[*Exit* Toby, Andrew, *and* Fabian.]

               I prithee, gentle friend,
Let thy fair wisdom, not thy passion, sway
In this uncivil and unjust extent[9]

45 Against thy peace. Go with me to my house,
And hear thou there how many fruitless pranks
This ruffian hath botched up,[10] that thou thereby
Mayst smile at this. Thou shalt not choose but go.

---

[4] straight—straightaway, at once.

[5] action of battery—lawsuit for assault.

[6] well fleshed—made eager by the taste of blood.

[7] malapert—impudent, saucy.

[8] Rudesby—unmannerly fellow, ruffian.

[9] extent—attack.

[10] botched up—clumsily contrived.

Olivia (Kathryn Meisle) protects Sebastian (Daniel Sunjata) in the Guthrie Theatre production.

Do not deny. Beshrew[11] his soul for me!

50 He started one poor heart of mine, in thee.[12]

Sebastian [*aside*]. What relish is in this? How runs the stream?

Or I am mad, or else this is a dream.

Let fancy still my sense in Lethe[13] steep;

If it be thus to dream, still let me sleep!

55 **Olivia.** Nay, come, I prithee. Would thou'dst be ruled by me!

Sebastian. Madam, I will.

Olivia.   O, say so, and so be!

[*They exit.*]

---

[11] Beshrew—curse.

[12] He started . . . in thee—He made my heart, which lies in you. (*Wordplay* on *heart* and *hart*, or deer; and on *start* as *startle*, or rouse an animal from its hiding place.)

[13] Lethe—river of forgetfulness in the underworld.

Act Four, Scene Two

Outside a darkened room in Olivia's house, Maria has Feste disguise himself as a priest named Sir Topas. He visits Malvolio, who has been locked in the dark room. Feste tells him he is mad if he thinks it is dark. Later, Feste reappears as himself and continues the jest, but in the end he agrees to bring Malvolio the materials to write a letter to Olivia.

Enter Maria *with a gown and a false beard, and* Feste.

Maria. Nay, I prithee, put on this gown and this beard; make him believe thou art Sir Topas the curate. Do it quickly. I'll call Sir Toby the whilst.

[*Exit* Maria.]

Feste. Well, I'll put it on, and I will **dissemble**[1] myself in 't, and I would I were the first that ever dissembled in such a gown. [*Puts on gown and beard.*] I am not tall enough to become the function well,[2] nor lean enough to be thought a good student;[3] but to be said an honest man and a good housekeeper goes as fairly as to say a careful man and a great scholar. The competitors[4] enter.

[*Enter* Sir Toby *and* Maria.]

Toby. Jove bless thee, Master Parson.

Feste. *Bonos dies,*[5] Sir Toby. For, as the old hermit of Prague, that never saw pen and ink, very wittily said to a niece of King Gorboduc,[6] "That that is, is"; so I, being Master Parson, am Master Parson; for what is "that" but "that," and "is" but "is"?

Toby. To him, Sir Topas.

Feste [*disguising his voice*]. What, ho, I say! Peace in this prison!

[*He approaches the door behind which* Malvolio *is confined.*]

Toby. The knave counterfeits well. A good knave.

Malvolio [*within*][7]. Who calls there?

Feste. Sir Topas the curate, who comes to visit Malvolio the lunatic.

---

[1] **dissemble**—disguise.

[2] become the function well—grace the priestly office.

[3] lean enough . . . good student—Scholars were proverbially thought not to get enough to eat.

[4] competitors—partners.

[5] *Bonos dies*—"Good day" in bad Latin.

[6] King Gorboduc—legendary king of England.

[7] *within*—Malvolio speaks from the room where he is confined.

Feste (Daniel Cooney) visits the imprisoned Malvolio (Dean Nolen) in the Yale Repertory Theatre production.

Malvolio. Sir Topas, Sir Topas, good Sir Topas, go to my lady—

20   **Feste.** Out, hyperbolical fiend![8] How vexest thou this man! Talkest thou nothing but of ladies?

Toby [*aside*]. Well said, Master Parson.

Malvolio. Sir Topas, never was man thus wronged. Good Sir Topas, do not think I am mad. They have laid me here in hideous darkness.—

25   **Feste.** Fie, thou dishonest Satan! I call thee by the most modest terms, for I am one of those gentle ones that will use the devil himself with courtesy. Sayst thou that house is dark?

Malvolio. As hell, Sir Topas.

---

[8] hyperbolical fiend—ranting devil (that Feste pretends possesses Malvolio).

I am no more mad than you are.

Feste. Why, it hath bay windows transparent as barricadoes,[9] and the
clerestories[10] toward the south-north are as lustrous as ebony; and yet
complainest thou of obstruction?

Malvolio. I am not mad, Sir Topas. I say to you this house is dark.

Feste. Madman, thou errest. I say there is no darkness but ignorance, in
which thou art more puzzled than the Egyptians in their fog.

Malvolio. I say this house is as dark as ignorance, though ignorance were
as dark as hell. And I say there was never man thus abused. I am no
more mad than you are. Make the trial of it in any constant question.[11]

Feste. What is the opinion of Pythagoras concerning wildfowl?[12]

Malvolio. That the soul of our grandam might haply[13] inhabit a bird.

Feste. What think'st thou of his opinion?

Malvolio. I think nobly of the soul, and no way approve his opinion.

Feste. Fare thee well. Remain thou still in darkness. Thou shalt hold th'
opinion of Pythagoras ere I will allow of thy wits,[14] and fear to kill a
woodcock lest thou dispossess the soul of thy grandam. Fare thee well.

[*He moves away from* Malvolio's *prison.*]

Malvolio. Sir Topas, Sir Topas!

Toby. My most exquisite Sir Topas!

Feste. Nay, I am for all waters.[15]

Maria. Thou mightst have done this without thy beard and gown.
He sees thee not.

Toby. To him in thine own voice, and bring me word how thou find'st
him. I would we were well rid of this knavery. If he may be conveniently delivered, I would he were, for I am now so far in offense with
my niece that I cannot pursue with any safety this sport to the
upshot.[16] Come by and by to my chamber.

---

[9] barricadoes—barricades, barriers.

[10] clerestories—windows in an upper wall.

[11] Make . . . question—Test me with any reasonable question.

[12] Pythagoras . . . wildfowl—referring to the Pythagorean doctrine of the transmigration of souls.

[13] haply—perhaps.

[14] allow of thy wits—agree that you are sane.

[15] for all waters—ready for anything.

[16] upshot—conclusion.

[*Exit* Toby *with* Maria.]

Feste [*singing as he approaches* Malvolio's *prison*].

55   *Hey, Robin, jolly Robin,*

       Tell me how thy lady does.

Malvolio. Fool!

Feste [*sings*]. *My lady is unkind, pardie.*[17]

Malvolio. Fool!

60 **Feste.** *Alas, why is she so?*

Malvolio. Fool, I say!

Feste. *She loves another*—Who calls, ha?

Malvolio. Good fool, as ever thou wilt deserve well at my hand, help me
      to a candle, and pen, ink, and paper. As I am a gentleman, I will live

65   to be thankful to thee for 't.

Feste. Master Malvolio?

Malvolio. Ay, good fool.

Feste. Alas, sir, how fell you beside your five wits?[18]

Malvolio. Fool, there was never man so notoriously abused. I am as well

70   in my wits, fool, as thou art.

Feste. But as well? Then you are mad indeed, if you be no better in your
      wits than a fool.

Malvolio. They have here propertied me,[19] keep me in darkness,
      send ministers to me—asses!—and do all they can to face me out

75   of my wits.

Feste. Advise you[20] what you say. The minister is here. [*He speaks in the
      voice of* Sir Topas.] Malvolio, Malvolio, thy wits the heavens restore!
      Endeavor thyself to sleep, and leave thy vain bibble-babble.

Malvolio. Sir Topas!

80 **Feste** [*as* Sir Topas]. Maintain no words with him, good fellow. [*In his own
      voice.*] Who, I, sir? Not I, sir. God b' wi' you, good Sir Topas. [*As* Sir
      Topas.] Marry, amen. [*In his own voice.*] I will, sir, I will.

---

[17] *pardie*—by God.

[18] fell you . . . wits—did you lose your wits, generally defined as common sense, fantasy, memory, judgment, and imagination.

[19] propertied me—stowed me away like a piece of furniture.

[20] Advise you—-consider well.

Malvolio. Fool! Fool! Fool, I say!

Feste. Alas, sir, be patient. What say you, sir? I am shent[21] for speaking
85   to you.

Malvolio. Good fool, help me to some light and some paper. I tell thee, I
     am as well in my wits as any man in Illyria.

Feste. Welladay that[22] you were, sir!

Malvolio. By this hand, I am. Good fool, some ink, paper, and light; and
90   convey what I will set down to my lady. It shall advantage thee more
     than ever the bearing of letter did.

Feste. I will help you to 't. But tell me true, are you not mad indeed, or
     do you but counterfeit?

Malvolio. Believe me, I am not. I tell thee true.

95 **Feste.** Nay, I'll ne'er believe a madman till I see his brains. I will fetch
     you light and paper and ink.

Malvolio. Fool, I'll requite it in the highest degree. I prithee, begone.

Feste [*sings*].

> *I am gone, sir,*
> *And anon, sir,*
100   *I'll be with you again,*
> *In a trice,[23]*
> *Like to the old Vice,*
>   *Your need to sustain;*

> *Who, with dagger of lath,[24]*
105 *In his rage and his wrath,*
>   *Cries, "Aha!" to the devil;*
> *Like a mad lad,*
> *Pare thy nails, dad.*
>   *Adieu, goodman[25] devil!"*

[*They exit.*]

---

[21] shent—rebuked.

[22] Welladay that—alas, if only.

[23] *trice*—moment.

[24] *dagger of lath*—comic weapon used by the character Vice to "trim" the devil's nails in morality plays.

[25] *goodman*—insult to Malvolio, ranking him below the level of a gentleman.

Act Four, Scene Three

In Olivia's garden, Sebastian is trying to work out why Olivia is so fond of him. She appears with a priest and asks Sebastian if he will *marry her. He agrees, and they enter the chapel to be formally engaged.*

Enter Sebastian *holding a pearl.*

Sebastian. This is the air; that is the glorious sun;
This pearl she gave me, I do feel 't and see 't;
And though 'tis wonder that enwraps me thus,
Yet 'tis not madness. Where's Antonio, then?
5   I could not find him at the Elephant;
Yet there he was, and there I found this credit,[1]
That he did range the town to seek me out.
His counsel now might do me golden service;
For though my soul disputes well with my sense[2]
10   That this may be some error, but no madness,
Yet doth this accident and flood of fortune
So far exceed all instance, all discourse,[3]
That I am ready to distrust mine eyes
And wrangle with my reason that persuades me
15   To any other trust[4] but that I am mad,—
Or else the lady's mad. Yet if 'twere so,
She could not sway her house, command her followers,
Take and give back affairs and their dispatch[5]
With such a smooth, discreet, and stable bearing
20   As I perceive she does. There's something in 't
That is deceivable. But here the lady comes.
    [*Enter* Olivia *and* Priest.]

---

[1] found this credit—learned.

[2] my soul disputes well with my sense—my reason and my senses both maintain.

[3] discourse—reasoning, logic.

[4] trust—belief.

[5] Take and give ... dispatch—Take business in hand and give instructions for its prompt execution.

Olivia. Blame not this haste of mine. If you mean well,
    Now go with me and with this holy man
    Into the chantry[6] by. There, before him,
25   And underneath that consecrated roof,
    Plight me[7] the full assurance of your faith,
    That my most jealous and too doubtful soul
    May live at peace. He shall conceal it
    Whiles[8] you are willing it shall come to note,
30   What time we will our celebration keep[9]
    According to my birth.[10] What do you say?
Sebastian. I'll follow this good man, and go with you,
    And, having sworn truth, ever will be true.
Olivia. Then lead the way, good father, and heavens so shine
35   That they may fairly note[11] this act of mine!
[They exit.]

---

[6] chantry—small private chapel.

[7] Plight me—pledge to me.

[8] Whiles—until.

[9] celebration keep—celebrate our marriage.

[10] birth—social rank.

[11] fairly note—look upon with favor.

Act Five, Scene One

Outside Olivia's house, Orsino and his followers have arrived. He instructs Feste to announce him. Antonio tells Orsino that he only came into Illyria out of his great love for Sebastian, and he again mistakes Cesario for him. Olivia welcomes the duke, but begs him not to press his love on her. Orsino becomes angry, threatening to kill Cesario whom he recognizes that Olivia loves. When Viola protests that she wishes only to stay with Orsino, Olivia in turn becomes upset. She sends for the priest who confirms that she is formally betrothed to Cesario, who Orsino now bitterly rejects. Sir Andrew rushes in searching for a doctor for his wounds and proclaiming that Cesario has attacked Sir Toby as well. Sebastian enters and the company is astonished to see the twins together.

Viola and Sebastian question each other until Viola admits that she is in disguise. Orsino realizes that the disguised Viola has often confessed her love for him. Olivia sends for Malvolio, who has caused the captain who saved Viola to be imprisoned. She remembers his madness, but Feste delivers a letter wherein Malvolio complains of his ill treatment and seems quite sane. As they await the steward, Orsino proposes to Viola and the couples agree to a double celebration. When Malvolio shows Olivia the forged letter, she tells him he has been deceived by a cruel trick, which Fabian explains. He adds that Sir Toby has now married Maria. Malvolio storms off, swearing he will get revenge. All go to prepare for the wedding celebration. Feste ends the play by singing a song as an epilogue.

Enter Feste *and* Fabian.

Fabian. Now, as thou lov'st me, let me see his letter.

Feste. Good Master Fabian, grant me another request.

Fabian. Anything.

Feste. Do not desire to see this letter.

5   **Fabian.** This is to give a dog and in recompense desire my dog again.
[*Enter* Duke Orsino, Viola, Curio, *and* Lords.]

Orsino. Belong you to the Lady Olivia, friends?

Feste. Ay, sir, we are some of her trappings.[1]

Orsino. I know thee well. How dost thou, my good fellow?

Feste. Truly, sir, the better for my foes and the worse for my friends.

10   **Orsino.** Just the contrary: the better for thy friends.

---

[1] trappings—belongings.

Feste. No, sir, the worse.

Orsino. How can that be?

Feste. Marry, sir, they praise me, and make an ass of me. Now my foes tell me plainly I am an ass, so that by my foes, sir, I profit in the knowl-
15 edge of myself, and by my friends I am abused. So that, conclusions to be as kisses, if your four negatives make your two affirmatives, why then the worse for my friends and the better for my foes.

Orsino. Why, this is excellent.

Feste. By my troth, sir, no, though it please you to be one of my friends.

20 **Orsino.** Thou shalt not be the worse for me. There's gold.

[*He gives* Feste *a coin*.]

Feste. But that it would be double-dealing, sir, I would you could make it another.

Orsino. O, you give me ill counsel.

Feste. Put your grace² in your pocket, sir, for this once, and let your flesh
25 and blood obey it.

Orsino. Well, I will be so much a sinner to be a double-dealer. There's another. [*He gives* Feste *another coin*.]

Feste. *Primo, secundo, tertio,*³ is a good play, and the old saying is, the third pays for all. The triplex, sir, is a good tripping measure, or the
30 bells of Saint Bennet,⁴ sir, may put you in mind—one, two, three.

Orsino. You can fool no more money out of me at this throw. If you will let your lady know I am here to speak with her, and bring her along with you, it may awake my bounty further.

Feste. Marry, sir, lullaby to your bounty till I come again. I go, sir, but I
35 would not have you to think that my desire of having is the sin of **covetousness.**⁵ But as you say, sir, let your bounty take a nap. I will awake it anon. [*Exit* Feste.]

[*Enter* Antonio *and* Officers.]

Viola. Here comes the man, sir, that did rescue me.

Orsino. That face of his I do remember well,
40 Yet when I saw it last, it was besmeared

---

² grace—virtue. Feste also puns on the customary way to address a duke, which is "your grace."

³ *Primo, secundo, tertio*—first, second, third; reference to a game of dice.

⁴ The triplex . . . Bennet—Triple time (in music) is good for dancing, just like the bells of the Church of St. Benedict in London.

⁵ **covetousness**—greed.

As black as Vulcan[6] in the smoke of war.
A baubling[7] vessel was he captain of,
For shallow draft and bulk unprizable,[8]
With which such scatheful grapple[9] did he make

45   With the most noble bottom[10] of our fleet
That very envy[11] and the tongue of loss
Cried fame and honor on him.—What's the matter?

First Officer. Orsino, this is that Antonio
That took the *Phoenix* and her freight from Candy,[12]

50   And this is he that did the *Tiger* board
When your young nephew Titus lost his leg.
Here in the streets, desperate of shame and state,[13]
In private brabble[14] did we apprehend him.

Viola. He did me kindness, sir, drew on my side,

55   But in conclusion put strange speech upon me.[15]
I know not what 'twas but distraction.[16]

Orsino. Notable pirate, thou saltwater thief,
What foolish boldness brought thee to their mercies
Whom thou in terms so bloody and so dear

60   Hast made thine enemies?

Antonio.   Orsino, noble sir,
Be pleased[17] that I shake off these names you give me.
Antonio never yet was thief or pirate,
Though, I confess, on base and ground enough
Orsino's enemy. A witchcraft drew me hither.

---

[6] Vulcan—Roman god of fire, blackened by the smoke of his forge.

[7] baubling—trifling.

[8] For shallow … unprizable—valueless because of its small size.

[9] scatheful grapple—damaging attack.

[10] bottom—ship.

[11] very envy—even enmity itself.

[12] Candy—island of Crete.

[13] desperate of shame and state—as if unconcerned with disgrace and danger.

[14] brabble—brawl.

[15] put strange speech upon me—spoke oddly to me.

[16] but distraction—unless it was madness.

[17] Be pleased—permit.

65   That most ingrateful boy there by your side
     From the rude sea's enraged and foamy mouth
     Did I redeem; a wreck past hope he was.
     His life I gave him and did thereto add
     My love, without retention or restraint,
70   All his in dedication. For his sake
     Did I expose myself, pure for his love,
     Into the danger of this adverse town,
     Drew to defend him when he was beset;
     Where, being apprehended, his false cunning,
75   Not meaning to partake with me in danger,
     Taught him to face me out of his acquaintance
     And grew a twenty years' removèd thing
     While one would wink;[18] denied me mine own purse,
     Which I had recommended to his use
80   Not half an hour before.

Viola. How can this be?

Orsino [*to* Antonio]. When came he to this town?

Antonio. Today, my lord; and for three months before,
     No interim, not a minute's vacancy,
85   Both day and night did we keep company.

[*Enter* Olivia *and* Attendants.]

Orsino. Here comes the countess. Now heaven walks on earth.—
     But for thee, fellow—fellow, thy words are madness.
     Three months this youth hath tended upon me—
     But more of that anon. [*To the* Officers.] Take him aside.

90   **Olivia** [*to* Orsino]. What would my lord, but that he may not have,
     Wherein Olivia may seem serviceable?—
     Cesario, you do not keep promise with me.

Viola. Madam?

Orsino. Gracious Olivia—

95   **Olivia.** What do you say, Cesario?—Good my lord—

Viola. My lord would speak. My duty hushes me.

---

[18] to face me . . . wink—brazenly deny that he knew me and in the twinkling of an eye became as distant as if we had not seen each other for twenty years.

Olivia. If it be aught to the old tune, my lord,
    It is as fat and fulsome[19] to mine ear
    As howling after music.

100 **Orsino.** Still so cruel?

Olivia.   Still so constant, lord.

Orsino. What, to perverseness? You uncivil lady,
    To whose ingrate and inauspicious[20] altars
    My soul the faithful'st offerings have breathed out
    That e'er devotion tendered! What shall I do?

105 **Olivia.** Even what it please my lord that shall become him.

Orsino. Why should I not, had I the heart to do it,
    Like to th' Egyptian thief at point of death
    Kill what I love?[21]—a savage jealousy
    That sometimes savors nobly. But hear me this:

110   Since you to nonregardance[22] cast my faith,
    And that I partly know the instrument
    That screws me from my true place in your favor,
    Live you the marble-breasted tyrant still.
    But this your minion,[23] whom I know you love,

115   And whom, by heaven I swear, I tender dearly,
    Him will I tear out of that cruel eye
    Where he sits crownèd in his master's spite.[24]—
    Come, boy, with me. My thoughts are ripe in mischief.
    I'll sacrifice the lamb that I do love,

120   To spite a raven's heart within a dove.[25] [*Going.*]

Viola. And I, most jocund,[26] apt, and willingly,
    To do you rest,[27] a thousand deaths would die.
[*Going.*]

---

[19] fat and fulsome—gross and distasteful.

[20] ingrate and inauspicious—ungrateful and unfavorable.

[21] Like . . . what I love—reference to a story in which an Egyptian robber captain who has fallen in love with his captive finds himself in danger of death at his enemies' hands and attempts to kill his beloved first.

[22] nonregardance—disregard, neglect.

[23] minion—darling (that is, Cesario).

[24] in his master's spite—in defiance of his master.

[25] I'll sacrifice . . . within a dove—I'll kill Cesario, who I love, to spite the black-hearted Olivia.

[26] jocund—cheerful, merry.

[27] do you rest—give you peace.

In the Guthrie Theatre production, Orsino (Peter Hermann) is enraged by Olivia's refusal to marry him.

Olivia. Where goes Cesario?

Viola.   After him I love
More than I love these eyes, more than my life,
More by all mores than e'er I shall love wife.
If I do feign, you witnesses above
Punish my life for tainting of my love!²⁸

Olivia. Ay me, detested! How am I **beguiled!**²⁹

Viola. Who does beguile you? Who does do you wrong?

Olivia. Hast thou forgot thyself? Is it so long?—
Call forth the holy father. [*Exit an* Attendant.]

Orsino [*to* Viola]. Come, away!

Olivia. Whither, my lord?—Cesario, husband, stay.

Orsino. Husband?

Olivia.   Ay, husband. Can he that deny?

125

130

---

²⁸ Punish my life . . . my love—Punish me with death for bringing my love into dishonor.
²⁹ **beguiled**—deceived.

Orsino [*to* Viola]. Her husband, sirrah?

Viola.   No, my lord, not I.

Olivia. Alas, it is the baseness of thy fear

  That makes thee strangle thy propriety.

  Fear not, Cesario. Take thy fortunes up;

  Be that thou know'st thou art, and then thou art

140 As great as that thou fear'st.

[*Enter* Priest.]

                                              O, welcome, father!

  Father, I charge thee by thy reverence

  Here to unfold—though lately we intended

  To keep in darkness what occasion now

  Reveals before 'tis ripe—what thou dost know

145 Hath newly passed between this youth and me.

Priest. A contract of eternal bond of love,

  Confirmed by mutual joinder of your hands,

  Attested by the holy close of lips,

  Strengthened by interchangement of your rings,

150 And all the ceremony of this compact

  Sealed in my function, by my testimony;

  Since when, my watch hath told me, toward my grave

  I have traveled but two hours.

Orsino [*to* Viola]. O thou dissembling cub! What wilt thou be

155 When time hath sowed a grizzle on thy case?[30]

  Or will not else thy craft so quickly grow

  That thine own trip[31] shall be thine overthrow?

  Farewell, and take her, but direct thy feet

  Where thou and I henceforth may never meet.

160 **Viola.** My Lord, I do protest—

Olivia.   O, do not swear!

  Hold little faith, though thou hast too much fear.

[*Enter* Sir Andrew.]

Andrew. For the love of God, a surgeon! Send one presently to Sir Toby.

Olivia. What's the matter?

---

[30] grizzle . . . case—grey hair on the skin (of a fox).

[31] trip—wrestling move in which one trips one's opponent.

Andrew. He's broke my head across, and has given Sir Toby a bloody
165   coxcomb³² too. For the love of God, your help! I had rather than forty
       pound I were at home.

Olivia. Who has done this, Sir Andrew?

Andrew. The count's gentleman, one Cesario. We took him for a coward,
       but he's the very devil incardinate.³³

170 **Orsino.** My gentleman, Cesario?

Andrew. 'Od's lifelings³⁴ here he is!—You broke my head for nothing,
       and that that I did, I was set on to do 't by Sir Toby.

Viola. Why do you speak to me? I never hurt you.
       You drew your sword upon me without cause,
175   But I bespake you fair, and hurt you not.

Andrew. If a bloody coxcomb be a hurt, you have hurt me. I think you set
       nothing by a bloody coxcomb.

       [*Enter* Toby *and* Feste.]

       Here comes Sir Toby, halting. You shall hear more. But if he had not
       been in drink, he would have tickled you othergates³⁵ than he did.

180 **Orsino.** How now, gentleman? How is 't with you?

Toby. That's all one. He's hurt me, and there's th' end on 't. [*To* Feste.]
       Sot, didst see Dick Surgeon, sot?

Feste. O, he's drunk, Sir Toby, an hour agone; his eyes were set at eight i'
       the morning.

185 **Toby.** Then he's a rogue, and a passy measures pavane.³⁶ I hate a
       drunken rogue.

Olivia. Away with him! Who hath made this havoc with them?

Andrew. I'll help you, Sir Toby, because we'll be dressed together.

Toby. Will you help? An ass-head and a coxcomb and a knave, a thin-
190   faced knave, a gull!

Olivia. Get him to bed, and let his hurt be looked to.

       [*Exit* Feste, Fabian, Sir Toby, *and* Sir Andrew.]

---

³² coxcomb—head.

³³ incardinate—mistake for "incarnate."

³⁴ 'Od's lifelings—by God's little lives (an oath).

³⁵ othergates—otherwise.

³⁶ passy measures pavane—slow and stately dance (possibly a comment on the doctor's slowness).

An apple cleft in two is not more twin
Than these two creatures.

[*Enter* Sebastian.]

Sebastian. I am sorry, madam, I have hurt your kinsman;
But, had it been the brother of my blood,
I must have done no less with wit and safety.[37]—

195   You throw a strange regard upon me,[38] and by that
I do perceive it hath offended you.
Pardon me, sweet one, even for the vows
We made each other but so late ago.

Orsino. One face, one voice, one habit, and two persons,

200   A natural perspective,[39] that is and is not!

Sebastian. Antonio, O my dear Antonio!
How have the hours racked and tortured me
Since I have lost thee!

Antonio. Sebastian are you?

Sebastian.   Fear'st thou that, Antonio?

205 **Antonio.** How have you made division of yourself?
An apple cleft in two is not more twin
Than these two creatures. Which is Sebastian?

Olivia. Most wonderful!

Sebastian [*seeing* Viola]. Do I stand there? I never had a brother;

210   Nor can there be that deity in my nature
Of here and everywhere.[40] I had a sister,
Whom the blind waves and surges have devoured.
Of charity, what kin are you to me?
What countryman? What name? What parentage?

215 **Viola.** Of Messaline. Sebastian was my father.
Such a Sebastian was my brother, too.

---

[37] with wit and safety—with due regard for my safety.

[38] throw a strange regard upon me—look at me as if I was a stranger.

[39] natural perspective—optical illusion produced by nature.

[40] Nor . . . everywhere—nor can I be everywhere at one time, like a god.

So went he suited to his watery tomb.
If spirits can assume both form and suit,
You come to fright us.

Sebastian. A spirit I am indeed,
220 But am in that dimension grossly clad
Which from the womb I did participate.
Were you a woman, as the rest goes even,
I should my tears let fall upon your cheek
And say, "Thrice welcome, drownèd Viola!"

225 **Viola.** My father had a mole upon his brow.

Sebastian. And so had mine.

Viola. And died that day when Viola from her birth
Had numbered thirteen years.

Sebastian. O, that record is lively in my soul!
230 He finishèd indeed his mortal act
That day that made my sister thirteen years.

Viola. If nothing lets[41] to make us happy both
But this my masculine usurped attire,
Do not embrace me till each circumstance
235 Of place, time, fortune, do cohere and jump[42]
That I am Viola—which to confirm
I'll bring you to a captain in this town
Where lie my maiden weeds,[43] by whose gentle help
I was preserved to serve this noble count.
240 All the occurrence of my fortune since
Hath been between this lady and this lord.

Sebastian [*to* Olivia]. So comes it, lady, you have been mistook.
But nature to her bias drew in that.[44]
You would have been contracted to a maid,
245 Nor are you therein, by my life, deceived.
You are betrothed both to a maid and man.

---

[41] lets—hinders.

[42] jump—coincide, agree.

[43] weeds—clothes.

[44] nature to her bias drew in that—nature followed her bent in that.

Orsino (Will Lyman) pledges to marry Viola (Marin Ireland) in this scene from the Hartt School production.

> **Orsino** [*to* Olivia]. Be not amazed; right noble is his blood.
>   If this be so, as yet the glass seems true,
>   I shall have share in this most happy wreck.
> 250   [*To* Viola.] Boy, thou hast said to me a thousand times
>   Thou never shouldst love woman like to me.[45]
> **Viola.** And all those sayings will I overswear,
>   And all those swearings keep as true in soul
>   As doth that orbèd continent the fire[46]
> 255   That severs day from night.
> **Orsino.** Give me thy hand.
>   And let me see thee in thy woman's weeds.
> **Viola.** The captain that did bring me first on shore
>   Hath my maid's garments. He upon some action
> 260   Is now in durance,[47] at Malvolio's suit,
>   A gentleman and follower of my lady's.

---

[45] like to me—as well as you love me.

[46] As doth . . . the fire—as the sun's sphere keeps the fire.

[47] in durance—in prison.

Olivia. He shall enlarge[48] him. Fetch Malvolio hither.

And yet, alas, now I remember me,

They say, poor gentleman, he's much distract.

[*Enter* Feste *with a letter, and* Fabian.]

265   A most extracting frenzy[49] of mine own

From my remembrance dearly banished his.

[*To* Feste.] How does he, sirrah?

Feste. Truly, madam, he holds Beelzebub at the stave's end as well as a

man in his case may do. He's here writ a letter to you. I should have

270   given 't you today morning. But as a madman's epistles are no

gospels, so it skills not much when they are delivered.[50]

Olivia. Open 't and read it.

Feste. Look then to be well edified when the fool delivers the madman.

[*He reads loudly.*] *By the Lord, madam—*

275   **Olivia.** How now, art thou mad?

Feste. No, madam, I do but read madness. An your ladyship will have it

as it ought to be, you must allow *vox*.[51]

Olivia. Prithee, read i' thy right wits.

Feste. So I do, madonna; but to read his right wits is to read thus.

280   Therefore perpend,[52] my princess, and give ear.

Olivia [*giving the letter to* Fabian]. Read it you, sirrah.

Fabian [*reads*]. *By the Lord, madam, you wrong me, and the world shall know it.*

Though you have put me into darkness and given your drunken cousin rule

over me, yet have I the benefit of my senses as well as your ladyship. I have

285   *your own letter that induced me to the semblance[53] I put on, with the which I*

doubt not but to do myself much right or you much shame. Think of me as you

please. I leave my duty a little unthought of, and speak out of my injury.[54]

                     The madly used Malvolio.

Olivia. Did he write this?

---

[48] enlarge—release.

[49] extracting frenzy—madness that took other things out of my mind.

[50] But on . . . delivered—Since a madman's letters are not to be taken as truth, so it makes little difference when they are delivered.

[51] allow *vox*—permit me to use the right voice.

[52] perpend—consider.

[53] *semblance*—costume suggested in the letter.

[54] *I leave . . . injury*—I am speaking not as your servant but as an injured party.

Malvolio (Dean Nolen) shows Maria's forged letter to Olivia in the Yale Repertory Theatre production.

290 **Feste.** Ay, madam.

Orsino. This savors not much of distraction.

Olivia. See him delivered, Fabian. Bring him hither.

[*Exit* Fabian.]

My lord, so please you, these things further thought on,

To think me as well a sister as a wife,[55]

295 One day shall crown th' alliance on 't, so please you,

Here at my house, and at my proper cost.

Orsino. Madam, I am most apt t' embrace your offer.

[*To* Viola.] Your master quits you; and for your service done him,

So much against the mettle of your sex,

300 So far beneath your soft and tender breeding,

And since you called me "master" for so long,

---

[55] as well . . . a wife—as good a sister-in-law as you were thinking of me as a wife.

Here is my hand. You shall from this time be
Your master's mistress.
Olivia.   A sister! You are she.
[*Enter* Fabian, *with* Malvolio.]
Orsino. Is this the madman?
Olivia.   Ay, my lord, this same.—
305   How now, Malvolio?
Malvolio.   Madam, you have done me wrong,
         Notorious wrong.
Olivia.   Have I, Malvolio? No.
Malvolio [*showing her a letter*].
         Lady, you have. Pray you, peruse that letter.
         You must not now deny it is your hand.
         Write from it,[56] if you can, in hand or phrase,
310   Or say 'tis not your seal, not your invention.
         You can say none of this. Well, grant it then,
         And tell me, in the modesty of honor,[57]
         Why you have given me such clear lights of favor?
         Bade me come smiling and cross-gartered to you,
315   To put on yellow stockings, and to frown
         Upon Sir Toby and the lighter[58] people?
         And, acting this in an obedient hope,
         Why have you suffered me to be imprisoned,
         Kept in a dark house, visited by the priest,
320   And made the most notorious geck and gull[59]
         That e'er invention played on? Tell me why?
Olivia. Alas, Malvolio, this is not my writing,
         Though, I confess, much like the character.
         But out of question, 'tis Maria's hand.
325   And now I do bethink me, it was she
         First told me thou wast mad; then cam'st in smiling,
         And in such forms which here were presupposed[60]
         Upon thee in the letter. Prithee, be content.

---

[56] from it—differently.

[57] in the modesty of honor—with the sense of propriety of an honorable person.

[58] lighter—lesser.

[59] geck and gull—dupe.

[60] presupposed—suggested beforehand.

This practice hath most shrewdly passed upon thee;[61]
330 But when we know the grounds and authors of it,
Thou shalt be both the plaintiff and the judge
Of thine own cause.

Fabian.　　　　　Good madam, hear me speak,
And let no quarrel nor no brawl to come
Taint the condition of this present hour,
335 Which I have wondered at. In hope it shall not,
Most freely I confess, myself and Toby
Set this device against Malvolio here,
Upon[62] some stubborn and uncourteous parts
We had conceived against him. Maria writ
340 The letter at Sir Toby's great importance,[63]
In recompense whereof he hath married her.
How with a sportful malice it was followed[64]
May rather pluck on laughter than revenge,
If that the injuries be justly weighed
345 That have on both sides passed.

Olivia [*to* Malvolio]. Alas, poor fool, how have they baffled thee!

Feste. Why, "some are born great, some achieve greatness, and some
have greatness thrown upon them." I was one, sir, in this interlude,
one Sir Topas, sir, but that's all one. "By the Lord, fool, I am not
350 mad." But do you remember? "Madam, why laugh you at such a
barren rascal? An you smile not, he's gagged." And thus the
whirligig of time[65] brings in his revenges.

Malvolio. I'll be revenged on the whole pack of you!

[*Exit* Malvolio.]

Olivia. He hath been most notoriously abused.

355 **Orsino.** Pursue him, and entreat him to a peace.
He hath not told us of the captain yet.
When that is known, and golden time convents,[66]

---

61 practice . . . thee—plot has maliciously tricked you.

62 Upon—in consequence of.

63 importance—importunity, urgent request.

64 followed—carried through.

65 whirligig of time—time's circling course. A whirligig is a toplike toy.

66 convents—suits.

For the rain it raineth every day.

A solemn combination shall be made
Of our dear souls.—Meantime, sweet sister,
360   We will not part from hence.—Cesario, come,
For so you shall be, while you are a man;
But when in other habits you are seen,
Orsino's mistress and his fancy's[67] queen.

[*Exit all but* Feste.]

Feste [*sings*]. *When that I was and a little tiny boy,*
365   *With hey, ho, the wind and the rain,*
A foolish thing was but a toy,
    For the rain it raineth every day.

But when I came to man's estate,
    With hey, ho, the wind and the rain,
370   *'Gainst knaves and thieves men shut their gate,*
    For the rain it raineth every day.

But when I came, alas, to wive,
    With hey, ho, the wind and the rain,
By swaggering could I never thrive,
375   *For the rain it raineth every day.*

But when I came unto my beds,
    With hey, ho, the wind and the rain,
With tosspots[68] still had drunken heads,
    For the rain it raineth every day.

380   *A great while ago the world begun,*
    With hey, ho, the wind and the rain,
But that's all one, our play is done,
    And we'll strive to please you every day.

[*Exit* Feste.]

---

[67] fancy's—love's.

[68] *tosspots*—drunkards.

Understanding the play

Act One

1. In Scene One, what kind of lover does Orsino seem to be?

2. In Scene Two, why does Viola want to go to Olivia's court? Why does she instead disguise herself as a man and go to Orsino's?

3. In Scene Three, why does Sir Toby not want Sir Andrew to leave Illyria?

4. In Scene Four, what is ironic about the task that Orsino sets for the disguised Viola?

5. In Scene Five, why does Feste say that Olivia is actually "the fool"?

6. How do Malvolio and Feste feel toward each other?

Act Two

1. In Scene One, why does Sebastian feel he must leave Antonio?

2. In Scene Two, why do you think Viola does not tell Malvolio that she didn't give Olivia a ring?

3. In Scene Three, why does Maria believe that her trick will fool Malvolio?

4. In Scene Four, Orsino twice contrasts men's and women's capacities to love (lines 34–37 and 89–97). How do the comparisons differ?

5. Why do you think Viola tells the story of her "sister" to Orsino?

6. In Scene Five, why do you think Malvolio is so quickly convinced that Olivia loves him?

Act Three

1. In Scene One, how does Feste explain his function as Olivia's jester? How does Viola see his role?

2. In Scene Two, how do Fabian and Sir Toby convince Sir Andrew not to leave?

3. In Scene Three, how does Antonio explain his concern about being found in Orsino's realm?

4. In Scene Four, how does Olivia react to Malvolio's dress and behavior?

5. Why does Antonio become so angry with Viola?

6. How does Viola react to Antonio's mistaking her for Sebastian?

Act Four

1. In Scene One, how does Sebastian react to Olivia's treatment of him?

2. In Scene Two, what has happened to Malvolio?

3. In his disguise as Sir Topas, how does Feste try to convince Malvolio that he is mad?

4. In Scene Three, why does Sebastian believe that Olivia is not mad?

Act Five

1. In Act Five, how does Antonio explain his willingness to risk being captured by his Illyrian enemies?

2. When Olivia refuses him once again, what does Orsino threaten to do?

3. Why do you think Sir Toby suddenly reveals his contempt for Sir Andrew?

4. Why do you think Viola and Sebastian are hesitant at first to recognize one another?

5. Once Orsino discovers that Viola is a girl, why do you think he is so willing to switch his affections from Olivia to her?

Analyzing the play

1. Shakespeare chose *What You Will* as the sub-title of this play. What phrases from the play do you feel might do a better job of capturing *Twelfth Night*'s meaning?

2. Most of the major characters in *Twelfth Night* are "in love" in one sense or another. Which of these emotions seem to you to be "true love"? What, in general, does this play seem to be saying about the nature of "true love"?

3. When Viola becomes aware that Olivia, thinking she is a man, has fallen in love with her, she observes, "Disguise, I see, thou are a wickedness." In *Twelfth Night,* what are the advantages and disadvantages of pretending to be someone you're not?

4. Related to the theme of disguise in *Twelfth Night* is the question of sexual identity. In the context of this play, what does it mean to be a man or a woman?

5. In Shakespeare's tragedies, "low" characters such as Sir Toby and Sir Andrew provide comic relief. What function do they serve in this comedy?

6. How would you sum up the "message" of *Twelfth Night* about how to live?

Writing projects

1. Most of the characters in *Twelfth Night* have love problems of one kind or another. Choose one character and write a short letter of advice, suggesting how to deal with their romantic difficulties.

2. Women tend to be far more important in Shakespeare's comedies than they are in his tragedies. Write an essay discussing how women dominate the action of *Twelfth Night.*

3. Malvolio is a puzzling figure who combines elements of the heroic, the comic, and the villainous. Write a character analysis of Malvolio that considers his actions (including his role as Olivia's steward), his thoughts, and how others act toward him.

4. Unlike the ancient country in the Balkan Peninsula, Shakespeare's Illyria is part Elizabethan England and part pure invention. Write a few brief entries for a "Traveler's Guide to Illyria." You might discuss the country's landscape, history, government, culture, and so on. Build on what you find in the play.

5. Write a brief news story about Antonio's sea fight against Orsino's galleys from the point of view of an Illyrian journalist.

6. Write the plot for a short sequel to *Twelfth Night* telling what happens to the various married couples in the future. Don't forget to include Sir Toby and Maria.

Performance projects

1. If you were directing *Twelfth Night*, how would you make the plot device of twins confused for one another convincing to the audience? Create some director's notes showing how to handle this problem.

2. If you were designing a production of *Twelfth Night,* how would you present Illyria? Decide on a concept and create some sketches for sets and costumes.

3. If you were playing Feste, how would you interpret the role? Would you stress absurdity? humor? melancholy? Create some actor's notes describing your interpretation of this role and include ideas for costuming and make-up.

4. Read Malvolio's letter to Olivia as you think it would be read by Feste, by Fabian, and by Malvolio himself.

5. Find contemporary songs that could serve in place of Feste's. Play them for the class and explain how they express the same themes as Shakespeare's originals.

Hamlet, Prince of Denmark

Introduction

Hamlet *is one of our central works of art. The play's story has been retold in many other art forms, its lines are familiar from frequent quotation, and everyone recognizes its melancholy, brooding hero. Each generation has been able to find in Hamlet a reflection of its own problems and fears. He has within himself the conflicting emotions that trouble all human minds. Hamlet's soliloquies—the* monologues he delivers—are Shakespeare's great dramatic innovation. The playwright used them to reveal his hero's emotions quickly and vividly and to present to the audience the internal process of examining and working out a moral problem. These glimpses into Hamlet's innermost feelings make him one of literature's most complete and sympathetic characters.

◀ Hamlet (Mark Rylance) struggles with his grief over his father's death in this scene from the 2000 production at London's Globe Theatre.

Plot

At its most basic level, Hamlet *is a story of revenge. Shortly before the play opens, the king of Denmark has died and been succeeded by his brother Claudius, who has also married the widowed queen. The play's major action is set in motion by the appearance of the Ghost, who tells the late king's* son, Hamlet, that his father was murdered by Claudius and to demand revenge. Hamlet first proceeds to convince himself of Claudius's guilt and then to enact revenge. As Claudius recognizes the danger Hamlet poses to him, a counterplot develops as the new king takes steps to destroy his nephew.

Another major action in the play involves Hamlet's troubled relations with his mother. Hamlet is outraged and disgusted by Gertrude's hasty remarriage, but she is in love with her new husband and cannot understand her son's anger. In a climactic scene, Hamlet first terrifies his mother with his violent behavior, and then fills her with guilt about her relationship with Claudius.

◄ In this scene from the 1987 production of *Hamlet* by Connecticut's Hartford Stage theater company, Gertrude (Pamela Payton-Wright) cannot understand why her son (Richard Thomas) continues to brood.

A third major action in Hamlet *involves the prince's equally troubled relationship with the other woman in his life, Ophelia, daughter of Polonius, the Lord Chamberlain. Ophelia's father and her brother Laertes warn her not to trust Hamlet's professions of love. She is torn by love and duty; when Hamlet accidentally kills Polonius, she goes mad and is drowned, perhaps a suicide. To avenge his father and sister, Laertes joins Claudius's plot against Hamlet.*

Hamlet (Mark Rylance, left) and Laertes (Mark Lockyer) are both grief-stricken at Ophelia's grave in the Globe Theatre production.

Settings and Characters

Most of Hamlet takes place at the Danish court at Elsinore castle. Much of the play is set at night or in dark interiors. One of the few scenes to be set in the daylight is Ophelia's funeral.

Hamlet completely dominates the play. Every other character is secondary, and each is defined essentially in relation to him. The major characters fall into several groups: (1) Claudius, Gertrude, and their courtiers, particularly Hamlet's former friends Rosencrantz and Guildenstern; (2) Polonius and his children, Ophelia and Laertes; (3) Hamlet's friend Horatio; (4) two Gravediggers who are the play's clowns; and (5) the Ghost.

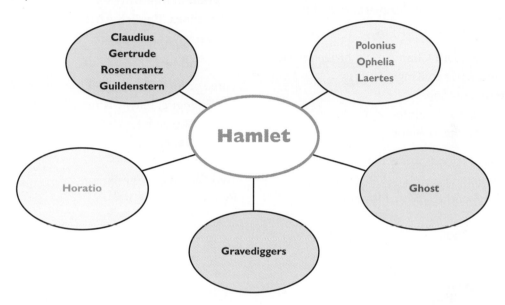

Themes

Hamlet is about death and about the ways that people react to it. When the play opens, the Danish court is in full celebration of a coronation and a wedding; but Hamlet is in black, still mourning his father's death. Hamlet has reacted to his father's death by giving up all of his former life. He was an athlete, a scholar, and an enthusiast of the theater, and he was deeply in love with Ophelia. Gertrude has reacted to her husband's death by finding love again rather than facing loneliness. Ophelia and Laertes will acknowledge death after their father's murder: she by falling into madness, he by caring only for revenge.

Throughout the play, Hamlet considers the question of what he must do. Death is the provocation, but Hamlet is unsure of how to act. He contemplates his every move and idea in the soliloquies that enable us to see a mind working out a problem. And behind it all is the fact made clear by Yorick's skull—that everyone ends as a corpse.

In Hamlet, Shakespeare also muses about the idea of acting or "playing"—of appearing different from reality. There is much deception in the play: Hamlet pretends to be mad; Rosencrantz and Guildenstern pretend to be the prince's friends; Claudius pretends to be a good king; Ophelia pretends to meet Hamlet by accident, and so on. And the play contains another play within it: Hamlet arranges for a troupe of actors to perform a play that resembles the murder of his deceased father to help him discover the truth about his uncle.

Characters

Ghost of Hamlet, the former King of
    Denmark
Claudius, King of Denmark, the former
    king's brother
Gertrude, Hamlet's mother, wife of
    the late king, now wife of Claudius
Hamlet, Prince of Denmark, son of the late
    king and of Gertrude

Polonius, Lord Chamberlain of Denmark,
    councilor to King Claudius
Laertes, his son
Ophelia, his daughter
Reynaldo, his servant

Horatio, friend of Hamlet
Rosencrantz and **Guildenstern,**
    boyhood friends of Hamlet

Voltimand, Cornelius, and **Osric,**
    courtiers
Bernardo, Francisco, and **Marcellus,**
    Danish soldiers

Fortinbras, prince of Norway
Captain in this army
Councilors, English Ambassadors,
    Servants, Musicians, Officers,
    Laertes's **Followers**

Three or four **Players,** taking the roles of
    Prologue, Player King, Player Queen,
    and Lucianus
Two **Messengers**
Sailor
Two **Clowns,** gravediggers
Priest

SCENE: *Denmark*

Act One, Scene One

*On a platform on top of the walls at Elsinore
castle, the sentries are changing. Horatio and
Marcellus join them. The new sentry, Bernardo,
tells Horatio of a ghost he has seen. The
Ghost, in the form of the late King Hamlet of
Denmark, enters but refuses to speak. Horatio
fears that the Ghost's appearance foretells a
great disaster. The Danes are preparing for
war because the young Norwegian prince
Fortinbras is threatening to try to recover lost
territory. The Ghost reappears, and the three
try to stop it from leaving. As morning dawns,
they decide that they must tell Prince Hamlet
what they have seen.*

Enter Bernardo *and* Francisco, *two sentinels, meeting.*

Bernardo. Who's there?

Francisco. Nay, answer me. Stand and unfold yourself.

Bernardo. Long live the King!

Francisco. Bernardo?

5   **Bernardo.** He.

Francisco. You come most carefully upon your hour.

Bernardo. 'Tis now struck twelve. Get thee to bed, Francisco.

Francisco. For this relief much thanks. 'Tis bitter cold,
    And I am sick at heart.

10   **Bernardo.** Have you had quiet guard?

Francisco. Not a mouse stirring.

Bernardo. Well, good night.
    If you do meet Horatio and Marcellus,
    The rivals of my watch,[1] bid them make haste.

[*Enter* Horatio *and* Marcellus.]

15   **Francisco.** I think I hear them.—Stand ho! Who is there?

Horatio. Friends to this ground.

Marcellus. And liegemen to the Dane.[2]

Francisco. Give you good night.

Marcellus. O, farewell, honest soldier. Who hath relieved you?

20   **Francisco.** Bernardo hath my place. Give you good night.

[*Exit* Francisco.]

Marcellus. Holla Bernardo!

Bernardo. Say, what, is Horatio there?

Horatio. A piece of him.

Bernardo. Welcome, Horatio.—Welcome, good Marcellus.

25   **Horatio.** What, has this thing appeared again tonight?

Bernardo. I have seen nothing.

Marcellus. Horatio says 'tis but our fantasy,
    And will not let belief take hold of him
    Touching this dreaded sight twice seen of us.

---

[1] rivals of my watch—fellow sentries.

[2] liegemen to the Dane—loyal subjects of the king of Denmark.

A stormy sea establishes the mood of the 1991 production of *Hamlet* by the Artists Repertory Theatre in Cambridge, Massachusetts.

30   Therefore I have entreated him along

With us to watch the minutes of this night,

That if again this **apparition**[3] come,

He may approve our eyes and speak to it.

Horatio. Tush, tush, 'twill not appear.

Bernardo.   Sit down awhile,

35   And let us once again **assail**[4] your ears,

That are so fortified against our story,

What we have two nights seen.

Horatio.   Well, sit we down,

And let us hear Bernardo speak of this.

---

[3] **apparition**—ghostly appearance.

[4] **assail**—attack.

Bernardo. Last night of all,

40   When yond same star that's westward from the pole
        Had made his course t' illume[5] that part of heaven
        Where now it burns, Marcellus and myself,
        The bell then beating one—

[*Enter* Ghost.]

Marcellus. Peace, break thee off! Look where it comes again!

45 **Bernardo.** In the same figure like the king that's dead.

Marcellus. Thou art a scholar. Speak to it, Horatio.

Bernardo. Looks he not like the king? Mark it, Horatio.

Horatio. Most like. It **harrows**[6] me with fear and wonder.

Bernardo. It would be spoke to.

Marcellus.   Speak to it, Horatio.

50 **Horatio.** What art thou that usurp'st this time of night,
        Together with that fair and warlike form
        In which the majesty of buried Denmark
        Did sometime march? By heaven, I charge thee, speak!

Marcellus. It is offended.

Bernardo.   See, it **stalks**[7] away.

55 **Horatio.** Stay! Speak, speak! I charge thee, speak!

[*Exit* Ghost.]

Marcellus. 'Tis gone and will not answer.

Bernardo. How now, Horatio? You tremble and look pale.
        Is not this something more than fantasy?
        What think you on 't?

60 **Horatio.** Before my God, I might not this believe
        Without the sensible and true avouch[8]
        Of mine own eyes.

Marcellus. Is it not like the king?

Horatio. As thou art to thyself.

65   Such was the very armor he had on
        When he the ambitious Norway combated.
        So frowned he once when, in an angry parle,[9]

---

[5] t' illume—to light.

[6] **harrows**—distresses.

[7] **stalks**—walks stiffly and proudly.

[8] avouch—testimony of my senses.

[9] parle—meeting.

He smote the sledded Polacks[10] on the ice.
'Tis strange.

70 **Marcellus.** Thus twice before, and jump[11] at this dead hour,
With martial stalk hath he gone by our watch.

Horatio. In what particular thought to work I know not,
But in the gross and scope of mine opinion
This bodes some strange eruption to our state.[12]

75 **Marcellus.** Good now, sit down, and tell me, he that knows,
Why this same strict and most observant watch
So nightly toils the subject of the land,[13]
And why such daily cast of brazen cannon
And foreign mart[14] for implements of war,

80 Why such impress of shipwrights,[15] whose sore task
Does not divide the Sunday from the week.
What might be toward, that this sweaty haste
Doth make the night joint-laborer with the day?
Who is 't that can inform me?

Horatio.   That can I;

85 At least, the whisper goes so. Our last king,
Whose image even but now appeared to us,
Was, as you know, by Fortinbras of Norway,
Thereto pricked on by a most emulate pride,[16]
Dared to the combat; in which our valiant Hamlet—

90 For so this side of our known world esteemed him—
Did slay this Fortinbras; who by a sealed compact
Well ratified by law and heraldry
Did forfeit, with his life, all those his lands
Which he stood seized[17] of, to the conqueror;

95 Against the which a moiety competent

---

[10] sledded Polacks—Polish soldiers in sleds.

[11] jump—precisely.

[12] In what . . . our state—While I am not certain what to think, my general idea is that this means some strange disturbance is going to happen in our country.

[13] toils . . . land—causes the subjects of this land to work.

[14] foreign mart—international trade.

[15] impress of shipwrights—forced service of builders of ships.

[16] Thereto . . . pride—impelled to do this by envious rivalry.

[17] seized—possessed.

Was gagèd[18] by our king, which had returned
To the inheritance of Fortinbras
Had he been vanquisher, as, by the same cov'nant
And carriage of the article designed,
His fell to Hamlet. Now, sir, young Fortinbras,   100
Of unimprovèd mettle[19] hot and full,
Hath in the skirts of Norway here and there
Sharked up a list of lawless resolutes[20]
For food and diet to some enterprise
That hath a stomach in 't,[21] which is no other—   105
As it doth well appear unto our state—
But to recover of us, by strong hand
And terms compulsatory,[22] those foresaid lands
So by his father lost. And this, I take it,
Is the main motive of our preparations,   110
The source of this our watch, and the chief head
Of this posthaste and rummage[23] in the land.

Bernardo. I think it be no other but e'en so.
Well may it sort that this portentous[24] figure
Comes armèd through our watch so like the king   115
That was and is the question of these wars.

Horatio. A mote[25] it is to trouble the mind's eye.
In the most high and palmy state of Rome,
A little ere the mightiest Julius fell,[26]
The graves stood tenantless, and the sheeted dead   120
Did squeak and gibber in the Roman streets;
As stars with trains of fire and dews of blood,
Disasters in the sun; and the moist star
Upon whose influence Neptune's empire stands[27]

---

[18] moiety . . . gagèd—equal portion was pledged.

[19] unimprovèd mettle—untried strength.

[20] in the skirts . . . resolutes—gathered from various outlying districts of Norway a number of desperados.

[21] hath a stomach in 't—requires courage.

[22] terms compulsatory—forced demands.

[23] head . . . rummage—cause of the hurry and activity.

[24] portentous—ominous.

[25] mote—small particle; speck.

[26] little ere . . . Julius fell—shortly before the assassination of Julius Caesar.

[27] moist star . . . empire stands—the moon that controls the seas.

125   Was sick almost to doomsday with eclipse.
      And even the like precurse of feared events,
      As **harbingers**[28] preceding still the fates
      And prologue to the omen coming on,
      Have heaven and earth together demonstrated
130   Unto our climatures[29] and countrymen.

[*Enter* Ghost.]

      But soft,[30] behold! Lo, where it comes again!

[Ghost *spreads his arms.*]

      I'll cross it, though it blast me. Stay, illusion!
      If thou hast any sound or use of voice,
      Speak to me!
135   If there be any good thing to be done
      That may to thee do ease and grace to me,
      Speak to me!
      If thou art privy to[31] thy country's fate,
      Which, happily[32] foreknowing may avoid,
140   O, speak!
      Or if thou hast uphoarded[33] in thy life
      Extorted treasure in the womb of earth,
      For which, they say, you spirits oft walk in death,
      Speak of it! [*The cock crows.*] Stay and speak!—
      Stop it, Marcellus.
145 **Marcellus.** Shall I strike at it with my partisan?[34]
Horatio. Do, if it will not stand.

[*They strike at it.*]

Bernardo.   'Tis here!
Horatio.   'Tis here!

[*Exit* Ghost.]

Marcellus. 'Tis gone.
      We do it wrong, being so majestical,

---

[28] **harbingers**—forerunners.

[29] climatures—geographic regions.

[30] soft—wait a minute.

[31] privy to—in on the secret of.

[32] happily—perhaps (haply); or luckily.

[33] uphoarded—hoarded up; stored away.

[34] partisan—long-handled spear.

To offer it the show of violence,
150   For it is as the air, invulnerable,
      And our vain blows malicious mockery.
Bernardo. It was about to speak when the cock crew.
Horatio. And then it started like a guilty thing
      Upon a fearful summons. I have heard
155   The cock, that is the trumpet to the morn,
      Doth with his lofty and shrill-sounding throat
      Awake the god of day, and at his warning,
      Whether in sea or fire, in earth or air,
      Th' extravagant and erring spirit hies[35]
160   To his confine, and of the truth herein
      This present object made probation.[36]
Marcellus. It faded on the crowing of the cock.
      Some say that ever 'gainst that season comes
      Wherein our Savior's birth is celebrated,
165   This bird of dawning singeth all night long,
      And then, they say, no spirit dare stir abroad,
      The nights are wholesome; then no planets strike,[37]
      No fairy takes, nor witch hath power to charm,
      So hallowed and so gracious is that time.
170   **Horatio.** So have I heard and do in part believe it.
      But look, the morn in russet mantle clad
      Walks o'er the dew of yon high eastward hill.
      Break we our watch up, and by my advice
      Let us impart what we have seen tonight
175   Unto young Hamlet; for upon my life,
      This spirit, dumb to us, will speak to him.
      Do you consent we shall acquaint him with it,
      As needful in our loves, fitting our duty?
Marcellus. Lets do 't, I pray, and I this morning know
180   Where we shall find him most conveniently.
      [*They exit.*]

---

[35] extravagant . . . hies—wandering ghost hurries.

[36] made probation—demonstrated.

[37] planets strike—heavenly bodies exert evil influence.

Act One, Scene Two

In an audience room in Elsinore castle, King Claudius, Denmark's new ruler, is holding court. In addition to succeeding his brother on the throne, he has married the late king's widow, Queen Gertrude. Claudius sends ambassadors to Norway's elderly king to warn him of Fortinbras's threatening plans. He grants Laertes, the son of the court chamberlain Polonius, leave to return to France; but Claudius denies Hamlet's request to return to the university at Wittenberg. He and Gertrude both urge Hamlet to give up his deep mourning. Left alone, Hamlet broods over his father's death and his mother's remarriage. He is angry and despairing. When Horatio, Marcellus, and Bernardo tell him about the Ghost, Hamlet decides to watch for it that night.

Flourish.[1] *Enter* Claudius, *king of Denmark,* Gertrude *the queen,* Councilors, Polonius *and his son* Laertes, Hamlet, *with others including* Voltimand *and* Cornelius.

King. Though yet of Hamlet our dear brother's death
 The memory be green, and that it us befitted
 To bear our hearts in grief, and our whole kingdom
 To be contracted in one brow of woe,
5 Yet so far hath discretion fought with nature
 That we with wisest sorrow think on him
 Together with remembrance of ourselves.
 Therefore our sometime sister, now our queen,
 Th' imperial jointress[2] to this warlike state
10 Have we—as 'twere with a defeated joy
 With an auspicious and a dropping[3] eye,
 With mirth in funeral and with **dirge**[4] in marriage,
 In equal scale weighing delight and dole[5]—
 Taken to wife. Nor have we herein barred
15 Your better wisdoms, which have freely gone

---

[1] *Flourish*—Trumpets sound.

[2] jointress—woman holding property jointly with her husband.

[3] auspicious . . . dropping—cheerful and weeping.

[4] **dirge**—funeral hymn or lament.

[5] dole—sorrow, grief.

With this affair along. For all, our thanks.
Now follows that you know. Young Fortinbras,
Holding a weak supposal of our worth,[6]
Or thinking by our late dear brother's death
20 Our state to be disjoint and out of frame,
Colleaguèd with this dream of his advantage,[7]
He hath not failed to pester us with message
Importing the surrender of those lands
Lost by his father, with all bonds of law,
25 To our most valiant brother. So much for him.
Now for ourself and for this time of meeting.
Thus much the business is: we have here writ
To Norway, uncle of young Fortinbras—
Who, impotent[8] and bed-rid, scarcely hears
30 Of this his nephew's purpose—to suppress
His further gait herein, in that the levies,
The lists, and full proportions are all made
Out of his subject;[9] and we here dispatch
You, good Cornelius, and you, Voltimand,
35 For bearers of this greeting to old Norway,
Giving to you no further personal power
To business with the king more than the scope
Of these dilated articles[10] allow.

[*He gives them a paper.*]

Farewell, and let your haste commend your duty.
40 **Cornelius, Voltimand.** In that, and all things, will we show our duty.
King. We doubt it nothing. Heartily farewell.

[*Exit* Voltimand *and* Cornelius]

And now, Laertes, what's the news with you?
You told us of some suit. What is 't, Laertes?
You cannot speak of reason to the Dane
45 And lose your voice. What wouldst thou beg, Laertes,
That shall not be my offer, not thy asking?

---

[6] weak . . . worth—low opinion of my ability.

[7] Colleaguèd . . . advantage—together with the hope of what he might gain.

[8] impotent—helpless.

[9] suppress . . . subject—stop his progress in this, since all the troops are drawn from his subjects.

[10] dilated articles—detailed terms.

A little more than kin,
and less than kind.

The head is not more native to the heart,
The hand more instrumental to the mouth,
Than is the throne of Denmark to thy father.
50 What wouldst thou have, Laertes?
Laertes.   My dread lord,
Your leave and favor to return to France,
From whence though willingly I came to Denmark
To show my duty in your coronation,
Yet now I must confess, that duty done,
55 My thoughts and wishes bend again toward France
And bow them to your gracious leave and pardon.
King. Have you your father's leave? What says Polonius?
Polonius. Hath, my lord, wrung from me my slow leave
By laborsome petition, and at last
60 Upon his will I sealed my hard[11] consent.
I do beseech you, give him leave to go.
King. Take thy fair hour, Laertes. Time be thine,
And thy best graces spend it at thy will!
But now, my cousin Hamlet and my son—
65 **Hamlet** [*aside*]. A little more than kin, and less than kind.[12]
King. How is it that the clouds still hang on you?
Hamlet. Not so, my lord. I am too much in the sun.[13]
Queen. Good Hamlet, cast thy nighted color off,
And let thine eye look like a friend on Denmark.
70 Do not forever with thy vailèd lids[14]
Seek for thy noble father in the dust.
Thou know'st 'tis common, all that lives must die,
Passing through nature to eternity.

---

[11] hard—reluctant.

[12] more . . . kind—Hamlet plays on the words *kin* and *kind*. *Kind* comes from *kin* and means similarity of character, nature, or race. Hamlet and Claudius are doubly related. Claudius is Hamlet's stepfather and uncle. But Hamlet's nature is not like Claudius's, nor does he feel kindness toward him.

[13] sun—pun on *son*.

[14] vailèd lids—downcast eyes.

Hamlet. Ay, madam, it is common.

Queen.   If it be,
75   Why seems it so particular with thee?

Hamlet. "Seems," madam? Nay, it is. I know not "seems."
       'Tis not alone my inky cloak, good mother,
       Nor customary suits of solemn black,
       Nor windy suspiration of forced breath,
80   No, nor the fruitful river in the eye,
       Nor the dejected havior of the visage,
       Together with all forms, moods, shapes of grief,
       That can denote me truly.[15] These indeed "seem,"
       For they are actions that a man might play.
85   But I have that within which passes show;
       These but the trappings and the suits of woe.

King. 'Tis sweet and commendable in your nature, Hamlet,
       To give these mourning duties to your father.
       But you must know your father lost a father,
90   That father lost, lost his, and the survivor bound
       In filial obligation for some term
       To do obsequious[16] sorrow. But to persever
       In obstinate condolement[17] is a course
       Of impious stubbornness. 'Tis unmanly grief.
95   It shows a will most incorrect to heaven,
       A heart unfortified, a mind impatient,
       An understanding simple and unschooled.
       For what we know must be and is as common
       As any the most vulgar thing to sense,
100   Why should we in our peevish opposition
       Take it to heart? Fie,[18] 'tis a fault to heaven,
       A fault against the dead, a fault to nature,
       To reason most absurd, whose common theme
       Is death of fathers, and who still hath cried,
105   From the first corpse till he that died today,
       "This must be so." We pray you, throw to earth

---

[15] 'Tis . . . truly—It's not only my black clothes, deep sighs, tears, sad looks, and other outward signs of grief that show how I really feel.

[16] obsequious—appropriate to funerals.

[17] obstinate condolement—stubborn grief.

[18] Fie—shame.

This unprevailing woe and think of us
As of a father; for let the world take note,
You are the most immediate to our throne,
110   And with no less nobility of love
Than that which dearest father bears his son
Do I impart toward you. For your intent
In going back to school in Wittenberg,
It is most retrograde[19] to our desire,
115   And we beseech you, bend you to remain
Here in the cheer and comfort of our eye,
Our chiefest courtier, cousin, and our son.

Queen. Let not thy mother lose her prayers, Hamlet.
I pray thee, stay with us. Go not to Wittenberg.

120 **Hamlet.** I shall in all my best obey you, madam.

King. Why, 'tis a loving and a fair reply.
Be as ourself in Denmark.—Madam, come.
This gentle and unforced accord of Hamlet
Sits smiling to my heart, in grace whereof
125   No jocund health that Denmark drinks today
But the great cannon to the clouds shall tell,
And the king's rouse the heaven shall bruit again,
Respeaking earthly thunder.[20] Come away.

[*Flourish. All exit but* Hamlet.]

Hamlet. O, that this too too sullied[21] flesh would melt,
130   Thaw, and resolve itself into a dew!
Or that the Everlasting had not fixed
His canon[22] 'gainst self-slaughter! O God, God,
How weary, stale, flat, and unprofitable
Seem to me all the uses of this world!

---

[19] retrograde—contrary.

[20] No jocund health . . . thunder—At each joyful toast the king drinks, a cannon will be fired so that the heavens will echo the noise.

[21] sullied—stained, defiled; often written as *solid*.

[22] canon—law.

Claudius (Laurence Ballard) and Gertrude (Katherine Ferrand) greet their courtiers in this scene from the 1989 production of *Hamlet* by Seattle's Intiman Theatre.

135　Fie on 't, ah fie! 'Tis an unweeded garden
　　That grows to seed. Things rank and gross in nature
　　Possess it merely. That it should come to this!
　　But two months dead—nay, not so much, not two.
　　So excellent a king, that was to this
140　Hyperion to a satyr,[23] so loving to my mother
　　That he might not beteem[24] the winds of heaven
　　Visit her face too roughly. Heaven and earth,
　　Must I remember? Why, she would hang on him
　　As if increase of appetite had grown
145　By what it fed on. And yet within a month—
　　Let me not think on 't; frailty, thy name is woman!—
　　A little month, or ere those shoes were old

---

23 was . . . Hyperion to a satyr—King Hamlet, compared to Claudius, was like the sun god compared to a creature that is half-goat, half-human.

24 might not beteem—would not allow.

With which she followed my poor father's body,
Like Niobe,[25] all tears, why she, even she—

150 O God, a beast, that wants discourse of reason,
Would have mourned longer—married with my uncle,
My father's brother, but no more like my father
Than I to Hercules. Within a month,
Ere yet the salt of most unrighteous tears

155 Had left the flushing in her gallèd[26] eyes,
She married. O, most wicked speed, to post
With such dexterity to incestuous[27] sheets!
It is not, nor it cannot come to good.
But break, my heart, for I must hold my tongue.

[*Enter* Horatio, Marcellus, *and* Bernardo.]

160 **Horatio.** Hail to your lordship!

Hamlet.   I am glad to see you well.
Horatio!—or I do forget myself.

Horatio. The same, my lord, and your poor servant ever.

Hamlet. Sir, my good friend; I'll change that name with you.
And what make you from[28] Wittenberg, Horatio?—

165 Marcellus.

Marcellus. My good lord.

Hamlet. I am very glad to see you. [*To* Bernardo.] Good even, sir.—
But what, in faith, make you from Wittenberg?

Horatio. A truant disposition, good my lord.

170 **Hamlet.** I would not hear your enemy say so,
Nor shall you do my ear that violence
To make it truster of your own report
Against yourself. I know you are no truant.
But what is your affair in Elsinore?

175 We'll teach you to drink deep ere you depart.

Horatio. My lord, I came to see your father's funeral.

Hamlet. I prithee,[29] do not mock me, fellow student.
I think it was to see my mother's wedding.

---

[25] Niobe—woman in Greek myth who wept endlessly for her dead children.

[26] gallèd—inflamed.

[27] incestuous—The marriage of a man to his brother's widow was so regarded until long after Shakespeare's time.

[28] what make you from—what are you doing away from.

[29] prithee—"I pray thee," a polite request.

> *He was a man. Take him for all in all,*
> *I shall not look upon his like again.*

Horatio. Indeed, my lord, it followed hard upon.

180　**Hamlet.** Thrift, thrift, Horatio! The funeral baked meats
　　　Did coldly furnish forth the marriage tables.
　　　Would I had met my dearest foe in heaven
　　　Or ever I had seen that day, Horatio!
　　　My father!—Methinks I see my father.

185　**Horatio.** Where, my lord?
　　　Hamlet.　　　　　　　　In my mind's eye, Horatio.
　　　Horatio. I saw him once. He was a goodly king.
　　　Hamlet. He was a man. Take him for all in all,
　　　I shall not look upon his like again.
　　　Horatio. My lord, I think I saw him yesternight.

190　**Hamlet.** Saw who?
　　　Horatio. My lord, the king your father.
　　　Hamlet.　　　　　　　　　The king my father?
　　　Horatio. Season your admiration for a while
　　　With an attent ear,[30] till I may deliver,
　　　Upon the witness of these gentlemen,

195　This marvel to you.
　　　Hamlet.　　　　　　For God's love, let me hear!
　　　Horatio. Two nights together had these gentlemen,
　　　Marcellus and Bernardo, on their watch,
　　　In the dead waste and middle of the night,
　　　Been thus encountered. A figure like your father,

200　Armèd at point exactly, cap-à-pie,[31]
　　　Appears before them, and with solemn march
　　　Goes slow and stately by them. Thrice he walked
　　　By their oppressed and fear-surprisèd eyes
　　　Within his truncheon's length,[32] whilst they, distilled

---

[30] Season . . . ear—Control your surprise for a moment and listen carefully.

[31] at . . . cap-à-pie—at every point from head to foot.

[32] truncheon's length—length of a short staff, carried here as a symbol of military command.

205 Almost to jelly with the act of fear,
Stand dumb and speak not to him. This to me
In dreadful secrecy impart they did,
And I with them the third night kept the watch,
Where, as they had delivered, both in time,
210 Form of the thing, each word made true and good,
The apparition comes. I knew your father;
These hands are not more like.

Hamlet.   But where was this?

Marcellus. My lord, upon the platform where we watch.

Hamlet. Did you not speak to it?

Horatio.   My lord, I did,
215 But answer made it none. Yet once methought
It lifted up its head and did address
Itself to motion, like as it would speak;
But even then the morning cock crew loud,
And at the sound it shrunk in haste away
220 And vanished from our sight.

Hamlet.   'Tis very strange.

Horatio. As I do live, my honored lord, 'tis true,
And we did think it writ down in our duty
To let you know of it.

Hamlet. Indeed, indeed, sirs. But this troubles me.
225 Hold you the watch tonight?

All.   We do, my lord.

Hamlet. Armed, say you?

All. Armed, my lord.

Hamlet. From top to toe?

All.   My lord, from head to foot.

Hamlet. Then saw you not his face?
230 **Horatio.** O, yes, my lord, he wore his beaver[33] up.

Hamlet. What, looked he frowningly?

Horatio. A **countenance**[34] more in sorrow than in anger.

Hamlet. Pale or red?

Horatio.   Nay, very pale.

---

[33] beaver—visor; front piece of a helmet.
[34] **countenance**—face.

Hamlet. And fixed his eyes upon you?

Horatio.   Most constantly.

235   **Hamlet.** I would I had been there.

Horatio.   It would have much amazed you.

Hamlet. Very like, very like. Stayed it long?

Horatio. While one with moderate haste might tell[35] a hundred.

Marcellus, Bernardo. Longer, longer.

Horatio. Not when I saw 't.

Hamlet.   His beard was grizzled—no?

240   **Horatio.** It was, as I have seen it in his life,
        A sable silvered.[36]

Hamlet.   I will watch tonight.
        Perchance[37] 'twill walk again.

Horatio.   I warrant it will.

Hamlet. If it assume my noble father's person,
        I'll speak to it, though hell itself should gape

245   And bid me hold my peace. I pray you all,
        If you have hitherto concealed this sight,
        Let it be tenable[38] in your silence still,
        And whatsoever else shall hap tonight,
        Give it an understanding but no tongue.

250   I will requite your loves. So, fare you well.
        Upon the platform, twixt eleven and twelve,
        I'll visit you.

All.   Our duty to your honor.

Hamlet. Your loves, as mine to you. Farewell.

[*All exit but* Hamlet.]
        My father's spirit—in arms! All is not well.

255   I doubt[39] some foul play. Would the night were come!
        Till then, sit still, my soul. Foul deeds will rise,
        Though all the earth o'erwhelm them, to men's eyes.

[*Exit* Hamlet.]

---

[35] tell—count.

[36] sable silvered—black with streaks of white.

[37] Perchance—perhaps, maybe.

[38] tenable—kept secret, held.

[39] doubt—suspect.

Act One, Scene Three

In Polonius's room in the castle, Laertes prepares to leave Elsinore. He counsels his sister, Ophelia, to be wary of Hamlet and his romantic attentions. Polonius, their father, lectures Laertes on acting prudently and maintaining appearances. After Laertes leaves, Polonius asks Ophelia what has happened between her and Hamlet. She describes Hamlet's promises of love. Polonius tells her not to believe what a prince says and orders her to avoid Hamlet's company.

Enter Laertes *and* Ophelia.

Laertes. My necessaries are embarked. Farewell.
 And, sister, as the winds give benefit
 And convoy is assistant,[1] do not sleep
 But let me hear from you.

Ophelia.   Do you doubt that?

5 **Laertes.** For Hamlet, and the trifling of his favor,
 Hold it a fashion and a toy in blood,[2]
 A violet in the youth of primy nature,[3]
 Forward, not permanent, sweet, not lasting,
 The perfume and suppliance of a minute[4]—
10 No more.

Ophelia. No more but so?

Laertes.   Think it no more.
 For nature, crescent, does not grow alone
 In thews and bulk, but as this temple waxes
 The inward service of the mind and soul
 Grows wide withal.[5] Perhaps he loves you now,
15 And now no soil nor cautel doth besmirch[6]

---

[1] convoy is assistant—ships are available.

[2] toy in blood—idle fancy; flirtation.

[3] in . . . nature—in the spring of its youthful nature.

[4] suppliance of a minute—minute's pastime.

[5] For nature. . . wide withal—For nature, growing, does not just grow in muscles and size, but as the body develops, the powers of mind and spirit grow along with it.

[6] soil . . . besmirch—no stain or deceit dirties.

The virtue of his will; but you must fear,
His greatness weighed, his will is not his own.
For he himself is subject to his birth.
He may not, as unvalued persons do,

20   Carve for himself, for on his choice depends
The safety and the health of this whole state,
And therefore must his choice be circumscribed
Unto the voice and yielding of that body
Whereof he is the head. Then, if he says he loves you,

25   It fits your wisdom so far to believe it
As he in his particular act and place
May give his saying deed, which is no further
Than the main voice of Denmark goes withal.[7]
Then weigh what loss your honor may sustain

30   If with too credent ear you list[8] his songs,
Or lose your heart, or your chaste treasure open
To his unmastered **importunity**.[9]
Fear it, Ophelia, fear it, my dear sister,
And keep you in the rear of your affection,

35   Out of the shot and danger of desire.
The chariest maid is prodigal[10] enough
If she unmask her beauty to the moon.
Virtue itself scapes not calumnious[11] strokes.
The canker galls the infants of the spring

40   Too oft before their buttons be disclosed,[12]
And, in the morn and liquid dew of youth
Contagious blastments are most imminent.[13]
Be wary then; best safety lies in fear.
Youth to itself rebels, though none else near.

---

[7] goes withal—allows.

[8] credent ear you list—believing ear you listen to.

[9] **importunity**—demand.

[10] chariest maid is prodigal—most modest girl is reckless.

[11] calumnious—injurious to a reputation.

[12] canker galls . . . disclosed—too often, the worm destroys the early spring blossoms before they are seen.

[13] Contagious . . . imminent—evil blights are most likely to occur.

45   **Ophelia.** I shall the effect of this good lesson keep
            As watchman to my heart. But, good my brother,
            Do not, as some ungracious pastors[14] do,
            Show me the steep and thorny way to heaven,
            Whiles like a puffed and reckless libertine
50   Himself the primrose path of dalliance treads,
            And recks not his own rede.[15]

      Laertes.   O, fear me not.

[*Enter* Polonius.]

            I stay too long. But here my father comes.
            A double blessing is a double grace.
            Occasion smiles upon a second leave.

55   **Polonius.** Yet here, Laertes? Aboard, aboard, for shame!
            The wind sits in the shoulder of your sail,
            And you are stayed for. There, my blessing with thee!
            And these few **precepts**[16] in thy memory
            Look thou character.[17] Give thy thoughts no tongue,
60   Nor any unproportioned thought his act.
            Be thou familiar, but by no means vulgar.
            Those friends thou hast, and their adoption tried,
            Grapple them unto thy soul with hoops of steel,
            But do not dull thy palm with entertainment
65   Of each new-hatched, unfledged courage.[18] Beware
            Of entrance to a quarrel, but being in,
            Bear 't that th' opposèd may beware of thee.
            Give every man thy ear, but few thy voice.
            Take each man's censure, but reserve thy judgment.
70   Costly thy habit as thy purse can buy,
            But not expressed in fancy; rich, not gaudy,

---

[14] ungracious pastors—wicked shepherds.

[15] Whiles like . . . own rede—while like a prideful youth you waste yourself in sin and do not listen to your own advice.

[16] **precepts**—rules of moral conduct.

[17] character—inscribe.

[18] But do . . . unfledged courage—but don't try to entertain every spirited young man you meet.

In this scene from the 1996 production of *Hamlet* by Boston's Huntington Theatre Company, Laertes (Thomas McCarthy) counsels his sister Ophelia (Natacha Roi).

> For the apparel oft proclaims the man,
> And they in France of the best rank and station
> Are of a most select and generous chief in that.
75   Neither a borrower nor a lender be,
> For loan oft loses both itself and friend,
> And borrowing dulls the edge of husbandry.[19]
> This above all: to thine own self be true,
> And it must follow, as the night the day,
80   Thou canst not then be false to any man.
> Farewell. My blessing season this in thee!

---

[19] husbandry—thrift; money management.

Laertes. Most humbly do I take my leave, my lord.

Polonius. The time invests you. Go, your servants tend.[20]

Laertes. Farewell, Ophelia, and remember well

85   What I have said to you.

Ophelia. 'Tis in my memory locked,

And you yourself shall keep the key of it.

Laertes. Farewell.

[*Exit* Laertes.]

90   **Polonius.** What is 't, Ophelia, he hath said to you?

Ophelia. So please you, something touching the Lord Hamlet.

Polonius. Marry,[21] well bethought.

'Tis told me he hath very oft of late

Given private time to you, and you yourself

Have of your audience been most free and bounteous.

95   If it be so—as so 'tis put on me,[22]

And that in way of caution—I must tell you

You do not understand yourself so clearly

As it behooves my daughter and your honor.

What is between you? Give me up the truth.

100   **Ophelia.** He hath, my lord, of late made many tenders[23]

Of his affection to me.

Polonius. Affection? Pooh! You speak like a green girl,

Unsifted[24] in such perilous circumstance.

Do you believe his "tenders," as you call them?

105   **Ophelia.** I do not know, my lord, what I should think.

Polonius. Marry, I will teach you. Think yourself a baby

That you have ta'en these tenders for true pay

Which are not sterling.[25] Tender yourself more dearly,

Or—not to crack the wind of the poor phrase,

110   Running it thus—you'll tender me a fool.[26]

---

[20] The time . . . tend—Time presses. Your servants wait.

[21] Marry—indeed (originally, an oath, "by the Virgin Mary").

[22] put on me—told to me.

[23] tenders—Here, *tenders* means "offers of affection." Later, Polonius makes a double pun. He speaks of *tenders* in the sense of "coins," or "legal tender." In his next sentence, he uses *tender* to mean "regard."

[24] Unsifted—untried.

[25] not sterling—not real.

[26] Tender . . . fool—present me with a fool, or present me with a baby.

Ophelia. My lord, he hath importuned me with love
    In honorable fashion.
Polonius. Ay, "fashion"[27] you may call it. Go to, go to.
Ophelia. And hath given countenance to his speech, my lord,
115   With almost all the holy vows of heaven.
Polonius. Ay, springes to catch woodcocks.[28] I do know,
    When the blood burns, how prodigal the soul
    Lends the tongue vows. These blazes, daughter,
    Giving more light than heat, extinct in both
120   Even in their promise as it is a-making,
    You must not take for fire. From this time
    Be something scanter of your maiden presence.
    Set your entreatments at a higher rate
    Than a command to parle.[29] For Lord Hamlet,
125   Believe so much in him that he is young,
    And with a larger tether may he walk
    Than may be given you. In few, Ophelia,
    Do not believe his vows, for they are brokers,
    Not of that dye which their investments show,
130   But mere implorators of unholy suits,
    Breathing like sanctified and pious bawds,
    The better to beguile.[30] This is for all:
    I would not, in plain terms, from this time forth
    Have you so slander any moment leisure
135   As to give words or talk with the Lord Hamlet.
    Look to 't, I charge you. Come your ways.
Ophelia. I shall obey, my lord.
[*They exit.*]

---

[27] fashion . . . "fashion"—The word can mean both "manners" and "pretense."

[28] springes to catch woodcocks—snares to catch stupid birds.

[29] Set . . . parle—Spend less time talking to Hamlet.

[30] for they are brokers . . . beguile—because they are salesmen who are not as honest as their clothes seem, but merely solicitors of sinful actions, speaking as if they are holy in order to entice.

Act One, Scene Four

On the platform on top of the walls of Elsinore castle, around midnight, Hamlet, Horatio, and Marcellus watch for the Ghost while the new king drinks and makes merry inside the castle.

The Ghost appears and beckons to Hamlet. Despite the attempts of Horatio and Marcellus to stop him, Hamlet follows.

Enter Hamlet, Horatio, *and* Marcellus.

Hamlet. The air bites shrewdly; it is very cold.

Horatio. It is a nipping and an eager air.

Hamlet. What hour now?

Horatio.   I think it lacks of twelve.

Marcellus. No, it is struck.

Horatio.   Indeed? I heard it not.

5   It then draws near the season
           Wherein the spirit held his wont to walk.

[*A flourish of trumpets sound, and two cannons go off within.*[1]]
           What does this mean, my lord?

Hamlet. The king doth wake tonight and takes his rouse,
           Keeps wassail, and the swagg'ring upspring reels;[2]

10   And as he drains his drafts of Rhenish[3] down,
           The kettledrum and trumpet thus bray out
           The triumph of his pledge.

Horatio.   Is it a custom?

Hamlet. Ay, marry, is 't,
           But to my mind, though I am native here

15   And to the manner born, it is a custom
           More honored in the breach than the observance.
           This heavy-headed revel east and west
           Makes us traduced and taxed of[4] other nations.

---

[1] *within*—offstage.

[2] *doth wake tonight . . . reels*—stays up late carousing with drink and dancing.

[3] Rhenish—Rhine wine.

[4] *traduced and taxed of*—humiliated and criticized by.

They clepe us drunkards, and with swinish phrase
20 Soil our addition.[5] And indeed it takes
From our achievements, though performed at height,
The pith and marrow of our attribute.[6]
So oft it chances in particular men,
That for some vicious mole of nature[7] in them,
25 As in their birth—wherein they are not guilty,
Since nature cannot choose his origin—
By their o'ergrowth of some complexion,
Oft breaking down the pales and forts of reason,
Or by some habit that too much o'erleavens
30 The form of plausive manners,[8] that these men,
Carrying, I say, the stamp of one defect,
Being nature's livery or fortune's star,[9]
His virtues else, be they as pure as grace,
As infinite as man may undergo,
35 Shall in the general censure take corruption
From that particular fault. The dram of evil
Doth all the noble substance of a doubt
To his own scandal.[10]

[*Enter* Ghost.]

Horatio.   Look, lord, it comes!

Hamlet. Angels and ministers of grace defend us!
40 Be thou a spirit of health or goblin damned,
Bring with thee airs from heaven or blasts from hell,
Be thy intents wicked or charitable,
Thou com'st in such a questionable shape
That I will speak to thee. I'll call thee "Hamlet,"
45 "King," "father," "Royal Dane." O, answer me!
Let me not burst in ignorance, but tell

---

[5] clepe ... addition—call us drunkards and disgrace our honor by calling us swine.

[6] pith ... attribute—essence of our reputation.

[7] mole of nature—natural fault.

[8] By their o'ergrowth ... manners—by the overdevelopment of some humor or emotion that often breaks down the restraint of reason, or some habit that spoils pleasing manners.

[9] Being ... star—whether they were born with it or got it by bad luck.

[10] The dram ... own scandal—A small amount of evil overpowers the good and destroys the man's reputation.

Why thy canonized bones, hearsèd[11] in death,
Have burst their cerements;[12] why the sepulcher[13]
Wherein we saw thee quietly **interred**[14]
50   Hath oped his ponderous and marble jaws
To cast thee up again. What may this mean,
That thou, dead corpse, again in complete steel,[15]
Revisits thus the glimpses of the moon,
Making night hideous, and we fools of nature
55   So horridly to shake our disposition
With thoughts beyond the reaches of our souls?
Say, Why is this? Wherefore? What should we do?

[*The* Ghost *beckons* Hamlet.]

Horatio. It beckons you to go away with it,
As if it some impartment did desire[16]
60   To you alone.

Marcellus.   Look with what courteous action
It waves you to a more removèd ground.
But do not go with it.

Horatio.   No, by no means.

Hamlet. It will not speak. Then I will follow it.

Horatio. Do not, my lord!

Hamlet.   Why, what should be the fear?
65   I do not set my life at a pin's fee,[17]
And for my soul, what can it do to that,
Being a thing immortal as itself?
It waves me forth again. I'll follow it.

Horatio. What if it tempt you toward the flood, my lord?
70   Or to the dreadful summit of the cliff
That beetles o'er[18] his base into the sea,

---

[11] hearsèd—buried.

[12] cerements—grave clothes.

[13] sepulcher—burial vault.

[14] **interred**—buried.

[15] complete steel—fully armored.

[16] some . . . desire—wanted to tell something.

[17] pin's fee—cost of a pin.

[18] beetles o'er—hangs over.

Something is rotten
in the state of Denmark.

And there assume some other horrible form
Which might deprive your sovereignty of reason
And draw you into madness? Think of it.
75　The very place puts toys of desperation,[19]
Without more motive, into every brain
That looks so many fathoms[20] to the sea
And hears it roar beneath.

Hamlet. It waves me still.—Go on, I'll follow thee.

80　**Marcellus.** You shall not go, my lord.

[*They try to stop him.*]

Hamlet.　　　　　　　　　　　　Hold off your hands!

Horatio. Be ruled. You shall not go.

Hamlet.　　　　　　　　　　My fate cries out,
And makes each petty artery in this body
As hardy as the Nemean lion's nerve.[21]
Still am I called. Unhand me, gentlemen.
85　By heaven, I'll make a ghost of him that lets me![22]
I say, away!—Go on, I'll follow thee.

[*Exit* Ghost *and* Hamlet.]

Horatio. He waxes[23] desperate with imagination.

Marcellus. Let's follow. 'Tis not fit thus to obey him.

Horatio. Have after. To what issue will this come?

90　**Marcellus.** Something is rotten in the state of Denmark.

Horatio. Heaven will direct it.

Marcellus.　　　　　　　　　Nay, let's follow him.

[*They exit.*]

---

[19] toys of desperation—desperate impulses; for example, inclinations to jump off.

[20] fathoms—units of depth equal to six feet; used to measure marine depths.

[21] Nemean lion's nerve—muscles of the lion killed by Hercules as one of his twelve labors.

[22] lets me—holds me back.

[23] waxes—grows more.

Act One, Scene Five

On the castle battlements, the Ghost tells Hamlet that he is the spirit of his father, condemned to walk the earth until he has done penance for his sins. He tells how Claudius murdered him as he lay sleeping. The Ghost charges Hamlet to avenge his death on Claudius but to spare Gertrude. The Ghost vanishes at dawn. Hamlet refuses to tell Horatio and Marcellus what the Ghost said but makes them swear never to reveal what they have seen or to comment on how he may act in the future.

Enter Ghost *and* Hamlet.

Hamlet. Whither wilt thou lead me? Speak. I'll go no further.
Ghost. Mark me.
Hamlet.　　　　I will.
Ghost.　　　　　　　My hour is almost come.
　　　When I to sulf'rous and tormenting flames
　　　Must render up myself.
Hamlet.　　　　　　　　Alas, poor Ghost!
5　**Ghost.** Pity me not, but lend thy serious hearing
　　　To what I shall unfold.
Hamlet. Speak. I am bound to hear.
Ghost. So art thou to revenge, when thou shalt hear.
Hamlet. What?
10　**Ghost.** I am thy father's spirit,
　　　Doomed for a certain term to walk the night,
　　　And for the day confined to fast[1] in fires,
　　　Till the foul crimes done in my days of nature
　　　Are burnt and purged away. But that I am forbid
15　　　To tell the secrets of my prison house,
　　　I could a tale unfold whose lightest word
　　　Would harrow up thy soul, freeze thy young blood,
　　　Make thy two eyes, like stars, start from their spheres,
　　　Thy knotted and combinèd locks to part,

[1] fast—do penance.

20	And each particular hair to stand on end
	Like quills upon the fretful porpentine.[2]
	But this eternal blazon[3] must not be
	To ears of flesh and blood. List,[4] list, O, list!
	If thou didst ever thy dear father love—
25	**Hamlet.** O God!
	Ghost. Revenge his foul and most unnatural murder.
	Hamlet. Murder?
	Ghost. Murder most foul, as in the best it is,
	But this most foul, strange, and unnatural.
30	**Hamlet.** Haste me to know 't, that I, with wings as swift
	As meditation or the thoughts of love,
	May sweep to my revenge.
	Ghost. I find thee apt;
	And duller shouldst thou be than the fat weed
	That roots itself in ease on Lethe[5] wharf,
35	Wouldst thou not stir in this. Now, Hamlet, hear.
	'Tis given out that, sleeping in my orchard,
	A serpent stung me. So the whole ear of Denmark
	Is by a forgèd process of my death
	Rankly abused. But know, thou noble youth,
40	The serpent that did sting thy father's life
	Now wears his crown.
	Hamlet. O, my prophetic soul! My uncle!
	Ghost. Ay, that incestuous, that adulterate beast,
	With witchcraft of his wit, with traitorous gifts—
45	O wicked wit and gifts, that have the power
	So to seduce!—won to his shameful lust
	The will of my most seeming-virtuous queen.
	O Hamlet, what a falling off was there!
	From me, whose love was of that dignity
50	That it went hand in hand even with the vow
	I made to her in marriage, and to decline

---

[2] porpentine—porcupine.

[3] eternal blazon—revealing of eternal things.

[4] List—listen.

[5] Lethe—river of forgetfulness in Hades, realm of the dead in Greek mythology.

The Ghost appears behind Hamlet (Campbell Scott) in the this scene from the Huntington Theatre production.

Upon a wretch whose natural gifts were poor
To those of mine!
But virtue, as it never will be moved,
55   Though lewdness court it in a shape of heaven,
So lust, though to a radiant angel linked,
Will **sate**[6] itself in a celestial bed
And prey on garbage.
But soft, methinks I scent the morning air.

---

[6] **sate**—gratify an appetite to the full; satiate.

60 Brief let me be. Sleeping within my orchard,
My custom always of the afternoon,
Upon my secure hour thy uncle stole,
With juice of cursèd hebona[7] in a vial,
And in the porches of my ears did pour
65 The leprous distillment, whose effect
Holds such an enmity with blood of man
That swift as quicksilver[8] it courses through
The natural gates and alleys of the body,
And with a sudden vigor it doth posset
70 And curd,[9] like eager[10] droppings into milk,
The thin and wholesome blood. So did it mine,
And a most instant tetter barked about,
Most lazar-like,[11] with vile and loathsome crust,
All my smooth body.
75 Thus was I, sleeping, by a brother's hand
Of life, of crown, of queen at once dispatched,
Cut off, even in the blossoms of my sin,
Unhouseled, disappointed, unaneled,[12]
No reck'ning made, but sent to my account
80 With all my imperfections on my head.
O, horrible! O, horrible, most horrible!
If thou hast nature in thee, bear it not.
Let not the royal bed of Denmark be
A couch for luxury and damnèd incest.
85 But, howsoever thou pursues this act,
Taint not thy mind, nor let thy soul contrive
Against thy mother aught. Leave her to heaven
And to those thorns that in her bosom lodge,

---

[7] hebona—ebony (which was believed in Shakespeare's time to be a poison).

[8] quicksilver—mercury, a poisonous silvery-white metallic element.

[9] posset . . . curd—curdle.

[10] eager—sour.

[11] most instant . . . lazar-like—sudden scabby eruption covered (my body), like leprosy.

[12] Unhouseled, disappointed, unaneled—without receiving final Christian rites.

To prick and sting her. Fare thee well at once.

90 The glowworm shows the matin[13] to be near,

And 'gins to pale his uneffectual fire.

Adieu, adieu, adieu! Remember me.

[*Exit* Ghost.]

Hamlet. O all you host of heaven! O earth! What else?

And shall I couple hell? O, fie! Hold, hold, my heart,

95 And you, my sinews,[14] grow not instant old,

But bear me stiffly up. Remember thee?

Ay, thou poor ghost, whiles memory holds a seat

In this distracted globe.[15] Remember thee?

Yea, from the table of my memory

100 I'll wipe away all trivial, fond[16] records,

All saws[17] of books, all forms, all pressures past

That youth and observation copied there,

And thy commandment all alone shall live

Within the book and volume of my brain,

105 Unmixed with baser matter. Yes, by heaven!

O most pernicious woman!

O villain, villain, smiling, damnèd villain!

My tables—meet it is I set it down[18]

That one may smile, and smile, and be a villain.

110 At least I am sure it may be so in Denmark.

[*Writing.*]

So, uncle, there you are. Now to my word.

It is "Adieu, adieu! Remember me."

I have sworn 't.

[*Enter* Horatio *and* Marcellus.]

Horatio. My lord, my lord!

115 **Marcellus.** Lord Hamlet!

Horatio. Heavens secure him!

---

[13] matin—morning.

[14] sinews—muscles.

[15] globe—head.

[16] trivial, fond—unimportant, foolish.

[17] saws—wise sayings.

[18] My tables . . . down—It is fitting that I write it on my tablet.

Hamlet. So be it.

Marcellus. Hillo, ho, ho,[19] my lord!

Hamlet. Hillo, ho, ho, boy! Come, bird, come.

120   **Marcellus.** How is 't, my noble lord?

Horatio.   What news, my lord?

Hamlet. O, wonderful!

Horatio. Good my lord, tell it.

Hamlet.   No, you will reveal it.

Horatio. Not I, my lord, by heaven.

Marcellus.   Nor I, my lord.

Hamlet. How say you, then. Would heart of man once think it?

125   But you'll be secret?

Horatio, Marcellus. Ay, by heaven, my lord.

Hamlet. There's never a villain dwelling in all Denmark
     But he's an arrant knave.[20]

Horatio. There needs no ghost, my lord, come from the grave

130   To tell us this.

Hamlet.   Why, right, you are in the right.
     And so, without more circumstance at all,
     I hold it fit that we shake hands and part,
     You as your business and desire shall point you—
     For every man hath business and desire,

135   Such as it is—and for my own poor part,
     I will go pray.

Horatio. These are but wild and whirling words, my lord.

Hamlet. I am sorry they offend you, heartily;
     Yes, faith, heartily.

Horatio.   There's no offense, my lord.

140   **Hamlet.** Yes, by Saint Patrick, but there is, Horatio,
     And much offense, too. Touching this vision here,
     It is an honest ghost, that let me tell you.
     For your desire to know what is between us,
     O'ermaster 't as you may. And now, good friends,

145   As you are friends, scholars, and soldiers,
     Give me one poor request.

---

[19] Hillo, ho, ho—This is a falconer's call to his hawk. Hamlet answers the same way.

[20] arrant knave—complete scoundrel.

Horatio. What is 't, my lord? We will.

Hamlet. Never make known what you have seen tonight.

Horatio, Marcellus. My lord, we will not.

150 **Hamlet.** Nay, but swear 't.

Horatio. In faith, my lord, not I.

Marcellus. Nor I, my lord, in faith.

Hamlet. Upon my sword.

[*He holds out his sword.*]

Marcellus. We have sworn, my lord, already.

155 **Hamlet.** Indeed, upon my sword, indeed.

Ghost [*cries under the stage*]. Swear.

Hamlet. Ha, ha, boy, sayst thou so? Art thou there, truepenny?[21]

Come on, you hear this fellow in the cellarage.

Consent to swear.

Horatio.   Propose the oath, my lord.

160 **Hamlet.** Never to speak of this that you have seen,

Swear by my sword.

Ghost [*beneath*]. Swear.

[*They put their hands on the sword hilt and swear.*]

Hamlet. *Hic et ubique?*[22] Then we'll shift our ground.

[*He moves to another spot.*]

Come hither, gentlemen,

And lay your hands again upon my sword.

165 Swear by my sword

Never to speak of this that you have heard.

Ghost [*beneath*]. Swear by his sword.

[*They swear.*]

Hamlet. Well said, old mole. Canst work i' th' earth so fast?

A worthy pioner![23]—Once more remove, good friends.

[*He moves again.*]

170 **Horatio.** O day and night, but this is wondrous strange!

---

[21] truepenny—trusty fellow.

[22] *Hic et ubique?*—Latin for "here and everywhere."

[23] pioner—digger, miner.

There are more things in heaven and earth, Horatio, than are dreamt of in your philosophy.

Hamlet. And therefore as a stranger give it welcome.
There are more things in heaven and earth, Horatio,
Than are dreamt of in your philosophy. But come;
Here, as before, never, so help you mercy,

175 How strange or odd some'er I bear myself—
As I perchance hereafter shall think meet
To put an antic disposition on[24]—
That you, at such times seeing me, never shall,
With arms encumbered thus, or this headshake,[25]

180 Or by pronouncing of some doubtful phrase
As "Well, well we know," or "We could, an if we would,"
Or "If we list[26] to speak," or "There be, an if they might,"
Or such **ambiguous**[27] giving-out, to note
That you know aught[28] of me—this do swear,

185 So grace and mercy at your most need help you.
Ghost [*beneath*]. Swear.
[*They swear.*]
Hamlet. Rest, rest, perturbèd spirit! So, gentlemen,
With all my love I do commend me to you;
And what so poor a man as Hamlet is

190 May do t' express his love and friending to you,
God willing, shall not lack. Let us go in together,
And still your fingers on your lips, I pray.
The time is out of joint. O cursèd spite
That ever I was born to set it right!
[*They wait for him to leave first.*]

195 Nay, come, let's go together.
[*They exit.*]

---

[24] As I . . . on—because in the future I may think it appropriate to act strangely.

[25] encumbered . . . headshake—with your arms folded or shaking your head in a knowing way.

[26] list—cared, wanted.

[27] **ambiguous**—uncertain, obscure.

[28] aught—anything.

Act Two, Scene One

***In Polonius's rooms in the castle, he is sending
his servant Reynaldo to go to France to spy
on Laertes. Ophelia rushes in to tell her
father that Hamlet has just confronted her
and acted as if he were insane. Polonius fears
that Hamlet has gone mad because Ophelia
refuses to see him. He takes Ophelia to see
the king.***

Enter Polonius *and* Reynaldo.

Polonius. Give him this money and these notes, Reynaldo.
[*He gives money and papers.*]
Reynaldo. I will, my lord.
Polonius. You shall do marvelous wisely, good Reynaldo,
    Before you visit him, to make inquire
5   Of his behavior.
Reynaldo.   My lord, I did intend it.
Polonius. Marry, well said, very well said. Look you, sir,
    Inquire me first what Danskers[1] are in Paris,
    And how, and who, what means, and where they keep,
    What company, at what expense; and finding
10   By this encompassment and drift of question[2]
    That they do know my son, come you more nearer
    Than your particular demands will touch it.[3]
    Take you, as 'twere,[4] some distant knowledge of him,
    As thus, "I know his father and his friends,
15   And, in part, him." Do you mark this, Reynaldo?
Reynaldo. Ay, very well, my lord.
Polonius. "And, in part, him, but," you may say, "not well.
    But if 't be he I mean, he's very wild,
    Addicted so and so," and there put on him
20   What forgeries you please—marry, none so rank
    As may dishonor him, take heed of that,

---

[1] Danskers—Danes.

[2] encompassment . . . question—round about talk.

[3] come you . . . touch it—you will learn more than you would by any direct question.

[4] Take you, as 'twere—pretend to.

But, sir, such wanton, wild, and usual slips
As are companions noted and most known
To youth and liberty.

Reynaldo. As gaming, my lord.

25 **Polonius.** Ay, or drinking, fencing, swearing,
Quarreling, drabbing[5]—you may go so far.

Reynaldo. My lord, that would dishonor him.

Polonius. Faith, no, as you may season it in the charge.
You must not put another scandal on him

30 That he is open to incontinency;[6]
That's not my meaning. But breathe his faults so quaintly
That they may seem the taints of liberty,
The flash and outbreak of a fiery mind,
A savageness in unreclaimèd blood,

35 Of general assault.[7]

Reynaldo. But, my good lord—

Polonius. Wherefore should you do this?

Reynaldo. Ay, my lord, I would know that.

Polonius. Marry, sir, here's my drift,

40 And I believe it is a fetch of wit.[8]
You, laying these slight sullies on my son,
As 'twere a thing a little soiled i' the working,
Mark you, your party in converse, him you would sound,
Having ever seen in the prenominate crimes[9]

45 The youth you breathe of guilty, be assured
He closes with you in this consequence:
"Good sir," or so, or "friend," or "gentleman,"
According to the phrase or the addition
Of man and country—

Reynaldo. Very good, my lord.

50 **Polonius.** And then, sir, does he this—he does—what was I about to say?
By the Mass, I was about to say something.
Where did I leave?

---

[5] drabbing—whoring.

[6] open to incontinency—habitually inclined to sexual indulgence.

[7] A savageness . . . assault—the wildness of youth, which all men have.

[8] fetch of wit—clever trick.

[9] prenominate crimes—aforementioned wrongdoings.

Reynaldo.   At "closes in the consequence."

Polonius. At "closes in the consequence,"—ay, marry—

  He closes thus: "I know the gentleman,
  I saw him yesterday, or th' other day,
  Or then, or then, with such or such, and as you say,
  There was he gaming, there o'ertook in 's rouse,
  There falling out at tennis," or perchance
  "I saw him enter such a house of sale,"
  Videlicet[10] a brothel, or so forth. See you now,
  Your bait of falsehood takes this carp of truth;[11]
  And thus do we of wisdom and of reach,
  With windlasses and with assays of bias,[12]
  By indirections find directions out.
  So by my former lecture and advice
  Shall you my son. You have me, have you not?

Reynaldo. My lord, I have.

Polonius.   God b' wi' you; fare you well.

Reynaldo. Good my lord.

Polonius. Observe his inclination in yourself.[13]

Reynaldo. I shall, my lord.

Polonius. And let him ply his music.

Reynaldo.   Well, my lord.

Polonius. Farewell.

[*Exit* Reynaldo.]

[*Enter* Ophelia.]

            How now, Ophelia, what's the matter?

Ophelia. O my lord, my lord, I have been so affrighted!

Polonius. With what, i' the name of God?

Ophelia. My lord, as I was sewing in my closet,[14]
  Lord Hamlet, with his doublet all unbraced,[15]
  No hat upon his head, his stockings fouled,
  Ungartered, and down-gyvèd[16] to his ankle,

---

[10] *Videlicet*—that is; namely.

[11] Your . . . truth—Your lure of lies catches the fish of truth.

[12] windlasses . . . bias—roundabout methods and indirect attempts.

[13] in yourself—directly, not in reports.

[14] closet—sitting room.

[15] doublet all unbraced—close-fitting jacket unfastened.

[16] down-gyvèd—fallen down.

Polonius (Robert Gerringer) comforts his daughter Ophelia
(Monique Fowler) after her frightening encounter with Hamlet
in this scene from the Hartford Stage production.

Pale as his shirt, his knees knocking each other,

80 And with a look so piteous in purport[17]
As if he had been loosèd out of hell
To speak of horrors—he comes before me.
Polonius. Mad for thy love?
Ophelia.   My lord, I do not know,
But truly I do fear it.
85 **Polonius.**   What said he?
Ophelia. He took me by the wrist and held me hard.
Then goes he to the length of all his arm,
And, with his other hand thus o'er his brow
He falls to such **perusal**[18] of my face

---

[17] purport—expression.
[18] **perusal**—careful examination.

As he would draw it. Long stayed he so.
90 At last, a little shaking of mine arm,
And thrice his head thus waving up and down,
He raised a sigh so piteous and profound
As it did seem to shatter all his bulk
And end his being. That done, he lets me go,
95 And, with his head over his shoulder turned
He seemed to find his way without his eyes,
For out o' doors he went without their helps,
And to the last bended their light on me.

Polonius. Come, go with me. I will go seek the king.
100 This is the very ecstasy[19] of love,
Whose violent property fordoes[20] itself
And leads the will to desperate undertakings
As oft as any passion under heaven
That does afflict our natures. I am sorry.
105 What, have you given him any hard words of late?

Ophelia. No, my good lord, but as you did command
I did repel his letters and denied
His access to me.

Polonius.   That hath made him mad.
I am sorry that with better heed and judgment
110 I had not coted[21] him. I feared he did but trifle
And meant to wrack thee. But beshrew my jealousy![22]
By heaven, it is as proper to our age
To cast beyond ourselves in our opinions
As it is common for the younger sort
115 To lack discretion.[23] Come, go we to the king.
This must be known, which, being kept close, might move
More grief to hide than hate to utter love.
Come.

[*They exit.*]

---

[19] ecstasy—madness.

[20] violent property fordoes—violent nature destroys.

[21] coted—observed.

[22] beshrew my jealousy—curse my suspicions.

[23] it is proper ... lack of discretion—old men are as given to thinking too much as young people are to thinking too little.

Act Two, Scene Two

In a room in Elsinore castle, Claudius and Gertrude ask Hamlet's boyhood friends Rosencrantz and Guildenstern to find out the cause of Hamlet's growing madness. They promise to do all they can for the king and queen. Voltimand and Cornelius, returned from Norway, report that the Norwegian king has stopped Fortinbras's preparations for war against Denmark. Claudius listens carefully to Polonius's theory that Hamlet's madness is the result of love and rejection. Claudius and Polonius decide to spy on a meeting between Hamlet and Ophelia. Polonius is left to arrange matters. Hamlet forces Rosencrantz and Guildenstern to admit that the king and queen sent for them. They express their worry about his recent behavior and hope that the arrival of his favorite company of actors will cheer him up. Polonius brings the players to Hamlet, and the prince asks their leader to recite a speech from an old play about the death of King Priam and the end of the Trojan War. Reciting the speech makes the actor weep tears appropriate to the text. Left alone, Hamlet is ashamed that he has shown less passion in avenging his father's murder than the actor did in playing a part. He decides to have the company perform a play that resembles his father's murder to test Claudius's guilt.

Flourish. Enter King Claudius *and* Queen Gertrude, Rosencrantz, Guildenstern, *and* Attendants.

King. Welcome, dear Rosencrantz and Guildenstern.
    Moreover that we much did long to see you,
    The need we have to use you did provoke
    Our hasty sending. Something have you heard
5   Of Hamlet's transformation, so call it,
    Sith nor[1] th' exterior nor the inward man
    Resembles that it was. What it should be,
    More than his father's death, that thus hath put him
    So much from th' understanding of himself,
10   I cannot dream of. I entreat you both
    That, being of so young days brought up with him,
    And sith so neighbored to his youth and havior,[2]

---

[1] Sith nor—since neither.

[2] havior—behavior.

That you vouchsafe your rest[3] here in our court
Some little time, so by your companies
15 To draw him on to pleasures, and to gather
So much as from occasion you may glean,[4]
Whether aught to us unknown afflicts him thus
That, opened, lies within our remedy.
Queen. Good gentlemen, he hath much talked of you,
20 And sure I am two men there is not living
To whom he more adheres.[5] If it will please you
To show us so much gentry[6] and good will
As to expend your time with us awhile
For the supply and profit of our hope,
25 Your visitation shall receive such thanks
As fits a king's remembrance.
Rosencrantz.   Both Your Majesties
Might, by the sovereign power you have of us,
Put your dread pleasures more into command
Than to entreaty.
Guildenstern.   But we both obey,
30 And here give up ourselves in the full bent[7]
To lay our service freely at your feet,
To be commanded.
King. Thanks, Rosencrantz and gentle Guildenstern.
Queen. Thanks, Guildenstern and gentle Rosencrantz.
35 And I beseech you instantly to visit
My too much changèd son. Go, some of you,
And bring these gentlemen where Hamlet is.
Guildenstern. Heavens make our presence and our practices
Pleasant and helpful to him!
Queen.   Ay, amen!
[*Exit* Rosencrantz *and* Guildenstern *with some* Attendants.]
[*Enter* Polonius.]

---

[3] vouchsafe your rest—agree to stay.

[4] glean—collect bit by bit.

[5] adheres—is attached to.

[6] gentry—courtesy, generosity.

[7] in the full bent—fully; totally.

	Polonius. Th' ambassadors from Norway, my good lord,
40	Are joyfully returned.
	King. Thou still hast been the father of good news.
	Polonius. Have I, my lord? I assure my good liege[8]
	I hold my duty, as I hold my soul,
45	Both to my God and to my gracious king;
	And I do think, or else this brain of mine
	Hunts not the trail of policy so sure
	As it hath used to do, that I have found
	The very cause of Hamlet's lunacy.
50	**King.** O, speak of that! That do I long to hear.
	Polonius. Give first admittance to th' ambassadors.
	My news shall be the fruit[9] to that great feast.
	King. Thyself do grace to them and bring them in.
	[*Exit* Polonius.]
	He tells me, my dear Gertrude, he hath found
55	The head and source of all your son's distemper.
	Queen. I doubt it is no other but the main,
	His father's death and our o'erhasty marriage.
	King. Well, we shall sift[10] him.
	[*Enter* Ambassadors Voltimand *and* Cornelius, *with* Polonius.]
	Welcome, my good friends!
	Say, Voltimand, what from our brother Norway?
60	**Voltimand.** Most fair return of greetings and desires.
	Upon our first, he sent out to suppress
	His nephew's levies, which to him appeared
	To be a preparation 'gainst the Polack,
	But, better looked into, he truly found
65	It was against Your Highness. Whereat grieved
	That so his sickness, age, and impotence
	Was falsely borne in hand, sends out arrests
	On Fortinbras, which he, in brief, obeys,
	Receives rebuke from Norway, and, in fine[11]
70	Makes vow before his uncle never more

---

[8] liege—sovereign.

[9] fruit—dessert.

[10] sift—examine thoroughly.

[11] in fine—in the end.

To give th' assay of arms against[12] Your Majesty.
Whereon old Norway, overcome with joy,
Gives him three-score thousand crowns in annual fee
And his commission to employ those soldiers,
75   So levied as before, against the Polack,
With an entreaty, herein further shown,

[*Giving a paper.*]

That it might please you to give quiet pass
Through your dominions for this enterprise,
On such regards of safety and allowance
80   As therein are set down.

King.   It likes us well,
And at our more considered time, we'll read,
Answer, and think upon this business.
Meantime, we thank you for your well-took labor.
Go to your rest. At night we'll feast together.
85   Most welcome home!

[*Exit* Voltimand *and* Cornelius.]

Polonius.   This business is well ended.
My liege, and madam, to **expostulate**[13]
What majesty should be, what duty is,
Why day is day, night night, and time is time,
Were nothing but to waste night, day, and time.
90   Therefore, since brevity is the soul of wit,
And tediousness the limbs and outward flourishes,
I will be brief. Your noble son is mad.
"Mad" call I it, for, to define true madness,
What is 't but to be nothing else but mad?
95   But let that go.

Queen.   More matter, with less art.

Polonius. Madam, I swear I use no art at all.
That he's mad, 'tis true; 'tis true 'tis pity,

---

[12] give . . . against—attack, assault.
[13] **expostulate**—make a speech about.

And pity 'tis 'tis true—a foolish figure,
But farewell it, for I will use no art.

100 Mad let us grant him, then, and now remains
That we find out the cause of this effect,
Or, rather say, the cause of this defect,
For this effect defective comes by cause.
Thus it remains, and the remainder thus.

105 Perpend.[14]
I have a daughter—have while she is mine—
Who, in her duty and obedience, mark,
Hath given me this. Now gather and surmise.

[*He reads the letter.*]

110 *To the celestial and my soul's idol, the most beautified Ophelia—*
That's an ill phrase, a vile phrase; "beautified" is a vile phrase. But
you shall hear. Thus:

[*He reads.*]

In her excellent white bosom, these, etc.

Queen. Came this from Hamlet to her?

Polonius. Good madam, stay awhile, I will be faithful.

[*He reads.*]

115   *Doubt thou the stars are fire,*
        Doubt that the sun doth move,
    Doubt truth to be a liar,
        But never doubt I love.

O dear Ophelia, I am ill at these numbers.[15] I have not art to reckon my
120 *groans. But that I love thee best, O most best, believe it. Adieu.*
    Thine evermore, most dear lady, whilst this machine is to him,[16] Hamlet.

This in obedience hath my daughter shown me,
And, more above, hath his solicitings,
As they fell out by time, by means, and place,
125 All given to mine ear.

King.   But how hath she received his love?

Polonius. What do you think of me?

King. As of a man faithful and honorable.

---

[14] **Perpend**—Consider carefully.

[15] *ill at these numbers*—unskilled at writing poetry.

[16] *whilst . . . him*—while I still occupy this body.

Polonius. I would fain[17] prove so. But what might you think,
When I had seen this hot love on the wing—

130   As I perceived it, I must tell you that,
Before my daughter told me—what might you,
Or my dear Majesty your queen here, think,
If I had played the desk or table book,[18]
Or given my heart a winking,[19] mute and dumb,

135   Or looked upon this love with idle sight?
What might you think? No, I went round to work,
And my young mistress thus I did bespeak:
"Lord Hamlet is a prince, out of thy star;
This must not be." And then I prescripts[20] gave her,

140   That she should lock herself from his resort,
Admit no messengers, receive no tokens.
Which done, she took the fruits of my advice;
And he, repellèd—short tale to make—
Fell into a sadness, then into a fast,

145   Thence to a watch, thence into a weakness,
Thence to a lightness, and by this declension[21]
Into the madness wherein now he raves,
And all we mourn for.

King [*to the* Queen].   Do you think 'tis this?

Queen. It may be, very like.

150   **Polonius.** Hath there been such a time—I would fain know that—
That I have positively said "'Tis so,"
When it proved otherwise?

King.   Not that I know.

Polonius. Take this from this,[22] if this be otherwise.
If circumstances lead me, I will find

155   Where truth is hid, though it were hid, indeed,
Within the center.

King.   How may we try it further?

---

[17] fain—willingly, gladly.

[18] If I . . . table book—if I had kept silent.

[19] given . . . winking—made my heart close its eyes to what I saw.

[20] prescripts—orders; instructions.

[21] declension—decline.

[22] Take this from this—Take my head from my neck.

Polonius. You know sometimes he walks four hours together

Here in the lobby.

Queen. So he does indeed.

Polonius. At such a time I'll loose my daughter to him.

[*To the* King.] Be you and I behind an arras[23] then.

Mark the encounter. If he love her not

And be not from his reason fall'n thereon,

Let me be no assistant for a state,

But keep a farm and carters.[24]

King. We will try it.

[*Enter* Hamlet *reading a book.*]

Queen. But look where sadly the poor wretch comes reading.

Polonius. Away, I do beseech you both, away.

I'll board him presently.[25] O, give me leave.

[*Exit* King *and* Queen *with* Attendants.]

How does my good Lord Hamlet?

Hamlet. Well, God-a-mercy.

Polonius. Do you know me, my lord?

Hamlet. Excellent well. You are a fishmonger.

Polonius. Not I, my lord.

Hamlet. Then I would you were so honest a man.

Polonius. Honest, my lord?

Hamlet. Ay, sir. To be honest, as this world goes, is to be one man picked out of ten thousand.

Polonius. That's very true, my lord.

Hamlet. For if the sun breed maggots in a dead dog, being a good kissing carrion[26]—Have you a daughter?

Polonius. I have, my lord.

Hamlet. Let her not walk i' the sun. Conception[27] is a blessing, but as your daughter may conceive, friend, look to 't.

Polonius [*aside*]. How say you by that? Still harping on my daughter. Yet he knew me not at first. He said I was a fishmonger. He is far gone.

---

[23] arras—screen of rich hanging tapestry.

[24] carters—wagon drivers.

[25] board him presently—speak to him immediately.

[26] good kissing carrion—flesh good enough for the sun to kiss.

[27] Conception—pun on *conception* meaning "understanding" and "getting pregnant."

185 　　And truly in my youth, I suffered much extremity for love, very near
　　　　this. I'll speak to him again.—What do you read, my lord?

Hamlet. Words, words, words.

Polonius. What is the matter,[28] my lord?

Hamlet. Between who?

190 **Polonius.** I mean, the matter that you read, my lord.

Hamlet. Slanders, sir; for the satirical rogue says here that old men have
　　　　gray beards, that their faces are wrinkled, their eyes purging thick
　　　　amber and plum-tree gum, and that they have a plentiful lack of wit,
　　　　together with most weak hams.[29] All which, sir, though I most power-
195 　　fully and potently believe, yet I told it not honesty to have it thus set
　　　　down, for yourself, sir, shall grow old as I am, if, like a crab you
　　　　could go backward.

Polonius [*aside*]. Though this be madness, yet there is method in 't.—Will
　　　　you walk out of the air, my lord?

200 **Hamlet.** Into my grave?

Polonius. Indeed, that's out of the air. [*Aside.*] How pregnant sometimes
　　　　his replies are! A happiness that often madness hits on, which reason
　　　　and sanity could not so prosperously be delivered of. I will leave him
　　　　and suddenly contrive the means of meeting between him and my
205 　　daughter.—My lord, I will take my leave of you.

Hamlet. You cannot, sir, take from me anything that I will more willingly
　　　　part withal[30]—except my life, except my life, except my life.

Polonius. Fare you well, my lord.

Hamlet [*aside*]. These tedious old fools!

[*Enter* Guildenstern *and* Rosencrantz.]

210 **Polonius.** You go to seek the Lord Hamlet. There he is.

Rosencrantz [*to* Polonius]. God save you, sir!

[*Exit* Polonius.]

Guildenstern. My honored lord!

Rosencrantz. My most dear lord!

Hamlet. My excellent good friends! How dost thou,
215 　　Guildenstern? Ah, Rosencrantz! Good lads, how do you both?

Rosencrantz. As the indifferent children of the earth.[31]

---

[28] matter—Polonius means "subject matter," but Hamlet pretends to understand it as "quarrel."

[29] hams—buttocks and thighs.

[30] withal—with.

[31] As the . . . earth—like ordinary men.

Guildenstern. Happy in that we are not overhappy.

On Fortune's cap we are not the very button.[32]

Hamlet. Nor the soles of her shoe?

220 **Rosencrantz.** Neither, my lord.

Hamlet. Then you live about her waist, or in the middle of her favors?

Guildenstern. Faith, her privates[33] we.

Hamlet. In the secret parts of Fortune? O, most true,

she is a strumpet.[34] What news?

225 **Rosencrantz.** None, my lord, but the world's grown honest.

Hamlet. Then is doomsday near. But your news is not true. Let me

question more in particular. What have you, my good friends,

deserved at the hands of Fortune that she sends you to prison hither?

Guildenstern. Prison, my lord?

230 **Hamlet.** Denmark's a prison.

Rosencrantz. Then is the world one.

Hamlet. A goodly one, in which there are many confines, wards, and

dungeons, Denmark being one o' th' worst.

Rosencrantz. We think not so, my lord.

235 **Hamlet.** Why then 'tis none to you, for there is nothing either good or

bad but thinking makes it so. To me, it is a prison.

Rosencrantz. Why then, your ambition makes it one. 'Tis too narrow for

your mind.

Hamlet. O God, I could be bounded in a nutshell and count myself a

240 king of infinite space, were it not that I have bad dreams.

Guildenstern. Which dreams, indeed, are ambition, for the very sub-

stance of the ambitious is merely the shadow of a dream.

Hamlet. A dream itself is but a shadow.

Rosencrantz. Truly, and I hold ambition of so airy and light a quality that

245 it is but a shadow's shadow.

Hamlet. Then are our beggars bodies, and our monarchs and out-

stretched heroes the beggars' shadows.[35] Shall we to the court? For,

by my fay,[36] I cannot reason.

---

[32] button—top.

[33] privates—intimates, friends; with a pun on "private parts," genitals.

[34] strumpet—whore.

[35] beggars bodies ... beggars' shadows—If ambition is a "shadow's shadow," kings and heroes, who are ruled by ambition, are only the shadows of beggars, who have no ambition.

[36] fay—faith.

Claudius (Richard Poe) greets Hamlet's friends Rosencrantz (Sheridan Crist) and Guildenstern (Nick Barmy) in this scene from the Hartford Stage production.

Rosencrantz, Guildenstern. We'll wait upon you.

250   **Hamlet.** No such matter. I will not sort you[37] with the rest of my servants, for, to speak to you like an honest man, I am most dreadfully attended. But, in the beaten way[38] of friendship, what make you at Elsinore?

Rosencrantz. To visit you, my lord, no other occasion.

255   **Hamlet.** Beggar that I am, I am even poor in thanks; but I thank you, and sure, dear friends, my thanks are too dear a halfpenny. Were you not sent for? Is it your own inclining? Is it a free visitation? Come, come, deal justly with me. Come, come. Nay, speak.

Guildenstern. What should we say, my lord?

260   **Hamlet.** Anything but to th' purpose. You were sent for, and there is a kind of confession in your looks which your modesties have not craft enough to color. I know the good king and queen have sent for you.

Rosencrantz. To what end, my lord?

---

[37] sort you—put you in the same class.
[38] beaten way—speaking friend to friend.

Hamlet. That you must teach me. But let me conjure you, by the rights
265   of our fellowship, by the consonancy of our youth,[39] by the obligation
of our ever-preserved love, and by what more dear a better proposer
could charge you withal: be even and direct with me whether you
were sent for or no.

Rosencrantz [*aside to* Guildenstern]. What say you?

270   **Hamlet** [*aside*]. Nay, then, I have an eye of you.—If you love me, hold
not off.

Guildenstern. My lord, we were sent for.

Hamlet. I will tell you why; so shall my anticipation prevent your discovery, and your secrecy to the king and queen molt no feather.[40] I
275   have of late—but wherefore I know not—lost all my mirth, forgone
all custom of exercises, and, indeed, it goes so heavily with my
disposition that this goodly frame, the earth, seems to me a sterile
promontory;[41] this most excellent **canopy**,[42] the air, look you, this
brave o'erhanging firmament,[43] this majestical roof, fretted with
280   golden fire, why, it appeareth nothing to me but a foul and pestilent
congregation[44] of vapors. What a piece of work is a man! How noble
in reason, how infinite in faculties, in form and moving how express
and admirable, in action how like an angel, in apprehension how like
a god! The beauty of the world, the **paragon**[45] of animals—and yet, to
285   me, what is this **quintessence**[46] of dust? Man delights not me—no,
nor woman neither, though by your smiling you seem to say so.

Rosencrantz. My lord, there was no such stuff in my thoughts.

Hamlet. Why did you laugh, then, when I said "Man delights not me"?

Rosencrantz. To think, my lord, if you delight not in man, what Lenten[47]
290   entertainment the players shall receive from you. We coted[48] them on
the way, and hither are they coming to offer you service.

---

[39] consonancy of our youth—harmony we enjoyed when we were younger.

[40] my anticipation . . . feather—my saying it first will stop your betraying the confidence of the king and queen.

[41] **promontory**—high ridge of land or rock jutting out into a body of water.

[42] **canopy**—high, overarching covering.

[43] firmament—sky.

[44] congregation—gathering.

[45] **paragon**—model of excellence.

[46] **quintessence**—very essence.

[47] Lenten—dismal.

[48] coted—passed.

Hamlet. He that plays the king shall be welcome. His Majesty shall have
tribute of me. The adventurous knight shall use his foil[49] and target,
the lover shall not sigh gratis,[50] the humorous man shall end his part
295 in peace, the clown shall make those laugh whose lungs are tickle o'
the sear,[51] and the lady[52] shall say her mind freely, or the blank verse
shall halt for 't. What players are they?

Rosencrantz. Even those you were wont to take such delight in, the
tragedians of the city.

300 **Hamlet.** How chances it they travel? Their residence, both in reputation
and profit, was better both ways.

Rosencrantz. I think their inhibition comes by the means of the late
innovation.[53]

Hamlet. Do they hold the same estimation they did when I was in the
305 city? Are they so followed?

Rosencrantz. No, indeed are they not.

Hamlet. How comes it? Do they grow rusty?

Rosencrantz. Nay, their endeavor keeps in the wonted[54] pace. But there
is, sir, an aerie of children, little eyases, that cry out on the top of
310 question and are most tyrannically clapped for 't.[55] These are now the
fashion, and so berattle the common stages[56]—so they call them—that
many wearing rapiers are afraid of goose quills[57] and dare scarce
come thither.

Hamlet. What, are they children? Who maintains 'em? How are they
315 escoted?[58] Will they pursue the quality no longer than they can sing?[59]
Will they not say afterwards, if they should grow themselves to
common players—as it is most like, if their means are no better—

---

[49] foil—light fencing sword.

[50] gratis—without reward.

[51] tickle o' the sear—easily made to laugh.

[52] lady—actor playing a female role.

[53] inhibition . . . late innovation—hindrance (to playing in the city) results from the new fashion (probably the companies of boy actors that had become popular).

[54] wonted—accustomed, usual.

[55] aerie . . . for 't—nest of young hawks (that is the child actors) that cry shrilly above others in controversy and are outrageously applauded for it.

[56] common stages—public theaters, like Shakespeare's Globe; the boy actors performed in private theaters.

[57] that many . . . goose quills—many gentlemen fear they will be satirized by those who write for the boy actors.

[58] escoted—financially supported.

[59] no longer than they can sing—only until their voices change.

their writers do them wrong to make them exclaim against their own succession?[60]

320 **Rosencrantz.** Faith, there has been much to-do on both sides, and the nation holds it no sin to tar[61] them to controversy. There was for a while no money bid for argument unless the poet and the player went to cuffs in the question.[62]

Hamlet. Is 't possible?

325 **Guildenstern.** O, there has been much throwing about of brains.

Hamlet. Do the boys carry it away?

Rosencrantz. Ay, that they do, my lord—Hercules and his load too.

Hamlet. It is not very strange; for my uncle is king of Denmark, and those that would make mouths at him while my father lived give twenty, forty, 330 fifty, a hundred ducats apiece for his picture in little.[63] 'Sblood,[64] there is something in this more than natural, if philosophy could find it out.

[*Flourish of trumpets within.*]

Guildenstern. There are the players.

Hamlet. Gentlemen, you are welcome to Elsinore. Your hands, come then. Th' appurtenance[65] of welcome is fashion and ceremony. Let me 335 comply with you in this garb,[66] lest my extent to the players, which, I tell you, must show fairly outwards, should more appear like entertainment than yours. You are welcome. But my uncle-father and aunt-mother are deceived.

Guildenstern. In what, my dear lord?

340 **Hamlet.** I am but mad north-north-west. When the wind is southerly, I know a hawk from a handsaw.[67]

[*Enter* Polonius.]

Polonius. Well be with you, gentlemen!

Hamlet [*aside to them*]. Hark you, Guildenstern, and you too; at each ear a hearer. That great baby you see there is not yet out of his swad-
345 dling clouts.

---

[60] succession—future.

[61] tar—incite.

[62] There was . . . the question—No plays could be sold unless they took up the quarrel between the children's poets and the adult players.

[63] picture in little—miniature portrait.

[64] 'Sblood—by God's blood (an oath).

[65] appurtenance—accessory.

[66] comply . . . garb—be courteous in this manner.

[67] I know . . . handsaw—that is, he can distinguish between things that are not alike.

Rosencrantz. Haply he is the second time come to them, for they say an old man is twice a child.

Hamlet. I will prophesy he comes to tell me of the players. Mark it.— [*Aloud.*] You say right, sir, o' Monday morning, 'twas then indeed.

350 **Polonius.** My lord, I have news to tell you.

Hamlet. My lord, I have news to tell you. When Roscius[68] was an actor in Rome—

Polonius. The actors are come hither, my lord.

Hamlet. Buzz, buzz![69]

355 **Polonius.** Upon my honor—

Hamlet. Then came each actor on his ass.

Polonius. The best actors in the world, either for tragedy, comedy, history, pastoral, pastoral-comical, historical-pastoral, tragical-historical, tragical-comical-historical-pastoral, scene individable, or poem

360 unlimited. Seneca cannot be too heavy, nor Plautus[70] too light. For the law of writ and the liberty,[71] these are the only men.

Hamlet. O Jephthah,[72] judge of Israel, what a treasure hadst thou!

Polonius. What a treasure had he, my lord?

Hamlet. Why,

365 *One fair daughter, and no more,*
The which he lovèd passing[73] well.

Polonius [*aside*]. Still on my daughter.

Hamlet. Am I not i' the right, old Jephthah?

Polonius. If you call me "Jephthah," my lord, I have a daughter that I love passing well.

370 **Hamlet.** Nay, that follows not.

Polonius. What follows then, my lord?

Hamlet. Why,

As by lot, God wot,[74]

and then, you know,

375 *It came to pass, as most like it was—*

---

[68] Roscius—most famous of Roman actors (died 62 B.C.).

[69] Buzz, buzz!—exclamation of impatience.

[70] Seneca . . . Plautus—two Roman playwrights, a tragedian and a comedian, respectively.

[71] law . . . liberty—for both regarding the rules and breaking them.

[72] Jephthah—According to the biblical story, Jephthah was forced to sacrifice his daughter when he swore that if God gave him victory in battle, he would sacrifice the next thing he met.

[73] *passing*—surpassingly.

[74] *As . . . wot*—as by chance, God knows.

the first row of the pious chanson[75] will show you more,
for look where my abridgement comes.

[*Enter the* Players.]

You are welcome, masters; welcome, all.—I am glad to see thee
well.—Welcome, good friends. O, old friend! Why, thy face is
380   valanced[76] since I saw thee last. Com'st thou to beard[77] me in
Denmark?—What, my young lady and mistress![78] By 'r Lady, your
ladyship is nearer to heaven than when I saw you last, by the altitude
of a chopine.[79] Pray God your voice, like a piece of uncurrent gold,
be not cracked within the ring.[80]—Masters, you are all welcome. We'll
385   e'en to 't like French falconers, fly at anything we see. We'll have a
speech straight. Come, give us a taste of your quality. Come, a passionate speech.

First Player. What speech, my good lord?

Hamlet. I heard thee speak me a speech once, but it was never acted, or
390   if it was, not above once; for the play, I remember, pleased not the
million; 'twas caviar to the general.[81] But it was—as I received it, and
others whose judgments in such matters cried in the top of[82] mine—
an excellent play, well digested in the scenes, set down with as much
modesty as cunning. I remember one said there were no sallets[83] in
395   the lines to make the matter savory, nor no matter in the phrase that
might indict the author of affectation, but called it an honest method,
as wholesome as sweet, and, by very much, more handsome than
fine. One speech in 't I chiefly loved. 'Twas Aeneas' tale to Dido,[84]
and thereabout of it especially when he speaks of Priam's slaughter.
400   If it live in your memory, begin at this line: let me see, let me see—
The rugged Pyrrhus,[85] *like th' Hyrcanian beast*[86]

---

[75] row . . . pious chanson—stanza of the holy song.

[76] valanced—fringed (bearded).

[77] beard—confront boldly.

[78] young . . . mistress—addressed to the boy actor who plays women's parts.

[79] chopine—thick-soled shoe.

[80] cracked within the ring—broken to the point where you can no longer play female roles. A coin with a crack extending far enough in from the edge to cross the circle surrounding the stamp of the sovereign's was unacceptable in exchange.

[81] caviar to the general—too good for the multitude.

[82] cried . . . top of—carried more authority than.

[83] sallets—spicy jokes.

[84] Aeneas . . . Dido—the Trojan hero Aeneas tells the story of the fall of Troy to Dido, queen of Carthage.

[85] Pyrrhus—son of Achilles who killed Priam, king of Troy, to avenge his father's death.

[86] Hyrcanian beast—tiger.

'Tis not so. It begins with Pyrrhus:

The rugged Pyrrhus, he whose sable[87] arms,
Black as his purpose, did the night resemble
405 *When he lay couchèd in the ominous horse,[88]*
Hath now this dread and black complexion smeared
With heraldry more dismal. Head to foot
Now is he total gules, horridly tricked[89]
With blood of fathers, mothers, daughters, sons,
410 *Baked and impasted with the parching streets,[90]*
That lend a tyrannous and a damnèd light
To their lord's murder. Roasted in wrath and fire,
And thus o'ersizèd with coagulate gore,[91]
With eyes like carbuncles,[92] the hellish Pyrrhus
415 *Old grandsire Priam seeks.*

So proceed you.

Polonius. 'Fore God, my lord, well spoken, with good accent
and good discretion.

First Player.   *Anon he finds him*
Striking too short at Greeks. His antique sword,
420 *Rebellious to his arm, lies where it falls*
Repugnant[93] to command. Unequal matched,
Pyrrhus at Priam drives, in rage strikes wide,
But with the whiff and wind of his fell[94] sword
Th' unnervèd[95] father falls. Then senseless Ilium,[96]
425 *Seeming to feel this blow, with flaming top*
Stoops to his base, and with a hideous crash
Takes prisoner Pyrrhus' ear. For, lo! His sword,

---

[87] *sable*—black.

[88] *horse*—Trojan Horse, huge wooden horse in which the Greeks hid so that they could get into Troy.

[89] *gules ... tricked*—red, horribly decorated.

[90] *Baked ... streets*—caked and crusted by the heat from the burning streets.

[91] *o'ersizèd with coagulate gore*—covered with clotted blood.

[92] *carbuncles*—deep red jewels believed to shine in the dark.

[93] *Repugnant*—resistant, hostile.

[94] *fell*—cruel.

[95] *unnervèd*—drained of strength.

[96] *Ilium*—fortress within Troy.

Which was declining on the milky head
Of reverend Priam, seemed i' th' air to stick.

430 *So as a painted tyrant Pyrrhus stood,*
And, like a neutral to his will and matter,[97]
Did nothing.
But as we often see against some storm
A silence in the heavens, the rack[98] stand still,
435 *The bold winds speechless, and the orb[99] below*
As hush as death, anon the dreadful thunder
Doth rend the region, so, after Pyrrhus' pause,
A rousèd vengeance sets him new a-work,
And never did the Cyclops' hammers[100] fall
440 *On Mars's armor forged for proof eterne[101]*
With less remorse than Pyrrhus' bleeding sword
Now falls on Priam.
Out, out, thou strumpet Fortune! All you gods
In general synod[102] take away her power!
445 *Break all the spokes and fellies[103] from her wheel,*
And bowl the round nave[104] down the hill of heaven
As low as to the fiends!

Polonius. This is too long.

Hamlet. It shall to the barber's with your beard.—Prithee, say on. He's
450 for a jig or a tale of bawdry,[105] or he sleeps. Say on, come to Hecuba.[106]

First Player. *But who, ah woe! had seen the moblèd[107] queen—*

Hamlet. "The moblèd queen?"

Polonius. That's good. "Moblèd queen" is good.

---

[97] *like . . . matter*—poised midway between intention and performance.

[98] *rack*—high cloud mass.

[99] *orb*—earth.

[100] *Cyclops' hammers*—hammers of legendary blacksmiths who forged thunderbolts for Jove, king of the Greco-Roman gods.

[101] *Mars's . . . proof eterne*—armor of the god of war, made to last forever.

[102] *synod*—council, assembly.

[103] *fellies*—rims.

[104] *nave*—hub of the wheel.

[105] *jig . . . bawdry*—mocking song and dance or scandalous tale.

[106] Hecuba—Priam's wife, queen of Troy.

[107] *moblèd*—muffled.

First Player. *Run barefoot up and down, threat'ning the flames*
455   *With bisson rheum,*[108] *a clout*[109] *upon that head*
         Where late the diadem[110] *stood, and, for a robe,*
         About her lank and all o'erteemed[111] *loins*
         A blanket, in the alarm of fear caught up—
         Who this had seen, with tongue in venom steeped,
460   *'Gainst Fortune's state would treason have pronounced.*
         But if the gods themselves did see her then
         When she saw Pyrrhus make malicious sport
         In mincing with his sword her husband's limbs,
         The instant burst of clamor that she made,
465   *Unless things mortal move them not at all,*
         Would have made milch[112] *the burning eyes of heaven,*
         And passion in the gods.

Polonius. Look whe'er he has not turned his color and has tears in 's eyes. Prithee, no more.

470 **Hamlet.** 'Tis well. I'll have thee speak out the rest of this soon.— Good my lord, will you see the players well bestowed? Do you hear, let them be well used, for they are the abstract and brief chronicles of the time. After your death you were better have a bad **epitaph**[113] than their ill report while you live.

475 **Polonius.** My lord, I will use them according to their desert.

Hamlet. God's bodikins,[114] man, much better! Use every man after his desert, and who shall 'scape whipping? Use them after your own honor and dignity. The less they deserve, the more merit is in your bounty. Take them in.

480 **Polonius.** Come, sirs.

[*Exit* Polonius.]

Hamlet. Follow him, friends. We'll hear a play tomorrow. [*As the* Players *start to leave,* Hamlet *detains the* First Player.] Dost thou hear me, old friend? Can you play *The Murder of Gonzago?*

---

[108] *bisson rheum*—blinding tears.

[109] *clout*—cloth.

[110] *diadem*—crown worn as a sign of royalty.

[111] *o'erteemed*—worn out by childbearing.

[112] *milch*—wet with tears, milky.

[113] **epitaph**—brief written poem or essay about a deceased person; inscription on a tombstone.

[114] God's bodikins—God's little body (a mild oath).

In this scene from the Hartford Stage production, Hamlet (Richard Thomas) listens as the First Player (Ted van Griethysen) performs a speech.

First Player. Ay, my lord.

485 **Hamlet.** We'll ha 't tomorrow night. You could, for a need, study a
speech of some dozen or sixteen lines, which I would set down and
insert in 't, could you not?

First Player. Ay, my lord.

Hamlet. Very well. Follow that lord—and look you mock him not.

490   [*Exit* First Player.] My good friends, I'll leave you till night. You are
welcome to Elsinore.

First Player. Good my lord.

Hamlet. Ay, so, goodbye to you.— [*Exit* Rosencrantz *and* Guildenstern.]
Now I am alone.

495   O, what a rogue and peasant slave am I!
    Is it not monstrous that this player here,
    But in a fiction, in a dream of passion,
    Could force his soul so to his own conceit

That from her working all his visage wanned,[115]

500 Tears in his eyes, distraction in his aspect,

A broken voice, and his whole function suiting

With forms to his conceit? And all for nothing!

For Hecuba!

What's Hecuba to him, or he to Hecuba,

505 That he should weep for her? What would he do

Had he the motive and the cue for passion

That I have? He would drown the stage with tears

And cleave the general ear with horrid speech,

Make mad the guilty and appall the free,

510 Confound the ignorant, and amaze indeed

The very faculties of eyes and ears. Yet I,

A dull and muddy-mettled rascal, peak

Like John-a-dreams, unpregnant of my cause,[116]

And can say nothing—no, not for a king

515 Upon whose property and most dear life

A damned defeat was made. Am I a coward?

Who calls me "villain"? Breaks my pate[117] across?

Plucks off my beard and blows it in my face?

Tweaks me by the nose? Gives me the lie i' the throat

520 As deep as to the lungs?[118] Who does me this?

Ha, 'swounds,[119] I should take it. For it cannot be

But I am pigeon-livered and lack gall[120]

To make oppression bitter, or ere this

I should have fatted all the region kites[121]

525 With this slave's offal.[122] Bloody, bawdy villain!

Remorseless, treacherous, lecherous, kindless villain!

O, vengeance!

Why, what an ass am I! This is most brave,

---

[115] dream . . . wanned—could make his imaginary emotion so powerful that his face grew pale.

[116] muddy-mettled . . . cause—dull-spirited rascal, mope, like an absent-minded fellow, unable to act on my cause.

[117] pate—head.

[118] Gives me . . . lungs?—calls me an absolute liar.

[119] 'swounds—by God's wounds (an oath).

[120] pigeon-livered . . . gall—cowardly and lack anger.

[121] fatted . . . kites—fed all the birds of prey in the sky.

[122] offal—entrails.

The play's the thing
Wherein I'll catch the conscience of the king.

530

535

540

545

550

That I, the son of a dear father murdered,
Prompted to my revenge by heaven and hell,
Must, like a whore, unpack my heart with words
And fall a-cursing like a very drab,
A scullion![123] Fie upon 't, foh!
About,[124] my brains!—Hum, I have heard
That guilty creatures sitting at a play
Have, by the very cunning of the scene,
Been struck so to the soul that presently
They have proclaimed their malefactions.[125]
For murder, though it have no tongue, will speak
With most miraculous organ. I'll have these players
Play something like the murder of my father
Before mine uncle. I'll observe his looks;
I'll tent[126] him to the quick. If he do blench,[127]
I know my course. The spirit that I have seen
May be the devil, and the devil hath power
T' assume a pleasing shape; yea, and perhaps,
Out of my weakness and my melancholy,
As he is very potent with such spirits,[128]
Abuses[129] me to damn me. I'll have grounds
More relative[130] than this. The play's the thing
Wherein I'll catch the conscience of the king.
[*He exits.*]

---

[123] scullion—kitchen servant.
[124] About—to work.
[125] malefactions—crimes, misdeeds.
[126] tent—probe.
[127] blench—flinch.
[128] spirits—emotional states.
[129] Abuses—deludes.
[130] relative—pertinent.

Act Three, Scene One

Rosencrantz and Guildenstern report to Claudius and Gertrude on their failure to find out why Hamlet is mad. Claudius and Polonius then hide so that they can overhear the meeting between Hamlet and Ophelia. Hamlet delivers his most famous soliloquy, "To be, or not to be," wondering whether it would be better to be dead and free from care or to be a man who must act and bear the consequences of his action. When he notices Ophelia, he is courteous, but when she tries to return his love letters and gifts, he grows increasingly angry, railing against love and marriage. He denies having loved her and tells her that she should enter a nunnery. After Hamlet leaves, Claudius decides that Hamlet's behavior is not caused by love. He decides to send Hamlet on an errand to England. Polonius persuades him not to act until Gertrude has talked with Hamlet after the play that evening.

Enter King Claudius, Queen Gertrude, Polonius, Ophelia, Rosencrantz, Guildenstern, *and* Lords.

King. And can you by no drift of conference[1]
    Get from him why he puts on this confusion,
    Grating so harshly all his days of quiet
    With turbulent and dangerous lunacy?

5   **Rosencrantz.** He does confess he feels himself distracted,
    But from what cause 'a will by no means speak.

Guildenstern. Nor do we find him forward to be sounded,[2]
    But with a crafty madness keeps aloof
    When we would bring him on to some confession

10   Of his true state.

Queen.   Did he receive you well?

Rosencrantz. Most like a gentleman.

Guildenstern. But with much forcing of his disposition.

Rosencrantz. Niggard of question,[3] but of our demands
    Most free in his reply.

15   **Queen.** Did you assay him to any pastime?

---

[1] drift of conference—direction of a conversation.

[2] forward . . . sounded—eager to be questioned.

[3] Niggard of question—careful with his words.

Rosencrantz. Madam, it so fell out that certain players
We o'erraught[4] on the way. Of these we told him,
And there did seem in him a kind of joy
To hear of it. They are here about the court,
20 And, as I think, they have already order
This night to play before him.
Polonius.   'Tis most true,
And he beseeched me to entreat Your Majesties
To hear and see the matter.
King. With all my heart, and it doth much content me
25 To hear him so inclined.
Good gentlemen, give him a further edge[5]
And drive his purpose into these delights.
Rosencrantz. We shall, my lord.
[*Exit* Rosencrantz, Guildenstern, *and* Lords.]
King.   Sweet Gertrude, leave us too,
For we have closely[6] sent for Hamlet hither,
30 That he, as 'twere by accident, may here
Affront[7] Ophelia.
Her father and myself, lawful espials,[8]
Will so bestow ourselves that, seeing unseen,
We may of their encounter frankly judge,
35 And gather by him, as he is behaved,
If 't be th' affliction of his love or no
That thus he suffers for.
Queen.   I shall obey you.
And for your part, Ophelia, I do wish
That your good beauties be the happy cause
40 Of Hamlet's wildness. So shall I hope your virtues
Will bring him to his wonted way again,
To both your honors.
Ophelia.   Madam, I wish it may.
[*Exit* Queen.]

---

[4] o'erraught—passed.

[5] edge—stimulus.

[6] closely—privately.

[7] Affront—meet face-to-face.

[8] espials—spies.

Polonius. Ophelia, walk you here.—Gracious, so please you,
We will bestow ourselves. [*Giving* Ophelia *a book*.] Read on this book,

45   That show of such an exercise may color
Your loneliness.[9] We are oft to blame in this—
'Tis too much proved—that with devotion's visage
And pious action we do sugar o'er
The devil himself.

50 **King** [*aside*]. O, 'tis too true!
How smart a lash that speech doth give my conscience!
The harlot's cheek, beautied with plast'ring art,
Is not more ugly to the thing that helps it
Than is my deed to my most painted word.[10]

55   O heavy burden!
Polonius. I hear him coming. Let's withdraw, my lord.
[*The* King *and* Polonius *withdraw*.]
[*Enter* Hamlet. Ophelia *pretends to read a book*.]
Hamlet. To be, or not to be, that is the question:
Whether 'tis nobler in the mind to suffer
The slings and arrows of outrageous fortune,

60   Or to take arms against a sea of troubles
And by opposing, end them. To die, to sleep—
No more—and by a sleep to say we end
The heartache and the thousand natural shocks
That flesh is heir to—'tis a consummation

65   Devoutly to be wished. To die, to sleep;
To sleep, perchance to dream. Ay, there's the rub,[11]
For in that sleep of death what dreams may come,
When we have shuffled off this mortal coil,[12]
Must give us pause. There's the respect

---

[9] That show . . . loneliness—that it will seem normal that you are alone.

[10] The harlot's cheek . . . painted word—A whore's face beneath her cosmetics is no uglier than my actions behind my words in public.

[11] rub—obstacle.

[12] shuffled . . . coil—freed ourselves from the turmoil of this life.

Robert Wilson is shown in his solo performance of *Hamlet* at Houston's Alley Theatre in 1995.

70   That makes calamity of so long life.

For who would bear the whips and scorns of time,

Th' oppressor's wrong, the proud man's contumely,[13]

The pangs of disprized love, the law's delay,

The insolence of office,[14] and the spurns

75   That patient merit of th' unworthy takes,

When he himself might his quietus make[15]

With a bare bodkin? Who would fardels[16] bear,

To grunt and sweat under a weary life,

But that the dread of something after death,

80   The undiscovered country from whose bourn[17]

No traveler returns, puzzles the will,

And makes us rather bear those ills we have

Than fly to others that we know not of?

Thus conscience does make cowards of us all;

85   And thus the native hue[18] of resolution

Is sicklied o'er with the pale cast of thought,

---

[13] contumely—insults.

[14] insolence of office—insolent behavior of officials.

[15] his quietus make—end or settle his own account.

[16] fardels—burdens.

[17] bourn—boundary.

[18] native hue—natural color.

And enterprises of great pitch and moment[19]
With this regard their currents turn awry
And lose the name of action.—Soft you now,
90   The fair Ophelia. Nymph, in thy orisons[20]
Be all my sins remembered.

Ophelia.   Good my lord,
How does Your Honor for this many a day?

Hamlet. I humbly thank you, well, well, well.

Ophelia. My lord, I have remembrances of yours,
95   That I have longèd long to redeliver.
I pray you, now receive them.

Hamlet. No, not I, I never gave you aught.

Ophelia. My honored lord, you know right well you did,
And with them words of so sweet breath composed
As made the things more rich. Their perfume lost,
100   Take these again, for to the noble mind
Rich gifts wax poor when givers prove unkind.
There, my lord.

Hamlet. Ha, ha! Are you honest?[21]

Ophelia. My lord?

Hamlet. Are you fair?

105   **Ophelia.** What means your lordship?

Hamlet. That if you be honest and fair, your honesty should admit no
discourse to your beauty.

Ophelia. Could beauty, my lord, have better commerce[22] than with honesty?

Hamlet. Ay, truly, for the power of beauty will sooner transform honesty
110   from what it is to a bawd than the force of honesty can translate
beauty into his likeness. This was sometime a **paradox,**[23] but now the
time gives it proof. I did love you once.

Ophelia. Indeed, my lord, you made me believe so.

Hamlet. You should not have believed me, for virtue cannot so inoculate
115   our old stock but we shall relish of it.[24] I loved you not.

---

[19] pitch and moment—height and importance.

[20] orisons—prayers.

[21] honest—chaste, modest, telling the truth (wordplay).

[22] commerce—dealings.

[23] **paradox**—seeming contradiction.

[24] virtue cannot . . . of it—Virtue can be grafted on sinful human nature, but the resulting fruit will still taste of sinfulness.

Ophelia. I was the more deceived.

Hamlet. Get thee to a nunnery.[25] Why wouldst thou be a breeder of sinners? I am myself indifferent honest, but yet I could accuse me of
such things that it were better my mother had not borne me: I am
very proud, revengeful, ambitious, with more offenses at my beck[26]
than I have thoughts to put them in, imagination to give them shape,
or time to act them in. What should such fellows as I do crawling
between earth and heaven? We are arrant knaves all; believe none of
us. Go thy ways to a nunnery. Where's your father?

Ophelia. At home, my lord.

Hamlet. Let the doors be shut upon him, that he may play the fool
nowhere but in 's own house. Farewell.

Ophelia. O, help him, you sweet heavens!

Hamlet. If thou dost marry, I'll give thee this plague for thy dowry: be
thou as chaste as ice, as pure as snow, thou shalt not escape
calumny.[27] Get thee to a nunnery, farewell. Or, if thou wilt needs
marry, marry a fool, for wise men know well enough what monsters
you make of them. To a nunnery, go, and quickly too. Farewell.

Ophelia. Heavenly powers, restore him!

Hamlet. I have heard of your paintings too, well enough. God hath given
you one face, and you make yourselves another. You jig and amble,
and you lisp, you nickname God's creatures and make your wanton-
ness your ignorance. Go to, I'll no more on 't. It hath made me mad. I
say we will have no more marriage. Those that are married already—
all but one—shall live. The rest shall keep as they are. To a nunnery, go.

[*Exit* Hamlet.]

Ophelia. O, what a noble mind is here o'erthrown!
The courtier's, soldier's, scholar's, eye, tongue, sword,
Th' expectancy and rose of the fair state,
The glass of fashion and the mold of form,[28]
Th' observed of all observers, quite, quite down!
And I, of ladies most deject and wretched,
That sucked the honey of his musicked vows,
Now see that noble and most sovereign reason

---

[25] nunnery—place where nuns live. The word was also used mockingly to mean "brothel."

[26] beck—call.

[27] **calumny**—slander.

[28] The glass . . . of form—the model of elegance and attractiveness.

150	Like sweet bells jangled, out of tune and harsh,
	That unmatched form and stature of blown youth
	Blasted with ecstasy.[29] O, woe is me,
	T' have seen what I have seen, see what I see!

[*Enter* King *and* Polonius.]

King. Love? His affections do not that way tend;

155	Nor what he spake, though it lacked form a little,
	Was not like madness. There's something in his soul
	O'er which his melancholy sits on brood,
	And I do doubt the hatch and the disclose
	Will be some danger; which for to prevent,
160	I have in quick determination
	Thus set it down: he shall with speed to England
	For the demand of our neglected tribute.
	Haply the seas and countries different,
	With variable objects, shall expel
165	This something-settled matter in his heart,
	Whereon his brains still beating puts him thus
	From fashion of himself. What think you on 't?

Polonius. It shall do well. But yet do I believe

	The origin and commencement of his grief
170	Sprung from neglected love.—How now, Ophelia?
	You need not tell us what Lord Hamlet said;
	We heard it all.—My lord, do as you please,
	But, if you hold it fit, after the play
	Let his queen-mother all alone entreat him
175	To show his grief. Let her be round[30] with him;
	And I'll be placed, so please you, in the ear
	Of all their conference. If she find him not,[31]
	To England send him, or confine him where
	Your wisdom best shall think.

180	**King.** It shall be so.
	Madness in great ones must not unwatched go.

[*They exit.*]

---

[29] blown . . . ecstasy—vigorous youth, blighted by madness.

[30] round—straightforward.

[31] find him not—does not learn his secret.

Act Three, Scene Two

In a hall in the castle, Hamlet coaches the actors on how to speak his new dialogue. He also asks Horatio to watch Claudius carefully during the play. As the audience arrives, Hamlet joins Ophelia and flirts with her, full of high spirits. At the beginning of the play, the actors mime the old king's murder and the queen's acceptance of the love of the murderer. Then the Player King and the Player Queen express their continuing love after thirty years of marriage. The Player King is old and sick, but his wife dismisses any idea that she might remarry after his death. He reminds her that promises are often forgotten as events change. She leaves him to rest. As he sleeps, his nephew enters and pours poison in his ear, plotting to become king. Claudius rises in horror and stops the play. Left alone, Hamlet and Horatio discuss the king's reaction to the play. Rosencrantz and Guildenstern tell Hamlet that Claudius is very angry and that Gertrude wishes to see him. When Guildenstern tries again to befriend Hamlet, he is told he is a liar. Polonius hurries Hamlet to the queen. As they go, Hamlet promises himself that he will not harm his mother but that he will speak sharply to her.

Enter Hamlet *and three of the* Players.

Hamlet. Speak the speech, I pray you, as I pronounced it to you, trippingly on the tongue. But if you mouth it, as many of our players do, I had as lief the town-crier spoke my lines. Nor do not saw the air too much with your hand, thus, but use all gently; for in the very torrent,

5   tempest, and, as I may say, whirlwind of your passion, you must acquire and beget a temperance that may give it smoothness. O, it offends me to the soul to hear a robustious periwig-pated[1] fellow tear a passion to tatters, to very rags, to split the ears of the groundlings,[2] who for the most part are capable of nothing but inexplicable dumb

10   shows and noise. I would have such a fellow whipped for o'erdoing Termagant. It out-Herods Herod.[3] Pray you, avoid it.

First Player. I warrant, Your Honor.

Hamlet. Be not too tame neither, but let your own discretion be your tutor. Suit the action to the word, the word to the action, with this

---

[1] robustious periwig-pated—boisterous, wig-wearing.

[2] groundlings—audience members who stood rather than sat, and consequently paid less to get in.

[3] Termagant . . . Herod—These are roles in medieval drama that are generally played with great noise and action. Termagant was an imaginary Muslim god; Herod was king of Judea.

15 special observance, that you o'erstep not the modesty of nature. For
anything so o'erdone is from the purpose of playing, whose end, both
at the first and now, was and is to hold as 'twere the mirror up to
nature, to show virtue her own feature, scorn her own image, and the
very age and body of the time his form and pressure.[4] Now this over-
20 done or come tardy[5] off, though it makes the unskillful laugh, cannot
but make the judicious grieve, the censure of the which one must in
your allowance o'erweigh a whole theater of others. O, there be players that I have seen play and heard others praise, and that highly, not
to speak it profanely, that, neither having th' accent of Christians nor
25 the gait of Christian, pagan, nor man, have so strutted and bellowed
that I have thought some of nature's journeymen had made men and
not made them well, they imitated humanity so abominably.

First Player. I hope we have reformed that indifferently[6] with us, sir.

Hamlet. O, reform it altogether. And let those that play your clowns
30 speak no more than is set down for them; for there be of them that
will themselves laugh, to set on some quantity of barren spectators to
laugh too, though in the meantime some necessary question of the
play be then to be considered. That's villainous and shows a most
pitiful ambition in the fool that uses it. Go make you ready.

[*Exit* Players.]

[*Enter* Polonius, Guildenstern, *and* Rosencrantz.]

35 How now, my lord, will the king hear this piece of work?

Polonius. And the queen too, and that presently.

Hamlet. Bid the players make haste.

[*Exit* Polonius.]

Will you two help to hasten them?

Rosencrantz. Ay, my lord.

[*Exit* Guildenstern, *and* Rosencrantz.]

Hamlet.   What ho, Horatio!

[*Enter* Horatio.]

40 **Horatio.** Here, sweet lord, at your service.

Hamlet. Horatio, thou art e'en as just a man
As e'er my conversation coped withal.[7]

---

[4] age . . . pressure—the present exactly as it is.

[5] tardy—inadequately.

[6] indifferently—fairly well.

[7] my conversation coped withal—I have ever met.

Horatio. O, my dear lord—

Hamlet. Nay, do not think I flatter,
For what advancement may I hope from thee
45 That no revenue hast but thy good spirits
To feed and clothe thee? Why should the poor be flattered?
No, let the candied[8] tongue lick absurd pomp,
And crook the pregnant[9] hinges of the knee
Where thrift may follow fawning. Dost thou hear?
50 Since my dear soul was mistress of her choice
And could of men distinguish her election
Hath sealed thee for herself. For thou hast been
As one, in suffering all, that suffers nothing,
A man that Fortune's buffets and rewards
55 Hast ta'en with equal thanks; and blessed are those
Whose blood and judgment are so well commeddled[10]
That they are not a pipe for Fortune's finger
To sound what stop she please. Give me that man
That is not passion's slave, and I will wear him
60 In my heart's core, ay, in my heart of heart,
As I do thee.—Something too much of this.—
There is a play tonight before the king.
One scene of it comes near the circumstance
Which I have told thee of my father's death.
65 I prithee, when thou seest that act afoot,
Even with the very comment of thy soul[11]
Observe my uncle. If his occulted[12] guilt
Do not itself unkennel in one speech,
It is a damnèd ghost that we have seen,
70 And my imaginations are as foul
As Vulcan's stithy.[13] Give him heedful note,
For I mine eyes will rivet to his face,

---

[8] candied—flattering.

[9] pregnant—ready to bend at any time.

[10] commeddled—mixed, blended.

[11] very comment of thy soul—most intense critical observation.

[12] occulted—deliberately hidden.

[13] Vulcan's stithy—forge of the Roman god of fire and metalworking.

And, after, we will both our judgments join
In censure of his seeming.[14]

Horatio.   Well, my lord.

75   If he steal aught the whilst this play is playing
And scape detecting, I will pay the theft.

[*Flourish. Enter trumpets and kettledrums,* King Claudius, Queen Gertrude,
Polonius, Ophelia, Rosencrantz, Guildenstern, *and other* Lords, *with*
Guards *carrying torches.*]

Hamlet. They are coming to the play. I must be idle. Get you a place.

King. How fares our cousin Hamlet?

Hamlet. Excellent, i' faith, of the chameleon's dish.[15] I eat the air,
80   promise-crammed. You cannot feed capons[16] so.

King. I have nothing with this answer, Hamlet. These words are not mine.[17]

Hamlet. No, nor mine now. [*To Polonius.*] My lord, you played once i' th'
university, you say?

Polonius. That did I, my lord, and was accounted a good actor.

85   **Hamlet.** What did you enact?

Polonius. I did enact Julius Caesar. I was killed i' the Capitol; Brutus
killed me.

Hamlet. It was a brute part of him to kill so capital a calf[18] there.—Be the
players ready?

90   **Rosencrantz.** Ay, my lord. They stay upon your patience.

Queen. Come hither, my dear Hamlet, sit by me.

Hamlet. No, good mother, here's metal more attractive.

Polonius [*to the* King]. O, ho, do you mark that?

Hamlet. Lady, shall I lie in your lap?

[*Lying down at Ophelia's feet.*]

95   **Ophelia.** No, my lord.

Hamlet. I mean, my head upon your lap?

Ophelia. Ay, my lord.

Hamlet. Do you think I meant country matters?[19]

---

[14] seeming—outward appearance.

[15] chameleon's dish—Chameleons were believed to live on air. Hamlet takes Claudius's word *fares* in the sense of "eats."

[16] capons—castrated cocks, fattened for the table.

[17] I have . . . not mine—I do not understand your answer. It is not a reply to my question.

[18] calf—fool.

[19] country matters—indecency.

Ophelia. I think nothing, my lord.

100 **Hamlet.** That's a fair thought to lie between maids' legs.

Ophelia. What is, my lord?

Hamlet. Nothing.

Ophelia. You are merry, my lord.

Hamlet. Who, I?

105 **Ophelia.** Ay, my lord.

Hamlet. O God, your only jig-maker. What should a man do but be merry? For look you how cheerfully my mother looks, and my father died within 's two hours.

Ophelia. Nay, 'tis twice two months, my lord.

110 **Hamlet.** So long? Nay then, let the devil wear black, for I'll have a suit of sables. O heavens! Die two months ago, and not forgotten yet? Then there's hope a great man's memory may outlive his life half a year. But, by 'r Lady, he must build churches, then, or else shall he suffer not thinking on, with the hobbyhorse, whose epitaph is "For O, for O,
115 the hobbyhorse is forgot."[20]

[*The trumpets sound. Dumb show*[21] *follows.*]

[*Enter a king and a queen very lovingly; the* queen *embracing him, and he her. She kneels, and makes show of protestation unto him. He takes her up, and leans his head upon her neck. He lies down upon a bank of flowers. She, seeing him asleep, leaves him. Soon another man comes in, takes off the king's crown, kisses it, pours poison in the king's ears, and leaves him. The queen returns, finds the king dead, makes passionate action. The poisoner, with some three or four men, comes in again, seeming to comfort her. The dead body is carried away. The poisoner woos the queen with gifts. She seems harsh for a while, but in the end she accepts his love.*]

[*Exit* Players.]

Ophelia. What means this, my lord?

Hamlet. Marry, this is miching mallico;[22] it means mischief.

Ophelia. Belike this show imports the argument of the play.

[*Enter* Prologue.]

Hamlet. We shall know by this fellow. The players cannot keep counsel;
120 they'll tell all.

Ophelia. Will he tell us what this show meant?

---

[20] hobbyhorse is . . . forgot—Hamlet quotes a song that regrets the forgotten hobby horse, a character in English folk dances.

[21] *Dumb show*—mime scene.

[22] miching mallico—sneaking mischief.

Hamlet. Ay, or any show that you will show him. Be not you ashamed to show, he'll not shame to tell you what it means.

Ophelia. You are naught,[23] you are naught. I'll mark the play.

125 **Prologue.** *For us, and for our tragedy,*
    Here stooping to your clemency,
    We beg your hearing patiently.

[*Exit* Prologue.]

Hamlet. Is this a prologue, or the posy of a ring?[24]

Ophelia. 'Tis brief, my lord.

130 **Hamlet.** As woman's love.

[*Enter* Player King *and* Player Queen.]

Player King. *Full thirty times hath Phoebus' cart gone round*
    Neptune's salt wash and Tellus' orbèd ground,[25]
    And thirty dozen moons with borrowed sheen
    About the world have times twelve thirties been,
135   *Since love our hearts and Hymen did our hands*
    Unite commutual[26] *in most sacred bands.*

Player Queen. *So many journeys may the sun and moon*
    Make us again count o'er ere love be done!
    But, woe is me! You are so sick of late,
140   *So far from cheer and from your former state,*
    That I distrust[27] *you. Yet, though I distrust,*
    Discomfort you, my lord, it nothing must.
    For women's fear and love hold quantity;
    In neither aught, or in extremity.
145   *Now, what my love is, proof hath made you know,*
    And as my love is sized, my fear is so.
    Where love is great, the littlest doubts are fear;
    Where little fears grow great, great love grows there.

Player King. *Faith, I must leave thee, love, and shortly too.*
150   *My operant powers their functions leave to do.*[28]
    And thou shalt live in this fair world behind,

---

[23] naught—naughty, indecent.

[24] posy of a ring—verse or motto inscribed in a ring.

[25] *Full thirty . . . orbèd ground*—thirty years. The sun has fully orbited the seas and earth thirty times.

[26] *Hymen . . . commutual*—the god of marriage united our hands mutually.

[27] *distrust*—fear for.

[28] *My operant . . . to do*—My bodily strength stops functioning.

Honored, beloved; and haply one as kind
For husband shalt thou—

Player Queen.   O, confound the rest!
Such love must needs be treason in my breast.
155 In second husband let me be accurst!
None wed the second but who killed the first.

Hamlet [*aside*]. Wormwood,[29] wormwood.

Player Queen. *The instances that second marriage move
Are base respects of thrift,[30] but none of love.*
160 *A second time I kill my husband dead
When second husband kisses me in bed.*

Player King. *I do believe you think what now you speak,
But what we do determine oft we break.
Purpose is but the slave to memory,*
165 *Of violent birth, but poor validity,
Which now, like fruit unripe, sticks on the tree,
But fall unshaken when they mellow be.
Most necessary 'tis that we forget
To pay ourselves what to ourselves is debt.*
170 *What to ourselves in passion we propose,
The passion ending, doth the purpose lose.
The violence of either grief or joy
Their own enactures[31] with themselves destroy.
Where joy most revels, grief doth most lament;*
175 *Grief joys, joy grieves, on slender accident.
This world is not for aye,[32] nor 'tis not strange
That even our loves should with our fortunes change;
For 'tis a question left us yet to prove,
Whether love lead fortune, or else fortune love.*
180 *The great man down, you mark his favorite flies;
The poor, advanced, makes friends of enemies.
And hitherto doth love on fortune tend,
For who not needs shall never lack a friend,
And who in want a hollow friend doth try*

---

[29] Wormwood—bitter, harsh; wormwood is a bitter herb.

[30] *base respects of thrift*—considerations only of worldly profit.

[31] *enactures*—fulfillment, enactment.

[32] *aye*—ever, always.

The Player King and Queen act out the murder of Hamlet's father in this scene from the American Repertory Theatre production.

<pre>
185   *Directly seasons[33] him his enemy.*
       But, orderly to end where I begun,
       Our wills and fates do so contrary run
       That our devices still[34] are overthrown;
       Our thoughts are ours, their ends none of our own.
190   *So think thou wilt no second husband wed,*
       But die thy thoughts when thy first lord is dead.
</pre>

Player Queen. *Nor earth to me give food, nor heaven light,*
Sport and repose lock from me day and night,
To desperation turn my trust and hope,
195 *An anchor's cheer[35] in prison be my scope!*
Each opposite that blanks the face of joy
Meet what I would have well and it destroy!
Both here and hence pursue me lasting strife
If, once a widow, ever I be wife!

200 **Hamlet.** If she should break it now!

Player King. *'Tis deeply sworn. Sweet, leave me here awhile.*
My spirits grow dull, and fain I would beguile
The tedious day with sleep.

Player Queen.   *Sleep rock thy brain,*
And never come mischance between us twain![36]

---

[33] *seasons*—ripens, converts into.

[34] *devices still*—plans always.

[35] *anchor's cheer*—hermit's food and drink.

[36] *twain*—two.

[He sleeps.]

[Exit Player Queen.]

205 **Hamlet.** Madam, how like you this play?

Queen. The lady doth protest too much, methinks.

Hamlet. O, but she'll keep her word.

King. Have you heard the argument? Is there no offense in 't?

Hamlet. No, no, they do but jest, poison in jest. No offense i' the world.

210 **King.** What do you call the play?

Hamlet. *The Mousetrap.* Marry, how? Tropically.[37] This play is the image
  of a murder done in Vienna. Gonzago is the duke's name, his wife,
  Baptista. You shall see anon. 'Tis a knavish piece of work, but what of
  that? Your Majesty and we that have free souls, it touches us not. Let
215 the galled jade wince, our withers are unwrung.[38]

[Enter Player as Lucianus.]

  This is one Lucianus, nephew to the King.

Ophelia. You are as good as a chorus,[39] my lord.

Hamlet. I could interpret between you and your love, if I could see the
  puppets dallying.

220 **Ophelia.** You are keen, my lord, you are keen.

Hamlet. It would cost you a groaning to take off mine edge.

Ophelia. Still better, and worse.[40]

Hamlet. So you mistake your husbands. Begin, murderer. Leave thy
  damnable faces and begin. Come, the croaking raven doth bellow
225 for revenge.

Lucianus. *Thoughts black, hands apt, drugs fit, and time agreeing,*
  Confederate season,[41] *else no creature seeing,*
  Thou mixture rank, of midnight weeds collected,
  With Hecate's ban[42] *thrice blasted, thrice infected,*
230 *Thy natural magic and dire property*[43]
  On wholesome life usurp immediately.

[He pours the poison into the Player King's ear.]

---

[37] Tropically—as a trope (a figure of speech).

[38] Let the galled . . . unwrung—Let guilty people wince; we have clean consciences. (A *galled jade* is a horse with sore skin; *withers* is the space between the horse's shoulder blades; *unwrung* means "not chafed.")

[39] chorus—character who explains the forthcoming action.

[40] Still better, and worse—More pointed, and less decent.

[41] *Confederate season*—suitable opportunity.

[42] *Hecate's ban*—curse of the goddess of witchcraft.

[43] *dire property*—terrible effect.

Hamlet. He poisons him i' the garden for his estate.[44] His name's
Gonzago. The story is extant, and written in very choice Italian. You
shall see anon how the murderer gets the love of Gonzago's wife.

[Claudius *rises.*]

235 **Ophelia.** The king rises.

Hamlet. What, frighted with false fire?[45]

Queen. How fares my lord?

Polonius. Give o'er the play.

King. Give me some light. Away!

240 **Polonius.** Lights, lights, lights!

[*All exit but* Hamlet *and* Horatio.]

Hamlet. *Why, let the strucken deer go weep,*
The hart ungallèd[46] play.
For some must watch, while some must sleep;
Thus runs the world away.

245 Would not this, sir, and a forest of feathers[47]—if the rest of my fortunes turn Turk with me[48]—with two Provincial roses on my razed
shoes,[49] get me a fellowship in a cry of players?[50]

Horatio. Half a share.

Hamlet. A whole one, I.

250 *For thou dost know, O Damon[51] dear,*
This realm dismantled was
Of Jove himself, and now reigns here
A very, very—pajock.[52]

Horatio. You might have rhymed.

255 **Hamlet.** O good Horatio, I'll take the ghost's word for a thousand
pound. Didst perceive?

Horatio. Very well, my lord.

Hamlet. Upon the talk of the poisoning?

Horatio. I did very well note him.

---

[44] estate—position as king.

[45] false fire—discharge of gun loaded with powder but no shot.

[46] *hart ungallèd*—unwounded male deer.

[47] forest of feathers—plumes worn by tragic actors.

[48] turn Turk with me—turn against me.

[49] Provincial roses . . . shoes—rosettes designed to look like a variety of French rose on my decoratively slashed shoes.

[50] fellowship . . . of players—partnership in a theater company.

[51] *Damon*—He was known, in Roman myth, for his great friendship with Pythias.

[52] *pajock*—peacock (in place of the rhyming word *ass*).

Hamlet. Aha! Come, some music! Come, the recorders.

> *For if the king like not the comedy,*
> *Why then, belike, he likes it not, perdy.*[53]

Come, some music.

[*Enter* Rosencrantz *and* Guildenstern.]

Guildenstern. Good my lord, vouchsafe me a word with you.

Hamlet. Sir, a whole history.

Guildenstern. The king, sir—

Hamlet. Ay, sir, what of him?

Guildenstern. Is in his retirement marvelous distempered.

Hamlet. With drink, sir?

Guildenstern. No, my lord, with choler.[54]

Hamlet. Your wisdom should show itself more richer to signify this to the doctor, for for me to put him to his purgation[55] would perhaps plunge him into more choler.

Guildenstern. Good my lord, put your discourse into some frame[56] and start not so wildly from my affair.

Hamlet. I am tame, sir. Pronounce.

Guildenstern. The queen, your mother, in most great affliction of spirit, hath sent me to you.

Hamlet. You are welcome.

Guildenstern. Nay, good my lord, this courtesy is not of the right breed. If it shall please you to make me a wholesome answer, I will do your mother's commandment. If not, your pardon and my return shall be the end of my business.

Hamlet. Sir, I cannot.

Rosencrantz. What, my lord?

Hamlet. Make you a wholesome answer. My wit's diseased. But, sir, such answer as I can make, you shall command, or rather, as you say, my mother. Therefore no more but to the matter. My mother, you say—

Rosencrantz. Then thus she says: your behavior hath struck her into amazement and admiration.[57]

---

[53] *perdy*—by God, from the French *par dieu.*

[54] choler—anger.

[55] purgation—act of purifying.

[56] frame—logical structure.

[57] admiration—wonder.

Hamlet. O wonderful son, that can so 'stonish a mother! But is there no sequel at the heels of this mother's admiration? Impart.

Rosencrantz. She desires to speak with you in her closet ere you go to bed.

Hamlet. We shall obey, were she ten times our mother. Have you any further trade with us?

Rosencrantz. My lord, you once did love me.

Hamlet. And do still, by these pickers and stealers.[58]

Rosencrantz. Good my lord, what is your cause of distemper? You do surely bar the door upon your own liberty if you deny your griefs to your friend.

Hamlet. Sir, I lack advancement.

Rosencrantz. How can that be, when you have the voice of the king himself for your succession in Denmark?

Hamlet. Ay, sir, but "While the grass grows"[59]—the proverb is something musty.

[*Enter the* Players *with recorders.*]

O, the recorders. Let me see one. [*He takes a recorder and turns to Guildenstern.*] To withdraw with you: why do you go about to recover the wind of me, as if you would drive me into a toil?[60]

Guildenstern. O, my lord, if my duty be too bold, love is too unmannerly.

Hamlet. I do not well understand that. Will you play upon this pipe?

Guildenstern. My lord, I cannot.

Hamlet. I pray you.

Guildenstern. Believe me, I cannot.

Hamlet. I do beseech you.

Guildenstern. I know no touch of it, my lord.

Hamlet. It is as easy as lying. Govern these ventages[61] with your fingers and thumb, give it breath with your mouth, and it will discourse most eloquent music. Look you, these are the stops.

Guildenstern. But these cannot I command to any utt'rance of harmony. I have not the skill.

Hamlet. Why, look you now, how unworthy a thing you make of me! You would play upon me, you would seem to know my stops, you would pluck out the heart of my mystery, you would sound me from

---

[58] pickers and stealers—hands.

[59] "While the grass grows"—The proverb usually ends "the horse starves."

[60] toil—trap.

[61] ventages—finger holes or stops on a recorder, a flute-like musical instrument.

my lowest note to the top of my compass,[62] and there is much music,
excellent voice, in this little organ, yet cannot you make it speak.
'Sblood, do you think I am easier to be played on than a pipe? Call
me what instrument you will, though you can fret me, you cannot
play upon me.

[*Enter* Polonius.]

God bless you, sir!

Polonius. My lord, the queen would speak with you, and presently.

Hamlet. Do you see yonder cloud that's almost in shape of a camel?

Polonius. By th' Mass and 'tis, like a camel indeed.

Hamlet. Methinks it is like a weasel.

Polonius. It is backed like a weasel.

Hamlet. Or like a whale.

Polonius. Very like a whale.

Hamlet. Then I will come to my mother by and by. [*Aside.*] They fool me
to the top of my bent.[63]—I will come by and by.

Polonius. I will say so.

[*Exit* Polonius.]

Hamlet. "By and by" is easily said. Leave me, friends.

[*All exit but* Hamlet.]

'Tis now the very witching time of night,
When churchyards yawn and hell itself breathes out
Contagion to this world. Now could I drink hot blood
And do such bitter business as the day
Would quake to look on. Soft, now to my mother.
O heart, lose not thy nature! Let not ever
The soul of Nero[64] enter this firm bosom.
Let me be cruel, not unnatural;
I will speak daggers to her, but use none.
My tongue and soul in this be hypocrites:
How in my words soever she be shent,[65]
To give them seals[66] never, my soul, consent!

[*He exits.*]

---

[62] compass—range.

[63] They fool . . . my bent—They make me play the fool to the limit of my ability.

[64] Nero—Roman emperor who had his mother executed.

[65] shent—rebuked.

[66] give them seals—confirm them by deeds.

Act Three, Scene Three

In a room in Elsinore, Claudius instructs Rosencrantz and Guildenstern to prepare to accompany Hamlet to England immediately. Polonius tells Claudius that he will spy on Hamlet's conversation with Gertrude. Claudius, left alone with his guilt, tries to pray. He says he cannot pray because he still enjoys the rewards of his evil deed. As Claudius kneels,

Hamlet steals up behind him and draws his sword. He stops himself from killing Claudius, as he fears that if Claudius dies at prayer, his soul will go to heaven. He decides to kill Claudius while the king is doing something sinful, so that his soul will go to hell. After Hamlet leaves, Claudius says he has not been able to pray.

Enter King Claudius, Rosencrantz, *and* Guildenstern.

King. I like him not, nor stands it safe with us
    To let his madness range. Therefore prepare you.
    I your commission will forthwith dispatch,
    And he to England shall along with you.
5   The terms of our estate may not endure
    Hazard so near 's as doth hourly grow
    Out of his brows.

Guildenstern.   We will ourselves provide.
    Most holy and religious fear it is
    To keep those many many bodies safe
10   That live and feed upon Your Majesty.

Rosencrantz. The single and peculiar life is bound
    With all the strength and armor of the mind
    To keep itself from noyance,[1] but much more
    That spirit upon whose weal[2] depends and rests
15   The lives of many. The cess[3] of majesty
    Dies not alone, but like a gulf doth draw
    What's near it with it; or it is a massy[4] wheel

---

[1] noyance—injury.
[2] weal—prosperity, happiness.
[3] cess—end, death.
[4] massy—massive.

O, my offense is rank! It smells to heaven.

Fixed on the summit of the highest mount,
To whose huge spokes ten thousand lesser things
20   Are mortised[5] and adjoined, which, when it falls,
Each small annexment, petty consequence,[6]
Attends the **boisterous**[7] ruin. Never alone
Did the king sigh, but with a general groan.

King. Arm you, I pray you, to this speedy voyage,
25   For we will fetters put about this fear,
Which now goes too free-footed.

Rosencrantz.   We will haste us.

[*Exit* Rosencrantz *and* Guildenstern.]

[*Enter* Polonius.]

Polonius. My lord, he's going to his mother's closet.
Behind the arras I'll convey myself
To hear the process. I'll warrant she'll tax him home,
30   And, as you said—and wisely was it said—
'Tis meet[8] that some more audience than a mother,
Since nature makes them partial, should o'erhear
The speech of vantage.[9] Fare you well, my liege.
I'll call upon you ere you go to bed
35   And tell you what I know.

King.   Thanks, dear my lord.

[*Exit* Polonius.]

O, my offense is rank! It smells to heaven.
It hath the primal eldest curse[10] upon 't,
A brother's murder. Pray can I not,
Though inclination be as sharp as will.

---

[5] mortised—fixed.

[6] Each small . . . consequence—every minor event.

[7] **boisterous**—noisy.

[8] meet—appropriate.

[9] of vantage—from an advantageous position (or perhaps in addition).

[10] the primal eldest curse—God's curse on Cain, who slew his brother Abel.

40	My stronger guilt defeats my strong intent,
	And, like a man to double business bound,
	I stand in pause where I shall first begin,
	And both neglect. What if this cursèd hand
	Were thicker than itself with brother's blood,
45	Is there not rain enough in the sweet heavens
	To wash it white as snow? Whereto serves mercy
	But to confront the visage of offense?
	And what's in prayer but this twofold force,
	To be forestallèd ere we come to fall,
50	Or pardoned being down? Then I'll look up.
	My fault is past. But O, what form of prayer
	Can serve my turn? "Forgive me my foul murder"?
	That cannot be, since I am still possessed
	Of those effects for which I did the murder:
55	My crown, mine own ambition, and my queen.
	May one be pardoned and retain th' offense?[11]
	In the corrupted currents of this world
	Offense's gilded hand may shove by justice,
	And oft 'tis seen the wicked prize itself
60	Buys out the law. But 'tis not so above.
	There is no shuffling, there the action lies
	In his true nature, and we ourselves compelled,
	Even to the teeth and forehead of our faults,
	To give in evidence.[12] What then? What rests?
65	Try what repentance can. What can it not?
	Yet what can it, when one cannot repent?
	O wretched state! O bosom black as death!
	O limèd[13] soul that, struggling to be free,
	Art more engaged! Help, angels! Make assay[14]
70	Bow, stubborn knees, and heart with strings of steel,
	Be soft as sinews of the newborn babe!
	All may be well.

---

[11] th' offense—the things gained, or fruits, of the offense.

[12] above . . . evidence—In heaven, there is no evasion. In God's court, we are compelled to give evidence, even against ourselves.

[13] limèd—caught (as in birdlime, a sticky substance used for catching birds).

[14] Make assay—Try hard.

In this scene from the 1964 Broadway production, Hamlet
(Richard Burton) considers whether to kill Claudius
(Alfred Drake) while he is praying.

[*He kneels.*]
[*Enter* Hamlet.]
Hamlet. Now might I do it pat,[15] now he is a-praying;
And now I'll do 't. [*He draws his sword.*] And so he goes to heaven,
75 And so am I revenged. That would be scanned:
A villain kills my father, and for that,
I, his sole son, do this same villain send
To heaven.
Why, this is hire and salary,[16] not revenge.

---

[15] pat—easily.
[16] hire and salary—something that should be paid for.

80 He took my father grossly, full of bread,
With all his crimes broad blown, as flush as May;
And how his audit stands who knows save heaven?[17]
But in our circumstance and course of thought
'Tis heavy with him. And am I then revenged,
85 To take him in the purging of his soul,
When he is fit and seasoned for his passage?
No!
Up, sword, and know thou a more horrid hent.[18]
[*He sheathes his sword.*]
When he is drunk asleep, or in his rage,
90 Or in th' incestuous pleasure of his bed,
At game, a-swearing, or about some act
That has no relish of salvation in 't—
Then trip him, that his heels may kick at heaven,
And that his soul may be as damned and black
95 As hell, whereto it goes. My mother stays.[19]
This physic[20] but prolongs thy sickly days.
[*Exit* Hamlet.]
King. My words fly up, my thoughts remain below.
Words without thoughts never to heaven go.
[*He exits.*]

---

[17] grossly . . . heaven—in a state of sin, with all his sins in full bloom, and how his final account with heaven stands, only heaven knows.

[18] know . . . horrid hent—be grasped at a more dreadful time.

[19] stays—awaits.

[20] physic—remedy (prayer).

Act Three, Scene Four

In Queen Gertrude's room, Polonius hides behind a hanging tapestry to spy on the queen and Hamlet. When Hamlet frightens his mother, and she calls fearfully for help, Polonius cries out. Thinking he is Claudius, Hamlet stabs Polonius. He then rebukes his mother for marrying his uncle, contrasting the virtues and vices of the two brothers. As his speech grows more and more vehement, the Ghost enters to remind Hamlet of his duty.

Gertrude cannot see the Ghost and pities Hamlet's madness. After the Ghost leaves, Hamlet explains his actions and tells her that she must face what she has done. He tells her to avoid Claudius's company and to tell him nothing of these events, but to let him think that Hamlet is simply mad. He reminds her that he is being sent to England and suspects that the mission is a plot against him. He exits, dragging Polonius's body.

Enter Queen Gertrude *and* Polonius.

Polonius. He will come straight. Look you lay home to him.[1]
  Tell him his pranks have been too broad to bear with,
  And that Your Grace hath screened and stood between
  Much heat and him. I'll silence me even here.
5 Pray you, be round with him.
Hamlet [*within*]. Mother, mother, mother!
Queen. I'll warrant you, fear me not.
  Withdraw, I hear him coming.
[Polonius *hides behind the arras.*]
[*Enter* Hamlet.]
Hamlet. Now, mother, what's the matter?
10 **Queen.** Hamlet, thou hast thy father much offended.
Hamlet. Mother, you have my father much offended.
Queen. Come, come, you answer with an idle tongue.
Hamlet. Go, go, you question with a wicked tongue.
Queen. Why, how now, Hamlet?
Hamlet.   What's the matter now?
15 **Queen.** Have you forgot me?

---

[1] lay home to him—scold him severely.

Hamlet.   No, by the rood,[2] not so:
            You are the queen, your husband's brother's wife,
            And—would it were not so!—you are my mother.

Queen. Nay, then, I'll set those to you that can speak.

Hamlet. Come, come, and sit you down; you shall not budge.

20   You go not till I set you up a glass
            Where you may see the inmost part of you.

Queen. What wilt thou do? Thou wilt not murder me?
            Help, ho!

Polonius [*behind the arras*]. What ho! Help!

25   **Hamlet** [*drawing his rapier*[3]]. How now? A rat? Dead for a ducat,[4] dead!

[*He thrusts his rapier through the arras.*]

Polonius [*behind the arras*]. O, I am slain!

[*He falls and dies.*]

Queen.   O me, what hast thou done?

Hamlet. Nay, I know not. Is it the king?

Queen. O, what a rash and bloody deed is this!

30   **Hamlet.** A bloody deed—almost as bad, good mother,
            As kill a king, and marry with his brother.

Queen. As kill a king!

Hamlet. Ay, lady, it was my word.

[*He parts the arras and pulls Polonius's body out.*]

            Thou wretched, rash, intruding fool, farewell!

35   I took thee for thy better. Take thy fortune.
            Thou find'st to be too busy[5] is some danger.—[*To* Queen Gertrude.]
            Leave wringing of your hands. Peace, sit you down,
            And let me wring your heart, for so I shall,
            If it be made of penetrable stuff,

40   If damnèd custom have not brazed it so
            That it be proof and bulwark against sense.[6]

Queen. What have I done, that thou dar'st wag thy tongue
            In noise so rude against me?

---

[2] rood—cross.

[3] *rapier*—small sword.

[4] Dead . . . ducat—Dead, I'll wager a gold coin.

[5] busy—officious, meddlesome.

[6] If damnèd custom. . . against sense—if the habit of evil has not hardened it so much that it is immune to feeling.

As Gertrude (Eileen Herlie) looks on, Hamlet (Laurence Olivier) prepares to stab Polonius in this scene from Olivier's 1947 film of the play.

Hamlet.   Such an act
            That blurs the grace and blush of modesty,
45   Calls virtue hypocrite, takes off the rose
            From the fair forehead of an innocent love
            And sets a blister there, makes marriage vows
            As false as dicers' oaths. O, such a deed
            As from the body of contraction[7] plucks
50   The very soul, and sweet religion makes
            A rhapsody of words! Heaven's face does glow
            O'er this solidity and compound mass
            With heated visage, as against the doom,
            Is thought-sick at the act.[8]

---

[7] body of contraction—marriage contract.

[8] Heaven's face ... act—Heaven's face grows red over the earth, as if judgment day had come, and is sick with horror at the act (that is, Gertrude's marriage).

Queen.   Ay me, what act,

55   That roars so loud and thunders in the index?[9]

Hamlet [*showing her two portraits*]. Look here upon this picture, and
          on this,

          The counterfeit presentment[10] of two brothers.

          See what a grace was seated on this brow:

          Hyperion's curls, the front of Jove himself,

60   An eye like Mars, to threaten and command,

          A station[11] like the herald Mercury

          New-lighted on a heaven-kissing hill—

          A combination and a form indeed

          Where every god did seem to set his seal

65   To give the world assurance of a man.

          This was your husband. Look you now what follows:

          Here is your husband, like a mildewed ear,[12]

          Blasting his wholesome brother. Have you eyes?

          Could you on this fair mountain leave to feed

70   And batten on this moor?[13] Ha, have you eyes?

          You cannot call it love, for at your age

          The heyday in the blood[14] is tame, it's humble,

          And waits upon the judgment; and what judgment

          Would step from this to this? Sense, sure, you have,

75   Else could you not have motion, but sure that sense

          Is apoplexed,[15] for madness would not err,

          Nor sense to ecstasy was ne'er so thralled,[16]

          But it reserved some quantity of choice

          To serve in such a difference. What devil was 't

80   That thus hath cozened you at hoodman-blind?[17]

---

[9] That roars . . . index—that receives such a violent introduction.

[10] counterfeit presentment—painted likenesses.

[11] station—bearing, manner in which one carries oneself.

[12] ear—ear of grain.

[13] batten on this moor—gorge on this barren land.

[14] heyday in the blood—excitement of passion.

[15] apoplexed—paralyzed.

[16] to ecstasy . . . thralled—never so enslaved to madness.

[17] cozened you at hoodman-blind—cheated you at blindman's bluff.

Eyes without feeling, feeling without sight,
Ears without hands or eyes, smelling sans[18] all,
Or but a sickly part of one true sense
Could not so mope. O shame, where is thy blush?
85   Rebellious hell,
If thou canst mutine[19] in a matron's bones,
To flaming youth let virtue be as wax
And melt in her own fire. Proclaim no shame
When the compulsive ardor gives the charge,
90   Since frost itself as actively doth burn,
And reason panders will.[20]

Queen.   O Hamlet, speak no more!
Thou turn'st mine eyes into my very soul,
And there I see such black and grainèd spots
As will not leave their tinct.[21]

Hamlet.   Nay, but to live
95   In the rank sweat of an enseamèd[22] bed,
Stewed in corruption, honeying and making love
Over the nasty sty!

Queen.   O, speak to me no more!
These words like daggers enter in my ears.
No more, sweet Hamlet!

Hamlet.   A murderer and a villain,
100   A slave that is not twentieth part the tithe[23]
Of your precedent lord, a vice[24] of kings,
A cutpurse[25] of the empire and the rule,
That from a shelf the precious diadem stole
And put it in his pocket!

Queen.   No more!

---

[18] sans—without.

[19] mutine—incite rebellion.

[20] Proclaim no . . . panders will—Do not call it a sin when the hot blood of youth is responsible for lechery, because here we see people of calmer age on fire for it, and reason aids desire instead of restraining it.

[21] leave their tinct—give up their color.

[22] enseamèd—dirty, fouled.

[23] tithe—one-tenth.

[24] vice—buffoon.

[25] cutpurse—pickpocket.

Gertrude (Marybeth Piel) fears Hamlet (Campbell Scott) has gone mad in this scene from the Hartford Stage production.

105 **Hamlet.** A king of shreds and patches[26]—
[*Enter* Ghost.]
　　Save me, and hover o'er me with your wings,
　　You heavenly guards!—What would your gracious figure?
Queen. Alas, he's mad!
Hamlet. Do you not come your tardy son to chide,
110 　　That, lapsed in time and passion, lets go by
　　Th' important acting of your dread command?
　　O, say!
Ghost. Do not forget. This visitation
　　Is but to whet[27] thy almost blunted purpose.

---

[26] of shreds and patches—clownish, alluding to the motley cloth worn by jesters.
[27] whet—sharpen.

115	But look, amazement on thy mother sits.
	O, step between her and her fighting soul!
	Conceit[28] in weakest bodies strongest works.
	Speak to her, Hamlet.
	Hamlet. How is it with you, lady?
120	**Queen.** Alas, how is 't with you,
	That you do bend your eye on vacancy,
	And with th' incorporal[29] air do hold discourse?
	Forth at your eyes your spirits wildly peep,
	And, as the sleeping soldiers in th' alarm,
	Your bedded hair, like life in excrements,[30]
125	Start up and stand on end. O gentle son,
	Upon the heat and flame of thy distemper[31]
	Sprinkle cool patience. Whereon do you look?
	Hamlet. On him, on him! Look you how pale he glares!
	His form and cause conjoined, preaching to stones,
130	Would make them capable.[32]—Do not look upon me,
	Lest with this piteous action you convert
	My stern effects. Then what I have to do
	Will want true color—tears perchance for blood.
	Queen. To whom do you speak this?
135	**Hamlet.** Do you see nothing there?
	Queen. Nothing at all, yet all that is I see.
	Hamlet. Nor did you nothing hear?
	Queen. No, nothing but ourselves.
	Hamlet. Why, look you there, look how it steals away!
140	My father, in his habit as he lived![33]
	Look where he goes even now out at the portal!
	[*Exit* Ghost.]
	Queen. This is the very coinage of your brain.
	This bodiless creation ecstasy
	Is very cunning in.

---

[28] Conceit—imagination.

[29] incorporal—immaterial.

[30] excrements—outgrowths, here hair.

[31] distemper—mental disturbance.

[32] His form . . . capable—His appearance and what he has to say would make stones able to listen.

[33] habit as he lived—dressed as he did when he lived.

145	**Hamlet.**　　　　　Ecstasy?

My pulse as yours doth temperately keep time,
And makes as healthful music. It is not madness
That I have uttered. Bring me to the test,
And I the matter will reword, which madness
Would gambol[34] from. Mother, for love of grace,
Lay not that flattering unction[35] to your soul
That not your trespass but my madness speaks.
It will but skin and film the ulcerous place,
Whiles rank corruption, mining[36] all within,
Infects unseen. Confess yourself to heaven,
Repent what's past, avoid what is to come,
And do not spread the compost on the weeds
To make them ranker. Forgive me this my virtue;
For in the fatness of these pursy times[37]
Virtue itself of vice must pardon beg,
Yea, curb and woo[38] for leave to do him good.
Queen. O Hamlet, thou hast cleft my heart in twain.
Hamlet. O, throw away the worser part of it,
And live the purer with the other half!
Good night. But go not to my uncle's bed.
Assume a virtue, if you have it not.
That monster, custom, who all sense doth eat,
Of habits devil, is angel yet in this,
That to the use of actions fair and good
He likewise gives a frock or livery
That aptly is put on.[39] Refrain tonight,
And that shall lend a kind of easiness
To the next **abstinence;**[40] the next more easy;
For use[41] almost can change the stamp of nature,

---

[34] gambol—start, jerk away.

[35] flattering unction—soothing ointment.

[36] mining—undermining.

[37] fatness . . . times—grossness of these sensual times.

[38] curb and woo—bow and entreat.

[39] frock . . . put on—a "habit" or customary garment easily put on without need of any decision.

[40] **abstinence**—holding back from some action; giving something up.

[41] use—habit.

And either . . .[42] the devil, or throw him out

175   With wondrous potency. Once more, good night;

And when you are desirous to be blest,

I'll blessing beg of you. For this same lord,

[*Pointing to* Polonius.]

I do repent; but heaven hath pleased it so

180   To punish me with this, and this with me,

That I must be their scourge and minister.[43]

I will bestow him, and will answer well

The death I gave him. So, again, good night.

I must be cruel only to be kind.

This bad begins, and worse remains behind.

185   One word more, good lady.

Queen.   What shall I do?

Hamlet. Not this by no means that I bid you do:

Let the bloat king tempt you again to bed,

Pinch wanton on your cheek, call you his mouse,

And let him, for a pair of reechy[44] kisses,

190   Or paddling in your neck with his damned fingers,

Make you to ravel[45] all this matter out,

That I essentially am not in madness,

But mad in craft. 'Twere good you let him know,

For who that's but a queen, fair, sober, wise,

195   Would from a paddock, from a bat, a gib,[46]

Such dear concernings hide? Who would do so?

No, in despite of sense and secrecy,

Unpeg the basket[47] on the house's top,

---

[42] And either . . .—A word seems to have been lost. Among possible words is "master."

[43] scourge and minister—the agent of heavenly justice against human crime.

[44] reechy—filthy.

[45] ravel—separate.

[46] paddock . . . gib—a toad, a bat, and a tomcat.

[47] Unpeg the basket—open the door of the cage.

Let the birds fly, and like the famous ape,

200   To try conclusions, in the basket creep

And break your own neck down.[48]

Queen. Be thou assured, if words be made of breath,

And breath of life, I have no life to breathe

What thou hast said to me.

205   **Hamlet.** I must to England. You know that?

Queen.   Alack,

I had forgot. 'Tis so concluded on.

Hamlet. There's letters sealed, and my two schoolfellows,

Whom I will trust as I will adders fanged,

They bear the mandate; they must sweep my way

210   And marshal me to knavery.[49] Let it work.

For 'tis the sport to have the enginer

Hoist with his own petard,[50] and 't shall go hard

But I will delve one yard below their mines

And blow them at the moon. O, 'tis most sweet

215   When in one line two crafts[51] directly meet.

This man shall set me packing.

I'll lug the guts into the neighbor room.

Mother, good night indeed. This counselor

Is now most still, most secret, and most grave,

220   Who was in life a foolish prating[52] knave—

Come, sir, to draw toward an end with you.—

Good night, mother.

[*They exit separately*, Hamlet *dragging* Polonius.]

---

[48] Let the . . . neck down—This is a reference to a lost story in which an ape tried to fly like a bird.

[49] they must . . . to knavery—they must lead me on and take me to some prepared treachery.

[50] to have. . . petard—to have the artilleryman blown up by his own explosive.

[51] When . . . two crafts—when a plot can have two different outcomes.

[52] prating—babbling, talking foolishly.

Act Four, Scene One

In a room in the castle, Queen Gertrude tells King Claudius that Hamlet is completely mad and in confusion killed Polonius. Claudius sends Rosencrantz and Guildenstern to recover the body and lay it in the chapel. He prepares to cover up the deed and Hamlet's madness.

Enter King Claudius *and* Queen Gertrude, *with* Rosencrantz *and* Guildenstern.

King. There's matter in these sighs, these profound heaves.
    You must translate; 'tis fit we understand them.
    Where is your son?
Queen. Bestow this place on us a little while.
[*Exit* Rosencrantz *and* Guildenstern.]
5   Ah, mine own lord, what have I seen tonight!
King. What, Gertrude? How does Hamlet?
Queen. Mad as the sea and wind when both contend
    Which is the mightier. In his lawless fit,
    Behind the arras hearing something stir,
10   Whips out his rapier, cries, "A rat, a rat!"
    And in this brainish apprehension[1] kills
    The unseen good old man.
King.   O heavy deed!
    It had been so with us, had we been there.
    His liberty is full of threats to all—
15   To you yourself, to us, to everyone.
    Alas, how shall this bloody deed be answered?
    It will be laid to us, whose providence[2]
    Should have kept short, restrained, and out of haunt
    This mad young man. But so much was our love,
20   We would not understand what was most fit,
    But, like the owner of a foul disease,
    To keep it from divulging,[3] let it feed

---

[1] brainish apprehension—crazy notion.
[2] laid . . . providence—charged to me, whose foresight.
[3] divulging—being revealed.

Even on the pith[4] of life. Where is he gone?

Queen. To draw apart the body he hath killed,

25   O'er whom his very madness, like some ore

    Among a mineral of metals base,

    Shows itself pure: he weeps for what is done.

King. O Gertrude, come away!

    The sun no sooner shall the mountains touch

30   But we will ship him hence, and this vile deed

    We must with all our majesty and skill

    Both countenance[5] and excuse.—Ho, Guildenstern!

[*Enter* Rosencrantz *and* Guildenstern.]

    Friends both, go join you with some further aid.

    Hamlet in madness hath Polonius slain,

35   And from his mother's closet hath he dragged him.

    Go seek him out, speak fair, and bring the body

    Into the chapel. I pray you, haste in this.

[*Exit* Rosencrantz *and* Guildenstern.]

    Come, Gertrude, we'll call up our wisest friends

    And let them know both what we mean to do

40   And what's untimely done so, haply slander

    Whose whisper o'er the world's diameter,

    As level as the cannon to his blank,[6]

    Transports his poisoned shot, may miss our name

    And hit the woundless air. O, come away!

45   My soul is full of discord and dismay.

[*They exit.*]

---

[4] pith—essence.

[5] countenance—recognize.

[6] As level . . . blank—as sure as a cannon hitting its target.

Act Four, Scene Two

In another room in the castle, Hamlet refuses to tell Rosencrantz and Guildenstern where he put the body. They take him to Claudius.

Enter Hamlet.

Hamlet. Safely stowed.

Rosencrantz, Guildenstern [*within*]. Hamlet! Lord Hamlet!

Hamlet. But soft, what noise? Who calls on Hamlet? O, here they come.

[*Enter* Rosencrantz *and* Guildenstern.]

Rosencrantz. What have you done, my lord, with the dead body?

5   **Hamlet.** Compounded it with dust, whereto 'tis kin.

Rosencrantz. Tell us where 'tis, that we may take it thence

And bear it to the chapel.

Hamlet. Do not believe it.

Rosencrantz. Believe what?

10   **Hamlet.** That I can keep your counsel and not mine own. Besides, to be demanded of a sponge, what replication should be made by the son of a king?[1]

Rosencrantz. Take you me for a sponge, my lord?

Hamlet. Ay, sir, that soaks up the king's countenance, his rewards, his

15   authorities. But such officers do the king best service in the end. He keeps them, like an ape, an apple in the corner of his jaw, first mouthed, to be last swallowed. When he needs what you have gleaned,[2] it is but squeezing you, and, sponge, you shall be dry again.

Rosencrantz. I understand you not, my lord.

20   **Hamlet.** I am glad of it. A knavish speech sleeps in a foolish ear.

Rosencrantz. My lord, you must tell us where the body is and go with us to the king.

---

[1] demanded . . . king—questioned by a sponge that soaks up royal favor, what reply should a king's son make?

[2] gleaned—learned.

In this scene from the Hartford Stage production, Hamlet (Richard Thomas) pretends to be mad to deceive Rosencrantz (Sheridan Crist) and Guildenstern (Nick Barmy).

> **Hamlet.** The body is with the king, but the king is not with the body.
>   The king is a thing—
> 25 **Guildenstern.** A "thing," my lord?
> **Hamlet.** Of nothing. Bring me to him. Hide fox, and all after![3]
> [*They exit, running.*]

---

[3] Hide fox, and all after—This is a line in some game resembling hide-and-seek.

Act Four, Scene Three

In another room in the castle, Claudius wonders how to deal with Hamlet. Rosencrantz reports that Hamlet will not tell them where Polonius's body is. Hamlet offers witty retorts to all of Claudius's questions. When Hamlet finally reveals the hiding place, Claudius insists that the prince must go to England immediately. Alone, Claudius reveals his plan. He hopes that the king of England, respecting Denmark's might, will grant him the favor of executing Hamlet.

Enter King Claudius, *and two or three* Attendants.

King. I have sent to seek him, and to find the body.
How dangerous is it that this man goes loose!
Yet must not we put the strong law on him.
He's loved of the distracted multitude,

5   Who like not in their judgment, but their eyes,
And, where 'tis so, th' offender's scourge is weighed,
But never the offense.[1] To bear all smooth and even,
This sudden sending him away must seem
Deliberate pause.[2] Diseases desperate grown

10   By desperate appliance[3] are relieved,
Or not at all.

[*Enter* Rosencrantz.]

        How now, what hath befall'n?

Rosencrantz. Where the dead body is bestowed, my lord,
We cannot get from him.

King.   But where is he?

Rosencrantz. Without,[4] my lord; guarded, to know your pleasure.

15 **King.** Bring him before us.

Rosencrantz.   Ho! Bring in the lord.

[*Enter* Hamlet *and* Guildenstern.]

---

[1] Who like . . . offense—When people love with their eyes, not their reason, they judge the punishment rather than the crime.

[2] must . . . pause—must be seen as long planned.

[3] appliance—remedy.

[4] Without—just outside.

King. Now, Hamlet, where's Polonius?

Hamlet. At supper.

King. At supper? Where?

Hamlet. Not where he eats, but where he is eaten. A certain convocation
of politic worms[5] are e'en at him. Your worm is your only emperor
for diet. We fat all creatures else to fat us, and we fat ourselves for
maggots. Your fat king and your lean beggar is but variable service[6]—
two dishes, but to one table. That's the end.

King. Alas, alas!

Hamlet. A man may fish with the worm that hath eat of a king and eat of
the fish that hath fed of that worm.

King. What dost thou mean by this?

Hamlet. Nothing but to show you how a king may go a progress through
the guts of a beggar.

King. Where is Polonius?

Hamlet. In heaven. Send thither to see. If your messenger find him not
there, seek him i' th' other place yourself. But if indeed you find him
not within this month, you shall nose him as you go up the stairs into
the lobby.

King [*to some* Attendants]. Go, seek him there.

Hamlet. He will stay till you come.

[*Exit* Attendants.]

King. Hamlet, this deed, for thine especial safety—
Which we do tender,[7] as we dearly grieve
For that which thou hast done—must send thee hence
With fiery quickness. Therefore prepare thyself.
The bark[8] is ready, and the wind at help,
Th' associates tend, and everything is bent
For England.

Hamlet.   For England?

King.   Ay, Hamlet.

---

[5] convocation of politic worms—assembly of crafty worms (referring to the Diet of Worms, a meeting at the city of Worms in 1521).

[6] variable service—different courses of a meal.

[7] tender—value.

[8] bark—sailing ship.

Hamlet.   Good.

King. So is it, if thou knew'st our purposes.

45   **Hamlet.** I see a cherub that sees them. But come, for England! Farewell,
dear mother.

King. Thy loving father, Hamlet.

Hamlet. My mother. Father and mother is man and wife,
Man and wife is one flesh, and so, my mother.—

50   Come, for England!

[*Exit* Hamlet.]

King. Follow him at foot;[9] tempt him with speed aboard.
Delay it not. I'll have him hence tonight.
Away! For everything is sealed and done
That else leans on[10] th' affair. Pray you, make haste.

[*Exit* Rosencrantz *and* Guildenstern.]

55   And, England,[11] if my love thou hold'st at aught[12]—
As my great power thereof may give thee sense,
Since yet thy cicatrice[13] looks raw and red
After the Danish sword, and thy free awe[14]
Pays homage to us—thou mayst not coldly set

60   Our sovereign process,[15] which imports at full,
By letters congruing to[16] that effect,
The present death of Hamlet. Do it, England,
For like the hectic[17] in my blood he rages,
And thou must cure me. Till I know 'tis done,

65   Howe'er my haps,[18] my joys were ne'er begun.

[*He exits.*]

---

[9] at foot—close behind.

[10] leans on—relates to.

[11] England—King of England.

[12] at aught—in any respect, at all.

[13] cicatrice—scar.

[14] free awe—voluntary show of respect.

[15] thou mayst . . . process—England must not disregard my royal command.

[16] congruing to—in accord with.

[17] hectic—continuous fever.

[18] Howe'er my haps—whatever my fortunes.

Act Four, Scene Four

On a plain in Denmark, Fortinbras, at the head of his army, sends one of his captains to ask Claudius for an escort to cross Danish land. Hamlet learns from the captain that the Norwegians are going to fight the Poles over a small tract of worthless land. Hamlet is struck both by their folly and by their bravery. He contrasts Fortinbras's ambition to act with his own continual hesitation. He accuses himself of cowardice and resolves to take bloody revenge for his father's death.

Enter Fortinbras, *a* Captain, *and* Soldiers, *marching.*

Fortinbras. Go, captain, from me greet the Danish king.
    Tell him that by his license Fortinbras
    Craves the conveyance¹ of a promised march
    Over his kingdom. You know the rendezvous.
5   If that His Majesty would aught with us,²
    We shall express our duty in his eye;
    And let him know so.
Captain. I will do 't, my lord.
Fortinbras. Go softly on.
[*All exit but the* Captain.]
[*Enter* Hamlet, Rosencrantz, Guildenstern, *and others.*]
10 **Hamlet.** Good sir, whose powers are these?
Captain. They are of Norway, sir.
Hamlet. How purposed, sir, I pray you?
Captain. Against some part of Poland.
Hamlet. Who commands them, sir?
15 **Captain.** The nephew to old Norway, Fortinbras.
Hamlet. Goes it against the main³ of Poland, sir,
    Or for some frontier?
Captain. Truly to speak, and with no addition,
    We go to gain a little patch of ground
20   That hath in it no profit but the name.

---

¹ conveyance—escort.

² would aught with us—have anything to do with us.

³ main—main territory.

In this scene from the 2001 production of *Hamlet* at The Shakespeare Theatre in Washington, D.C., Fortinbras (Jovan Rameau, right) leads his army into Denmark.

To pay five ducats,[4] five, I would not farm it;
Nor will it yield to Norway or the Pole
A ranker rate, should it be sold in fee.[5]
Hamlet. Why, then the Polack never will defend it.
25 **Captain.** Yes, it is already garrisoned.[6]
Hamlet. Two thousand souls and twenty thousand ducats
Will not debate the question of this straw.[7]
This is th' impostume[8] of much wealth and peace,
That inward breaks, and shows no cause without
30 Why the man dies. I humbly thank you, sir.
Captain. God b' wi' you, sir.
[*Exit* Captain.]
Rosencrantz. Will 't please you go, my lord?
Hamlet. I'll be with you straight. Go a little before.
[*All exit except* Hamlet.]
How all occasions do inform against[9] me
35 And spur my dull revenge! What is a man,
If his chief good and market of his time
Be but to sleep and feed? A beast, no more.
Sure He that made us with such large discourse,

---

[4] To pay five ducats—for an annual rent of five gold coins.

[5] A ranker . . . in fee—a higher rate if it were sold outright.

[6] garrisoned—occupied by soldiers.

[7] debate the . . . this straw—settle such a foolish matter.

[8] impostume—abscess.

[9] inform against—accuse.

Looking before and after,[10] gave us not

40 That capability and godlike reason

To fust[11] in us unused. Now, whether it be

Bestial **oblivion**,[12] or some **craven**[13] scruple

Of thinking too precisely on th' event—

A thought which, quartered, hath but one part wisdom

45 And ever three parts coward—I do not know

Why yet I live to say "This thing's to do,"

Sith I have cause, and will, and strength, and means

To do 't. Examples gross as earth[14] exhort me:

Witness this army of such mass and charge,

50 Led by a delicate and tender prince,

Whose spirit with divine ambition puffed

Makes mouths at the invisible event,[15]

Exposing what is mortal and unsure

To all that fortune, death, and danger dare,

55 Even for an eggshell. Rightly to be great

Is not to stir without great argument,

But greatly to find quarrel in a straw

When honor's at the stake. How stand I, then,

That have a father killed, a mother stained,

60 Excitements of my reason and my blood,

And let all sleep, while to my shame I see

The imminent death of twenty thousand men

That for a fantasy and trick of fame

Go to their graves like beds, fight for a plot

65 Whereon the numbers cannot try the cause,[16]

Which is not tomb enough and continent

To hide the slain? O, from this time forth

My thoughts be bloody or be nothing worth!

[*He exits.*]

---

[10] Sure . . . after—surely God that made us with reasoning power that looks into the past and future.

[11] fust—grow moldy.

[12] **oblivion**—forgetfulness.

[13] **craven**—cowardly.

[14] gross as earth—obvious as the earth.

[15] Makes mouths . . . invisible event—treats the future scornfully.

[16] Whereon the . . . the cause—which isn't large enough to let the opposing armies engage upon it.

Act Four, Scene Five

In a room in Elsinore castle, Gertrude, hearing that Ophelia is mad, tries to comfort her; but Ophelia is oblivious to the world and sings about death and betrayal. Claudius and Gertrude are saddened that grief seems to have snapped her mind. Claudius is also dismayed that the Danish people seem to blame him for Polonius's death. Laertes has returned and is stirring up the population. When a mob attacks the castle, Laertes confronts the king and queen, prepared to avenge his father's death. Claudius tells Laertes that he had nothing to do with Polonius's death. When Laertes sees Ophelia, he is devastated. Claudius promises that he can explain everything.

Enter Horatio, Queen Gertrude, *and a* Gentleman.

Queen. I will not speak with her.
Gentleman.   She is importunate,
    Indeed distract.[1] Her mood will needs be pitied.
Queen. What would she have?
Gentleman. She speaks much of her father, says she hears
5   There's tricks i' the world, and hems, and beats her heart,
    Spurns enviously at straws,[2] speaks things in doubt
    That carry but half sense. Her speech is nothing,
    Yet the unshapèd use of it doth move
    The hearers to collection; they yawn at it,[3]
10   And botch[4] the words up fit to their own thoughts,
    Which, as her winks and nods and gestures yield them,
    Indeed would make one think there might be thought,
    Though nothing sure, yet much unhappily.
Horatio. 'Twere good she were spoken with, for she may strew
15   Dangerous conjectures in ill-breeding[5] minds.
Queen. Let her come in.
[*Exit* Gentleman.]

---

[1] importunate . . . distract—very persistent, in fact deeply agitated.

[2] Spurns . . . straws—takes angry offense at trifles.

[3] Her speech . . . yawn at it—What she says makes no sense, but its formlessness makes the hearers try to draw conclusions from it; they gape eagerly (as if to swallow).

[4] botch—patch together.

[5] ill-breeding—conceiving ill thoughts, prone to think the worst.

[*Aside.*] To my sick soul, as sin's true nature is,

    Each toy seems prologue to some great amiss.[6]

    So full of artless jealousy is guilt,

20   It spills itself in fearing to be spilt.

[*Enter* Ophelia, *distracted.*]

Ophelia. Where is the beauteous Majesty of Denmark?

Queen. How now, Ophelia?

Ophelia [*sings*].

    How should I your true-love know

      From another one?

25   *By his cockle hat and staff,*

      And his sandal shoon.[7]

Queen. Alas, sweet lady, what imports this song?

Ophelia. Say you? Nay, pray you, mark.

    [*Sings.*] *He is dead and gone, lady,*

30   *He is dead and gone;*

    At his head a grass-green turf,

      At his heels a stone.

    O, ho!

Queen. Nay, but Ophelia—

35 **Ophelia.** Pray you, mark.

    [*Sings.*] *White his shroud as the mountain snow—*

[*Enter* King Claudius.]

Queen. Alas, look here, my lord.

Ophelia [*sings*]. *Larded*[8] *with sweet flowers;*

    Which bewept to the ground did not go

40   *With true-love showers.*[9]

King. How do you, pretty lady?

Ophelia. Well, God 'ild you![10] They say the owl was a baker's daughter.[11]

    Lord, we know what we are, but know not what we may be. God be

    at your table!

---

[6] *toy . . . amiss*—trifle seems like the start of a disaster.

[7] *cockle hat and staff . . . shoon*—symbols of a pilgrim. A hat with a cockle shell on it showed that a pilgrim had been to the Shrine of St. James of Campostella in Spain. *Shoon* is an archaic word for shoes.

[8] *Larded*—adorned.

[9] *true-love showers*—tears.

[10] God 'ild you—God yield (that is, reward) you.

[11] baker's daughter—allusion to the legend of a baker's daughter whom Jesus turned into an owl because she did not generously respond to his request for bread.

45   **King.** Conceit upon[12] her father.

Ophelia. Pray let's have no words of this, but when they ask you what it
means, say you this:

[*Sings.*] *Tomorrow is Saint Valentine's day*
       All in the morning betime,
50   *And I a maid at your window,*
       To be your Valentine.
    Then up he rose and donned his clothes,
       And dupped[13] the chamber door,
    Let in the maid, that out a maid
55   *Never departed more.*

King. Pretty Ophelia—

Ophelia. Indeed, without an oath, I'll make an end on 't:

[*Sings.*] *By Gis[14] and by Saint Charity,*
       Alack, and fie for shame!
60   *Young men will do 't, if they come to 't;*
       By Cock,[15] they are to blame.
    Quoth she, "Before you tumbled me,
       You promised me to wed."

He answers:

       "So would I ha' done, by yonder sun,
65   *An thou hadst not come to my bed."*

King. How long hath she been thus?

Ophelia. I hope all will be well. We must be patient, but I cannot choose
but weep to think they would lay him i' the cold ground. My brother
70   shall know of it. And so I thank you for your good counsel. Come,
my coach! Good night, ladies, good night, sweet ladies,
good night, good night.

[*Exit* Ophelia.]

King [*to* Horatio]. Follow her close. Give her good watch, I pray you.

[*Exit* Horatio.]

    O, this is the poison of deep grief. It springs
75   All from her father's death—and now behold!

---

[12] Conceit upon—She is thinking about.

[13] *dupped*—opened.

[14] *Gis*—contraction of "Jesus."

[15] *Cock*—substitution for "God" in oaths.

When sorrows come, they come not single spies, But in battalions.

O Gertrude, Gertrude,
When sorrows come, they come not single spies,
But in battalions. First, her father slain;
Next, your son gone, and he most violent author

80 Of his own just remove; the people muddied,[16]
Thick, and unwholesome in their thoughts and whispers
For good Polonius' death, and we have done but greenly,[17]
In hugger-mugger to inter him;[18] poor Ophelia
Divided from herself and her fair judgment,

85 Without the which we are pictures or mere beasts;
Last, and as much containing as all these,
Her brother is in secret come from France,
Feeds on this wonder, keeps himself in clouds,
And wants not buzzers[19] to infect his ear

90 With pestilent speeches of his father's death,
Wherein necessity, of matter beggared,
Will nothing stick our person to arraign
In ear and ear. O my dear Gertrude, this,
Like to a murdering piece,[20] in many places

95 Gives me superfluous death.
[*A noise within.*]
Queen. Alack, what noise is this?
King. Attend!
Where is my Switzers?[21] Let them guard the door.
[*Enter a* Messenger.]
What is the matter?

---

[16] muddied—confused.

[17] we have . . . greenly—I have acted unwisely.

[18] hugger-mugger to inter him—to bury him secretly and hastily, without proper ceremony.

[19] wants not buzzers—does not lack gossipers.

[20] murdering piece—cannon that fires grapeshot.

[21] Switzers—Swiss guards.

Messenger. Save yourself, my lord!

100 The ocean, overpeering of his list,
   Eats not the flats with more impetuous haste
   Than young Laertes, in a riotous head,
   O'erbears your officers.[22] The rabble call him "lord,"
   And, as the world were now but to begin,
105 Antiquity forgot, custom not known,
   The ratifiers and props of every word,
   They cry, "Choose we! Laertes shall be king!"
   Caps, hands, and tongues applaud it to the clouds,
   "Laertes shall be king, Laertes king!"

[*A noise of shouting within.*]

110 **Queen.** How cheerfully on the false trail they cry!
   O, this is counter,[23] you false Danish dogs!

King. The doors are broke.

[*Enter* Laertes *with* Followers.]

Laertes. Where is this king?—Sirs, stand you all without.

All. No, let's come in.

115 **Laertes.** I pray you, give me leave.

All. We will, we will.

Laertes. I thank you. Keep the door. [*Exit* Followers.]
   O thou vile king,
   Give me my father!

120 **Queen** [*restraining him*]. Calmly, good Laertes.

Laertes. That drop of blood that's calm proclaims me bastard,
   Cries "cuckold" to my father,[24] brands the harlot
   Even here, between the chaste unsmirchèd brow
   Of my true mother.

King. What is the cause, Laertes,
125 That thy rebellion looks so giant-like?
   Let him go, Gertrude. Do not fear our person.
   There's such divinity doth hedge[25] a king
   That treason can but peep to what it would,

---

[22] ocean . . . officers—Laertes and his rebellious force are overpowering the king's officers as fast as an ocean overflows its shores and floods the lowlands.

[23] counter—on the wrong scent.

[24] Cries . . . father—tells my father that he had an unfaithful wife (that is, I am not his son).

[25] hedge—protect.

Acts little of his will.—Tell me, Laertes,

130   Why thou art thus incensed.—Let him go, Gertrude.
Speak, man.

Laertes. Where is my father?

King.   Dead.

Queen.   But not by him.

King. Let him demand his fill.

Laertes. How came he dead? I'll not be juggled with.

135   To hell, allegiance! Vows, to the blackest devil!
Conscience and grace, to the profoundest pit!
I dare damnation. To this point I stand,
That both the worlds I give to negligence,
Let come what comes, only I'll be revenged

140   Most throughly for my father.

King. Who shall stay you?

Laertes. My will, not all the worlds.
And for my means, I'll husband them²⁶ so well
They shall go far with little.

King.   Good Laertes,

145   If you desire to know the certainty
Of your dear father, is 't writ in your revenge
That, swoopstake,²⁷ you will draw both friend and foe,
Winner and loser?

Laertes. None but his enemies.

King.   Will you know them, then?

150 **Laertes.** To his good friends thus wide I'll ope my arms,
And, like the kind life-rendering pelican
Repast them with my blood.²⁸

King.   Why, now you speak
Like a good child and a true gentleman.
That I am guiltless of your father's death,

155   And am most sensibly in grief for it,

---

²⁶ husband them—use them thriftily.

²⁷ swoopstake—indiscriminately.

²⁸ pelican . . . blood—The female pelican was believed to feed her young with her own blood.

In this scene from the Hartford Stage production, Laertes (Stephen Pelinski) attempts to comfort his sister Ophelia (Monique Flower), who has gone mad from grief over their father's death.

It shall as level to your judgment 'pear
As day does to your eye.
[*A noise within.*] Let her come in.

Laertes. How now, what noise is that?

[*Enter* Ophelia.]

160   **Laertes.** O heat, dry up my brains! Tears seven times salt
Burn out the sense and virtue of mine eye!
By heaven, thy madness shall be paid with weight[29]
Till our scale turn the beam.[30] O rose of May!
Dear maid, kind sister, sweet Ophelia!

---

[29] paid with weight—avenged.
[30] turn the beam—tilt in our favor.

165　　　　O heavens, is 't possible a young maid's wits
　　　　　Should be as mortal as an old man's life?
　　　　　Nature is fine in[31] love, and, where 'tis fine,
　　　　　It sends some precious instance of itself
　　　　　After the thing it loves.
170　　**Ophelia** [*sings*]. *They bore him barefaced on the bier,*[32]
　　　　　　　Hey non nonny, nonny, hey nonny,
　　　　　　　And in his grave rained many a tear—
　　　　　Fare you well, my dove!
　　　　Laertes. Hadst thou thy wits and didst persuade revenge,
175　　　　It could not move thus.
　　　　Ophelia. You must sing "A-down a-down," and you "Call him a-down-a."
　　　　　O, how the wheel[33] becomes it! It is the false steward that stole his
　　　　　master's daughter.
　　　　Laertes. This nothing's more than matter.[34]
180　　**Ophelia.** There's rosemary, that's for remembrance. Pray you, love,
　　　　　remember. And there is pansies, that's for thoughts.
　　　　Laertes. A document in madness, thoughts and remembrance fitted.
　　　　Ophelia. There's fennel for you, and columbines.[35] There's rue[36] for you,
　　　　　and here's some for me; we may call it herb of grace o' Sundays. You
185　　　　must wear your rue with a difference.[37] There's a daisy. I would give
　　　　　you some violets,[38] but they withered all when my father died. They
　　　　　say he made a good end—[*Sings.*] *For bonny sweet Robin is all my joy.*
　　　　Laertes. Thought and afflictions, passion, hell itself,
　　　　　She turns to favor and to prettiness.
190　　**Ophelia** [*sings*]. *And will 'a not come again?*
　　　　　　　And will he not come again?
　　　　　　　No, no, he is dead.
　　　　　　　Go to thy deathbed,

---

[31] fine in—refined by.

[32] *bier*—transport for a corpse.

[33] wheel—refrain or chorus.

[34] This nothing's. . . matter—This mad talk is more eloquent than lucid speech.

[35] fennel . . . columbines—These plants are symbols of flattery and ingratitude, respectively.

[36] rue—This plant is a symbol of sorrow or repentance.

[37] with a difference—to represent a different cause of sorrow.

[38] daisy . . . violets—The daisy is the symbol of untruth, lies; violets are a symbol of faithfulness.

                    He never will come again.
195   *His beard was as white as snow,*
                    All flaxen was his poll.[39]
                        He is gone, he is gone,
                        And we cast away moan.
                    God ha' mercy on his soul!
200   And of all Christian souls, I pray God. God b' wi' you.
                [*Exit* Ophelia, *followed by* Gertrude.]

Laertes. Do you see this, O God?

King. Laertes, I must commune with your grief,
                Or you deny me right. Go but apart,
                Make choice of whom your wisest friends you will,
205   And they shall hear and judge 'twixt you and me.
                If by direct or by collateral[40] hand
                They find us touched, we will our kingdom give,
                Our crown, our life, and all that we call ours
                To you in satisfaction; but if not,
210   Be you content to lend your patience to us,
                And we shall jointly labor with your soul
                To give it due content.

Laertes.   Let this be so.
                His means of death, his obscure funeral—
                No trophy, sword, nor hatchment[41] o'er his bones,
215   No noble rite, nor formal **ostentation**[42]—
                Cry to be heard, as 'twere from heaven to earth,
                That I must call 't in question.

King.   So you shall,
                And where th' offense is, let the great ax fall.
                I pray you, go with me.
                [*They exit.*]

---

[39] *poll*—head.
[40] collateral—as an accessory.
[41] hatchment—memorial showing the coat of arms of a person who has recently died.
[42] **ostentation**—ceremony.

Act Four, Scene Six

In another room in the castle, sailors bring Horatio a letter from Hamlet. It explains that on the journey to England, pirates attacked Hamlet's boat and that he escaped with them. He asks Horatio to join him immediately.

Enter Horatio *and others.*

Horatio. What are they that would speak with me?

Gentleman. Seafaring men, sir. They say they have letters for you.

Horatio. Let them come in.

[*Exit* Gentleman.]

     I do not know from what part of the world

5   I should be greeted, if not from Lord Hamlet.

[*Enter* Sailors.]

First Sailor. God bless you, sir.

Horatio. Let Him bless thee too.

First Sailor. He shall, sir, an 't please Him. There's a letter for you, sir. It came from th' ambassador that was bound for England—if your

10   name be Horatio, as I am let to know it is.

[*He gives* Horatio *a letter.*]

Horatio [*reads*]. *Horatio, when thou shalt have overlooked this, give these fellows some means to the king. They have letters for him. Ere we were two days old at sea, a pirate of very warlike appointment[1] gave us chase. Finding ourselves too slow of sail, we put on a compelled valor, and in the grapple[2] I*

15   *boarded them. On the instant, they got clear of our ship, so I alone became their prisoner. They have dealt with me like thieves of mercy, but they knew what they did: I am to do a good turn for them. Let the king have the letters I have sent, and repair thou[3] to me with as much speed as thou wouldest fly*

---

[1] *pirate . . . appointment*—well-equipped pirate ship.

[2] *grapple*—struggle.

[3] *repair thou*—come.

death. I have words to speak in thine ear will make thee dumb, yet are they
20 *much too light for the bore of the matter.*[4] *These good fellows will bring thee*
where I am. Rosencrantz and Guildenstern hold their course for England. Of
them I have much to tell thee. Farewell.

He that thou knowest thine, Hamlet.

Come, I will give you way for these your letters,
And do 't the speedier that you may direct me
25 To him from whom you brought them.
[*They exit.*]

---

[4] *too light ... matter*—too light for the caliber of the gun (that is, inadequate).

Act Four, Scene Seven

In a room in the castle, Claudius has convinced Laertes of his innocence and explains
that he could not punish Hamlet because
both Gertrude and the public adore the
prince. Laertes demands revenge. When letters
arrive from Hamlet announcing that he will
return to court tomorrow, Claudius prepares a
plot. He tells Laertes that Hamlet is jealous of
his renown as a fencer. Claudius plans to bring
them together in a fencing match, and Laertes
says he will poison his sword. To be sure that
Hamlet is killed, Claudius will poison the wine
he offers Hamlet. A cry is heard, and Gertrude
interrupts them to announce that Ophelia
has drowned.

Enter King Claudius *and* Laertes.

King. Now must your conscience my acquittance seal,
    And you must put me in your heart for friend,
    Sith you have heard, and with a knowing ear,
    That he which hath your noble father slain
5   Pursued my life.

Laertes.   It well appears. But tell me
    Why you proceeded not against these feats
    So criminal and so capital[1] in nature,
    As by your safety, greatness, wisdom, all things else,
    You mainly were stirred up.

King.   O, for two special reasons,
10   Which may to you perhaps seem much unsinewed,[2]
    But yet to me they're strong. The queen his mother
    Lives almost by his looks, and for myself—
    My virtue or my plague, be it either which—
    She is so conjunctive[3] to my life and soul
15   That, as the star moves not but in his sphere,
    I could not but by her. The other motive
    Why to a public count[4] I might not go

---

[1] capital—deadly; deserving death.

[2] unsinewed—weak.

[3] conjunctive—closely joined.

[4] count—accounting, judgment.

Is the great love the general gender[5] bear him,
Who, dipping all his faults in their affection,
20 Work like the spring that turneth wood to stone,
Convert his gyves[6] to graces, so that my arrows,
Too slightly timbered for so loud a wind,
Would have reverted to my bow again
But not where I had aimed them.

25 **Laertes.** And so have I a noble father lost,
A sister driven into desp'rate terms,
Whose worth, if praises may go back again,
Stood challenger on mount of all the age
For her perfections. But my revenge will come.

30 **King.** Break not your sleeps for that. You must not think
That we are made of stuff so flat and dull
That we can let our beard be shook with danger
And think it pastime. You shortly shall hear more.
I loved your father, and we love ourself,
35 And that, I hope, will teach you to imagine—

[*Enter a* Messenger *with letters.*]

How now? What news?

Messenger.   Letters, my lord, from Hamlet:
This to Your Majesty, this to the queen.

[*He gives* Claudius *letters.*]

King. From Hamlet? Who brought them?

Messenger. Sailors, my lord, they say. I saw them not.
40 They were given me by Claudio. He received them
Of him that brought them.

King.   Laertes, you shall hear them.—
Leave us.

[*Exit* Messenger.]

[Claudius *reads.*] *High and mighty, you shall know I am set naked[7] on your
kingdom. Tomorrow shall I beg leave to see your kingly eyes, when I shall,*
45 *first asking your pardon, thereunto recount the occasion of my sudden and
more strange return.*   Hamlet.

---

[5] general gender—common people.

[6] Convert his gyves—transform his fetters (shackles, confining chains).

[7] *naked*—defenseless.

What should this mean? Are all the rest come back?
Or is it some abuse, and no such thing?

Laertes. Know you the hand?

King.   'Tis Hamlet's character.[8] "Naked!"
50   And in a postscript here he says "alone."
            Can you advise me?

Laertes. I am lost in it, my lord. But let him come.
            It warms the very sickness in my heart
            That I shall live and tell him to his teeth,
55   "Thus didst thou."

King.   If it be so, Laertes—
            As how should it be so? How otherwise?—
            Will you be ruled by me?

Laertes.   Ay, my lord,
            So you will not o'errule me to a peace.

King. To thine own peace. If he be now returned,
60   As checking at[9] his voyage, and that he means
            No more to undertake it, I will work him
            To an exploit, now ripe in my device,[10]
            Under the which he shall not choose but fall;
            And for his death no wind of blame shall breathe,
65   But even his mother shall uncharge the practice[11]
            And call it accident.

Laertes.   My lord, I will be ruled,
            The rather if you could devise it so
            That I might be the organ.[12]

King.   It falls right.
            You have been talked of since your travel much,
70   And that in Hamlet's hearing, for a quality
            Wherein they say you shine. Your sum of parts
            Did not together pluck such envy from him

---

[8] character—handwriting.

[9] checking at—refusing to continue.

[10] device—planning.

[11] uncharge the practice—fail to see any blame.

[12] organ—instrument, agent.

As did that one, and that, in my regard,
Of the unworthiest siege.[13]

75 **Laertes.** What part is that, my lord?

King. A very ribbon in the cap of youth,
Yet needful too, for youth no less becomes
The light and careless livery that it wears
Than settled age his sables and his weeds[14]

80 Importing health and graveness. Two months since
Here was a gentleman of Normandy.
I have seen myself, and served against, the French,
And they can well on horseback,[15] but this gallant
Had witchcraft in 't. He grew unto his seat,

85 And to such wondrous doing brought his horse
As had he been encorpsed and demi–natured
With the brave beast.[16] So far he topped my thought
That I in forgery of shapes and tricks
Come short of what he did.

Laertes.   A Norman was 't?

90 **King.** A Norman.

Laertes. Upon my life, Lamord.

King.   The very same.

Laertes. I know him well. He is the brooch indeed
And gem of all the nation.

King. He made confession of you,

95 And gave you such a masterly report
For art and exercise in your defense,
And for your rapier most especial,
That he cried out 'twould be a sight indeed
If one could match you. Th' escrimers[17] of their nation,

100 He swore, had neither motion, guard, nor eye
If you opposed them. Sir, this report of his
Did Hamlet so envenom with his envy
That he could nothing do but wish and beg

---

[13] unworthiest siege—least important position.

[14] for youth . . . weeds—clothes of youth are as becoming to them as rich clothes are becoming to older wearers.

[15] can well on horseback—are excellent riders.

[16] encorpsed . . . beast—as though the horse and he made a single body, like a centaur (half-man, half-horse).

[17] escrimers—fencers.

Your sudden coming o'er, to play with you.
105 Now, out of this—

Laertes. What out of this, my lord?

King. Laertes, was your father dear to you?
Or are you like the painting of a sorrow,
A face without a heart?

Laertes. Why ask you this?

King. Not that I think you did not love your father,
110 But that I know love is begun by time,
And that I see, in passages of proof,
Time qualifies the spark and fire of it
There lives within the very flame of love

Claudius (Ted van Griethuysen, right) plots with Laertes (Bo Foxworth)
to kill Hamlet in this scene from The Shakespeare Theatre production.

A kind of wick or snuff[18] that will abate it,

115 And nothing is at a like goodness still,[19]

For goodness, growing to a pleurisy,[20]

Dies in his own too much. That we would do,

We should do when we would; for this "would" changes

And hath abatements and delays as many

120 As there are tongues, are hands, are accidents,

And then this "should" is like a spendthrift sigh,

That hurts by easing. But, to the quick o' th' ulcer:[21]

Hamlet comes back. What would you undertake

To show yourself in deed your father's son

125 More than in words?

Laertes.   To cut his throat i' the church.

King. No place, indeed, should murder sanctuarize;[22]

Revenge should have no bounds. But good Laertes,

Will you do this? Keep close within your chamber.

Hamlet, returned, shall know you are come home.

130 We'll put on those shall praise[23] your excellence

And set a double varnish on the fame

The Frenchman gave you, bring you, in fine, together,

And wager on your heads. He, being remiss,[24]

Most generous, and free from all contriving,

135 Will not peruse the foils, so that with ease,

Or with a little shuffling, you may choose

A sword unbated,[25] and in a pass of practice

Requite him for your father.

Laertes.   I will do 't,

And for that purpose I'll anoint my sword.

140 I bought an unction of a mountebank[26]

So mortal that, but dip a knife in it,

---

[18] snuff—charred part of a candle's wick.

[19] nothing is ... goodness still—nothing remains forever at the same pitch of perfection.

[20] pleurisy—excess.

[21] quick o' th' ulcer—main point.

[22] murder sanctuarize—offer asylum to a murderer.

[23] put ... praise—incite those who will praise.

[24] remiss—careless.

[25] unbated—not blunted (that is, still sharp).

[26] unction of a mountebank—ointment from a traveling quack doctor.

Where it draws blood no cataplasm[27] so rare,
Collected from all simples that have virtue
Under the moon, can save the thing from death

145 That is but scratched withal.[28] I'll touch my point
With this contagion, that if I gall him slightly,
It may be death.[29]

King.   Let's further think of this,
Weigh what convenience both of time and means
May fit us to our shape. If this should fail,

150 And that our drift look through our bad performance,[30]
'Twere better not **assayed**.[31] Therefore this project
Should have a back or second, that might hold
If this did blast in proof.[32] Soft, let me see.
We'll make a solemn wager on your cunnings—

155 I ha't!
When in your motion you are hot and dry—
As make your bouts more violent to that end—
And that he calls for drink, I'll have prepared him
A chalice for the nonce,[33] whereon but sipping,

160 If he by chance escape your venomed stuck,
Our purpose may hold there.

[*A cry within.*]

                    But stay, what noise?

[*Enter* Queen Gertrude.]

Queen. One woe doth tread upon another's heel,
So fast they follow. Your sister's drowned, Laertes.

Laertes. Drowned! O, where?

165 **Queen.** There is a willow grows askant[34] the brook,
That shows his hoar[35] leaves in the glassy stream;

---

[27] cataplasm—medicine in a bandage, poultice.

[28] Collected . . . withal—made from herbs so deadly that anything scratched with it cannot be saved from death.

[29] if . . . death—if I graze him, he'll die.

[30] drift look . . . bad performance—Our plot is exposed through poor execution.

[31] **assayed**—tried.

[32] blast in proof—blow up in the testing.

[33] chalice for the nonce—cup for the occasion.

[34] askant—sideways over.

[35] hoar—gray.

Therewith fantastic garlands did she make
Of crowflowers, nettles, daisies, and long purples,
That liberal shepherds give a grosser name,
But our cold maids do "dead men's fingers" call them. 170
There on the pendent boughs[36] her coronet weeds[37]
Clamb'ring to hang, an envious sliver[38] broke,
When down her weedy trophies and herself
Fell in the weeping brook. Her clothes spread wide,
And mermaid-like awhile they bore her up, 175
Which time she chanted snatches of old lauds,[39]
As one incapable of her own distress,
Or like a creature native and endued[40]
Unto that element. But long it could not be
Till that her garments, heavy with their drink, 180
Pulled the poor wretch from her melodious lay[41]
To muddy death.

Laertes.　　　　　Alas, then she is drowned?

Queen. Drowned, drowned.

Laertes. Too much of water hast thou, poor Ophelia,
And therefore I forbid my tears. But yet 185
It is our trick;[42] nature her custom holds,
Let shame say what it will. [*He weeps.*] When these are gone,
The woman will be out. Adieu, my lord.
I have a speech of fire that fain would blaze,
But that this folly drowns it. 190

[*Exit* Laertes.]

King.　　　　　　　　Let's follow, Gertrude.
How much I had to do to calm his rage!
Now fear I this will give it start again;
Therefore let's follow.

[*They exit.*]

---

[36] pendent boughs—hanging branches.

[37] coronet weeds—crown of flowers.

[38] envious sliver—malicious branch.

[39] lauds—hymns.

[40] endued—used to.

[41] lay—song.

[42] It is our trick—Weeping is our natural way.

Act Five, Scene One

In a churchyard, two gravediggers are preparing for Ophelia's funeral. Hamlet tries to find out who the grave is for. The digger shows him the just-upturned skull of the old jester Yorick. Hamlet reminisces about playing with the jester in his youth and notes that we all must come to dust in the earth. Ophelia's funeral procession enters, and Hamlet and Horatio hide themselves to learn what has happened. Laertes is angry that the funeral rites are short, but it is feared that Ophelia committed suicide. Hamlet, learning about her death and seeing Laertes leap into the grave, rushes forward and proclaims his own grief and love for Ophelia. He and Laertes come to blows, but Claudius counsels Laertes to save his anger for later.

Enter two Clowns[1] *with spades and mattocks.*

First Clown. Is she to be buried in Christian burial, when she willfully seeks her own salvation?

Second Clown. I tell thee she is. Therefore make her grave straight. The crowner hath sat on her, and finds it Christian burial.[2]

5   **First Clown.** How can that be, unless she drowned herself in her own defense?

Second Clown. Why, 'tis found so.

First Clown. It must be *se offendendo*,[3] it cannot be else. For here lies the point: if I drown myself wittingly, it argues an act, and an act hath

10   three branches—it is to act, to do, and to perform. Argal,[4] she drowned herself wittingly.

Second Clown. Nay, but hear you, goodman delver[5]—

First Clown. Give me leave. Here lies the water; good. Here stands the man; good. If the man go to this water and drown himself, it is, will

15   he, nill he,[6] he goes, mark you that. But if the water come to him and drown him, he drowns not himself. Argal, he that is not guilty of his own death shortens not his own life.

---

[1] Clowns—rustics; here, the gravediggers.

[2] The crowner ... burial—The coroner has conducted a formal inquest and brought in a verdict that she should have a Christian burial.

[3] *se offendendo*—blunder for *se defendendo,* Latin for "in self-defense."

[4] Argal—blunder for *ergo,* Latin for "therefore."

[5] delver—digger.

[6] will he, nill he—willy-nilly (that is, will he, will he not).

Second Clown. But is this law?

First Clown. Ay, marry, is 't—crowner's quest[7] law.

20 **Second Clown.** Will you ha' the truth on 't? If this had not been a gentle-woman, she should have been buried out o' Christian burial.

First Clown. Why, there thou sayst. And the more pity that great folk should have count'nance[8] in this world to drown or hang themselves, more than their even-Christian.[9] Come, my spade. There is no ancient 25 gentlemen but gard'ners, ditchers, and grave-makers. They hold up[10] Adam's profession.

Second Clown. Was he a gentleman?

First Clown. He was the first that ever bore arms.

Second Clown. Why, he had none.

30 **First Clown.** What, art a heathen? How dost thou understand the Scripture? The Scripture says Adam digged. Could he dig without arms? I'll put another question to thee. If thou answerest me not to the purpose, confess thyself[11]—

Second Clown. Go to.

35 **First Clown.** What is he that builds stronger than either the mason, the shipwright, or the carpenter?

Second Clown. The gallows-maker, for that frame outlives a thousand tenants.

First Clown. I like thy wit well, in good faith. The gallows does well. But 40 how does it well? It does well to those that do ill. Now, thou dost ill to say the gallows is built stronger than the church. Argal, the gallows may do well to thee. To 't again, come.

Second Clown. "Who builds stronger than a mason, a shipwright, or a carpenter?"

45 **First Clown.** Ay, tell me that, and unyoke.[12]

Second Clown. Marry, now I can tell.

First Clown. To 't.

---

[7] crowner's quest—coroner's inquest.

[8] count'nance—legal approval.

[9] even-Christian—fellow Christians.

[10] hold up—continue.

[11] confess thyself—This is usually completed by "and be damned."

[12] unyoke—stop working.

Second Clown. Mass, I cannot tell.

[*Enter* Hamlet *and* Horatio *at a distance.*]

First Clown. Cudgel thy brains no more about it, for your dull ass will
not mend his pace with beating. And, when you are asked this question next, say "a grave-maker." The houses he makes lasts till
doomsday. Go, get thee in and fetch me a stoup[13] of liquor.

[*Exit* Second Clown. First Clown *digs.*]

[*Sings.*]

> *In youth, when I did love, did love,*
> *Methought it was very sweet,*
> *To contract—O[14]—the time for—a—my behove,[15]*
> *O, methought there—a—was nothing—a—meet.*

Hamlet. Has this fellow no feeling of his business, he sings in grave-
making?

Horatio. Custom hath made it in him a property of easiness.

Hamlet. 'Tis e'en so. The hand of little employment hath the daintier sense.

First Clown [*sings*].

> *But age with his stealing steps*
> *Hath clawed me in his clutch,*
> *And hath shipped me into the land,*
> *As if I had never been such.*

[*He throws up a skull.*]

Hamlet. That skull had a tongue in it and could sing once. How the
knave jowls[16] it to the ground, as if 'twere Cain's jawbone, that did
the first murder! This might be the pate of a politician, which this ass
now o'erreaches, one that would circumvent God, might it not?

Horatio. It might, my lord.

Hamlet. Or of a courtier, which could say, "Good morrow, sweet lord! How
dost thou, sweet lord?" This might be my Lord Such-a-one that praised
my Lord Such-a-one's horse when he meant to beg it, might it not?

---

13 stoup—cup.

14 *O*—The "O"s and "a"s may be the grunts of the gravedigger as he works, or they may be part of the song, which makes
little sense.

15 *behove*—advantage.

16 jowls—throws.

Horatio. Ay, my lord.

Hamlet. Why, e'en so, and now my Lady Worm's, chapless,[17] and
knocked about the mazard[18] with a sexton's[19] spade. Here's fine revo-
lution, an we had the trick to see 't. Did these bones cost no more the
breeding but to play at loggets[20] with them? Mine ache to think on 't.

First Clown [*sings*].

> *A pickax and a spade, a spade,*
> *For and a shrouding sheet;*
> *O, a pit of day for to be made*
> *For such a guest is meet.*

[*He throws up another skull.*]

Hamlet. There's another. Why may not that be the skull of a lawyer?
Where be his quiddities now, his quillities,[21] his cases, his tenures,[22]
and his tricks? Why does he suffer this mad knave now to knock
him about the sconce[23] with a dirty shovel and will not tell him of his
action of battery? Hum, this fellow might be in 's time a great buyer
of land, with his statutes, his recognizances,[24] his fines, his double
vouchers,[25] his recoveries. Is this the fine of his fines and the recovery
of his recoveries, to have his fine pate full of fine dirt? Will his
vouchers vouch him no more of his purchases, and double ones
too, than the length and breadth of a pair of indentures?[26] The very
conveyances[27] of his lands will scarcely lie in this box, and must th'
inheritor himself have no more, ha?

Horatio. Not a jot more, my lord.

Hamlet. Is not parchment made of sheepskins?

Horatio. Ay, my lord, and of calves' skins too.

---

[17] chapless—lacking a lower jaw.

[18] mazard—head.

[19] sexton's—belonging to an employee of a church responsible for its upkeep.

[20] loggets—game in which wooden pins are thrown at a stake.

[21] quiddities. . . quillities—subtleties, quibbles.

[22] tenures—titles to real estate.

[23] sconce—head.

[24] statutes. . . recognizances—bonds securing debts by attaching land and property.

[25] double vouchers—documents, signed by two persons, guaranteeing title to real estate.

[26] pair of indentures—contracts. Hamlet also refers to the two rows of teeth in the skull.

[27] conveyances—documents relating to transfer of property.

Hamlet. They are sheep and calves which seek out assurance in that. I will speak to this fellow.—Whose grave's this, sirrah?[28]

First Clown. Mine, sir.

[*Sings.*]

100 　　　　　*O, pit of clay for to be made*
　　　　　　For such a guest is meet.

Hamlet. I think it be thine, indeed, for thou liest in 't.

First Clown. You lie out on 't, sir, and therefore 'tis not yours. For my part, I do not lie in 't, yet it is mine.

105 **Hamlet.** Thou dost lie in 't, to be in 't and say it is thine. 'Tis for the dead, not for the quick;[29] therefore thou liest.

First Clown. 'Tis a quick lie, sir; 'twill away again from me to you.

Hamlet. What man dost thou dig it for?

First Clown. For no man, sir.

110 **Hamlet.** What woman, then?

First Clown. For none, neither.

Hamlet. Who is to be buried in 't?

First Clown. One that was a woman, sir, but, rest her soul, she's dead.

Hamlet. How absolute the knave is! We must speak by the card,[30] or

115 **equivocation**[31] will undo us. By the Lord, Horatio, this three years I have took note of it: the age is grown so picked that the toe of the peasant comes so near the heel of the courtier, he galls his kibe.[32]— How long hast thou been grave-maker?

First Clown. Of all the days i' the year, I came to 't that day that our last

120 King Hamlet overcame Fortinbras.

Hamlet. How long is that since?

First Clown. Cannot you tell that? Every fool can tell that. It was that very day that young Hamlet was born—he that is mad and sent into England.

125 **Hamlet.** Ay, marry, why was he sent into England?

First Clown. Why, because 'a was mad. He shall recover his wits there, or if he do not, 'tis no great matter there.

---

[28] sirrah—form of address to an inferior.

[29] quick—living.

[30] by the card—precisely.

[31] **equivocation**—ambiguity; words with double meaning used to mislead.

[32] the age . . . his kibe—The age has become so refined that peasants walk so close to courtiers that they rub their sore heels.

Hamlet. Why?

First Clown. 'Twill not be seen in him there. There the men are as mad
as he.

Hamlet. How came he mad?

First Clown. Very strangely, they say.

Hamlet. How "strangely"?

First Clown. Faith, e'en with losing his wits.

Hamlet. Upon what ground?

First Clown. Why, here in Denmark. I have been sexton here, man and
boy, thirty years.

Hamlet. How long will a man be i' th' earth ere he rot?

First Clown. Faith, if he be not rotten before he die—as we have many
pocky corpses nowadays that will scarce hold the laying in[33]—he
will last you some eight year or nine year. A tanner[34] will last you
nine year.

Hamlet. Why he more than another?

First Clown. Why, sir, his hide is so tanned with his trade that he will
keep out water a great while, and your water is a sore decayer of
your whoreson dead body.

[*He picks up a skull.*]

Here's a skull now hath lien you[35] i' th' earth three-and-twenty years.

Hamlet. Whose was it?

First Clown. A whoreson mad fellow's it was. Whose do you think it was?

Hamlet. Nay, I know not.

First Clown. A pestilence on him for a mad rogue! He poured a flagon of
Rhenish[36] on my head once. This same skull, sir, was, sir, Yorick's
skull, the king's jester.

Hamlet. This?

First Clown. E'en that.

Hamlet. Let me see.

[*He takes the skull.*]

---

[33] pocky . . . laying in—corpses of people with the pox (syphilis) that barely hold together long enough to be buried.

[34] tanner—leather worker.

[35] lien you—lain.

[36] flagon of Rhenish—vessel containing Rhine wine.

Hamlet (Kevin Kline) studies the skull of the king's jester, Yorick, in this scene from the 1986 production of *Hamlet* by the New York Shakespeare Festival.

Alas, poor Yorick! I knew him, Horatio—a fellow of infinite jest, of most excellent fancy. He hath bore me on his back a thousand times, and now how abhorred in my imagination it is! My gorge rises at it. Here hung those lips that I have kissed I know not how oft. Where be your gibes now? your gambols?[37] your songs? your flashes of merriment that were wont to set the table on a roar? Not one now to mock your own grinning? Quite chapfallen?[38] Now get you to my lady's chamber and tell her, let her paint an inch thick, to this favor[39] she must come. Make her laugh at that.—Prithee, Horatio, tell me one thing.

160

165

---

[37] gambols—playful skipping.

[38] chapfallen—without a lower jaw; punning on *chapfallen*, "downcast."

[39] favor—appearance.

Horatio. What's that, my lord?

Hamlet. Dost thou think Alexander[40] looked o' this fashion i' th' earth?

Horatio. E'en so.

Hamlet. And smelt so? Pah!

[*He puts down the skull.*]

170   **Horatio.** E'en so, my lord.

Hamlet. To what base uses we may return, Horatio! Why may not imagination trace the noble dust of Alexander till he find it stopping a bunghole?[41]

Horatio. 'Twere to consider too curiously[42] to consider so.

175   **Hamlet.** No, faith, not a jot, but to follow him thither with modesty enough, and likelihood to lead it. As thus: Alexander died, Alexander was buried, Alexander returneth to dust, the dust is earth, of earth we make loam,[43] and why of that loam whereto he was converted might they not stop a beer barrel?

180   Imperious Caesar, dead and turned to clay,

Might stop a hole to keep the wind away.

O, that that earth which kept the world in awe

Should patch a wall t' expel the winter's flaw!

[*Enter* Priest, *leading a funeral procession that includes the body of* Ophelia, Laertes, *and* King Claudius *and* Queen Gertrude *with their* Attendants.]

But soft, but soft awhile! Here comes the king,

185   The queen, the courtiers. Who is this they follow?

And with such maimèd[44] rites? This doth betoken

The corpse they follow did with desperate hand

Fordo[45] its own life. 'Twas of some estate.[46]

Couch we awhile and mark.

[Hamlet *and* Horatio *conceal themselves.* Ophelia's body is taken to the grave.]

---

[40] Alexander—Alexander the Great.

[41] bunghole—hole in a keg of beer.

[42] curiously—precisely; elaborately.

[43] loam—mixture of moistened clay with sand used to make plaster.

[44] maimèd—incomplete.

[45] Fordo—destroy.

[46] estate—high rank.

190   **Laertes.** What ceremony else?

Hamlet. That is Laertes, a very noble youth. Mark.

Laertes. What ceremony else?

Priest. Her obsequies[47] have been as far enlarged

As we have warranty.[48] Her death was doubtful,

195   And but that great command o'ersways the order,

She should in ground unsanctified been lodged

Till the last trumpet.[49] For charitable prayers,

Shards,[50] flints, and pebbles should be thrown on her.

Yet here she is allowed her virgin crants,[51]

200   Her maiden strewments,[52] and the bringing home

Of bell and burial.

Laertes. Must there no more be done?

Priest.   No more be done.

We should profane the service of the dead

To sing a requiem and such rest to her

205   As to peace-parted souls.

Laertes.   Lay her i' th' earth,

And from her fair and unpolluted flesh

May violets spring! I tell thee, churlish[53] priest,

A ministering angel shall my sister be

When thou liest howling.[54]

210   **Hamlet** [*to* Horatio].   What, the fair Ophelia!

Queen [*scattering flowers*]. Sweets to the sweet! Farewell.

I hoped thou shouldst have been my Hamlet's wife.

I thought thy bride-bed to have decked, sweet maid,

And not t' have strewed thy grave.

---

[47] obsequies—funeral rites.

[48] warranty—authority for.

[49] last trumpet—end of the world; Judgment Day.

[50] Shards—broken bits of pottery.

[51] crants—wreaths and garlands.

[52] maiden strewments—flowers scattered on the grave of an unmarried girl.

[53] churlish—having a bad disposition, surly.

[54] howling—in hell.

As Ophelia's brother Laertes (Curzon Dobell) holds her body in his arms, Hamlet (Zlejko Ivanek) prepares to leap into her grave in this scene from the 1988 production of *Hamlet* at Minneapolis's Guthrie Theatre.

Laertes. O, treble[55] woe

215   Fall ten times treble on that cursèd head
    Whose wicked deed thy most ingenious sense
    Deprived thee of!—Hold off the earth awhile,
    Till I have caught her once more in mine arms.
[He leaps into the grave and embraces Ophelia.]
    Now pile your dust upon the quick and dead,
220   Till of this flat a mountain you have made
    T' o'ertop old Pelion or the skyish head
    Of blue Olympus.[56]

---

[55] treble—threefold.
[56] Pelion . . . Olympus—sacred mountains in ancient Greece.

Hamlet [*coming forward*]. What is he whose grief
   Bears such an emphasis, whose phrase of sorrow
225   Conjures the wandering stars and makes them stand
   Like wonder-wounded hearers? This is I,
   Hamlet the Dane.
Laertes [*grappling with him*]. The devil take thy soul!
Hamlet. Thou pray'st not well.
230   I prithee, take thy fingers from my throat,
   For though I am not splenitive[57] and rash,
   Yet have I in me something dangerous,
   Which let thy wisdom fear. Hold off thy hand.
King. Pluck them asunder.
235 **Queen.** Hamlet! Hamlet!
All. Gentlemen!
Horatio. Good my lord, be quiet.
[Hamlet *and* Laertes *are separated.*]
Hamlet. Why, I will fight with him upon this theme
   Until my eyelids will no longer wag!
240 **Queen.** O my son, what theme?
Hamlet. I loved Ophelia. Forty thousand brothers
   Could not with all their quantity of love
   Make up my sum. What wilt thou do for her?
King. O, he is mad, Laertes.
245 **Queen.** For love of God, forbear him.
Hamlet. 'Swounds, show me what thou'lt do.
   Woo't[58] weep? Woo't fight? Woo't fast? Woo't tear thyself?
   Woo't drink up eisel?[59] Eat a crocodile?
   I'll do 't. Dost thou come here to whine?
250   To outface me with leaping in her grave?
   Be buried quick with her, and so will I.
   And if thou prate of mountains, let them throw
   Millions of acres on us, till our ground,

---

[57] splenitive—impetuous.
[58] Woo't—will you.
[59] eisel—vinegar.

	Singeing his pate against the burning zone,[60]
255	Make Ossa[61] like a wart! Nay, an thou'lt mouth,
	I'll rant as well as thou.

Queen.   This is mere madness,
   And thus awhile the fit will work on him;
   Anon, as patient as the female dove
   When that her golden couplets are disclosed,[62]

260   His silence will sit drooping.

Hamlet.   Hear you, sir.
   What is the reason that you use me thus?
   I loved you ever. But it is no matter.
   Let Hercules himself do what he may,
   The cat will mew, and dog will have his day.

[*Exit* Hamlet.]

265   **King.** I pray thee, good Horatio, wait upon him.

[*Exit* Horatio.]

King [*to* Laertes]. Strengthen your patience in our last night's speech;
   We'll put the matter to the present push.—
   Good Gertrude, set some watch over your son.—
   This grave shall have a living[63] monument.

270   An hour of quiet shortly shall we see;
   Till then, in patience our proceeding be.

[*They exit.*]

---

[60] burning zone—sun's orbit.

[61] Ossa—another mountain in Greece.

[62] When that . . . are disclosed—when her chicks are hatched.

[63] living—lasting.

Act Five, Scene Two

In a hall of the castle, Hamlet explains to Horatio how he discovered the orders for his murder and turned them against Rosencrantz and Guildenstern. Osric, a silly courtier, tells Hamlet that Claudius has wagered on his fencing skill in a match against Laertes. Hamlet agrees to take the challenge and the court assembles for the fight. Hamlet apologizes to Laertes. Claudius suggests a toast be drunk if Hamlet scores any of the first three hits and promises him a rare pearl. When Hamlet scores the first hit, Claudius places the pearl, which is poison, in a cup and asks Hamlet to drink. He declines. Gertrude drinks from the cup before Claudius can stop her.

The fight continues and Laertes wounds Hamlet with the poisoned sword. Hamlet forces an exchange of weapons and Laertes is wounded with his own poisoned blade. The queen dies, and the dying Laertes admits all the treachery. Hamlet stabs the king and forces the poisoned wine down his throat. Dying, Hamlet asks Horatio to make sure the world learns the truth. Hamlet has heard about Fortinbras's victorious return and tells Horatio that Fortinbras will make a good king. After Hamlet dies, Fortinbras arrives and is shocked by what he sees. He orders a military funeral for Hamlet and prepares to claim the crown of Denmark.

Enter Hamlet *and* Horatio.

Hamlet. So much for this, sir. Now shall you see the other.[1]
    You do remember all the circumstance?
Horatio. Remember it, my lord!
Hamlet. Sir, in my heart there was a kind of fighting
5   That would not let me sleep. Methought I lay
    Worse than the mutines in the bilboes.[2] Rashly—
    And praised be rashness for it—let us know
    Our indiscretion sometimes serves us well
    When our deep plots do pall,[3] and that should learn us
10   There's a divinity that shapes our ends,
    Rough-hew them how we will[4]—
Horatio.   That is most certain.

---

[1] see the other—hear the other news.
[2] mutines in the bilboes—mutineers in shackles.
[3] pall—lose force, come to nothing.
[4] There's . . . will—No matter how crudely we shape our designs, Fate puts the finishing touch to them.

There's a divinity that shapes our ends, Rough-hew them how we will.

Hamlet. Up from my cabin,
My sea-gown scarfed about me, in the dark
Groped I to find out them,[5] had my desire,
15 Fingered their packet,[6] and in fine withdrew
To mine own room again, making so bold,
My fears forgetting manners, to unseal
Their grand commission; where I found, Horatio—
Ah royal knavery!—an exact command,
20 Larded with many several sorts of reasons
Importing[7] Denmark's health and England's too,
With, ho! such bugs and goblins in my life,
That on the supervise, no leisure bated,
No, not to stay the grinding of the ax,[8]
25 My head should be struck off.

Horatio.   Is 't possible?

Hamlet [*giving him a document*]. Here's the commission. Read it at more
leisure.
But wilt thou hear now how I did proceed?

Horatio. I beseech you.

30 **Hamlet.** Being thus benetted round with villainies—
Ere I could make a prologue to my brains,
They had begun the play—I sat me down,
Devised a new commission, wrote it fair.
I once did hold it, as our statists[9] do,
35 A baseness[10] to write fair, and labored much
How to forget that learning, but, sir, now

---

[5] them—Rosencrantz and Guildenstern.

[6] Fingered their packet—stole their letters.

[7] Importing—relating to.

[8] such bugs . . . ax—terrifying things in prospect if I were allowed to live, that on reading, without delay, not even to sharpen the ax.

[9] statists—statesmen, public officials.

[10] I once . . . baseness—I once believed, as most statesmen do, it was a lower-class skill.

It did me yeoman's[11] service. Wilt thou know
Th' effect of what I wrote?

Horatio.   Ay, good my lord.

Hamlet. An earnest conjuration from the king,

40   As England was his faithful tributary,
     As love between them like the palm might flourish,
     As peace should still her wheaten garland wear
     And stand a comma[12] 'tween their amities,
     And many suchlike ases of great charge,

45   That, on the view and knowing of these contents,
     Without debatement further, more or less,
     He should those bearers put to sudden death,
     Not shriving time[13] allowed.

Horatio.   How was this sealed?

Hamlet. Why, even in that was heaven ordinant.[14]

50   I had my father's signet in my purse,
     Which was the model of that Danish seal;
     Folded the writ up in the form of th' other,
     Subscribed it, gave 't th' impression, placed it safely,
     The changeling[15] never known. Now, the next day

55   Was our sea fight, and what to this was sequent[16]
     Thou knowest already.

Horatio. So Guildenstern and Rosencrantz go to 't.

Hamlet. Why, man, they did make love to this employment.
     They are not near my conscience.[17] Their defeat

60   Does by their own insinuation[18] grow.
     'Tis dangerous when the baser nature comes
     Between the pass and fell incensèd points
     Of mighty opposites.[19]

Horatio.   Why, what a king is this!

---

[11] yeoman's—solid, substantial.

[12] comma—connection, link.

[13] shriving time—time for confession and absolution.

[14] ordinant—guiding me.

[15] changeling—substituted letter.

[16] sequent—next.

[17] They . . . conscience—I don't feel guilty about them.

[18] insinuation—intervention.

[19] pass . . . opposites—thrust of fierce, angry swords of mighty opponents.

Hamlet. Does it not, think thee, stand me now upon—

    He that hath killed my king and whored my mother,

65   Popped in between th' election[20] and my hopes,

    Thrown out his angle for my proper life,

    And with such cozenage[21]—is 't not perfect conscience

    To quit him with this arm? And is 't not to be damned

    To let this canker of our nature come

70   In further evil?

Horatio. It must be shortly known to him from England

    What is the issue of the business there.

Hamlet. It will be short. The **interim**[22] is mine,

    And a man's life's no more than to say "one."

75   But I am very sorry, good Horatio,

    That to Laertes I forgot myself,

    For by the image of my cause I see

    The portraiture of his. I'll court his favors.

    But, sure, the bravery[23] of his grief did put me

80   Into a tow'ring passion.

Horatio.   Peace, who comes here?

[*Enter* Osric, *a courtier.*]

Osric. Your lordship is right welcome back to Denmark.

Hamlet. I humbly thank you, sir. [*To Horatio.*] Dost know this waterfly?[24]

Horatio [*aside to Hamlet*]. No, my good lord.

Hamlet [*aside to Horatio*]. Thy state is the more gracious, for 'tis a vice to

85   know him. He hath much land and fertile. Let a beast be lord of

    beasts, and his crib shall stand at the king's mess.[25] 'Tis a chough,[26]

    but, as I say, spacious in the possession of dirt.

Osric. Sweet lord, if your lordship were at leisure, I should impart a

    thing to you from His Majesty.

90   **Hamlet.** I will receive it, sir, with all diligence of spirit.

    Put your bonnet[27] to his right use; 'tis for the head.

---

[20] th' election—In Denmark, the king was chosen by election.

[21] cozenage—trickery.

[22] **interim**—interval between events.

[23] bravery—boastful expression.

[24] waterfly—fluttering creature.

[25] beast . . . mess—Even a beast that owned many cattle (as Osric does) could dine with the king.

[26] chough—jackdaw, chatterer.

[27] bonnet—hat.

Osric. I thank your lordship, it is very hot.

Hamlet. No, believe me, 'tis very cold. The wind is northerly.

Osric. It is indifferent cold, my lord, indeed.

95 **Hamlet.** But yet methinks it is very sultry and hot for my complexion.

Osric. Exceedingly, my lord. It is very sultry, as 'twere—I cannot tell how. My lord, His Majesty bade me signify to you that he has laid a great wager on your head. Sir, this is the matter—

Hamlet. I beseech you, remember.

100 [Hamlet *motions to* Osric *to put on his hat.*]

Osric. Nay, good my lord, for my ease, in good faith. Sir, here is newly come to court Laertes—believe me, an absolute gentleman, full of most excellent differences, of very soft society and great showing.[28] Indeed, to speak feelingly of him, he is the card or calendar of gentry, for you shall find in him the continent of what part[29] a gentleman

105 would see.

Hamlet. Sir, his definement suffers no perdition[30] in you, though I know to divide him inventorially would dozy th' arithmetic of memory, and yet but yaw neither in respect of his quick sail.[31] But, in the verity of extolment,[32] take him to be a soul of great article, and his infusion of

110 such dearth and rareness as, to make true diction of him, his semblable is his mirror and who else would trace him his umbrage, nothing more.[33]

Osric. Your lordship speaks most infallibly of him.

Hamlet. The concernancy, sir? Why do we wrap the gentleman in our

115 more rawer breath?[34]

Osric. Sir?

Horatio [*aside to* Hamlet]. Is 't not possible to understand in another tongue? You will do 't, sir, really.

---

[28] of very . . . great showing—of good manners and splendid appearance. Osric speaks in an affected, imprecise way, and Hamlet answers him in an even more exaggerated way.

[29] the continent . . . part—one who contains every quality.

[30] perdition—loss.

[31] to divide . . . quick sail—In mockingly affected language, Hamlet says that to list his good qualities would make our memories dizzy, and even if we did, our list would be clumsy compared to his excellence.

[32] in the . . . extolment—to praise him truly.

[33] a soul . . . nothing more—Laertes is such a fine man that only his mirror can give a true picture of him. Everything else is nothing more than a shadow.

[34] The concernancy . . . breath?—The relevance, sir? Why are we talking about him?

Hamlet. What imports the nomination[35] of this gentleman?

Osric. Of Laertes?

120 **Horatio** [*to* Hamlet]. His purse is empty already; all 's golden words
are spent.

Hamlet. Of him, sir.

Osric. I know you are not ignorant—

Hamlet. I would you did, sir. Yet, in faith, if you did, it would not much
125 approve me. Well, sir?

Osric. You are not ignorant of what excellence Laertes is—

Hamlet. I dare not confess that, lest I should compare with him in excellence. But to know a man well were to know himself.

Osric. I mean, sir, for his weapon. But in the imputation laid on him by
130 them, in his meed he's unfellowed.[36]

Hamlet. What's his weapon?

Osric. Rapier and dagger.

Hamlet. That's two of his weapons. But, well.

Osric. The king, sir, hath wagered with him six Barbary horses, against
135 the which he has impawned,[37] as I take it, six French rapiers and
poniards,[38] with their assigns, as girdle, hangers, and so.[39] Three of
the carriages,[40] in faith, are very dear to fancy, very responsive to the
hilts, most delicate carriages, and of very liberal conceit.[41]

Hamlet. What call you the carriages?

140 **Horatio** [*aside to* Hamlet]. I knew you must be edified by the margent[42]
ere you had done.

Osric. The carriages, sir, are the hangers.

Hamlet. The phrase would be more **germane**[43] to the matter if we could
carry a cannon by our sides. I would it might be "hangers" till then.

---

[35] nomination—naming.

[36] meed . . . unfellowed—merit he is unmatched.

[37] impawned—staked.

[38] poniards—daggers.

[39] assigns . . . and so—accessories, such as sword belt, attaching straps, and so on.

[40] carriages—affected word for *hangers*, or attaching straps.

[41] liberal conceit—fanciful design.

[42] edified by the margent—instructed by marginal notes.

[43] **germane**—relevant.

<table>
<tr><td>145</td><td>But, on. Six Barbary horses against six French swords, their assigns, and three liberal-conceited carriages; that's the French bet against the Danish. Why is this "impawned," as you call it?</td></tr>
</table>

145 But, on. Six Barbary horses against six French swords, their assigns, and three liberal-conceited carriages; that's the French bet against the Danish. Why is this "impawned," as you call it?

Osric. The king, sir, hath laid, sir, that in a dozen passes between yourself and him, he shall not exceed you three hits. He hath laid on twelve
150 for nine, and it would come to immediate trial, if your lordship would vouchsafe the answer.[44]

Hamlet. How if I answer no?

Osric. I mean, my lord, the opposition of your person in trial.

Hamlet. Sir, I will walk here in the hall. If it please His Majesty, it is the
155 breathing time[45] of day with me. Let the foils be brought, the gentleman willing, and the king hold his purpose, I will win for him, an I can. If not, I will gain nothing but my shame and the odd hits.

Osric. Shall I deliver you so?

Hamlet. To this effect, sir, after what flourish your nature will.

160 **Osric.** I commend my duty to your lordship.

Hamlet. Yours, yours. [*Exit* Osric.] He does well to commend it himself. There are no tongues else for 's turn.

Horatio. This lapwing[46] runs away with the shell on his head.

Hamlet. He did comply with his dug[47] before he sucked it. Thus has he—
165 and many more of the same breed that I know the drossy[48] age dotes on—only got the tune of the time and, out of an habit of encounter, a kind of yeasty[49] collection, which carries them through and through the most fanned and winnowed[50] opinions; and do but blow them to their trial, the bubbles are out.

170 [*Enter a* Lord.]

Lord. My lord, His Majesty commended him to you by young Osric, who brings back to him that you attend him in the hall. He sends to know if your pleasure hold to play with Laertes, or that you will take longer time.

---

[44] vouchsafe the answer—accept the challenge. Hamlet chooses to understand it differently.

[45] breathing time—exercise period.

[46] lapwing—newly fledged bird that was thought to run off with part of the eggshell still on its head.

[47] comply with his dug—bow to his mother's breast.

[48] drossy—worthless.

[49] yeasty—frothy.

[50] fanned and winnowed—select and refined.

There is a special providence in the fall of a sparrow.

Hamlet. I am constant to my purposes. They follow the king's pleasure.
175   If his fitness speaks, mine is ready now or whensoever, provided I be
so able as now.

Lord. The king and queen and all are coming down.

Hamlet. In happy time.

Lord. The queen desires you to use some gentle entertainment[51] to
180   Laertes before you fall to play.

Hamlet. She well instructs me.

[*Exit* Lord.]

Horatio. You will lose, my lord.

Hamlet. I do not think so. Since he went into France, I have been in continual practice. I shall win at the odds. But thou wouldst not think
185   how ill all's here about my heart; but it is no matter.

Horatio. Nay, good my lord—

Hamlet. It is but foolery, but it is such a kind of gaingiving[52] as would
perhaps trouble a woman.

Horatio. If your mind dislike anything, obey it. I will forestall their
190   repair[53] hither and say you are not fit.

Hamlet. Not a whit, we defy augury.[54] There is a special providence in
the fall of a sparrow.[55] If it be not now, 'tis not to come; if it be not to
come, it will be now; if it be not now, yet it will come. The readiness
is all. Since no man of aught he leaves knows, what is 't to leave
195   betimes?[56] Let be.

[*A table prepared. Enter* Musicians *with trumpets and drums;* Officers *with
cushions;* King Claudius, Queen Gertrude, Osric, *and* Courtiers; Servants
carrying foils, daggers, and wine; and Laertes.]

---

[51] use some gentle entertainment—receive him in a friendly way.

[52] gaingiving—misgiving.

[53] repair—coming.

[54] augury—omens.

[55] providence . . . sparrow—allusion to a quotation from the New Testament, Matthew 10:29: "Are not two sparrows sold for a farthing and one of them shall not fall on the ground without your Father."

[56] since . . . betimes—Since no one has knowledge of what he leaves behind, what does it matter to die early?

King. Come, Hamlet, come and take this hand from me.

[*The* King *puts Laertes's hand into Hamlet's.*]

Hamlet [*to* Laertes]. Give me your pardon, sir. I have done you wrong,
　　But pardon 't as you are a gentleman. This presence knows,
　　And you must needs have heard, how I am punished
200　　With a sore distraction. What I have done
　　That might your nature, honor, and exception
　　Roughly awake, I here proclaim was madness.
　　Was 't Hamlet wronged Laertes? Never Hamlet.

Hamlet (Zlejko Ivanek) scores a hit in his fencing match with Laertes (Curzon Dobell) in this scene from the Guthrie Theatre production.

If Hamlet from himself be ta'en away,

205 And when he's not himself does wrong Laertes,

Then Hamlet does it not, Hamlet denies it.

Who does it, then? His madness. If 't be so,

Hamlet is of the faction[57] that is wronged;

His madness is poor Hamlet's enemy.

210 Sir, in this audience

Let my disclaiming from a purposed evil

Free me so far in your most generous thoughts

That I have shot my arrow o'er the house

And hurt my brother.

Laertes.   I am satisfied in nature,

Whose motive in this case should stir me most

To my revenge. But in my terms of honor

I stand aloof and will no reconcilement

Till by some elder masters of known honor

I have a voice and precedent of peace

To keep my name ungored.[58] But till that time

I do receive your offered love like love,

And will not wrong it.

Hamlet.   I embrace it freely,

And will this brothers' wager frankly play.

Give us the foils. Come on.

Laertes.   Come, one for me.

Hamlet. I'll be your foil,[59] Laertes. In mine ignorance

Your skill shall, like a star i' the darkest night,

Stick fiery off[60] indeed.

Laertes.   You mock me, sir.

Hamlet. No, by this hand.

King. Give them the foils, young Osric. Cousin Hamlet,

You know the wager?

Hamlet.   Very well, my lord.

Your Grace has laid the odds o' the weaker side.

---

[57] faction—group.

[58] name ungored—reputation uninjured.

[59] foil—background against which you will shine; punning on *foil*, "a blunted sword."

[60] Stick fiery off—blaze out in contrast.

King. I do not fear it; I have seen you both.

But, since he is bettered, we have therefore odds.

Laertes. This is too heavy. Let me see another.

235   [*He exchanges his foil for the sharper, poisoned blade.*]

Hamlet. This likes me well. These foils have all a length?

[*They prepare to play.*]

Osric. Ay, my good lord.

King. Set me the stoups of wine upon that table.

If Hamlet give the first or second hit,

Or quit in answer of the third exchange,[61]

240   Let all the battlements their ord'nance[62] fire.

The king shall drink to Hamlet's better breath,

And in the cup an union[63] shall he throw

Richer than that which four successive kings

In Denmark's crown have worn. Give me the cups,

245   And let the kettle[64] to the trumpet speak,

The trumpet to the cannoneer without,

The cannons to the heavens, the heaven to earth,

"Now the King drinks to Hamlet." Come, begin.

[*Trumpets sound.*]

And you, the judges, bear a wary eye.

250   **Hamlet.** Come on, sir.

Laertes.   Come, my lord.

[*They play.* Hamlet *scores a hit.*]

Hamlet.   One.

Laertes.   No.

Hamlet.   Judgment!

Osric. A hit, a very palpable hit.

[*Drum, trumpets, and cannons fire.*]

Laertes.   Well, again.

---

[61] quit in . . . third exchange—pay back by taking the third pass.

[62] ord'nance—artillery.

[63] union—large pearl.

[64] kettle—kettledrum.

King. Stay, give me drink.—Hamlet, this pearl is thine.

Here's to thy health.

[*He drinks, and drops a pearl in Hamlet's cup. Drums, trumpet, and cannon shot.*]

255 Give him the cup.

Hamlet. I'll play this bout first. Set it by awhile.

Come. [*They play.*] Another hit; what say you?

Laertes. A touch, a touch, I do confess 't.

King. Our son shall win.

Queen. He's fat and scant of breath.

260 Here, Hamlet, take my napkin, rub thy brows.

The queen carouses to thy fortune, Hamlet.

[*She lifts the poisoned cup.*]

Hamlet. Good madam!

King. Gertrude, do not drink.

Queen. I will, my lord, I pray you pardon me.

[*She drinks.*]

King [*aside*]. It is the poisoned cup. It is too late.

Hamlet. I dare not drink yet, madam; by and by.

265 **Queen.** Come, let me wipe thy face.

Laertes [*to* Claudius]. My lord, I'll hit him now.

King. I do not think 't.

Laertes [*aside*]. And yet it is almost against my conscience.

Hamlet. Come, for the third, Laertes. You do but dally.

I pray you, pass with your best violence;

270 I am afeard you make a wanton⁶⁵ of me.

Laertes. Say you so? Come on.

[*They play.*]

Osric. Nothing neither way.

Laertes. Have at you now!

[Laertes *wounds* Hamlet; *then, in scuffling,* Hamlet *forces a change of rapiers and wounds* Laertes.]

King. Part them! They are incensed.

Hamlet. Nay, come, again.

275 [Queen Gertrude *falls.*]

Osric. Look to the Queen there, ho!

---

⁶⁵ afeard . . . wanton—afraid that you are treating me like a spoiled child.

Horatio. They bleed on both sides. How is it, my lord?

Osric. How is 't, Laertes?

Laertes. Why, as a woodcock to mine own springe, Osric,
    I am justly killed with mine own treachery.

Hamlet. How does the queen?

280 **King.**   She swoons to see them bleed.

Queen. No, no, the drink, the drink! O my dear Hamlet—
    The drink, the drink! I am poisoned.

[*She dies.*]

Hamlet. O villainy! Ho! Let the door be locked!
    Treachery! Seek it out.

[Laertes *falls. Exit* Osric.]

Laertes. It is here, Hamlet. Hamlet, thou art slain.

285   No med'cine in the world can do thee good;
    In thee there is not half an hour's life.
    The treacherous instrument is in thy hand,
    Unbated and envenomed.[66] The foul practice
    Hath turned itself on me. Lo, here I lie,

290   Never to rise again. Thy mother's poisoned.
    I can no more. The king, the king's to blame.

Hamlet. The point envenomed too? Then, venom, to thy work.

[*He stabs* Claudius.]

All. Treason! Treason!

King. O, yet defend me, friends! I am but hurt.

295 **Hamlet** [*forcing* Claudius *to drink the poison*]. Here, thou incestuous,
        murderous, damnèd Dane,
    Drink off this potion. Is thy union here?
    Follow my mother.

[Claudius *dies.*]

Laertes.   He is justly served.

300   It is a poison tempered by himself
    Exchange forgiveness with me, noble Hamlet.
    Mine and my father's death come not upon thee,
    Nor thine on me!

[*He dies.*]

---

[66] Unbated and envenomed—sharp and poisoned.

Hamlet (Campbell Scott) forces Claudius to drink his own poison in this scene from the Huntington Theatre production.

Hamlet. Heaven make thee free of it! I follow thee.—
305   I am dead, Horatio. Wretched queen, adieu!
      You that look pale and tremble at this chance,
      That are but mutes or audience to this act,
      Had I but time—as this fell sergeant,[67] Death,
      Is strict in his arrest. O, I could tell you—
310   But let it be.—Horatio, I am dead;
      Thou livest. Report me and my cause aright
      To the unsatisfied.

---

[67] fell sergeant—arresting officer.

If thou didst ever hold me in thy heart,
Absent thee from felicity awhile.

Horatio.   Never believe it.
I am more an antique Roman[68] than a Dane.
Here's yet some liquor left.

[*He attempts to drink from the poisoned cup. Hamlet prevents him.*]

Hamlet.   As thou'rt a man,
315 Give me the cup! Let go! By heaven, I'll ha 't.
O God, Horatio, what a wounded name,
Things standing thus unknown, shall I leave behind me!
If thou didst ever hold me in thy heart,
Absent thee from felicity[69] awhile,
320 And in this harsh world draw thy breath in pain
To tell my story.

[*A march afar off and a shot within.*]

What warlike noise is this?

[*Enter Osric.*]

Osric. Young Fortinbras, with conquest come from Poland,
To th' ambassadors of England gives
325 This warlike volley.

Hamlet.   O, I die, Horatio!
The potent poison quite o'ercrows[70] my spirit.
I cannot live to hear the news from England,
But I do prophesy th' election lights
On Fortinbras. He has my dying voice.[71]
330 So tell him, with th' occurrents more and less
Which have solicited[72]—the rest is silence.

[*He dies.*]

---

[68] antique Roman—one who will commit suicide on such an occasion.

[69] Absent . . . felicity—keep yourself from the happiness of death.

[70] o'ercrows—triumphs over.

[71] voice—vote.

[72] occurrents . . . solicited—occurrences that have brought on.

Horatio (Jeffrey Hayenga) embraces the dying Hamlet (Richard Thomas) in the final scene of the Hartford Stage production.

Horatio. Now cracks a noble heart. Good night, sweet prince,
And flights of angels sing thee to thy rest!
[*March within.*]
Why does the drum come hither?

335 [*Enter* Fortinbras, *with the* English Ambassadors
with drum, flags, and Attendants.]

Fortinbras. Where is this sight?

Horatio. What is it you would see?
If aught of woe or wonder, cease your search.

Fortinbras. This quarry cries on havoc.[73] O proud Death,

340 What feast is toward in thine eternal cell,
That thou so many princes at a shot
So bloodily hast struck?

First Ambassador. The sight is dismal,
And our affairs from England come too late.
The ears are senseless that should give us hearing,

345 To tell him his commandment is fulfilled,
That Rosencrantz and Guildenstern are dead.
Where should we have our thanks?

Horatio. Not from his mouth,
Had it th' ability of life to thank you.
He never gave commandment for their death.

350 But since, so jump upon this bloody question,[74]
You from the Polack wars, and you from England,
Are here arrived, give order that these bodies
High on a stage be placèd to the view,
And let me speak to th' yet unknowing world

355 How these things came about. So shall you hear

---

[73] This quarry . . . havoc—This heap of corpses proclaims a massacre.

[74] jump . . . question—precisely at the time of this bloody quarrel.

Of carnal, bloody, and unnatural acts,
Of accidental judgments, casual slaughters,
Of deaths put on by cunning and forced cause,
And, in this upshot, purposes mistook
360 Fall'n on th' inventors' heads. All this can I
Truly deliver.
Fortinbras.   Let us haste to hear it,
And call the noblest to the audience.
For me, with sorrow I embrace my fortune.
I have some rights of memory[75] in this kingdom,
365 Which now to claim my vantage[76] doth invite me.
Horatio. Of that I shall have also cause to speak,
And from his mouth whose voice will draw on more.
But let this same be presently performed,
Even while men's minds are wild, lest more mischance
On plots and errors happen.
370 **Fortinbras.**   Let four captains
Bear Hamlet, like a soldier, to the stage,
For he was likely, had he been put on,[77]
To have proved most royal; and for his passage,
The soldiers' music and the rite of war
375 Speak loudly for him.
Take up the bodies. Such a sight as this
Becomes the field,[78] but here shows much amiss.
Go bid the soldiers shoot.
[*They exit, marching, bearing off the dead bodies; a peal of ordinance is shot off.*]

---

[75] rights of memory—traditional rights.

[76] my vantage—my presence at a moment when the throne is empty.

[77] put on—put to the test.

[78] Becomes the field—befits the field of battle.

Understanding the Play

Act One

1. What is the function of Scene One? What do we learn?

2. Why is Hamlet so angry and despairing in Scene Two? What state of mind does the syntax of his "O, that this too too sullied flesh" soliloquy (lines 129–159) indicate?

3. In Scene Three, why is Laertes so fearful about Ophelia's relationship with Hamlet?

4. What is Polonius's advice to Laertes? What is your opinion of its value?

5. In Scenes Four and Five, what do Hamlet's reactions to the Ghost tell about the prince's state of mind?

Act Two

1. In Scene One, what is the point of Polonius's complicated instructions to Reynaldo?

2. In Scene Two, why is Claudius pleased by the ambassadors' news?

3. What are Rosencrantz and Guildenstern like? What is your opinion of their feelings for Hamlet?

4. What does Hamlet's discussion of the theater companies indicate about his state of mind?

5. What does the First Player's performance of the speech tell Hamlet? Why is he so struck by it?

Act Three

1. In Scene One, what is Hamlet's dilemma in his famous "To be or not to be" speech? What can you infer about his character from his concerns?

2. Why does Hamlet attack Ophelia so viciously? What is he really angry about?

3. In Scene Two, how does Claudius react to the play within the play? How does Gertrude react?

4. In Scene Three, why does Hamlet decide not to kill Claudius while the king is praying?

5. In Scene Four, how does Hamlet convince his mother that he is not mad? What does he instruct her to do?

Act Four

1. In Scene One, why does Gertrude say that Hamlet is mad when she reports the murder of Polonius? What does this say about her?

2. After the murder of Polonius, does Claudius think that Hamlet is actually mad? What is the evidence for your answer?

3. In Scene Five, why does the public blame Claudius for Polonius's death? How does this reflect on Claudius's right to rule?

4. In Scene Seven, do you think that Ophelia committed suicide or died accidentally? Explain your reasoning.

Act Five

1. In Scene One, what is it that Yorick's skull reminds Hamlet of? How does he receive the knowledge?

2. What does Hamlet finally express clearly in the scene at Ophelia's funeral?

3. In Scene Two, do you think that Hamlet was justified in causing the death of Rosencrantz and Guildenstern? Explain your reasoning.

4. Why does Hamlet ask Laertes' pardon before they fight? What is your opinion of his sincerity?

5. Why do you think Fortinbras orders a military funeral for Hamlet?

Analyzing the Play

1. What is the central moral problem presented in *Hamlet?* How does Hamlet eventually resolve it?

2. Why do you think that Shakespeare presented humorous elements such as the gravediggers and Osric in what is essentially a tragedy? What do the various humorous elements add to *Hamlet?*

3. In *Hamlet,* Shakespeare is presenting a great variety of ideas in opposition, such as the ambition of Fortinbras versus the passivity of Hamlet or the actual governing of the king versus the melancholy of Hamlet. Make a list of all the oppositions you can find in the play. Remember that Shakespeare carefully contrasted many of the characters.

4. Compare and contrast the madness of Ophelia with that of Hamlet. What distinguishes the ways they act?

5. A revenge play is a tragic drama in which the hero rights a wrong. In what ways is *Hamlet* a revenge play?

Writing Projects

1. Hamlet is the central figure of the play, but Shakespeare has presented a number of other figures who are obvious parallels to him. Choose Laertes, Fortinbras, or Horatio, and write a short essay comparing and contrasting them with Hamlet.

2. One of the famous lines in *Hamlet* is that "Something is rotten in the state of Denmark." Running through the play is the theme that below the healthy surface, things are diseased or sick. Write a short essay pointing out all the elements in *Hamlet* that show a surface health but that reflect the disease wasting Denmark.

3. Write a letter from Ophelia to her brother describing her reactions to their father's death and Hamlet's rejection of her. Think about her emotions before you write, and then let her pour them out to her beloved brother.

4. Hamlet is an extremely rounded figure as Shakespeare presents him. Using what you know, write a short story describing how a contemporary Hamlet would react to his father's death and his mother's remarriage so soon after. Change whatever elements from the original you need to in order to create a modern picture of the hero.

Performance Projects

1. Write a short dialogue between Ophelia and Gertrude, in which the two of them discuss Hamlet, their love for him, and their fears. With another student, perform your dialogue for the class.

2. *Hamlet* was written to be performed in modern dress in Shakespeare's day. If you were going to restage *Hamlet,* where would you set it? Consider what the play will gain and lose by restaging. Do a presentation for the class on how you are going to perform the play, and why.

3. The play-within-the-play is a powerful device in *Hamlet.* Working in a group, act out *The Mousetrap* for the rest of the class. Add whatever dialogue is necessary to finish up the scene that is interrupted in the play. Stage it in whatever manner you think will best express the action.

4. Working with a partner, create a news interview of Horatio after the play has ended. One of you will play Horatio, the other the interviewer. Write the dialogue, and then perform the skit of Horatio trying to get Hamlet's story out.

Shakespeare on Film

Film versions of Shakespeare's plays go back to the earliest days of the movies. The approaches taken by filmmakers have ranged from simply recording a theatrical performance to taking full advantage of the cinema's techniques, such as close-ups, filming on location, and special effects.

▲
In 1935, German director Max Reinhardt recreated his Broadway production of *A Midsummer Night's Dream* for Hollywood. The lavish film version featured James Cagney as Bottom and Joe E. Brown as Flute, shown here in the scene where the two Athenian tradesmen perform their absurd version of the classical love story of Pyramus and Thisbe.

A year later, Hollywood produced another of Shakespeare's comedies, *As You Like It,* starring German actress Elisabeth Bergner as Rosalind and English actor Laurence Olivier as Orlando.

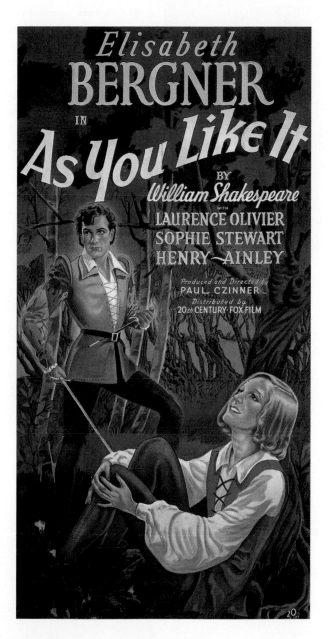

A filmmaker sometimes chooses a particular play of Shakespeare because it seems to have something important to say at that moment in history. During World War II, actor Laurence Olivier (shown here), directed his first film, creating and starring in a stirring version of Shakespeare's patriotic play *Henry V*. Beginning as a theatrical performance at Shakespeare's Globe theater, the film gradually becomes realistic as the scene shifts to warfare in France.

▲
In an unusual bit of casting, Italian director Franco Zeffirelli used action star Mel Gibson to play Hamlet in his 1991 film version of Shakespeare's most famous play.

◀ Actor-director Orson Welles merged parts of Shakespeare's *Henry IV, Parts 1 and 2, Henry V, Richard III,* and *The Merry Wives of Windsor* into *Chimes at Midnight* (1966), which deals with one of the playwright's greatest comic creations, Sir John Falstaff. Welles himself (shown here) played Falstaff.

Japanese director Akira Kurosawa retold *Macbeth* in *Throne of Blood* (1957), a film about an ambitious, ruthless samurai who murders his lord. Here, actress Isuju Yamada, who plays the samurai's wife, is driven mad by guilt over their deed. ▶

Filmmakers sometimes use one of Shakespeare's plays the way he used his own sources, as the basis on which to build a completely original work. In 1957, *The Tempest* was remade as a science-fiction film called *Forbidden Planet*, with a scientist and robot in place of Prospero and Ariel.
▼

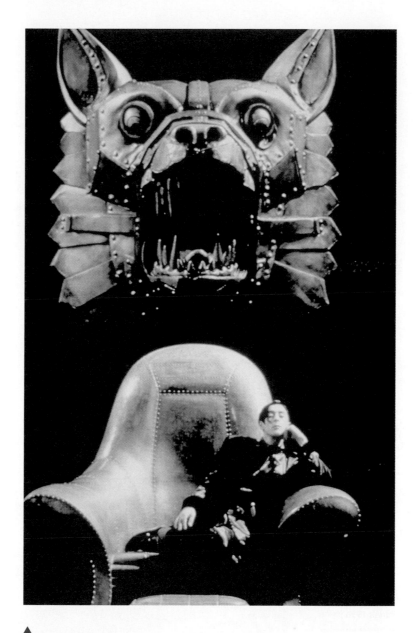

American director Julie Taymor has a theatrical background as a scenic and costume designer. This is strongly evident in *Titus* (1999), her adaptation of Shakespeare's *Titus Andronicus*, a bloody revenge play set in ancient Rome. Here, Alan Cumming, as the depraved emperor Saturninus, sits on his throne beneath a ferocious image of a wolf, a symbol of Rome's power.

◄ The most popular modern adaptation of Shakespeare's most popular play is *West Side Story* (1960), a musical based on *Romeo and Juliet*. The 1961 film version of *West Side Story* won the Oscar for best picture. Here, actor Russ Tamblyn is seen as the leader of a New York street gang.

Like *West Side Story*, Australian director Baz Luhrmann's 1996 version of *Romeo and Juliet* also had a contemporary setting with the Capulets and Montagues as members of warring street gangs. ►

▲

Another recent version of Shakespeare with a contemporary setting was Michael Almereyda's *Hamlet* (2000). Here, Steve Zahn and Dechan Thurman are seen as Rosencrantz and Guildenstern.

Some of the most interesting Shakespeare films of recent years have been the work of English actor and director Kenneth Branagh. Among them is his lively 1993 film version of Shakespeare's witty battle of the sexes, *Much Ado About Nothing.* ▶

English director Trevor Nunn gave his 1996 version of Shakespeare's *Twelfth Night* a 19th-century setting. Here, Malvolio (Nigel Hawthorne), believing that Olivia loves him, goes into raptures.
▼

Heath Ledger and Julia Stiles are the battling lovers in *10 Things I Hate About You* (1999), a film adaptation of Shakespeare's comedy *The Taming of the Shrew*.

Macbeth

Introduction

Macbeth *is a fast-paced murder story set in medieval Scotland—a time as distant and remote from Shakespeare's era as his period is from ours. His play was based on a historical event that had become very timely.* Macbeth *was written in 1606 when England's new king, James I, had been on the throne for just three years. James was descended from Banquo, a historical figure who is one of the main characters in* Macbeth. *The king was the patron of Shakespeare's acting company, so flattery was certainly one of the playwright's intentions. But the play's themes also would have been of real interest to the young king. James was also king of Scotland and was very concerned with cementing relations between the two countries he ruled. He was also fascinated by witchcraft and had written a book on the subject in 1597. Moreover, a spectacular plot against the king's life had been foiled in 1605, and London was full of rumors of treason and assassination. Shakespeare mixed all these contemporary elements into his play, creating a gripping story of ambition, bloodshed, horror, and the supernatural.*

Plot

At the center of the play is the courageous Macbeth, who has won great honors on the battlefield but is driven by his ambitious wife to murder his way to the throne of Scotland. He is encouraged in this by the prophecies of three witches. In the first part of the play, Macbeth is contrasted with King Duncan and Banquo, who have different ideas about loyalty and honor.

◀ A blood-soaked Macbeth (Alec Baldwin) returns from murdering his king in this scene from the 1998 production of *Macbeth* at New York's Joseph Papp Public Theater.

Once Macbeth is king, he is haunted by the need to maintain his position. He murders his opponents and is willing to commit any crime. Many Scots go into exile to escape his tyranny. Macbeth is no longer led by his wife's ambition but rather by his trust in the prophecies of the witches.

◄ In this scene from the 2000 production of *Macbeth* by the Hartford Stage Company, Macbeth (Denis O'Hare) and his wife (Stephanie Roth-Haberle) find no satisfaction in achieving their ambitions.

The final part of the play depicts Macbeth's growing isolation and the alliance of nobles who defeat him. They are led by Macduff, who, in another contrast to Macbeth, is both brave and loyal. In the play's climax, Macduff kills Macbeth in battle and helps to crown Duncan's son Malcolm as king.

Macbeth (Philip Goodwin) battles Macduff (Edward Gero) in this scene from the 1988 production of *Macbeth* by The Shakespeare Theatre in Washington, D.C. ▶

Settings and Characters

The action of Macbeth takes place almost entirely at several castles in Scotland. It is a very dark play, dominated by fierce storms, torch-lit rooms, gloomy forests, the din of battle, and supernatural appearances.

Macbeth is at the center of the play, which he completely dominates. (He delivers two-thirds of the lines.) The other major characters either draw Macbeth toward evil or stand as a contrast to him. Lady Macbeth and the three Witches pull Macbeth toward dark deeds. Duncan, his son Malcolm, and his followers Banquo and Macduff, stand as foils to Macbeth in his evil and treachery.

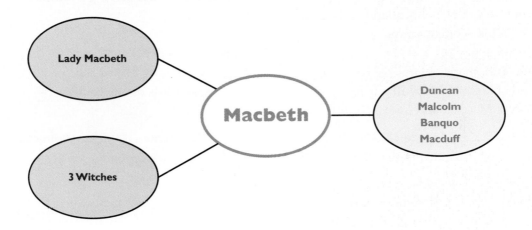

Themes

Macbeth is a play about ambition, action, and honor. Macbeth, a courageous warrior, is driven to dark crime by his own ambition and by his wife's questioning of his courage. Shakespeare comments on the ideals of honor and loyalty by beginning and ending the play with the appearance of a well-intentioned ruler whose fighting is done by others. Macbeth wins a great battle for Duncan, but he is unsatisfied with his reward and so murders Duncan and takes the crown. At the end, Macduff wins another great battle, but he returns the crown to the rightful king. Macbeth and Banquo are also contrasts. Like Macbeth, Banquo is offered a great future by the witches; but, unlike Macbeth, he fears to dwell on the prophecy as it might lead him into evil.

Macbeth has many noble qualities—courage, resolve, and decisiveness. After Lady Macbeth goads him into murdering the king, she becomes consumed by guilt and cannot act further. But Macbeth clearly grasps what he has done and continues to act forcefully, knowing that more evil cannot any further condemn him. Macbeth's rivals also act forcefully. Macduff risks his family to do what is right for Scotland. Shakespeare is praising those who can act but also asking the audience to focus on what it is that allows good men to do right.

One of the key elements of Macbeth is the interaction of the natural and supernatural worlds. The play is set in motion by the three witches, who stir up Macbeth's ambition with promises of glory. The witches, along with ghosts and spirits, continually drive the action forward; and Scotland is plagued by supernatural disasters during Macbeth's reign. Normality returns only with his death. The play is set at a time when "darkness does the face of earth entomb," and strange sightings and phenomena are common.

Characters

Duncan, king of Scotland
Malcolm and **Donalbain,** his sons

Macbeth, thane of Glamis, later thane of
    Cawdor, later king of Scotland
Lady Macbeth, Macbeth's wife

Banquo, a thane of Scotland and a general
    in the Scottish army
Fleance, his son
Macduff, thane of Fife
Lady Macduff, Macduff's wife
Son of Macduff and Lady Macduff

Lennox, Ross, Menteith, Angus, and
    Caithness, thanes and noblemen of
    Scotland

Siward, earl of Northumberland, com-
    mander of the English army, uncle of
    Malcolm and Donalbain

Young Siward, his son
Seyton, an officer attending Macbeth
English Doctor
Scottish Doctor
Gentlewoman, attending Lady Macbeth
Captain, an officer serving Duncan
Porter
Old Man
Three **Murderers**
Three **Witches** or **Weird Sisters**
Hecate, goddess of witchcraft
Apparitions

Lords, Gentlemen, Officers, Soldiers,
    Servants, Attendants, and
    Messengers

SCENE: *Scotland and England*

Act One, Scene One

As a storm rages on a deserted plain, three witches meet and predict that they will meet Macbeth when a battle with an invading army is over.

Thunder and lightning. Enter three Witches.

First Witch. When shall we three meet again?
    In thunder, lightning, or in rain?
Second Witch. When the hurlyburly's[1] done,
    When the battle's lost and won.
5   **Third Witch.** That will be ere the set of sun.
First Witch. Where the place?
Second Witch. Upon the heath.[2]
Third Witch. There to meet with Macbeth.
First Witch. I come, Graymalkin![3]
10   **Second Witch.** Paddock calls.
Third Witch. Anon![4]
All. Fair is foul, and foul is fair.
    Hover through the fog and filthy air.
[*They exit.*]

---

[1] hurlyburly's—noisy confusion is.

[2] heath—open uncultivated stretch of land covered with low shrubs or plants; a moor.

[3] Graymalkin . . . Paddock—cat and toad that are the witches' familiars. A familiar is an attendant spirit, often taking animal form.

[4] Anon—right away.

Act One, Scene Two

At King Duncan's camp near the battlefield, a wounded captain tells the king that a rebel army was victorious until Macbeth and Banquo fearlessly counterattacked. Macbeth fought his way through the enemy forces and killed their leader. Then the Thane of Ross arrives to report that Macbeth has defeated invading Norwegian forces, which were assisted by a Scottish traitor, the Thane of Cawdor. Duncan orders that Macbeth be given Cawdor's title and lands.

Alarum within.[1] *Enter* King Duncan, Malcolm, Donalbain, Lennox, *with* Attendants, *meeting a bleeding* Captain.

Duncan. What bloody man is that? He can report,
As seemeth by his **plight**,[2] of the revolt
The newest state.

Malcolm.   This is the sergeant
Who like a good and hardy soldier fought

5   'Gainst my captivity. Hail, brave friend!
Say to the king the knowledge of the broil[3]
As thou didst leave it.

Captain.   Doubtful it stood,
As two spent swimmers that do cling together
And choke their art. The merciless Macdonwald—

10   Worthy to be a rebel, for to that
The multiplying villainies of nature
Do swarm upon him—from the Western Isles
Of kerns and gallowglasses[4] is supplied;
And Fortune, on his damnèd quarrel smiling,

15   Showed like a rebel's whore. But all's too weak;
For brave Macbeth—well he deserves that name—
Disdaining Fortune, with his brandished steel,
Which smoked with bloody execution,

---

[1] *Alarum within*—Trumpets sound offstage, a signal that soldiers should arm themselves.
[2] **plight**—situation of difficulty or peril.
[3] broil—battle.
[4] kerns and gallowglasses—light and heavy-armed foot soldiers.

　　　　　Like valor's minion,[5] carved out his passage

20　　　Till he faced the slave,

　　　　　Which ne'er shook hands nor bade farewell to him

　　　　　Till he unseamed him from the nave to th' chops,[6]

　　　　　And fixed his head upon our battlements.

Duncan. O valiant cousin, worthy gentleman!

25　　**Captain.** As whence the sun 'gins his reflection

　　　　　Shipwrecking storms and direful thunders break,

　　　　　So from that spring whence comfort seemed to come

　　　　　Discomfort swells.[7] Mark,[8] King of Scotland, mark.

　　　　　No sooner justice had, with valor armed,

30　　　Compelled these skipping kerns to trust their heels

　　　　　But the Norweyan lord, surveying vantage,

　　　　　With furbished[9] arms and new supplies of men,

　　　　　Began a fresh assault.

Duncan. Dismayed not this our captains, Macbeth and

35　　　Banquo?

Captain. Yes, as sparrows eagles, or the hare the lion.

　　　　　If I say sooth, I must report they were

　　　　　As cannons overcharged with double cracks,[10]

　　　　　So they doubly redoubled strokes upon the foe.

40　　　Except they meant to bathe in reeking wounds

　　　　　Or memorize another Golgotha,[11]

　　　　　I cannot tell—

　　　　　But I am faint. My gashes cry for help.

Duncan. So well thy words become thee as thy wounds;

45　　　They smack of honor both.—Go get him surgeons.

[*Exit* Captain, *attended.*]

[*Enter* Ross *and* Angus.]

　　　　　Who comes here?

---

[5] minion—favorite.

[6] unseamed . . . chops—split him open from the navel to the jaw.

[7] As whence . . . swells—Just as when the sun turns back from its southward progression during winter, bringing the spring, storms come; so now when things seemed promising, trouble grew.

[8] Mark—Notice.

[9] furbished—polished.

[10] cracks—charges of gunpowder.

[11] memorize another Golgotha—make as famous for slaughter as the place where Jesus was crucified, as told in the Bible.

King Duncan (Brian Thompson) questions the wounded Captain (Christopher Evan Welch) about the battle in this scene from the 1992 production of *Macbeth* by Seattle's Intiman Theatre.

Malcolm.   The worthy Thane[12] of Ross.

Lennox. What a haste looks through his eyes!
          So should he look that seems to speak things strange.

Ross. God save the king!

50   **Duncan.** Whence cam'st thou, worthy thane?

Ross. From Fife, great King,
          Where the Norweyan banners flout the sky
          And fan our people cold.
          Norway himself, with terrible numbers,

55   Assisted by that most disloyal traitor,
          The Thane of Cawdor, began a dismal conflict,
          Till that Bellona's bridegroom, lapped in proof,[13]
          Confronted him with self-comparisons,
          Point against point, rebellious arm 'gainst arm,

60   Curbing his lavish spirit, and to conclude,
          The victory fell on us.

Duncan.   Great happiness!

Ross.   That now
          Sweno, the Norways' king, craves composition;
          Nor would we deign him burial of his men
          Till he disbursèd at Saint Colme's Inch[14]

65   Ten thousand dollars to our general use.

Duncan. No more that Thane of Cawdor shall deceive
          Our bosom interest. Go pronounce his present death,
          And with his former title greet Macbeth.

Ross. I'll see it done.

70   **Duncan.** What he hath lost noble Macbeth hath won.
          [*They exit.*]

---

[12] Thane—ancient Scottish title for the most important men in Scotland next to the king.

[13] Till that . . . proof—until Macbeth, clad in strong armor. (Bellona was the Roman goddess of war.)

[14] Saint Colme's Inch—Inchcolm, a small island in the Firth of Forth.

Act One, Scene Three

In a bare, windy place, the witches discuss how to punish a woman who has offended one of them. Macbeth and Banquo enter. The witches first greet Macbeth by his title, Thane of Glamis, but then as Thane of Cawdor and one who soon shall be king. Banquo asks if they can promise him future glory too. After telling him that his children shall be kings, the witches suddenly vanish. Ross and Angus bring the victorious generals the king's thanks; they hail Macbeth as the Thane of Cawdor. Macbeth now wonders how he might become king and decides that fate will lead him where it will. Macbeth and Banquo agree to discuss these events later.

Thunder. Enter the three Witches.

First Witch. Where hast thou been, sister?

Second Witch. Killing swine.

Third Witch. Sister, where thou?

First Witch. A sailor's wife had chestnuts in her lap,

5   And munched, and munched, and munched. "Give me," quoth I.

    "Aroint thee,[1] witch!" the rump-fed runnion[2] cries.

    Her husband's to Aleppo gone, master o' the *Tiger;*

    But in a sieve I'll thither sail,

    And, like a rat without a tail,

10   I'll do, I'll do, and I'll do.

Second Witch. I'll give thee a wind.

First Witch. Thou'rt kind.

Third Witch. And I another.

First Witch. I myself have all the other,

15   And the very ports they blow,

    All the quarters that they know

    I' the shipman's card.[3]

    I'll drain him dry as hay.

    Sleep shall neither night nor day

20   Hang upon his penthouse lid.[4]

---

[1] Aroint thee—be gone.

[2] rump-fed runnion—mangy creature fed on garbage.

[3] shipman's card—sailor's compass.

[4] penthouse lid—eyelid.

He shall live a man forbid.
Weary sev'nnights, nine times nine,
Shall he dwindle, peak, and pine.
Though his bark cannot be lost,

25   Yet it shall be tempest-tossed.
Look what I have.

Second Witch. Show me, show me!

First Witch. Here I have a pilot's thumb,
Wrecked as homeward he did come.

[*Drum within.*]

30   **Third Witch.** A drum, a drum!
Macbeth doth come.

All. The Weird[5] Sisters, hand in hand,
Posters of the sea and land,
Thus do go about, about,

35   Thrice to thine, and thrice to mine,
And thrice again, to make up nine.
Peace! The charm's wound up.

[*Enter* Macbeth *and* Banquo.]

Macbeth. So foul and fair a day I have not seen.

Banquo. How far is't called to Forres?—What are these,

40   So withered and so wild in their attire,
That look not like th' inhabitants o' th' Earth
And yet are on 't?— Live you? Or are you aught
That man may question? You seem to understand me
By each at once her chappy[6] finger laying

45   Upon her skinny lips. You should be women,
And yet your beards forbid me to interpret
That you are so.

Macbeth.   Speak, if you can. What are you?

First Witch. All hail, Macbeth! Hail to thee, Thane of Glamis!

Second Witch. All hail, Macbeth! Hail to thee, Thane of Cawdor!

50   **Third Witch.** All hail, Macbeth, that shalt be king hereafter!

Banquo. Good sir, why do you start and seem to fear
Things that do sound so fair?—I' the name of truth,
Are ye fantastical, or that indeed

---

[5] Weird—fateful, fate-determining, supernatural.
[6] chappy—chapped.

Which outwardly ye show? My noble partner
55   You greet with present grace and great prediction
        Of noble having and of royal hope,
        That he seems rapt withal. To me you speak not.
        If you can look into the seeds of time
        And say which grain will grow and which will not,
60   Speak, then, to me, who neither beg nor fear
        Your favors nor your hate.
First Witch. Hail!
Second Witch. Hail!
Third Witch. Hail!
65 **First Witch.** Lesser than Macbeth, and greater.
Second Witch. Not so happy,[7] yet much happier.
Third Witch. Thou shalt get[8] kings, though thou be none.
        So all hail, Macbeth and Banquo!
First Witch. Banquo and Macbeth, all hail!
70 **Macbeth.** Stay, you imperfect speakers, tell me more!
        By Sinel's death I know I am Thane of Glamis,
        But how of Cawdor? The Thane of Cawdor lives
        A prosperous gentleman; and to be king
        Stands not within the prospect of belief,
75   No more than to be Cawdor. Say from whence
        You owe this strange intelligence, or why
        Upon this blasted heath you stop our way
        With such prophetic greeting? Speak, I charge you.
[Witches *vanish*.]
Banquo. The earth hath bubbles, as the water has,
80   And these are of them. Whither are they vanished?
Macbeth. Into the air; and what seemed corporal[9] melted,
        As breath into the wind. Would they had stayed!
Banquo. Were such things here as we do speak about?
        Or have we eaten on the insane root
85   That takes the reason prisoner?
Macbeth. Your children shall be kings.
Banquo.   You shall be king.

---

[7] happy—fortunate.
[8] get—beget, sire.
[9] corporal—of the body; real.

Macbeth. And Thane of Cawdor too. Went it not so?

Banquo. To th' selfsame tune and words.—Who's here?

[*Enter Ross and Angus.*]

Ross. The king hath happily received, Macbeth,
90   The news of thy success; and when he reads
     Thy personal venture in the rebels' fight,
     His wonders and his praises do contend
     Which should be thine or his. Silenced with that,
     In viewing o'er the rest o' the selfsame day
95   He finds thee in the stout Norweyan ranks,
     Nothing afeard of what thyself didst make,
     Strange images of death. As thick as tale,
     Came post with post, and every one did bear
     Thy praises in his kingdom's great defense,
100   And poured them down before him.

Angus.   We are sent
     To give thee from our royal master thanks,
     Only to herald thee into his sight,
     Not pay thee.

Banquo (left) and Macbeth encounter the three Witches.

Why do you dress me in borrowed robes?

Ross. And, for an earnest of a greater honor,
105   He bade me, from him, call thee Thane of Cawdor;
      In which addition, hail, most worthy thane,
      For it is thine.
Banquo.   What, can the devil speak true?
Macbeth. The Thane of Cawdor lives. Why do you dress me
      In borrowed robes?
Angus.   Who was the thane lives yet,
110   But under heavy judgment bears that life
      Which he deserves to lose. Whether he was combined
      With those of Norway, or did line the rebel
      With hidden help and vantage, or that with both
      He labored in his country's wrack,[10] I know not;
115   But treasons capital, confessed and proved,
      Have overthrown him.
Macbeth [*aside*]. Glamis, and Thane of Cawdor!
      The greatest is behind. [*To Ross and Angus.*] Thanks
           for your pains.
      [*Aside to Banquo.*] Do you not hope your children shall be kings,
120   When those that gave the Thane of Cawdor to me
      Promised no less to them?
Banquo [*to Macbeth*].   That, trusted home,
      Might yet enkindle[11] you unto the crown,
      Besides the Thane of Cawdor. But 'tis strange;
      And oftentimes to win us to our harm
125   The instruments of darkness tell us truths,
      Win us with honest trifles, to betray 's
      In deepest consequence.—
      Cousins, a word, I pray you.
Macbeth [*aside*]. Two truths are told,
130   As happy prologues to the swelling act
      Of the imperial theme.—I thank you, gentlemen.

---

[10] wrack—ruin.

[11] enkindle—set on fire, act as a catalyst.

[*Aside.*] This supernatural soliciting
Cannot be ill, cannot be good. If ill,
Why hath it given me earnest of success
135　Commencing in a truth? I am Thane of Cawdor.
If good, why do I yield to that suggestion
Whose horrid image doth unfix my hair
And make my seated heart knock at my ribs,
Against the use of nature? Present fears
140　Are less than horrible imaginings.
My thought, whose murder yet is but fantastical,
Shakes so my single state of man
That function is smothered in surmise,
And nothing is but what is not.[12]

145　**Banquo.** Look how our partner's rapt.

Macbeth [*aside*]. If chance will have me king, why, chance may crown me
Without my stir.

Banquo.　　　　New honors come upon him,
Like our strange garments, cleave not to their mold[13]
But with the aid of use.

Macbeth [*aside*].　　　　Come what come may,
150　Time and the hour runs through the roughest day.

Banquo. Worthy Macbeth, we stay upon your leisure.

Macbeth. Give me your favor. My dull brain was wrought
With things forgotten. Kind gentlemen, your pains
Are registered where every day I turn
155　The leaf to read them. Let us toward the king.
[*Aside to* Banquo.] Think upon what hath chanced,
　　and at more time,
The **interim**[13] having weighed it, let us speak
Our free hearts each to other.

Banquo [*to* Macbeth]. Very gladly.

160　**Macbeth** [*to* Banquo]. Till then, enough.—Come, friends
[*They exit.*]

---

[12] My thought . . . not—Just the thought of murder so overwhelms me that my whole being is given over to this imagined action, and nothing exists for me but the imaginary.

[13] cleave not to their mold—do not fit the body's form.

[14] **interim**—interval of time between two events.

Act One, Scene Four

At King Duncan's palace at Forres, he lavishes praise on Macbeth and Banquo for the victory. Duncan then names his son Malcolm as heir to the throne. The company retires to Macbeth's castle, and as they go, Macbeth muses that Malcolm now stands in his way to the throne.

Flourish.[1] *Enter* King Duncan, Lennox, Malcolm, Donalbain, *and* Attendants.

Duncan. Is execution done on Cawdor? Are not
　　Those in commission yet returned?

Malcolm.　　　　　　　　　　　　My liege,[2]
　　They are not yet come back. But I have spoke
　　With one that saw him die, who did report
5　　That very frankly he confessed his treasons,
　　Implored Your Highness' pardon, and set forth
　　A deep repentance. Nothing in his life
　　Became him like the leaving it. He died
　　As one that had been studied in his death
10　　To throw away the dearest thing he owed
　　As 'twere a careless trifle.

Duncan.　　　　　　　　　　There's no art
　　To find the mind's construction in the face.
　　He was a gentleman on whom I built
　　An absolute trust.
[*Enter* Macbeth, Banquo, Ross, *and* Angus.]
　　　　　　　　　　　　O worthiest cousin!
15　　The sin of my ingratitude even now
　　Was heavy on me. Thou art so far before
　　That swiftest wing of **recompense**[3] is slow
　　To overtake thee. Would thou hadst less deserved,
　　That the proportion both of thanks and payment

---

[1] *Flourish*—trumpets sound.
[2] liege—lord.
[3] **recompense**—repayment.

20 Might have been mine! Only I have left to say,
   More is thy due than more than all can pay.

Macbeth. The service and the loyalty I owe,
   In doing it, pays itself. Your Highness' part
   Is to receive our duties; and our duties
25 Are to your throne and state children and servants,
   Which do but what they should by doing everything
   Safe toward[4] your love and honor.

Duncan.   Welcome hither!
   I have begun to plant thee and will labor
   To make thee full of growing. —Noble Banquo,
30 That hast no less deserved, nor must be known
   No less to have done so, let me enfold thee
   And hold thee to my heart.

Banquo.   There if I grow,
   The harvest is your own.

Duncan.   My plenteous joys,
   Wanton[5] in fullness, seek to hide themselves
35 In drops of sorrow.—Sons, kinsmen, thanes,
   And you whose places are the nearest, know
   We will establish our estate upon
   Our eldest, Malcolm, whom we name hereafter
   The Prince of Cumberland;[6] which honor must
40 Not unaccompanied invest[7] him only,
   But signs of nobleness, like stars, shall shine
   On all deservers.—From hence to Inverness,[8]
   And bind us further to you.

Macbeth. The rest is labor which is not used for you.
45 I'll be myself the **harbinger**[9] and make joyful
   The hearing of my wife with your approach;
   So humbly take my leave.

Duncan.   My worthy Cawdor!

---

[4] **Safe toward**—protective of.

[5] **Wanton**—unrestrained.

[6] **Prince of Cumberland**—title of the heir to the Scottish throne.

[7] **invest**—clothe; adorn.

[8] **Inverness**—site of Macbeth's castle.

[9] **harbinger**—forerunner.

> *Stars, hide your fires;*
> *Let not light see my black and deep desires.*

Macbeth [*aside*]. The Prince of Cumberland! That is a step
    On which I must fall down or else o'erleap,
50   For in my way it lies. Stars, hide your fires;
    Let not light see my black and deep desires.
    The eye wink at the hand; yet let that be
    Which the eye fears, when it is done, to see.
[*He exits.*]
Duncan. True, worthy Banquo. He is full so valiant,
55   And in his commendations I am fed;
    It is a banquet to me. Let's after him,
    Whose care is gone before to bid us welcome.
    It is a peerless kinsman.
[*Flourish. They exit.*]

Act One, Scene Five

In Macbeth's castle at Inverness, Lady Macbeth reads a letter from her husband describing what has happened. A messenger announces that the king and his followers are soon to arrive at Inverness to celebrate the victory. When Macbeth enters, Lady Macbeth hails him and tells him to prepare himself for great deeds but to keep his desires hidden.

     Enter Lady Macbeth, *alone, with a letter.*

Lady Macbeth [*reads*]. "They met me in the day of success; and I have
     learned by the perfect'st report they have more in them than mortal
     knowledge. When I burned in desire to question them further, they
     made themselves air, into which they vanished. Whiles I stood rapt
5   in the wonder of it came missives from the king, who all-hailed me
     'Thane of Cawdor,' by which title, before, these Weird Sisters saluted
     me, and referred me to the coming on of time with 'Hail, king that
     shalt be!' This have I thought good to deliver thee, my dearest partner
     of greatness, that thou might'st not lose the dues of rejoicing by being
10   ignorant of what greatness is promised thee. Lay it to thy heart,
     and farewell."
     Glamis thou art, and Cawdor, and shalt be
     What thou art promised. Yet do I fear thy nature;
     It is too full o' the milk of human kindness
15   To catch the nearest way. Thou wouldst be great,
     Art not without ambition, but without
     The illness should attend it. What thou wouldst highly,
     That wouldst thou holily; wouldst not play false,
     And yet wouldst wrongly win. Thou'd'st have, great Glamis,
20   That which cries "Thus thou must do," if thou have it,
     And that which rather thou dost fear to do
     Than wishest should be undone. Hie[1] thee hither,
     That I may pour my spirits in thine ear
     And chastise with the valor of my tongue
25   All that impedes thee from the golden round

---

[1] Hie—hurry.

Which fate and metaphysical aid doth seem
To have thee crowned withal.

[*Enter a* Messenger.]

                                           What is your tidings?

Messenger. The king comes here tonight.

Lady Macbeth.   Thou'rt mad to say it!
Is not thy master with him, who, were 't so,
30   Would have informed for preparation?

Messenger. So please you, it is true. Our thane is coming.
One of my fellows had the speed of him,
Who, almost dead for breath, had scarcely more
Than would make up his message.

Lady Macbeth.   Give him tending;
35   He brings great news.

[*Exit* Messenger.]

                             The raven himself is hoarse
That croaks the fatal entrance of Duncan
Under my battlements. Come, you spirits
That tend on **mortal**[2] thoughts, unsex me here
And fill me from the crown to the toe top-full
40   Of direst cruelty! Make thick my blood;
Stop up th' access and passage to remorse,
That no compunctious visitings of nature
Shake my fell purpose, nor keep peace between
Th' effect and it! Come to my woman's breasts
45   And take my milk for gall, you murdering ministers,
Wherever in your sightless substances
You wait on nature's mischief! Come, thick night,
And pall thee in the dunnest smoke of hell,
That my keen knife see not the wound it makes,
50   Nor heaven peep through the blanket of the dark
To cry "Hold, hold!"

[*Enter* Macbeth.]

                       Great Glamis! Worthy Cawdor!
Greater than both by the all-hail hereafter!
Thy letters have transported me beyond

---

[2] **mortal**—deadly.

Lady Macbeth (Stephanie Roth-Haberle) is delighted by her husband's letter in this scene from the Hartford Stage Company production.

This ignorant present, and I feel now
55　　　The future in the instant.
Macbeth.　　　　　　　　My dearest love,
　　　Duncan comes here tonight.
Lady Macbeth. And when goes hence?
Macbeth. Tomorrow, as he purposes.
Lady Macbeth.　　　　　　　　O, never
　　　Shall sun that morrow see!
　　　Your face, my thane, is as a book where men
60　　　May read strange matters. To beguile the time,
　　　Look like the time; bear welcome in your eye,
　　　Your hand, your tongue. Look like th' innocent flower,
　　　But be the serpent under 't. He that's coming
　　　Must be provided for; and you shall put
65　　　This night's great business into my dispatch,
　　　Which shall to all our nights and days to come
　　　Give solely sovereign sway and masterdom.
Macbeth. We will speak further.
Lady Macbeth.　　　　　　　Only look up clear.
　　　To alter favor ever is to fear.[3]
70　　　Leave all the rest to me.
　　　[*They exit.*]

---

[3] look . . . fear—appear calm; to change expression will create suspicion.

Act One, Scene Six

King Duncan and his followers arrive at Macbeth's castle. The king and Lady

Macbeth exchange courtesies before he enters the castle.

Hautboys[1] *and torches. Enter* King Duncan, Malcolm, Donalbain, Banquo, Lennox, Macduff, Ross, Angus, *and* Attendants.

Duncan. This castle hath a pleasant seat.[2] The air
    Nimbly and sweetly recommends itself
    Unto our gentle senses.
Banquo.   This guest of summer,
    The temple-haunting martlet, does approve

5   By his loved mansionry that the heaven's breath
    Smells wooingly here.[3] No jutty, frieze,
    Buttress, nor coign of vantage[4] but this bird
    Hath made his **pendent**[5] bed and procreant[6] cradle.
    Where they most breed and haunt, I have observed

10   The air is delicate.
[*Enter* Lady Macbeth.]
Duncan.   See, see, our honored hostess!
    The love that follows us sometimes is our trouble,
    Which still we thank as love. Herein I teach you
    How you shall bid God 'ild[7] us for your pains,
    And thank us for your trouble.
Lady Macbeth.   All our service

15   In every point twice done, and then done double,
    Were poor and single business[8] to contend

---

[1] *Hautboys*—powerful wind instruments designed for outdoor ceremonies.

[2] seat—location.

[3] This guest . . . here—This summer bird, the martin, which usually nests in churches, shows by building nests here that the weather is mild in this area.

[4] frieze . . . vantage—various sections of a building's exterior.

[5] **pendent**—hanging.

[6] procreant—producing offspring.

[7] God 'ild—God yield.

[8] single business—weak service.

Against those honors deep and broad wherewith
Your Majesty loads our house. For those of old,
And the late dignities heaped up to them,
20   We rest your hermits.[9]

Duncan.   Where's the Thane of Cawdor?
We coursed him at the heels, and had a purpose
To be his purveyor,[10] but he rides well,
And his great love, sharp as his spur, hath helped him
To his home before us. Fair and noble hostess,
25   We are your guest tonight.

Lady Macbeth.   Your servants ever
Have theirs, themselves, and what is theirs in compt
To make their audit at Your Highness' pleasure,
Still to return your own.[11]

Duncan.   Give me your hand.
Conduct me to mine host. We love him highly,
30   And shall continue our graces towards him.
By your leave, hostess.

[*They exit.*]

---

[9] rest your hermits—will remain your hermits; that is, will pray for you like holy men.

[10] coursed . . . purveyor—followed swiftly after him, hoping to be like a servant sent ahead to provide for entertainment.

[11] Your servants . . . your own—Those who serve you hold their own servants and all their possessions in trust from you. Your servants are at your disposal whenever you wish, ready always to render back to you what is yours.

Act One, Scene Seven

In a room in the castle, Macbeth tells himself why it would be a terrible thing to murder Duncan and thus betray his king, kinsman, and guest. He tells Lady Macbeth his thoughts, but she tells him he is a coward, afraid to act on his desires. She suggests a plan to murder Duncan, which Macbeth accepts.

Hautboys and torches. Enter a Butler *and* Servants *with dishes and service. They pass across the stage. Then enter* Macbeth.

Macbeth. If it were done when 'tis done, then 'twere well
It were done quickly. If th' assassination
Could trammel up[1] the consequence, and catch
With his surcease[2] success—that but this blow
5   Might be the be-all and the end-all here,
But here, upon this bank and **shoal**[3] of time,
We'd jump the life to come. But in these cases
We still have judgment here, that we but teach
Bloody instructions, which, being taught, return
10   To plague th' inventor. This even-handed justice
Commends th' ingredience of our poisoned chalice[4]
To our own lips. He's here in double trust:
First, as I am his kinsman and his subject,
Strong both against the deed; then, as his host,
15   Who should against his murderer shut the door,
Not bear the knife myself. Besides, this Duncan
Hath borne his faculties so meek, hath been
So clear in his great office, that his virtues
Will plead like angels, trumpet-tongued, against
20   The deep damnation of his taking-off;
And Pity, like a naked newborn babe

---

[1] trammel up—prevent, restrain.

[2] surcease—death, coming to an end.

[3] **shoal**—shallow place in a body of water.

[4] chalice—cup or goblet.

Striding the blast, or heaven's cherubin,[5] horsed
Upon the sightless couriers of the air,
Shall blow the horrid deed in every eye,
That tears shall drown the wind. I have no spur
To prick the sides of my intent, but only
Vaulting ambition, which o'erleaps itself
And falls on th' other—

[*Enter* Lady Macbeth.]

How now, what news?

Lady Macbeth. He has almost supped. Why have you left the chamber?

Macbeth. Hath he asked for me?

Lady Macbeth.   Know you not he has?

Macbeth. We will proceed no further in this business.
He hath honored me of late, and I have bought
Golden opinions from all sorts of people,
Which would be worn now in their newest gloss,
Not cast aside so soon.

Lady Macbeth.   Was the hope drunk
Wherein you dressed yourself?[6] Hath it slept since?
And wakes it now, to look so green and pale
At what it did so freely? From this time
Such I account thy love. Art thou afeard
To be the same in thine own act and valor
As thou art in desire? Wouldst thou have that
Which thou esteem'st the ornament of life,
And live a coward in thine own esteem,
Letting "I dare not" wait upon "I would,"
Like the poor cat i' th' adage?[7]

Macbeth.   Prithee, peace!
I dare do all that may become a man;
Who dares do more is none.

Lady Macbeth.   What beast was 't, then,
That made you break this enterprise to me?
When you durst do it, then you were a man;

---

[5] Striding . . . cherubin—mounted on the wind, or an angel.

[6] Was the hope . . . dressed yourself—Did your ambition cease when you gained these honors?

[7] cat i' th' adage—In the proverb, the cat would eat fish but will not wet her feet.

But screw your courage to the sticking place
And we'll not fail.

And, to be more than what you were, you would
Be so much more the man. Nor time nor place
Did then adhere, and yet you would make both.
They have made themselves, and that their fitness now
55 Does unmake you. I have given suck, and know
How tender 'tis to love the babe that milks me;
I would, while it was smiling in my face,
Have plucked my nipple from his boneless gums
And dashed the brains out, had I so sworn as you
60 Have done to this.

Macbeth. If we should fail?

Lady Macbeth. We fail?

But screw your courage to the sticking place
And we'll not fail. When Duncan is asleep—
Whereto the rather shall his day's hard journey
Soundly invite him—his two chamberlains
65 Will I with wine and wassail so convince[8]
That memory, the warder of the brain,
Shall be a fume, and the receipt of reason
A limbeck[9] only. When in swinish sleep
Their drenchèd natures lies as in a death,
70 What cannot you and I perform upon
Th' unguarded Duncan? What not put upon
His spongy[10] officers, who shall bear the guilt
Of our great quell?[11]

Macbeth. Bring forth men-children only!
For thy undaunted mettle[12] should compose

---

[8] wassail so convince—drink so overpower.
[9] limbeck—device for distilling drinks.
[10] spongy—soaked; that is, drunken.
[11] quell—killing.
[12] mettle—spirit, temperament.

75   Nothing but males. Will it not be received,
      When we have marked with blood those sleepy two
      Of his own chamber and used their very daggers,
      That they have done 't?

Lady Macbeth.   Who dares receive it other,
      As we shall make our griefs and clamor roar
80   Upon his death?

Macbeth.   I am settled, and bend up
      Each corporal agent to this terrible feat.
      Away, and mock the time with fairest show.
      False face must hide what the false heart doth know.

[*They exit.*]

In this scene from the Hartford Stage production, Lady Macbeth (Stephanie Roth-Haberle) advises her husband (Denis O'Hare) to "screw his courage to the sticking place."

Act Two, Scene One

In the castle, Macbeth meets Banquo and his son Fleance late at night. Banquo says he is still troubled by the witches' prophecy, which Macbeth pretends he has forgotten. Macbeth tells Banquo that he will give him honors should Banquo support him in a time of need. Banquo agrees but makes no commitments before they part. As Macbeth prepares to commit the murder, he imagines that he sees a bloody dagger floating in the air, drawing him to Duncan's room. A bell sounds to indicate that Lady Macbeth has completed her preparations. Macbeth exits to murder Duncan.

Enter Banquo *and* Fleance *with a torch before him.*

Banquo. How goes the night, boy?

Fleance. The moon is down. I have not heard the clock.

Banquo. And she goes down at twelve.

Fleance.   I take 't, 'tis later, sir.

Banquo. Hold, take my sword. There's
            husbandry[1] in heaven;

5   Their candles are all out. Take thee that too.
           A heavy summons lies like lead upon me,
           And yet I would not sleep. Merciful powers,
           Restrain in me the cursèd thoughts that nature
           Gives way to in repose!

[*Enter* Macbeth, *and a* Servant *with a torch.*]
                                    Give me my sword.

10   Who's there?

Macbeth. A friend.

Banquo. What, sir, not yet at rest? The king's abed.
           He hath been in unusual pleasure,
           And sent forth great largess to your offices.[2]

15   This diamond he greets your wife withal,
           By the name of most kind hostess, and shut up
           In measureless content.

---

[1] husbandry—economy.

[2] largess to your offices—gifts to your servants.

In the Intiman Theatre production, Macbeth (Daniel Reichart) confronts the phantom dagger on his way to murder Duncan.

Macbeth.   Being unprepared,
Our will became the servant to defect,
Which else should free have wrought.

Banquo.   All's well.
20 I dreamt last night of the three Weird Sisters.
To you they have showed some truth.

Macbeth.   I think not of them.
Yet, when we can entreat an hour to serve,
We would spend it in some words upon that business,
If you would grant the time.

Banquo.   At your kind'st leisure.

25 **Macbeth.** If you shall cleave to my consent when 'tis,[3]
It shall make honor for you.

Banquo.   So I lose none
In seeking to augment it, but still keep
My bosom franchised[4] and allegiance clear,
I shall be counseled.

Macbeth.   Good repose the while!

30 **Banquo.** Thanks, sir. The like to you.
[*Exit* Banquo *with* Fleance.]

Macbeth [*to* Servant]. Go bid thy mistress, when my drink is ready,
She strike upon the bell. Get thee to bed.
[*Exit* Servant.]

---

[3] cleave . . . 'tis—support me when the time comes.
[4] franchised—free (from guilt).

Is this a dagger which I see before me,
The handle toward my hand? Come, let me clutch thee.
35 I have thee not, and yet I see thee still.
Art thou not, fatal vision, sensible
To feeling as to sight? Or art thou but
A dagger of the mind, a false creation,
Proceeding from the heat-oppressèd brain?
40 I see thee yet, in form as palpable
As this which now I draw.
Thou marshal'st me the way that I was going,
And such an instrument I was to use.
Mine eyes are made the fools o' th' other senses,
45 Or else worth all the rest. I see thee still,
And on thy blade and dudgeon gouts[5] of blood,
Which was not so before. There's no such thing.
It is the bloody business which informs
Thus to mine eyes. Now o'er the one-half world
50 Nature seems dead, and wicked dreams abuse
The curtained sleep. Witchcraft celebrates
Pale Hecate's offerings, and withered Murder,
Alarumed by his sentinel, the wolf,
Whose howl's his watch, thus with his stealthy pace,
55 With Tarquin's[6] ravishing strides, towards his design
Moves like a ghost. Thou sure and firm-set earth,
Hear not my steps which way they walk, for fear
Thy very stones prate of my whereabouts
And take the present horror from the time
60 Which now suits with it. Whiles I threat, he lives;
Words to the heat of deeds too cold breath gives.
[*A bell rings.*]
I go, and it is done. The bell invites me.
Hear it not, Duncan, for it is a knell[7]
That summons thee to heaven or to hell.
[*He exits.*]

---

[5] dudgeon gouts—handle drops.

[6] Hecate's . . . Tarquin's—Hecate was goddess of witchcraft; Tarquin was an Etruscan who raped the Roman woman Lucretia.

[7] knell—bell rung slowly for a death.

Act Two, Scene Two

In the castle, Lady Macbeth says she has drugged the grooms guarding Duncan. When Macbeth appears, he is full of remorse. He has the bloody daggers that he should have left in Duncan's room as evidence against the grooms. Lady Macbeth tells him she is disgusted by his unmanliness and puts the daggers back in the grooms' room. When she returns, she urges Macbeth, who is paralyzed with horror, to wash the blood from his hands. They hear knocking at the gate.

Enter Lady Macbeth.

Lady Macbeth. That which hath made them drunk hath made me bold;
    What hath quenched them hath given me fire. Hark! Peace!
    It was the owl that shrieked, the fatal bellman,
    Which gives the stern'st good-night. He is about it.[1]
5   The doors are open; and the **surfeited**[2] grooms
    Do mock their charge with snores. I have drugged their possets,[3]
    That death and nature do contend about them
    Whether they live or die.
Macbeth [*within*].   Who's there? What, ho!
Lady Macbeth. Alack, I am afraid they have awaked,
10   And 'tis not done. Th' attempt and not the deed
    Confounds us. Hark!—I laid their daggers ready;
    He could not miss 'em. Had he not resembled
    My father as he slept, I had done 't.
[*Enter* Macbeth.]
    My husband!
15 **Macbeth.** I have done the deed. Didst thou not hear a noise?
Lady Macbeth. I heard the owl scream and the crickets cry.
    Did not you speak?
Macbeth. When?
Lady Macbeth. Now.
20 **Macbeth.** As I descended?

---

[1] He . . . it—that is, Macbeth is murdering the king.
[2] **surfeited**—having eaten and drunk to excess.
[3] possets—hot bedtime drinks.

Lady Macbeth. Ay.

Macbeth. Hark! Who lies i' the second chamber?

Lady Macbeth. Donalbain.

Macbeth. This is a sorry sight.

25 **Lady Macbeth.** A foolish thought, to say a sorry sight.

Macbeth. There's one did laugh in 's sleep, and one cried "Murder!"
  That they did wake each other. I stood and heard them.
  But they did say their prayers, and addressed them
  Again to sleep.

Lady Macbeth.   There are two lodged together.

30 **Macbeth.** One cried "God bless us!" and "Amen!" the other,
  As they had seen me with these hangman's hands.
  List'ning their fear, I could not say "Amen"
  When they did say "God bless us!"

Lady Macbeth. Consider it not so deeply.

35 **Macbeth.** But wherefore could not I pronounce "Amen"?
  I had most need of blessing, and "Amen"
  Stuck in my throat.

Lady Macbeth.   These deeds must not be thought
  After these ways; so, it will make us mad.

Macbeth. Methought I heard a voice cry "Sleep no more!

40 Macbeth does murder sleep," the innocent sleep,
  Sleep that knits up the raveled sleave[4] of care,
  The death of each day's life, sore labor's bath,
  Balm of hurt minds, great nature's second course,
  Chief nourisher in life's feast—

Lady Macbeth.   What do you mean?

45 **Macbeth.** Still it cried "Sleep no more!" to all the house;
  "Glamis hath murdered sleep, and therefore Cawdor
  Shall sleep no more; Macbeth shall sleep no more."

Lady Macbeth. Who was it that thus cried? Why, worthy thane,
  You do unbend your noble strength to think
50 So brainsickly of things. Go get some water
  And wash this filthy witness from your hand.—
  Why did you bring these daggers from the place?
  They must lie there. Go, carry them and smear
  The sleepy grooms with blood.

---

[4] raveled sleave—tangled threads.

Macbeth.   I'll go no more.

55   I am afraid to think what I have done;
       Look on 't again I dare not.

Lady Macbeth.   Infirm of purpose!
       Give me the daggers. The sleeping and the dead
       Are but as pictures. 'Tis the eye of childhood
       That fears a painted devil. If he do bleed,

60   I'll gild[5] the faces of the grooms withal,
       For it must seem their guilt.

---

[5] gild—smear.

Refusing to return to the murdered Duncan's bedchamber with the bloody daggers, Macbeth (Denis O'Hare) surrenders them to his wife (Stephanie Roth-Haberle) in this scene from the Hartford Stage Company production.

Will all great Neptune's ocean wash this blood Clean from my hand?

[*She exits. Knocking within.*]

Macbeth.   Whence is that knocking?
How is 't with me, when every noise appalls me?
What hands are here? Ha! They pluck out mine eyes.
Will all great Neptune's ocean wash this blood
65 Clean from my hand? No, this my hand will rather
The multitudinous seas incarnadine,[6]
Making the green one red.

[*Enter* Lady Macbeth.]

Lady Macbeth. My hands are of your color, but I shame
To wear a heart so white. [*Knock.*] I hear a knocking
70 At the south entry. Retire we to our chamber.
A little water clears us of this deed.
How easy is it, then! Your constancy
Hath left you unattended.[7] [*Knock.*] Hark! More knocking.
Get on your nightgown, lest occasion call us
75 And show us to be watchers. Be not lost
So poorly in your thoughts.

Macbeth. To know my deed, 'twere best not know myself.

[*Knock.*]

Wake Duncan with thy knocking! I would thou couldst!

[*They exit.*]

---

[6] incarnadine—turn blood-red.

[7] constancy . . . unattended—courage has left you.

Act Two, Scene Three

At the castle gate, a drunken porter slowly goes to answer the knocking. He imagines himself guarding the gates of hell. Macduff and Lennox enter to call for the king. Macbeth comes to greet them. When Macduff discovers the murder, his shouts awaken the castle's guests. Macbeth kills the blood-covered grooms. The assembled lords agree to hunt out the truth of the horror. Duncan's sons, fearing for their own lives, decide to escape, Malcolm to England, and Donalbain to Ireland.

Enter a Porter. *Knocking within.*

Porter. Here's a knocking indeed! If a man were porter of hell gate, he should have old turning the key.¹ [*Knock.*] Knock, knock, knock! Who's there, i' the name of Beelzebub?² Here's a farmer that hanged himself on th' expectation of plenty. Come in time! Have napkins enough about you; here you'll sweat for 't. [*Knock.*] Knock, knock! Who's there, in th' other devil's name? Faith, here's an **equivocator**,³ that could swear in both the scales against either scale, who committed treason enough for God's sake, yet could not equivocate to heaven. O, come in, equivocator. [*Knock.*] Knock, knock, knock! Who's there? Faith, here's an English tailor come hither for stealing out of a French hose. Come in, tailor. Here you may roast your goose. [*Knock.*] Knock, knock! Never at quiet! What are you? But this place is too cold for hell. I'll devil-porter it no further. I had thought to have let in some of all professions that go the primrose⁴ way to th' everlasting bonfire. [*Knock.*] Anon, anon! [*Opens the gate.*] I pray you, remember the porter.

[*Enter* Macduff *and* Lennox.]

Macduff. Was it so late, friend, ere you went to bed,
That you do lie so late?

Porter. Faith, sir, we were carousing till the second cock; and drink, sir, is a great provoker of three things.

Macduff. What three things does drink especially provoke?

---

¹ old . . . key—plenty of key turning.
² Beelzebub—prince of devils.
³ **equivocator**—one who avoids making explicit statements.
⁴ primrose—easy or full of pleasure.

Porter. Marry, sir, nose-painting, sleep, and urine. Lechery, sir, it provokes and unprovokes: it provokes the desire, but it takes away the performance. Therefore much drink may be said to be an equivocator with lechery: it makes him and it mars him; it sets him on and it takes him off; it persuades him and disheartens him; makes him stand to and not stand to; in conclusion, equivocates him in a sleep and, giving him the lie, leaves him.

Macduff. I believe drink gave thee the lie last night.

Porter. That it did, sir, i' the very throat on me. But I requited him for his lie, and, I think, being too strong for him, though he took up my legs sometimes, yet I made a shift to cast him.

Macduff. Is thy master stirring?

[*Enter* Macbeth.]

Our knocking has awaked him. Here he comes.

[*Exit* Porter.]

Lennox. Good morrow, noble sir.

Macbeth.   Good morrow, both.

Macduff. Is the king stirring, worthy thane?

The porter (Ken Granthman) in the Hartford Stage Company production considers the nature of "equivocation."

Macbeth.   Not yet.

Macduff. He did command me to call timely on him.
    I have almost slipped the hour.

Macbeth.   I'll bring you to him.

Macduff. I know this is a joyful trouble to you,
    But yet 'tis one.

40   **Macbeth.** The labor we delight in physics[5] pain.
    This is the door.

Macduff.   I'll make so bold to call,
    For 'tis my limited service.[6]

[*Exit* Macduff.]

Lennox. Goes the king hence today?

Macbeth. He does; he did appoint so.

45   **Lennox.** The night has been unruly. Where we lay,
    Our chimneys were blown down, and, as they say,
    Lamentings heard i' th' air, strange screams of death,
    And prophesying with accents terrible
    Of dire combustion and confused events

50   New hatched to th' woeful time. The obscure bird[7]
    Clamored the livelong night. Some say the earth
    Was feverous and did shake.

Macbeth.   'Twas a rough night.

Lennox. My young remembrance cannot parallel
    A fellow to it.

[*Enter* Macduff.]

Macduff.   O, horror, horror, horror!

55   Tongue nor heart cannot conceive nor name thee!

Macbeth and Lennox. What's the matter?

Macduff. Confusion now hath made his masterpiece!
    Most **sacrilegious**[8] murder hath broke ope
    The Lord's **anointed**[9] temple and stole thence

60   The life o' the building!

Macbeth. What is 't you say? The life?

---

[5] physics—cures.

[6] limited service—appointed duty.

[7] obscure bird—owl.

[8] **sacrilegious**—grossly disrespectful.

[9] **anointed**—divinely chosen.

Lennox. Mean you His Majesty?

Macduff. Approach the chamber and destroy your sight
   With a new Gorgon.[10] Do not bid me speak;
65   See, and then speak yourselves.

[*Exit* Macbeth *and* Lennox.]

                                    Awake, awake!
   Ring the alarum bell. Murder and treason!
   Banquo and Donalbain, Malcolm, awake!
   Shake off this downy sleep, death's counterfeit,
   And look on death itself! Up, up, and see
70   The great doom's image! Malcolm, Banquo,
   As from your graves rise up and walk like sprites
   To countenance[11] this horror! Ring the bell.

[*Bell rings.*]

[*Enter* Lady Macbeth.]

Lady Macbeth. What's the business,
   That such a hideous trumpet calls to parley[12]
75   The sleepers of the house? Speak, speak!

Macduff. O gentle lady,
   'Tis not for you to hear what I can speak.
   The repetition in a woman's ear
   Would murder as it fell.

[*Enter* Banquo.]

                              O Banquo, Banquo,
80   Our royal master's murdered!

Lady Macbeth.   Woe, alas!
   What, in our house?

Banquo.   Too cruel anywhere.—
   Dear Duff, I prithee, contradict thyself
   And say it is not so.

[*Enter* Macbeth, Lennox, *and* Ross.]

Macbeth. Had I but died an hour before this chance
85   I had lived a blessèd time; for from this instant
   There's nothing serious in mortality.
   All is but toys. Renown and grace is dead;

---

[10] Gorgon—monster with a hideous face whose look turned beholders to stone.

[11] countenance—see.

[12] parley—conference between enemies.

The wine of life is drawn, and the mere lees[13]
Is left this vault[14] to brag of.

[*Enter* Malcolm *and* Donalbain.]

90   **Donalbain.** What is amiss?

Macbeth.   You are, and do not know 't.
The spring, the head, the fountain of your blood
Is stopped; the very source of it is stopped.

Macduff. Your royal father's murdered.

Malcolm.   O, by whom?

Lennox. Those of his chamber, as it seemed, had done 't.

95   Their hands and faces were all badged with blood;
So were their daggers, which unwiped we found
Upon their pillows. They stared and were distracted;
No man's life was to be trusted with them.

Macbeth. O, yet I do repent me of my fury,

100   That I did kill them.

Macduff.   Wherefore did you so?

Macbeth. Who can be wise, amazed, temp'rate and furious,
Loyal and neutral, in a moment? No man.
Th' expedition of my violent love
Outran the pauser, reason. Here lay Duncan,

105   His silver skin laced with his golden blood,
And his gashed stabs looked like a breach in nature
For ruin's wasteful entrance; there the murderers,
Steeped in the colors of their trade, their daggers
Unmannerly breeched[15] with gore. Who could refrain

110   That had a heart to love, and in that heart
Courage to make's love known?

Lady Macbeth.   Help me hence, ho!

Macduff. Look to the lady.

Malcolm [*aside to* Donalbain]. Why do we hold our tongues,
That most may claim this argument for ours?

115   **Donalbain** [*aside to* Malcolm]. What should be spoken here, where our fate,
Hid in an auger hole, may rush and seize us?
Let's away. Our tears are not yet brewed.[16]

---

[13] lees—dregs.

[14] vault—the earth (with a pun on "wine vault").

[15] breeched—covered.

[16] Our . . . brewed—We haven't time for weeping.

Malcolm [*aside to* Donalbain]. Nor our strong sorrow upon the foot of
    motion.[17]

Banquo. Look to the lady.

[Lady Macbeth *is carried out.*]

120   And when we have our naked frailties hid,[18]

    That suffer in exposure, let us meet

    And question this most bloody piece of work

    To know it further. Fears and **scruples**[19] shake us.

    In the great hand of God I stand, and thence

125   Against the undivulged pretense I fight

    Of treasonous malice.

Macduff.   And so do I.

All.   So all.

Macbeth. Let's briefly put on manly readiness

    And meet i' the hall together.

All.   Well contented.

[*Exit all but* Malcolm *and* Donalbain.]

Malcolm. What will you do? Let's not consort with them.

130   To show an unfelt sorrow is an office

    Which the false man does easy. I'll to England.

Donalbain. To Ireland, I. Our separated fortune

    Shall keep us both the safer. Where we are,

    There's daggers in men's smiles; the near in blood,

135   The nearer bloody.[20]

Malcolm.   This murderous shaft that's shot

    Hath not yet lighted, and our safest way

    Is to avoid the aim. Therefore to horse,

    And let us not be dainty of[21] leave-taking,

    But shift away. There's warrant in that theft

140   Which steals itself when there's no mercy left.

[*They exit.*]

---

[17] upon . . . motion—ready to act.

[18] naked . . . hid—bodies clothed.

[19] **scruples**—doubts, suspicions.

[20] near . . . bloody—that is, those next in line to the throne are most likely to be murdered.

[21] dainty of—polite about.

Act Two, Scene Four

Outside the castle, a short time later, an old man tells Ross about the strange events that happened on the night the king was murdered. Macduff says that Malcolm and Donalbain have fled and are suspected of bribing the grooms to murder the king. Ross says that Macbeth has gone to be crowned king. Ross will follow him, but Macduff resolves to return home.

Enter Ross *with an* Old Man.

Old Man. Threescore and ten[1] I can remember well,
　　Within the volume of which time I have seen
　　Hours dreadful and things strange, but this sore night
　　Hath trifled former knowings.

Ross. 　　　　　　　　　　　Ha, good father,
5　　Thou seest the heavens, as troubled with man's act,
　　Threatens his bloody stage.[2] By th' clock 'tis day,
　　And yet dark night strangles the traveling lamp.[3]
　　Is 't night's predominance or the day's shame
　　That darkness does the face of earth entomb
10　　When living light should kiss it?

Old Man. 　　　　　　　　　　'Tis unnatural,
　　Even like the deed that's done. On Tuesday last
　　A falcon, tow'ring in her pride of place,
　　Was by a mousing owl hawked at and killed.

Ross. And Duncan's horses—a thing most strange and certain—
15　　Beauteous and swift, the minions of their race,
　　Turned wild in nature, broke their stalls, flung out,
　　Contending 'gainst obedience, as they would
　　Make war with mankind.

Old Man. 　　　　　　　　'Tis said they eat each other.

Ross. They did so, to th' amazement of mine eyes
20　　That looked upon 't.

---

[1] Threescore and ten—seventy years.

[2] stage—the earth.

[3] traveling lamp—the sun.

[Enter Macduff.]

Here comes the good Macduff.—

How goes the world, sir, now?

Macduff. Why, see you not?

Ross. Is 't known who did this more than bloody deed?

Macduff. Those that Macbeth hath slain.

Ross. Alas the day,

What good could they pretend?

Macduff. They were **suborned**.[4]

25   Malcolm and Donalbain, the King's two sons,

Are stol'n away and fled, which puts upon them

Suspicion of the deed.

Ross. 'Gainst nature still!

Thriftless ambition, that will ravin up[5]

Thine own life's means! Then 'tis most like

30   The sovereignty will fall upon Macbeth.

Macduff. He is already named and gone to Scone[6]

To be invested.

Ross. Where is Duncan's body?

Macduff. Carried to Colmekill,[7]

The sacred storehouse of his predecessors

35   And guardian of their bones.

Ross. Will you to Scone?

Macduff. No, cousin, I'll to Fife.[8]

Ross. Well, I will thither.

Macduff. Well, may you see things well done there. Adieu,

Lest our old robes sit easier than our new!

Ross. Farewell, father.

40   **Old Man.** God's benison[9] go with you, and with those

That would make good of bad, and friends of foes!

[They exit.]

---

[4] **suborned**—bribed; hired.

[5] ravin up—devour ravenously.

[6] Scone—site of the coronation of Scottish kings.

[7] Colmekill—Iona, an island off the coast of Scotland where the Scottish kings were buried.

[8] Fife—Macduff is Thane of Fife.

[9] benison—blessing.

Act Three, Scene One

In the king's palace at Forres, Banquo wonders if Macbeth murdered his way to the throne. The new king, Macbeth, interrupts his thoughts and insists that Banquo join him at a feast. Banquo intends to go riding but promises to return in time. After dismissing his followers, Macbeth considers again the witches' prophecy that Banquo's heirs will succeed Macbeth on the throne. Macbeth arranges for two men to murder Banquo and Fleance on their ride.

Enter Banquo.

Banquo. Thou hast it now—king, Cawdor, Glamis, all
As the weird women promised, and I fear
Thou played'st most foully for 't. Yet it was said
It should not stand in thy posterity,
5   But that myself should be the root and father
Of many kings. If there come truth from them—
As upon thee, Macbeth, their speeches shine—
Why, by the verities on thee made good,
May they not be my oracles as well
10   And set me up in hope? But hush, no more.

[*Sennet*[1] *sounded. Enter Macbeth as King; Lady Macbeth as Queen; Lennox, Ross, Lords, and Attendants.*]

Macbeth. Here's our chief guest.

Lady Macbeth.   If he had been forgotten,
It had been as a gap in our great feast
And all-thing unbecoming.

Macbeth. Tonight we hold a solemn supper, sir,
15   And I'll request your presence.

Banquo.   Let Your Highness
Command upon me, to the which my duties
Are with a most **indissoluble**[2] tie
Forever knit.

Macbeth. Ride you this afternoon?

Banquo.   Ay, my good lord.

---

[1] Sennet—trumpet call.

[2] **indissoluble**—permanent, binding.

20   **Macbeth.** We should have else desired your good advice,
        Which still hath been both grave and prosperous,
        In this day's council; but we'll take tomorrow.
        Is 't far you ride?
     Banquo. As far, my lord, as will fill up the time
25   'Twixt this and supper. Go not my horse the better,
        I must become a borrower of the night
        For a dark hour or **twain**.³
     Macbeth. Fail not our feast.
     Banquo. My lord, I will not.
30   **Macbeth.** We hear our bloody cousins are bestowed
        In England and in Ireland, not confessing
        Their cruel **parricide**,⁴ filling their hearers
        With strange invention. But of that tomorrow,
        When therewithal we shall have cause of state
35   Craving us jointly. Hie you to horse. Adieu,
        Till you return at night. Goes Fleance with you?
     Banquo. Ay, my good lord. Our time does call upon 's.
     Macbeth. I wish your horses swift and sure of foot,
        And so I do commend you to their backs.
40   Farewell.
     [*Exit* Banquo.]
        Let every man be master of his time
        Till seven at night. To make society
        The sweeter welcome, we will keep ourself
        Till suppertime alone. While then, God be with you!
     [*Exit all but* Macbeth *and a* Servant.]
45   Sirrah,⁵ a word with you. Attend those men
        Our pleasure?
     Servant. They are, my lord, without the palace gate.
     Macbeth. Bring them before us.
     [*Exit* Servant.]
                                    To be thus⁶ is nothing,
        But to be safely thus.—Our fears in Banquo

---

³ **twain**—two.

⁴ **parricide**—murder of one's father.

⁵ Sirrah—form of address to a servant or child.

⁶ thus—that is, king.

Macbeth (Daniel Reichart) speaks to his servant as the two murderers wait in the background in this scene from the Intiman Theatre production.

50   Stick deep, and in his royalty of nature
Reigns that which would be feared. 'Tis much he dares;
And to that **dauntless**[7] temper of his mind
He hath a wisdom that doth guide his valor
To act in safety. There is none but he
55   Whose being I do fear, and under him
My genius is rebuked, as it is said
Mark Antony's was by Caesar.[8] He chid[9] the sisters
When first they put the name of king upon me,
And bade them speak to him. Then, prophet-like,
60   They hailed him father to a line of kings.
Upon my head they placed a fruitless crown

---

[7] **dauntless**—fearless.
[8] Mark Antony's was by Caesar—reference to Augustus Caesar, who defeated Mark Antony at the battle of Actium in 31 B.C.
[9] chid—scolded.

And put a barren scepter in my gripe,
Thence to be wrenched with an unlineal hand,
No son of mine succeeding. If 't be so,

65 For Banquo's issue have I filed[10] my mind;
For them the gracious Duncan have I murdered,
Put **rancors**[11] in the vessel of my peace
Only for them, and mine eternal jewel
Given to the common enemy of man

70 To make them kings, the seeds of Banquo kings!
Rather than so, come fate into the list,[12]
And champion me to th' utterance![13]—Who's there?

[*Enter* Servant *and two* Murderers.]

Now go to the door, and stay there till we call.

[*Exit* Servant.]

Was it not yesterday we spoke together?

75 **Murderers.** It was, so please Your Highness.

Macbeth.   Well then, now
Have you considered of my speeches? Know
That it was he, in the times past, which held you
So under fortune, which you thought had been
Our innocent self. This I made good to you

80 In our last conference, passed in probation[14] with you
How you were borne in hand, how crossed, the instruments,
Who wrought with them, and all things else that might
To half a soul and to a notion crazed[15]
Say, "Thus did Banquo."

First Murderer.   You made it known to us.

85 **Macbeth.** I did so, and went further, which is now
Our point of second meeting. Do you find
Your patience so predominant in your nature
That you can let this go? Are you so gospeled[16]

---

[10] filed—defiled.

[11] **rancors**—bitter resentments.

[12] list—place of combat.

[13] to th' utterance—to the end.

[14] passed in probation—went over the proof.

[15] To half . . . crazed—to a half-wit or a lunatic.

[16] gospeled—full of religious spirit.

<pre>
                To pray for this good man and for his issue,
        90   Whose heavy hand hath bowed you to the grave
                And beggared yours forever?
</pre>

First Murderer.   We are men, my liege.

Macbeth. Ay, in the catalogue ye go for men,

<pre>
                As hounds and greyhounds, mongrels, spaniels, curs,
                Shoughs, water-rugs, and demi-wolves[17] are clept[18]
        95   All by the name of dogs. The valued file
                Distinguishes the swift, the slow, the subtle,
                The housekeeper, the hunter, every one
                According to the gift which bounteous nature
                Hath in him closed, whereby he does receive
        100   Particular addition from the bill[19]
                That writes them all alike; and so of men.
                Now, if you have a station in the file,
                Not i' the worst rank of manhood, say 't,
                And I will put that business in your bosoms
        105   Whose execution takes your enemy off,
                Grapples you to the heart and love of us,
                Who wear our health but sickly in his life,
                Which in his death were perfect.
</pre>

Second Murderer.   I am one, my liege,

<pre>
                Whom the vile blows and buffets[20] of the world
        110   Hath so incensed that I am reckless what
                I do to spite the world.
</pre>

First Murderer.   And I another,

<pre>
                So weary with disasters, tugged with fortune,
                That I would set my life on any chance
                To mend it or be rid on 't.
</pre>

Macbeth.   Both of you

<pre>
        115   Know Banquo was your enemy.
</pre>

Both Murderers.   True, my lord.

---

[17] Shoughs, water-rugs, and demi-wolves—rough-haired lap dogs, long-haired water dogs, and crossbreeds of dog and wolf.

[18] clept—called.

[19] addition . . . bill—distinction or qualification in the inventory.

[20] buffets—beatings.

Macbeth. So is he mine, and in such bloody distance[21]
    That every minute of his being thrusts
    Against my near'st of life. And though I could
    With barefaced power sweep him from my sight
120   And bid my will **avouch**[22] it, yet I must not,
    For certain friends that are both his and mine,
    Whose loves I may not drop, but wail his fall
    Who I myself struck down. And thence it is
    That I to your assistance do make love,
125   Masking the business from the common eye
    For **sundry**[23] weighty reasons.
Second Murderer.   We shall, my lord,
    Perform what you command us.
First Murderer.   Though our lives—
Macbeth. Your spirits shine through you.[24] Within this hour at most
    I will advise you where to plant yourselves,
130   Acquaint you with the perfect spy[25] o' the time,
    The moment on 't, for 't must be done tonight,
    And something from the palace; always thought
    That I require a clearness.[26] And with him—
    To leave no rubs nor botches in the work—
135   Fleance his son, that keeps him company,
    Whose absence is no less material to me
    Than is his father's, must embrace the fate
    Of that dark hour. Resolve yourselves apart;
    I'll come to you anon.
140 **Both Murderers.** We are resolved, my lord.
    Macbeth. I'll call upon you straight. Abide within.
[*Exit* Murderers.]
    It is concluded. Banquo, thy soul's flight,
    If it find heaven, must find it out tonight.
[*He exits.*]

---

[21] bloody distance—mortal enmity.

[22] **avouch**—justify.

[23] **sundry**—various.

[24] spirits . . . you—courage is evident.

[25] spy—lookout, observation point.

[26] thought . . . clearness—borne in mind that I must remain free of suspicion.

Act Three, Scene Two

In the palace at Forres, Lady Macbeth and Macbeth talk of their unhappiness. Lady Macbeth tells Macbeth not to appear to be unhappy. He describes his fears that their throne is not safe. Macbeth agrees to seem happy that evening, and he also asks her to pay special attention to Banquo. He does not tell her of the murder set in motion.

Enter Lady Macbeth *and a* Servant.

Lady Macbeth. Is Banquo gone from court?

Servant. Ay, madam, but returns again tonight.

Lady Macbeth. Say to the king I would attend his leisure
    For a few words.

Servant.   Madam, I will.

[*Exit Servant.*]

Lady Macbeth.   Naught's had, all's spent,
5   Where our desire is got without content.
    'Tis safer to be that which we destroy
    Than by destruction dwell in doubtful joy.

[*Enter* Macbeth.]

    How now, my lord? Why do you keep alone,
    Of sorriest fancies your companions making,
10   Using those thoughts which should indeed have died
    With them they think on? Things without all remedy
    Should be without regard. What's done is done.

Macbeth. We have scorched the snake, not killed it.
    She'll close[1] and be herself, whilst our poor malice
15   Remains in danger of her former tooth.
    But let the frame of things disjoint, both the worlds suffer,[2]
    Ere we will eat our meal in fear and sleep
    In the affliction of these terrible dreams
    That shake us nightly. Better be with the dead,
20   Whom we, to gain our peace, have sent to peace,

---

[1] close—heal.

[2] let the frame . . . suffer—let the universe itself fall apart and both heaven and earth perish.

O, full of scorpions is my mind, dear wife!

Than on the torture of the mind to lie
In restless ecstasy. Duncan is in his grave;
After life's fitful fever he sleeps well.
Treason has done his worst; nor steel, nor poison,
25 Malice domestic, foreign levy,[3] nothing
Can touch him further.

Lady Macbeth.   Come on,
Gentle my lord, sleek o'er your rugged looks.
Be bright and jovial among your guests tonight.

Macbeth. So shall I, love, and so, I pray, be you.
30 Let your remembrance apply to Banquo;
Present him eminence, both with eye and tongue—
Unsafe the while, that we
Must lave our honors in these flattering streams[4]
And make our faces vizards[5] to our hearts,
35 Disguising what they are.

Lady Macbeth.   You must leave this.

Macbeth. O, full of scorpions is my mind, dear wife!
Thou know'st that Banquo and his Fleance lives.

Lady Macbeth. But in them nature's copy's not eterne.[6]

Macbeth. There's comfort yet; they are assailable.
40 Then be thou **jocund.**[7] Ere the bat hath flown
His cloistered flight, ere to black Hecate's summons
The shard-borne beetle with his drowsy hums
Hath rung night's yawning peal, there shall be done
A deed of dreadful note.

Lady Macbeth.   What's to be done?

45 **Macbeth.** Be innocent of the knowledge, dearest chuck,
Till thou applaud the deed. Come, seeling[8] night,

---

[3] levy—armies.

[4] Unsafe . . . streams—since we are still unsafe, we must clean our reputations in streams of flattery.

[5] vizards—masks.

[6] eterne—eternal, perpetual.

[7] **jocund**—lighthearted, happy.

[8] seeling—blinding.

Scarf up the tender eye of pitiful day,
And with thy bloody and invisible hand
Cancel and tear to pieces that great bond
50 Which keeps me pale! Light thickens,
And the crow makes wing to th' rooky wood;
Good things of day begin to droop and drowse,
Whiles night's black agents to their preys do rouse.—
Thou marvel'st at my words, but hold thee still.
55 Things bad begun make strong themselves by ill.
So, prithee, go with me.

[*They exit.*]

Act Three, Scene Three

Outside the castle, the two murderers are joined by a third. Banquo is murdered, but Fleance escapes.

Enter three Murderers.

First Murderer. But who did bid thee join with us?

Third Murderer.   Macbeth.

Second Murderer. He needs not our mistrust, since he delivers
Our offices and what we have to do
To the direction just.[1]

First Murderer.   Then stand with us.
5   The west yet glimmers with some streaks of day.
Now spurs the lated traveler **apace**[2]
To gain the timely inn, and near approaches
The subject of our watch.

---

[1] He needs . . . just—Macbeth should not be mistrustful, since he gave us our orders, and we plan to follow his directions exactly.
[2] **apace**—rapidly.

Third Murderer. Hark, I hear horses.

Banquo [*within*]. Give us a light there, ho!

Second Murderer. Then 'tis he. The rest

10   That are within the note of expectation

     Already are i' the court.

First Murderer. His horses go about.

Third Murderer. Almost a mile; but he does usually—

     So all men do—from hence to th' palace gate

     Make it their walk.

[*Enter* Banquo, *and* Fleance *with a torch.*]

Second Murderer. A light, a light!

Third Murderer. 'Tis he.

15 **First Murderer.** Stand to 't.

Banquo. It will be rain tonight.

First Murderer. Let it come down!

[*They attack* Banquo.]

Banquo. O, treachery! Fly, good Fleance, fly, fly, fly!

     Thou mayst revenge.—O slave!

[*He dies.* Fleance *escapes.*]

Third Murderer. Who did strike out the light?

First Murderer. Was 't not the way?

20 **Third Murderer.** There's but one down; the son is fled.

Second Murderer. We have lost best half of our affair.

First Murderer. Well, let's away and say how much is done.

[*They exit.*]

Act Three, Scene Four

At the banquet in the castle, one of the murderers reports to Macbeth that Banquo is dead but that Fleance has escaped. Macbeth returns to the feast and is telling the guests how much he regrets Banquo's absence when the missing man's bloody ghost appears at the table, invisible to all but Macbeth, who cries out. Lady Macbeth has to calm the company. With the ghost's exit, Macbeth recovers his composure and is proposing a toast to Banquo when the ghost reappears. Macbeth rages against the dead who will not stay in their graves. His wife sends the guests away. When he calms, Macbeth decides to see the witches again. He foresees a future of more violence.

Banquet prepared. Enter Macbeth, Lady Macbeth, Ross, Lennox, Lords, *and* Attendants.

Macbeth. You know your own degrees;[1] sit down. At first
    And last, the hearty welcome.

Lords.   Thanks to Your Majesty.

Macbeth. Ourself will mingle with society
    And play the humble host.

5   Our hostess keeps her state,[2] but in best time
    We will require her welcome.

Lady Macbeth. Pronounce it for me, sir, to all our friends,
    For my heart speaks they are welcome.

[*Enter* First Murderer *to the door.*]

Macbeth. See, they encounter thee with their hearts' thanks.

10   Both sides are even. Here I'll sit i' the midst.
    Be large in mirth; anon we'll drink a measure
    The table round. [*He goes to the* Murderer.]
    There's blood upon thy face.

Murderer. 'Tis Banquo's, then.

15 **Macbeth.** 'Tis better thee without than he within.
    Is he dispatched?

Murderer. My lord, his throat is cut. That I did for him.

---

[1] degrees—relative status; thus, where you should sit.

[2] keeps her state—stays on her throne.

Macbeth. Thou art the best o' the cutthroats.
　　　　Yet he's good that did the like for Fleance;
20　　　If thou didst it, thou art the nonpareil.[3]

Murderer. Most royal sir, Fleance is 'scaped.

Macbeth [*aside*]. Then comes my fit again. I had else been perfect,
　　　　Whole as the marble, founded as the rock,
　　　　As broad and general as the casing[4] air.
25　　　But now I am cabined, cribbed, confined, bound in
　　　　To **saucy**[5] doubts and fears. But Banquo's safe?

Murderer. Ay, my good lord. Safe in a ditch he bides,
　　　　With twenty trenchèd gashes on his head,
　　　　The least a death to nature.

Macbeth.　　　　　　　　　Thanks for that.
30　　　There the grown serpent lies; the worm that's fled
　　　　Hath nature that in time will venom breed,
　　　　No teeth for th' present. Get thee gone. Tomorrow
　　　　We'll hear ourselves[6] again.

[*Exit Murderer.*]

Lady Macbeth.　　　　　　　　My royal lord,
　　　　You do not give the cheer. The feast is sold
35　　　That is not often vouched, while 'tis a-making,
　　　　'Tis given with welcome.[7] To feed were best at home;
　　　　From thence, the sauce to meat is ceremony;
　　　　Meeting were bare without it.

[*Enter the* Ghost of Banquo, *and sits in* Macbeth's *place.*]

Macbeth.　　　　　　　　　Sweet remembrancer!—
　　　　Now, good digestion wait on appetite,
40　　　And health on both!

Lennox.　　　　　　　May 't please Your Highness sit?

Macbeth. Here had we now our country's honor roofed
　　　　Were the graced person of our Banquo present,
　　　　Who may I rather challenge for unkindness
　　　　Than pity for mischance.

---

[3] nonpareil—one without equal.

[4] casing—enveloping.

[5] **saucy**—sharp, impudent.

[6] hear ourselves—confer.

[7] The feast ... welcome—Unless the guests are often assured of their welcome, a feast is not better than a meal one pays for.

Ross. His absence, sir,

45 Lays blame upon his promise. Please 't Your Highness

To grace us with your royal company?

Macbeth. The table's full.

Lennox. Here is a place reserved, sir.

Macbeth. Where?

50 **Lennox.** Here, my good lord. What is 't that moves Your Highness?

Macbeth. Which of you have done this?

Lords. What, my good lord?

Macbeth. Thou canst not say I did it. Never shake

Thy gory locks at me.

Ross. Gentlemen, rise. His Highness is not well.

55 **Lady Macbeth.** Sit, worthy friends. My lord is often thus,

And hath been from his youth. Pray you, keep seat.

The fit is momentary; upon a thought

He will again be well. If much you note him

You shall offend him and extend his passion.

60 Feed, and regard him not.— Are you a man?

Macbeth. Ay, and a bold one, that dare look on that

Which might appall the devil.

Lady Macbeth. O, proper stuff!

This is the very painting of your fear.

This is the air-drawn dagger which, you said,

65 Led you to Duncan. O, these flaws and starts,

Impostors to true fear, would well become

A woman's story at a winter's fire,

Authorized by her grandam. Shame itself!

Why do you make such faces? When all's done,

70 You look but on a stool.

Macbeth. Prithee, see there!

Behold, look! Lo, how say you?

Why, what care I? If thou canst nod, speak too.

In this scene from the Intiman Theatre production, Macbeth (Daniel Reichart) is horrified when he sees the ghost of the murdered Banquo.

If charnel houses[8] and our graves must send
Those that we bury back, our monuments
75   Shall be the maws of kites.[9]
[*Exit* Ghost.]
Lady Macbeth. What, quite unmanned in folly?
Macbeth. If I stand here, I saw him.
Lady Macbeth.   Fie, for shame!
Macbeth. Blood hath been shed ere now, i' th' olden time,
Ere humane statute purged the gentle weal;[10]
80   Ay, and since too, murders have been performed
Too terrible for the ear. The time has been

---

[8] charnel houses—depositories for bones or bodies.
[9] our monuments . . . kites—Our burial vaults shall be the stomachs of birds of prey.
[10] Ere . . . weal—before the laws cleansed society of violence.

That, when the brains were out, the man would die,
And there an end; but now they rise again
With twenty mortal murders on their crowns,
85 And push us from our stools. This is more strange
Than such a murder is.

Lady Macbeth.   My worthy lord,
Your noble friends do lack you.

Macbeth.   I do forget.
Do not muse at me, my most worthy friends;
I have a strange infirmity, which is nothing
90 To those that know me. Come, love and health to all!
Then I'll sit down.—Give me some wine. Fill full.

[*Enter* Ghost.]

I drink to the general joy o' th' whole table,
And to our dear friend Banquo, whom we miss.
Would he were here! To all, and him, we thirst,
95 And all to all.

Lords.   Our duties and the pledge.

Macbeth [*seeing the* Ghost].
Avaunt,[11] and quit my sight! Let the earth hide thee!
Thy bones are marrowless, thy blood is cold;
Thou hast no speculation in those eyes
Which thou dost glare with!

Lady Macbeth.   Think of this, good peers,
100 But as a thing of custom. 'Tis no other;
Only it spoils the pleasure of the time.

Macbeth [*to the* Ghost]. What man dare, I dare.
Approach thou like the rugged Russian bear,
The armed rhinoceros, or th' Hyrcan[12] tiger;
105 Take any shape but that, and my firm nerves
Shall never tremble. Or be alive again
And dare me to the desert with thy sword.
If trembling I inhabit then, protest me
The baby of a girl. Hence, horrible shadow!
110 Unreal mock' ry, hence! [*Exit* Ghost.]

---

[11] Avaunt—begone.

[12] Hyrcan—of Hyrcania, an ancient region near the Caspian Sea.

It will have blood, they say;
blood will have blood.

Why, so; being gone,
I am a man again.—Pray you, sit still.

Lady Macbeth. You have displaced the mirth, broke the good meeting
With most admired[13] disorder.

Macbeth.   Can such things be,
115   And overcome us like a summer's cloud,
Without our special wonder? You make me strange
Even to the disposition that I owe,[14]
When now I think you can behold such sights
And keep the natural ruby of your cheeks
120   When mine is blanched with fear.

Ross.   What sights, my lord?

Lady Macbeth. I pray you, speak not. He grows worse and worse;
Question enrages him. At once, good night.
Stand not upon the order of your going,
But go at once.

Lennox.   Good night, and better health
125   Attend His Majesty!

Lady Macbeth.   A kind good night to all!

[*Exit all but* Macbeth *and* Lady Macbeth.]

Macbeth. It will have blood, they say; blood will have blood.
Stones have been known to move, and trees to speak;
Augures and understood relations have
By maggot pies and choughs and rooks brought forth
130   The secret'st man of blood.[15] What is the night?

Lady Macbeth. Almost at odds with morning, which is which.

Macbeth. How sayst thou, that Macduff denies his person
At our great bidding?

Lady Macbeth.   Did you send to him, sir?

---

[13] admired—amazing.

[14] strange . . . owe—seem strange to myself.

[15] Augures . . . blood—Omens and hidden knowledge of the most secret murderer have been revealed through speaking birds.

Macbeth. I hear it by the way, but I will send.
135   There's not a one of them but in his house
       I keep a servant fee'd.[16] I will tomorrow—
       And betimes[17] I will—to the Weird Sisters.
       More shall they speak, for now I am bent to know
       By the worst means the worst. For mine own good
140   All causes shall give way. I am in blood
       Stepped in so far that, should I wade no more,
       Returning were as tedious as go o'er.
       Strange things I have in head, that will to hand,
       Which must be acted ere they may be scanned.[18]
145 **Lady Macbeth.** You lack the season of all natures, sleep.
    Macbeth. Come, we'll to sleep. My strange and self-abuse
       Is the initiate fear[19] that wants hard use.
       We are yet but young in deed.
    [*They exit.*]

---

[16] fee'd—paid to spy.

[17] betimes—early.

[18] ere . . . scanned—before I have time to think about them.

[19] initiate fear—fear felt by a beginner.

Act Three, Scene Five

On the deserted plain, Hecate, goddess of witchcraft, scolds the three witches for their actions with Macbeth. [Many scholars believe that this scene was not written by Shakespeare, but was added later.]

Thunder. Enter the three Witches, *meeting* Hecate.

First Witch. Why, how now, Hecate? You look angerly.

Hecate. Have I not reason, beldams[1] as you are?
Saucy and overbold, how did you dare
To trade and traffic with Macbeth
5   In riddles and affairs of death,
And I, the mistress of your charms,
The close contriver of all harms,
Was never called to bear my part
Or show the glory of our art?
10   And, which is worse, all you have done
Hath been but for a wayward son,
Spiteful and wrathful, who, as others do,
Loves for his own ends, not for you.
But make amends now. Get you gone,
15   And at the pit of Acheron[2]
Meet me i' the morning. Thither he
Will come to know his destiny.
Your vessels and your spells provide,
Your charms and everything beside.
20   I am for th' air. This night I'll spend
Unto a dismal and a fatal end.
Great business must be wrought ere noon.
Upon the corner of the moon
There hangs a vap'rous drop profound;
25   I'll catch it ere it come to ground,

---

[1] beldams—hags.

[2] Acheron—river of sorrow in Hades; here, hell itself.

And that, distilled by magic sleights,[3]
Shall raise such artificial sprites
As by the strength of their illusion
Shall draw him on to his confusion.

30   He shall spurn fate, scorn death, and bear
His hopes 'bove wisdom, grace, and fear.
And you all know, security
Is mortals' chiefest enemy.

[Music and a song within, "Come away, come away," *etc.]*

Hark! I am called. My little spirit, see,

35   Sits in a foggy cloud and stays for me.

[Exit Hecate.]

First Witch. Come, let's make haste. She'll soon be back again.

[They exit.]

---

[3] sleights—tricks.

Act Three, Scene Six

In the palace at Forres, Lennox and another lord discuss Banquo's death and politics in Scotland. Both believe Macbeth to be guilty. The lord tells Lennox that Macduff has gone to England to join Malcolm, who has raised an army to invade Scotland. Macbeth is also preparing for war.

Enter Lennox *and another* Lord.

Lennox. My former speeches have but hit your thoughts,[1]
  Which can interpret farther. Only I say
  Things have been strangely borne.[2] The gracious Duncan
  Was pitied of Macbeth; marry,[3] he was dead.
5 And the right valiant Banquo walked too late,
  Whom you may say, if 't please you, Fleance killed,
  For Fleance fled. Men must not walk too late.
  Who cannot want the thought[4] how monstrous
  It was for Malcolm and for Donalbain
10 To kill their gracious father? Damnèd fact!
  How it did grieve Macbeth! Did he not straight
  In pious rage the two delinquents tear
  That were the slaves of drink and thralls[5] of sleep?
  Was not that nobly done? Ay, and wisely too;
15 For 'twould have angered any heart alive
  To hear the men deny 't. So that I say
  He has borne all things well; and I do think
  That had he Duncan's sons under his key—
  As, an't[6] please heaven, he shall not—they should find
20 What 'twere to kill a father. So should Fleance.
  But peace! For from broad words, and 'cause he failed

---

[1] My former . . . thoughts—What I have been saying agrees with your own thinking.

[2] Only . . . borne—I'll only add, strange things have happened.

[3] marry—indeed (originally an oath, "by the Virgin Mary").

[4] want the thought—fail to think.

[5] thralls—slaves.

[6] an't—if it.

His presence at the tyrant's feast, I hear
Macduff lives in disgrace. Sir, can you tell
Where he bestows himself?

Lord.   The son of Duncan,
25   From whom this tyrant holds the due of birth,
Lives in the English court, and is received
Of the most pious Edward[7] with such grace
That the **malevolence**[8] of fortune nothing
Takes from his high respect. Thither Macduff
30   Is gone to pray the holy king, upon his aid,
To wake Northumberland and warlike Siward,
That by the help of these—with Him above
To ratify the work—we may again
Give to our tables meat, sleep to our nights,
35   Free from our feasts and banquets bloody knives,
Do faithful homage, and receive free honors—
All which we pine for now. And this report
Hath so exasperate the king that he
Prepares for some attempt of war.

40 **Lennox.** Sent he to Macduff?

Lord. He did, and with an absolute "Sir, not I,"
The cloudy messenger turns me his back
And hums,[9] as who should say, "You'll **rue**[10] the time
That clogs[11] me with this answer."

Lennox.   And that well might
45   Advise him to a caution, t' hold what distance
His wisdom can provide. Some holy angel
Fly to the court of England and unfold
His message ere he come, that a swift blessing
May soon return to this our suffering country
50   Under a hand accursed!

Lord.   I'll send my prayers with him.

[*They exit.*]

---

[7] Edward—Edward the Confessor, King of England (1042–1066).

[8] **malevolence**—ill-will.

[9] cloudy . . . hums—scowling messenger turns his back and grumbles.

[10] **rue**—regret, feel sorrow.

[11] clogs—burdens.

Act Four, Scene One

In a cave, the witches are brewing a powerful potion in a cauldron, or large pot. When Macbeth questions them, they raise three spirits who advise him to fear Macduff, that no man born of a woman can harm him, and that he will only be defeated when Birnam Wood comes to Dunsinane Hill (site of Macbeth's castle). When Macbeth asks if Banquo's heirs will rule Scotland, the witches show him eight spirits with crowns and a ninth, the blood-covered Banquo, who indicates they are his descendants. The witches vanish, and Macbeth learns from Lennox that Macduff has fled to England. He resolves to attack Macduff's castle and kill his family. (Many scholars believe that this scene, or parts of it, was not written by Shakespeare.)

Thunder. Enter the three Witches.

First Witch. Thrice the brinded[1] cat hath mewed.
Second Witch. Thrice, and once the hedgepig[2] whined.
Third Witch. Harpier[3] cries, "'Tis time, 'tis time!"
First Witch. Round about the cauldron go;
5   In the poisoned entrails throw.
     Toad, that under cold stone
     Days and nights has thirty-one
     Sweltered venom, sleeping got,
     Boil thou first i' the charmèd pot.
10 **All.** Double, double, toil and trouble;
     Fire burn, and cauldron bubble.
     Second Witch. Fillet[4] of a fenny snake,
     In the cauldron boil and bake;
     Eye of newt and toe of frog,
15   Wool of bat and tongue of dog,
     Adder's fork[5] and blindworm's sting,
     Lizard's leg and owlet's wing,

---

[1] brinded—striped.
[2] hedgepig—hedgehog.
[3] Harpier—name of a familiar spirit.
[4] **Fillet**—slice.
[5] fork—tongue.

Double, double, toil and trouble; Fire burn, and cauldron bubble.

For a charm of powerful trouble,
Like a hell-broth boil and bubble.

20 **All.** Double, double, toil and trouble;
Fire burn, and cauldron bubble.

Third Witch. Scale of dragon, tooth of wolf,
Witches' mummy, maw and gulf
Of the ravined salt-sea shark,[6]

25 Root of hemlock digged i' the dark,
Liver of blaspheming Jew,
Gall of goat, and slips of yew[7]
Slivered in the moon's eclipse,
Nose of Turk and Tartar's lips,

30 Finger of birth-strangled babe
Ditch-delivered by a drab,[8]
Make the gruel thick and slab.[9]
Add thereto a tiger's chaudron[10]
For th' ingredience of our cauldron.

35 **All.** Double, double, toil and trouble;
Fire burn, and cauldron bubble.

Second Witch. Cool it with a baboon's blood,
Then the charm is firm and good.

[*Enter* Hecate.]

Hecate. O, well done! I commend your pains,

40 And everyone shall share i' the gains.
And now about the cauldron sing
Like elves and fairies in a ring,
Enchanting all that you put in.

---

[6] maw ... shark—stomach and gullet of the always hungry shark.

[7] slips of yew—cuttings of a tree planted in graveyards and associated with mourning.

[8] drab—whore.

[9] slab—sticky.

[10] chaudron—entrails.

[*Music and a song: "Black spirits," etc.*]

[*Exit* Hecate.]

Second Witch. By the pricking of my thumbs,

45   Something wicked this way comes.

[*Knocking.*]

        Open, locks,

        Whoever knocks!

[*Enter* Macbeth.]

Macbeth. How now, you secret, black, and midnight hags?

    What is 't you do?

All.   A deed without a name.

50 **Macbeth.** I conjure you, by that which you profess,

    Howe'er you come to know it, answer me.

    Though you untie the winds and let them fight

    Against the churches, though the yeasty waves

    Confound and swallow navigation up,

55   Though bladed corn be lodged[11] and trees blown down,

    Though castles topple on their warders'[12] heads,

    Though palaces and pyramids do slope

    Their heads to their foundations, though the treasure

    Of nature's germens[13] tumble all together,

60   Even till destruction sicken, answer me

    To what I ask you.

First Witch.   Speak.

Second Witch.   Demand.

Third Witch.   We'll answer.

First Witch. Say if thou'dst rather hear it from our mouths

    Or from our masters.

Macbeth.   Call 'em. Let me see 'em.

    Pour in sow's blood, that hath eaten

65   Her nine farrow;[14] grease that's sweaten

    From the murderer's gibbet[15] throw

    Into the flame.

---

[11] bladed corn be lodged—unripe corn be knocked over.

[12] warders'—watchmens'.

[13] germens—seeds.

[14] farrow—litter of pigs.

[15] gibbet—gallows.

All.   Come high or low,
    Thyself and office deftly show!
[*Thunder. First Apparition, an armed head.*]
Macbeth. Tell me, thou unknown power—
First Witch.   He knows thy thought.
70   Hear his speech, but say thou naught.
    First Apparition. Macbeth! Macbeth! Macbeth! Beware Macduff,
        Beware the Thane of Fife. Dismiss me. Enough.
[*He descends.*]

The three Witches (left to right, Jeanne Sakata, Mary Louise Wilson, and Katherine Hiler) gather around their cauldron in the 1989 production of *Macbeth* by the New York Shakespeare Festival.

Macbeth. Whate'er thou art, for thy good caution, thanks;

Thou hast harped[16] my fear aright. But one word more—

75 **First Witch.** He will not be commanded. Here's another,

More potent than the first.

[*Thunder. Second Apparition,* a bloody child.]

Second Apparition. Macbeth! Macbeth! Macbeth!

Macbeth. Had I three ears, I'd hear thee.

Second Apparition. Be bloody, bold, and resolute; laugh to scorn

80 The power of man, for none of woman born

Shall harm Macbeth.

[*Descends.*]

Macbeth. Then live, Macduff; what need I fear of thee?

But yet I'll make assurance double sure,

And take a bond of fate. Thou shalt not live,

85 That I may tell pale-hearted fear it lies,

And sleep in spite of thunder.

[*Thunder. Third Apparition,* a child crowned, with a tree in his hand.]

                            What is this

That rises like the issue of a king

And wears upon his baby brow the round

And top of sovereignty?

All.   Listen, but speak not to 't.

90 **Third Apparition.** Be lion-mettled,[17] proud, and take no care

Who chafes, who frets, or where conspirers are.

Macbeth shall never vanquished be until

Great Birnam Wood to high Dunsinane Hill

Shall come against him.

[*Descends.*]

Macbeth.   That will never be.

95 Who can impress the forest, bid the tree

Unfix his earthbound root? Sweet bodements,[18] good!

Rebellious dead, rise never till the wood

Of Birnam rise, and our high-placed Macbeth

Shall live the lease of nature, pay his breath

---

[16] harped—touched on, guessed.

[17] lion-mettled—brave as a lion.

[18] bodements—prophecies.

100   To time and mortal custom. Yet my heart
       Throbs to know one thing. Tell me, if your art
       Can tell so much: shall Banquo's issue ever
       Reign in this kingdom?
All.   Seek to know no more.
Macbeth. I will be satisfied. Deny me this,
105   And an eternal curse fall on you! Let me know.
[*Hautboys.*]
       Why sinks that cauldron? And what noise is this?
First Witch. Show!
Second Witch. Show!
Third Witch. Show!
110 **All.** Show his eyes, and grieve his heart;
       Come like shadows, so depart!
[*A show of eight kings, the eighth king with a glass in his hand and* Banquo *last.*]
Macbeth. Thou art too like the spirit of Banquo. Down!
       Thy crown does sear mine eyeballs. And thy hair,
       Thou other gold-bound brow, is like the first.
115   A third is like the former.—Filthy hags,
       Why do you show me this? A fourth? Start, eyes!
       What, will the line stretch out to th' crack of doom?
       Another yet? A seventh? I'll see no more.
       And yet the eighth appears, who bears a glass
120   Which shows me many more; and some I see
       That twofold balls and treble scepters[19] carry.
       Horrible sight! Now I see 'tis true,
       For the blood-boltered[20] Banquo smiles upon me
       And points at them for his. [Apparitions *descend.*]
                                  What, is this so?
125 **First Witch.** Ay, sir, all this is so. But why
       Stands Macbeth thus amazedly?
       Come, sisters, cheer we up his sprites
       And show the best of our delights.
       I'll charm the air to give a sound,

---

[19] twofold balls and treble scepters—the two orbs and three scepters used by James I, king of England, when the play was written. The orbs represent his rule over Scotland and England; the scepters represent his claim to the thrones of Great Britain, France, and Ireland.

[20] blood-boltered—hair matted with blood.

130   While you perform your antic round,

That this great king may kindly say

Our duties did his welcome pay.

[*Music. The* Witches *dance, and vanish.*]

Macbeth. Where are they? Gone? Let this **pernicious**[21] hour

Stand aye accursèd in the calendar!

135   Come in, without there!

[*Enter* Lennox.]

Lennox.   What's Your Grace's will?

Macbeth. Saw you the Weird Sisters?

Lennox.   No, my lord.

Macbeth. Came they not by you?

Lennox.   No, indeed, my lord.

Macbeth. Infected be the air whereon they ride,

And damned all those that trust them! I did hear

140   The galloping of horse. Who was 't came by?

Lennox. 'Tis two or three, my lord, that bring you word

Macduff is fled to England.

Macbeth.   Fled to England!

Lennox. Ay, my good lord.

Macbeth [*aside*]. Time, thou anticipat'st my dread exploits.

145   The flighty[22] purpose never is o'ertook

Unless the deed go with it. From this moment

The very firstlings of my heart shall be

The firstlings of my hand.[23] And even now,

To crown my thoughts with acts, be it thought and done:

150   The castle of Macduff I will surprise,

Seize upon Fife, give to th' edge o' the sword

His wife, his babes, and all unfortunate souls

That trace him in his line. No boasting like a fool;

This deed I'll do before this purpose cool.

155   But no more sights!—Where are these gentlemen?

Come, bring me where they are.

[*They exit.*]

---

[21] **pernicious**—destructive, wicked.

[22] flighty—fleeting.

[23] firstlings . . . my hand—first desires of my heart will be the first actions of my hands.

Act Four, Scene Two

At Macduff's castle in Fife, Ross comforts Lady Macduff. After Ross leaves, she bemoans her state to her son, who will not believe that his father is either dead or a traitor. A messenger warns Lady Macduff that she is in danger. But before she can escape, Macbeth's assassins arrive and kill the whole family.

Enter Lady Macduff, *her* Son, *and* Ross.

Lady Macduff. What had he done to make him fly the land?

Ross. You must have patience, madam.

Lady Macduff.   He had none.
His flight was madness. When our actions do not,
Our fears do make us traitors.

Ross.   You know not
15   Whether it was his wisdom or his fear.

Lady Macduff. Wisdom? To leave his wife, to leave his babes,
His mansion, and his titles in a place
From whence himself does fly? He loves us not,
He wants the natural touch;[1] for the poor wren,
10   The most diminutive of birds, will fight,
Her young ones in her nest, against the owl.
All is the fear and nothing is the love,
As little is the wisdom, where the flight
So runs against all reason.

Ross.   My dearest coz,[2]
15   I pray you, school yourself. But, for your husband,
He is noble, wise, judicious, and best knows
The fits o' the season.[3] I dare not speak much further,
But cruel are the times when we are traitors
And do not know ourselves, when we hold rumor
20   From what we fear, yet know not what we fear,

---

[1] wants . . . touch—lacks the feelings natural to a husband and father.

[2] coz—cousin (meaning any kinswoman).

[3] fits . . . season—disturbances of the times.

But float upon a wild and violent sea
Each way and none. I take my leave of you;
Shall not be long but I'll be here again.
Things at the worst will cease, or else climb upward

25   To what they were before.—My pretty cousin,
Blessing upon you!

Lady Macduff. Fathered he is, and yet he's fatherless.

Ross. I am so much a fool, should I stay longer
It would be my disgrace and your discomfort.

30   I take my leave at once.

[*Exit* Ross.]

Lady Macduff. Sirrah, your father's dead;
And what will you do now? How will you live?

Son. As birds do, Mother.

Lady Macduff.   What, with worms and flies?

Son. With what I get, I mean; and so do they.

35 **Lady Macduff.** Poor bird! Thou'dst never fear
The net nor lime, the pitfall nor the gin.[4]

Son. Why should I, Mother? Poor birds they are not set for.
My father is not dead, for all your saying.

Lady Macduff. Yes, he is dead. How wilt thou do for a father?

40 **Son.** Nay, how will you do for a husband?

Lady Macduff. Why, I can buy me twenty at any market.

Son. Then you'll buy 'em to sell again.

Lady Macduff. Thou speak'st with all thy wit,
And yet, i' faith, with wit enough for thee.

45 **Son.** Was my father a traitor, Mother?

Lady Macduff. Ay, that he was.

Son. What is a traitor?

Lady Macduff. Why, one that swears and lies.

Son. And be all traitors that do so?

---

[4] net . . . gin—traps for catching birds. Lime is a sticky substance put on branches to snare birds; a gin is a snare.

Lady Macduff (Amy Perry) and her son (Torrey Hanson) discuss her husband's flight to England in the Intiman Theatre production.

50 **Lady Macduff.** Every one that does so is a traitor,
And must be hanged.

Son. And must they all be hanged that swear and lie?

Lady Macduff. Every one.

Son. Who must hang them?

55 **Lady Macduff.** Why, the honest men.

Son. Then the liars and swearers are fools, for there are
liars and swearers enough to beat the honest men and
hang up them.

Lady Macduff. Now, God help thee, poor monkey!

60 But how wilt thou do for a father?

Son. If he were dead, you'd weep for him; if you would
not, it were a good sign that I should quickly have a new father.

Lady Macduff. Poor prattler,[5] how thou talk'st!

[*Enter a* Messenger.]

65

Messenger. Bless you, fair dame! I am not to you known,
    Though in your state of honor I am perfect,[6]
    I doubt some danger does approach you nearly.
    If you will take a homely man's advice,
    Be not found here. Hence with your little ones!
    To fright you thus, methinks, I am too savage;

70

    To do worse to you were fell[7] cruelty,
    Which is too nigh your person. Heaven preserve you!
    I dare abide no longer.

[*Exit* Messenger.]

Lady Macduff.   Whither should I fly?
    I have done no harm. But I remember now
    I am in this earthly world, where to do harm

75

    Is often laudable, to do good sometimes
    Accounted dangerous folly. Why then, alas,
    Do I put up that womanly defense
    To say I have done no harm?

[*Enter* Murderers.]

                What are these faces?

First Murderer. Where is your husband?

80

Lady Macduff. I hope in no place so unsanctified
    Where such as thou mayst find him.

First Murderer.   He's a traitor.

Son. Thou liest, thou shag-haired villain!

First Murderer.   What, you egg?

[*Stabbing him.*]
    Young fry[8] of treachery!

Son.   He has killed me, Mother.
    Run away, I pray you!

[*Dies.*]

[*Exit* Lady Macduff *crying "Murder!" followed by the* Murderers.]

---

[5] prattler—one who babbles meaninglessly.

[6] in . . . perfect—I well know position of honor.

[7] fell—fierce.

[8] fry—child.

Act Four, Scene Three

At the English king's palace, Macduff finds Malcolm and urges him to fight Macbeth. Because he fears betrayal, Malcolm pretends to be unfit to rule. Macduff's great distress for Scotland at this news convinces Malcolm of his loyalty, and he announces that an army is prepared for the fight against Macbeth. Ross tells them that many Scots are already in open revolt. He also tells Macduff that his family has been murdered. Macduff swears to avenge them.

Enter Malcolm *and* Macduff.

Malcolm. Let us seek out some desolate shade, and there
    Weep our sad bosoms empty.

Macduff.   Let us rather
    Hold fast the mortal sword, and like good men
    Bestride our downfall'n birthdom.[1] Each new morn

5   New widows howl, new orphans cry, new sorrows
    Strike heaven on the face, that it resounds
    As if it felt with Scotland and yelled out
    Like syllable of dolor.[2]

Malcolm.   What I believe, I'll wail;
    What know, believe; and what I can **redress**,[3]

10   As I shall find the time to friend, I will.
    What you have spoke, it may be so, perchance.
    This tyrant, whose sole name blisters our tongues,
    Was once thought honest. You have loved him well;
    He hath not touched you yet. I am young; but something

15   You may deserve of him through me, and wisdom
    To offer up a weak, poor, innocent lamb
    T' appease an angry god.

Macduff. I am not treacherous.

Malcolm.   But Macbeth is.
    A good and virtuous nature may recoil

---

[1] birthdom—native land.

[2] dolor—sadness.

[3] **redress**—set right.

	20	In an imperial charge.[4] But I shall crave your pardon.
		That which you are my thoughts cannot transpose;
		Angels are bright still, though the brightest[5] fell.
		Though all things foul would wear the brows of grace,
		Yet grace must still look so.

Macduff.   I have lost my hopes.

25 **Malcolm.** Perchance even there where I did find my doubts.
Why in that rawness left you wife and child,
Those precious motives, those strong knots of love,
Without leave-taking? I pray you,
Let not my jealousies be your dishonors,
30 But mine own safeties. You may be rightly just,
Whatever I shall think.

Macduff.   Bleed, bleed, poor country!
Great tyranny, lay thou thy basis sure,
For goodness dare not check thee; wear thou thy wrongs,
The title is affeered![6] Fare thee well, lord.
35 I would not be the villain that thou think'st
For the whole space that's in the tyrant's grasp,
And the rich East to boot.

Malcolm.   Be not offended.
I speak not as in absolute fear of you.
I think our country sinks beneath the yoke;
40 It weeps, it bleeds, and each new day a gash
Is added to her wounds. I think withal[7]
There would be hands uplifted in my right;
And here from gracious England have I offer
Of goodly thousands. But, for all this,
45 When I shall tread upon the tyrant's head,
Or wear it on my sword, yet my poor country
Shall have more vices than it had before,
More suffer, and more sundry ways than ever,
By him that shall succeed.

Macduff.   What should he be?

---

[4] recoil . . . charge—give way to a king's command.

[5] the brightest—Lucifer, the angel who was cast out of heaven for pride and became the ruler of hell.

[6] title is affeered—Macbeth's title to the crown is confirmed.

[7] withal—in addition, at the same time.

Malcolm. It is myself I mean, in whom I know
    All the particulars of vice so grafted[8]
    That, when they shall be opened, black Macbeth
    Will seem as pure as snow, and the poor state
    Esteem him as a lamb, being compared
    With my confineless harms.
      Macduff.   Not in the legions
    Of horrid hell can come a devil more damned
    In evils to top Macbeth.
      Malcolm.   I grant him bloody,
    Luxurious, **avaricious**,[9] false, deceitful,
    Sudden,[10] malicious, smacking of every sin
    That has a name. But there's no bottom, none,
    In my voluptuousness. Your wives, your daughters,
    Your matrons, and your maids could not fill up
    The cistern[11] of my lust, and my desire
    All continent impediments[12] would o'erbear
    That did oppose my will. Better Macbeth
    Than such an one to reign.
      Macduff.   Boundless intemperance
    In nature is a tyranny; it hath been
    Th' untimely emptying of the happy throne
    And fall of many kings. But fear not yet
    To take upon you what is yours. You may
    Convey your pleasures in a spacious plenty,
    And yet seem cold, the time you may so hoodwink.[13]
    We have willing dames enough. There cannot be
    That vulture in you to devour so many
    As will to greatness dedicate themselves,
    Finding it so inclined.
      Malcolm.   With this there grows
    In my most ill-composed affection such

---

[8] grafted—joined or mixed.

[9] **avaricious**—greedy.

[10] Sudden—violent.

[11] cistern—tank for holding water.

[12] continent impediments—restraining limits, barriers.

[13] hoodwink—blindfold; deceive.

A stanchless[14] avarice that, were I king,
I should cut off the nobles for their lands,
80 Desire his jewels, and this other's house,
And my more-having would be as a sauce
To make me hunger more, that I should forge
Quarrels unjust against the good and loyal,
Destroying them for wealth.

Macduff. This avarice
85 Sticks deeper, grows with more pernicious root
Than summer-seeming[15] lust, and it hath been
The sword[16] of our slain kings. Yet do not fear;
Scotland hath foisons[17] to fill up your will
Of your mere own. All these are portable,
90 With other graces weighed.

Malcolm. But I have none. The king-becoming graces,
As justice, verity, temp'rance, stableness,
Bounty, perseverance, mercy, lowliness,
Devotion, patience, courage, fortitude,
95 I have no relish of them, but abound
In the division of each several crime,
Acting it many ways. Nay, had I power, I should
Pour the sweet milk of **concord**[18] into hell,
Uproar the universal peace, confound
100 All unity on earth.

Macduff. O Scotland, Scotland!

Malcolm. If such a one be fit to govern, speak.
I am as I have spoken.

Macduff. Fit to govern?
No, not to live.—O nation miserable,
With an untitled tyrant bloody-sceptered,
105 When shalt thou see thy wholesome days again,
Since that the truest issue of thy throne
By his own interdiction stands accursed

---

[14] stanchless—unable to be satisfied.

[15] summer-seeming—appropriate to youth.

[16] sword—cause of overthrow.

[17] foisons—resources; plenty.

[18] **concord**—harmony or agreement.

And does blaspheme his breed?[19] Thy royal father
Was a most sainted king. The queen that bore thee,
110 Oft'ner upon her knees than on her feet,
Died every day she lived. Fare thee well.
These evils thou repeat'st upon thyself
Hath banished me from Scotland.—O my breast,
Thy hope ends here!

Malcolm.   Macduff, this noble passion,
115 Child of integrity, hath from my soul
Wiped the black scruples, reconciled my thoughts
To thy good truth and honor. Devilish Macbeth
By many of these trains hath sought to win me
Into his power, and modest wisdom plucks me
120 From overcredulous haste.[20] But God above
Deal between thee and me! For even now
I put myself to thy direction and
Unspeak mine own detraction, here **abjure**[21]
The taints and blames I laid upon myself
125 For strangers to my nature. I am yet
Unknown to woman, never was forsworn,
Scarcely have coveted what was mine own,
At no time broke my faith, would not betray
The devil to his fellow, and delight
130 No less in truth than life. My first false speaking
Was this upon myself. What I am truly
Is thine and my poor country's to command—
Whither indeed, before thy here-approach,
Old Siward with ten thousand warlike men,
135 Already at a point, was setting forth.
Now we'll together; and the chance of goodness
Be like our **warranted**[22] quarrel!—Why are you silent?

Macduff. Such welcome and unwelcome things at once
'Tis hard to reconcile.

[*Enter a* Doctor.]

140 **Malcolm.** Well, more anon.—Comes the king forth, I pray you?

---

[19] **blaspheme his breed**—disgrace his family line.

[20] **trains . . . haste**—tricks has tried to trap me, and common sense keeps me from believing too quickly.

[21] **abjure**—renounce under oath, forswear.

[22] **warranted**—just.

Exiles at the English court, Malcolm (Thomas Gibson, left) and Macduff (William Converse-Roberts) talk about Macbeth's tyranny in Scotland in the New York Shakespeare Festival production.

Doctor. Ay, sir. There are a crew of wretched souls
    That stay his cure. Their malady convinces
    The great essay of art; but at his touch—
    Such **sanctity**[23] hath heaven given his hand—
145   They presently amend.
Malcolm.   I thank you, Doctor.
[*Exit* Doctor.]
Macduff. What's the disease he means?
Malcolm.   'Tis called the evil.[24]
    A most miraculous work in this good king,
    Which often, since my here-remain in England,
    I have seen him do. How he solicits heaven
150   Himself best knows; but strangely-visited people,
    All swoll'n and ulcerous, pitiful to the eye,
    The mere despair of surgery, he cures,
    Hanging a golden stamp about their necks
    Put on with holy prayers; and 'tis spoken,
155   To the succeeding royalty he leaves
    The healing benediction.[25] With this strange virtue
    He hath a heavenly gift of prophecy,

[23] **sanctity**—holiness.
[24] the evil—scrofula, a form of tuberculosis that the king's touch was thought to heal.
[25] benediction—blessing.

And sundry blessings hang about his throne

That speak him full of grace.

[*Enter* Ross.]

Macduff. See who comes here.

160 **Malcolm.** My countryman, but yet I know him not.

Macduff. My ever-gentle cousin, welcome hither.

Malcolm. I know him now. Good God betimes remove

The means that makes us strangers!

Ross. Sir, amen.

Macduff. Stands Scotland where it did?

Ross. Alas, poor country,

165 Almost afraid to know itself. It cannot

Be called our mother, but our grave; where nothing

But who knows nothing is once seen to smile;

Where sighs and groans and shrieks that rend the air

Are made, not marked; where violent sorrow seems

170 A modern ecstasy.[26] The dead man's knell

Is there scarce asked for who, and good men's lives

Expire before the flowers in their caps,

Dying or ere they sicken.

Macduff. O, relation

Too nice, and yet too true!

Malcolm. What's the newest grief?

175 **Ross.** That of an hour's age doth hiss[27] the speaker;

Each minute teems a new one.

Macduff. How does my wife?

Ross. Why, well.

Macduff. And all my children?

Ross. Well too.

Macduff. The tyrant has not battered at their peace?

Ross. No, they were well at peace when I did leave 'em.

180 **Macduff.** Be not a niggard[28] of your speech. How goes 't?

Ross. When I came hither to transport the tidings

Which I have heavily borne, there ran a rumor

Of many worthy fellows that were out,

---

[26] modern ecstasy—commonplace feeling.

[27] hiss—cause to be hissed (for repeating stale news).

[28] niggard—stingy person, miser.

Which was to my belief witnessed the rather,[29]

185 For that I saw the tyrant's power afoot.

Now is the time of help. [*To* Malcolm.] Your eye in Scotland

Would create soldiers, make our women fight,

To **doff**[30] their dire distresses.

Malcolm.   Be 't their comfort

We are coming thither. Gracious England hath

190 Lent us good Siward and ten thousand men;

An older and a better soldier none

That Christendom gives out.

Ross.   Would I could answer

This comfort with the like! But I have words

That would be howled out in the desert air,

195 Where hearing should not latch[31] them.

Macduff.   What concern they?

The general cause? Or is it a fee-grief[32]

Due to some single breast?

Ross.   No mind that's honest

But in it shares some woe, though the main part

Pertains to you alone.

Macduff.   If it be mine,

200 Keep it not from me. Quickly let me have it.

Ross. Let not your ears despise my tongue forever,

Which shall possess them with the heaviest sound

That ever yet they heard.

Macduff.   Hum! I guess at it.

Ross. Your castle is surprised, your wife and babes

205 Savagely slaughtered. To relate the manner

Were, on the quarry of these murdered deer,

To add the death of you.

Malcolm.   Merciful heaven!

What, man, ne'er pull your hat upon your brows;

Give sorrow words. The grief that does not speak

210 Whispers the o'erfraught heart and bids it break.

Macduff. My children too?

---

[29] witnessed the rather—made the more likely.

[30] **doff**—put off, get rid of.

[31] latch—catch.

[32] fee-grief—private sorrow.

Ross.   Wife, children, servants, all

    That could be found.

Macduff.   And I must be from thence!

    My wife killed too?

Ross.   I have said.

Malcolm.   Be comforted.

    Let's make us medicines of our great revenge

215   To cure this deadly grief.

Macduff. He has no children. All my pretty ones?

    Did you say "all"? O hell-kite! All?

    What, all my pretty chickens and their dam

    At one fell swoop?

220   **Malcolm.** Dispute it like a man.

Macduff.   I shall do so;

    But I must also feel it as a man.

    I cannot but remember such things were,

    That were most precious to me. Did heaven look on

    And would not take their part? Sinful Macduff,

225   They were all struck for thee! Naught that I am,

    Not for their own demerits, but for mine,

    Fell slaughter on their souls. Heaven rest them now!

Malcolm. Be this the whetstone[33] of your sword. Let grief

    Convert to anger, blunt not the heart, enrage it.

230   **Macduff.** O, I could play the woman with mine eyes

    And braggart with my tongue! But, gentle heavens,

    Cut short all intermission. Front to front

    Bring thou this fiend of Scotland and myself;

    Within my sword's length set him. If he scape,[34]

235   Heaven forgive him too!

Malcolm.   This tune goes manly.

    Come, go we to the king. Our power is ready;

    Our lack is nothing but our leave. Macbeth

    Is ripe for shaking, and the powers above

    Put on their instruments. Receive what cheer you may.

240   The night is long that never finds the day.

    [They exit.]

---

[33] whetstone—hard stone for sharpening tools.

[34] scape—escape.

Act Five, Scene One

In a room in Macbeth's castle at Dunsinane, a doctor and a gentlewoman who attends Lady Macbeth watch as she sleepwalks. As she washes her hands in the air, Lady Macbeth cries out that she will never clean the blood from them. The doctor fears that nothing can help her.

Enter a Doctor of Physic *and a* Waiting Gentlewoman.

Doctor. I have two nights watched with you, but can perceive no truth in your report. When was it she last walked?

Gentlewoman. Since His Majesty went into the field,[1] I have seen her rise from her bed, throw her nightgown upon her, unlock her closet, take forth paper, fold it, write upon 't, read it, afterwards seal it, and again return to bed; yet all this while in a most fast sleep.

Doctor. A great **perturbation**[2] in nature, to receive at once the benefit of sleep and do the effects of watching! In this slumbery agitation, besides her walking and other actual performances, what, at any time, have you heard her say?

Gentlewoman. That, sir, which I will not report after her.

Doctor. You may to me, and 'tis most meet you should.

Gentlewoman. Neither to you nor anyone, having no witness to confirm my speech.

[*Enter Lady Macbeth, with a taper.*]

Lo you, here she comes! This is her very guise,[3] and, upon my life, fast asleep. Observe her. Stand close.

Doctor. How came she by that light?

Gentlewoman. Why, it stood by her. She has light by her continually. 'Tis her command.

Doctor. You see her eyes are open.

Gentlewoman. Ay, but their sense are shut.

Doctor. What is it she does now? Look how she rubs her hands.

---

[1] into the field—to war.
[2] **perturbation**—agitation.
[3] guise—usual behavior.

Gentlewoman. It is an accustomed action with her to seem thus washing her hands. I have known her continue in this a quarter of an hour.

Lady Macbeth. Yet here's a spot.

Doctor. Hark, she speaks. I will set down what comes from her, to satisfy my remembrance the more strongly.

Lady Macbeth. Out, damned spot! Out, I say! One—two—why then, 'tis time to do 't. Hell is murky—Fie, my lord, fie, a soldier, and afeard? What need we fear who knows it, when none can call our power to account? Yet who would have thought the old man to have had so much blood in him?

Doctor. Do you mark that?

Lady Macbeth. The Thane of Fife had a wife. Where is she now?—What, will these hands ne'er be clean?—No more o' that, my lord, no more o' that; you mar all with this starting.

Doctor. Go to, go to. You have known what you should not.

Gentlewoman. She has spoke what she should not, I am sure of that. Heaven knows what she has known.

Lady Macbeth. Here's the smell of the blood still. All the perfumes of Arabia will not sweeten this little hand. O, O, O!

Doctor. What a sigh is there! The heart is sorely charged.

Gentlewoman. I would not have such a heart in my bosom for the dignity of the whole body.

Doctor. Well, well, well.

Gentlewoman. Pray God it be, sir.

Doctor. This disease is beyond my practice. Yet I have known those which have walked in their sleep who have died holily in their beds.

Lady Macbeth. Wash your hands, put on your nightgown; look not so pale! I tell you yet again, Banquo's buried. He cannot come out on 's grave.

Doctor. Even so?

Lady Macbeth. To bed, to bed! There's knocking at the gate. Come, come, come, come, give me your hand. What's done cannot be undone. To bed, to bed, to bed!

[*Exit* Lady Macbeth.]

Doctor. Will she go now to bed?

Gentlewoman. Directly.

Her mind unsettled by guilt, Lady Macbeth (Stephanie Roth-Haberle)
sleepwalks in the Hartford Stage Company production.

60   **Doctor.** Foul whisp'rings are abroad. Unnatural deeds
       Do breed unnatural troubles. Infected minds
       To their deaf pillows will discharge their secrets.
       More needs she the divine[4] than the physician.
       God, God forgive us all! Look after her;
65   Remove from her the means of all annoyance,
       And still keep eyes upon her. So, good night.
       My mind she has mated,[5] and amazed my sight.
       I think, but dare not speak.
       Gentlewoman.   Good night, good Doctor.
       [*They exit.*]

---

[4] divine—priest or minister.
[5] mated—bewildered, stupefied.

Act Five, Scene Two

Near Macbeth's castle at Dunsinane, a group of Scottish lords are on their way to join Malcolm, Macduff, Siward (the general sent by the king of England), and the army at *Birnam Wood. They discuss Macbeth's crimes and are prepared to die to save Scotland from a tyrant.*

Drum and Colors.[1] *Enter* Menteith, Caithness, Angus, Lennox, *and* Soldiers.

Menteith. The English power is near, led on by Malcolm,
His uncle Siward, and the good Macduff.
Revenges burn in them, for their dear causes
Would to the bleeding and the grim alarm

5   Excite the mortified man.[2]

Angus.   Near Birnam Wood
Shall we well meet them. That way are they coming.

Caithness. Who knows if Donalbain be with his brother?

Lennox. For certain, sir, he is not. I have a file
Of all the gentry. There is Siward's son,

10   And many unrough youths that even now
Protest their first of manhood.

Menteith.   What does the tyrant?

Caithness. Great Dunsinane he strongly fortifies.
Some say he's mad, others that lesser hate him
Do call it valiant fury. But for certain

15   He cannot buckle his distempered[3] cause
Within the belt of rule.

Angus.   Now does he feel
His secret murders sticking on his hands;
Now minutely revolts upbraid his faith-breach.[4]
Those he commands move only in command,[5]

---

[1] *Colors*—flags.

[2] Excite the mortified man—Call the dead to battle.

[3] distempered—diseased, sick.

[4] minutely . . . faith-breach—every minute new revolts shame his treachery.

[5] in command—because they are ordered to.

20   Nothing in love. Now does he feel his title
      Hang loose about him, like a giant's robe
      Upon a dwarfish thief.

Menteith.   Who, then, shall blame
      His pestered senses to recoil and start,
      When all that is within him does condemn
25   Itself for being there?

Caithness.   Well, march we on
      To give obedience where 'tis truly owed.
      Meet we the med'cine of the sickly weal,[6]
      And with him pour we in our country's purge[7]
      Each drop of us.

Lennox.   Or so much as it needs
30   To dew the sovereign flower and drown the weeds.
      Make we our march towards Birnam.

      [*They exit, marching.*]

---

[6] med'cine of the sickly weal—doctor (that is, Malcolm) for our sick commonwealth.

[7] purge—cleansing, but also bloodletting.

Act Five, Scene Three

Inside Macbeth's castle, Macbeth receives reports of the opposing armies. The prophecies have convinced him that Malcolm and the armies cannot harm him. When he asks the doctor to cure his wife of her growing madness, *the doctor replies that he has no cure. As he puts on his armor, Macbeth asks the doctor whether his science can cure Scotland of the English, as he will do with arms.*

Enter Macbeth, Doctor, *and* Attendants.

Macbeth. Bring me no more reports. Let them fly all!
    Till Birnam Wood remove to Dunsinane,
    I cannot taint with fear. What's the boy Malcolm?
    Was he not born of woman? The spirits that know

5   All mortal consequences have pronounced me thus:
    "Fear not, Macbeth. No man that's born of woman
    Shall e'er have power upon thee." Then fly, false thanes,
    And mingle with the English epicures![1]
    The mind I sway by[2] and the heart I bear

10   Shall never sag with doubt nor shake with fear.
[*Enter* Servant.]
    The devil damn thee black, thou cream-faced loon!
    Where got'st thou that goose look?

Servant. There is ten thousand—

Macbeth.   Geese, villain?

Servant.   Soldiers, sir.

Macbeth. Go prick thy face and over-red thy fear,

15   Thou lily-livered boy. What soldiers, patch?[3]
    Death of thy soul! Those linen cheeks of thine
    Are counselors to fear. What soldiers, whey-face?

Servant. The English force, so please you.

Macbeth. Take thy face hence. [*Exit* Servant.] Seyton!—I am sick at heart

20   When I behold—Seyton, I say!—This push

---

[1] epicures—lovers of luxury.

[2] sway by—rule myself by.

[3] patch—fool.

> # *My way of life is fall'n into the sere,*
> # *the yellow leaf.*

Will cheer me ever, or disseat[4] me now.
I have lived long enough. My way of life
Is fall'n into the sere,[5] the yellow leaf,
And that which should accompany old age,

25 As honor, love, obedience, troops of friends,
I must not look to have, but in their stead
Curses, not loud but deep, mouth-honor,[6] breath
Which the poor heart would fain deny and dare not.—
Seyton!

[*Enter* Seyton.]

30 **Seyton.** What's your gracious pleasure?

Macbeth.   What news more?

Seyton. All is confirmed, my lord, which was reported.

Macbeth. I'll fight till from my bones my flesh be hacked.
Give me my armor.

Seyton.   'Tis not needed yet.

Macbeth. I'll put it on.

35 Send out more horses. Skirr[7] the country round.
Hang those that talk of fear. Give me mine armor.
How does your patient, Doctor?

Doctor.   Not so sick, my lord,
As she is troubled with thick-coming fancies
That keep her from her rest.

Macbeth.   Cure her of that.

40 Canst thou not minister to a mind diseased,
Pluck from the memory a rooted sorrow,
Raze out the written troubles of the brain,

---

[4] disseat—dethrone.
[5] sere—dry and withered.
[6] mouth-honor—empty flattery.
[7] Skirr—search quickly, scour.

And with some sweet oblivious antidote[8]

Cleanse the stuffed bosom of that perilous stuff

45   Which weighs upon the heart?

Doctor.   Therein the patient

Must minister to himself.

Macbeth. Throw physic[9] to the dogs! I'll none of it.

Come, put mine armor on. Give me my staff.

[Attendants *arm him.*]

Seyton, send out.—Doctor, the thanes fly from me—

50   Come, sir, dispatch.—If thou couldst, Doctor, cast

The water of my land, find her disease,[10]

And purge it to a sound and **pristine**[11] health,

I would applaud thee to the very echo,

That should applaud again.—Pull 't off, I say.—

55   What rhubarb, senna, or what purgative drug

Would scour these English hence? Hear'st thou of them?

Doctor. Ay, my good lord. Your royal preparation

Makes us hear something.

Macbeth.   Bring it after me.—

I will not be afraid of death and bane,[12]

60   Till Birnam Forest come to Dunsinane.

[*Exit all but the* Doctor.]

Doctor. Were I from Dunsinane away and clear,

Profit again should hardly draw me here.

[*He exits.*]

---

[8] oblivious antidote—remedy causing forgetfulness.

[9] physic—medicine.

[10] cast the water ... disease—diagnose the disease that afflicts Scotland.

[11] **pristine**—pure.

[12] bane—fatal injury or ruin.

Act Five, Scene Four

In Birnam Wood, Malcolm orders the soldiers to cut and carry branches to conceal their numbers.

Drum and flags. Enter Malcolm, Siward, Macduff, Young Siward, Menteith, Caithness, Angus, Lennox, Ross, *and* Soldiers, *marching.*

Malcolm. Cousins, I hope the days are near at hand
    That chambers[1] will be safe.
Menteith.   We doubt it nothing.
Siward. What wood is this before us?
Menteith.   The wood of Birnam.
Malcolm. Let every soldier **hew**[2] him down a **bough**[3]
5   And bear 't before him. Thereby shall we shadow
    The numbers of our host and make discovery
    Err in report of us.
Soldiers.   It shall be done.
Siward. We learn no other but the confident tyrant
    Keeps still in Dunsinane and will endure
10   Our setting down before 't.
Malcolm.   'Tis his main hope;
    For, where there is advantage to be given,
    Both more and less have given him the revolt,[4]
    And none serve with him but constrainèd things
    Whose hearts are absent too.
Macduff.   Let our just **censures**[5]
15   Attend the true event, and put we on
    Industrious soldiership.

---

[1] chambers—our homes.
[2] **hew**—cut down.
[3] **bough**—large branch.
[4] where . . . revolt—when they can, both lords and soldiers have deserted.
[5] **censures**—strong disapproval.

Siward.   The time approaches

That will with due decision make us know

What we shall say we have and what we owe.

Thoughts speculative their unsure hopes relate,

20   But certain issue strokes must arbitrate—[6]

Towards which advance the war.

[*They exit, marching.*]

---

[6] **what . . . arbitrate**—what we lay claim and what we actually possess. Talking about the event in advance is just guesswork; only battle can settle the issue.

In the Hartford Stage production, the troops of Macbeth's enemies disguise themselves with tree branches, fulfilling the Witches' prophecy that he would be safe until Birnam Wood came to his stronghold at Dunsinane.

Despairing, Macbeth (Raul Julia) embraces his dead wife (Melinda Mullins) in the New York Shakespeare Festival production.

That lies like truth. "Fear not, till Birnam Wood
45 Do come to Dunsinane," and now a wood
Comes toward Dunsinane. Arm, arm, and out!
If this which he avouches does appear,
There is nor flying hence nor tarrying here.
I 'gin to be aweary of the sun,
50 And wish th' estate o' the world were now undone.
Ring the alarum bell! Blow wind, come wrack,
At least we'll die with harness on our back.
[*They exit.*]

Act Five, Scene Six

Outside Macbeth's castle, Malcolm, Siward, and Macduff make their plan for the battle to come.

Drum and Colors. Enter Malcolm, Siward, Macduff, and their Soldiers, with branches.

Malcolm. Now near enough. Your leafy screens throw down,
And show like those you are.—You, worthy uncle,
Shall with my cousin, your right noble son,
Lead our first battle. Worthy Macduff and we
5   Shall take upon 's what else remains to do,
According to our order.[1]

Siward.   Fare you well.
Do we but find the tyrant's power tonight,
Let us be beaten if we cannot fight.

Macduff. Make all our trumpets speak! Give them all breath,
10   Those **clamorous**[2] harbingers of blood and death.
[*They exit. Trumpets sound.*]

---

[1] **order**—plan of attack.

[2] **clamorous**—noisy.

Act Five, Scene Seven

On the battlefield, Macbeth meets and kills Young Siward. On another part of the battlefield, Macduff searches for Macbeth. Siward announces to Malcolm that the day is won and Macbeth's followers are surrendering.

Enter Macbeth.

Macbeth. They have tied me to a stake. I cannot fly,
But bearlike I must fight the course.[1] What's he
That was not born of woman? Such a one
Am I to fear, or none.

[*Enter* Young Siward.]

5   **Young Siward.** What is thy name?

Macbeth. Thou'lt be afraid to hear it.

Young Siward. No, though thou call'st thyself a hotter name
Than any is in hell.

Macbeth.   My name's Macbeth.

Young Siward. The devil himself could not pronounce a title
10   More hateful to mine ear.

Macbeth.   No, nor more fearful.

Young Siward. Thou liest, abhorrèd tyrant! With my sword
I'll prove the lie thou speak'st.

[*They fight, and* Young Siward *is killed.*]

Macbeth.   Thou wast born of woman.
But swords I smile at, weapons laugh to scorn,
Brandished by man that's of a woman born.

[*Exit* Macbeth.]

[*Alarums. Enter* Macduff.]

15   **Macduff.** That way the noise is. Tyrant, show thy face!
If thou beest slain, and with no stroke of mine,
My wife and children's ghosts will haunt me still.
I cannot strike at wretched kerns, whose arms
Are hired to bear their staves. Either thou, Macbeth,

---

[1] tied . . . course—Macbeth compares himself to a bear tied to a post (as in Elizabethan sport of bairbaiting) and attacked by dogs.

20   Or else my sword with an unbattered edge
           I sheathe again undeeded. There thou shouldst be;
           By this great clatter, one of greatest note
           Seems bruited.[2] Let me find him, Fortune,
           And more I beg not.

           [*Exit* Macduff. *Alarums.*]

           [*Enter* Malcolm *and* Siward.]

25   **Siward.** This way, my lord. The castle's gently rendered:[3]
           The tyrant's people on both sides do fight,
           The noble thanes do bravely in the war,
           The day almost itself professes yours,
           And little is to do.

           Malcolm.   We have met with foes

30   That strike beside us.[4]

           Siward.   Enter, sir, the castle.

           [*They exit. Alarum.*]

---

[2] bruited—announced.

[3] gently rendered—surrendered without a fight.

[4] strike beside us—fight on our side.

Act Five, Scene Eight

On another part of the battlefield, Macduff and Macbeth fight. Macbeth is unbeatable until Macduff says he was cut from his mother's womb and so is not of a woman born. Macbeth is then afraid to continue fighting, only does so when Macduff tells him that, if he surrenders, he will be displayed as a public spectacle. They fight again, and Macduff kills him.

Inside the castle, Ross announces Young Siward's death. Siward is comforted to learn that his son died honorably. Macduff enters with Macbeth's head and hails Malcolm as king. The new king honors the assembled company, promising to thank them by ruling well.

Why should I play the Roman fool and die On mine own sword?

Enter Macbeth.

Macbeth. Why should I play the Roman fool[1] and die
        On mine own sword? Whiles I see lives, the gashes
        Do better upon them.
[*Enter* Macduff.]
Macduff.   Turn, hellhound, turn!
Macbeth. Of all men else I have avoided thee.
5   But get thee back! My soul is too much charged
        With blood of thine already.
Macduff.   I have no words;
        My voice is in my sword, thou bloodier villain
        Than terms can give thee out!
[*They fight. Alarums.*]
Macbeth.   Thou losest labor.
        As easy mayst thou the intrenchant[2] air
10   With thy keen sword impress as make me bleed.
        Let fall thy blade on vulnerable crests;[3]
        I bear a charmèd life, which must not yield
        To one of woman born.
Macduff.   Despair thy charm,
        And let the angel[4] whom thou still hast served
15   Tell thee, Macduff was from his mother's womb
        Untimely ripped.
Macbeth. Accursèd be that tongue that tells me so,
        For it hath cowed my better part of man!
        And be these juggling[5] fiends no more believed
20   That palter with us in a double sense,[6]

---

[1] Roman fool—It was traditional for defeated Roman generals to take their own lives.

[2] intrenchant—incapable of being cut.

[3] crests—helmets.

[4] angel—bad angel, evil spirit.

[5] juggling—deceiving.

[6] palter . . . sense—fool us with wordplay.

Lay on, Macduff, and damned be him that first cries, "Hold, enough!

That keep the word of promise to our ear
And break it to our hope. I'll not fight with thee.

Macduff. Then yield thee, coward,
And live to be the show and gaze o' the time!
25 We'll have thee, as our rarer monsters are,
Painted upon a pole, and underwrit,
"Here may you see the tyrant."

Macbeth.   I will not yield
To kiss the ground before young Malcolm's feet
And to be baited with the rabble's curse.
30 Though Birnam Wood be come to Dunsinane,
And thou opposed, being of no woman born,
Yet I will try the last. Before my body
I throw my warlike shield. Lay on, Macduff,
And damned be him that first cries, "Hold, enough!"

[*They exit, fighting. Alarums.*]

[*They enter fighting, and* Macbeth *is killed.* Macduff *exits, carrying Macbeth's body. Flourish. Enter, with Drum and Colors,* Malcolm, Siward, Ross, Thanes, *and* Soldiers.]

35 **Malcolm.** I would the friends we miss were safe arrived.

Siward. Some must go off; and yet, by these I see
So great a day as this is cheaply bought.

Malcolm. Macduff is missing, and your noble son.

Ross. Your son, my lord, has paid a soldier's debt.
40 He only lived but till he was a man,
The which no sooner had his prowess confirmed
In the unshrinking station where he fought,
But like a man he died.

Siward.   Then he is dead?

Ross. Ay, and brought off the field. Your cause of sorrow
45 Must not be measured by his worth, for then
It hath no end.

Siward.   Had he his hurts before?

Ross. Ay, on the front.

Siward. Why then, God's soldier be he!
Had I as many sons as I have hairs
I would not wish them to a fairer death.
50   And so, his knell is knolled.[7]

Malcolm. He's worth more sorrow
And that I'll spend for him.

Siward. He's worth no more.
They say he parted well and paid his score,
And so, God be with him! Here comes newer comfort.

[*Enter* Macduff, *with Macbeth's head.*]

Macduff. Hail, King! For so thou art. Behold where stands
55   Th' usurper's cursèd head. The time is free.
I see thee compassed with thy kingdom's pearl,[8]
That speak my salutation in their minds,
Whose voices I desire aloud with mine:
Hail, King of Scotland!

60 **All.** Hail, King of Scotland! [*Flourish.*]

Malcolm. We shall not spend a large expense of time
Before we reckon with your several loves
And make us even with you. My thanes and kinsmen,
Henceforth be earls, the first that ever Scotland
65   In such an honor named. What's more to do
Which would be planted newly with the time,
As calling home our exiled friends abroad
That fled the snares of watchful tyranny,
Producing forth the cruel ministers
70   Of this dead butcher and his fiendlike queen—
Who, as 'tis thought by self and violent hands
Took off her life—this, and what needful else
That calls upon us, by the grace of Grace
We will perform in measure, time, and place.
75   So, thanks to all at once and to each one,
Whom we invite to see us crowned at Scone.

[*Flourish. All exit.*]

---

[7] knell is knolled—funeral bell is rung, tolled.

[8] compassed . . . pearl—surrounded by the noblest of your kingdom.

Understanding the Play

Act One

1. Who are the enemies that Duncan's army is fighting at the start of the play?

2. In Scene Two, what is Macbeth's reaction to being hailed "Thane of Cawdor"? How does it differ from Banquo's reaction?

3. In Scene Five, how does Lady Macbeth react to the news of the battle and the witches' prophecy?

4. In Scene Seven, why does Macbeth want to go back on the plan to kill Duncan? How does his wife change his mind?

Act Two

1. Why is Banquo unable to sleep in Scene One? What does Macbeth ask of him, and how does he respond?

2. In Scene Two, what does Lady Macbeth do with the bloody daggers?

3. In Scene Three, why is the porter so slow in answering the knocking at the gate?

4. Why does Macbeth slay the grooms? How does his stated reason differ from his real reason?

5. Why do Malcolm and Donalbain flee Scotland?

6. In Scene Four, what do the events noted by the Old Man and Ross suggest about the state of things in Scotland?

Act Three

1. In Scene One, why does Banquo suspect Macbeth of Duncan's murder? What does he plan to do?

2. Why has Macbeth grown to hate Banquo? How does he convince the murderers to kill Banquo and Fleance?

3. In Scene Two, why is Lady Macbeth unhappy as queen? Why do you think Macbeth does not tell her of his plot to murder Banquo?

4. In Scene Four, how does the company react to Macbeth's outbursts at Banquo's ghost?

Act Four

1. In Scene One, what does Macbeth learn from the spirits in the cave?

2. What effect does the spirits' information have on Macbeth? What does it spur him to do?

3. In Scene Two, how does Lady Macduff respond to her husband's flight? How does her son respond?

4. In Scene Three, why does Malcolm not welcome Macduff at first? What changes his mind?

5. How does Malcolm test Macduff?

Act Five

1. In Scene One, why does Lady Macbeth walk in her sleep? What does the doctor learn from observing her?

2. In Scene Three, why does Macbeth not fear Malcolm or his growing army?

3. In Scene Five, how does Macbeth react to his wife's death?

4. What brings Macbeth out of the castle to fight Malcolm and his army? How would you describe this act?

5. In Scene Eight, how does Siward react to his son's death?

6. Why is Malcolm's speech a good ending for the play?

Analyzing the Play

1. At the beginning of the play, Lady Macbeth spurs her husband on to murder Duncan. At what point in the play does she cease to influence Macbeth? Who takes over this role? Why do you think Shakespeare shifts the plot this way?

2. What purposes does the porter serve in Act Two, Scene Three? How does he help to create the atmosphere at Macbeth's castle?

3. Do you think Malcolm will make a good king for Scotland? Explain your answer.

4. Shakespeare called *Macbeth* a tragedy. A tragedy is generally defined as the story of a noble hero's downfall, often caused by a flaw in the hero's character. Do you think *Macbeth* is a tragedy or something else? Which elements of the play are tragic and which are not?

Writing Projects

1. In Act One, Scene Five, Lady Macbeth receives a letter from her husband describing the battle, his meeting with the witches, and his new honors. Write your own version of this letter, explaining the day's events as well as your own hopes and fears.

2. What do you think motivates Lady Macbeth, and how does her motivation evolve over the course of the play? Write a sequence of very short diary entries for her. Begin with the day before the battle and end near her death. You should have an entry for all the major events that involve Lady Macbeth.

3. Choose either Duncan, Banquo, or Macduff and write a short essay comparing and contrasting him with Macbeth.

4. Over the centuries, many productions of *Macbeth* have added a speech for Macbeth after he has been mortally wounded by Macduff. Write Macbeth's dying words. Think carefully about what you want Macbeth to express—remorse, defiance, anger or some other feeling.

5. Write an aphorism that sums up what you think is the ultimate message of *Macbeth*—for example, "Ambition and contentment seldom mix" or "Your good name is all you have." Explain how your aphorism sums up the many sides of the story.

Performance Projects

1. Choose one of the scenes between Macbeth and his wife; with a partner, rewrite it in modern English. You and your partner should then read your new version to the class.

2. How would you costume the characters in your own production of *Macbeth*? Would you choose medieval dress, modern dress, the styles of Shakespeare's time, or some other style? Write a description of the costume requirements for your production. Or, if you prefer, you can instead create images of the main characters in the costumes of your choosing.

3. *Macbeth* is a play that has very little light or sunshine in it. Much of it is set at night, during storms, and inside castles or caves. Go through the play and note the lighting needs of each of the scenes. Explain how you are going to create the right overall atmosphere for the various settings of the play.

4. Choose one of Macbeth's great speeches—Act One, Scene Seven, lines 1–28; Act Two, Scene One, lines 33–64; Act Five, Scene Five, lines 17–28—and practice reading it aloud. Then perform it for the class in two very different interpretations (for example, fast and slow, with an accent or without, excitedly or in a monotone).

The Tempest

Introduction

The Tempest *is a play about magic—
both white and black. The main character,
Prospero, is a powerful magician living in
exile on an enchanted island. He is able to
control the forces of nature, command spirits,
and even summon up the dead. However,
Prospero's magic is at the opposite extreme
from witchcraft. The evidence of black magic
is also present in the play in the character
of Prospero's servant, Caliban, a half-human
monster who is the son of a witch. Caliban's
dead mother, Sycorax, though also powerful,
was wholly evil in the exercise of her magic,
whose source was the devil.*

A crouching Caliban (Jack Willis) unwillingly obeys his master Prospero (Paul Freeman) in this scene from the 1995
production of *The Tempest* by the American Repertory Theatre of Cambridge, Massachusetts.

Plot

*Twelve years before the the action of the play starts,
Prospero had been the duke of Milan. Because he
allowed himself to become completely absorbed
in the study of magic, Prospero lost his dukedom
through a conspiracy between his brother, Antonio,
and Alonso, the king of Naples. Prospero was put
to sea with his infant daughter, Miranda, in a ship
that was meant to sink. Instead, they landed on an
island inhabited only by spirits and the half-human
Caliban. There, Prospero used his magic to release
the spirit Ariel, who had been imprisoned by Sycorax,
and Ariel became his servant. After an unsuccessful
attempt to civilize Caliban, Prospero made him a
servant too. Prospero used the ensuing years to
educate his growing daughter.*

As the play opens, Prospero has become aware that his enemies Antonio and Alonso are on a ship passing near the island. He raises a terrible storm, and the ship seems about to sink. The passengers abandon it and make their way to the island in separate groups. Coming ashore alone, Alonso's son, Ferdinand, meets and falls in love with Miranda; but Prospero, pretending to believe that Ferdinand is a spy, puts him under a spell and forces him to work. Alonso, fearful that his son is dead, searches for him. Antonio persuades Alonso's brother, Sebastian, to take advantage of the situation, kill Alonso, and become king. Their plot is foiled, however, by Ariel's intervention.

◄ With daggers raised, Antonio (left) and Sebastian prepare to kill Alonso and his counselor Gonzalo in this scene from the 1988 production of *The Tempest* by the Seattle Repertory Theatre.

Meanwhile, two of Alonso's servants, Trinculo and Stephano, meet Caliban, who, tasting their wine, befriends them. They all get drunk, and Caliban persuades Stephano to kill Prospero and take over the island. The three set out to do that, but Ariel lures them into a swamp. Prospero agrees to the marriage of Ferdinand and Miranda, and celebrates their betrothal with a magical entertainment. When Alonso finally meets Prospero, he finds that Ferdinand is indeed alive and joyfully agrees to the young people's marriage and Prospero's reinstatement as duke of Milan. Prospero forgives his brother and reveals that the ship is safe. At the close, Prospero frees Ariel and renounces magic. The island becomes Caliban's once more.

In the American Repertory Theatre production, (left to right) Caliban (Jack Willis), Stephano (Charles Levin), and Trinculo (Thomas Derrah) drunkenly plot against Prospero; invisible to them, Ariel (Benjamin Evett) stands and listens. ▶

Settings and Characters

The setting of The Tempest *is an otherwise uninhabited island in the Mediterranean Sea.*

The time is close to Shakespeare's own day. The main characters fall into two groups:

On the Island	From the Ship	
Prospero, a powerful magician and the rightful duke of Milan	**Alonso,** king of Naples	**Gonzalo,** an old councilor
Miranda, his daughter	**Ferdinand,** his son	**Trinculo,** a jester
Ariel, a spirit	**Sebastian,** his brother	**Stephano,** a butler
Caliban, a half-human monster	**Antonio,** Prospero's brother and the present duke of Milan	

Themes

The Tempest *is one of Shakespeare's late comedies (often classified as "romances"). These works differ in theme from his earlier comedies, such as* A Midsummer Night's Dream *and* Twelfth Night, *in several significant ways. The late comedies give less attention to the problems of young lovers and more to those of parents and children. In* The Tempest, *this concern is expressed in Prospero's efforts to be an educator. This effort is successful in the case of his daughter, but fails with Caliban.*

Another theme of The Tempest *is the basic character of human nature. Are human beings naturally good or naturally bad? Although the play is set on an island in the Mediterranean Sea, the background is the exploration of the Americas, which was very much of interest to the English when Shakespeare wrote his play in 1611. He makes several references to literature dealing with voyages to the New World. The most important is to the essay "On Cannibals" by the French writer Michel de Montaigne (1533–1592). Montaigne presents the American Indians as free from the vices of civilization and therefore naturally good. Shakespeare based the name of his character Caliban on the word* cannibal, *and presents in him a less optimistic picture of uncivilized human nature, partly good and partly bad.*

Because The Tempest *is about magic, another major theme is the difference between illusion and reality. Through his magic, Prospero creates a series of illusions—first to defeat his enemies and later to solemnize the love match between Ferdinand and Miranda. In the end, he questions whether the world itself is not an illusion:*

We are such stuff
As dreams are made on, and our little life
Is rounded with a sleep.

Characters

Alonso, king of Naples

Sebastian, his brother

Prospero, the rightful duke of Milan

Antonio, his brother, the usurping duke of Milan

Ferdinand, son to the king of Naples

Gonzalo, an honest old councilor

Adrian and Francisco, lords

Caliban, a savage and deformed slave

Trinculo, a jester

Stephano, a drunken butler

Master of a ship

Boatswain

Mariners

Miranda, daughter to Prospero

Ariel, an airy spirit

Spirits, who take the roles of:

Iris, Ceres, Juno, Nymphs, Reapers

Other Spirits attending on Prospero

SCENE: *An uninhabited island*

Act One, Scene One

A terrible storm is raging. Thunder roars and lightning flashes around a ship, which is in danger of sinking. The mariners work hard to steer, tend the sails, and keep the ship afloat. The boatswain angrily orders the passengers to go back to their cabins because they are in the way, but some insist on coming back on deck and an argument takes place. When the ship finally appears to begin to sink, all the characters think they are going to die.

A tempestuous noise of thunder and lightning heard. Enter a Shipmaster *and a* Boatswain.[1]

Master. Boatswain!

Boatswain. Here, master. What cheer?

Master. Good,[2] speak to the mariners. Fall to 't yarely,[3] or we run ourselves aground. Bestir, bestir! [*Exit* Master.]

---

[1] Boatswain—ship's officer in charge of the crew, rigging, anchors, etc.

[2] Good—good man.

[3] Fall to 't yarely—Get about your work quickly.

What cares these roarers
for the name of king?

[*Enter* Mariners.]

5   **Boatswain.** Heigh, my hearts! Cheerly, cheerly, my hearts! Yare, yare! Take in the topsail. Tend to the master's whistle.—Blow till thou burst thy wind, if room enough! [4]

[*Enter* Alonso, Sebastian, Antonio, Ferdinand, Gonzalo, *and others.*]

Alonso. Good boatswain, have care. Where's the master? Play the men. [5]

Boatswain. I pray now, keep below.

10   **Antonio.** Where is the master, bos'n?

Boatswain. Do you not hear him? You mar our labor. Keep your cabins! You do assist the storm.

Gonzalo. Nay, good, be patient.

Boatswain. When the sea is. Hence! What cares these roarers for the
15   name of king? [6] To cabin! Silence! Trouble us not.

Gonzalo. Good, yet remember whom thou hast aboard.

Boatswain. None that I more love than myself. You are a councilor; if you can command these elements to silence and work the peace of the present, [7] we will not hand a rope more. Use your authority. If you
20   cannot, give thanks you have lived so long and make yourself ready in your cabin for the mischance of the hour, if it so hap.—Cheerly, good hearts!—Out of our way, I say. [*Exit* Boatswain.]

Gonzalo. I have great comfort from this fellow. Methinks he hath no
25   drowning mark upon him. His complexion is perfect gallows. [8] Stand fast, good Fate, to his hanging! Make the rope of his destiny our cable, [9] for our own doth little advantage. If he be not born to be hanged, our case is miserable. [*Exit* Passengers.]

[*Enter* Boatswain.]

---

[4] Blow . . . enough—Wind, you can blow until you burst, as long as we have enough sea room to avoid running aground.

[5] Play the men—Make the men do their work.

[6] What cares . . . king?—What do the wind and the sea care if a king is aboard?

[7] work . . . present—bring peace to our present circumstances.

[8] Methinks . . . gallows—He is not likely to drown because his appearance shows he was born to be hanged.

[9] cable—ship's anchor chain.

In this scene from the 1995 production of *The Tempest* by the New York Shakespeare Festival, the mariners struggle to save their ship from the storm raised by Prospero.

Boatswain. Down with the topmast! Yare! Lower, lower! Bring her to try
30 wi' the main course.[10] [*A cry within.*[11]] A plague upon this howling!
They are louder than the weather or our office.[12]
[*Enter* Sebastian, Antonio, *and* Gonzalo.]
Yet again? What do you here? Shall we give o'er and drown?
Have you a mind to sink?
Sebastian. A pox o'[13] your throat, you bawling, blasphemous,
35 incharitable dog!
Boatswain. Work you, then.
Antonio. Hang, cur! Hang, you whoreson, **insolent**[14] noisemaker! We are
less afraid to be drowned than thou art.

---

[10] Bring ... course—Use the mainsail to keep the ship close to the wind.
[11] *within*—offstage.
[12] office—work, duties.
[13] pox o'—curses on.
[14] **insolent**—disrespectful.

Gonzalo. I'll warrant him for drowning,[15] though the ship were no

40   stronger than a nutshell and as leaky as an unstanched wench.

Boatswain. Lay her ahold,[16] ahold! Set her two courses. Off to sea again!

     Lay her off!

[*Enter* Mariners *wet.*]

Mariners. All lost! To prayers, to prayers! All lost!

[*Exit* Mariners.]

Boatswain. What, must our mouths be cold?[17]

45 **Gonzalo.** The king and prince at prayers! Let's assist them,

     For our case is as theirs.

Sebastian.   I am out of patience.

Antonio. We are merely cheated of our lives by drunkards.

     This wide-chopped[18] rascal! Would thou mightst lie drowning

     The washing of ten tides![19]

Gonzalo.   He'll be hanged yet,

50   Though every drop of water swear against it

     And gape at wid'st to glut him.[20]

[*A confused noise within:*] "Mercy on us"—

     "We split, we split!"—"Farewell, my wife and children!"—

     "Farewell, brother!"—"We split, we split, we split!"

[*Exit* Boatswain.]

55 **Antonio.** Let's all sink wi' the king.

Sebastian. Let's take leave of him.

[*Exit* Sebastian *with* Antonio.]

Gonzalo. Now would I give a thousand furlongs of sea for an acre of

     barren ground: long heath, brown furze,[21] anything. The wills above

     be done! But I would fain[22] die a dry death.

[*He exits.*]

---

[15] warrant . . . drowning—guarantee that he won't drown.

[16] ahold—close to the wind.

[17] What . . . cold—Must we die?

[18] wide-chopped—big-mouthed.

[19] lie . . . tides—Pirates were hanged onshore and left hanging until three tides had washed over them.

[20] gape . . . him—open their widest to swallow him.

[21] long heath, brown furze—long heather, brown gorse, that is, weeds.

[22] fain—rather.

Act One, Scene Two

On the island, Miranda worries about the people on the ship. She begs Prospero to stop the storm, if it is caused by his magic. Prospero tells her not to worry and explains how they came to the island. He concludes by telling her that fate has now put his enemies in his power. Prospero then charms Miranda asleep and summons the spirit Ariel, who reports that he has caused all the shipwrecked people to land in separate groups that don't know of the others' survival. Ariel then asks Prospero for his freedom. The magician first becomes angry, accusing Ariel of ingratitude; but he then promises to free him in two days. Prospero wakes Miranda and they visit Caliban, who curses them both for taking the island from him. Prospero commands him to fetch fuel. Led by Ariel, who is invisible, Ferdinand discovers Miranda and falls in love with her. Prospero pretends to believe that Ferdinand is a spy and puts him to work under a spell.

Enter Prospero *and* Miranda.

Miranda. If by your art, my dearest father, you have
Put the wild waters in this roar, **allay**[1] them.
The sky, it seems, would pour down stinking pitch,
But that the sea, mounting to th' welkin's cheek,[2]
5   Dashes the fire out. O, I have suffered
With those that I saw suffer! A brave[3] vessel,
Who had, no doubt, some noble creature in her,
Dashed all to pieces. O, the cry did knock
Against my very heart! Poor souls, they perished.
10   Had I been any god of power, I would
Have sunk the sea within the earth or ere[4]
It should the good ship so have swallowed and
The fraughting souls[5] within her.

---

[1] **allay**—calm; quiet.
[2] welkin's cheek—sky's face.
[3] brave—splendid.
[4] or ere—before.
[5] fraughting souls—people carried.

Prospero.   Be collected.[6]
No more amazement. Tell your piteous heart
15   There's no harm done.
Miranda.   O, woe the day!
Prospero.   No harm.
I have done nothing but in care of thee,
Of thee, my dear one, thee, my daughter, who
Art ignorant of what thou art, naught knowing
Of whence I am,[7] nor that I am more better
20   Than Prospero, master of a full poor cell,[8]
And thy no greater father.
Miranda.   More to know
Did never meddle with my thoughts.
Prospero.   'Tis time
I should inform thee farther. Lend thy hand
And pluck my magic garment from me. So,

[*Lays down his mantle.*]

25   Lie there, my art.—Wipe thou thine eyes. Have comfort.
The direful spectacle of the wrack,[9] which touched
The very virtue of compassion in thee,
I have with such provision in mine art
So safely ordered that there is no soul—
30   No, not so much perdition as an hair
Betid to any creature in the vessel[10]
Which thou heard'st cry, which thou saw'st sink. Sit down,
For thou must now know farther.
Miranda.   You have often
Begun to tell me what I am, but stopped
35   And left me to a bootless inquisition,[11]
Concluding, "Stay, not yet."
Prospero.   The hour's now come;
The very minute bids thee ope thine ear.

---

[6] collected—calm.

[7] naught . . . I am—knowing nothing of where I came from.

[8] full poor cell—very simple cave or cottage, like a hermit's cell.

[9] direful . . . wrack—terrible sight of the wrecked boat.

[10] I have . . . vessel—I have taken precautions to work my magic so that no one on the ship will lose even a hair.

[11] bootless inquisition—useless questioning.

Obey, and be attentive. Canst thou remember
A time before we came unto this cell?
40 I do not think thou canst, for then thou wast not
Out three years old.

Miranda. Certainly, sir, I can.

Prospero. By what? By any other house or person?
Of anything the image tell me that
Hath kept with thy remembrance.[12]

Miranda. 'Tis far off,
45 And rather like a dream than an assurance
That my remembrance warrants.[13] Had I not
Four or five women once that tended me?

Prospero. Thou hadst, and more, Miranda. But how is it
That this lives in thy mind? What seest thou else
50 In the dark backward and abysm of time?[14]
If thou rememb'rest aught ere thou cam'st here,
How thou cam'st here thou mayst.[15]

Miranda. But that I do not.

Prospero. Twelve year since, Miranda, twelve year since,
Thy father was the duke of Milan and
55 A prince of power.

Miranda. Sir, are not you my father?

Prospero. Thy mother was a piece of virtue, and
She said thou wast my daughter, and thy father
Was duke of Milan, and his only heir
And princess no worse issued.

Miranda. O the heavens!
60 What foul play had we, that we came from thence?
Or blessèd was 't we did?

Prospero. Both, both, my girl.
By foul play, as thou sayst, were we heaved thence,
But blessedly holp[16] hither.

---

[12] Of anything . . . remembrance—Tell me anything you remember.

[13] rather . . . warrants—more like a dream than a sure memory.

[14] backward . . . time—gulf or chasm of the past.

[15] If thou . . . mayst—If you remember anything before you came here, perhaps you remember how you came.

[16] holp—helped.

Prospero (Rick Tutor) tells Miranda (Kari McGee) how they came to the island in this scene
from the 1998 production of *The Tempest* by the Seattle Children's Theatre.

Miranda.   O, my heart bleeds
          To think o' the teen that I have turned you to,[17]
65   Which is from my remembrance! Please you, farther.
Prospero. My brother and thy uncle, called Antonio—
          I pray thee, mark me—that a brother should
          Be so **perfidious**![18]—he whom next thyself
          Of all the world I loved, and to him put
70   The manage of my state, as at that time
          Through all the seigniories it was the first,[19]
          And Prospero the prime[20] duke, being so reputed
          In dignity, and for the liberal arts
          Without a parallel. Those being all my study,

---

[17] teen . . . to—trouble that I've caused you.

[18] **perfidious**—treacherous; guilty of betraying trust.

[19] Through . . . first—It was the most important of the city-states.

[20] prime—first in rank.

75	The government I cast upon my brother
	And to my state grew stranger, being transported
	And rapt in secret studies.[21] Thy false uncle—
	Dost thou attend me?

Miranda. Sir, most heedfully.

Prospero. Being once perfected how to grant suits,

80	How to deny them, who t' advance, and who
	To trash for overtopping, new created
	The creatures that were mine, I say, or changed 'em,
	Or else new formed 'em, having both the key
	Of officer and office, set all hearts i' the state
85	To what tune pleased his ear, that now he was
	The ivy which had hid my princely trunk
	And sucked my verdure out on 't.[22] Thou attend'st not.

Miranda. O, good sir, I do.

Prospero. I pray thee, mark me.

	I, thus neglecting worldly ends, all dedicated
90	To closeness and the bettering of my mind
	With that which, but by being so retired,
	O'erprized all popular rate,[23] in my false brother
	Awaked an evil nature; and my trust,
	Like a good parent, did beget of him
95	A falsehood in its contrary as great
	As my trust was, which had indeed no limit,
	A confidence sans[24] bound. He being thus lorded
	Not only with what my revenue yielded
	But what my power might else exact, like one
100	Who, having into truth by telling of it,
	Made such a sinner of his memory
	To credit his own lie, he did believe
	He was indeed the duke, out o' the substitution

---

[21] transported . . . studies—fascinated and carried away by the study of the magic arts.

[22] Being . . . out on 't—Once he (Antonio) had become skilled in how to grant or deny requests and whom to support or hold back for being overly ambitious, he got new followers or changed the loyalties of my followers. Since he had the power of office, he could tell everyone what he wanted, so that he, like ivy on a tree, covered me and sapped my strength.

[23] With that . . . rate—with study that, even if it had not kept me so secluded, would be beyond the understanding of ordinary people.

[24] sans—without.

And executing th' outward face of royalty

105   With all **prerogative.**[25] Hence his ambition growing—

Dost thou hear?

Miranda.   Your tale, sir, would cure deafness.

Prospero. To have no screen between this part he played

And him he played it for, he needs will be

Absolute Milan.[26] Me, poor man, my library

110   Was dukedom large enough. Of temporal royalties

He thinks me now incapable; confederates—

So dry he was for sway—wi' the king of Naples

To give him annual tribute, do him homage,

Subject his coronet to his crown, and bend

115   The dukedom, yet unbowed—alas, poor Milan!—

To most ignoble stooping.[27]

Miranda.   O the heavens!

Prospero. Mark his condition and th' event,[28] then tell me

If this might be a brother.

Miranda.   I should sin

To think but nobly of my grandmother.

120   Good wombs have borne bad sons.

Prospero.   Now the condition.

This King of Naples, being an enemy

To me **inveterate,**[29] hearkens my brother's suit,

Which was that he, in lieu o' the premises[30]

Of homage and I know not how much tribute,

125   Should presently extirpate[31] me and mine

Out of the dukedom, and confer fair Milan,

With all the honors, on my brother. Whereon,

A treacherous army levied, one midnight

Fated to th' purpose did Antonio open

---

[25] **prerogative**—right, privilege.

[26] Absolute Milan—actual duke of Milan.

[27] Of temporal . . . stooping—He thought that I was now incapable of the responsibilities of a ruler, and he was so thirsty for power that he arranged with the king of Naples that Milan—which had always been independent—would honor him and pay him an annual tribute.

[28] condition . . . event—compact and the outcome.

[29] **inveterate**—deep-rooted; long-standing.

[30] lieu . . . premises—return for he pledge.

[31] presently extirpate—immediately drive away.

130	The gates of Milan, and, i' the dead of darkness,
	The ministers for the purpose hurried thence
	Me and thy crying self.

Miranda.   Alack, for pity!
I, not remembering how I cried out then,
Will cry it o'er again. It is a hint

135 That wrings mine eyes to 't.[32]

Prospero.   Hear a little further,
And then I'll bring thee to the present business
Which now's upon 's, without the which this story
Were most **impertinent**.[33]

Miranda.   Wherefore did they not
That hour destroy us?

Prospero.   Well demanded, wench.

140 My tale provokes that question. Dear, they durst not,
So dear the love my people bore me, nor set
A mark so bloody on the business, but
With colors fairer painted their foul ends.[34]
In few, they hurried us aboard a bark,[35]

145 Bore us some leagues to sea, where they prepared
A rotten carcass of a butt,[36] not rigged,
Nor tackle, sail, nor mast, the very rats
Instinctively have quit it. There they hoist us,
To cry to th' sea that roared to us, to sigh

150 To th' winds whose pity, sighing back again,
Did us but loving wrong.

Miranda.   Alack, what trouble
Was I then to you!

Prospero.   O, a cherubin[37]
Thou wast that did preserve me. Thou didst smile,—
Infusèd with a **fortitude**[38] from heaven,

---

[32] hint . . . to 't—occasion that brings tears to my eyes.

[33] **impertinent**—irrelevant; not to the point.

[34] With colors . . . ends—made their evil goals seem more attractive.

[35] In few . . . bark—In short, they quickly put us on a ship.

[36] butt—that is, a boat no better than a wooden tub.

[37] cherubin—angel.

[38] **fortitude**—strength.

Sit still, and hear the last
of our sea sorrow.

155   When I have decked the sea with drops full salt,[39]
        Under my burden groaned, which raised in me
        An undergoing stomach,[40] to bear up
        Against what should ensue.

Miranda.   How came we ashore?

Prospero. By providence divine.

160   Some food we had, and some fresh water, that
        A noble Neapolitan, Gonzalo,
        Out of his charity, who being then appointed
        Master of this design, did give us, with
        Rich garments, linens, stuffs, and necessaries,

165   Which since have steaded much.[41] So, of his gentleness,
        Knowing I loved my books, he furnished me
        From mine own library with volumes that
        I prize above my dukedom.

Miranda.   Would I might
        But ever see that man!

Prospero.   Now I arise.

[_Puts on his robe._]

170   Sit still, and hear the last of our sea sorrow.
        Here in this island we arrived, and here
        Have I, thy schoolmaster, made thee more profit[42]
        Than other princess' can, that have more time
        For vainer hours and tutors not so careful.

175 **Miranda.** Heavens thank you for 't! And now, I pray you, sir—
        For still 'tis beating in my mind—your reason
        For raising this sea storm?

Prospero.   Know thus far forth:
        By accident most strange, bountiful Fortune,

---

[39] decked . . . salt—covered the sea with my salty tears.

[40] undergoing stomach—courage; a sustaining spirit.

[41] steaded much—been of great use.

[42] made thee more profit—caused you to learn more.

Prospero (Patrick Stewart) gently puts Miranda (Carrie Preston) to sleep in this scene from the New York Shakespeare Festival production.

Now my dear lady, hath mine enemies
180   Brought to this shore; and by my prescience
I find my zenith doth depend upon
A most auspicious star, whose influence
If now I court not, but omit, my fortunes
Will ever after droop.[43] Here cease more questions.
185   Thou art inclined to sleep. 'Tis a good dullness,
And give it way. I know thou canst not choose.
[Miranda *sleeps.*] Come away, servant, come! I am ready now.
Approach, my Ariel, come.
[*Enter* Ariel.]
Ariel. All hail, great master! Grave sir, hail! I come
190   To answer thy best pleasure. Be 't to fly,
To swim, to dive into the fire, to ride
On the curled clouds, to thy strong bidding task
Ariel and all his quality.[44]

---

[43] **by my prescience . . . droop**—By my foresight, I find that the high point of my fortune depends on a star that will bring success. If I do not act now, my fortune will never be good.

[44] **to thy . . . quality**—Make demands on the abilities of Ariel and his fellow spirits to do what you want.

Prospero.   Hast thou, spirit,
    Performed to point the tempest that I bade thee?

195 **Ariel.** To every article.
    I boarded the king's ship. Now on the beak,
    Now in the waist, the deck, in every cabin,
    I flamed amazement.[45] Sometimes I'd divide
    And burn in many places. On the topmast,
200   The yards, and bowsprit would I flame distinctly,
    Then meet and join. Jove's lightning, the precursors
    O' the dreadful thunderclaps, more momentary
    And sight-outrunning were not.[46] The fire and cracks
    Of sulfurous roaring the most mighty Neptune[47]
205   Seem to besiege and make his bold waves tremble,
    Yea, his dread trident shake.

Prospero.   My brave spirit!
    Who was so firm, so constant, that this coil[48]
    Would not infect his reason?

Ariel.   Not a soul
    But felt a fever of the mad and played
210   Some tricks of desperation. All but mariners
    Plunged in the foaming brine and quit the vessel,
    Then all afire with me. The king's son, Ferdinand,
    With hair up-staring—then like reeds, not hair—
    Was the first man that leapt; cried, "Hell is empty,
215   And all the devils are here!"

Prospero.   Why, that's my spirit!
    But was not this nigh shore?

Ariel.   Close by, my master.

Prospero. But are they, Ariel, safe?

Ariel.   Not a hair perished.
    On their sustaining garments not a blemish,
    But fresher than before; and, as thou bad'st me,
220   In troops I have dispersed them 'bout the isle.
    The king's son have I landed by himself,

---

[45] flamed amazement—caused terror with artificial fire.

[46] Jove's lightning ... were not—The lightning bolts of the king of the gods, which foretell thunder to follow, could not have been faster or harder to follow with the eyes.

[47] Neptune—Roman god of the sea, who carries a three-pronged spear (trident) as a symbol of power.

[48] coil—disturbance.

Whom I left cooling of the air with sighs
In an odd angle of the isle, and sitting,
His arms in this sad knot.

[*He folds his arms.*]

Prospero.   Of the king's ship,
The mariners, say how thou hast disposed,
And all the rest o' the fleet.

Ariel.   Safely in harbor
Is the king's ship. In the deep nook, where once
Thou called'st me up at midnight to fetch dew
From the still-vexed Bermoothes,[49] there she's hid;
The mariners all under hatches stowed,
Who, with a charm joined to their suffered labor,
I have left asleep. And for the rest o' the fleet,
Which I dispersed, they all have met again
And are upon the Mediterranean float[50]
Bound sadly home for Naples,
Supposing that they saw the king's ship wrecked
And his great person perish.

Prospero.   Ariel, thy charge
Exactly is performed. But there's more work.
What is the time o' the day?

Ariel.   Past the mid season.

Prospero. At least two glasses.[51] The time twixt six and now
Must by us both be spent most preciously.

Ariel. Is there more toil? Since thou dost give me pains,
Let me remember thee what thou hast promised,
Which is not yet performed me.

Prospero.   How now? Moody?
What is 't thou canst demand?

Ariel.   My liberty.

Prospero. Before the time be out? No more!

Ariel.   I prithee,
Remember I have done thee worthy service,
Told thee no lies, made thee no mistakings, served

---

49 still-vexed Bermoothes—always-stormy Bermudas.

50 float—sea.

51 Past . . . glasses—two hours (hourglasses) past noon (2 P.M.).

Without or grudge or grumblings. Thou did promise
250 To bate[52] me a full year.

Prospero. Dost thou forget
From what a torment I did free thee?

Ariel. No.

Prospero. Thou dost, and think'st it much to tread the ooze
Of the salt deep,
To run upon the sharp wind of the north,
255 To do me business in the veins o' the earth
When it is baked with frost.

Ariel. I do not, sir.

Prospero. Thou liest, malignant thing! Hast thou forgot
The foul witch Sycorax, who with age and envy
Was grown into a hoop?[53] Hast thou forgot her?

260 **Ariel.** No, sir.

Prospero. Thou hast. Where was she born? Speak. Tell me.

Ariel. Sir, in Argier.[54]

Prospero. O, was she so? I must
Once in a month recount what thou hast been,
Which thou forget'st. This damned witch Sycorax,
265 For mischiefs manifold and sorceries terrible
To enter human hearing, from Argier,
Thou know'st, was banished. For one thing she did
They would not take her life.[55] Is not this true?

Ariel. Ay, sir.

270 **Prospero.** This blue-eyed hag was hither brought with child
And here was left by th' sailors. Thou, my slave,
As thou report'st thyself, was then her servant,
And, for thou wast a spirit too delicate
To act her earthy and abhorred commands,
275 Refusing her grand hests,[56] she did confine thee,
By help of her more potent ministers
And in her most unmitigable[57] rage,

---

[52] bate—deduct.

[53] grown into a hoop—bent over.

[54] Argier—Algiers, an African seaport on the Mediterranean.

[55] For one . . . life—because she was pregnant, they would not execute her.

[56] hests—commands.

[57] unmitigable—not capable of being lessened.

Into a cloven[58] pine, within which rift
Imprisoned thou didst painfully remain
280 A dozen years; within which space she died
And left thee there, where thou didst vent thy groans
As fast as mill wheels strike. Then was this island—
Save for the son that she did litter here,
A freckled whelp, hag-born—not honored with
A human shape.

285 **Ariel.** Yes, Caliban, her son.

Prospero. Dull thing, I say so! He, that Caliban
Whom now I keep in service. Thou best know'st
What torment I did find thee in. Thy groans
Did make wolves howl, and penetrate the breasts
290 Of ever-angry bears. It was a torment
To lay upon the damned, which Sycorax
Could not again undo. It was mine art,
When I arrived and heard thee, that made gape
The pine and let thee out.

Ariel. I thank thee, master.

295 **Prospero.** If thou more murmur'st, I will rend an oak
And peg thee in his knotty entrails[59] till
Thou hast howled away twelve winters.

Ariel. Pardon, master.
I will be correspondent[60] to command
And do my spriting gently.

Prospero. Do so, and after two days
300 I will discharge thee.

Ariel. That's my noble master!
What shall I do? Say what? What shall I do?

Prospero. Go make thyself like a nymph o' the sea.[61] Be subject
To no sight but thine and mine, invisible

---

[58] cloven—split.

[59] If thou . . . entrails—If you complain any more, I will split an oak tree and imprison you in its tough insides.

[60] correspondent—obedient.

[61] nymph o' the sea—sea nymphs were minor sea goddesses in the form of beautiful maidens.

Thou poisonous slave, got by the devil himself Upon thy wicked dam, come forth!

To every eyeball else. Go take this shape
305 And hither come in 't. Go, hence with **diligence!**[62]
[*Exit* Ariel.]
Awake, dear heart, awake! Thou hast slept well.
Awake!

Miranda. The strangeness of your story put
Heaviness in me.

Prospero.   Shake it off. Come on,
310 We'll visit Caliban, my slave, who never
Yields us kind answer.

Miranda.   'Tis a villain, sir,
I do not love to look on.

Prospero.   But, as 'tis,
We cannot miss[63] him. He does make our fire,
Fetch in our wood, and serves in offices
315 That profit us.—What ho! Slave! Caliban!
Thou earth, thou! Speak.

Caliban [*within*].   There's wood enough within.

Prospero. Come forth, I say! There's other business for thee.
Come, thou tortoise! When?
[*Enter* Ariel *like a water nymph.*]
Fine apparition! My quaint Ariel,
320 Hark in thine ear.
[*He whispers.*]

Ariel.   My lord, it shall be done. [*Exit* Ariel.]

Prospero. Thou poisonous slave, got by the devil himself
Upon thy wicked dam,[64] come forth!
[*Enter* Caliban.]

---

[62] **diligence**—careful, constant effort.

[63] miss—do without.

[64] dam—mother.

Miranda (Kari McGee) expresses her contempt for Caliban (Amy Thone) in this scene from the Seattle Children's Theatre production.

Caliban. As wicked dew as e'er my mother brushed
With raven's feather from unwholesome fen[65]
325   Drop on you both! A southwest[66] blow on ye
And blister you all o'er!
Prospero. For this, be sure, tonight thou shalt have cramps,
Side-stitches that shall pen thy breath up. Urchins
Shall forth at vast of night that they may work
330   All exercise on thee.[67] Thou shalt be pinched
As thick as honeycomb, each pinch more stinging
Than bees that made 'em.
Caliban.   I must eat my dinner.
This island's mine by Sycorax, my mother,
335   Which thou tak'st from me. When thou cam'st first,

---

[65] fen—swamp.

[66] southwest—wind thought to bring disease.

[67] Urchins . . . on thee—goblins in the form of hedgehogs will come out in the dark of night to torment you.

This island's mine by Sycorax, my mother, Which thou tak'st from me.

Thou strok'st me and made much of me, wouldst give me
Water with berries in 't, and teach me how
To name the bigger light, and how the less,
That burn by day and night.[68] And then I loved thee
340   And showed thee all the qualities o' th' isle,
The fresh springs, brine pits, barren place and fertile.
Cursed be I that did so! All the charms
Of Sycorax, toads, beetles, bats, light on you!
For I am all the subjects that you have,
345   Which first was mine own king; and here you sty me[69]
In this hard rock, whiles you do keep from me
The rest o' th' island.

Prospero.   Thou most lying slave,
Whom stripes[70] may move, not kindness! I have used thee,
Filth as thou art, with humane care, and lodged thee
350   In mine own cell, till thou didst seek to violate
The honor of my child.[71]

Caliban. O ho, O ho! Would't had been done!
Thou didst prevent me; I had peopled else
This isle with Calibans.

Miranda.   Abhorrèd slave,
355   Which any print of goodness wilt not take,
Being capable of all ill! I pitied thee,
Took pains to make thee speak, taught thee each hour
One thing or other. When thou didst not, savage,
Know thine own meaning, but wouldst gabble like
360   A thing most brutish, I endowed thy purposes[72]
With words that made them known. But thy vile race,

---

[68] To name . . . night—to name the sun and the moon.

[69] sty me—pen me up as if in a pigsty.

[70] stripes—lashes; beatings.

[71] till thou . . . child—until you tried to rape Miranda.

[72] purposes—meanings; ideas.

Though thou didst learn, had that in 't which good natures
Could not abide to be with. Therefore wast thou
Deservedly confined into this rock,
365   Who hadst deserved more than a prison.

Caliban. You taught me language, and my profit on 't
Is I know how to curse. The red plague rid you
For learning me your language!

Prospero.   Hagseed, hence!
Fetch us in fuel, and be quick, thou'rt best,
370   To answer other business.[73] Shrugg'st thou, malice?
If thou neglect'st or dost unwillingly
What I command, I'll rack thee with old cramps,
Fill all thy bones with aches, make thee roar
That beasts shall tremble at thy din.

Caliban.   No, pray thee.
375   [*Aside.*] I must obey. His art is of such power
It would control my dam's god, Setebos,[74]
And make a vassal[75] of him.

Prospero.   O, slave, hence!
[*Exit* Caliban.]
[*Enter* Ferdinand; *and* Ariel, *invisible, playing and
singing.* Ferdinand *does not see* Prospero *and* Miranda.]
Ariel. [*Sings.*] *Come unto these yellow sands,*
     And then take hands;
380   *Curtsied when you have, and kissed*
     The wild waves whist;[76]
Foot it featly[77] *here and there,*
     And, sweet sprites, bear
The burden.[78] *Hark, hark!*
385   [*Burden, dispersedly,*[79] *within.*] *Bow-wow.*
The watchdogs bark.

---

[73] answer other business—perform other duties.

[74] Setebos—god of the Patagonians, Indians from a region of South America, now Argentina.

[75] vassal—servant.

[76] *whist*—silent.

[77] *Foot it featly*—dance with agility.

[78] *bear . . . burden*—sing the refrain.

[79] *dispersedly*—from different sides; not in unison.

Full fathom five thy father lies,
Of his bones are coral made.

                  [Burden, dispersedly.] Bow-wow.

                  Hark, hark! I hear

                  The strain of strutting chanticleer[80]

390   *Cry Cock-a-diddle-dow.*

Ferdinand. Where should this music be? I' th' air or th' earth?

     It sounds no more; and sure it waits upon

     Some god o' th' island. Sitting on a bank,

     Weeping again the king my father's wrack,

395   This music crept by me upon the waters,

     Allaying both their fury and my passion

     With its sweet air. Thence I have followed it,

     Or it hath drawn me rather. But 'tis gone.

     No, it begins again.

400 **Ariel** [*sings*]. *Full fathom five thy father lies.*

         Of his bones are coral made.

     Those are pearls that were his eyes.

         Nothing of him that doth fade

     But doth suffer a sea change

405   *Into something rich and strange.*

     Sea nymphs hourly ring his knell.

[Burden within.] Ding dong.

     Hark, now I hear them, ding dong bell.

Ferdinand. The ditty does remember my drowned father.

410   This is no mortal business, nor no sound

     That the earth owes. I hear it now above me.

Prospero [*to* Miranda]. The fringèd curtains of thine eye advance

     And say what thou seest yond.[81]

Miranda.   What is 't? A spirit?

     Lord, how it looks about! Believe me, sir,

415   It carries a brave form. But 'tis a spirit.

---

[80] *strain . . . chanticleer*—tune of the strutting rooster.

[81] The fringèd . . . yond—Raise your eyelids and tell me what you see over there.

Ferdinand (Scott Ripley) muses over his father's fate in this scene from the American Repertory Theatre production.

Prospero. No, wench, it eats and sleeps and hath such senses
As we have, such. This gallant which thou seest
Was in the wreck; and, but he's something stained
With grief—that's beauty's canker[82]—thou mightst call him
A goodly person. He hath lost his fellows
420 And strays about to find 'em.
Miranda.   I might call him
A thing divine, for nothing natural
I ever saw so noble.
Prospero [*aside*].   It goes on, I see,
As my soul prompts it.—
425 [*To* Ariel.] Spirit, fine spirit, I'll free thee
Within two days for this.
Ferdinand [*seeing* Miranda]. Most sure, the goddess
On whom these airs attend!—Vouchsafe my prayer
May know[83] if you remain upon this island,
430 And that you will some good instruction give
How I may bear me here. My prime request,
Which I do last pronounce, is—O you wonder!—
If you be maid or no?

---

[82] beauty's canker—cankerworm, spoiler of beauty.
[83] Vouchsafe . . . know—grant my prayer so that I may know.

Miranda.   No wonder, sir,
But certainly a maid.

Ferdinand.   My language? Heavens!
435   I am the best of them that speak this speech,
Were I but where 'tis spoken.[84]

Prospero [*coming forward*]. How? The best?
What wert thou if the king of Naples heard thee?

Ferdinand. A single thing, as I am now, that wonders
440   To hear thee speak of Naples. He does hear me,
And that he does I weep. Myself am Naples,
Who with mine eyes, never since at ebb,[85] beheld
The king my father wrecked.

Miranda.   Alack, for mercy!

Ferdinand. Yes, faith, and all his lords, the duke of Milan
And his brave son being twain.[86]

445   **Prospero** [*aside*].   The duke of Milan
And his more braver daughter could control thee,
If now 'twere fit to do 't.[87] At the first sight
They have changed eyes.[88]—Delicate Ariel,
I'll set thee free for this. [*To Ferdinand.*] A word, good sir.
450   I fear you have done yourself some wrong. A word!

Miranda [*aside*]. Why speaks my father so ungently? This
Is the third man that e'er I saw, the first
That e'er I sighed for. Pity move my father
To be inclined my way!

Ferdinand.   O, if a virgin,
455   And your affection not gone forth, I'll make you
The queen of Naples.

Prospero.   Soft,[89] sir! One word more.
[*Aside.*] They are both in either's powers. But this swift business
I must uneasy make, lest too light winning
460   Make the prize light. [*To Ferdinand.*] One word more: I charge thee

---

[84] I am . . . spoken—If I were home, where my language is spoken, I would be king of Naples.

[85] myself . . . never since at ebb—I myself am king of Naples, whose eyes that have not stopped crying since then.

[86] twain—two. Antonio's son never appears anywhere else in the play.

[87] The duke . . . do 't—The real duke of Milan (myself) and his more splendid daughter could prove you wrong, if now were the proper time to do it.

[88] changed eyes—fallen in love.

[89] Soft—wait.

That thou attend me. Thou dost here usurp[90]
The name thou ow'st not, and hast put thyself
Upon this island as a spy, to win it
From me, the lord on 't.

Ferdinand.   No, as I am a man.

Miranda. There's nothing ill can dwell in such a temple.

465   If the ill spirit have so fair a house,
Good things will strive to dwell with 't.

Prospero.   Follow me.—
[*To* Miranda.] Speak not you for him; he's a traitor.—
[*To* Ferdinand.] Come,
I'll manacle thy neck and feet together.

470   Sea water shalt thou drink. Thy food shall be
The fresh-brook mussels, withered roots, and husks
Wherein the acorn cradled. Follow.

Ferdinand.   No!
I will resist such entertainment[91] till
Mine enemy has more power.

[*He draws his sword, but is charmed from moving.*]

Miranda.   O dear father,

475   Make not too rash a trial of him, for
He's gentle, and not fearful.

Prospero.   What, I say,
My foot my tutor?[92]—Put thy sword up, traitor,
Who mak'st a show but dar'st not strike, thy conscience
Is so possessed with guilt. Come from thy ward,[93]

480   For I can here disarm thee with this stick
And make thy weapon drop.

Miranda Beseech you, father!

Prospero. Hence! Hang not on my garments.

Miranda.   Sir, have pity!
I'll be his surety.

Prospero.   Silence! One word more

485   Shall make me chide thee, if not hate thee. What,

---

[90] usurp—steal.

[91] entertainment—treatment.

[92] My foot my tutor—Should a subordinate part of me (my child) be my teacher?

[93] ward—defensive position.

An **advocate**[94] for an impostor? Hush!
Thou think'st there is no more such shapes as he,
Having seen but him and Caliban. Foolish wench,
To the most of men this is a Caliban,
And they to him are angels.

490 **Miranda.** My affections
Are then most humble. I have no ambition
To see a goodlier man.

Prospero [*to* Ferdinand]. Come on, obey.
Thy nerves are in their infancy again
And have no vigor in them.

495 **Ferdinand.** So they are.
My spirits, as in a dream, are all bound up.
My father's loss, the weakness which I feel,
The wreck of all my friends, nor this man's threats
To whom I am subdued, are but light to me,
500 Might I but through my prison once a day
Behold this maid. All corners else o' th' earth
Let liberty make use of. Space enough
Have I in such a prison.

Prospero [*aside*]. It works. [*To* Ferdinand.] Come on.—
Thou hast done well, fine Ariel!—[*To* Ferdinand.]
Follow me.
[*To* Ariel.] Hark what thou else shalt do me.

505 **Miranda** [*to* Ferdinand]. Be of comfort.
My father's of a better nature, sir,
Than he appears by speech. This is unwonted[95]
Which now came from him.

Prospero [*to* Ariel]. Thou shalt be as free
As mountain winds; but then exactly do
All points of my command.

Ariel. To th' syllable.

510 **Prospero.** [*to* Ferdinand].
Come, follow. [*To* Miranda.] Speak not for him.
[*They exit.*]

---

[94] **advocate**—spokesperson; defender.

[95] **unwonted**—unusual; unaccustomed.

Act Two, Scene One

In another part of the island, Gonzalo and Adrian try to convince the others to be happy because they are still alive, but King Alonso mourns his son because he is sure that Ferdinand is dead. To distract the king, Gonzalo describes the ideal society he would establish on the island if he ruled it. As the men debate what they should do, Ariel magically puts all of them to sleep, except Sebastian and Antonio. Antonio suggests that because Ferdinand must have drowned, Sebastian is next in line to be king of Naples—if Alonso were dead. They pull out their swords to kill Alonso and Gonzalo, but Ariel wakes Gonzalo, and his cries wake the others. Sebastian and Antonio explain their unsheathed swords by saying that they were frightened by a loud noise. The men scatter to search the island.

Enter Alonso, Sebastian, Antonio, Gonzalo, Adrian, Francisco, *and others.*

Gonzalo [*to* Alonso]. Beseech you,[1] sir, be merry. You have cause,
    So have we all, of joy, for our escape
    Is much beyond our loss. Our hint of woe
    Is common; every day some sailor's wife,
5   The masters of some merchant, and the merchant,
    Have just our theme of woe. But for the miracle,
    I mean our preservation, few in millions
    Can speak like us. Then wisely, good sir, weigh
    Our sorrow with our comfort.

Alonso.   Prithee, peace.

10 **Sebastian** [*aside to* Antonio]. He receives comfort like cold porridge.

Antonio [*aside to* Sebastian]. The visitor will not give him o'er so.[2]

Sebastian. Look, he's winding up the watch of his wit; by and by
    it will strike.

Gonzalo [*to* Alonso]. Sir—

15 **Sebastian** [*aside to* Antonio]. One. Tell.[3]

Gonzalo. When every grief is entertained that's offered, comes to
    th' entertainer—

---

[1] Beseech you—I pray you that is, please.

[2] The visitor . . . so—The one bringing comfort will not give up on him.

[3] Tell—Keep count.

Sebastian. A dollar.[4]

Gonzalo. Dolor comes to him, indeed. You have spoken truer
   than you purposed.

Sebastian. You have taken it wiselier than I meant you should.

Gonzalo [*to* Alonso]. Therefore, my lord—

Antonio. Fie, what a spendthrift is he of his tongue!

Alonso [*to* Gonzalo]. I prithee, spare.[5]

Gonzalo. Well, I have done. But yet—

Sebastian [*aside to* Antonio]. He will be talking.

Antonio [*aside to* Sebastian]. Which, of he or Adrian,
   for a good wager, first begins to crow?[6]

Sebastian. The old cock.

Antonio. The cockerel.

Sebastian. Done. The wager?

Antonio. A laughter.

Sebastian. A match!

Adrian. Though this island seem to be desert—

Antonio. Ha, ha, ha!

Sebastian. So, you're paid.

Adrian. Uninhabitable and almost **inaccessible**[7] —

Sebastian. Yet—

Adrian. Yet—

Antonio. He could not miss 't.

Adrian. It must needs be of subtle, tender, and delicate temperance.[8]

Antonio. Temperance was a delicate wench.

Sebastian. Ay, and a subtle, as he most learnedly delivered.

Adrian. The air breathes upon us here most sweetly.

Sebastian. As if it had lungs, and rotten ones.

Antonio. Or as 'twere perfumed by a fen.

Gonzalo. Here is everything advantageous to life.

Antonio. True, save means to live.[9]

Sebastian. Of that there's none, or little.

---

[4] dollar—widely circulated coin; the German thaler and the Spanish piece of eight. Gonzalo puns on *dolor*, "sadness."

[5] spare—stop; spare me.

[6] Which . . . crow—Do you want to bet whether Gonzalo or Adrian will speak first?

[7] **inaccessible**—unable to be reached.

[8] It must . . . temperance—It must have a mild climate. Antonio puns on *Temperance*, a girl's name.

[9] save means to live—except for ways to stay alive.

50   **Gonzalo.** How lush and lusty the grass looks! How green!

Antonio. The ground indeed is tawny.

Sebastian. With an eye of green in 't.

Antonio. He misses not much.

Sebastian. No. He doth but mistake the truth totally.

55   **Gonzalo.** But the rarity of it is—which is indeed almost beyond credit—

Sebastian. As many vouched rarities[10] are.

Gonzalo. That our garments, being, as they were, drenched in the sea,
hold notwithstanding their freshness and glosses, being rather new-
dyed than stained with salt water.

60   **Antonio.** If but one of his pockets could speak, would it not say he lies?[11]

Sebastian. Ay, or very falsely pocket up[12] his report.

Gonzalo. Methinks our garments are now as fresh as when we put them
on first in Afric, at the marriage of the king's fair daughter Claribel to
the king of Tunis.[13]

65   **Sebastian.** 'Twas a sweet marriage, and we prosper well in our return.

Adrian. Tunis was never graced before with such a **paragon**[14] to
their queen.

Gonzalo. Not since widow Dido's[15] time.

Antonio [*aside to* Sebastian]. Widow? A pox o' that!

70   How came that "widow" in? Widow Dido!

Sebastian. What if he had said "widower Aeneas" too? Good Lord, how
you take it!

Adrian [*to* Gonzalo]. "Widow Dido" said you? You make me study of
that. She was of Carthage, not of Tunis.

75   **Gonzalo.** This Tunis, sir, was Carthage.

Adrian. Carthage?

Gonzalo. I assure you, Carthage.

Antonio. His word is more than the miraculous harp.

Sebastian. He hath raised the wall, and houses too.[16]

---

[10] vouched rarities—sights that are unusual but claimed to be true.

[11] If but . . . lies—Antonio suggests that Gonzalo's pocket would prove him a liar because it is still wet.

[12] pocket up—conceal; suppress.

[13] Tunis—seaport on the north coast of Africa (Afric).

[14] **paragon**—perfect example; ideal.

[15] Dido's—In Roman mythology, she was the queen of Carthage (an ancient city near the site of Tunis). She was deserted by her lover, the Trojan hero Aeneas.

[16] His word . . . houses too—reference to Amphion's harp, with which he raised the walls of legendary Thebes. Gonzalo has bettered him by raising not only the walls but the entire city with his words.

80 **Antonio.** What impossible matter will he make easy next?

Sebastian. I think he will carry this island home in his pocket and give it his son for an apple.

Antonio. And, sowing the kernels[17] of it in the sea, bring forth more islands.

85 **Gonzalo.** Ay.

Antonio. Why, in good time.

Gonzalo [*to* Alonso]. Sir, we were talking that our garments seem now as fresh as when we were at Tunis at the marriage of your daughter, who is now queen.

90 **Antonio.** And the rarest that e'er came there.

Sebastian. Bate,[18] I beseech you, widow Dido.

Antonio. O, widow Dido? Ay, widow Dido.

Gonzalo. Is not, sir, my doublet as fresh as the first day I wore it? I mean, in a sort.

95 **Antonio.** That "sort" was well fished for.

Gonzalo. When I wore it at your daughter's marriage.

Alonso. You cram these words into mine ears against
The stomach of my sense. Would I had never
Married my daughter there! For, coming thence,
100 My son is lost and, in my rate,[19] she too,
Who is so far from Italy removed
I ne'er again shall see her. O thou mine heir
Of Naples and of Milan, what strange fish
Hath made his meal on thee?

Francisco.   Sir, he may live.
105 I saw him beat the surges[20] under him
And ride upon their backs. He trod the water,
Whose **enmity**[21] he flung aside, and breasted
The surge most swoll'n that met him. His bold head
'Bove the **contentious**[22] waves he kept, and oared
110 Himself with his good arms in lusty stroke

---

[17] kernels—seeds.

[18] Bate—except for.

[19] in my rate—as far as I'm concerned.

[20] surges—waves.

[21] **enmity**—hostility; antagonism.

[22] **contentious**—quarrelsome.

To th' shore, that o'er his wave-worn basis bowed,
As stooping to relieve him.[23] I not doubt
He came alive to land.

Alonso.   No, no, he's gone.

Sebastian [*to* Alonso]. Sir, you may thank yourself for this great loss,
115   That would not bless our Europe with your daughter,
But rather loose her to an African,
Where she at least is banished from your eye,
Who hath cause to wet the grief on 't.[24]

Alonso.   Prithee, peace.

Sebastian. You were kneeled to and importuned otherwise
120   By all of us, and the fair soul herself
Weighed between loathness and obedience at
Which end o' the beam should bow.[25] We have lost your son,
I fear, forever. Milan and Naples have
More widows in them of this business' making
125   Than we bring men to comfort them.
The fault's your own.

Alonso.   So is the dear'st[26] o' the loss.

Gonzalo. My lord Sebastian,
The truth you speak doth lack some gentleness
And time to speak it in. You rub the sore
130   When you should bring the plaster.[27]

Sebastian.   Very well.

Antonio. And most chirurgeonly.[28]

Gonzalo [*to* Alonso]. It is foul weather in us all, good sir,
When you are cloudy.

Sebastian [*to* Antonio]. Foul weather?

Antonio [*to* Sebastian].   Very foul.

135 **Gonzalo.** Had I plantation[29] of this isle, my lord—

---

[23] that o'er . . . him—that bent down over its eroded base as if stooping to help him.

[24] Where she . . . grief on 't—You have a reason to weep for her, who is too far away for you to see her.

[25] You were . . . bow—All of us begged you on our knees not to insist on the marriage. Claribel herself was undecided between her unwillingness to marry and her duty to obey you.

[26] dear'st—most precious (or most bitter) part.

[27] plaster—medicated bandage.

[28] chirurgeonly—like a surgeon.

[29] Had I plantation—if I were the colonizer. But Antonio puns by taking the word in its other sense.

I would with such perfection govern, sir, T' excel the Golden Age.

Antonio He'd sow 't with nettle seed.

Sebastian.   Or docks, or mallows.

Gonzalo. And were the king on 't, what would I do?

Sebastian. Scape being drunk for want of wine.[30]

Gonzalo. I' the commonwealth I would by contraries

140   Execute all things;[31] for no kind of traffic

Would I admit; no name of magistrate;

Letters should not be known; riches, poverty,

And use of service, none; contract, succession,

Bourn, bound of land, tilth,[32] vineyard, none;

145   No use of metal, corn, or wine, or oil;

No occupation; all men idle, all,

And women too, but innocent and pure;

No sovereignty—

Sebastian.   Yet he would be king on 't.

Antonio. The latter end of his commonwealth forgets the beginning.

150 **Gonzalo.** All things in common nature should produce

Without sweat or endeavor. Treason, felony,

Sword, pike, knife, gun, or need of any engine[33]

Would I not have; but nature should bring forth,

Of its own kind, all foison,[34] all abundance,

155   To feed my innocent people.

Sebastian. No marrying 'mong his subjects?

Antonio. None, man, all idle—whores and knaves.

Gonzalo. I would with such perfection govern, sir,

T' excel the Golden Age.

Sebastian.   Save His Majesty!

---

[30] Scape ... wine—Never get drunk because there is no wine.

[31] I would ... things—I would do all things opposite to the ways they are usually done.

[32] Bourn ... tilth—land ownership, farming.

[33] engine—instrument of war.

[34] foison—plenty.

160   **Antonio.** Long live Gonzalo!

Gonzalo.   And—do you mark me, sir?

Alonso. Prithee, no more. Thou dost talk nothing to me.

Gonzalo. I do well believe Your Highness, and did it to minister occasion
       to these gentlemen, who are of such sensible and nimble lungs that
       they always use to laugh at nothing.[35]

165   **Antonio.** 'Twas you we laughed at.

Gonzalo. Who in this kind of merry fooling am nothing to you. So you
       may continue, and laugh at nothing still.

Antonio. What a blow was there given!

Sebastian. An it had not fallen flatlong.[36]

170   **Gonzalo.** You are gentlemen of brave mettle; you would lift the
       moon out of her sphere[37] if she would continue in it five weeks
       without changing.

[*Enter* Ariel (*invisible*) *playing solemn music.*]

Sebastian. We would so, and then go a-batfowling.[38]

Antonio. Nay, good my lord, be not angry.

175   **Gonzalo.** No, I warrant you, I will not adventure my discretion so
       weakly.[39] Will you laugh me asleep? For I am very heavy.

Antonio. Go sleep, and hear us.[40]

[*All sleep except* Alonso, Sebastian, *and* Antonio.]

Alonso. What, all so soon asleep? I wish mine eyes
       Would, with themselves, shut up my thoughts. I find

180   They are inclined to do so.

Sebastian.   Please you, sir,
       Do not omit the heavy offer of it.[41]
       It seldom visits sorrow; when it doth,
       It is a comforter.

---

[35] to minister . . . nothing—to provide an opportunity for these gentlemen, who are so witty and sensitive that they laugh at anything.

[36] An it . . . flatlong—if it had not fallen harmlessly (with the flat of the sword).

[37] You are . . . sphere—You are gentlemen of such spirit that you would move the moon from its orbit.

[38] go a-batfowling—go hunting birds at night with a lantern and stick.

[39] I will . . . weakly—I won't risk my reputation for so slight a cause (by getting angry at your jokes).

[40] hear us—listen to our laughter.

[41] Do not . . . of it—Don't fight off sleep.

Antonio.   We two, my lord,
        Will guard your person while you take your rest,
185   And watch your safety.

Alonso.   Thank you. Wondrous heavy.

[Alonso *sleeps. Exit* Ariel.]

Sebastian. What a strange drowsiness possesses them!

Antonio. It is the quality o' the climate.

Sebastian.   Why
        Doth it not then our eyelids sink? I find not
        Myself disposed to sleep.

In this scene from the Seattle Repertory Theatre production, Antonio (left) attempts to persuade Sebastian to conspire with him against Alonso.

Antonio.   Nor I. My spirits are nimble.

190   They fell together all, as by consent;
         They dropped as by a thunderstroke. What might,
         Worthy Sebastian, O, what might—? No more.
         And yet methinks I see it in thy face,
         What thou shouldst be. Th' occasion speaks thee,[42] and

195   My strong imagination sees a crown
         Dropping upon thy head.

Sebastian.   What, art thou waking?[43]

Antonio. Do you not hear me speak?

Sebastian.   I do, and surely
         It is a sleepy language, and thou speak'st
         Out of thy sleep. What is it thou didst say?

200   This is a strange repose, to be asleep
         With eyes wide open—standing, speaking, moving—
         And yet so fast asleep.

Antonio.   Noble Sebastian,
         Thou let'st thy fortune sleep, die rather; wink'st
         Whiles thou art waking.[44]

Sebastian.   Thou dost snore distinctly;

205   There's meaning in thy snores.

Antonio. I am more serious than my custom. You
         Must be so too, if heed me; which to do
         Trebles thee o'er.[45]

Sebastian.   Well, I am standing water.

Antonio. I'll teach you how to flow.

Sebastian.   Do so. To ebb

210   Hereditary sloth instructs me.[46]

Antonio.   O,
         If you but knew how you the purpose cherish
         Whiles thus you mock it! How, in stripping it,
         You more invest it! Ebbing men, indeed,

---

[42] Th' occasion speaks thee—The opportunity of the moment calls you.

[43] What . . . waking?—Are you awake, or are you asleep and dreaming?

[44] wink'st . . . waking—Although you are awake, you shut your eyes (to your opportunity).

[45] You . . . o'er—You must also be more serious than usual if you pay attention to me, which would make you three times more powerful.

[46] To ebb . . . me—Natural laziness and the position of a younger brother who cannot inherit make me inclined to fall back.

            Most often do so near the bottom run

215   By their own fear or sloth.[47]

Sebastian.   Prithee, say on.

            The setting of thine eye and cheek proclaim

            A matter from thee, and a birth indeed

            Which throes thee much to yield.[48]

Antonio.   Thus, sir:

            Although this lord[49] of weak remembrance—this

220   Who shall be of as little memory

            When he is earthed[50]—hath here almost persuaded—

            For he's a spirit of persuasion, only

            Professes to persuade[51]—the king his son's alive,

            'Tis as impossible that he's undrowned

225   As he that sleeps here swims.

Sebastian.   I have no hope[52]

            That he's undrowned.

Antonio.   O, out of that "no hope"

            What great hope have you! No hope that way is

            Another way so high a hope that even

            Ambition cannot pierce a wink beyond,

230   But doubt discovery there.[53] Will you grant with me

            That Ferdinand is drowned?

Sebastian.   He's gone.

Antonio.   Then tell me,

            Who's the next heir of Naples?

Sebastian.   Claribel.

Antonio. She that is Queen of Tunis; she that dwells

            Ten leagues beyond man's life; she that from Naples

235   Can have no note, unless the sun were post—

---

[47] If you ... sloth—If you only realized how much importance you give to ambition by the act of making fun of it. The more you tear it down, the more you build it up. Men without a sense of adventure may run aground and miss the tide of fortune.

[48] birth ... yield—idea that is paining you to express.

[49] this lord—Gonzalo.

[50] earthed—buried.

[51] only ... persuade—his only function is to persuade.

[52] hope—expectation.

[53] Ambition ... there—Even ambition can't see any further than that hope of the crown, but it's unsure of itself in seeing even that far and dazzled by daring to think so high.

The Man i' the Moon's too slow—till newborn chins
Be rough and razorable;[54] she that from whom
We all were sea-swallowed, though some cast again,
And by that destiny to perform an act

240   Whereof what's past is prologue, what to come
In yours and my discharge.[55]

Sebastian. What stuff is this? How say you?
'Tis true my brother's daughter's queen of Tunis,
So is she heir of Naples, 'twixt which regions

245   There is some space.

Antonio.   A space whose ev'ry cubit
Seems to cry out, "How shall that Claribel
Measure us back to Naples? Keep in Tunis,
And let Sebastian wake." Say this were death
That now hath seized them, why, they were no worse

250   Than now they are. There be that[56] can rule Naples
As well as he that sleeps, lords that can prate
As amply and unnecessarily
As this Gonzalo. I myself could make
A chough of as deep chat.[57] O, that you bore

255   The mind that I do! What a sleep were this
For your advancement! Do you understand me?

Sebastian. Methinks I do.

Antonio.   And how does your content
Tender your own good fortune?

Sebastian.   I remember
You did **supplant**[58] your brother Prospero.

Antonio.   True.

260   And look how well my garments sit upon me,
Much feater[59] than before. My brother's servants
Were then my fellows. Now they are my men.

---

[54] She that . . . razorable—she who lives farther away than the journey of a lifetime; she who will receive no news from Naples unless the sun serves as messenger because the moon is too slow; she who lives so far away that babies become old enough to shave in the time that news takes to travel the distance.

[55] discharge—performance.

[56] There be that—there are people who.

[57] I myself . . . chat—I could teach a crow or jackdaw to talk with as much sense.

[58] **supplant**—replace, take the place of; also, displace, uproot.

[59] feater—more elegant.

Here lies your brother,
No better than the earth he lies upon.

Sebastian. But, for your conscience?

Antonio. Ay, sir, where lies that? If 'twere a kibe,

265   'Twould put me to my slipper; but I feel not

This deity in my bosom.[60] Twenty consciences

That stand twixt me and Milan, candied be they

And melt ere they molest![61] Here lies your brother,

No better than the earth he lies upon,

270   If he were that which now he's like—that's dead,

Whom I, with this obedient steel, three inches of it,

Can lay to bed forever; whiles you, doing thus,

To the perpetual wink for aye might put[62]

This ancient morsel, this Sir Prudence, who

275   Should not upbraid our course. For all the rest,

They'll take suggestion as a cat laps milk.

They'll tell the clock to any business that

We say befits the hour.

Sebastian.   Thy case, dear friend,

Shall be my precedent. As thou gott'st Milan,

280   I'll come by Naples. Draw thy sword. One stroke

Shall free thee from the tribute which thou payest,

And I the king shall love thee.

Antonio.   Draw together,

And when I rear my hand, do you the like

To fall it on Gonzalo.

Sebastian.   O, but one word.

[*They talk apart.*]

[*Enter Ariel (invisible), with music and song.*]

---

[60] If 'twere . . . bosom—If it were a sore heel, it would cause me to wear slippers, but I don't feel any pangs of conscience in my heart.

[61] candied . . . molest—May they be frozen and melt before they cause trouble.

[62] To the perpetual . . . put—put to sleep forever.

Ariel (Benjamin Evett) warns the sleeping Gonzalo (Alvin Epstein) about the threat against him and Alonso in this scene from the American Repertory Theatre production.

285   **Ariel** [*to* Gonzalo]. My master through his art foresees the danger
       That you, his friend, are in, and sends me forth—
       For else his project dies—to keep them living.
    [*Sings in* Gonzalo's *ear.*]
        While you here do snoring lie,
        Open-eyed conspiracy
290   *His time*[63] *doth take.*

---

[63] time—opportunity.

> *If of life you keep a care,*
> *Shake off slumber, and beware.*
> > *Awake, awake!*

Antonio. Then let us both be sudden.

295 **Gonzalo** [*waking*]. Now, good angels preserve the King!

[*He wakes* Alonso. *The others wake.*]

Alonso. Why, how now, ho! Awake? Why are you drawn?
    Wherefore this ghastly looking?

Gonzalo.   What's the matter?

Sebastian. Whiles we stood here securing your repose,[64]
    Even now, we heard a hollow burst of bellowing

300   Like bulls, or rather lions. Did 't not wake you?
    It struck mine ear most terribly.

Alonso.   I heard nothing.

Antonio. O, 'twas a din to fright a monster's ear,
    To make an earthquake! Sure it was the roar
    Of a whole herd of lions.

305 **Alonso.** Heard you this, Gonzalo?

Gonzalo. Upon mine honor, sir, I heard a humming,
    And that a strange one too, which did awake me.
    I shaked you, sir, and cried. As mine eyes opened,
    I saw their weapons drawn. There was a noise,

310   That's verily.[65] 'Tis best we stand upon our guard,
    Or that we quit this place. Let's draw our weapons.

Alonso. Lead off this ground, and let's make further search
    For my poor son.

Gonzalo.   Heavens keep him from these beasts!
    For he is, sure, i' th' island.

Alonso.   Lead away.

315 **Ariel** [*aside*]. Prospero my lord shall know what I have done.
    So, king, go safely on to seek thy son.

[*They exit separately.*]

---

[64] securing your repose—guarding your sleep.

[65] verily—true.

Act Two, Scene Two

On another part of the island, Caliban curses Prospero for sending spirits to torment him. He thinks Trinculo is a spirit and hides from him under his cloak. Trinculo wonders what kind of strange creature Caliban is. He hides under Caliban's cloak to shelter from a new storm. Stephano, drunk, sees Caliban and Trinculo hiding and thinks he's found a rare four-legged animal. Trinculo and Stephano greet each other warmly, each having thought the other dead. Caliban, tasting some wine that Stephano salvaged from the wreck, thinks the drink heavenly and the man a god. He swears to serve Stephano.

Enter Caliban *carrying a load of wood. A noise of thunder heard.*

Caliban. All the infections that the sun sucks up
From bogs, fens, flats, on Prosper fall, and make him
By inchmeal[1] a disease! His spirits hear me,
And yet I needs must curse. But they'll nor pinch,
5   Fright me with urchin-shows, pitch me i' the mire,
Nor lead me, like a firebrand, in the dark
Out of my way, unless he bid 'em. But
For every trifle are they set upon me,
Sometimes like apes, that mow[2] and chatter at me
10   And after bite me; then like hedgehogs, which
Lie tumbling in my barefoot way and mount
Their pricks at my footfall. Sometimes am I
All wound with adders, who with cloven tongues
Do hiss me into madness.
[*Enter* Trinculo.]
               Lo, now, lo!
15   Here comes a spirit of his, and to torment me
For bringing wood in slowly. I'll fall flat.
Perchance he will not mind me.[3]
[*He lies down and covers himself with a cloak.*]

---

[1] By inchmeal—inch by inch.

[2] mow—make faces.

[3] Perchance . . . mind me—Maybe he won't notice me.

Misery acquaints a man with strange bedfellows.

Trinculo. Here's neither bush nor shrub to bear off any weather at all.
And another storm brewing, I hear it sing i' the wind. Yond same
black cloud, yond huge one, looks like a foul bombard[4] that would
shed his liquor. If it should thunder as it did before, I know not where
to hide my head. Yond same cloud cannot choose but fall by pailfuls.
What have we here, a man or a fish? Dead or alive? A fish, he smells
like a fish—a very ancient and fishlike smell, a kind of not-of-the-
newest Poor John.[5] A strange fish! Were I in England now, as once I
was, and had but this fish painted, not a holiday fool there but would
give a piece of silver. There would this monster make a man. Any
strange beast there makes a man.[6] When they will not give a doit[7] to
relieve a lame beggar, they will lay out ten to see a dead Indian.
Legged like a man, and his fins like arms! Warm, o' my troth![8] I do
now let loose my opinion, hold it no longer: this is no fish, but an
islander, that hath lately suffered by a thunderbolt. [_Thunder._] Alas,
the storm is come again! My best way is to creep under his
gaberdine.[9] There is no other shelter hereabout. Misery acquaints a
man with strange bedfellows. I will here shroud[10] till the dregs of the
storm be past.

[_He creeps under Caliban's cloak, his head at Caliban's feet._]

[_Enter_ Stephano, _singing, a bottle in his hand._]

Stephano. _I shall no more to sea, to sea,_

Here shall I die ashore—

This is a very scurvy[11] tune to sing at a man's funeral.
Well, here's my comfort. [_Drinks._]

---

[4] foul bombard—dirty leather jug.

[5] Poor John—cheap, salted fish.

[6] Were I . . . man—If I were back in England, and advertised this fish on a painted sign or billboard, every fool on a holiday
would pay to see it. This monster would make a man rich there, as can any strange beast.

[7] doit—tiny coin.

[8] Warm, o' my troth!—Still alive, by my faith!

[9] gaberdine—cloak.

[10] shroud—take shelter.

[11] scurvy—contemptible.

[*Sings.*]

> The Master, the swabber, the Boatswain, and I,
> The gunner and his mate,
> Loved Mall, Meg, and Marian, and Margery,
> But none of us cared for Kate.
> For she had a tongue with a tang,
> Would cry to a sailor, "Go hang!"
> She loved not the savor of tar nor of pitch,
> Yet a tailor might scratch her where'er she did itch.
> Then to sea, boys, and let her go hang!

This is a scurvy tune too. But here's my comfort.

[*Drinks.*]

Caliban. Do not torment me! O!

Stephano. What's the matter? Have we devils here? Do you put tricks upon 's with savages and men of Ind?[12] Ha? I have not scaped drowning to be afeard now of your four legs. For it hath been said, "As proper a man as ever went on four legs cannot make him give ground," and it shall be said so again while Stephano breathes at' nostrils.

Caliban. This spirit torments me! O!

Stephano. This is some monster of the isle with four legs, who hath got, as I take it, an ague.[13] Where the devil should he learn our language? I will give him some relief, if it be but for that. If I can recover him and keep him tame and get to Naples with him, he's a present for any emperor that ever trod on neat's leather.[14]

Caliban. Do not torment me, prithee. I'll bring my wood home faster.

Stephano. He's in his fit now and does not talk after the wisest. He shall taste of my bottle. If he have never drunk wine afore, it will go near to remove his fit. If I can recover him and keep him tame, I will not take too much[15] for him. He shall pay for him that hath him, and that soundly.[16]

---

[12] Ind—India.

[13] ague—fever and shakes.

[14] trod ... leather—wore cowhide shoes.

[15] I will ... much—I will ask whatever price I like.

[16] soundly—dearly; that is, whoever buys him will pay a lot for him.

Caliban. Thou dost me yet but little hurt; thou wilt anon,[17] I know it by
  thy trembling. Now Prosper works upon thee.

Stephano. Come on your ways. Open your mouth. Here is that which
  will give language to you, cat.[18] Open your mouth. This will shake
  your shaking, I can tell you, and that soundly. [Caliban *drinks.*] You
  cannot tell who's your friend. Open your chaps again.

Trinculo. I should know that voice. It should be—but he is drowned, and
  these are devils. O, defend me!

Stephano. Four legs and two voices—a most delicate monster! His forward voice now is to speak well of his friend; his backward voice is to
  utter foul speeches and to detract. If all the wine in my bottle will
  recover him, I will help his ague. Come. [Caliban *drinks.*] Amen! I will
  pour some in thy other mouth.

Trinculo. Stephano!

Stephano. Doth thy other mouth call me? Mercy, mercy! This is a devil,
  and no monster. I will leave him. I have no long spoon.[19]

Trinculo. Stephano! If thou beest Stephano, touch me and speak to me,
  for I am Trinculo—be not afeard—thy good friend Trinculo.

Stephano. If thou beest Trinculo, come forth. I'll pull thee by the lesser
  legs. If any be Trinculo's legs, these are they. [*Pulling him out from
  under Caliban's cloak.*] Thou art very Trinculo indeed! How cam'st thou
  to be the siege of this mooncalf?[20] Can he vent Trinculos?

Trinculo. I took him to be killed with a thunderstroke. But art thou not
  drowned, Stephano? I hope now thou art not drowned. Is the storm
  overblown? I hid me under the dead mooncalf's gaberdine for fear of
  the storm. And art thou living, Stephano? O Stephano, two
  Neapolitans scaped![21]

Stephano. Prithee, do not turn me about. My stomach is not constant.

Caliban [*aside*]. These be fine things, an if they be not spirits that's a
  brave god, and bears **celestial**[22] liquor. I will kneel to him.

---

[17] anon—soon; presently.

[18] give . . . cat—reference to the proverb, "Good liquor will make a cat speak."

[19] I have . . . spoon—reference to the proverb, "Anyone who dines with the devil had better use a long spoon."

[20] siege . . . mooncalf—excrement of this monstrous creature.

[21] scaped—escaped.

[22] **celestial**—heavenly.

Stephano. How didst thou scape? How cam'st thou hither? Swear by this
    bottle how thou cam'st hither. I escaped upon a butt of sack[23] which
    the sailors heaved o'erboard—by this bottle, which I made of the bark
    of a tree with mine own hands since I was cast ashore.

Caliban. I'll swear upon that bottle to be thy true subject, for the liquor is
    not earthly.

Stephano. [*to* Trinculo]. Here. Swear then how thou escapedst.

Trinculo. Swum ashore, man, like a duck. I can swim like a duck, I'll
    be sworn.

Stephano. Here, kiss the book.[24] [Trinculo *drinks*.] Though thou canst
    swim like a duck, thou art made like a goose.

Trinculo. O Stephano, hast any more of this?

Stephano. The whole butt, man. My cellar is in a rock by th' seaside,
    where my wine is hid.—How now, mooncalf? How does thine ague?

Caliban. Hast thou not dropped from heaven?

Stephano. Out o' the moon, I do assure thee. I was the man i' the moon
    when time was.

Caliban. I have seen thee in her, and I do adore thee. My mistress showed
    me thee, and thy dog, and thy bush.[25]

Stephano. Come, swear to that. Kiss the book. I will furnish it anon with
    new contents. Swear.

[Caliban *drinks*.]

Trinculo. By this good light, this is a very shallow monster! I afeard of
    him? A very weak monster! The man i' the moon? A most poor
    credulous[26] monster! Well drawn, monster, in good sooth![27]

Caliban. [*to* Stephano]. I'll show thee every fertile inch o' th' island,
    And I will kiss thy foot. I prithee, be my god.

Trinculo. By this light, a most perfidious and drunken monster! When 's
    god's asleep, he'll rob his bottle.

Caliban. I'll kiss thy foot. I'll swear myself thy subject.

Stephano. Come on then. Down, and swear.

[Caliban *kneels*.]

---

[23] butt of sack—barrel of Spanish white wine.

[24] kiss the book—have a drink (with a joking reference to kissing the Bible when swearing an oath).

[25] thy dog . . . bush—In folklore, the man in the moon had a dog and a thornbush.

[26] **credulous**—believing too easily.

[27] Well drawn . . . sooth—You have taken a good, long drink, in truth.

130 **Trinculo.** I shall laugh myself to death at this puppy-headed monster.
A most scurvy monster! I could find in my heart to beat him—
Stephano. Come, kiss.
Trinculo. But that the poor monster's in drink. An abominable monster!
Caliban. I'll show thee the best springs. I'll pluck thee berries.
135 I'll fish for thee and get thee wood enough.
A plague upon the tyrant that I serve!
I'll bear him no more sticks, but follow thee,
Thou wondrous man.
Trinculo. A most ridiculous monster, to make a wonder of a poor drunkard!

Stephano (David Sabin, standing, right) tells Trinculo (Floyd King) where he has hidden the rest of his wine while Caliban (Chad Coleman) looks on in the 1997 production of *The Tempest* by The Shakespeare Theatre in Washington, D.C.

'Ban, 'Ban, Ca—Caliban
Has a new master. Get a new man!

140 **Caliban.** I prithee, let me bring thee where crabs[28] grow,
And I with my long nails will dig thee pignuts,
Show thee a jay's nest, and instruct thee how
To snare the nimble marmoset.[29] I'll bring thee
To clustering filberts, and sometimes I'll get thee
145 Young scamels[30] from the rock. Wilt thou go with me?
Stephano. I prithee now, lead the way without any more talking.—
Trinculo, the king and all our company else being drowned, we will
inherit here.—Here, bear my bottle.—Fellow Trinculo, we'll fill him
by and by again.
150 **Caliban** [*sings drunkenly*]. *Farewell, master, farewell, farewell!*
Trinculo. A howling monster; a drunken monster!
Caliban. *No more dams I'll make for fish,*
Nor fetch in firing
At requiring,
155 *Nor scrape trenchering,[31] nor wash dish.*
'Ban, 'Ban, Ca—Caliban
Has a new master. Get a new man!
Freedom, high-day! High-day, freedom! Freedom,
high-day, freedom!
160 **Stephano.** O brave monster! Lead the way.
[*They exit.*]

---

[28] crabs—crab apples.

[29] marmoset—small monkey.

[30] scamels—shellfish.

[31] *scrape trenchering*—scrape wooden dishes, to clean them.

Act Three, Scene One

In front of Prospero's cave, later that day, Ferdinand comments that his labor, though enforced, is pleasurable when he thinks of Miranda. She tells him to rest for a while. They exchange loving words, and Ferdinand admits he is a prince—perhaps a king, if his father is dead. Then they vow to marry, not knowing that Prospero is watching them do exactly what he had hoped they would do.

Enter Ferdinand, *carrying a log.*

Ferdinand. There be some sports are painful, and their labor
    Delight in them sets off.[1] Some kinds of baseness
    Are nobly undergone, and most poor matters
    Point to rich ends. This my mean task
5   Would be as heavy to me as **odious**,[2] but
    The mistress which I serve quickens what's dead
    And makes my labors pleasures. O, she is
    Ten times more gentle than her father's crabbed,
    And he's composed of harshness. I must remove
10   Some thousands of these logs and pile them up,
    Upon a sore injunction.[3] My sweet mistress
    Weeps when she sees me work and says such baseness
    Had never like executor.[4] I forget;
    But these sweet thoughts do even refresh my labors,
15   Most busiest when I do it.
    [*Enter* Miranda; *and* Prospero *at a distance, unseen.*]
Miranda.   Alas now, pray you,
    Work not so hard. I would the lightning had
    Burnt up those logs that you are enjoined[5] to pile!
    Pray, set it down and rest you. When this burns,
    'Twill weep for having wearied you. My father

---

[1] There be … sets off—Some games are tiring, but our enjoyment in them makes up for the weariness.
[2] **odious**—hateful.
[3] sore injunction—harsh command.
[4] such baseness … executor—such lowly, menial work as was never before done by so noble a person.
[5] enjoined—commanded.

20   Is hard at study. Pray now, rest yourself.
      He's safe for these three hours.

Ferdinand.   O most dear mistress,
      The sun will set before I shall discharge
      What I must strive to do.

Miranda.   If you'll sit down,
      I'll bear your logs the while. Pray, give me that.
25   I'll carry it to the pile.

Ferdinand.   No, precious creature,
      I had rather crack my sinews, break my back,

Miranda (Jessalyn Gilsig) and Ferdinand (Scott Ripley) pledge their love to each other in this scene from the American Repertory Theatre production.

> *For several virtues*
> *Have I liked several women.*

Than you should such dishonor undergo
While I sit lazy by.

Miranda.   It would become me
As well as it does you, and I should do it
30   With much more ease, for my good will is to it,
And yours it is against.

Prospero [*aside*].   Poor worm, thou art infected![6]
This visitation shows it.

Miranda.   You look wearily.

Ferdinand. No, noble mistress, 'tis fresh morning with me
When you are by at night. I do beseech you—
35   Chiefly that I might set it in my prayers,
What is your name?

Miranda.   Miranda—O my father,
I have broke your hest to say so.[7]

Ferdinand.   Admired Miranda![8]
Indeed the top of admiration, worth
What's dearest to the world! Full many a lady
40   I have eyed with best regard, and many a time
Th' harmony of their tongues hath into bondage
Brought my too diligent ear. For several virtues
Have I liked several women, never any
With so full soul but some defect in her
45   Did quarrel with the noblest grace she owed,
And put it to the foil.[9] But you, O you,
So perfect and so peerless, are created
Of every creature's best!

---

[6] Poor ... infected—Miranda, you have fallen in love.

[7] I have ... say so—I have broken your order not to tell my name.

[8] Admired Miranda—pun on her name, since *Miranda* means "wondered at."

[9] never ... foil—There was never a woman who was so perfect that she didn't have some defect that fought and defeated her best quality.

Miranda.   I do not know
          One of my sex, no woman's face remember,
50   Save, from my glass, mine own. Nor have I seen
          More that I may call men than you, good friend,
          And my dear father. How features are abroad
          I am skilless of,[10] but, by my modesty,
          The jewel in my dower,[11] I would not wish
55   Any companion in the world but you;
          Nor can imagination form a shape,
          Besides yourself, to like of. But I prattle
          Something too wildly, and my father's **precepts**[12]
          I therein do forget.
Ferdinand.   I am in my condition
60   A prince, Miranda; I do think, a king—
          I would, not so!—and would no more endure
          This wooden slavery than to suffer
          The flesh-fly blow my mouth.[13] Hear my soul speak:
          The very instant that I saw you did
65   My heart fly to your service, there resides
          To make me slave to it, and for your sake
          Am I this patient log-man.
Miranda.   Do you love me?
Ferdinand. O heaven, O earth, bear witness to this sound,
          And crown what I profess with kind event[14]
70   If I speak true! If hollowly, invert
          What best is boded me to mischief.[15] I
          Beyond all limit of what else i' the world
          Do love, prize, honor you.
Miranda [*weeping*].   I am a fool
          To weep at what I am glad of.

---

[10] How features . . . skilless of—I don't know what people look like in other places.

[11] dower—dowery, property a bride brings to her husband.

[12] **precepts**—rules; teachings.

[13] flesh-fly . . . mouth—flesh-eating fly foul my dead mouth with its eggs.

[14] kind event—favorable outcome.

[15] If hollowly . . . mischief—If I speak insincerely, turn my best possible future into evil.

Fair encounter
Of two most rare affections!

Prospero [*aside*].   Fair encounter
75   Of two most rare affections! Heavens rain grace
            On that which breeds between 'em!
Ferdinand.   Wherefore weep you?
Miranda. At mine unworthiness, that dare not offer
            What I desire to give, and much less take
            What I shall die to want. But this is trifling,
80   And all the more it seeks to hide itself
            The bigger bulk it shows. Hence, bashful cunning,
            And prompt me, plain and holy innocence!
            I am your wife, if you will marry me;
            If not, I'll die your maid. To be your fellow[16]
85   You may deny me, but I'll be your servant
            Whether you will or no.
Ferdinand.   My mistress, dearest,
            And I thus humble ever.
Miranda.   My husband, then?
Ferdinand. Ay, with a heart as willing
            As bondage e'er of freedom. Here's my hand.
90   **Miranda.** And mine, with my heart in 't. And now farewell
            Till half an hour hence.
Ferdinand.   A thousand thousand!
[*Exit* Ferdinand *and* Miranda *separately.*]
Prospero. So glad of this as they I cannot be,
            Who are surprised withal; but my rejoicing
            At nothing can be more. I'll to my book,
95   For yet ere suppertime must I perform
            Much business appertaining.[17] [*He exits.*]

___

[16] fellow—equal; companion.

[17] appertaining—related to what is happening.

Act Three, Scene Two

On another part of the island, Trinculo and Caliban quarrel, and Stephano takes Caliban's side. Caliban persuades Stephano to kill Prospero, marry Miranda, and become king of the island. Ariel, who has heard the plot, says he will tell Prospero. He plays music to lead the conspirators off.

Enter Caliban, Stephano, *and* Trinculo.

Stephano [*to* Trinculo]. Tell not me. When the butt is out, we will drink water, not a drop before. Therefore bear up and board 'em.[1] Servant monster, drink to me.

Trinculo. Servant monster? The folly[2] of this island! They say there's but
5   five upon this isle. We are three of them; if th' other two be brained like us, the state totters.[3]

Stephano. Drink, servant monster, when I bid thee. Thy eyes are almost set in thy head.

[Caliban *drinks.*]

Trinculo. Where should they be set else? He were a brave monster indeed
10   if they were set in his tail.

Stephano. My man-monster hath drowned his tongue in sack. For my part, the sea cannot drown me. I swam, ere I could recover the shore, five and thirty leagues off and on, by this light. Thou shalt be my lieutenant, monster, or my standard.[4]

15   **Trinculo.** Your lieutenant, if you list,[5] he's no standard.

Stephano. We'll not run, Monsieur Monster.

Trinculo. Nor go neither. But you'll lie like dogs, and yet say nothing neither.

Stephano. Mooncalf, speak once in thy life, if thou beest a good mooncalf.

---

[1] bear . . . 'em—stand firm and attack (naval jargon); that is, take a drink.

[2] folly—stupidity.

[3] if th' other . . . totters—If the other two people on this island have the same intelligence as we do, the government is in trouble.

[4] standard—flag-bearer. Trinculo puns that Caliban is "no standard"; that is, he's not able to stand up.

[5] list—prefer.

20   **Caliban.** How does thy honor? Let me lick thy shoe.
        I'll not serve him. He is not valiant.
    Trinculo. Thou liest, most ignorant monster. I am in case to jostle a
        constable.[6] Why, thou debauched fish, thou! Was there ever man
        a coward that hath drunk so much sack as I today? Wilt thou
25   tell a monstrous lie, being but half a fish and half a monster?
    Caliban. Lo, how he mocks me! Wilt thou let him, my lord?
    Trinculo. "Lord," quoth he? That a monster should be such a natural![7]
    Caliban. Lo, lo, again! Bite him to death, I prithee.
    Stephano. Trinculo, keep a good tongue in your head. If you prove a
30   mutineer—the next tree![8] The poor monster's my subject, and he
        shall not suffer indignity.
    Caliban. I thank my noble lord. Wilt thou be pleased
        To hearken once again to the suit I made to thee?
    Stephano. Marry, will I. Kneel and repeat it. I will
35   stand, and so shall Trinculo.
    [*Enter* Ariel, *invisible.*]
    Caliban. As I told thee before, I am subject to a tyrant,
        A sorcerer, that by his cunning hath
        Cheated me of the island.
    Ariel [*mimicking* Trinculo]. Thou liest.
40   **Caliban.** Thou liest, thou jesting monkey, thou!
        I would my valiant master would destroy thee.
        I do not lie.
    Stephano. Trinculo, if you trouble him any more in 's tale, by this
        hand, I will supplant some of your teeth.
45   **Trinculo.** Why, I said nothing.
    Stephano. Mum, then, and no more.—Proceed.
    Caliban. I say by sorcery he got this isle;
        From me he got it. If thy greatness will
        Revenge it on him—for I know thou dar'st,
50   But this thing[9] dare not—

---

[6] I am . . . constable—I'm in a fit condition (that is, drunk enough) to challenge a policeman.

[7] natural—simpleton.

[8] the next tree—You'll hang from the next tree.

[9] this thing—Trinculo.

Stephano. That's most certain.

Caliban. Thou shalt be lord of it, and I'll serve thee.

Stephano. How now shall this be compassed?[10] Canst thou bring me
　　to the party?

55　**Caliban.** Yea, yea, my lord. I'll yield him thee asleep,
　　While thou mayst knock a nail into his head.

Ariel [*mimicking* Trinculo]. Thou liest; thou canst not.

Caliban. What a pied[11] ninny's this!—Thou scurvy patch![12]—
　　I do beseech thy greatness, give him blows

60　　And take his bottle from him. When that's gone
　　He shall drink naught but brine, for I'll not show him
　　Where the quick freshes[13] are.

Stephano. Trinculo, run into no further danger. Interrupt the
　　monster one word further and, by this hand, I'll turn my mercy out

65　　o' doors and make a stockfish[14] of thee.

Trinculo. Why, what did I? I did nothing. I'll go farther off.

Stephano. Didst thou not say he lied?

Ariel [*mimicking* Trinculo]. Thou liest.

Stephano. Do I so? Take thou that. [*He beats* Trinculo.]

70　　As you like this, give me the lie another time.

Trinculo. I did not give the lie. Out o' your wits and hearing too? A
　　pox o' your bottle! This can sack and drinking do. A murrain[15] on
　　your monster, and the devil take your fingers!

Caliban. Ha, ha, ha!

75　**Stephano.** Now, forward with your tale. [*To* Trinculo.]
　　Prithee, stand further off.

Caliban. Beat him enough. After a little time
　　I'll beat him too.

Stephano. [*to* Trinculo]. Stand farther.—Come, proceed.

---

[10] compassed—brought about; achieved.

[11] pied—in motley, the many-colored patchwork costume traditionally worn by jesters.

[12] patch—fool.

[13] quick freshes—fresh-water springs.

[14] stockfish—cod dried and then beaten before cooking.

[15] murrain—plague.

Stephano (seated at right) forces a reluctant Trinculo to carry Caliban on his shoulders in this scene from the 2000 production of *The Tempest* by Boston's Commonwealth Shakespeare Company.

80   **Caliban.** Why, as I told thee, 'tis a custom with him
I' th' afternoon to sleep. There thou mayst brain him,
Having first seized his books, or with a log
Batter his skull, or paunch him with a stake,
Or cut his weasand[16] with thy knife. Remember
85   First to possess his books, for without them
He's but a sot,[17] as I am, nor hath not
One spirit to command. They all do hate him

---

[16] paunch ... weasand—stab him in the stomach or cut his windpipe.
[17] sot—fool.

The isle is full of noises, sounds, and sweet airs, that give delight and hurt not.

As rootedly as I. Burn but his books.

He has brave utensils[18]—for so he calls them—

90 Which, when he has a house, he'll deck withal.[19]

And that most deeply to consider is

The beauty of his daughter. He himself

Calls her a **nonpareil**.[20] I never saw a woman

But only Sycorax my dam and she;

95 But she as far surpasseth Sycorax

As great'st does least.

Stephano. Is it so brave a lass?

Caliban. Ay, lord. She will become thy bed, I warrant,

And bring thee forth brave brood.[21]

100 **Stephano.** Monster, I will kill this man. His daughter and I will be

king and queen—save Our Graces!—and Trinculo and thyself shall be

viceroys.[22] Dost thou like the plot, Trinculo?

Trinculo. Excellent.

Stephano. Give me thy hand. I am sorry I beat thee. But, while thou

105 liv'st, keep a good tongue in thy head.

Caliban. Within this half hour will he be asleep.

Wilt thou destroy him then?

Stephano.   Ay, on mine honor.

Ariel [*aside*]. This will I tell my master.

Caliban. Thou mak'st me merry; I am full of pleasure.

110 Let us be jocund. Will you troll the catch

You taught me but whilere?[23]

Stephano. At thy request, monster, I will do reason, any reason.—

Come on, Trinculo, let us sing. [*Sings.*]

---

[18] utensils—furnishings.

[19] deck withal—decorate with.

[20] **nonpareil**—someone or something without equal.

[21] bring . . . brood—bear you fine children.

[22] viceroys—royal governors.

[23] Let us . . . whilere—Let's be merry. Will you sing the round you taught me a while ago?

> *Flout 'em and scout 'em*
115 > *And scout 'em and flout 'em!*[24]
> *Thought is free.*

Caliban. That's not the tune.

[Ariel *plays the tune on a tabor*[25] *and pipe.*]

Stephano. What is this same?

Trinculo. This is the tune of our catch, played by the picture of
120   Nobody.

Stephano. If thou beest a man, show thyself in thy likeness. If thou
        beest a devil, take 't as thou list.

Trinculo. O, forgive me my sins!

Stephano. He that dies pays all debts.[26] I defy thee.
125   Mercy upon us!

Caliban. Art thou afeard?

Stephano. No, monster, not I.

Caliban. Be not afeard. The isle is full of noises,
        Sounds, and sweet airs, that give delight and hurt not.
130   Sometimes a thousand twangling instruments
        Will hum about mine ears, and sometimes voices
        That, if I then had waked after long sleep,
        Will make me sleep again; and then, in dreaming,
        The clouds methought would open and show riches
135   Ready to drop upon me, that when I waked
        I cried to dream again.

Stephano. This will prove a brave kingdom to me, where I shall have my
        music for nothing.

Caliban. When Prospero is destroyed.
140 **Stephano.** That shall be by and by. I remember the story.

Trinculo. The sound is going away. Let's follow it, and after do our work.

Stephano. Lead, monster; we'll follow.—I would I could see this taborer!
        He lays it on.[27]

Trinculo. Wilt come? I'll follow, Stephano.

[*They exit following Ariel's music.*]

---

[24] *Flout . . . 'em*—Scoff at them and belittle them.

[25] *tabor*—small drum.

[26] He . . . debts—If I have to die, that will end my debts and obligations (a proverb).

[27] taborer . . . it on—drummer. He plays with spirit.

Act Three, Scene Three

On another part of the island, Alonso and his attendants, tired of searching for Ferdinand, sit to rest. Antonio reminds Sebastian of his resolve to kill Alonso. Prospero makes a banquet appear by magic, but when the men attempt to eat, Ariel, disguised as a monster, accuses Alonso, Sebastian, and Antonio of deposing Prospero and exposing him and Miranda to the sea. Alonso, sure now that his son is dead, sets out to join him in death. Gonzalo urges the other men to follow and prevent the king from doing anything rash.

Enter Alonso, Sebastian, Antonio, Gonzalo, Adrian, Francisco, *and* Mariners.

Gonzalo. By 'r lakin,[1] I can go no further, sir.
　　My old bones aches. Here's a maze trod indeed
　　Through forthrights and meanders![2] By your patience,
　　I needs must rest me.

Alonso. 　　　　　　　　Old lord, I cannot blame thee,
5　　Who am myself attached with weariness,
　　To th' dulling of my spirits. Sit down and rest.
　　Even here I will put off my hope, and keep it
　　No longer for my flatterer.[3] He is drowned
　　Whom thus we stray to find, and the sea mocks
10　　Our frustrate search on land. Well, let him go.

Antonio [*aside to* Sebastian]. I am right glad that he's so out of hope.
　　Do not, for one repulse,[4] forgo the purpose
　　That you resolved t' effect.

Sebastian [*aside to* Antonio].　The next advantage
15　　Will we take throughly.

Antonio [*aside to* Sebastian].Let it be tonight,
　　For now they are oppressed with travel, they
　　Will not, nor cannot, use such vigilance
　　As when they are fresh.

---

[1] By 'r lakin—by our little Lady (the Virgin Mary).

[2] Here's . . . meanders—We have walked back and forth on straight and crooked paths as if we were in a maze.

[3] Even here . . . flatterer—Now I will give up hope and no longer let it flatter me or cheer me up.

[4] for one repulse—because of having been stopped once.

Now I will believe
That there are unicorns.

Sebastian [*aside to* Antonio]. I say tonight. No more.

[*Solemn and strange music. Enter* Prospero *on the top,[5] invisible.*]

20 **Alonso.** What harmony is this? My good friends, hark!

Gonzalo. Marvelous sweet music!

[*Enter several strange shapes, bringing in a banquet. They dance about it with gentle actions of salutations; and inviting the King, etc. to eat, they depart.*]

Alonso. Give us kind keepers,[6] heavens! What were these?

Sebastian. A living drollery.[7] Now I will believe

    That there are unicorns; that in Arabia

25   There is one tree, the phoenix' throne,[8] one phoenix

    At this hour reigning there.

Antonio.   I'll believe both;

    And what does else want credit, come to me

    And I'll be sworn 'tis true. Travelers ne'er did lie,

    Though fools at home condemn 'em.

Gonzalo.   If in Naples

30   I should report this now, would they believe me

    If I should say I saw such islanders?

    For, certes,[9] these are people of the island,

    Who, though they are of monstrous shape, yet note

    Their manners are more gentle, kind, than of

35   Our human generation you shall find

    Many, nay, almost any.

Prospero [*aside*].   Honest lord,

    Thou hast said well, for some of you there present

    Are worse than devils.

---

[5] *top*—on an upper level of the tiring-house.

[6] keepers—guardian angels.

[7] drollery—amusing entertainment.

[8] phoenix' throne—nest of the mythical bird supposed to die in fire every few centuries, to be reborn from its own ashes.

[9] certes—certainly.

In this scene from the Commonwealth Shakespeare Company production, Alonso and the other courtiers are presented with a magical banquet that abruptly vanishes.

Alonso.   I cannot too much muse[10]
Such shapes, such gesture, and such sound, expressing—
Although they want the use of tongue—a kind
Of excellent dumb discourse.
Prospero [*aside*].   Praise in departing.[11]
Francisco. They vanished strangely.
Sebastian.   No matter, since
They have left their viands[12] behind, for we have stomachs.
Will 't please you taste of what is here?

40

---

[10] I cannot . . . muse—I can't be amazed enough at.

[11] Praise in departing—Save your praise until the visit is ended.

[12] viands—food and drink.

You are three men of sin.

Alonso.   Not I.

45 **Gonzalo.** Faith, sir, you need not fear. When we were boys
Who would believe that there were mountaineers
Dewlapped like bulls, whose throats had hanging at 'em
Wallets of flesh? Or that there were such men
Whose heads stood in their breasts? Which now we find

50 Each putter-out of five for one will bring us
Good warrant of.[13]

Alonso.   I will stand to and feed,
Although my last[14]—no matter, since I feel
The best is past. Brother, my lord the Duke,
Stand to, and do as we.

[Alonso, Sebastian, *and* Antonio *approach the table.*]

[*Thunder and lightning. Enter* Ariel, *like a harpy,*[15] *claps his wings upon the table, and with a quaint device*[16] *the banquet vanishes.*]

55 **Ariel.** You are three men of sin, whom Destiny,
That hath to instrument this lower world
And what is in 't, the never-surfeited sea
Hath caused to belch up you,[17] and on this island
Where man doth not inhabit, you 'mongst men

60 Being most unfit to live. I have made you mad;
And even with suchlike valor, men hang and drown
Their proper selves. [Alonso, Sebastian, *and* Antonio *draw their swords.*]
                        You fools! I and my fellows
Are ministers of Fate. The elements
Of whom your swords are tempered may as well

65 Wound the loud winds, or with bemocked-at stabs
Kill the still-closing waters, as diminish

---

[13] Each . . . warrant of—every traveler brings us back claims of. Travelers deposited a sum of money before they departed. If they returned, it was repaid fivefold. If they didn't; it was forfeited.

[14] Although my last—even if it proves to be my last meal.

[15] *harpy*—mythological creature that is part woman and part bird (talons and wings).

[16] *quaint device*—ingenious stage effect.

[17] whom . . . up you—whom Fate, which controls this lower world and its creatures, has caused the ever-hungry sea to spit out.

One dowl that's in my plume.[18] My fellow ministers
Are like **invulnerable**.[19] If you could hurt,
Your swords are now too massy[20] for your strengths

70 And will not be uplifted. But remember,
For that's my business to you, that you three
From Milan did supplant good Prospero;
Exposed unto the sea, which hath requit it,[21]
Him and his innocent child, for which foul deed

75 The powers, delaying, not forgetting, have
Incensed[22] the seas and shores, yea, all the creatures,
Against your peace. Thee of thy son, Alonso,
They have bereft; and do pronounce by me
Ling'ring perdition, worse than any death

80 Can be at once, shall step by step attend
You and your ways, whose wraths to guard you from,
Which here, in this most desolate isle, else falls
Upon your heads, is nothing but heart's sorrow
And a clear life ensuing.[23]

85 [*He vanishes in thunder; then, to soft music, enter the shapes again, and dance,*
with mocks and mows,[24] *and carrying out the table.*]

Prospero. Bravely the figure of this harpy hast thou
Performed, my Ariel; a grace it had, devouring.[25]
Of my instruction hast thou nothing bated[26]
In what thou hadst to say. So, with good life
And observation strange, my meaner ministers

90 Their several kinds have done.[27] My high charms work,

---

[18] dowl . . . plume—tiny feather in my plumage.

[19] **invulnerable**—not capable of being harmed.

[20] massy—heavy.

[21] requit it—avenged the deed.

[22] **Incensed**—enraged; made very angry.

[23] Thee . . . ensuing—They have taken your son from you, Alonso, and tell you, through me, that you shall not die quickly but slowly and painfully here on this desolate island, unless you avoid the anger of these heavenly powers by being truly sorry and living a pure life from now on.

[24] *with mocks and mows*—gesturing and making faces.

[25] a grace . . . devouring—You gracefully caused the banquet to disappear (with a pun on *grace*, a blessing before eating).

[26] bated—omitted; held back.

[27] So . . . done—So have my other servants played their parts well, with lifelike appearances and fine attention to detail.

And these mine enemies are all knit up
In their distractions.[28] They now are in my power;
And in these fits I leave them, while I visit
Young Ferdinand, whom they suppose is drowned,
95 And his and mine loved darling. [*Exit* Prospero *and* Ariel *above.*]
Gonzalo. I' the name of something holy, sir, why stand you
In this strange stare?
Alonso. O, it[29] is monstrous, monstrous!
Methought the billows spoke and told me of it,
The winds did sing it to me, and the thunder,
100 That deep and dreadful organ pipe, pronounced
The name of Prospero; it did bass my trespass.[30]
Therefor my son i' th' ooze is bedded, and
I'll seek him deeper than e'er plummet[31] sounded,
And with him there lie mudded. [*Exit* Alonso.]
105 **Sebastian.** But one fiend at a time,
I'll fight their legions o'er.
Antonio. I'll be thy second.
[*Exit* Sebastian *and* Antonio.]
Gonzalo. All three of them are desperate. Their great guilt,
Like poison given to work a great time after,
Now 'gins to bite the spirits. I do beseech you,
That are of suppler joints,[32] follow them swiftly
110 And hinder them from what this ecstasy[33]
May now provoke them to.
Adrian. Follow, I pray you.
[*They all exit.*]

---

[28] knit . . . distractions—bound up in their madness.

[29] it—that is, my sin.

[30] bass my trespass—proclaim my sin like a bass note in music.

[31] plummet—weight attached to a line for sounding, or testing, the depth of water.

[32] That are . . . joints—you who are younger and faster.

[33] ecstasy—fit of madness.

Act Four, Scene One

In front of Prospero's cave, later that day, Prospero tells Ferdinand that he has passed his test well and gives him permission to marry Miranda. Prospero tells Ariel to bring the island's spirits to stage a masque, an elaborate show with music, dance, and fantastic costumes, in which goddesses from classical myth bless the marriage of the young lovers. But he abruptly stops the masque to prepare for Caliban and his fellow conspirators by hanging up fine clothes to distract them. Stephano and Trinculo take the clothes despite Caliban's urging that killing Prospero is more important. But Prospero changes spirits into hounds that drive the three conspirators away.

Enter Prospero, Ferdinand, *and* Miranda.

Prospero. If I have too **austerely**[1] punished you,
    Your compensation makes amends, for I
    Have given you here a third[2] of mine own life,
    Or that for which I live; who once again
5   I tender[3] to thy hand. All thy vexations
    Were but my trials of thy love, and thou
    Hast strangely stood the test. Here, afore heaven,
    I **ratify**[4] this my rich gift. O Ferdinand,
    Do not smile at me that I boast of her,
10   For thou shalt find she will outstrip all praise
    And make it halt behind her.

Ferdinand.   I do believe it
    Against an oracle.[5]

Prospero. Then, as my gift and thine own acquisition
    Worthily purchased, take my daughter. But
15   If thou dost break her virgin-knot before

---

[1] **austerely**—harshly.

[2] a third—Miranda; possibly, a third of "that for which I live," the other two being his studies and his dukedom.

[3] tender—offer.

[4] **ratify**—confirm.

[5] Against an oracle—even if a god's priest or priestess should claim otherwise.

All sanctimonious[6] ceremonies may
With full and holy rite be ministered,
No sweet aspersion[7] shall the heavens let fall
To make this contract grow; but barren hate,
20   Sour-eyed disdain, and discord shall bestrew
The union of your bed with weeds so loathly
That you shall hate it both. Therefore take heed,
As Hymen's lamps[8] shall light you.

Ferdinand.   As I hope
For quiet days, fair issue,[9] and long life,
25   With such love as 'tis now, the murkiest den,
The most opportune place, the strong'st suggestion
Our worser genius can[10] shall never melt
Mine honor into lust, to take away
The edge of that day's celebration
30   When I shall think or Phoebus' steeds are foundered
Or Night kept chained below.[11]

Prospero.   Fairly spoke.
Sit then and talk with her. She is thine own.
What, Ariel! My industrious servant, Ariel!

[*Enter* Ariel.]

Ariel. What would my potent master? Here I am.

35   **Prospero.** Thou and thy meaner fellows your last service
Did worthily perform, and I must use you
In such another trick. Go bring the rabble,[12]
O'er whom I give thee power, here to this place.
Incite them to quick motion, for I must

---

[6] sanctimonious—sacred.

[7] aspersion—dew; shower.

[8] Hymen's lamps—torches carried in a wedding procession.

[9] fair issue—fine children.

[10] the strong'st . . . can—strongest temptation an evil spirit may be capable of producing.

[11] or Phoebus' . . . below—either that the horses are lame that pull the chariot of the sun god or that the night is being kept prisoner. In other words, Ferdinand will be impatient for their wedding night to arrive.

[12] rabble—Ariel's helpers, the "meaner fellows" just mentioned.

40   Bestow upon the eyes of this young couple
        Some vanity of mine art.[13] It is my promise,
        And they expect it from me.

Ariel.   Presently?

Prospero. Ay, with a twink.

Ariel. Before you can say "Come" and "Go,"
45   And breathe twice, and cry "So, so,"
        Each one, tripping on his toe,
        Will be here with mop and mow.
        Do you love me, master? No?

Prospero. Dearly, my delicate Ariel. Do not approach
50   Till thou dost hear me call.

Ariel.   Well; I conceive.[14] [*Exit* Ariel.]

Prospero [*to* Ferdinand]. Look thou be true; do not give dalliance
        Too much the rein.[15] The strongest oaths are straw
        To the fire i' the blood. Be more **abstemious,**[16]
        Or else good night your vow!

Ferdinand.   I warrant you, sir,
55   The white cold virgin snow upon my heart
        Abates the ardor of my liver.[17]

Prospero.   Well.—
        Now come, my Ariel! Bring a corollary,
        Rather than want a spirit.[18] Appear, and pertly!—
        No tongue! All eyes! Be silent.

[*Soft music.*]

[*Enter* Iris.[19]]

---

[13] vanity . . . art—illusion that shows my magic.

[14] conceive—understand.

[15] do not . . . rein—Don't flirt too freely.

[16] **abstemious**—moderate; self-controlled.

[17] ardor . . . liver—my innocence cools my passion. The liver was thought to be the source of the passions.

[18] Bring . . . spirit—Bring extra spirits rather than lack one that is needed.

[19] Iris—in classical mythology, goddess of the rainbow and female messenger of the gods. Here, she is the messenger of Juno, wife of Jupiter, king of the gods. Juno is the "queen o' the sky" in line 70. Ceres is the goddess of agriculture.

As Prospero (Patrick Stewart) reclines in the foreground, Ferdinand (Paul Whitthorne) and Miranda (Carrie Preston) are entertained by a masque performed by spirits in this scene from the New York Shakespeare Festival production.

60	**Iris.** Ceres, most bounteous lady, thy rich leas[20]
	Of wheat, rye, barley, vetches, oats, and peas;
	Thy turfy mountains, where live nibbling sheep,
	And flat meads thatched with stover, them to keep;
	Thy banks with pionèd and twillèd brims,[21]
65	Which spongy April at thy hest betrims
	To make cold nymphs chaste crowns; and thy broom groves,
	Whose shadow the dismissèd bachelor loves,
	Being lass-lorn;[22] thy poll-clipped vineyard;
	And thy sea marge, sterile and rocky hard,
70	Where thou thyself dost air: the queen o' the sky,
	Whose watery arch and messenger am I,
	Bids thee leave these, and with her sovereign grace,

[20] leas—fields; meadows.

[21] meads ... brims—fields covered with forage to feed the sheep; the banks of your streams, eroded by the swift current but protected by tangled roots.

[22] lass-lorn—having lost his sweetheart.

Here on this grass plot, in this very place
To come and sport. Her peacocks fly amain.[23]

[Juno *descends slowly in her chariot.*]

75   Approach, rich Ceres, her to entertain.

[*Enter* Ceres.]

Ceres. Hail, many-colored messenger, that ne'er
Dost disobey the wife of Jupiter,
Who with thy saffron wings upon my flowers
Diffusest honey drops, refreshing showers,
80   And with each end of thy blue bow dost crown
My bosky acres and my unshrubbed down,[24]
Rich scarf to my proud earth. Why hath thy queen
Summoned me hither to this short-grassed green?

Iris. A contract of true love to celebrate,
85   And some donation freely to estate[25]
On the blest lovers.

Ceres.   Tell me, heavenly bow,
If Venus or her son, as thou dost know,
Do now attend the queen? Since they did plot
The means that dusky Dis my daughter got,
90   Her and her blind boy's scandaled company
I have forsworn.[26]

Iris.   Of her society
Be not afraid. I met her deity
Cutting the clouds towards Paphos,[27] and her son
Dove-drawn with her. Here thought they to have done
95   Some wanton charm[28] upon this man and maid,
Whose vows are that no bed-right shall be paid
Till Hymen's torch be lighted; but in vain.
Mars's hot minion[29] is returned again;

---

[23] Her peacocks fly amain—The peacocks (Juno's symbol) that pull her chariot fly at full speed.

[24] My bosky . . . down—my wooded acres and my treeless uplands.

[25] estate—give; bestow.

[26] If Venus . . . forsworn—Are Venus (goddess of love) or her son (Cupid, pictured blindfolded), with Juno? Since they helped Dis (god of the underworld) to kidnap my daughter (Persephone), I have refused to associate with such disgraceful people.

[27] Paphos—city on the island of Cyprus, sacred to Venus.

[28] wanton charm—lustful spell.

[29] Mars's hot minion—Venus, the lover of Mars, god of war.

Her waspish-headed son has broke his arrows,
100 Swears he will shoot no more, but play with sparrows
And be a boy right out.

[Juno *alights.*]

Ceres.   Highest queen of state,
Great Juno, comes; I know her by her gait.

Juno. How does my bounteous sister? Go with me
To bless this twain, that they may prosperous be,
105 And honored in their issue. [*They sing.*]

Juno. *Honor, riches, marriage blessing,*
Long continuance, and increasing,
Hourly joys be still upon you!
Juno sings her blessings on you.

110 **Ceres.** *Earth's increase, foison plenty,*[30]
Barns and garners never empty,
Vines with clustering bunches growing,
Plants with goodly burden bowing;
Spring come to you at the farthest
115 *In the very end of harvest!*
Scarcity and want shall shun you,
Ceres' blessing so is on you.

Ferdinand. This is a most majestic vision, and
Harmonious charmingly. May I be bold
120 To think these spirits?

Prospero.   Spirits, which by mine art
I have from their confines called to enact
My present fancies.

Ferdinand.   Let me live here ever!
So rare a wondered father and a wife
Makes this place paradise.

[Juno *and* Ceres *whisper, and send* Iris *on employment.*]

Prospero.   Sweet now, silence!
125 Juno and Ceres whisper seriously.
There's something else to do. Hush and be mute,
Or else our spell is marred.

---

[30] *foison plenty*—rich harvest.

We are such stuff
As dreams are made on.

Iris. You nymphs, called naiads,[31] of the windring brooks,
With your sedged crowns and ever-harmless looks,
130 Leave your crisp channels, and on this green land
Answer your summons, Juno does command.
Come, temperate nymphs, and help to celebrate
A contract of true love. Be not too late.

[*Enter some* Nymphs.]
You sunburned sicklemen,[32] of August weary,
135 Come hither from the furrow and be merry.
Make holiday; your rye-straw hats put on,
And these fresh nymphs encounter every one
In country footing.[33]

[*Enter some* Reapers, *properly habited. They join with the* Nymphs *in a grace-ful dance, towards the end wherof* Prospero *starts suddenly, and speaks. After which, in a strange, hollow, and confused noise, they heavily vanish.*]

Prospero [*aside*]. I had forgot that foul conspiracy
140 Of the beast Caliban and his confederates
Against my life. The minute of their plot
Is almost come. [*To the* Spirits.] Well done! Avoid; no more!

Ferdinand. This is strange. Your father's in some passion
That works him strongly.

Miranda.   Never till this day
145 Saw I him touched with anger so distempered.

Prospero. You do look, my son, in a moved sort,[34]
As if you were dismayed. Be cheerful, sir.
Our revels[35] now are ended. These our actors,
As I foretold you, were all spirits and

---

[31] naiads—minor goddesses of lakes or rivers.

[32] sicklemen—harvesters.

[33] footing—dancing.

[34] in a moved sort—disturbed.

[35] revels—entertainments.

In this scene from the New York Shakespeare Festival production, Prospero (Patrick Stewart) becomes enraged when he remembers Caliban's conspiracy with Stephano and Trinculo.

150   Are melted into air, into thin air;
                 And, like the baseless fabric of this vision,
                 The cloud-capped towers, the gorgeous palaces,
                 The solemn temples, the great globe itself,
                 Yea, all which it inherit,[36] shall dissolve,
155   And, like this insubstantial pageant faded,
                 Leave not a rack[37] behind. We are such stuff
                 As dreams are made on, and our little life
                 Is rounded with a sleep. Sir, I am vexed.

[36] the great . . . inherit—the earth (with a pun on the Globe theater) and all who occupy it now or in the future.
[37] rack—wisp of cloud.

Bear with my weakness. My old brain is troubled.
160   Be not disturbed with my infirmity.
       If you be pleased, retire into my cell
       And there repose. A turn or two I'll walk
       To still my beating mind.
        Ferdinand, Miranda.   We wish your peace.
        [*Exit* Ferdinand *and* Miranda.]
        Prospero. Come with a thought! I thank thee, Ariel. Come.
        [*Enter* Ariel.]
165   **Ariel.** Thy thoughts I cleave to.[38] What's thy pleasure?
        Prospero.   Spirit,
       We must prepare to meet with Caliban.
        Ariel. Ay, my commander. When I presented Ceres,
       I thought to have told thee of it, but I feared
       Lest I might anger thee.
170   **Prospero.** Say again, where didst thou leave these varlets?[39]
        Ariel. I told you, sir, they were red-hot with drinking;
       So full of valor that they smote[40] the air
       For breathing in their faces, beat the ground
       For kissing of their feet; yet always bending
175   Towards their project. Then I beat my tabor,
       At which, like unbacked[41] colts, they pricked their ears,
       Advanced their eyelids, lifted up their noses
       As they smelt music. So I charmed their ears
       That calflike they my lowing followed[42] through
180   Toothed briers, sharp furzes, pricking gorse, and thorns,
       Which entered their frail shins. At last I left them
       I' the filthy-mantled[43] pool beyond your cell,
       There dancing up to th' chins, that the foul lake
       O'erstunk their feet.

---

[38] cleave to—cling to.

[39] varlets—scoundrels.

[40] smote—beat at.

[41] unbacked—untamed.

[42] calflike . . . followed—followed my music as a calf follows the sounds of its mother's voice.

[43] filthy-mantled—covered with slime.

Prospero.   This was well done, my bird.

185   Thy shape invisible retain thou still.

        The trumpery[44] in my house, go bring it hither,

        For stale[45] to catch these thieves.

Ariel.   I go, I go. [*Exit* Ariel.]

Prospero. A devil, a born devil, on whose nature

        Nurture can never stick; on whom my pains,

190   Humanely taken, all, all lost, quite lost!

        And as with age his body uglier grows,

        So his mind cankers.[46] I will plague them all,

        Even to roaring.

[*Enter Ariel, laden with glistering[47] apparel, etc.*]

        Come, hang them on this line.[48]

[Prospero *and Ariel* remain, invisible. Enter *Caliban, Stephano, and* Trinculo, *all wet.*]

Caliban. Pray you, tread softly, that the blind mole may

195   Not hear a footfall. We now are near his cell.

Stephano. Monster, your fairy, which you say is a harmless

        fairy, has done little better than played the jack with us.[49]

Trinculo. Monster, I do smell all horse piss, at which my nose is

        in great indignation.

200 **Stephano.** So is mine. Do you hear, monster? If I should take a

        displeasure against you, look you—

Trinculo. Thou wert but a lost monster.

Caliban. Good my lord, give me thy favor still.

        Be patient, for the prize I'll bring thee to

205   Shall hoodwink this mischance.[50] Therefore speak softly.

        All's hushed as midnight yet.

Trinculo. Ay, but to lose our bottles in the pool!

Stephano. There is not only disgrace and dishonor in that, monster,

        but an infinite loss.

---

[44] trumpery—showy clothing.

[45] stale—bait.

[46] cankers—grows malignant.

[47] glistering—glittering.

[48] line—linden (lime) tree.

[49] played the jack with us—made fools out of us.

[50] hoodwink this mischance—cover up this misfortune and so put it out of your notice.

Trinculo. That's more to me than my wetting. Yet this is your
    harmless fairy, monster!

Stephano. I will fetch off my bottle, though I be o'er ears for my labor.[51]

Caliban. Prithee, my king, be quiet. Seest thou here,
    This is the mouth o' the cell. No noise, and enter.
    Do that good mischief which may make this island
    Thine own forever, and I thy Caliban
    For aye thy foot-licker.

Stephano. Give me thy hand. I do begin to have bloody thoughts.

Trinculo [*seeing the finery*]. O King Stephano! O peer! O worthy
    Stephano! Look what a wardrobe here is for thee!

Caliban. Let it alone, thou fool, it is but trash.

Trinculo. O ho, monster! We know what belongs to a frippery.[52] O
    King Stephano! [*He puts on a gown.*]

Stephano. Put off that gown, Trinculo. By this hand,
    I'll have that gown.

Trinculo. Thy Grace shall have it.

Caliban. The dropsy drown this fool! What do you mean
    To dote thus on such luggage?[53] Let 't alone
    And do the murder first. If he awake,
    From toe to crown he'll fill our skins with pinches,
    Make us strange stuff.

Stephano. Be you quiet, monster.—Mistress line, is
    not this my jerkin? [*He takes a leather jacket down.*] Now is the jerkin
    under the line.[54] Now, jerkin, you are like to lose your
    hair and prove a bald jerkin.

Trinculo. Do, do! We steal by line and level,[55] an 't like
    Your Grace.

Stephano. I thank thee for that jest. Here's a garment for 't. Wit shall not
go unrewarded while I am king of this country. "Steal by line and level"
is an excellent pass of pate.[56] There's another garment for 't.

210

215

220

225

230

235

240

---

[51] I will . . . labor—I'll get my bottle back, even if I have to dive underwater.

[52] frippery—used clothing store.

[53] The dropsy . . . luggage—May dropsy (a disease) suffocate this fool! Why are you bothering with such trash?

[54] under the line—under the lime tree, with a pun on *line* "equator." Travelers who went south of the equator on long sea voyages were believed to lose their hair from diseases such as scurvy.

[55] by line and level—methodically, as if by means of the carpenter's plumb line and level.

[56] pass of pate—witty play on words.

Trinculo. Monster, come, put some lime[57] upon your fingers, and away
with the rest.

Caliban. I will have none on 't. We shall lose our time

245   And all be turned to barnacles,[58] or to apes

    With foreheads villainous low.

Stephano. Monster, lay to your fingers. Help to bear this away
where my hogshead of wine is, or I'll turn you out of my kingdom.
Go to, carry this.

250 **Trinculo.** And this.

Stephano. Ay, and this.

[*They load* Caliban *with more and more garments.*]

[*A noise of hunters heard. Enter divers* Spirits, *in shape of dogs and hounds,
hunting them about,* Prospero *and* Ariel *setting them on.*]

Prospero. Hey, Mountain, hey!

Ariel. Silver! There it goes, Silver!

Prospero. Fury, Fury! There, Tyrant, there! Hark! Hark!

[Caliban, Stephano, *and* Trinculo *are driven out.*]

255   Go, charge my goblins that they grind their joints

    With dry convulsions, shorten up their sinews

    With agèd cramps, and more pinch-spotted make them

    Than pard or cat o' mountain.[59]

Ariel.   Hark, they roar!

Prospero. Let them be hunted soundly. At this hour

260   Lies at my mercy all mine enemies.

    Shortly shall all my labors end, and thou

    Shalt have the air at freedom. For a little

    Follow, and do me service.

[*They exit.*]

---

[57] lime—birdlime; sticky substance (to give Caliban sticky fingers for theft).

[58] barnacles—geese.

[59] grind . . . mountain—give them cramps like those of old age and pinch them so they have more spots than a leopard or wildcat.

Act Five, Scene One

In front of Prospero's cave, later that day, he says he will give up magic after he accomplishes his goals. Ariel leads in Alonso and his followers, still in a trance. Prospero accuses Antonio of being treacherous, yet he forgives him. Dressing himself in his robes as duke of Milan, Prospero breaks the spell over Alonso and his party. Alonso asks Prospero's pardon and gives up his claim to tribute from Milan.

In return, Prospero shows him that Ferdinand is alive and introduces him to Miranda. Alonso blesses their marriage. Ariel leads in the ship's master and boatswain, who report that their ship is somehow whole and seaworthy. Prospero tells everyone that he will explain these strange events; then he pardons Caliban, sets Ariel free, and gives up magic.

Enter Prospero *in his magic robes, with his staff, and* Ariel.

Prospero. Now does my project gather to a head.
    My charms crack not, my spirits obey, and time
    Goes upright with his carriage.[1]—How's the day?
Ariel. On the sixth hour, at which time, my lord,
5   You said our work should cease.
Prospero.   I did say so,
    When first I raised the tempest. Say, my spirit,
    How fares the king and 's followers?
Ariel.   Confined together
    In the same fashion as you gave in charge,
    Just as you left them; all prisoners, sir,
10   In the line grove which weather-fends your cell.[2]
    They cannot budge till your release. The king,
    His brother, and yours abide all three distracted,
    And the remainder mourning over them,
    Brim full of sorrow and dismay, but chiefly
15   Him that you termed, sir, the good old Lord Gonzalo.
    His tears runs down his beard like winter's drops
    From eaves of reeds. Your charm so strongly works 'em

---

[1] time . . . carriage—Time's burden is not so heavy now, and he can walk upright.
[2] line . . . cell—grove of lime trees that surrounds and protects your cave from bad weather.

The rarer action is

In virtue than in vengeance.

That if you now beheld them, your affections
Would become tender.

Prospero.   Dost thou think so, spirit?

20 **Ariel.** Mine would, sir, were I human.

Prospero.   And mine shall.
Hast thou, which art but air, a touch, a feeling
Of their afflictions, and shall not myself,
One of their kind, that relish all as sharply
Passion as they, be kindlier moved than thou art?[3]

25 Though with their high wrongs I am struck to the quick,
Yet with my nobler reason 'gainst my fury
Do I take part. The rarer action is
In virtue than in vengeance.[4] They being penitent,
The sole drift of my purpose doth extend

30 Not a frown further. Go release them, Ariel.
My charms I'll break, their senses I'll restore,
And they shall be themselves.

Ariel.   I'll fetch them, sir.

[_Exit_ Ariel.]

[Prospero _traces a magic circle with his staff._]

Prospero. Ye elves of hills, brooks, standing lakes, and groves,
And ye that on the sands with printless foot

35 Do chase the ebbing Neptune, and do fly him
When he comes back; you demi-puppets that
By moonshine do the green sour ringlets make,
Whereof the ewe not bites; and you whose pastime
Is to make midnight mushrooms, that rejoice

40 To hear the solemn curfew;[5] by whose aid,

---

[3] Hast . . . art—If you, who are only an airy spirit, can feel so strongly about their discomforts, shouldn't I, who am human and who feels human passions as strongly as they do, pity them even more than you?

[4] The rarer . . . vengeance—It is nobler to show compassion than to take revenge.

[5] you demi-puppets . . . curfew—you elves and fairies, who make fairy rings in the grass at night, which sheep never graze from; and who make mushrooms appear overnight, who are happy to hear the evening bell ringing.

In a 1986 production of *The Tempest* by New York City's Classic Stage Company, Prospero uses his magic staff to lift his spell from Alonso and the other courtiers.

Weak masters though ye be, I have bedimmed
The noontide sun, called forth the mutinous winds,
And, twixt the green sea and the azured vault[6]
Set roaring war; to the dread rattling thunder
45 Have I given fire, and rifted[7] Jove's stout oak
With his own bolt; the strong-based promontory
Have I made shake, and by the spurs[8] plucked up
The pine and cedar; graves at my command
Have waked their sleepers, oped, and let 'em forth
50 By my so **potent**[9] art. But this rough magic
I here **abjure,**[10] and when I have required

---

[6] azured vault—blue sky.

[7] rifted—split.

[8] spurs—roots.

[9] **potent**—powerful.

[10] **abjure**—reject; formally give up.

But this rough magic
I here abjure.

Some heavenly music—which even now I do—
To work mine end upon their senses that
This airy charm is for, I'll break my staff,
Bury it certain fathoms in the earth,
55   And deeper than did ever plummet sound
I'll drown my book.

[*Solemn music.*]

[*Here enters* Ariel *before; then* Alonso, *with a frantic gesture, attended by*
Gonzalo; Sebastian *and* Antonio *in like manner, attended by* Adrian *and*
Francisco. *They all enter the circle which* Prospero *had made, and there stand
charmed; which* Prospero *observing, speaks.*]

A solemn air, and the best comforter
To an unsettled fancy,[11] cure thy brains,
60   Now useless, boiled within thy skull! There stand,
For you are spell-stopped.—
Holy Gonzalo, honorable man,
Mine eyes, e'en sociable to the show of thine,
Fall fellowly drops.[12] The charm dissolves apace,
65   And as the morning steals upon the night,
Melting the darkness, so their rising senses
Begin to chase the ignorant fumes that mantle[13]
Their clearer reason.—O good Gonzalo,
My true preserver, and a loyal sir
70   To him thou follow'st! I will pay thy graces
Home[14] both in word and deed.—Most cruelly
Didst thou, Alonso, use me and my daughter.
Thy brother was a furtherer[15] in the act.—

---

[11] fancy—imagination.
[12] Mine eyes . . . drops—My eyes cry tears that are companions to your tears.
[13] mantle—cover up.
[14] pay . . . Home—repay your favors fully.
[15] furtherer—accomplice.

Thou art pinched[16] for 't now, Sebastian. Flesh and blood,

75 You, brother mine, that entertained ambition,
Expelled **remorse**[17] and nature, whom, with Sebastian,
Whose inward pinches therefore are most strong,
Would here have killed your king, I do forgive thee,
Unnatural though thou art.—Their understanding

80 Begins to swell, and the approaching tide
Will shortly fill the reasonable shore
That now lies foul and muddy.[18] Not one of them
That yet looks on me, or would know me.—Ariel,
Fetch me the hat and rapier in my cell.

[*Exit* Ariel *and returns immediately.*]

85 I will discase me and myself present
As I was sometime Milan.[19]—Quickly, spirit!
Thou shalt ere long be free.

[Ariel *sings and helps to attire him.*]

Ariel. *Where the bee sucks, there suck I.*

In a cowslip's bell I lie;

90 *There I couch[20] when owls do cry.*

On the bat's back I do fly

After summer merrily.

Merrily, merrily shall I live now

Under the blossom that hangs on the bough.

95 **Prospero.** Why, that's my dainty Ariel! I shall miss thee,
But yet thou shalt have freedom. So, so, so.
To the king's ship, invisible as thou art.
There shalt thou find the mariners asleep
Under the hatches. The master and the boatswain

100 Being awake, enforce them to this place,
And presently, I prithee.

---

[16] pinched—punished.

[17] **remorse**—deep and painful regret for doing something.

[18] the approaching . . . muddy—The waters of reason will soon return to fill your minds, which now are empty.

[19] I will . . . Milan—I will take off these magic robes and show myself as I used to be, the duke of Milan.

[20] *couch*—lie; cuddle up.

Ariel. I drink the air before me and return
  Or ere[21] your pulse twice beat. [*Exit* Ariel.]

Gonzalo. All torment, trouble, wonder, and amazement
105   Inhabits here. Some heavenly power guide us
  Out of this fearful country!

Prospero [*to* Alonso].   Behold, sir king,
  The wrongèd duke of Milan, Prospero.
  For more assurance that a living prince
  Does now speak to thee, I embrace thy body,
110   And to thee and thy company I bid
  A hearty welcome.

Alonso.   Whe'er thou be'st he or no,
  Or some enchanted trifle[22] to abuse me,
  As late I have been, I not know. Thy pulse
  Beats as of flesh and blood; and, since I saw thee,
115   Th' affliction of my mind amends, with which
  I fear a madness held me. This must crave—
  An if this be at all—a most strange story.[23]
  Thy dukedom I resign, and do entreat
  Thou pardon me my wrongs. But how should Prospero
120   Be living, and be here?

Prospero [*to* Gonzalo]. First, noble friend,
  Let me embrace thine age, whose honor cannot
  Be measured or confined.

Gonzalo.   Whether this be
  Or be not, I'll not swear.

Prospero.   You do yet taste
125   Some subtleties o' th' isle, that will not let you
  Believe things certain. Welcome, my friends all!
  [*Aside to* Sebastian *and* Antonio.] But you, my brace[24] of lords, were
    I so minded,

---

[21] Or ere—before.

[22] trifle—magic trick.

[23] This must . . . story—If all this is actually happening, there must be a strange explanation for it.

[24] brace—pair.

I here could pluck His Highness' frown upon you
And justify you traitors. At this time
130   I will tell no tales.

Sebastian. The devil speaks in him.

Prospero. No.
[*To* Antonio.] For you, most wicked sir, whom to call brother
Would even infect my mouth, I do forgive
Thy rankest fault, all of them and require
My dukedom of thee, which perforce[25] I know
135   Thou must restore.

Alonso. If thou be'st Prospero,
Give us particulars of thy preservation,
How thou hast met us here, whom three hours since
Were wrecked upon this shore; where I have lost—
How sharp the point of this remembrance is!—
140   My dear son Ferdinand.

Prospero. I am woe[26] for 't, sir.

Alonso. Irreparable is the loss, and Patience
Says it is past her cure.

Prospero. I rather think
You have not sought her help, of whose soft grace,
For the like loss, I have her sovereign aid
145   And rest myself content.

Alonso. You the like loss?

Prospero. As great to me as late, and supportable
To make the dear loss, have I means much weaker
Than you may call to comfort you;[27] for I
Have lost my daughter.

Alonso. A daughter?
150   O heavens, that they were living both in Naples,
The king and queen there! That they were, I wish
Myself were mudded in that oozy bed
Where my son lies!—When did you lose your daughter?

---

[25] perforce—of necessity.

[26] woe—sorry.

[27] As great . . . you—My loss is as great to me as it is recent, but I have fewer means to comfort me than you have.

In the American Repertory Theatre production, Prospero (Paul Freeman) reveals Ferdinand (Scott Ripley) and Miranda (Jessalyn Gilsig) playing chess.

Prospero. In this last tempest. I perceive these lords
155   At this encounter do so much admire[28]
     That they devour their reason, and scarce think
     Their eyes do offices of truth, their words
     Are natural breath.[29]—But, howsoever you have
     Been jostled from your senses, know for certain
160   That I am Prospero and that very duke
     Which was thrust forth of Milan, who most strangely
     Upon this shore, where you were wrecked, was landed
     To be the lord on 't. No more yet of this,
     For 'tis a chronicle of day by day,[30]

---

[28] admire—marvel.

[29] That they . . . breath—that they are dumbfounded and scarcely believe what their eyes tell them or that their words come naturally.

[30] a chronicle . . . day—story that will take days to tell.

165   Not a relation for a breakfast, nor

Befitting this first meeting. [*To Alonso.*] Welcome, sir.

This cell's my court. Here have I few attendants,

And subjects none abroad. Pray you, look in.

My dukedom since you have given me again,

170   I will **requite**[31] you with as good a thing,

At least bring forth a wonder to content ye

As much as me my dukedom.

[*Here* Prospero *discovers,*[32] Ferdinand *and* Miranda, *playing at chess.*]

Miranda. Sweet lord, you play me false.

Ferdinand.   No, my dearest love,

I would not for the world.

175   **Miranda.** Yes, for a score of kingdoms you should wrangle,

And I would call it fair play.

Alonso.   If this prove

A vision of the island, one dear son

Shall I twice lose.

Sebastian.   A most high miracle!

Ferdinand.

Though the seas threaten, they are merciful;

180   I have cursed them without cause. [*Kneels.*]

Alonso.   Now, all the blessings

Of a glad father compass thee about!

Arise, and say how thou cam'st here.

Miranda.   O, wonder!

How many goodly creatures are there here!

How beauteous mankind is! O brave new world

185   That has such people in 't!

Prospero.   'Tis new to thee.

---

[31] **requite**—repay.

[32] discovers—reveals (perhaps by drawing a curtain).

Alonso [*to* Ferdinand]. What is this maid with whom thou wast at play?
    Your eld'st acquaintance cannot be three hours.
    Is she the goddess that hath severed us,
    And brought us thus together?

Ferdinand.   Sir, she is mortal,

190   But by immortal providence she's mine.
    I chose her when I could not ask my father
    For his advice, nor thought I had one. She
    Is daughter to this famous duke of Milan,
    Of whom so often I have heard renown,

195   But never saw before; of whom I have
    Received a second life; and second father
    This lady makes him to me.

Alonso.   I am hers.
    But O, how oddly will it sound that I
    Must ask my child forgiveness!

Prospero.   There, sir, stop.

200   Let us not burden our remembrances with
    A heaviness that's gone.

Gonzalo.   I have inly wept,
    Or should have spoke ere this. Look down, you gods,
    And on this couple drop a blessèd crown!
    For it is you that have chalked forth the way[33]

205   Which brought us hither.

Alonso.   I say "Amen," Gonzalo!

Gonzalo. Was Milan thrust from Milan, that his issue
    Should become kings of Naples? O, rejoice
    Beyond a common joy, and set it down
    With gold on lasting pillars: in one voyage

210   Did Claribel her husband find at Tunis,
    And Ferdinand, her brother, found a wife
    Where he himself was lost; Prospero his dukedom
    In a poor isle; and all of us ourselves
    When no man was his own.[34]

---

[33] chalked . . . way—marked the pathway.

[34] and all . . . own—We found ourselves again after we had lost our senses.

Alonso [*to Ferdinand and* Miranda]. Give me your hands.
 215
    Let grief and sorrow still embrace his heart

    That doth not wish you joy!

Gonzalo.   Be it so! Amen!

[*Enter* Ariel, *with the* Master *and* Boatswain *amazedly following.*]

    O, look, sir, look, sir! Here is more of us.

    I prophesied, if a gallows were on land,

220   This fellow could not drown.—Now, blasphemy,

    That swear'st grace o'erboard, not an oath on shore?[35]

    Hast thou no mouth by land? What is the news?

Boatswain. The best news is that we have safely found

    Our king and company. The next, our ship

225   Which, but three glasses since, we gave out split,[36]

    Is tight and yare and bravely rigged as when

    We first put out to sea.

Ariel [*aside to* Prospero]. Sir, all this service

    Have I done since I went.

230 **Prospero** [*aside to* Ariel]. My tricksy[37] spirit!

Alonso. These are not natural events. They strengthen

    From strange to stranger. Say, how came you hither?

Boatswain. If I did think, sir, I were well awake,

    I'd strive to tell you. We were dead of sleep,

235   And—how we know not—all clapped under hatches,

    Where but even now, with strange and several noises

    Of roaring, shrieking, howling, jingling chains,

    And more diversity of sounds, all horrible,

    We were awaked; straightway at liberty,

240   Where we, in all her trim, freshly beheld

    Our royal, good, and gallant ship, our master

    Cap'ring to eye her.[38] On a trice,[39] so please you,

---

[35] Now, blasphemy . . . shore—Now, you swearer of oaths (the boatswain), who banished heavenly grace from the ship with your swearing, have you no curses now that you're onshore?

[36] three glasses . . . split—three hours ago we reported to be broken apart.

[37] tricksy—crafty.

[38] Cap'ring . . . her—dancing for joy to see her.

[39] On a trice—in a moment.

Even in a dream, were we divided from them
And were brought moping[40] hither.

Ariel [*aside to* Prospero].   Was 't well done?

245   **Prospero** [*aside to* Ariel]. Bravely, my diligence.[41] Thou shalt be free.

Alonso. This is as strange a maze as e'er men trod,
        And there is in this business more than nature
        Was ever conduct of. Some oracle
        Must **rectify**[42] our knowledge.

Prospero.   Sir, my liege,

250   Do not infest your mind with beating on
        The strangeness of this business. At picked leisure,
        Which shall be shortly, single I'll resolve you,
        Which to you shall seem probable, of every
        These happened accidents;[43] till when, be cheerful

255   And think of each thing well. [*Aside to* Ariel.]
        Come hither, spirit.
        Set Caliban and his companions free.
        Untie the spell. [*Exit* Ariel.] How fares my gracious sir?
        There are yet missing of your company

260   Some few odd lads that you remember not.

[*Enter* Ariel, *driving in* Caliban, Stephano, *and* Trinculo, *in their
stolen apparel.*]

Stephano. Every man shift for all the rest, and let no man take care
        for himself; for all is but fortune. Coragio, bully monster, coragio![44]

Trinculo. If these be true spies[45] which I wear in my head, here's a
        goodly sight.

265   **Caliban.** O Setebos, these be brave spirits indeed!
        How fine my Master is! I am afraid
        He will chastise me.

---

[40] moping—in a daze.

[41] diligence—here, careful and thorough worker.

[42] **rectify**—improve; set straight.

[43] single . . . accidents—I will explain to you privately every one of these events until they seem understandable to you.

[44] Every man . . . coragio!—Let every man be responsible for all the others and not just for himself, for we are all in the hands of fate. Have courage, my fine monster!

[45] true spies—eyes that see the truth.

Sebastian. Ha, ha!
What things are these, my lord Antonio?
270   Will money buy 'em?

Antonio.   Very like. One of them
Is a plain fish, and no doubt marketable.

Prospero. Mark but the badges[46] of these men, my lords,
Then say if they be true. This misshapen knave,
His mother was a witch, and one so strong
275   That could control the moon, make flows and ebbs,
And deal in her command without her power.
These three have robbed me, and this demidevil—
For he's a bastard one—had plotted with them
To take my life. Two of these fellows you
280   Must know and own. This thing of darkness I
Acknowledge mine.

Caliban.   I shall be pinched to death.

Alonso. Is not this Stephano, my drunken butler?

Sebastian. He is drunk now. Where had he wine?

Alonso. And Trinculo is reeling ripe. Where should they
285   Find this grand liquor that hath gilded 'em?[47]
[*To* Trinculo.] How cam'st thou in this pickle?

Trinculo. I have been in such a pickle since I saw you last that, I
fear me, will never out of my bones. I shall not fear flyblowing.[48]

Sebastian. Why, how now, Stephano?

290 **Stephano.** O, touch me not! I am not Stephano, but a cramp.

Prospero. You'd be king o' the isle, sirrah?[49]

Stephano. I should have been a sore one, then.

Alonso [*pointing to* Caliban].
This is a strange thing as e'er I looked on.

Prospero. He is as disproportioned in his manners
295   As in his shape. [*To* Caliban.] Go, sirrah, to my cell.

---

[46] badges—the stolen clothing and jewelry.

[47] gilded 'em—flushed their faces.

[48] I have been . . . flyblowing—Trinculo puns on *pickle,* "predicament," and *pickle,* "salt brine for preserving." He will not fear being eaten by maggots from fly eggs because he has been pickled like preserved meat.

[49] sirrah—form of address to an inferior.

Take with you your companions. As you look

To have my pardon, trim it[50] handsomely.

Caliban. Ay, that I will, and I'll be wise hereafter

And seek for grace. What a thrice-double ass

300 Was I to take this drunkard for a god

And worship this dull fool!

Prospero.   Go to. Away!

Alonso. Hence, and bestow your luggage where you found it.

Sebastian. Or stole it, rather.

[*Exit* Caliban, Stephano, *and* Trinculo.]

Prospero. Sir, I invite Your Highness and your train

305 To my poor cell, where you shall take your rest

For this one night, which, part of it, I'll waste

With such discourse[51] as, I not doubt, shall make it

Go quick away: the story of my life,

And the particular accidents gone by

310 Since I came to this isle. And in the morn

I'll bring you to your ship, and so to Naples,

Where I have hope to see the nuptual[52]

Of these our dear-belovèd solemnized;

And thence retire me to my Milan, where

Every third thought shall be my grave.

315 **Alonso.**   I long

To hear the story of your life, which must

Take the ear strangely.

Prospero.   I'll deliver all;

And promise you calm seas, **auspicious**[53] gales,

And sail so expeditious that shall catch

320 Your royal fleet far off.[54] [*Aside to* Ariel.] My Ariel, chick,

That is thy charge. Then to the elements

Be free, and fare thou well!—Please you, draw near.

[*All except* Prospero *exit.*]

---

[50] trim it—Put it in order.

[51] discourse—storytelling.

[52] nuptual—wedding.

[53] **auspicious**—favorable.

[54] sail . . . far off—sailing so efficiently and speedily that you will be able to catch up with the rest of your fleet (now on its way back to Naples).

Standing within a magic circle, Prospero (Rick Tutor) delivers his epilogue at the close of the Seattle Children's Theatre production.

Epilogue

Prospero asks the audience for its applause.

Spoken by Prospero.

Now my charms are all o'erthrown,
And what strength I have 's mine own,
Which is most faint. Now, 'tis true,
I must be here confined by you
5　Or sent to Naples. Let me not,
Since I have my dukedom got
And pardoned the deceiver, dwell
In this bare island by your spell,
But release me from my bands
10　With the help of your good hands.[1]
Gentle breath of yours my sails
Must fill, or else my project fails,
Which was to please. Now I want[2]
Spirits to enforce, art to enchant,
15　And my ending is despair,
Unless I be relieved by prayer,
Which pierces so that it assaults
Mercy itself, and frees all faults.
As you from crimes would pardoned be,
20　Let your indulgence[3] set me free.
　　[*He exits.*]

---

[1] But release . . . hands—Prospero continues the theme of magic spells: He must remain on this island until his own spell is broken by the audience's applause.

[2] want—lack.

[3] indulgence—humoring approval; forgiveness of sin.

Understanding the Play

Act One

1. In Scene One, how do the passengers treat the ship's crew? How does the crew treat the passengers?

2. In Scene Two, what is Miranda's reaction to Prospero's story?

3. What evidences of Prospero's magic do we see in Act One?

4. How did Ariel come to be in Prospero's service? Why does he stay?

5. Who is Caliban? How did he come to be in Prospero's service?

6. How does Ferdinand react to meeting Miranda? How does she react to meeting him?

7. What are Prospero's secret plans for Ferdinand and Miranda?

Act Two

1. In Scene One, how does Gonzalo try to cheer Alonso up? How does Alonso react?

2. What does Sebastian accuse Alonso of?

3. Why does Ariel put the men to sleep? Why does he wake them up?

4. In Scene Two, why does Caliban swear allegiance to Stephano?

Act Three

1. In Scene One, why is Ferdinand willing to endure the labors imposed by Prospero?

2. In Scene Two, what does Caliban persuade Stephano and Trinculo to do? Why does he do this, and why do they agree?

3. How does Prospero demonstrate his magic abilities in Scene Three? What is his purpose here?

4. Why do you suppose Prospero has Ariel accuse Alonso, Sebastian, and Antonio of their crimes instead of doing it himself?

5. How do the reactions of Gonzalo, Alonso, Sebastian, and Antonio to these strange events differ? Who appears to be most affected by what he experiences?

6. What does Gonzalo fear at the end of the scene?

Act Four

1. How does Prospero compensate Ferdinand for his punishment?

2. What message do the spirits playing Ceres and Juno bring to Ferdinand and Miranda? Why are they appropriate characters to bring this message?

3. How do Prospero and Ariel plan to spoil Caliban's plot against Prospero? How well does this plan work?

Act Five

1. Prospero says, "The rarer action is/In virtue than in vengeance" (lines 27–28). What does he mean by this? How do his actions reflect his belief?

2. How does Prospero greet the king and the nobles? How do they respond to him?

3. What threat does Prospero make to Sebastian and Antonio? Why do you think he does so?

4. What do we now learn actually happened to the boat and its crew?

5. How does Prospero punish Caliban, Stephano, and Trinculo? Does this seem appropriate?

6. In the Epilogue, how does Prospero's request fit the spirit of the play?

Analyzing the Play

1. One of the basic themes of *The Tempest* is education. Compare the method and results of Prospero's schooling of Miranda with those of his effort to teach Caliban.

2. Analyze the character of Caliban as an example of uncivilized human nature. What are his good and bad qualities? How does his morality compare to that of the "civilized" characters?

3. What do you think is the purpose of the low-comedy scenes with Caliban, Stephano, and Trinculo?

4. Some critics have seen in the character of Prospero an image of Shakespeare himself. What elements in *The Tempest* do you think support this interpretation?

Writing Projects

1. Write a flashback scene that dramatizes either how Prospero, newly arrived on the island, saves Ariel from his imprisonment in a "cloven pine" or how he first encounters Caliban and tries to teach him. First reread parts of the play in which the characters discuss these events. Then use your imagination to create the actions and the dialogue.

2. Write a character sketch of Prospero. What do his actions suggest about his character? How does he describe himself? How do other characters speak about him and act toward him?

3. Imagine that Miranda keeps a diary. Using her voice, write some entries for this diary. Start with one or two entries before the events of this day. How does she spend her time? What interests her or displeases her? Then write one or more entries for this amazing day.

4. Write an essay on the theme of giving and taking, as it is expressed in *The Tempest*.

Who takes what from whom? How are those actions punished? Who gives? Is such action rewarded? Conclude with a generalization that sums up how Shakespeare seems to have regarded the theme.

Performance Projects

1. With a partner, perform Act Three, Scene One. (Because most of Prospero's lines are asides, you can simply leave them out.) Remember that Ferdinand and Miranda have just met an hour earlier. How can you express your growing love without becoming too passionate too soon?

2. Draw and color a costume design or clothe a costume doll for either Ariel or Caliban, or for both of them. Remember that Ariel is essentially a spirit of air and that Caliban is the child of an evil witch. How will the costumes you design for them reflect their characters and their behavior?

3. Find some dance music from Shakespeare's time. Choose one piece and play it several times. Experiment with movement that seems appropriate for the music. Choreograph a dance that might be used as part of the masque in Act Four. Include a partner if you wish. Finally, perform your dance for an audience of your classmates.

4. The Elizabethan stage was capable of some special effects, such as using overhead machinery to lower Juno in her chariot through a trapdoor in the ceiling in Act Four. Design a chariot for Juno and make a model of it. First, consider its construction: what size, shape, materials, and support would it need to carry a person? Then consider its decoration: What colors, symbols, and so on would signify to an audience that this is the chariot of the queen of the gods?

Sonnets

Introduction

The sonnet is the best-known and one of the most challenging short poetic forms in Western literature. In a sonnet of his own, the 19th-century English poet Dante Gabriel Rossetti defined the form as "a moment's monument." The sonnet's brevity favors the concentrated expression of an idea or feeling. As a result, a typical sonnet theme has been some aspect of love. But the form has also been used to express a broad range of other themes such as nature and reflections on history. Since its appearance in Renaissance Italy, the sonnet has been a form used by some of the finest European and American poets. Among the most famous sonneteers in English have been Shakespeare, John Milton, William Wordsworth, John Keats, Elizabeth Barrett Browning, Henry Wadsworth Longfellow, Edwin Arlington Robinson, Edna St. Vincent Millay, and W. H. Auden.

Sonnets Before Shakespeare

The word sonnet comes from Italian and means "a little sound," that is, a short poem. The sonnet form originated in Italy, probably in the 1200s. The Italian poet Francis Petrarch (1304–1374) popularized the form by writing a highly influential sequence of sonnets exploring his feelings for his beloved, Laura. The sonnet form spread throughout Europe during the Renaissance.

Sonnets became very popular in England in the 1590s. The Elizabethan poets followed Petrarch's lead in writing sonnet sequences celebrating the women they admired. Two famous examples are Astrophel and Stella (1591) by Sir Philip Sidney (1554–1586) and Amoretti (1595) by Edmund Spenser (c.1552–1599).

Shakespeare's Sonnets

Shakespeare's sonnets were first published in 1609, although some had been known in manuscript copies in the 1590s. Shakespeare would have read both Sidney and Spenser. He clearly showed his awareness of the sonnet form in Romeo and Juliet (probably written in 1595) when he made the young lovers recite a sonnet to each other at their first meeting. As this suggests, sonnets often tell the story of the love between a man and a woman. Shakespeare's sonnets give this a new twist by bringing in a third party, making the situation a love triangle, a situation familiar in his comedies, such as Twelfth Night.

There are 154 sonnets of Shakespeare, which fall into two broad groups. Sonnets 1 through 126 are addressed to a young nobleman, for whom the speaker (the "I" of the poems) declares his love. The young man is urged to marry, so that his beauty will survive in that of his children. Sonnets 127 through 152 are addressed to a woman (the "Dark Lady"), who is said in Sonnet 144 to have been the mistress of the young man as well as of the speaker. The last two poems, Sonnets 153 and 154, are not part of either of these groups.

Despite many suggestions, neither the young man nor the Dark Lady can be identified. It is not even certain that they are real persons; they may simply be invented. We should also be careful of assuming that the speaker of the poems is Shakespeare.

Structure of the Shakespearean Sonnet

Almost all Shakespeare's sonnets follow a similar pattern:
- There are fourteen lines.
- Each line is in iambic pentameter (see page 13).
- The sonnet is broadly divided into the first eight lines (or octave) and the last six (or sestet).
- Within this division, there are three groups of four lines each (or quatrains) and the final two lines, which rhyme with each other (a couplet).
- The rhyme scheme is: abab (first quatrain), cdcd (second quatrain), efef (third quatrain), gg (couplet).

These divisions were used by Shakespeare to structure an argument. The first quatrain states a major idea. The second states another. The third brings the two ideas together. The couplet provides a neat conclusion, or summary. Frequently, each of these stages in the argument is also a complete sentence. Words such as and, but, or so draw attention to the structural logic of the poem.

Examining Sonnet 55

It is important to remember that a Shakespearean sonnet, although it presents a structure of ideas, is not a kind of essay. The sonnet's ideas are developed through a series of images, which need to be carefully studied. Look at Sonnet 55:

Not marble nor the gilded monuments
Of princes shall outlive this pow'rful rhyme,
But you shall shine more bright in these contents
Than unswept stone, besmeared with sluttish time.
When wasteful war shall statues overturn,
And broils root out the work of masonry,
Nor Mars his sword nor war's quick fire shall burn
The living record of your memory.
'Gainst death and all-oblivious enmity
Shall you pace forth; your praise shall still find room,
Even in the eyes of all posterity
That wear this world out to the ending doom.
    So, till the judgment that yourself arise,
    You live in this, and dwell in lovers' eyes.

The English artist Nicholas Hilliard (1547–1619), a contemporary of Shakespeare, painted this young man. The speaker in the Sonnets celebrates this type of Elizabethan male beauty in his beloved. ▶

First, consider the idea presented in each division of the sonnet.

- First quatrain: This poem will last longer than apparently much more solid memorials, so it will be a better way of commemorating you.
- Second quatrain: Although the poem is only a piece of paper, it will survive the threat of destruction by war or fire, which will be fatal to buildings or statues.
- Third quatrain: You will even outlive your own death, by being made immortal in the poem. Your memory will endure until the Last Judgment.
- Couplet: On Judgment Day, you will be resurrected from death; but until then, you can live on in this poem and in the emotion of love that others feel from reading it.

Second, examine Shakespeare's use of language. The vocabulary of the sonnet is fairly simple, but its language is vigorous and effective. Notice the emphasis that comes from the alliteration in "unswept stone, besmeared with sluttish time"; or the energy of the verb "root out." Much of the sonnet's compactness comes from balancing phrases; for example, "Nor Mars his sword nor war's quick fire"; or, in the last line, "You live in this and dwell in lover's eyes."

Finally, respond to the sonnet as a whole. The speaker makes an outrageous claim. How can a fragile piece of paper last longer than brass or marble? Yet words are not subject to decay, neglect, or physical damage. A poem in a book exists in many copies, which may be read by many people, so there is a better chance still of its survival. The young man will die physically, but his youth and beauty will live on in the poem and be renewed every time someone reads it. In the end, we cannot disagree with what the sonnet says, because we prove it to be true by reading it. The young man does indeed survive only in these lines, and lives on today because we think of him when we read Shakespeare!

◀ Painted by the English artist George Gower (c. 1540–1596) in 1573, this portrait of an English noblewoman shows the golden hair and fair complexion that marked the Elizabethan ideal of female beauty.

Sonnet 15

When I consider every thing that grows
Holds in perfection but a little moment,
That this huge stage[1] presenteth naught[2] but shows
Whereon the stars in secret influence comment;[3]
When I perceive that men as[4] plants increase,
Cheerèd and checked[5] even by the selfsame sky,
Vaunt in their youthful sap,[6] at height decrease,[7]
And wear their brave state out of memory;[8]
Then the conceit of this inconstant stay[9]
Sets you most rich in youth before my sight,
Where wasteful Time debateth with Decay[10]
To change your day of youth to sullied night;
    And, all in war[11] with Time for love of you,
    As he takes from you I engraft you new.[12]

[1] this huge stage—this world.

[2] naught—nothing.

[3] in secret . . . comment—affect mysteriously (the belief that underlies astrology).

[4] as—like.

[5] Cheerèd and checked—applauded and hissed; that is, urged on and held back.

[6] Vaunt in . . . sap—boast about their youthful vigor.

[7] at height decrease—as soon as they reach full maturity, begin to decline.

[8] And wear . . . memory—wear out their splendid condition until it is forgotten.

[9] conceit . . . stay—idea of this changeable duration.

[10] wasteful . . . Decay—Time and Decay join forces.

[11] in war—fighting hard.

[12] engraft you new—renew you by grafting; give you new life through verse.

Sonnet 18

Shall I compare thee to a summer's day?
Thou art more lovely and more temperate.
Rough winds do shake the darling buds of May,
And summer's lease hath all too short a date.[1]
Sometimes too hot the eye of heaven[2] shines,
And often is his gold complexion dimmed;
And every fair from fair[3] sometimes declines,
By chance or nature's changing course untrimmed.[4]
But thy eternal summer shall not fade
Nor lose possession of that fair thou ow'st;[5]
Nor shall Death brag thou wanderest in his shade,
When in eternal lines[6] to time thou grow'st.[7]
    So long as men can breathe or eyes can see,
    So long lives this, and this gives life to thee.

[1] lease . . . date—allotted time is too short.

[2] eye of heaven—sun.

[3] fair from fair—beautiful person from beauty.

[4] untrimmed—stripped of ornament and beauty.

[5] fair thou ow'st—beauty you have.

[6] lines—poetry.

[7] to time thou grow'st—you become incorporated into time, engrafted on it.

Sonnet 19

Devouring Time, blunt thou the lion's paws,
And make the earth devour her own sweet brood;
Pluck the **keen**[1] teeth from the fierce tiger's jaws,
And burn the long-lived phoenix[2] in her blood;
Make glad and sorry seasons as thou fleet'st,[3]
And do whate'er thou wilt, swift-footed Time,
To the wide world and all her fading sweets.
But I forbid thee one most heinous crime:
O, carve not with thy hours my love's fair brow,
Nor draw no lines there with thine antique[4] pen;
Him in thy course untainted[5] do allow
For beauty's pattern to succeeding men.
    Yet, do thy worst, old Time. Despite thy wrong,
    My love shall in my verse ever live young.

[1] **keen**—sharp.
[2] phoenix—mythological bird that is consumed alive ("in her blood") by fire and then reborn in the ashes. The phoenix is a symbol of immortality.
[3] fleet'st—hurry.
[4] antique—old; fantastic.
[5] untainted—unaltered.

Sonnet 23

As an unperfect actor[1] on the stage
Who with his fear is put beside[2] his part,
Or some fierce thing **replete**[3] with too much rage,
Whose strength's abundance weakens his own heart,[4]
So I, for fear of trust,[5] forget to say
The perfect ceremony of love's rite,
And in mine own love's strength seem to decay,
O'ercharged with burden of mine own love's might.
O, let my books be then the eloquence
And dumb presagers[6] of my speaking breast,
Who plead for love and look for **recompense**[7]
More than that tongue that more hath more expressed.[8]
    O, learn to read what silent love hath writ.
    To hear with eyes belongs to love's fine wit.[9]

[1] unperfect actor—actor who has not learned his lines.
[2] beside—out of.
[3] **replete**—overfilled.
[4] heart—courage.
[5] for fear of trust—mistrusting myself.
[6] dumb presagers—silent messengers.
[7] **recompense**—payment in return.
[8] more hath more expressed—has more often expressed more.
[9] wit—intelligence.

Sonnet 29

When in disgrace with Fortune and men's eyes
I all alone beweep[1] my outcast state,
And trouble deaf heaven with my bootless[2] cries,
And look upon myself and curse my fate,
Wishing me like to one more rich in hope,
Featured[3] like him, like him with friends possessed,
Desiring this man's art and that man's scope,[4]
With what I most enjoy contented least;
Yet in these thoughts myself almost despising,
Haply I think on thee, and then my state
(Like to the lark at break of day arising
From **sullen**[5] earth) sings hymns at heaven's gate,
    For thy sweet love remembered such wealth brings,
    That then I scorn to change my state with kings.

[1] beweep—weep over, mourn.
[2] bootless—useless.
[3] Featured—that is, handsome.
[4] scope—range of mind.
[5] **sullen**—dull, heavy.

Sonnet 30

When to the sessions of sweet silent thought
I summon up remembrance of things past,
I sigh[1] the lack of many a thing I sought,
And with old woes new wail my dear Time's waste.[2]
Then can I drown an eye, unused to flow,[3]
For precious friends hid in death's dateless[4] night,
And weep afresh love's long since canceled[5] woe,
And moan th' expense[6] of many a vanished sight.
Then can I grieve at grievances foregone,[7]
And heavily from woe to woe tell o'er[8]
The sad account of fore-bemoanèd moan,
Which I new pay as if not paid before.
    But if the while I think on thee, dear friend,
    All losses are restored and sorrows end.

[1] sigh—sigh for.
[2] new wail . . . waste—be freshly sad at Time's destruction of things precious to me.
[3] unused to flow—not used to shedding tears.
[4] dateless—endless.
[5] canceled—paid in full.
[6] expense—loss.
[7] grievances foregone—former sorrows.
[8] tell o'er—count again.

Sonnet 35

No more be grieved at that which thou hast done.
Roses have thorns, and silver fountains mud,
Clouds and eclipses stain both moon and sun,
And loathsome canker[1] lives in sweetest bud.
All men make faults, and even I in this,
Authorizing thy trespass with compare,[2]
Myself corrupting, salving thy amiss,[3]
Excusing thy sins more than thy sins are.[4]
For to thy sensual fault I bring in sense[5]—
Thy adverse party is thy advocate[6]—
And 'gainst myself a lawful plea commence.
Such civil war is in my love and hate
    That I an accessary[7] needs must be
    To that sweet thief which sourly robs from me.

[1] canker—cankerworm that destroys flowers.
[2] authorizing . . . compare—justifying your misdeeds by comparison.
[3] Myself corrupting . . . thy amiss—bring blame on myself by excusing your sins.
[4] are—deserve.
[5] sense—logical argument, reason.
[6] Thy . . . advocate—Your opponent is your defender.
[7] accessary—accomplice.

Sonnet 55

Not marble, nor the gilded monuments
Of princes shall outlive this pow'rful rhyme,
But you shall shine more bright in these contents[1]
Than unswept stone[2] besmeared with sluttish[3] time.
When wasteful war shall statues overturn,
And broils[4] root out the work of masonry,
Nor Mars his sword[5] nor war's quick fire shall burn
The living record of your memory.
'Gainst death and all-oblivious enmity[6]
Shall you pace forth; your praise shall still find room
Even in the eyes of all posterity
That wear this world out to the ending doom.[7]
    So, till the judgment that yourself arise,[8]
    You live in this, and dwell in lovers'[9] eyes.

[1] these contents—contents of my poem.
[2] Than unswept stone—than in a memorial stone on a church's floor that has not been swept.
[3] sluttish—neglectful, dirtying.
[4] broils—quarrels, battles.
[5] Mars his sword—sword of Mars, the god of war.
[6] death . . . enmity—forgetfulness caused by death, the enemy of all.
[7] wear . . . doom—outlasts from now until the end of the world (Doomsday).
[8] till the judgement . . . arise—until Judgment Day raises you from the dead.
[9] lovers'—admirers'.

Sonnet 65

Since[1] brass, nor stone, nor earth, nor boundless sea,
But[2] sad mortality o'ersways their power,
How with this rage[3] shall beauty hold[4] a plea,
Whose action is no stronger than a flower?
O, how shall summer's honey breath hold out
Against the wrackful[5] siege of battering days,
When rocks impregnable[6] are not so stout,[7]
Nor gates of steel so strong, but Time decays?[8]
O fearful meditation! Where, alack,[9]
Shall Time's best jewel from Time's chest lie hid?[10]
Or what strong hand can hold his swift foot back?
Or who his spoil[11] of beauty can forbid?
    O, none, unless this miracle have might,
    That in black ink my love may still shine bright.

[1] Since—since neither.

[2] But—but that.

[3] with this rage—against this destructive power.

[4] hold—maintain.

[5] wrackful—wrecking, destructive.

[6] impregnable—unbreakable.

[7] stout—strong.

[8] decays—undermines them; causes them to decay.

[9] alack—exclamation of sorrow.

[10] from Time's ... hid—conceal itself so that it won't be hidden away in Time's storage chest.

[11] spoil—plunder.

Sonnet 71

No longer mourn for me when I am dead
Than you shall hear the surly sullen bell[1]
Give warning to the world that I am fled
From this vile world, with vilest worms to dwell.
Nay, if you read this line, remember not
The hand that writ it, for I love you so
That I in your sweet thoughts would be forgot
If thinking on me then should make you woe.[2]
O, if, I say, you look upon this verse
When I perhaps compounded am with clay,
Do not so much as my poor name rehearse,
But let your love even with my life decay,
    Lest the wise world should look into your moan
    And mock you with[3] me after I am gone.

[1] surly ... bell—rude, gloomy bell tolled when a person dies.

[2] If thinking ... woe—if thinking about me should cause you pain.

[3] with—because of; for loving.

Sonnet 73

That time of year thou mayst in me behold[1]
When yellow leaves, or none, or few, do hang
Upon those boughs[2] which shake against the cold,
Bare ruined choirs[3] where late[4] the sweet birds sang.
In me thou seest the twilight of such day
As after sunset fadeth in the west,
Which by and by black night doth take away,
Death's second self, that seals up[5] all in rest.
In me thou seest the glowing of such fire
That on the ashes of his[6] youth doth lie
As the deathbed whereon it must expire,
Consumed with that which it was nourished by.
    This thou perceiv'st, which makes thy love more
        strong,
    To love that well which thou must leave ere long.

[1] behold—see.
[2] boughs—branches.
[3] choirs—part of churches set apart for the choirs (singers) in a service.
[4] late—lately; recently. (Many churches were torn down in the reign of Henry VIII.)
[5] seals up—closes.
[6] his—its.

Sonnet 106

When in the chronicle of wasted[1] time
I see descriptions of the fairest wights,[2]
And beauty making beautiful old rhyme
In praise of ladies dead and lovely knights,
Then, in the blazon[3] of sweet beauty's best,
Of hand, of foot, of lip, of eye, of brow,
I see their antique pen would have expressed
Even such a beauty as you master[4] now.
So all their praises are but prophecies
Of this our time, all you prefiguring;[5]
And, for[6] they looked but with divining[7] eyes,
They had not skill enough your worth to sing.
    For we,[8] which now behold these present days,
    Have eyes to wonder, but lack tongues to praise.

[1] wasted—used up, past.
[2] wights—people.
[3] blazon—record of virtues and excellencies (a heraldic metaphor).
[4] master—have, possess.
[5] you prefiguring—representing you beforehand.
[6] for—because.
[7] divining—prophetic, foretelling.
[8] For we—for even we.

Sonnet 116

Let me not to the marriage of true minds
Admit impediments.[1] Love is not love
Which alters when it alteration finds,
Or bends with the remover to remove.
O, no, it is an ever-fixéd mark[2]
That looks on **tempests**[3] and is never shaken;
It is the star to every wandering bark,[4]
Whose worth's unknown, although his height be taken.[5]
Love's not Time's fool, though rosy lips and cheeks
Within his bending sickle's compass[6] come;
Love alters not with his brief hours and weeks,
But bears it out even to the edge of doom.[7]
　　　If this be error and upon me proved,
　　　I never writ, nor no man ever loved.

[1] Admit impediments—allow consideration of obstructions, hindrances.
[2] mark—object that helps navigation.
[3] **tempests**—fierce storms.
[4] star … bark—North Star to every wandering boat.
[5] Whose worth's … taken—whose value to sailors is beyond estimation, even though the star's position is known.
[6] Time's … compass—range of the curved blade of Time's scythe.
[7] bears … doom—survives to the end of time.

Sonnet 130

My mistress' eyes are nothing like the sun;
Coral is far more red than her lips' red;
If snow be white, why then her breasts are dun;[1]
If hairs be wires, black wires grow on her head.
I have seen roses damasked,[2] red and white,
But no such roses see I in her cheeks;
And in some perfumes is there more delight
Than in the breath that from my mistress reeks.
I love to hear her speak, yet well I know
That music hath a far more pleasing sound.
I grant I never saw a goddess go;[3]
My mistress, when she walks, treads on the ground.
　　　And yet, by heaven, I think my love as rare
　　　As any she belied with false compare.[4]

[1] dun—plain brown, mouse colored.
[2] damasked—mingled red and white.
[3] go—walk.
[4] any she … compare—any woman misrepresented by false comparison.

Sonnet 138

When my love swears that she is made of truth,[1]
I do believe her, though I know she lies,
That she might think me some untutored[2] youth,
Unlearnèd in the world's false subtleties.
Thus vainly thinking that she thinks me young,
Although she knows my days are past the best,
Simply I credit[3] her false-speaking tongue;
On both sides thus is simple truth suppressed.
But wherefore says she not she is unjust?[4]
And wherefore say not I that I am old?
O, love's best habit[5] is in seeming trust,
And age in love loves not to have years told.[6]
    Therefore I lie with[7] her, and she with me,
    And in our faults by lies we flattered be.

[1] truth—fidelity, faithfulness.
[2] untutored—inexperienced, without learning.
[3] Simply I credit—foolishly I believe.
[4] wherefore ... unjust?—why does she not say she is unfaithful?
[5] habit—appearance, clothing.
[6] age ... told—an older person in love doesn't like having years counted (or revealed).
[7] lie with—lie to or sleep with.

Sonnet 140

Be wise as thou art cruel; do not press[1]
My tongue-tied patience with too much disdain,[2]
Lest sorrow lend me words, and words express
The manner of my pity-wanting pain.[3]
If I might teach thee wit,[4] better it were,
Though not to love, yet, love, to tell me so,[5]
As testy sick men, when their deaths be near,
No news but health from their physicians know.
For if I should despair, I should grow mad,
And in my madness might speak ill of thee.
Now this ill-wresting[6] world is grown so bad,
Mad slanderers by mad ears believèd be.
    That I may not be so,[7] nor thou belied,[8]
    Bear thine eyes straight, though thy proud
        heart go wide.[9]

[1] press—oppress.
[2] disdain—scorn.
[3] manner ... pain—nature of my pain, which you don't pity.
[4] wit—wisdom.
[5] better it were ... me so—It would be better to tell me that you love me even if you do not.
[6] ill-wresting—misinterpreting everything as worse.
[7] I may not be so—I may not be a "mad slanderer" or believed to be one.
[8] belied—defamed, slandered.
[9] wide—astray (like an arrow that misses its target).

Sonnet 146

Poor soul, the center of my sinful earth,[1]
Thrall to[2] these rebel powers that thee array,[3]
Why dost thou pine within and suffer dearth,[4]
Painting thy outward walls[5] so costly gay?
Why so large cost, having so short a lease,
Dost thou upon thy fading mansion spend?
Shall worms, inheritors of this excess,
Eat up thy charge?[6] Is this thy body's end?
Then, soul, live thou upon thy servant's loss,
And let that pine to aggravate thy store;[7]
Buy terms divine in selling hours of dross;[8]
Within be fed, without be rich no more.
    So shalt thou feed on Death, that feeds on men,
    And Death once dead, there's no more dying then.

---

[1] sinful earth—body.

[2] Thrall to—under the control of. (This is one of several possibilities that take the place of a printer's error.)

[3] rebel powers . . . array—rebellious body that you dress up.

[4] dearth—spiritual want.

[5] outward walls—body, dressed in expensive clothes and cosmetics.

[6] charge—body put in your charge, for which you are responsible, and on which you have spent so much.

[7] that . . . store—body starves to increase your spirit (or your stock of riches).

[8] Buy . . . dross—buy ages of immortality by giving up (selling) hours of wasteful luxury.

Understanding the Poems

Sonnets 15, 18, and 19

1. In Sonnet 15, what are Time and Decay attacking?

2. What solution does the speaker propose?

3. In Sonnet 18, why does the speaker not want to compare his love to a summer's day?

4. Why will the speaker's love have an "eternal summer"?

5. What is the "heinous crime" that the speaker forbids in Sonnet 19?

Sonnets 23, 29, and 30

1. What does Sonnet 23 do that the speaker cannot?

2. What does the speaker mean by the "perfect ceremony of love's rite" in line 6?

3. Why is the speaker "in disgrace" in Sonnet 29?

4. What is the mood of the speaker in Sonnet 30?

5. What are the speaker's grievances?

Sonnets 35, 55, and 65

1. What has happened between the speaker and the listener in Sonnet 35?

2. What is motivating the speaker?

3. In Sonnet 55, why does the speaker feel his poem will outlast monuments and statues?

4. What are the opposites presented in Sonnet 65?

5. What does "Time's chest" represent and how is it defeated in this case?

Sonnets 71, 73, and 106

1. What is the speaker's fear in Sonnet 71?

2. In Sonnet 73, to what does the speaker compare his time of life?

3. Why will his beloved's love for him grow stronger?

4. What does the speaker in Sonnet 106 say is the difference between old and contemporary writers?

5. Why are the old writers' poems called "prophecies" in line 9?

Sonnets 116, 130, and 138

1. In Sonnet 116, why does the speaker say that love is "an ever-fixéd mark"?

2. What is the speaker saying is ruled by Time in lines 9–10?

3. Why does the speaker in Sonnet 130 reject "false compare"?

4. Why do the speaker and his love lie to each other in Sonnet 138?

5. What is "seeming trust" in line 11?

Sonnets 140 and 146

1. Why does the speaker in Sonnet 140 say that it would be better for his love to speak to him of love?

2. How can sorrow "lend me words"?

3. What are the two meanings of mad in line 9?

4. How does the speaker contrast the body and the soul in Sonnet 146?

5. What does it mean to "live upon thy servant's loss"?

Analyzing the Poems

1. Who do you think is the speaker in the Sonnets?

2. What is the general tone of the sonnets? In which sonnets does it change to match specific subject matter?

3. How are Sonnets 116 and 140 alike and different in what they say about love and lovers' actions?

4. How does the speaker of the sonnets feel about the value of art and literature? What is his view of the power of verse?

5. Most of the sonnets deal with the relationship between love and time. How does the way in which Shakespeare treats this relationship change in these poems? How does it remain the same?

Writing About the Poems

1. Choose one of the sonnets and write a five-paragraph summary of what the poem says. Be sure to include all of the shades of meaning that Shakespeare introduces.

2. Sonnets 130, 138, 140, and 146 are thought by scholars to be addressed to a different person—a woman known as "The Dark Lady"—than the earlier sonnets. Write an essay describing what is different in tone, language, imagery, and ideas between these two groups of poems.

3. Choose one of the sonnets and imagine that you received it from the writer. Write a response back describing your reactions to what it says.

4. Write a short essay discussing how Shakespeare employs one of the following in the Sonnets: the seasons, time, war, writing or performing, animals, or music.

5. Write your own sonnet. Reread the introduction to the sonnet and then map out what you want to say in each quatrain and the couplet. Now write your fourteen lines being sure to get the rhythm and rhyme correct.

Glossary of Literary and Theater Terms

act major division of a play. See **scene**.

alliteration repetition of consonant sounds at the beginnings of words or within words.

aside short speech or comment that is delivered by a character to the audience, but that is beyond the hearing of other characters who are present.

blank verse unrhymed verse in which each line has five accented syllables; the verse pattern in which Shakespeare wrote many of his plays.

caesura pause in the middle of a verse line.

cast of characters list of all the characters in a play.

character person, animal, or other being that takes part in the action of a literary work. Events center on the lives of one or more characters, referred to as main characters. The other characters, called minor characters, interact with the main characters and help move the action along.

climax decisive point in a dramatic plot when the central conflict must be resolved in one way or another.

comedy dramatic work that is light and often humorous in tone, usually ending happily with a peaceful resolution of the main conflict.

comic relief amusing episode in a serious or tragic drama that is introduced to relieve tension.

conflict struggle between opposing forces that is the basis of a plot. An **external conflict** pits a character against fate, nature, society, or another character; an internal conflict is between opposing forces within a character.

couplet two lines of verse that may rhyme or have complementary rhythms.

dialogue conversation between two or more characters in a literary work. In drama, the story is told almost exclusively through dialogue.

drama type of literature that is primarily written to be performed for an audience.

dramatic unities characteristics of time, place, and action that defined classical drama: a play was to present only one principal action occupying only one day and showing only what could be observed by a spectator sitting in one place.

epilogue a concluding speech that follows the action of a play.

exposition beginning part of a play, in which a dramatist explains the basic situation of the drama, identifies the setting, introduces the characters, establishes the mood and tone, and provides any important background information.

external conflict See **conflict**.

falling action part of a plot that follows and shows the effects of the climax. As the falling action begins, the suspense is over, but the effects of the decision or action that caused the climax are not yet fully worked out.

First Folio first substantially complete edition of Shakespeare's works, published in 1623.

foil character whose traits contrast with those of another character.

Globe theater eight-sided playhouse built in 1598 where most of Shakespeare's plays were performed.

history play one of a cycle of plays by Shakespeare based on the lives of English kings.

iambic pentamenter ten-syllable verse line that has five stresses, on the second, fourth, sixth, eighth, and tenth syllable. See **blank verse**.

imagery words and phrases that create vivid sensory experiences for the reader.

internal conflict See **conflict**.

irony in drama, a contrast between what characters expect to happen and what actually happens, between what a character says and what is meant, or between what the characters know and what the audience knows.

masque type of lavish dramatic spectacle that was a feature of entertainments at the English court in the early 1600s. Masques were plays on pastoral and mythical themes that featured music, dance, large casts (many courtiers took part), beautiful scenery, extravagant costumes, and elaborate stagecraft.

monologue long speech spoken by a single character to himself or herself, or to the audience. See **soliloquy**.

mood emotional response created by a literary work. See **tone**.

octave the first eight lines of a sonnet. See **sestet**.

Pit in Shakespeare's Globe theater, the open area in front of the stage which provided standing room for those who couldn't afford a seat in the surrounding galleries.

plot action or storyline of a play.

prologue introduction to a play. A prologue may be in the form of a monologue by a character.

prop object used in a play.

prose in a play, dialogue without meter.

protagonist main character in a literary work.

pun play on words that involves different sense of the same word or the similar sense or sound of different words.

quatrain group of four lines of poetry.

resolution or dénouement final part of a plot, which follows—and often blends with—the falling action, completes the resolution of the conflict, and ties up loose ends.

rhyme scheme pattern of rhymes in a poem. A rhyme scheme can be desribed by using a different letter to represent each rhyming sound.

rising action in a plot, the events that lead to the climax by adding complications or expanding the conflict. Suspense usually builds during the rising action.

scene subdivision of an act in a drama. Each scene usually establishes a separate time or place.

sestet last six lines of a sonnet. See **octave**.

setting the time and place of the action of a play.

soliloquy monologue in which a character speaks his or her private thoughts aloud and appears to be unaware of the audience.

sonnet fourteen-line poem made up of three quatrains and couplet. The **rhyme scheme** for a Shakespearean sonnet is *abab cdcd efef gg*.

stage directions dramatist's instructions for performing a play. Usually set in italics, stage directions are located at the beginning of a play and throughout the text.

stress syllable in a word that receives the most emphasis from the speaker.

thrust stage a stage with the audience sitting on two or three sides of the acting area.

tiring-house in Elizabethan theaters such as Shakespeare's Globe, the three-story structure that contained the various acting areas, as well as the performers' dressing rooms. (*Tiring* is a shortened form of *attiring*, "dressing.") Forming the back of the different stages, the façade of the tiring house was the theater's permanent set.

tone writer's attitude, either stated or unstated, to his or her subject matter. See **mood**.

tragedy form of drama in which the main character suffers disaster.

tragic hero main character of a tragedy.

wordplay witty or clever dialogue. See **pun**.

Texts

Notes and text to "Romeo and Juliet" from *The Complete Works of Shakespeare, 4th ed.* by David Bevington. Copyright © 1997 by Addison-Wesley Educational Publishers, Inc. Reprinted by permission of Pearson Education, Inc.

Notes and text to "Macbeth" from *The Complete Works of Shakespeare, 4th ed.* by David Bevington. Copyright © 1997 by Addison-Wesley Educational Publishers, Inc. Reprinted by permission of Pearson Education, Inc.

Evans, G. Blackmore (Editor), *The Riverside Shakespeare.* Copyright © 1974 by Houghton Mifflin Company. Used with permission.

Illustrations

Positions of illustrations on a page are indicated by these abbreviations: (T) top, (C) center, (B) bottom, (L) left, (R) right.

3 Century Fox/The Kobal Collection. **4T** Jennifer Lester/Theatre Pix. **4B** The Kobal Collection. **5T** T. Charles Erickson/Theatre Pix. **5B** Donald Cooper/Shakespeare's Globe. **6B** Shakespeare Birthplace Trust, Stratford-Upon-Avon. **6T** Shakespeare Birthplace Trust, Stratford-Upon-Avon. **7T** The Granger Collection, New York. **7B** North Wind. **9B** The Granger Collection, New York. **8T** Bettmann/Corbis. **9TL** The Granger Collection, New York. **9TR** The Granger Collection, New York. **9B** Illustration by C. Walter Hodges from *William Shakespeare: The Complete Works*, edited by Alfred Harbage, copyright © 1969 by Penguin Books, Inc. **10T** Donald Cooper/Shakespeare's Globe. **10B** The Granger Collection, New York. **11** Shakespeare Birthplace Trust, Stratford-Upon Avon. **12** T. Charles Erickson/Theatre Pix. **13** Chris Bennion/Theatre Pix. **14** George Karger/Pix Inc./TimePix. **15** Jennifer Lester/Theatre Pix. **17** Chris Bennion/Theatre Pix. **18T** Chris Bennion/Theatre Pix. **18B** T. Charles Erickson/Theatre Pix. **24** Jennifer Lester/Theatre Pix. **38** T. Charles Erickson/

Theatre Pix. **49** Richard Feldman/Theatre Pix. **59** T. Charles Erickson/Theatre Pix. **61** Jennifer Lester/Theatre Pix. **66** Jennifer Lester/Theatre Pix. **73** Jennifer Lester/Theatre Pix. **80** T. Charles Erickson/Theatre Pix. **86** T. Charles Erickson/Theatre Pix. **93** Jennifer Lester/Theatre Pix. **98** Jennifer Lester/Theatre Pix. **106** Michael Brosilow/Theatre Pix. **116** T. Charles Erickson/Theatre Pix. **122** T. Charles Erickson/Theatre Pix. **127** Jennifer Lester/Theatre Pix. **132** Richard Anderson/The Shakespeare Theatre. **141** T. Charles Erickson/Theatre Pix. **144** T. Charles Erickson/Theatre Pix. **148** Richard Feldman/Theatre Pix. **153** Martha Swope/TimePix. **154T** Jennifer Lester/Theatre Pix. **154B** Jennifer Lester/Theatre Pix. **163** Chris Bennion/Theatre Pix. **168** T. Charles Erickson/Theatre Pix. **173** Jennifer Lester/Theatre Pix. **181** T. Charles Erickson/Theatre Pix. **184** Jennifer Lester/Theatre Pix. **189** Chris Bennion/Theatre Pix. **191** Jennifer Lester/Theatre Pix. **194** Jennifer Lester/Theatre Pix. **198** Michal Daniel/Theatre Pix. **201** T. Charles Erickson/Theatre Pix. **206** Chris Bennion/Theatre Pix. **209** T. Charles Erickson/Theatre Pix. **212** T. Charles Erickson/Theatre Pix. **216** T. Charles Erickson/Theatre Pix. **219** T. Charles Erickson/Theatre Pix. **233** Richard Feldman/Theatre Pix. **238** T. Charles Erickson/Theatre Pix. **243** Michal Daniel/Theatre Pix. **244T** Richard Feldman/Theatre Pix. **244B** John Tramper/Shakespeare's Globe. **252** Jennifer Lester/Theatre Pix. **264** Jennifer Lester/Theatre Pix. **271** Jennifer Lester/Theatre Pix. **277** Richard Feldman/Theatre Pix. **283** Jennifer Lester/Theatre Pix. **289** Chris Bennion/Theatre Pix. **294** Chris Bennion/Theatre Pix. **299** Richard Feldman/Theatre Pix. **302** T. Charles Erickson/Theatre Pix. **309** T. Charles Erickson/Theatre Pix. **317** Jennifer Lester/Theatre Pix. **320** Michal Daniel/Theatre Pix. **325** Martha Swope/TimePix. **331** Michal Daniel/Theatre Pix. **338** Jennifer Lester/Theatre Pix. **345** Richard Feldman/Theatre Pix. **352** Jennifer Lester/Theatre Pix. **356** Martha Swope/TimePix. **357L** Terry Smith/TimePix. **357R** The National Theatre London/The Bridgeman Art Library. **358L** Martha Swope/

TimePix. **358R** John Swope/TimePix. **359** Richard Feldman/Theatre Pix. **360T** The Kobal Collection. **360B** Richard Feldman/Theatre Pix. **361T** Jennifer Lester/Theatre Pix. **361B** T. Charles Erickson/Theatre Pix. **362T** George Karger/TimePix. **362B** The Kobal Collection. **363** John Tramper/Shakespeare's Globe. **364** T. Charles Erickson/Theatre Pix. **365L** Eileen Darby/TimePix. **365R** T. Charles Erickson/Theatre Pix. **367** Fine Line/MPTV. **368T** T. Charles Erickson/Theatre Pix. **368B** Shakespeare Birthplace Trust. **375** T. Charles Erickson/Theatre Pix. **379** Michal Daniel/Theatre Pix. **385** Kevin Sprague. **391** Michal Daniel/Theatre Pix. **401** Chris Bennion/Theatre Pix. **404** T. Charles Erickson/Theatre Pix. **408** T. Charles Erickson/Theatre Pix. **415** Chris Bennion/Theatre Pix. **423** Kevin Sprague. **433** T. Charles Erickson/Theatre Pix. **440** Jennifer Lester/Theatre Pix. **446** Michal Daniel/Theatre Pix. **448** T. Charles Erickson/Theatre Pix. **459** Michal Daniel/Theatre Pix. **464** Jennifer Lester/Theatre Pix. **466** T. Charles Erickson/Theatre Pix. **473** John Tramper/Shakespeare's Globe. **474T** Jennifer Lester/Theatre Pix. **474B** Shakespeare's Globe. **478** T. Charles Erickson/Theatre Pix. **489** Chris Bennion/Theatre Pix. **497** T. Charles Erickson/Theatre Pix. **506** T. Charles Erickson/Theatre Pix. **515** Jennifer Lester/Theatre Pix. **526** Jennifer Lester/Theatre Pix. **535** T. Charles Erickson/Theatre Pix. **541** T. Charles Erickson/Theatre Pix. **552** Richard Feldman/Theatre Pix. **561** George Silk/TimePix. **565** Nat Farbman/TimePix. **568** T. Charles Erickson/Theatre Pix. **576** Jennifer Lester/Theatre Pix. **581** Carol Rosegg/Shakespeare Theatre. **589** Jennifer Lester/Theatre Pix. **598** Carol Rosegg/Shakespeare Theatre. **608** Martha Swope/TimePix. **611** Michal Daniel/Theatre Pix. **622** Michal Daniel/Theatre Pix. **627** T. Charles Erickson/Theatre Pix. **629** Jennifer Lester/Theatre Pix. **634** The Kobal Collection. **635** The Kobal Collection. **636T** The Kobal Collection. **636B** The Kobal Collection. **637** The Kobal Collection. **638T** The Kobal Collection. **638B** The Kobal Collection. **639** The Kobal Collection. **640T** Gjon Mili/TimePix. **640B** The Kobal Collection. **641** The Kobal Collection. **642T** The Kobal Collection. **642B** The Kobal Collection. **643** The Kobal Collection. **645** Michal Daniel/Theatre Pix. **646T** Jennifer Lester/Theatre Pix. **646B** Joan Marcus/Shakespeare Theatre. **652** Chris Bennion/Theatre Pix. **656** Joe Cocks Studio/Shakespeare Centre Library. **664** T. Charles Erickson/Theatre Pix. **670** T. Charles Erickson/Theatre Pix. **672** Chris Bennion/Theatre Pix. **676** T. Charles Erickson/Theatre Pix. **679** Jennifer Lester/Theatre Pix. **688** Chris Bennion/Theatre Pix. **699** Chris Bennion/Theatre Pix. **710** Martha Swope/TimePix. **716** Chris Bennion/Theatre Pix. **723** Martha Swope/TimePix. **729** Jennifer Lester/Theatre Pix. **736** Jennifer Lester/Theatre Pix. **739** Martha Swope/TimePix. **749** T. Charles Erickson/Theatre Pix. **750T** Chris Bennion/Theatre Pix. **750B** T. Charles Erickson/Theatre Pix. **754** Michal Daniel/Theatre Pix. **759** Chris Bennion/Theatre Pix. **764** Michal Daniel/Theatre Pix. **770** Chris Bennion/Theatre Pix. **774** T. Charles Erickson/Theatre Pix. **785** Chris Bennion/Theatre Pix. **790** Charles Erickson/Theatre Pix. **797** Carol Rosegg/Shakespeare Theatre. **800** T. Charles Erickson/Theatre Pix. **807** Richard Feldman/Theatre Pix. **812** Richard Feldman/Theatre Pix. **819** Michal Daniel/Theatre Pix. **823** Michal Daniel/Theatre Pix. **830** Richard Feldman/Theatre Pix. **835** T. Charles Erickson/Theatre Pix. **842** Chris Bennion/Theatre Pix. **848** The Granger Collection, New York. **849** The Granger Collection, New York.

Every effort has been made to secure complete rights and permissions for all texts and illustrations presented herein. Updated acknowledgements, if needed, will appear in subsequent printings.